D0075855

CHARGES TO THE GRAND JURY

CHARGES TO THE GRAND JURY 1689–1803

edited by

GEORGES LAMOINE

CAMDEN FOURTH SERIES
VOLUME 43

LONDON
OFFICES OF THE ROYAL HISTORICAL SOCIETY
UNIVERSITY COLLEGE LONDON
GOWER STREET WC1E 6BT
1992

British Library Cataloguing in Publication Data

Charges to the Grand Jury, 1689–1803. –
(Royal Historical Society: Camden Fourth Series; Vol. 43)
I. Lamoine, Georges II. Series 344.1

ISBN 0.86193–130.0

Printed and bound in Great Britain by
Butler & Tanner Ltd, Frome and London

CONTENTS

ACKNOWLEDGEMENTS

Because this book could not have been made possible without the help of a number of institutions in England and Ireland, thanks and acknowledgments are due to the following, for permission to reprint or print the texts of the *Charges* held in their respective collections:

The British Library for the following: Sir M.D., Lord Stamford, Lovell, Bulstrode, Cocks 1 & 2, W. Cowper, Montagu, Ryder, Dolins, Gonson, J... P..., Marlay, H. Fielding, Marriott, Sir J. Hawkins, Mainwaring, Partridge, Jacson, Day, Harvey, Chedworth, Sir J. Eyre, Lord Kenyon, D. George, Grose, Gwillim; the Bodleian Library, Oxford, for Corsellis & Bayley; the Cambridge University Library: Squire Law Library, for Witton, Ryder and Berwick; the King's Inn Library Dublin: Aston; the Bristol Public Library, for W. Cann and R. Burke; the Norfolk Record Office: the National Trust, Blincking Hall, Aylsham, and Sir Ronald Preston, Beeston Hall, Beeston St. Lawrence, near Wroxham, Norwich respectively for the two series of mss texts; and for Jodrell and Charles Harvey; the Surrey Record Office: Mr. J. R. More-Molyneux of Loseley Park for the mss of the Guilford 1736 series; the Greater London Record Officer and History Library (with acknowledgements to H.M. Stationary Office), for the text of Sir John Fielding; the Gloucester Public Library, for the Foley Charges; The Guildhall Library, Aldermanbury, London; the London Record Office; Mr. K. H. Rogers and the Wiltshire County Record Office, the Exeter Cathedral Library, the Wiltshire Archæological and Natural History Society, the Lancashire County Council and Mr. K. Hall, for information.

The Public Record Office, Kew, by permission of the Controller of H.M. Stationary Office, to quote the documents in H.O. 42/ 22 and 42/ 23, and P.C. 2/ 137.

The Photographic Service of the British Library, Reference Division, for their permanent help with material queries.

Special thanks are also due to colleagues, friends, correspondants, who have kindly undertaken to check on, or supply, information on various aspects of these texts: The Librarians and the Assistant Librarians of King's Inn Library, Dublin, of Bristol Reference Library (Mr. Langley and Miss Bridge), of Gloucester Public Library (Mrs. Voyce and Mr. Hyatt), of the Greater London Record Office and History Library (Miss Coburn), of the Guildhall Library London, the staff of these institutions, the staff of the Bristol, Norfolk (Miss J. Kennedy), Surrey, Essex (Miss J.T. Smith), Cambridge (Dr. D.M. Owen for the Ely Ecclesiastical

Records) record offices, my colleague and friend Prof. P-G. Boucé, of the university of Paris III La Sorbonne nouvelle. Nor should I forget the staff of all the other county record offices who looked for texts of *Charges* in their own collections, and could find none. Last but not least, special thanks are due to Professor H. T. Dickinson, of Edinburgh University, for his friendly advice and suggestions while reading the typescript at an early stage, and without whose encouragement the book would not have been published. Nor should the Literary Editor, Dr. J. Ramsden, be forgotten for his help with the final details.

INTRODUCTION

History and geography

The idea of collecting the texts of the *Charges* into one book grew ten years ago as I was trying to find material that could give light and information on the judicial system of England in the 18th century. It is quite possible that some other texts are still forgotten in mss, in private libraries or in family collections, but county record offices and public libraries offered all the texts they had. Obviously, I cannot claim to have given *all* the Charges still extant in England, Wales and Ireland because I have not been able to carry out personal research in each of the above mentioned record offices and libraries.

The first texts given here are contemporary with the Glorious Revolution,[1] the last ones were delivered during the years following the peace of Amiens; the period covered extends beyond 1799, because we have a series of texts by the same hand from 1797 until 1803, although it is not quite complete. To go beyond this date would have meant taking in all the *Charges* delivered in the early 19th century. Evidently there survive in libraries *Charges* for earlier ages, the 16th and the 17th centuries, but the period chosen corresponds mainly to my personal field of research, and to the interest of reading these as documents as further sources of social history, for a period of considerably increasing wealth and population in Great Britain. It was the time of the largest development of overseas trade before the Industrial Revolution made its impact fully felt. It would also be interesting to try and measure how much the influence of the Enlightenment could soften the rigour of the law, whereas the Bloody Code became more and more severe for those who transgressed the sacred notion of property. The answer is probably to be looked for, and found, in the attitudes of the many juries who underrated the number of thefts, versus the lawmakers who passed more and more acts punishing known offences, or who invented new forms of offences, in response to new forms of delinquency.

Although all of them are called *Charges to the Grand Jury*, the distinction is to be made between those delivered at (General) Quarter-Sessions of the Peace, and those intended to be heard by the session of Oyer and Terminer and General Gaol Delivery, or Assizes. In the former case the court would try offences that were not capital either at the common law

[1] All dates quoted in new style.

or made so by statute; they were misdemeanours, or felonies not capital, mostly theft under all its possible forms, which often resulted in fines, imprisonment, or transportation for a term or for life. The latter case would on the contrary try the major crimes that would lead the offenders to the gallows: murder under its various legal forms (wilful murder, manslaughter, self defence, chance medley, etc) high or petty treason, arson, sodomy and rape, and later on in the century, forgery increasingly. An example of the distinction between the two sorts of sessions is to be found in Foley, Epiphany 1801. But a special case of Grand Jury is that of Sir James Eyre's before the King's Bench, or that of Lord Kenyon.

Most of the *Charges* are Quarter-Sessions ones, even if one may find that there is no direct relevance in contents, in either case, to the nature of the court then addressed. The proportion is 10 for Oyer and Terminer, out of a total of 76, or nearly 13%. There is no explanation of the fact that Q-S. Charges are kept in this proportion (87%), unless we remember that Q-S. were held four times a year, and that the commissions of Oyer & Terminer were normally issued twice a year, and that, not in every county, Northern counties being sometimes visited by Judges once a year only. On the other hand these sessions came round rather regularly in London, about every six weeks or so, because of the number of people there were to try both within the jurisdiction of the City's magistrates and the development of the Middlesex suburbs. Although, as has been said, these *Charges* were delivered in many different places of the kingdom, the proportion can be explained by the fact that several series contain a relatively high number of texts in succession: the Norfolk series I and II, the Foley Gloucester series, which are all Quarter-Sessions and must be taken separately into account. This also explains why these are published here as a series, irrespective of dates, although all others are given in chronological order. Either an absence of dates makes it difficult to give each text its real place, or erroneous dates had to be corrected, but could not be ascertained. Because of this special aspect it was thought preferable to give these texts as a continuous series. There is one example only of a magistrate having given a charge both to a grand jury of the Q-S, and of Oyer and Terminer (Day, in Dublin).

Few of these texts concern Ireland (6), the rest representing many parts of England. London, with its encroachments into Middlesex, has an important share, with 19 Charges representing 25% of the total, since towards the close of the century, the metropolis accounted for one-eighth of the population of England; but if we cannot speak of an equitable distribution over the kingdom, there is no exclusive concentration on London: Cambridge, Ely, Bristol, Norwich, Salford, Gloucester, Guildford, Chester, Berwick, and the counties of Leicester, Essex, Devon, Wiltshire, Yorkshire, Lincolnshire are represented. The reason why there seems no have been no charge printed for the sessions of gaol delivery and Oyer and Terminer in the Old Bailey is, that apparently the same juries served at the Q-S held in the Guildhall, and then immediately after when the gaol delivery sessions began, which brought about the adjournment of the Q-S. They were therefore given no charge, since the charge had been given at the Q-S. by the presiding magistrate.[1]

These texts belong to various periods of English history: the Revolution and its immediate aftermath, Queen Anne's reign, then those of the three Georges, with one particular number of them concentrated on the months of January-February 1793, these speeches being delivered a few days before or after the execution of Louis XVI. In the latter case, the author's reaction is quite perceptible, when the text was printed after the news of the king's death had reached England, in the early days of February '93. One is directly concerned with the 1794 political trials against the partisans of the French Revolution; a few more given in Ireland are concerned with the French influence over the Irish trying once more to revolt against English rule.

From the political point of view, there is little doubt that most orators had adopted the tenets of the Glorious Revolution: their insistence on the Whig principles which led William to the throne are expressed in almost constant terms, circumstances only creating the variable elements. The chronological sequence covers the first months of the Revolution, the last years of Anne's whig ministry, then the short-lived tory government of Harley, the coming of George I, the taking over of power by Robert Walpole and his nearly 20 years of uninterrupted rule, the continuation of the whig domination until the accession of George III and the new tory ascendency, down to 1803.

The majority of these Charges was printed, "at the request of the Grand Jury..." Only three series are manuscript, one kept in Guildford Muniment Room, and two in Norfolk Archives. The Norfolk texts cover two different periods, 1709–11 in the first case, 1752–67 in the second. For these later texts, there are at times great difficulties in deciphering the handwriting, often charged with superscriptions, themselves being crossed out and reworded. For the printed texts most are pamphlets, being often bound together in the *Tracts* volumes of the B. L.; two are printed on a broadsheet or a newspaper front page. Only one is a book of its own containing the Foley charges (Gloucester). There is considerable variation in size, the shortest one being 6 pages long, the most lengthy one running to over 60 pages. Sir John Astry's *Charge to all*

[1] See J. M. Beattie, "London Juries in the 1690s," 223, n. 17 in: J. S. Cockburn & T. A. Green, eds., *Twelve Good Men and True, The Criminal Trial Jury in England, 1200–1800* (Princeton, N.J.: Princeton U.P., 1988). – The same article contains interesting evidence as to the simultaneity of the London Q-S. and Gaol delivery and O. & T. sessions, 222–23.

Juries ... (1703) has not been included, as being far too long and too general.

Nature of the documents

R. Witton seems to have been the only author who cared to give his audience an explanation as to the origin of the judicial necessity of giving a charge, but unfortunately he gives no date; he only mentions the first practice of delivering them in writing to the jury, and states that the tradition died away of confining it to paper. One would normally expect these texts to answer the definition of them given by Giles Jacob's *New Law Dictionary* (5th ed., 1750, no page number) under ' Chapiters':

> Signifies in our Common Law a Summary of such Matters as are to be enquired of, or presented before Justices in Eyre, Justices of Assize, or of Peace, in their Sessions delivered by the Mouth of the Justice in his Charge to the Inquest.

More precise is the explanation supplied by *The Oxford Companion to Law*, the charge being

> A judge's explanation to a jury, at the conclusion of the hearing of evidence, of the relevant law, of the issues for their consideration, the onus of proof, the effect of finding certain facts to have been proved and other matters which they must consider when reaching their verdict on the evidence.[1]

This is perhaps what, paradoxically, makes the interest of these texts today: if they had been only concerned with dry legal matters, they would probably be useful to students or specialists of things past only. A number of the magistrates indeed played the game, and instructed the jury, on the three main sorts of offences for which an English subject could be tried (see below). There ensued the lists of offences, either capital or not, the former being far more numerous than the latter, and the scale of punishments. This can be found, e.g.under the pens of W. Bulstrode, Sir John Gonson, J. Mountagu, H. Fielding the playwright-novelist-cum magistrate. Such texts make up one category of *Charges*, from their contents.

Another group, more numerous, is constituted of texts of a more strongly affirmed political tone. Beside the lawful and judicial occasion which the sessions afforded, the magistrate had to convince the audience, beyond the immediate range of the jury, of political truths and necessities. Indeed a session, whatever its name, brought together a great concourse of people of the country, and two at least of the authors here quoted insist on the fact that they speak not exclusively to the jury, but that

[1] ed. D.M. Walker (OUP, 1980), p. 206. See R. Burke.

beyond the twelve persons legally concerned they address the public at large. It must be quite clear that the J.P.s, and more particularly the Westminster Judges, not only 'took the assizes' as they went on their respective circuits, but that doing so, they brought along with them the instructions of Government in criminal as well as in political matters (see Lovell, p. 7: "At the Judges setting out from London,..." and below, about the post-1792 charges). This was of course nothing new: it was noted, e.g. for the reign of Elizabeth, when "The judges of assize on their twice-yearly circuits conveyed the Crown's wishes to local governors, supervising their activities and reporting back to the Privy Council on the conduct of county business."[1] In the *Charge* of Sir John Gonson, dated 3 July 1729, the Jurors thanked the magistrate for

> A most Eloquent and Useful Charge, tending to the good Government, not only of this City and Liberty but also to the Universal Guidance and Directions of all Persons whatsoever, in Execution of the several Offices and Trusts in them respectively reposed.

James Mountagu's text, of 1720, is as illuminating on the subject. Nash Grose's short address to Hertforshire jurymen, in 1796, was intended to make it widely known that any attempt at stealing foodstuff and provisions would be made a capital offence, in these years of dearth and political difficulties in Europe, and that such offenders were to expect no mercy either from the court and the jury, or from the king's ultimate power of pardoning. He insisted on the fact that the session was a particularly suitable moment to make it publicly known.

The third category is that composed of the 1792–93 and post–1793 charges, all marked by the strong anti-revolutionary spirit of those years.

Political aspects

Most magistrates felt that they were obliged to vindicate "the ways of God to Man," in explaining why a government over men was necessary. They assigned its prime origins to the depravity of man after the Fall, and made it clear that strength would be the reigning rule if laws were not permitted to regulate the passions and violence of man. This reminds us very much of the political theories inherited from the mid- and late 17th century, with Hobbes's and Locke's theoretical state of nature and the notion of civil contract (Gonson 4, Guilford 1740). Hence this definition: "the true end of government is the protection of society" (Norfolk 1710). The first text by Sir M.D. completes the previous definition, explaining the use of the meeting of the grand jury: "the preservation of the peace in matters ecclesiastical as well as civil."

[1] Penry Williams, "The Crown and the Counties" in: Chr. Haigh, ed., *The Reign of Elizabeth* (London: Macmillan, 1984) 126.

The word 'party,' whenever it is mentioned, is criticised as a factor of division of H.M.'s subjects (cf Mountagu, Guilford 1741, Hawkins 1770 'faction'), but not a word is said of the magistrate's own leanings; must we understand that they spoke in public in their official capacity, leaving aside their personal convictions, and that they might speak another language in times of general elections? This is not certain, and the mode of appointing J.P.s and judges leaves little doubt that they were reliable props of the government in the provinces. Since the years had confirmed the settlement of the revolution and of the Hanoverian succession, J.P.s had to make the best of it, if they did not overtly agree with it. But it is striking to see how many times the sacred character of kingship and of the king's person is emphasised, under a régime which had fought the hereditary character and the divine right theory of the previous dynasty. Let us remember that ardent supporters of William, 'the great Deliverer', (cf Mountagu, 47) took great care to have it spread and believed, that the prince of Orange had been sent Heaven-sent to restore liberties and save the Protestant religion from Papism, D. Defoe's *True-Born Englishman* being the first and best example of it. Thus was the sacred character of monarchy restored, and regularly defended to the subjects, with totally different political aims. A man like Henry Fielding, whose other writings cannot make him suspect of Jacobite sympathies or leanings, insists on the sacredness of the king's majesty in 1749. We might also conclude that the monarchical principle remained the same as before, but being applied to a different man and a new dynasty, it served a slightly different purpose and a different group of men, and remained valid when the conditions of its application were acceptable. The patriarchal character of the monarchy is clearly recalled to the attention of the jury by Sir Nash Grose, who called the king's proclamation against vice and immorality, "a parental admonition" (1796, p. 9).

When following the chronological order of these texts, we note that there was a necessity of convincing the audience of the legitimacy of the sovereign, from William and Mary down to George II, the problem being not mentioned any longer after 1760 (Hawkins 1770, p. 13, "the security with which H.M. holds his crown…"). Considering the publicity given to the sessions, the importance of the Magistrate's speech to the crowd, always restless and ready to riot, could be considerable, and its impact was expected to have its full weight. From the enormously learned speech of Lord Stamford, with all its notes borrowed from chronicle-writers and historians, to the more humble style of Mr. Baron Lovell, the question of the post-revolutionary settlement was obviously the main point on which to focus. The arguments were easy enough to put forward: no Papism, the defence of the Englishman's birthrights, no more Stuart absolutism. Whether under William or under his sister-in-law and rightful successor, one may feel the fear of plotting and scheming, and one thinks of Thackeray's *Henry Esmond* revisited. The magistrate also had to prevent the spreading of fanatic preaching after the trial of Dr. Sacheverell in the late days of 1709 (cf Lovell) and the early weeks of 1710. Because we have no text written immediately during or after the two Jacobite risings of 1715 and 1745 we have no directly relevant commentary on the events.

For the post 1789-period, few footnotes will be found added to the texts, for giving more of them would have implied writing a full comment on those events, and this is not the aim of this book. Therefore it is assumed that the reader would be at least familiar with the main issues and events of this much-troubled area of European history, and with British history as well. Let me simply recall that a handful of partisans of the new French system were violently denounced in Edmund Burke's *Reflections on the Revolution in France* (1790), that Thomas Paine's *The Rights of Man* was the Bible of the new creed, that a war of pamphlets raged until 1794–95 on both sides, that Paine was tried *in abstentia*, and that members of the London Corresponding Society were tried in London in October 1794 for high treason, but that they were acquitted, partly on account of the vigorous address sent by William Godwin on their behalf to the principal newspapers just before the trial opened. This was one of the cases when the choice and the reaction of the jury were of paramount importance: the government could not carry the day, neither had it been able to do so in far different circumstances, when James II had wished to try the Bishops in revolt against his Declaration of Indulgence. Other trials in Scotland were less favourable to the accused, and a few died as a consequence, either in jail, or on their way out to the new colony of Botany Bay (see Robert Southey's poem on the subject). The charges given in Ireland naturally allude to the attempted revolution of the United Irishmen with the help of French spies and forces.

Some characteristic features

Before examining the special points of interest of these pages, the reader should remember that magistrates had to deliver their speeches quite regularly, and that the heart of the matter remained much the same from one session to the next. The nature of the offences being well-known and categorised, only the number of prisoners to be tried could change, from one calendar year to the next. Only circumstances, and the evidence about cases, changed. Therefore it is not surprising that the same magistrate should more or less repeat the same thing, and should make the same comments on similar subjects in recurring situations, unless in the meantime a new statute was added to the Book. Hence the sometimes repetitive aspect of a few of these texts for Gonson, Bulstrode, etc. Yet, they managed to improve on the text, so as not to bore the jury, or one would simply refer the jury to his previously printed text. The same thing can be said of the Old Bailey proceedings, where all that we would consider as ritual remained unchanged, only names, circumstances and verdicts and sentences being changeable. Still, when one goes through the whole series, one will be able to notice the evolution of the Code, and both the increase of the new offences, and of the penalties attached to them.

One characteristic feature of the 18th century was the firm belief that England had reached the perfection of the civilized world, or nearly so (see Grose, p. 13). It would be useless to quote all the authors who, generally speaking, did write in this way. If the novelist or the playwright staged (nearly) perfect English characters, and their opposites, and French or Frenchified people, and even after the 1760's, Macaronis, the J.P. was proud of being (very often) a member of the ruling class of England. He would then repeat session after session, that the Constitution of England was the envy of the world for its mixture of the three traditional types of governments, the aristocratic, the democratic, and the monarchic, blended into a unique example throughout the ages. Nearly every single text says so under one form or another (cf Mountagu).The balance between the three separate heads of power was again very much insisted on (Norfolk 1749). This was shown even better in a comparison with the Continent, and as naturally, with France first and foremost before 1789, since the glory of Louis XIV's reign had marked Europe with the sign of French military power, with grandeur, and also absolutism (cf Gonson 3, W. Cann, H. Fielding, 1749 comparing English Liberty with French Bastilles, *lettres de cachet*, and the Inquisition). Hawkins 1770 went so far as to say that no country could compare its laws with those of England, and it would be interesting to make a study of the influence of Blackstone's candidly admiring book over these Charges.The Constitution meant several things, since it was used to mean the governing process of the country, its policy, the several parts of the political power (King, Lords, and Commons), the relations between them, and those between the former and the rest of the people; no J. P. (or any of his contemporaries) had any hesitation in writing "the constitution of government,"[1] or in understanding the exact scope of the expression (cf Gonson 1-4, H. Fielding). It also meant the Established Church, the laws, and everything pertaining to the administration of the country. England is blessed with a monarch who will make the Law of the country his will, thus contrasting with the Stuarts, or even with Louis XIV ("l'Etat, c'est moi"); he and his family are paragons of virtues, to a point which may be amusing: when one reads the panegyric of George I then that of George II, at once with the *Memoirs* of Lord Hervey, for

[1] See the opening lines of H. Fielding's *An Enquiry into the Causes of the late Increase of Robbers*..., 1751, ed. G. Lamoine (Toulouse: P.U.M., 1989)

example, it is difficult for us to find both to be portraits of the same character. It is true that most people listening to a magistrate in court would not have known the book written by the courtier. The *Media via* of the Church made this *ecclesia* the most perfect church of Christendom, which means in fact the most perfect religious organisation in the history of the world. None of the excesses of puritanism, none of the enormities of the church of Rome and its political ambitions. These texts might have been inspired by Hooker's *Ecclesiatical Polity* and Swift's *A Tale of a Tub* at once. They nearly all contained a patriotic note focusing on the mildness of the laws (everything being measured by the standards of its own times), the excellence of the constitution, the virtues of a gentle prince, and the qualities of the clergy.

Indeed a large number of the magistrates took pride in recalling the antiquity of the system of trial by juries (Astry, Gonson 2, 3, H. Fielding, Day 2, Jodrell); they emphasised the ancient and respectable character of the jury, taken as a part of the constitution. Dolins reminded them that because of their local origins, they were supposed to know every thing in and about their neighbourhood. The text Norfolk 1741 called the grand jury 'the primum mobile and spring' of justice, repeated in 1742 as 'first spring'. Marriott could rightly say in Cambridge: "With you, Gentlemen, as a Grand Jury, the laws begin and end." This was evident insofar as when a jury found a bill not true, the accusation fell. Richard Burke, Edmund's brother and Recorder of the City and County of Bristol, said the grand jury was granted "the sacred Office of Protector and Guardian of Innocence" and that they played the part of the public Accuser. Though most magistrates alluded to the antiquity of the system of trial by jury, they were not sure of its exact origins, and would speak of its ancient existence, as if the adjective were a guarantee in itself of historic truth. One text goes as far as to call the trial by jury a 'Gothic institution', thus following a well-established custom of attributing a Northern origin to most elements of the political system, and to the population of England, according to the myth of the Northern Hive then prevailing. Swift said the same thing of the origin of Parliament, revering the wisdom of the 'Gothic institution'. Whether they tried to show the Saxon origin of the trial by jury, or to propose a Norman beginning, they insisted on the fact that trial by jury was the greatest safety of the subject, protecting his life and property from all violence and encroachment either from the rich and powerful, or from the poor and the needy (cf Day 1). "The Law is respecter of no person," and none is above the law. It would probably be very difficult to say whether the practice always justified the theory. But lawyers very much insisted that the rights of the English subject existed at least since Magna Carta was signed, and were confirmed by 39 Car. II c. 2, the *Habeas Corpus Amendment Act.* These texts probably represent the clearest explanation of how the system of trial by two successive juries was working: the grand jury deciding whether in their opinion there was evidence enough to send the accused party to take his trial (H. Fielding: "there is a probable cause for his Accusation"), the petty jury trying then the heart of the matter. The first jury was then playing the part undertaken to-day by a police commissioner, or detectives, or the French juge d'instruction; the second one, under the supervision of the judge, who saw to it that the law was respected in the form as well as in the spirit, were really those who passed judgment on the accused: their verdict was literally a matter of life and death in the most serious cases. The judge only followed their verdict: acquitted, he was to be set free; guilty, he was to be punished according to his desert. The petty jury could also find an "extenuation of the offence," that is, they underrated the amount of damage claimed in case of theft, so that for example the person found guilty of a theft over 40 shillings should not be hanged. (This was called the 'pious perjury.' cf Astry, 15, 21, and Hawkins 1770.) The charges also insist on the fact that the jurors were respectable members of the community, and substantial freeholders or farmers (cf Aston, Jodrell). This is an interesting indication of the social class from which the sheriff would return the jurors for each session. As some few lists of jurors are added to the Charges (cf Bulstrode 1–3, Mountagu, Dolins, Gonson 1–5, J. Fielding, Bayley[1]) we can check that the same jurors were not permanently present at each session; it is true that some surnames would recur rather frequently, and the use of the intitals is not enough to know whether J. is John, James, Jonathan, etc. in a same family. I myself had the occasion to meet this difficulty when looking at some of the Quarter-Sessions Papers of the City and County of Bristol for the 18th century. Unfortunately the trade, occupation or calling of the jurors is not given together with their names.

The task of a grand jury was double: to try either by inquest and accusation, or by presentment; this second mode was different since it carried along with it the responsibilty of accusing one's neighbours, or 'peaching' on them, to speak like J. Gay in *The Beggar's Opera*. The definitions of Presentment and Indictment are made quite clear in Astry, H. Fielding (p. 22) Hawkins 1770 (p. 10). Accusing someone of swearing in public, of being drunk, of working on Sundays, of being a regular customer at late hours in an ale-house, or betting and gambling in a gaming-house, or worst of all, of being seen in a bawdy house, made the jury the guardians of public morality. H. Fielding did not hesitate to write: "Grand Juries, Gentlemen, are in Reality the only Censors of this Nation ...they are the Correctors of Manners..." (63). This was perhaps not a pleasant task, from our point of view; but apparently the subjects

[1] One only text gives the list of the members of the bench. One jury is a special jury of constables.

of Anne or of King George had no such scruples, since the jury were the most respectable members of the community, and they found in their self-righteousness the reason for denouncing any thing that was felt to be 'a breach of the peace.' Hawkins 1780 says *totiisdem verbis*, "to this extensive Jurisdiction,...the Law has added the Correction of the public Manners, and has given you Authority to inquire of and present Offences *contra bonos mores*..." p. 29. What does not appear in the *Charges* is the fact that an indictment invariably opened with the reciting of the facts for which a person was charged, followed by the formula: "For that thou, John Smith, of the parish of X..., not having the fear of God before thine eyes, didst on the ...nth day of... wilfully and feloniously commit the said crime..." No wonder if in the eyes of a few magistrates, crime and sin were still mingled into one and same notion of an offence "against the peace of the king, his crown and his dignity," that is against God. Thus some of these texts could appear to-day as regular handbooks of morals: Bulstrode 1, which denounced "prophane cursing and swearing, this great and crying Sin (p. 9)", 2, 3 against fornication. In many parishes of the kingdom grand juries regularly presented strolling actors as rogues and vagabonds, both out of fear of, and anger against, "the nurseries of the Devil," as the stage was called, but pursuant to the many Acts passed at least since the reign of Elizabeth. If charges have no positive trace of it (Bulstrode 1 (pp. 34–36), 3), presentments still subsist (for example in Bristol archives), showing how the magistrates endeavoured to discourage strolling actors from setting up their booth in their towns or cities by sending them to jail. So in the eyes of a few magistrates, the separation of the temporal (the King's justice) and the spiritual (considering every offence as a sin) was perhaps not quite so clear-cut as we might think it was.

Another characteristic of these texts is the regularity with which the magistrates all insisted on the rank, the wealth, the respectability of the men composing the grand juries. Whether they were impanelled for the grand jury of Quarter-Sessions or for that of Oyer and Terminer, these documents bear out other opinions on the flattering position of a grand jury man, by comparison with that of petty juror. It was not so much the fact of being addressed as 'Gentlemen' by the magistrate, as the being reminded that they were men of substance, rank, position, influence and experience. Obviously, those impanelled to sit on the grand jury were those in the forefront of local and communal life.[1]

The *Charges* will also reveal the at times incredible catalogue of offences and the corresponding punishments from the end of the 17th to the last years of the 18th centuries. Reading some of these pages in detail will reveal how antiquated the whole fabric was and remained (until the

[1] Cf J. S. Cockburn & Th. A. Green, *Twelve Good Men and True*... (Princeton U.P., 1988) ch. 9 & 10, passim.

Victorian era), leaving behind it this infamous name in English history of the Bloody Code. Any reader familiar with E. P. Thompson's study *Whigs and Hunters* will remember the development of criminal legislation in the course of the 18th century, and the severe punishment meted out for a sometimes trifling offence: the Riot Act, the systematic transportation for a theft under twelve pence, the gallows for a theft of £ 2, etc.[1] The comparison of the number of pages devoted to capital offences, and the not capital ones, is particularly revealing in the case of Gonson and his contemporaries. Only a systematic study over the years of such records as are preserved for Q-S and Oyer and Terminer, such as The Old Bayley proceedings, could show if the number of persons charged with offences, the nature of the offences, corresponded to the increase permanently denounced by the partisans of an ever greater severity towards offenders.[2] In relation to the punishment of offences against private property, the number of the definitions of attacks against it, stealing 'from the person', 'putting him in fear,' or in a house, at night or in the day-time, etc. has much to say for the care with which private property was defended, and thus *de facto* made more sacred (Burke, 14: "Property was declared to be sacred," Grose, 9) than the life of a man. Indeed, when comparing the price to be paid for a small theft (hanging) and for a wilful murder, the obvious conclusion is, that there was no scale of punishment proportioned to the nature of the offence. If readers of *Moll Flanders* have known this for a long time, they will find here the reason why it was so. The three main headings under which all offences were classed were: against God and his Church, against the King, his family, his government, and his servants in the broadest sense of the term; against one's fellow-subjects, including attempts against the life, property and honour of one's neighbour. This division, first to be found in Astry's general Charge not given here, is taken up again in nearly every text (Bulstrode, Cowper, Ryder, Dolins, Gonson, Henry & John Fielding), except in Guildford 1736 and ff. where there are reduced to two: "moral and civil justice." Moral justice includes cursing, swearing, breaking the Sabbath, drunkenness, bawdry, and all offences against the Church of England; civil justice comprises of necessity all the rest. In fact, many a magistrate made drunkenness a leading factor of criminality and denounced it as an abominable vice, the origin of many others and at the root of all crimes (Cocks 1, Guilford 1738, 1741 'crying immorality')[3].

[1] E.P. Thompson, *Whigs and Hunters*, 1975 (Peregrine Books edition, 1977).

[2] In this field statistical data are nearly impossible to obtain; the 18th century figures collected by Sir Theodore Janssen were destroyed during World War II; see G. Lamoine, ed., *Bristol Gaol Delivery Fiats 1741–1799* (Bristol Record Society, vol. XL, 1989), and *Littérature et justice pénale en Angleterre au 18e siècle* (Paris: Didier-Erudition, 1987), iv, 132–37.

[3] Before the act of Parliament passed under James I so often quoted hereafter, there had been attempts at legislating (e.g. in Coventry and York) "against the preference of the

Hawkins 1770 counts two sorts of offences only, those capital or those finable, the latter including imprisonment. The magistrate who delivered the Charge at Berwick (1754) insisted on the necessity of eliminating perjury, as particularly obnoxious to the functioning of justice, since accusers and witnesses were on oath.[1] He also gives interesting definitions of 'assault, 'battery', and 'affrays', and a more unexpected one of 'riot' (it concerned three persons...), since the 1714 Riot Act construed it felony for *twelve* people or more to assemble. The numerous sorts of thieving make a rather impressive list of offences and, naturally enough, against this there was one of corresponding punishments. Needless to say, to-day we do not understand the necessity of such cruel and useless repression as then existed, but the century had not yet grasped the simple reality that the social structure of the time was responsible for most of its criminality, in spite of Defoe's repeated warnings from the point of view of a potential social danger, and that of religious justice between Christian men and brethren. Later on, the translation of Beccaria's small book does not seem to have had a real influence on those who could modify and improve the judicial system

The *Charges* will also reveal to readers not familiar with the books by B. & S. Webb or more modern studies, or with W. Lambarde's *Eirenarcha* (1581) the sometimes overburdening task of the Jury: they had to be informed of the state of the county, hundreds and various parishes. They had to present such parishes as did not repair or keep up their streets, bridges and highways, pavements, hedges and ditches; the London ones had to think of the cleansing of the bed of the Thames, of being severe to coachmen driving to the public danger; other juries were reminded that the streets of Dublin were encumbered with the litter resulting from pulling down old houses and building new ones. The administration of the Poor Law, although in the hands of the Overseers of the Poor and the Churchwardens, also concerned the Grand Jury in more than one way, and Foley's texts are illuminating in this respect, for they show both the influence that the Jurors could exert as private individuals, and the official control that they had to keep over the whole process. These latter texts are particularly interesting insofar as they are a mixture of the judicial, the administrative, and the humane points of view. Particular attention is brought to the balance between a necessary control, so as not to waste the parochial funds, and the generosity of the attitude recommending positive and preventive action in the interests of the poor, and not only in those of the ratepayers. The fact that no other text gives

---

'poorest sorte' ' to sytte all daye in halehouse...' " cf D.M. Palliser, *The Age of Elizabeth* (Longman, 1983) iii, 62.

[1] H. Fielding had already denounced perjury and false witnesses in his *Enquiry into the Causes of the late Increase of Robbers*, only a few years earlier.

as much thought to the poor and the application of the Law in their favour does not bear out the genuine attention contained in Foley's words; the time, money, and books devoted to the problem in the neighbouring county of Bristol until c.1825 will confirm the great care taken by the authorities concerned. Everyday life is also evoked with the serious problem of food, victualling, etc, on market-places and market-days, with the necessity of having weights and measures checked against possible fraud, that of preventing the prices of foodstuff from going up artificially by regrating, forestalling, etc. Such offences were abolished as such around 1835.

A number of other subjects can be found more or less recurrent in these pages. Politics and religious problems were inseparable, and some echoes of the older quarrels can be still heard on the subject.

Sir M.D., probably a fairly young man by 1688, alludes to marprelates, jesuits and Hooker. Although the last-mentioned name will be found, often quoted *passim*, marprelates and jesuits are strongly reminiscent of the late Elizabethan years, with the quarrels over *Martin Parprelate*, and the late anti-Catholic Acts of Elizabeth's reign. When the political problem of the succession after Anne became more acute, and Jacobite activities were a threat to the Settlement, Lovell mentioned again the danger of Papism, and so did Mountagu still later. Roman Catholicism being inseparable from the settlement, we also find appeals against the Pretender under the pen of Cocks (1 & 2), defending the right of Parliament to settle the crown, Cowper, Ryder; the later texts simply take it for granted that George II is the rightful king in spite of what can be said or written. Sir M.D. again overtly mentions Charles I as the martyr king, being the only one to do so in these terms. Only Witton, in a rather unexpected manner, strongly criticised Oliver Cromwell, the regicides, and the régime of the Commonwealth.

The jurors and the audience were read a number of official texts at each session; two at least are mentioned here: the king's commission appointing so-and-so to sit at Q-S, or to take the assize, that is, to be a judge of Oyer and Terminer and general gaol delivery (Mountagu); if only one document alludes to it, it was a compulsory practice, without which the trial could be halted on the ground of a technical flaw. More often shall we find that the queen's or the king's proclamation was read in public (Astry, quoting Q. Anne's text, Cocks 1, Cowper, Mountagu, Guilford 1741, Aston, Marriot) about the necessity of promoting virtue and discouraging vice and profaneness.[1] As for the later texts from 1792 onwards, their object being partly to wage a psychological war against Paine and his supporters, naturally enough reading the king's proclamation "against seditious pamphlets" and other wicked books was part

[1] For which texts see infra.

of the ritual: Jodrell, wishing the jury to suppress libels called it "the triumph of law over the efforts of sedition (12)". Whatever the date, we may note that jurors were always invited to suppress anti-governmental publications, in spite of the 'liberty of the press' so much boasted of (Gonson 3, Guilford 1738, "seditious libels against government"). The line was drawn at an overt opposition to the policy of the country and the social fabric of the time, and to write, as Paine had done, that the British Parliament did not really represent the whole of the population, was not to avail oneself of the liberty of the press, but high-treason. Mainwaring mentions two proclamations, that of 21 May 1792, and one of December 1793 on the same subject. The part conclusion drawn by Cocks 1, that religious-minded and God-fearing subjects were law-abiding citizens, is to be seen in the same light. Sir William Ashhurst's text was found so convincing, that it was translated even into Welsh to be distributed in that language.

One last note about the post-1792 texts is that they read like copies of one text, distributed over the counties of England, written as if by one hand to be repeated by many mouths. There was in fact one text, most likely copies of it being sent out by the government to each county, to be delivered in public:

> His Majesty has commanded his J.P.s to address the several Grand Juries throughout his Kingdom at this present general Quarter-Session...,

the Rev. S. Partridge said on 14 Jan. 1793. This further corresponds to the contents of the Proclamation issued "the 21st of May 1792, at the Court of the Queen's House,"[P.R.O. P.C. 2 / 137, pp. 26-28]:

> Whereas divers wicked and seditious writings have been printed, pubished, and industriously dispersed, tending to excite Tumult and disorder by endeavouring to raise groundless Jealousies and Discontents... in the Minds of our faithful and loving subjects...
>
> We therefore being resolved, as far as in Us lies, to suppress the wicked and seditious Practices aforesaid, and to deter all Persons from following so pernicious an Example, have thought, by the advice of our Privy Council, to issue this Our Royal Proclamation, solemnly warning all our loving Subjects,
>
> And we strictly charge and command All our Magistrates in and throughout our Kingdom of Great-Britain, that they do make diligent Enquiry in Order to discover the Authors and Printers of such wicked and seditious writings......

It is certain that orders were sent out under the direction of Lord Grenville; but if no copy of this letter could be traced, scores of answers to it can be read in the Home Office Papers, (P.R.O., H.O. 42/22;

f. 516): one example is the letter from the Earl of Mount Edgecumbe, 25 Nov. 1792,

My Lord,
I have had the honor to receive your Lordships letter of the 24th communicating his Majesty's directions relative to the Charge to be given to the Grand Jury at the next Quarter Sessions of the Peace for the County of Cornwall, on the subject of the seditious writings so industriously spread about, which command shall be punctually obey'd.
Your Lordship shall be furnish'd with as accurate a List as I can promise, of the separate Jurisdictions.
I have the honor to be with great respect,
My Lord, Your Lordships
Most obedient and most humbe Servt.
Right Hon[ble] Lord Grenville &c.

In the same box 42 / 22 there could be found f. 531, a letter from Hatfield, 26 Nov. 1792, beginning with: "In obedience to HMs commands...", and it will also supply the list of acting magistrates; f. 533 from W. Bullocks, Clerk of the Peace for Essex, that will send the list of separate jurisdictions; f. 554, from the Earl of Upper Ossory, Aysthill Park, 27 Nov. 92: "communicating to me H.Ms information concerning the renewal of the circulation of wicked and seditions writings, and also the King's directions that it should be given in charge to the Grand Jury at the next ensuing Quarter Session of the peace for the County of Bedford, to make enquiry and presentments thereof; in order that the Authors, Printers, publishers and Distributors of all such wicked and seditious writings as aforesaid, may be severally dealt with for their said offences according to law...;" f. 565 from Earl Stamford, Envil, 28th Nov. 92: "I have order'd copies of it to be transmitted to all the acting magistrates in the County of Chester...;" f. 569, from the Earl of Radnor, at Grafton St., 28 Nov.; f. 594, from the Duke of Dorset, 29 Nov.; f. 596, from Lord Viscount Bateman, Shabdon, 29 Nov.; f. 610, from the Earl of Bute, 29 Nov.; f. 614–17, from Lord Digby, Sherborne Castle [Dorset] 30 Nov., together with a list of boroughs, Hundreds and Liberties; f. 617, from the Earl of Hardwick, New Cavendish St., Nov. 30, "My Lord, I had the honour of your Lordship's letter a few days since, and in order to apprise the Farmers and Yeomanry of the County, of whom the Juries at the Quarter Session are composed, of the wish of Government and of the expediency of presenting the distributors of seditious publications, I sent it to the Printer of the County Paper..."

In Box H.O. 42/23 similar letters are to be found: f. 107, 3 Dec. 92, from John Vaughan, Esq., Golden Grove; f. 126, 4 Dec. from the Duke of Bolton, Hackwood, Southampton, together with nine such other letters respectively from the Duke of Marlborough, the Chester Clerk of the Peace for the County, the Earl of Berkeley, Earl Poulett, the Earl of Hertford, the Mayors of Canterbury (with an issue of *The Kentish Gazette*, n°2552, giving the text of the Royal Proclamation of 1 Dec.), and of Yarmouth, the Duke of Beaufort, the Mayor of Wycombe. There can therefore subsist no doubt as to the origin of the texts, and we know that they were either hand copied or printed and sent to the chairman of each court of Q-S, and that they were even inserted in the local newspapers for everybody to be informed.

The *Charges* delivered by the Rev. Foley in Gloucester contain similar allusions to riots, obviously provoked by problems of the price of food and other provisions, and difficulties connected with the poor, with wages and the hardships brought about by severe winters, and a scarcity of grain. But various printed sources were scanned in vain for reference to these riots in Gloucestershire.

The *Charges* very often request the jury to enquire into the ways and doings of petty officers such as constables or watchmen in parishes, and jailers, bailiffs, etc. with a special concern for extortion of fees: this was current malpractice throughout the kingdom at least before the publication of J. Howard's *State of the Prisons*, and repeated efforts throughout the 18th century could not really eradicate this particular failure of the system (Bulstrode 1). The same text Bulstrode 1 is the first to note that witchcraft is no longer to be considered as a major offence from the penal point of view, which indicates an evolution of English thought on this painful problem.

Gonson 1 (5), Aston (23: "restraining this Inquiry to the reading of certain written Papers", Day 2), invited the jury *not* to be satisfied in their enquiry on the possible guilt of a prisoner, with written depositions and affidavits, but insisted on the necessity of a public oral examination. This was consistent with the idea that justice was not to be hidden behind veils, as in France, but rendered in open light. Now it is interesting that the same request to a jury should be made at nearly seventy years' distance, and in two different towns, since apparently the said practice was still being carried on in both kingdoms. It would be left for a specialist to say whether this was often to be found, where, and why. The most usual sources of information of the time do mention the use of written records admissible in court as evidence, but on the understanding that they were written proofs; they are not mentioned as being the transcript of previous oral evidence given before the committing magistrate, or as a letter instead of the witness in person. [1]

[1] See G. Jacob, *New Law Dictionary*, under: evidence, examination: "the Accusers must be bound to appear and give Evidence at the next Assise, & to which the Examinations must

The role of the judges is explained in more detail in a few texts (Astry, Lovell, and others) as differing from that of the jury on legal grounds; the late post-1792 texts give a different ring: the magistrate invites the jury to side with him, the governement and the nation, in order to suppress the seditious libels, pamphlets etc that infest the country, in favour of Paine's ideas and book. They depart from the traditional attitude of non-commitment of the judge in front of the jury. Special circumstances called for special attitudes, adapted to the times.

A few odd notes can be met on various subjects. Cocks 2, three years after the event had taken place, commented on the failure of the South-Sea Bubble. William Cann fully expatiated on the rights and liberties of the Englishman, which may be understandable since Bristol, as a County in its own right, enjoyed the privilege of having not only a Court of Q-S, but of Oyer & Terminer and General Gaol Delivery. Sir John Gonson gave very precise explanations on the statute of high treason (25 Edw. III), Dolins on the offences made capital by statute or being so at Common Law. J… P… in 1736, under the government of Robert Walpole,wrote that England was prosperous, a land of plenty. In the same year, the magistrate of Guildford made allusions to Property and Prerogative being abused as pretences for oppression and sedition. Was this a note about some social unrest or sleeping radicalism, or a timid note of social justice? Probably the same magistrate dismissed in a rather amusing hotch-potch of three sentences, towards the end of his text, all the offences consisting in criticism of the government, riots, forcible entries, public nuisances about the highways. It probably means that the texts as we have them in mss were rather memos than full texts, this being confirmed by the number of abbreviations and old-fashioned use of 'y^{e}' and 'y^{t}'. Henry Fielding enumerated several causes of offences and among them he assailed 'Balls, Assemblies, Fairs,' and all the luxurious forms of pleasure which abounded in the London of George II's reign. We find here what he expanded in his *An Enquiry into the Cause…* when he had more time and space to develop the argument to its full weight. But he could evidently not rank theatre-going as one of these causes, even if he showed himself careful of the morality of young people…

On the question of over numerous beggars in Dublin raised by Aston, a recent essay on the subject shows that the propensity of the poor to resort to the city was heightened by crop failures or other economic

be certified." – Evidence: "Is used in the law for some Proof, by Testimony of Men on Oath, or by Writings or Records." R. Burn, *The J.P. and Parish Officer*, 2 vols. (1755): I, 286–94, v: Of the manner of giving Evidence: 1.– The evidence both for and against a prisoner ought to be on oath. 4.– In cases of life, no evidence is to be given against a prisoner, but in his presence. 2 *Hawk.* 428. 7.– A witness shall not be permitted to read his evidence, but he may look upon his notes to refresh his memory. *St. Tr.* V, 4, 45."

factors. Now, 1763–64 (and 1766-67) were years of particular crisis, which may explain Aston's remark.[1] We could compare the notes made by Burke in Bristol, and Foley in Gloucester at the same time that the number of criminals to be tried was on the decrease, but that seems to be more of a coincidence than a tendency. Even if Burke remarked on the "regulated manners of the lower classes of Citizens," which implies that the upper classes could never be found at the bar of the Court, some of his wishes are well in keeping with the line policy of his family: religion and morals are the bases of civil peace, (therefore brothels should be closed down as source of immorality) and every pro-libertarian thought of the time ought to be suppressed. The last indication he supplies is that the Charge was delivered before the Bills be brought in for the jury to examine them.

More generally, a number of Charges contain one often-repeated notion, that the magistrates, the Legislature, and any other authority, have acted in such a way, or have taken such or such a decision, for 'the public good.' Probably no idea could be more specifically said to belong to the eighteenth century, than this notion of public good, which can be found in all sorts of literary texts such as *Gulliver's Travels*, to begin with. Whether to justify the protection of property, of order and peace in the kingdom, or to explain the necessity of having a government, of protecting the king and royal family from the crime of high treason, or the subject from the violence of the subject, everything was done in the name of that principle, the public good. It may sound oddly contradictory with the harsh punishments inflicted on individuals, to assume that transporting or hanging persons for the theft of one petticoat or a dozen handkerchiefs, was enforcing the notion of public good; but however critical we may be to-day of English society at the time, we have to bear in mind that society was seen as a whole, where even the poorest and most unfortunate subjects were taken into account, since the Poor Laws dealt with them. Hence the notion that the division between rich and poor was a reasonable balance to maintain. All depends on one's interpretation of the public good: was the public the whole body of the nation, was it only the ruling class, did it consist in the belief that individuals had to be protected fot the greater benefit of the collectivity? It seems that the several hypotheses are to be found in these pages. For the sake of truth in trials, the prisoner had no counsel; but 'the magistrate shall be counsel for the prisoner'; a convicted felon may be an abandoned wretch, a most profligate man, etc; but gaolers must not demand unjust fees from him. See the interest in a correct execution of the Poor Laws,

[1] See Joseph O' Carroll, "Contemporary Attitudes towards the Homeless Poor 1725–75," in D. Dickson, ed., *The Gorgeous Mask: Dublin 1700–1850* (Dublin, 1987) Information kindly supplied by the Assistant Librarian of King's Inn Library.

shown by the Rev. Foley. The question remains open. Nor should we forget the expression "a useful member of the community, [or] of society." In connection with the question of the Poor, it means that they must not be left idle when they could be useful by their work; it can also refer to some persons convicted, who should not be hanged, for they too could be useful by their work. This is to be found in the discussion on the uselessness of the death penalty, which deprives H.M. of as many subjects, who could, again, be reclaimed and be made "useful members...." One text deserves special attention for the clear exposition of the necessity of having a religious belief besides civil laws: Hawkins 1770 states, p. 22, that civil punishments are not strong enough to prevent men from committing offences and crimes, and that the fear of a punishment in the other world is a powerful deterrent. We might conclude that by 1770 people, including acting magistrates, were convinced that the death penalty was no longer useful as a warning against offending. Alas, it had long ceased to be so, and the whole century witnessed the debates between the partisans of a very few executions, duly carried out when passed on the criminals, and those who wanted hanging *en masse*, in order to show more examples. Without reflecting in the least on the author's own morals or piety, it might also be taken as a sign that religion was no longer viewed as the Word of God, but as a psychological means of keeping the King's peace, on top of the man-made laws. The rest of the passage ending p. 24, saying that it is the civil magistrate's interest to promote the interests of religion, and the mention of political reasons, seems to take the reader far away from purely religious grounds. But Hawkins's words would probably not be construed in this way at the time. At last, his text of 1780 seems also to imply that private morality is at the lowest, since religion needs the public support of the state: without this support, "it is much to be questioned whether we should have any Religion at all".

Note on the text

The texts have been carefully reprinted as they were, together with their title-pages. In some cases, a few things have been slightly altered or added, such as page numbers when the orignal ones were obviously wrong; original misprints were retained and shown as such. In the case of the Stamford Speech, the very long Latin quotations have not been given, since he gave the English translation for them. In Norfolk 1749–56, a great many difficulties could not be solved, and guesses or tentative transcriptions are sometimes the only solution. There has been no suppression of ye and yt, etc. in the old manuscript form. One alteration is, that of printing '£' what is written 'l' or 'lb'. Otherwise the mss texts were transcribed such as they are, abbreviated words not being fully developed. In all cases the original page sequence is shown between [ ].

Two series of texts created some difficulty in ascertaining their correct dates: those in Norwich manuscripts, and those by the Rev. Foley. For the first series, only the handwritten notes can be followed as to the years, but not always as to the particular sessions, since no printed version can establish any date of publication. For the latter series the printed edition does give dates, but there are obvious discrepancies (see footnotes), and the early nineteenth-century editor was aware of the difficulty of giving correct dates for each text. Because I have not been able to be more positive than he, I will only make suppositions, based on the fact that in Gloucester, the dates of the sessions were as follows:

	1797	1798	1801
Epiphany	10-12th Jan.	9-11th Jan.	13-16th Jan.
Easter	25th April	17-18th April	14-16th April
Trinity	11th July	10-12th July	14-16th July
Michaelmas	3rd October	2-4th October	6-8th October.

References to the sovereigns' proclamations are to be found in various Charges. In order to avoid repetitions, here are the texts alluded to in brief:

William and Mary: *A Proclamation for preventing & punishing Immorality & Prophaneness*... (24. 02. 1698, repeated 09. 12. 1699)

Anne: *A Proclamation for the Encouragement of Piety & Virtue, & for the Preventing & Punishing of Vice*, 26. 03. 1702; *A Proclamation for the Encouragement of Piety & Virtue, & for the Preventing & Punishing of Vice, Prophaneness & Immorality*, 25. 02. 1703.

George I: The King's Proclamation: *By the King.A Proclamation for the Encouragement of Piety & Virtue*, ... 05. 01. 1715; reprinted 1727.

George II: *By the King. A Proclamation for the Encouragement of Piety & Virtue*, ...05. 07. 1727.

George III: *A Proclamation for the Encouragement of Piety & Virtue, & for the Preventing & Punishing of Vice, Prophaneness & Immorality*, 31. 10. 1760; 01. 06. 1787; another edition, 1806, 1817.

H. M.'s Proclamation of the 21st of May, 1792 against seditious writings...etc.

The authors

The magistrates who delivered these Charges could be classed into two groups at least: those who were trained lawyers (judges, serjeants-at-law), and those who had no professional background. The latter are by far the more numerous; they were men who, by their wealth, influence and/or connections, social position in their own county or towns, and their interest in public affairs, were naturally appointed J.P.s by the government. Some of them were also M.P.s, which means that they had a fairly comprehensive view of political, public and administrative life. Within this group we also find laymen and clergymen. But the texts here given are not quantitatively representative of the whole century, for there was a fairly large number of reverend magistrates on the benches of counties and large cities (and this increasingly as the century drew on), to which newspapers, novels and plays will bear witness.

Rather surprisingly, for some of those who did not play a prominent part in public life otherwise, it is difficult to find detailed biographical information. In the cases of the three mss batches, only guesses can be offered, since there is no certainty as to the handwriting: was it the author's, or a clerk's or a copist's? Even in the Greater London Record Office and History Library, little information could be found on the curricula of Middlesex magistrates. For those who, through various circumstances, found their way in to the columns of the *Dictionary of National Biography*, or Burke's *Peerage* or *Baronetcies of England...*, the reader is requested to see the corresponding pages. Here is given only the scantiest information necessary to situate the magistrates in the century.

Sir M. D: the suggestion made by the Library of Gray's Inn is that he was Sir Marmaduke Carrell, called to the bar in 1680, an 'Ancient' of Gray's Inn in 1688, and a Bencher in 1701. We should rather think of Sir Matthew Dudley, of Clapton, Northamptonshire (the only son of Sir William, b. 1597, d. 1670) second baronet in 1670. By 1683 he was sheriff of Northamptonshire. See J. Swift, *Journal to Stella*, ed. H. Williams, 2 vols. (Oxford: Clarendon Press, 1963). I, 11 & index, passim. A "violent Whig" in Swift's own terms.

Earl of Stamford (1654–1720) *D. N. B.*

Nicholas Corsellis (1661–1728). Lincoln College, Oxford, 1679; Lincoln's Inn, 1687; represented Colchester in Parliament, 1714–15. Lord of the manors of Wivenhoe and Layer Marner. See *The Essex Review*, vol. xviii, "The Corsellis Legend", by the Rev. A. Clark; G.M.G. Cullum, "Pedigree of... Corsellis" (*Misc. Gen. Hist.*. 5th ser. i (1916) 6.)

Norfolk 1709–11: possibly Ashe Widham, M.P., of Felbrigg, (c. 1671/72–1749).

Sir Salathiel Lovell (1619–1713) *D. N. B.*

Sir Richard Cocks, 4th baronet, of Dumbleton, b.circa. 1658 (?) succeeded his grandfather, sat for his county in 3 successive parliaments, was High Sheriff of Gloucestershire in 1692, was Deputy-Lieutenant for the county in 1694; was engaged in the Bangorian controversy c. 1720. See J.V.

Somers Cocks, *A History of the Cocks Family*, part 4, 98–101.

Whitelocke Bulstrode, (1650–1724) *D.N.B.*

William Cowper, ?

James Mountagu, (1673/4–d. 1747), of Lackham in Lacock, an active J.P. in 1736.

Samuel Ryder

Sir Daniel Dolins, d. 22 April 1728, of Hackney, J.P. for Midlesex. See: W.A.Shaw, *The Knights of England,* (1906) vol. 2, 282.; A. Boyer, *The Political State of G-B,* (1728) vol. 35, 415.

Sir John Gonson, called to the bar of the Inner Temple, 3 July 1715; knighted 14 May 1722; a J.P. for Westminster; d. 7 Jan. 1765. *London Magazine*, vol. 34, p. 54; Shaw, ut supra; *A Calendar of the Inner Temple Records*, vol. 4, p. 8. Probably represented in one of Hogarth's plates of *The Harlot's Progress.*

Sir William Cann, d. 28 March 1753. Succeeded his brother Sir Robert, High Sheriff of Gloucestershire, in 1748; 27 Feb. 1720–21, steward of the court of the Sheriff's or Tolzey court; resigned his stewardship on being appointed Town Clerk in July 1731. From 1743 (Latimer, 253, gives Nov. 1744), incapacitated by illness until his death. *Felix Farley's Bristol Journal* for 24–31 March 1753, "Yesterday died in an advanced Age, at his Seat at Clifton, Sir William Cann, Bart. Town-Clerk of this City; which Place he enjoy'd upward of twenty Years." A. Beaven, *Bristol Lists: municipal and miscellaneous* (Bristol, 1909) 235, 237, 281.

J... P...: unidentifiable.

Guilford 1736: Perhaps Sir William More-Molyneux of Loseley (1690–1760), made a J.P. by 9 Aug. 1720. It is possible that he also wrote the 1748 and Post 1757 ones, but they may have been copied by a menial.

Richard Witton: connected with the Milner family by marriage, 1713; see C. R. Markham, *The great Lord Fairfax* (London, 1870).

Henry (and Sir John) Fielding: (1707–54) – Sir John: (1721–80). *D.N.B.*

Norfolk 1749–67: presumably Jacob Preston of Beeston St. Lawrence (d. 1753) and/or his son Isaac (d. 1768).

Sir Richard Aston: (1717–78). *D.N.B.* But an interesting point is, that he was noticed for his unremitting attempts at preventing the jury from relying on written depositions, instead of oral examinations of witnesses. The practice remained unaltered until 1836. F. Erlington Ball, *The Judges in Ireland*, 1221–1921 (London: 1926), vol.II, 148–49.

Sir James Marriott: (1730?–1803). *D.N.B.* See D.A. Winstanley, *The University of Cambridge in the 18th Century*, C.U.P., 1958,. pp. 66–7, 130–32, 271–81, 282–97.

Sir John Hawkins: (1719–89) *D.N.B.*

William Mainwaring ?

Charles Partridge: (1750–1817); Obituary in *Gentleman's Magazine*, vol. 87, part 2, 186, 198. Foster, *Alumni Oxinienses,* 1715–1886, vol. 3 p. 1077. Corpus Christi, Oxford 1768, a demy of Magdalen College 1771–74, a fellow of that college 1774–82. BA 1772, MA 1775; 1785, was instituted to the vicarage of Boston, and in 1797 also held that of Wigtoft-cum-Quadring. Was Chairman of Q-S for the Hundreds of Kirton and Skirbeck.

Robert Day: (1746–1841). See F. Erlington Ball, II, 181–82, 229. A student of law at Dublin University, 1761, Middle Temple 1764, B.A. 1766, called to the Bar 1774, doctor of law 1780; a member for Tuam, 1783; chairman of the Q-S in Dublin County 1790, king's counsel 1790, King's Bench 1798, when he attended the special commission after the 1798 rebellion.

The Rev. Roger Jacson ?

Henry Jodrell: (1750–1814). Born at Duffield?; lived at Bayfield Hall, Norfolk. 1797 elected MP for Great Yarmouth, 1802, 1806, 1807 sat for Bramber. Appointed Recorder of Great Yarmouth in 1792 on the recommendation of the member of the borough; "Jodrell is the fittest person you can have: he has for some years past acquitted himself with credit as one of the chairmen of the Q-S. He is of a very quiet and obliging disposition." In 1813 he resigned his office so that he should not have to pass sentence of death on a man tried for the murder of his wife. Ch.J. Palmer, *The History of Great Yarmouth* (Great Yarmouth, L. A. Meall, 1856).

Lord Chedworth: (1754–1804) *D.N.B.*

Charles Harvey ?

Richard Burke: (1733–94)

Sir James Eyre: (1734–99) *D. N. B.*

Lord Kenyon: (1732–1802) *D. N. B.*

Thomas Bayley: b. 1744 of a Nonconformist Manchester family, educated at Edinburgh; corresponded with J. Wilkes, whose principles on justice he retained; his influence must have been considerable: since Manchester had no Q-S., the Salford justices tried the city's criminal cases. He must have died c. 1802, since *Biographical Memoirs of the late Th.B. Bayley, Esq...* were published in Manchester, 1802. See Margaret De Lacy, *Prison Reform in Lancashire, 1700-1850*, Chetham Society, vol. 33, 3rd series (Manchester 1986) 70-73, & 240 for bibliographical sources.

Denis George: (circa 1753?–1821). called to the bar Dublin, 1776, Recorder of Dublin 1785, a baron of the Exchequer, 1798.

Sir Nash Grose: (1740–1814) *D. N. B.*

Henry Gwillim: (1760?–1837) chief justice of the Isle of Ely in 1794. Probably born in Hereford; Christchurch College, Oxford, 1776; BA 1779, MA 1783; a barrister at Middle Temple from 1787; a judge at Madras, knighted in 1808. Cf T. Bentham, *Abbey and Convent of Ely,* (1812) II, 39: "Sir Henry Gwyllim knight, one of his Majesty's judges of the Supreme Court and was appointed Chief Justice of the Isle by Bishop James Yorke on the resignation of Mr. Charles Yorke." Yorke was Bishop of St David's between 1774 and 1779 and one of the sons of Lord Chancellor Hardwicke. See the best account of the jurisdiction of the Bishops in the Isle, in Edward Miller, *Victoria County History of Cambridgeshire*, IV, 1-27.

The Rev. John Foley: (1745–28 Nov. 1803). Obituary: *Gloucester Journal*, Monday 5 December 1803, and *Gentleman's Magazine*, 1803, part 2, 1189. Fellow of Brasenose College; 1782, rector of Christ Church, Spitalfields, Middlesex. March 1782, vicar of Newent, Worcestershire, at the death of the Rev. Dr. Foley, Dean of Worcester. In the commission of the peace for the counties of Gloucester, Worcester and Hereford. Deputy-Lieutenant for Gloucestershire, and one of the chairmen of the Q-S.

"He possessed a very accurate knowledge of the Statute laws of his country, with the adjudged cases thereon; ... the seasonable and humane charges to the Grand Juries,... his benevolent and unremitting endeavours for the good of his fellow-creatures ..." *Gloucester Journal,* Monday 30 Jan. 1797, "It is with pleasure that the Rev. Mr. Foley, Chairman of our late Quarter-Sessions, has consented to the publication of his charge, in compliance with the unanimous wish of the Bench." *Oxford Alumni, 1715–1886*, p. 473: matriculated 22.5.1760, aged 15; BA 1764, MA 1766, proctor 1777.

The text for *Berwick* bears no indication, and it has not been possible to identify its author.

If biographical data are at times scarce on the authors of these pages, it seems that behind their official masks, behind the legal jargon which Swift railed at so much, we may come to know the men a little better, and their preoccupations with the difficulty of maintaining the king's peace and order in their respective towns, cities or counties. Their wish to reduce religious differences, even it often boiled down to conformity, to rally around their king, to preserve the existing social order sometimes at the price of so many sufferings and deaths in order to protect private property, the wish to preserve, according to Edmund Burke's formula, 'mores majorum' after 1792, should not make them only servants of the crown and the government. The most remarkable amongst them did try and bring Parliament to deal with problems left over from previous reigns and generations; their humane treatment of the poor shows that they were men, with their foibles and qualities. Because they transcribed into legal technicalities the links between the Crown and the subjects in an important period of English history, these texts are worth reading today. They also represent part of a code of the multifarious types of human relations between all categories of subjects, irrespective of their rank, class and level of fortune on the one hand, and between the men of property and the less wealthy on the other hand; they therefore assist us in reading with more profit and insight other documents which help us understand the relations existing between neighbour and neighbour, between husband and wife, master and servant, such as the proceedings of the Old Bailey or of other courts, gaol delivery fiats and Oyer and Terminer, nisi prius records, or records of quarter sessions of the peace, wherever they still exist, at a time when society grew more and more complex in the organisation of its relations. Since now historians are rightly more preoccupied than their predecessors with the study of human relations within groups, they might help make students more familiar with this aspect of English civilisation in the 18th century, and be considered as complementary documents to the understanding of social history on the one hand, and of literature and other aspects of Great Britain in that fascinating age.

A CHARGE AT **The General Quarter Sessions of the Peace** Held for **The COUNTY of CAMBRIDGE,** AT **The Castle of** *Cambridge*, On Thursday the seventeenth day of January, Anno Domini 1688/9. **By Sir *M. D.* of *Grey* 's -Inn.**[1]

Li. *Non desunt Theologi qui ad tumultus Classicum canant.*

Ge. *Istos ego statuerem in prima Acie.* Erasm.[2] Licensed Febr. the 1st. 1688/9 *London* printed for *Randal Taylor* near *Stationers-hall*, *Anno Dom.* 1689.

Gentlemen

The great occasion of our meeting here is, for Preservation of the Peace in matters Ecclesiastical as well as Civil: By matters Ecclesiastical is meant matters of the Church, and by the Church is meant the Church of *England* as 'tis by Law Established in this Kingdom, the Constitutions of which are undoubtedly the best of any now in practice in any other part of the Christian World, as coming nearest to that Forme of divine Worship which was taught by our Blessed Saviour and his Apostles, and which indeed is a Member of that very Church which was at Unity with it self for some Centuries after Christ's Ascension, as making the whole Scriptures the Rule of our Faith; as believing and acknowledging for Orthodox, the Doctrines of the prime Primitive Fathers, and the Four first General Councils.

It were mightily to be wondred at, how it should come to pass that such Disorders afterwards should arise, were it not that it pleased God for the sins of mortal Men, in after Ages (as it appears he did the ***JEWS*** in the Old Testament) to suffer them to follow their own wicked Imaginations.

The first moving steps to those Confusions that seem obvious to humane understanding, were, That the Christians in succeeding times growing very Conversant with the Writings of the Ancient heathen Philosophers, learnt thereby very subtle ways of Cavellling and Disputing with one another about empty Notions and Uncertainties, and by degrees falling from those Nicer Speculations, they came to make Religion the Subject matter of their Debates; the Consequence of that *Disputandi pruritus* was soon found to be *Ecclesiæ Scabies*; for, those of them that vainly assumed to themselves Conquest in Disputation [3] afterwards, boldly took upon them to work Innovations in Religion, and broaching new Doctrines never heard of in the Primitive Church, giving out at the same time, that the Holy Sciptures onely could not make Men wise enough

[1] Sir Matthew Dudley. See Introd., Notes on Authors.

[2] *Opera Omnia D. Erasmi Rotterdami*, 13 vols.Amsterdam: North Holland Pub. C°, 1969-83. Vol. III, ed. Halkin, Bierlaire, Hoven, *Familiaria Colloquia*, "Alia", p. 135: "Livinus: Imo non desunt theologi, qui frigidam suffundant, et ad hos tumultus classiam canant."

to Salvation, but we must take along with us these Wild Notions to help us in our way to Heaven.

Now, I say, why these Enthusiastick Dreams or pretended Traditions of fancifull Men, warranted by nothing but their own Authorities, should crowd in amongst us, and become Articles of our Christian Faith, I confess is beyond my poor Capacity to comprehend.

But as it is a sad and serious Truth, that these false Doctrines have for many Ages influenced that part of the Christian Church which is grown to a proud and mighty Empire, so it is as true that the ways and means used to aggrandize this Power has been, as our Histories very plentifully tell us, through the most horrible Rapines, the most grievous Bloudsheds, the most dreadfull Persecutions imaginable; a deep Consideration of which, caused a noble Historian of ours to declare, that Certainly there was nothing more to be lamented, than the private Contention, the passionate Dispute, the personal Hatred, and the perpetual War, Massacres and Murthers, for Religion among Christians.

With us begun our famous Reformation or Re-establishing of the old Religion amongst us (though the ground work laid in the preceeding Reign) in the time of KING *EDWARD* the Sixth, through the greatest Care of that Excellent Prince, and the very Reverend and Learned Prelates of those times; Cherished it was with very happy Progressions during his short Reign, but suddenly again Eclipsed by QUEEN *MARY*'s coming to the Throne. Every one has heard, and therefore [4] I shall not need repeat the bloudy persecutions and prosecutions of those times. Let it therefore suffice to say, that many to avoid the Cruelties inflicted then on Protestants were forced to leave their native Countrey and seek shelter abroad for safety of their Lives. But this Reign likewise being but short, our Religion was restored again with full strength and vigour by that ever Renowned QUEEN *ELIZABETH*.

Now every Man had it in his power to be happy, in enjoying the blessed Sun-shine and Tranquility of a peacefull Regimen; but such it seems were the Iniquities even of those times, that the restless Spirits of some Men, and especially of those that were returned fome from their places of refuge abroad, that they began to preach forth certain new-fangled Doctrines, which they had pick'd up in a foreign Countrey, and to set them in opposition to the established Religion.

In ANSWER, and to appease, if possible, these MARPRELATES[1], who were full of petulant Disputation, and Contention, arose Reverend Mr. *Hooker*,[2] and with his learned and judicious Pen stated the whole Matter, that those things, as he says, might not pass as in a Dream.

[1] An allusion to the Martin Marprelate Tracts, 1588-9, a scurrilous and hilarious indictment of the bishops by Puritan anonymous writers.

[2] Richard Hooker (1554?-1600), author of *Of the Laws of Ecclesiastical Politie*, 1594-97.

It must not be omitted, that the PRIESTS and JESUITS would be sure to put in for their share, and whose Disciples 'tis possible some of the former were; therefore with most indefatigable Industry they lay'd about them, though all their desperate Attempts, as well as private Insinuations, as their other Plots and Contrivances, then proved ineffectual.

Against these *Boutefeus*[1] the Wisedom of those times thought it necessary to enact sanguinary Laws, which, if they had been at all times since strictly executed upon them, might have prevented many bitter Troubles that have happened since. [5

I cannot leave them without remembring what *Machiavel* writes in his Letter to *Zenobio*, that if Princes shall Perform this Business by halves, and leave any root of this CLERGY or PRIEST-CRAFT as it now is in the ground, or if they do not wholly extirpate this sort of Men, then I must foretell, that they will find themselves deceived in their Expectations, and that the least *Fibra* of this Plant will overrun against the whole Vineyard of the Lord.

Thus we see in this transitory World it has not been possible, even in the best of these later times, for our Holy Religion to move on a steddy and even Course, but that her Waters have been troubled with furious and tempestuous Blasts of Adversity.

But let us notwithstanding, every one in his station, resolve to hold fast to this Profession, which is likely to procure us an eternal Peace; let us in the future Course of our lives shew our selves True Christians, that thereby we may procure the Powers of Heaven to overshadow and protect us; let us, I say, hold fast to that Religion which our Learned KING *JAMES* the First made publick profession of in his Adress to all Christian Princes; which that ever blessed Saint in Heaven, KING CHARLES the First said he had fully tryed, and after much search concluded it to be the best in the world, and therefore charged his Son to persevere in it, as coming nearest to God's Word for Doctrine, and to the primitive Examples of Government; It teaches us how to grow in Vertue and Goodness; it instructs us in acts of Charity, Patience, Longsuffering, Loving and Bearing with the Infirmities of one another; let us therefore be at unity with our selves; one more let us all conform, I say, to the establish'd Government of our Church; let us for the future resolve to avoid all vain Dis-[6] putations and Scriblings; and let us persevere in the same, to the end that time may come which Reverend Mr. *Hooker* speaks of, when three words uttered with Charity and Meekness shall receive a far more blessed reward than three thousand Volumes written with disdainful sharpness of Wit.

I should now come to speak of the Civil Power or that Legal Admin-

[1] French = fire-brand.

istration of Justice peculiar to this Kingdom; which is *Jus suum cuique tribuere.*[1]

But there having been many Discourses of that nature formerly in this place by Gentlemen whose Learning and Abilities I have infinitely more reason to value than my own, I shall for this time spare you and my self that trouble,

Gentlemen,

You that are the Enquest for this County, &c.

[1] Lat. = to give every one his right.

THE **SPEECH** OF THE RIGHT HONOURABLE **THOMAS** EARL OF **STAMFORD,** Lord *Gray* of *GROOBY*, &c. AT THE General Quarter-Sessions held for the County of *LEICESTER*, at Michaelmas, 1690. His Lordship being made CUSTOS ROTULORUM for the said County by the Late Lord Commissioners of the Great Seal.

Non partum Studiis agimur, sed sumpsimus Arma.
Rode, Caper, Vitem, tamen hinc cum Stabis ad Aras,
In tua quod fundi, Cornus possit, erit.

LONDON: Printed for Richard Baldwin, near the Oxford-Arms in Warwick Lane. MDCXCII.

A 2

TO

ALL Impartial **READERS**.

THIS IS now principally Addressed to you, because I know you will read, not with biass'd Understanding, nor Minds preposs'd or warpt, but with unprejudiced Candour and Fairness; and will put that natural and genuine Construction on this most Noble Author's[1] *Speech, which, considering the sincerity of his Intentions, it ought to receive; which were (when it was spoken, and continues the same now it is Printed) no other than to support and justifie the Legal proceedings of the late Convention and Parliament, in the placing Their present Majesties on the Throne of their Ancestors, That being* (Ultimum necessitatis Praesidium, *as* Grotius'*s words are*, i.e. *) *the last Refuge in that extream Necessity the Government was then brought to, by Those **Evil Councellors, Judges and Ministers, who had been imployed by the Late King, to subvert and extirpate the Protestant Religion, and the Laws and Liberties of this Kingdom, in ways so open and violent, that (as* Suetonius *saith*) vix referri, audirive, nedum credi fas est, *it is scarce allowable either to be related, or heard, and much less to be believed.*

This was the Design, and the only Design (as his Lordship hath often assured me) of his giving this Charge at the general Quarter Sessions, to inform the Ignorant, to satisfy the then Scrupulous, and to convince, if possible, the Obstinate and Factious, and to bring them over to a hearty Submission and Obedience to the present Establishment.

But instead of meeting with this good effect designed, these last discontented and froward Gentlemen, still retaining their old Enslaving *Principles, or drinking in with them, the modern Conceits of some* Clergy-men, who are *fond of their*

[1] Thomas Gray, 2nd Earl of Stamford, 1654-1720. He was a friend of the first Earl of Shaftesbury, and one of the first noblemen to join William in Nottingham. In 1694 he was made a Privy Counsellor. After the accession of Queen Anne, he was dismissed from all his appointments and offices, but was made President of the Board of Trade, 1707–1711. This text is the first plea *in situ* (among this collection) in favour of all that the Glorious Revolution could represent, after the departure of James.

unintelligible Speculations, have industriously been labouring to asperse this Noble English *Peer (through their ignorance of our Government, not to say worse) under the false ignominious Character of a* Commonwealths-man; *and to misrepresent his Speech for a* Comble *of Republican Principles.*

This Impudent Aspersion has extended farther than the Bounds of that County wherein this Charge was given; His Lordship hath heard the same Traduction of him has slily been whispered in Royal Palaces.

This is a most wicked Piece of Malice in whosoever are guilty of it, and so much the more dangerous, the higher any are in Station, and the nearer to the Person of their Soveraign in their constant attendances on him; 'for those who have the Ear of the Prince, and are almost continually with him may by specious Informations and disguising Truths, influence him to approve or reject Persons and Things, according to their various Aspects given by them. Such will be sure only to have a Charity for themselves, that shall extend no farther than their own separate Interests; whosoever will not come overto them, and make their Paces, shall not fail to be blacken'd with any odious Name (be it that of a Commonwealths-man) *which they think will provoke a Prince against them.*

This is a bold Liberty indeed; but I would fain know if any one will say (after K. James *had withdrawn himself, and taken away the Seals with him) that his Lordship was a* Commonwealths-man, *in Voting the* Abdication, *and* Vacancy *of the Throne? Or in opposing the Regency so zealously as he did, and indeavouring to set HIM upon the Throne, who came and was successfull, in delivering this Nation from Popish Tyrany, and Slavery à la mode de France? Or in so strenuously labouring the* Bill *that afterwards* recognized and acknowledged *their Majesties to be our* Lawful *and* Rightful *Sovereigns*[1]*? (which to say, were in effect to say, That the resetling of a Legal Monarchy, when brought into Confusion, is to introduce a* Commonwealth). *And if these are not* Commonwealth Principles (*which say it who dare) I challenge any one to alledge any other grounds for so unworthy an Aspersion.*

*His Lordship's design by this Speech was, in my Opinion, to do a great deel of good, by setting People right in their understandings, as to Government, That *** Monarchy is not of meer* Divine Right, *but by* Humane Consent; *and by shewing them, that in all the steps to this happy Settlement, the* Assembled Estates *did govern themselves by the* Laws and Rules *of this* Ancient Constitution.

To do himself Right, His Lordship hath given me leave to Print it, with the Addition of these collected Authorities, *and if any will take Exceptions to the* Speech, *as not being consonant to our* Establishment, *and the Laws of* England; *I would desire them to answer the Notes in the* Appendix, *by which it is justified, so far forth as it can be pretended to be liable to the aforesaid Exceptions.*

I am sure all those, who have the Honour of a through Acquaintance with his Lordship, know very well this to be a just Character *of him, That He hath a most*

[1] Those two adjectives were an important constitutional point in the election of William and Mary as sovereigns. Cf p. 1 of the text itself.

Sacred Regard to Truth and Integrity in all the ways of his Conversation, and that, notwithstanding what he hath met with in the whole course of his Life, yet nothing could alienate him from the true Interests of his Prince and Countrey, *which not only gives a bright Lustre to his great Birth, but is a much more shining Grace and Ornament to his greater Life.*

Ipsa quidem Virtus precium sibi.

* Grot. de Jure Belli & Pacis. lib. I c. 4 n. 7.

** Act I W. and M. declaring the Rights and Liberties of the Subject, and Setling the Successors of the Crown. Sueton. in Vit. Tiber. n. 44.

***Dominium & Praelatio (says Tho. Aquinas) introducta sunt ex Jure humano. secunda secundae quest. 10. Art. 10 in Conclusione. And again, Dominium introductum est de Jure gentium, quod est jus humanum. secunda secundae quaest. 12. Art. 2. Conclus.

I

THE SPEECH OF THE RIGHT HONOURABLE THOMAS EARL OF STAMFORD, &c.

Gentlemen of the Jury

There being some men in this Kingdom, who are so injurious to Themselves, their Countrey, and the Establish'd Religion they profess, that they will not allow Their present Majesties King *William* and Queen *Mary*, to be the Lawful and Rightful King and Queen of these Realms, notwithstanding the great Consent of the whole Nation, by their Representatives in Parliament, [2] hath most solemnly Declared them so: I think therefore it will not be altogether a Mispence either of your or my time (before I come to the Articles of your Charge) to acquaint you, how persons at first united themselves into Government.

When Numbers of Men were got together, they, for their own Preservation, and general Good, soon agreed among themselves, to chuse some one, or more, to be their Judge, or Judges, of Right and Wrong, and to give remedy to the injured and oppressed; to call them together to consult about the weighty Affairs of their Government, to head them against any Foreign or Common Enemy, to reconcile Differences amongst themselves, and to defend both their Persons and Goods in Peace by Rules of Law. (a)

For there was never yet any Civilized Nation, either of ancient or later days, to be found, either by the Discovery of the *Indies*, or elsewhere, where men living together, had not some kind of Magistrate or Magistrates to govern them, by their own consent.

But there is a sort of men amongst us, who by the cunning Insinuations of some disaffected persons, are prevailed upon to believe that the very *Species* of Governement is of *Divine Right*; [3] but I must needs tell them, That to me it seems contradictory to the Nature, as well as destructive to the very End and Being of Government.

For if we consider that we are all equal by the state of Nature[1], and by that there can be no superiority, or subordination one above another; there can be nothing more rational, than that Creatures of the same Species and Rank promiscuously born to all the same advantages of Nature, and the use of the same faculties, should also be equal one amongst another; and were it not for the corruption and viciousness of Degenerate men, there would be no need of any other State; for every one in that State is both Judge and Executioner of the Law of Nature, which is to punish according to the Offence committed; but men being partial to themselves, Passion and Revenge is very apt to carry them too far in their own Cases, as well as Negligence and Unconcernedness is apt to make too remiss in other mens.

This made every one willing to give up his single Power of Rule to one or more, as they thought most fit and convenient for the Publick Good; and he or they to govern by such Rules as the Community or those Authorised [B 2–4] by them to that purpose should agree on, with intention in every on the better to preserve himself, his Liberty and Property; but not as those Persons would have it, who (b) flatter Monarchs in Authority, *That they may do what they please, because they have Power to do more than others*; as if rational Creatures can be supposed, when free, to put themselves into Subjection to another for their own harm, which were to put themselves into a worse Condition than in the state of Nature, wherein they had Liberty to defend their Lives and Properties against the Invasions of all Mankind; whereas by giving themselves up to the Absolute Arbitrary Power of any man, they at the same time Disarm themselves, and Arm him, to make what Prey of them he pleaseth, whenever he hath a mind to it.

I must confess, if there were but one sort of Government in the world, I should less blame the Confidence of these men; because they would have something more to say for their Opinion: For tho I own that Government in general is of Divine Right, yet the particular species cannot be so, because there are so many sorts of them (which I will briefly run [5] over), and so many several Laws fitted for them, that it cannot with the least colour of Reason be said, that either God or Nature made them, but it was the Industry of man, as occasion required, and God permitted them.

For can any one say, that God and Nature did not concur as well with

[1] The ideas expressed in Locke's *Treatise of Government*, 1690.

Italy when it had but one Prince, as now when it hath so many; the like with *Germany* and *Switzerland*, which was once one Commonwealth under the Marquesses and Dukes of *Austria*, and now are divided into Thirteen Cantons, or Commonwealths, under Popular Magistrates of their own?

To come to our own Nation; *England* also was first governed by one or more King under the *Britains*, and then became a Province under the *Roman* Emperors, and afterwards was divided into a *Heptarchy*, or Seven Kingdoms, at once under the *Saxons*; after that, under the *English-Saxons*, *Danes*, and *Norman* Kings, it became a Limited Monarchy, as it now continues under their present Majesties; all this by God's Providence and Permission (not by peculiar Divine Designation) who suffered his own people the *Jews* to be under divers manners of Governments, at different times: at first under Patriarchs; as *Abraham, Isaac* and *Jacob*; then under Captains, [6] as *Moses, Joshua*, and the like; then under Judges, as *Othoniel, Ehud*, and *Gideon*; then under High Priests, as *Ely* and *Samuel*; then under Kings, as *Saul*, and *David*, and the rest; then, under Captains and High Priests again, until they were brought under the Power of the *Romans*.

After this, I hope none can doubt but that as to all the just forms of Civil Government, God doth concur with what the Community thinks fit to order and direct for the publick good.

Some there are, that vainly affirm *Monarchies to be so divinely Hereditary*, that the people have nothing to do to resist or remove any Monarch, altho never so cruel or Tyrannical over his Subjects; which is a Doctrine (I think) was never believed in former Ages; as I hope I shall plainly make to appear in my following Discourse, from the usage and practice of this and several other Kingdoms and Countries; which being done, I hope all men (I am sure *All* that have a hearty love and value for Liberty and Property) will be satisfied that K. *William* and Queen *Mary* are our Rightful and Lawful King and Queen of these Realms; and that what hath been done in relation to the late King *James*, and the placing this present King and Queen upon the Throne, is nothing more than what hath been oft times practised in former Ages in this [7] and other Kingdoms; and that the like Changes in Government have been, I shall endeavour to make out by several Instances.

And first I will begin with foreign Nations, in which I will be as short as possible.

There were in *France* made two great Changes in the Royal line, the first from the Race of *Pharamond* to the Line of *Pepin*; the second from that of *Pepin* to *Hugo Capet*, whose Posterity enjoy it to this day.

(c) *Childerick* the third was deprived for his evil Government by the States of the Kingdom, and *Pepin* chosen King in his stead; and as long as his Race proved brave Kings, and acted for the Common Good, they were continued Kings; *Lewis* the Third, and *Charles*, Sirnamed the *Gross*, were both deprived by the States of *France* for their ill Government, and such who were thought more worthy appointed in their stead. This all their Historians agree in. (d)

Those who write of *Spain*, do say, that *Flaveo Suintilla* (e) was deprived for his evil Government, together with all his Posterity, and *Sissinando* chosen in his Room.

Don Pedro (f) Sirnamed the *Cruel*, for his injurious Proceedings with his Subjects, was Dethroned; the *Spaniards* called in his Bastard Bro-[8] ther *Henry* that lived in *France* (who came to their assistance and slew *Don Pedro* hand to hand) and they chose him King, whose Posterity reigns now.

In *Portugal* Don *Sancho* the Second was deprived by the Universal consent of the *Portugueses*, and Don *Alonso* his Brother set up in his stead (g 1.2.)

Christierne King of *Denmark* for his intolerable Cruelty was deprived, and his Wife and three Children disinherited, and his Uncle *Frederick* was chosen King. (h)

In *Scotland* the Nobility and Gentry took up Arms against *Durstus* their King for his Intolerable Cruelty, and slew him and his Confederates in Battel, and put his Sons by, and chose *Even* his Brother, King, who leaving a Bastard Son, called *Gillo*, the Kingdom was conferred upon him.

Crathy Cinthus having surprized and slain *Donald* for his Cruelty and Tyranny, was Unanimously chosen King. And,

Ethus for his ill Government was deprived, and *Gregory* was made King in his stead. (i)

As for *England*, I will mention some few before the Conquest (vulgarly called so) who were (k) *Archigallo*, (l) *Emerian*, (m) *Vortigern*, (n) *Sigebert*, King of the *West-Saxons*. (o) *Beornred*, and (p) *Alured* King of *Northumberland*, all these were deprived of their Thrones, for their cruel and evil Govern-[9] ment, and others more worthy put in their steads.

King (q) *Edwin* being deprived for his unjust Government, the Crown was given to his Brother *Edgar*, who proved a most incomparable Prince.

There are several such Instances, among which were *Egbert*, who obtained the Crown, tho not next in blood; and as for *Adelstan*, he was Illegitimate.

After the reputed Conquest, you will find that upon the death of *William* the first, his Eldest Son *Robert* was put by, and (r) *William Rufus* his Brother, and the Third Son, was Elected King. After his death his younger Brother (s) *Henry* the First tho not the next Heir, was chosen King by the peoples full consent, tho not summoned by Writ. Next (t) *Stephen* was chosen King against the Right of *Maude* the Daughter of *Henry* the First; then (u) *Henry* the Second against the Right of his Mother *Maude* then living. After the death of (w) *Richard* the First, (x) *John* (Earl of *Moreton*) was Elected King, and *Arthur* the right Heir disinherited. (y)

Henry the 3. was chosen against the Right of *Eleanor*, Prince *Arthur's* Sister. At the death of *Henry* the Third, the (z) States of the Kingdom met, and settled the Government by appointing Officers, and doing what else was necessary for the defence of the Realm. And (aa) *Edward* the [10] Fourth was declared King by the people, his first Parliament Recognizing his Title to the Crown, *Henry* the Sixth then living.

Tho I could go on farther, yet I will stop here, because I have mentioned enough to put it past all contradiction, even by the most prejudiced, That the *several Forms* of Government are not of *Divine Right*, though Government it self be. And also, that our present King *William*, and Queen *Mary*, are our Rightful and Lawful King and Queen of these Realms; and that none can be friends to Government in general, nor to this wonderful and happy Revolution, who go about to maintain the contrary, or take the Oaths to this Government with any Mental Reservation, or particular explanation.

I could wish there were no such men in this Kingdom; but yet it is too plain there are amongst us such as do not care what fire and heat they cause, so that they can but warm themselves by it.

I beg your pardon, Gentlemen, that I have kept you so long; nor would I have done it, but that I thought it proper to acquaint you with the nature of Governments in general, as well as the *Rightfulness* and *Lawfulness* of This, before I came to tell you the parts that you are to act, [11] and the business you are to do to support it and your selves, which is to present all those that are guilty of Treasons, which are either High or Petty Treason. High Treason is compassing or imagining the death of the King or Queen, and declaring the same by open deed, or overt act; Killing the Chancellor, or Treasurer, Justice of the one or other Bench, or other Justices in Eyre, or of Assize, or Oyer and Terminer, in their places doing their Offices; Counterfeiting the Great or Privy Seal; Counterfeiting, Clipping, Washing, or filing of the Current Money of this Realm for lucre or gain; absolving the Subjects from their Obedience, or reconciling them to the Obedience of the Church of Rome, in both the Reconciler or Reconciled.

Petty Treason is, when a Servant kills his Master or Mistress, the Wife her Husband, &c. and Misprisions of Treasons are those that conceal any sort of Treasons, or harbour the Traytors, knowing them to be such.

Murder, under its several Denominations, whether the person did kill another out of malice, or by accident, or by defending of himself, the Law is so tender and careful for the loss of a Man, that it requires an Inquisition to be made after, that so the offence may be punished according to its nature. [12]

All sorts of Robberies, whether on the Road, or in Houses, open, or shut; the stealing of Horses, or other Cattel, abroad or elsewhere; and to prevent that and other loose and idle Living, the Law does provide

Punishments for Poachers or Destroyers of Hares, or Partridges, Pheasants, Rabbets, and Deer, in, and out of Parks; Alehouses or Tipling-Houses, which receive and entertain lewd and idle Persons at unseasonable and unsual hours; vagabonds and sturdy Beggars; all Constables for neglecting their Duties, or taking more than their Dues; and other Officers, as Registers, Clerks, and Bayliffs; the Law is so careful to prevent men in Office from oppressing the People, that there can be no Oppression it does not take notice of to punish. I must yet add this, That tho I have omitted several Particulars, yet that does not excuse you from Presenting of all other Offences which come to your knowledge; which I doubt not but you will do without either Favour, Affection, or Malice: So you will perform your Oaths justly and uprightly, and do God Honour, the King Service, and your Selves and Countrey Right: And so I leave you to your Enquiry.

NOTES

(a) *Mihi quidem non apud* Medos *solum (ut ait* Herodotus) *sed etiam apud Majores nostres fruendae Justitiae causa videntur olim bene morati Reges constituti. Nam cum premeretur initio mutltitudo ab ius qui Majores opes habebant, ad unum aliquem confugiebant virtute praestantem, qui cum prohiberet injuria tenuiores, aequitate constituenda summos cum infimis pari Jure retinebat.* Eamdem *constituendarum* Legum *fuit causa, qua* Regum. *Jus enim semper quaesitum est aequabile: neque enim aliter esset jus. Id si ab une justo & bono viro consequabantur: eo erant contenti: cum id minus contingeret; Leges sunt inventae, quae cum omnibus semper una atque eadem voce loquerentur. Ergo hoc quidem perspicuum est,* eos ad imperandum deligi solitos, quorum de Justitia magna esset Opinio multitudinis. *Adjuncto vero hoc, ut iidem etiam prudentes haberentur: nihil erat quod homines his Auctoribus non posse consequi se arbitrarentur.* Cicero. *de Offic. lib.* 2.[1] which I find thus translated by Sir *Roger L'Estrange*. '*Herodotus* tells us, That the *Medians* chose their Kings originally for the probity of their *manners*, and in hope of enjoying the benefits of *Common Justice*: which I am persuaded was the end and practice likewise of our Predecessors. For when in old time, the Weaker were oppressed by the Stronger, the People presently betook themselves to one more Excellent than the rest, for their Protector: and it was his part to relieve the distressed, and to make such provisions, that common Right be done indifferently betwixt all Parties. And in the making of their *Laws*, they had the same prospect, as in the choice of their *Kings*; the thing propounded, was an *Equal*, and a *Common Right*; and in truth, it could be no Right, without being so qualified. If under the Administration of some *one man* that was *just*, and *good*, they attained that end, they were well contented there to rest; but in case of failing, there were Laws invented, which to all under them, and at all times, should pronounce one and the same Sentence. This now is clear, That *in all Elections the People have still had a care to pitch upon him for their Governour, that was most reverenced for his Justice*; always provided that he were a man of prudence too. And what is it that a Nation would not believe it self

[1] Considering the length of this text, the text of the Latin quotations has been suppressed except if it is not translated into English.

able to compass under so Auspicious a Conduct? 'Sir R. *L'Estrange*'s Translation, p. 101, 102.

Neither can any man with reason think, but that the first Institution of Kings, a sufficient consideration wherefore their Power should always depend on that from which it did always flow by Original Influence of Power, from the Body unto the King, is the cause of Kings dependency in Power upon the Body. By Dependency we mean Subordination and Subjection. A manifest Token of which Dependecy may be this; As there is no more certain Argument that Lands are held under any as Lords, than if we see that such Lands in defect of Heirs fall unto them [14] by Escheat: in like manner it doth follow rightly, That seeing Dominion, when there is none to inherit it, returneth unto the Body; therefore they which before were Inheritors thereof, did hold it with dependency upon the Body; so that by the comparing the Body with the Head, as touching Power, it seemeth always to reside in both; fundamentally and radically in the one, in the other derivatively; in the one the habit, in the other the act of Power. *Hooker's Eccles. Policy, Book 8, fol.* 455.

(b) *Occurit alia* Adulatorum *Turba prudentia nomine commendata, qui ut se in Gratiam Regum* insinuent *illis persuadent* eos esse supra Leges; *& paulo post, Nunquam in Regnis & Civitatibus* homines scelerati *defuerunt, nec hodie desunt, qui Principes erroribus turbulentis* inficiant, *quibus illi quidem annumerandi sunt, qui* cum se Jure consultos existimari velint, *Regibus persuadent*, illos omnino solutos esse. Legibus Osorius,[1] *lib.* 5. De Regis Institutione; which may be thus render'd.

There is another Race of *Flatterers*, that set up for *Statists*, that will needs recommend themselves by their pretended *super-fine* Prudentials, and to *insinuate* themselves into the favour of their Kings, will be persuading of them that *They are above the Laws* ; and (a little after, says he) there never wanting such *base* and *vile Wretches* as these in Kingdoms and Cities, nor yet are, who labour to *infect* Princes, with such pernicious Errors, among whom, those are to be put upon the file of account, that, *when they would fain be esteemed and reckoned most trusty Councellors*, will be persuading Kings that they altogether free and loose from the Laws.

But the Lord Chancellor *Bacon*, among many other Excellent Councels to the then Duke of *Buckingham*, wisely cautioned him in these words; viz 'In respect of the King your Master, you must be wary that you give him *true Information*; and if the matter concern him in his *Government*, that you do not flatter him; if you do, You are as great a *Traytor* in the *Court of Heaven*, as he that draws his Sword against him. *Caballa of Lett.* f. 41.

King *James* I. gives these sort of Persons no better names than those of *Vipers* and *Pests* to their *Prince*, and the *Commonwealth*. 'For (saith he) a King governing in a setled Kingdom, leaves to be a King, and degenerates into a Tyrant, as soon as he leaves off to rule according to his Laws. *In his Speech to his Parliament*, 1609. *in his Works*, 531.

(c) *Childerick* the Third, after Ten years reign, was deposed by Pope *Zachary*, at the request of the whole Nobility and Clergy of *France*; or rather his Deprivation was by them, and confirmed by the Pope, to whom they alledged this Reason for their so doing, as *Girard* sets down in both his *French Chronicles*, the Large one, and the Abbreviation, *viz*. 'That their Oath to *Childerick* was to honour, serve,

[1] Osorio de Fonseca, bishop of Silves.

and obey, maintain and defend him against all Men, as long as he was just, religious, valiant, clement, and would resist the Enemies of the Crown, punished the wicked, and conserve the good, and defend the Christian Faith. And forasmuch as these Promises (said they) were conditional, they ought not to hold, or bind longer, than they were reciprocally observed on both parts; which seeing they were not on the part of *Childerick*, they would not be any longer his Subjects, and desired *Zachary* to absolve them from their Oaths, which he did, and by this means *Childerick* was deposed, and put into a Monastery, where he died. In his place *Pepin* was *chosen*, and crowned King, whose Posterity [15] reigned for almost 200 years after him, until *Hugo Capet* was put into the same Throne by the same Authority of the Commonwealth; and *Charles of Lorraine*, last of the race of *Pepin*, for the Evil Satisfaction which the *French* Nation had of him, was put by it, and kept Prisoner during his Life, in the Castle of *Orleance*.

Hugo Capet was chosen King of France, notwithstanding the apparent Right of *Charles* of *Lorrain*, who was the next Heir of *Lewis V.* by reason that the said Charles seemed too much linked to the Interests of the *Germans*, who at that time were Enemies to *France*. *Guil. de Nangis*, *ad An.* 987. and others in *du Chesne*. [1]

(d) *Lewis* XI of *France*, the most unbridled Monarch that ever was; in his Rosary of War,[2] composed by him a little before his death, for the use of his Son Charles VIII. writes thus, 'When Kings or Princes have no respect to the Laws, they take from the People what they ought to leave them possessed of, and do not give them what they ought to have; and in so doing, *they make their People Slaves, and thereby lose the Name of a King*.

Wherefore the incomparable Hooker tells us that, 'There is the best Established Dominion, where the Law doth most rule the King.' *Eccles. Polit. lib. 8. fo.* 443.

(e) About the Year of *Christ* 630. we read of a Legal King named *Flaveo Suintilla*, put down and deprived, both He and his Posterity, in the Fourth National Council of *Toledo*, holden in the Year of our Lord 633. according to *Ambrosio Morales*; and one *Sissinando* confirmed in his place, notwithstanding that *Suintilla* was at the beginning of his Reign, a very good King, and much commended by *Isodorus*, Archbishop of *Sevill.* (*Isid. in Hist. Hisp.*)[3] who yet in the said Council was the first man that *subscribed* to his Deprivation. *Council. Tolet.* 4. *cap.* 4. *Ambrosio Morales, lib.* 11. *cap.* 17. [4]

And the Fathers of that Councel (after Matters of Religion, and Reformation of Manners, which they handled in 73 Chapters) in the end, and Last Chapter came to handle Matters of State also. And first of all they do *confirm* the *Deposition* of *Suintilla*, together with his Wife, Brother, and Children, and all for his great Wickedness, which in the Concil is recounted; and they do deprive them, not only of any Title to the Crown, but also of all other Goods and Possessions, Moveables and Immoveables, saving only which the new King's Mercy would bestow upon them. *Council. Tolet.* 4. *cap.* 74.

[1] Probably André du Chesne, chronicle writer, a monk of the Abbey of St. Denis, died 1302. See *Chronique latine...* ed. H. Géraud, 2 vols (Paris: J. Renouard, 1843–44).

[2] *Le Rozier des Guerres, composé par le feu roy Louis XI...pour Mgr le Dauphin Charles.* (Paris: N. Beron, 1616).

[3] *Chronicon D. Isidori, archiep. hisp.* (Taurini: J.B. Bevilaqua, 1593).

[4] Probably *La Corònica general de España...que continuava A. de M.*, 2 vols. (Madrid: Alacala de Ilenares...1574-77)

(f) This Don Pedro, called the Cruel, tho otherwise he was legally possess'd of the Crown, as Son and Heir to King, *Don Alonso* the Twelfth, and had reigned among his Subjects 18 years, yet for his evil and barbarous Government over them, about the Year of our Saviour 1368. they resolved to *depose*, and so sent for a Bastard Brother of his, named *Henry*, that lived in France, requesting him that he would come with some *Frenchmen* to assist them in that Act, and take the Crown upon himself, which he did, and by the help of the *Spaniards*, and *French* Soldiers, he drove the said *Pedro* out of *Spain*, and he himself was crowned. *Estevan de Garibay*. lib. 14. cap. 40, 41.[1]

Before him, as the same Author acquaints us, about the Year 1282. One *Don Alonso*, the Eleventh of that name, King of *Castile* and *Leon*, succeeded his Father *Fernando* the Saint, and himself obtained the Sirname of *Sabio* and *Astrologo*, for his excellent Learning in that Art, as may appear by the Astronomical Tables that at this day go under his name. This man, for his *evil* [16] *Government*, and especially for *Tyranny* used towards two Nephews of his, was deposed of his Kingdom by *a publick Act of Parliament* in the Town of *Valladolid*, after he had reigned 30 years, and his Son *Don Sancho* the Fourth, was Crowned in his Place, who for his valiant Acts was Sirnamed *El Bravo*, and it turned to the great benefit and advantage of the Common-wealth: *Garib. lib.* 13. *de la Hist. de Esp. cap.* 15.

(g.1) *An.* 1243. All was in combustion in *Portugal*, by the negligence and baseness of their King *Don Sancho Capello*, who was wholly given to his Wife's humours, hated of the *Portugals*, and himself disliked for her sake; for many Malefactors and insolent persons were supported by her, who grew daily more audacious in their Excess, without fear of Justice, which was trodden under foot for their respect; For these Considerations, and her Barrenness too, all the Noblemen of the Kingdom desired to have the Queen (called *Mencia*) separated and sent out of *Portugal*: For effecting whereof, they made a great instance at *Rome*, but neither Exhortation, Admonition, nor Commandment, nor Censure could prevail, the King so doting on her, that he would not leave her; which the Portugals perceiving, some of them presumed to seize on her in the City of *Coimbra*, and conducted her into *Gallicia*, from whence she never more returned to *Portugal*. Not content therewith, they sought to depose the King from His Royal Dignity too for his ill Government, and to advance his Brother, *Don Alphonso*, to the Regal Throne in his place; whom the Estates Assembled, made Regent of *Portugal*, leaving only the Title of King to his Brother: Which fact of the Estates; the Pope in the Council of *Lyons*, Authorized by his Apostolick Power, with which the King being displeased, abandoned his Realm, and retired into *Castile*. *General Hist. of Spain, Lib.* 11. *f.* 377, 378.

(g.2) *Don Sancho* II. Sirnam'd *Capello*, fourth King of *Portugal*, (Legitimate Son and Heir to *Don Alonso*, Sirnamed *El Gardo*, third King thereof) after he had reigned 34 years, was deprived for his Defects in Government, by the Universal Consent of all *Portugal*; *Garib. lib.* 4 *de Hist. Portugal. cap.* 19 and this his Deprivation from all Kingly Rule and Authority (leaving him only the bare Name of King) was approved by a General Council in *Lyons*, Pope *Innocent IV*, being there present, who at the Petition and Instance of the whole Realm of *Portugal* by their

[1] *Los XL Libros del Compendio historial de la Chronicas y unviersal Historiade todos los reynos de Esp*.... 2 vols.(Anveres: C. Planino,1571)

Ambassadors, the Archbishop of *Braga*, Bishop of *Comibra* [sic], and divers of the Nobility, sent to *Lyons* for that purpose, did authorize the said State of *Portugal* to put in Supream Government *Don Alonso* his Brother, who was at the time Earl of *Bulloign* in *Picardy*, by right of his Wife; and so the *Portugueses* did, and a little after they deprived their said King, and did drive him out of his Realm into *Castile* where he spent the rest of his days in banishment, and died in *Toledo* without ever returning. And this Decree of the Council and Pope at *Lyons*, for authorizing of this Fact, is extant in the 6th Book of Decretals in print. *Lib. 6. Decret tit. 6. de Supplenda. cap. Grand. 1.*

(h) *Christierne* the Second, King of *Denmark*, was thrust out of his Kingdom for his intolerable Cruelty, Tyranny, and Breach of his Subjects Privileges; which he endeavouring to regain, was taken Prisoner by his Uncle *Frederick*, Duke of *Scleswick* and *Holstein*, and committed Prisoner to *Sunderburge* in *Holsatia*, where he died in Chains: *Frederick* was elected King in his place (upon certain Articles [17] and Conditions which he was sworn unto before his Coronation) in a general Assembly of the States held at *Hafnia, An.* 1524. in and by which Assembly, *Christierne* was solemnly deposed, and a Declaration Made, Printed, and Published in the name of all the States of *Denmark*, wherein they express the Cause, why they renounced their Faith and Obedience to *Christierne*, sworn unto him upon certain Conditions which he had broken, and Elected *Frederick*; which Declaration is recorded in *David Chytraeus*,[1] his *Chr. Sax. lib.* 10. p.301, to 312. *Sleid. lib.* 4 Hist. *An.* 1532.

(i) Amongst the many Examples the *Scotch* Historians do afford us of *Abdicated Kings*, none is so remarkable as that of King *James* the 3d; who endeavouring to introduce an Arbitrary Government, and to support it by a Soveraign Power; after the Violation of all the solemn promises he made to the contrary; at last the *Nobility and Gentry* in great Number assembled themselves together, having the young Prince, his eldest Son, then about Sixteen Years of Age at their Head, to oppose his designs: They hapned to meet in the Field of *Stirling*, where the King had the misfortune to be *deserted* and *slain*, whereupon the Prince was declared King, and in a *free Parliament* soon after call'd, the business of the field *of Sterling* was fully debated, and *by the unanimous consent of the Three Estates, it was declared and adjudged*, That those that were slain in the said Field of Sterling in the assistance and defence of the late King, had fallen by their own deserving, and justly suffered the punishment of their rashness; That the Conquerors were innocently guilty of the Blood there shed, and fairly acquitted of any pursuit. The Act of Parliament, that condemns the Arbitrary proceedings of the said King James 3. *Fines and Forfeits most of the Nobility and Gentry there stood by him at the Battel of* Sterling, in which he fell, and justifies and *clears all those that fought against him in the defence of their Laws and Liberties*, is to be seen amongst the Scotch *Acts of Parliament*, Printed by Authority of *Mary* Queen of *Scots, An.* 1567. of which, see more in *Buchanan Drummund*'s History of the Five *James*. *Leslaeus*, in his *Historia de gestis Scotorum*, and others. [2]

[1] *Davidis Chytraei operum tomus quartus, Saxonia,ab anno A.C. 1500 usque ad 1599 recognita*...(Sumtibus H. Grossii: Lispiæ, 1599) fol.

[2] Buchanan Drummond's Hist. of the Five James: It ought to be William Drummond, *History of Scotland, from the Year 1423, until the year 1542. Containing the Lives and Reigns of James*

Nay, the very Emperors themselves, when they infringed the Rules of Government which they have sworn inviolably to observe, and violated the Fundamental Laws of the Empire, the States have opposed and resisted them, and finally deprived them of the Empire. The *German* Lawyers have always held, and do still hold it for a certain Truth, That when they abuse their Power, for the overturning of the State, or for invading the Rights of the Princes of the Empire, That it is a *Right inherent in the Empire*, to deprive them of their Imperial Dignity, and to confer the same on another. This is declared by *Lampadius*, *Arnizaeus*, *Diderick*, *Conringius*, and many others.[1]

The Emperor *Wenceslaus* was deposed by the Electors of the Empire in the year 1400. after that he had been twice taken Prisoner, and had been exhorted by the State, to amend and take up from his irregular actings. *Aventin. lib. 7. Annalium & Cuspinian. in Vita Venceslai.* [2]

(k) *Archigallo*, one of our Ancient *British* Kings in times of Paganisme, giving himself to all dissentions and strife, imagining Causes against his Nobles, to put them from their Goods and Dignities, setting up ignoble persons in their places, and plucking away by sinister, wrongful means from the Rich their Wealth and Goods, by [18] which he enriched himself, and impoverished his Subjects: They *of one assent* lastly took and deprived him of all Kingly Honour and Dignity, when he had Reigned almost five years, making his brother *Elidurus*, King of *Britain* by one Assent, in the year of the World 4915. who after five years good Reign, feigning himself sick, Assembled the Barons of the Land, and by his discreet words, and bearing loving carriage, persuaded them to restore *Archigallo* to his former Honour and Regalty: And thereupon assembling a *Council* of his Britons at *Caerbrank*, or *York*, he caused such means to be made to the *Commons*, that in Conclusion, when *Elidurus* had Ruled the Land five years as King, he resigned there his Crown and all Kingly Power to *Archigallo*; who being thus restored to his Kingly Dignity, by *joint consent of the People*, remembered well what evil life that before that time he had led, and the punishment he had suffered for the same; wherefore in eschewing of like danger, he changed all his old Conditions, and became a good and right wise Man, Ministring to the People Equity and Justice, and bare himself so Nobly again towards his Lords and Rulers under him of his Lands, that he was beloved and dreaded of all his Subjects, and so continued during the Term of his Natural Life. *Fabian*'s Chronicle, 2d part. L. 15. *chap.* 39, 40, 41. [3]

Hollinshead writes thus of him, *Archigallo*, the Second Son of *Merindus*, and Brother to *Gorbonianus*, was admitted King of *Britain* in the year 3686. but he followed not the steps of his Brother, but giving himself to dissension and stryfe,

---

the I... London: 1655. Leslaeus: *De origine, moribus, et rebus gestis Scotorum libri decem... Authore Ioanne Leslaeo.* Romae: 1578 [John Lesley, Scot, 1527-96, Bishop of Ross]

[1] *Jacobus Lampadius, Tractaus de constitutilone imperii Romano-Germanici*, (Lugduni Batavorum: 1634). in-16°.- *De Republica Romano-Germanica.* (Helmestadii, n.d.) - Henningus Arnisaeus, (d. 1635–36?) physician, philosopher and political writer, *De autoritate principum in populum semper inviolabili...*, (Francofurti: A. Eichorus, 1612). See *Allgemeine Deutsche Biographie* (Leipzig: Duncken & Humbolt, 1875) vol. I, 575. See the same for Veit Theodorus or Diderick, (1509–1549); vol. 5, 196–7; Hermannus Conringius, vol. IV, 446–51.(1606–81)

[2] Johannes Aventinus, *Annalium Boiorum libri septem* (Ingolstadii: Weissenhornios, 1554)?

[3] Robert Fabian, d. 1513, *The Concordance of Histories*, 1516.

ymagined Causes against his Nobles, that he might displace them, and set such in their rowmths [sic] as were Men of base Byrth, and of evil Condytyons. Also he sought by unlawful means to bereave his wealthy Subjects of their Goods and Riches, so to inrich himself, and impoverish his People: For the which his inordinate doings, his Nobles conspired against him, *and finally deprived him of all His Honour and Kingly Dignity*, after he had Reigned the space of one year.

Elidurus, the 3d Son to *Merindus*, was, *by one Assent of the* Britains, *chosen* to Reign over them in his Brother's stead, after the Creation of the World 3687. but he being a Prince, doubted lest he should do otherwise than became him, if he did not care for his Brother *Archigallo*'s Estate; therefore he shewed wonderful diligence in travelling with the Nobles of the Realm, to have his Brother restored to the Crown again. One day happening to hunt in the Wood called *Calater*, near *York*, he found his Brother *Archigallo* wandring there in the thickest part of it, whom in most loving manner he conveyed secretly home to his House, in the City of *Aldud,* otherwise called *Acliud*; shortly after, feigning himself sick, He sent to Assemble his Barons, who being come at the day appointed, He called one after another into his Privy-Chamber, and so effectually managed them, that he prevailed with them to further him to their powers to reduce the Kingdom into his Brother *Archigallo*'s hands.

Then he assembled a Council at *York*, where he so used the matter with the *Commons*, that in Conclusion, when the said *Elidurus* had Govern'd the Land well and honourably for three years, he resigned wholy his Crown and Kingly Title, unto his Brother *Archigallo,* who was received of the Britayns agayn as King, by this mediation of his brother *Elidurus*. This Restitution made *Archigallo* become a new Man, to Reign in surety, and by using himself uprightly in the Administration of Justice towards both the Nobles and Commons of the Realm, that he was beloved and dreaded of [19] all his Subjects, during all the remainder of his Life, which was Ten years. *Holishead, f.* 3O. *Col.* 2, 31, *Col.* 1 & 2. Printed 1577.

Geoffrey of Monmouth gives this relation of him: ... *Galf. Monumet. L* 3. *c.* 17. *f.* 21, 22.[1]

(l) *Emerian*, an old *British* King, for misgoverning of his People, was deposed by them in the sixth year of his Reign, and *Ydwallo* proclaimed King in his stead. *Hollinshead*, indeed, does but just mention him, saying, That He being far unlike his immediate Predecessor, and Brother *Margam*, in manners, was Deposed in the sixth year of his Reign, *Fol.* 32. *Col.* 2. *l.* 48.

Geoffrey of Monmouth gives this Account... *Galf. Monum. f.* 22. *c.* 19.

Fabian only mentions his name, and says, He was deprived for his Cruelness, *Fab. 2* d Part, Chap. 46. p. 17 b.

(m) *Vortigern*, saith *Speed, f.* 263. among the many molestations of the *Scots* and *Picts*, was *Ordained* supream [20] Governor of these Affairs; and to that end, with the *Britains* full consent was *Elected* their King.

But *Stow* writes, that for the Love he bore to *Rowen* the *Saxon*, he was Divorced from his Lawful Wife, by whom he had three Sons; for which deed well ner all the *Britains* forsook him. *Vodine*, Archbishop of *London*, a Man of singular Devotion, and good Life, by the advice of *Vortimer*, went to *Vortigern*, and said to him, that he had not done as a Christian Prince, in departing from his Lawful Wife, and

[1] Galf. Monum.: *Chronicon Galfridi le Baker de Swynbroke*, ed. E.M. Thomson (Oxford, 1889)?

taking another Woman, whose Father was an Enemy to the Christain Faith, and also went about to Conquer the Crown of *Britain*. Then said *Vortigern*, I was not wise when I brought the Saxons to help me against mine Enemies; but I was more unwise, when I was taken with the inordinate lust of the Daughter of *Hengist*: I know that mine Empire will be terrible, except I repent me with speed, and turn to God.

Hengist, hearing *Vortiger* make this Lamentation, blamed him, for that He believed the persuasions of a prophane Man, of feigned Life, (as he termed him) and forthwith slew the good Archbishop *Vodine*, and many other Priests and religious Persons. All the Churches in *Kent* were polluted with Blood, the Nuns, with other Religious persons, were by force put from their Houses and Goods, and constrained to pollution of their Bodies.

The *Britains* considering the daily repair of the *Saxons* into this Realm, shewed to their King the Jeopardy that might thereof ensue; and advertised him of the danger, but all was in vain; for *Vortiger*, by reason of his Wife; bare such favour to the *Saxons*, that he would in no wise hear the Counsel of his Subjects; wherefore they *with one mind* deprived of his Royal Dignity, when he had Reigned Six years, and *Ordained* to be their King, *Vortimer*, his eldest Son. *Stow* 's Chron. *Fol.* 51,52.

Mr. Rastell, in his Chronicle, says, after Vortiger had married *Engist* his Daughter, called *Ronwen*, and gave to *Engest* the Countrey of *Kent*, wherefore the *Britains* were wroth, and put down *Vortigerus*, and crowned *Vortimer*, his Son, King, the year of Christ iiiiclxiiii. and *Ronwen* causing him to be Poysoned, the *Britains* by common assent made *Vortiger* King again.

Nennius, the most Ancient *English* Historian after *Gildas*, tells us, that *Vortigerne*, was *deposed* by St. *Germaine*, and the *Council* of the *Britains*, because he had Married his own Daughter, who placed his Son *Vortimer* upon the Throne. And as Fabian tells us, He was *by Assent* of the *Britains*, made King of *Britain*, in the year of our Lord 464. *Fab. p.* 36. a.

Daniel says, the *British* Nobility combined themselves against *Vortigern*, (the Author of the Improvident Admission of *Hengist* and *Horsa*, the Leaders of the *Saxons*;) who, after his marriage with the Daughter, or Niece of Hengist, an exceeding Beautiful Lady (brought over of purpose to work on the dotage of this dissolute Prince) drew in so many of their own populous and military Nation, that in short time, of Servants they became Masters, to contemn their Entertainers, and commit many Insolencies; whereupon *the Nobility Deposed Vortigerne, and Elected Vortimer* his Son, a Prince of great worth. *Dan. Hist. fol.* 7.[1]

Geoffrey of Monmouth writes thus of him, … *Galf. Monumet.* lib. 6. cap. 13. fol. 44, 45; …Id. ibid. cap. 14., cap. 15 [21]- …Id. Lib. 8. cap. 2. fol.54. *Vid. Mat. Westm. fol.*90.

Henry Huntingdon tells us … Lib. 2. fol. 178. a, lin. 35.

Mr. *Ralph Hollinshed*, in his History of *England*, hath much the same Story of *Vortigern*, Fol. 122. Col. 1, 2.

(n) *Sigebert*, King of the West-Saxons, (tho his Parentage is obscure and unknown yet) made his Vices [22] sufficiently apparent and manifest; for he, wallowing in all sensual pleasures, added Exactions and Cruelties upon his Subjects, and being Tyrannous towards them, did set aside, and change Ancient Laws and Customs

[1] Daniel: Samuel Daniel's *Collection of the historie of England*. London: N. Okes, 1618.

after his own Lust; of which vicious Life, when he was lovingly admonished by his most faithful Councellor, a worthy Earl, called *Cumbra*, so far was his mind from abandoning his Impious Courses, that he caused that Noble Person to be cruelly slain: Whereupon *the Peers* and *the Commons*, seeing their Estates and Lives were every day in danger, and that their Laws so notoriously violated, [*Convenerunt proceres Regni cum populo Universo*] Assembled altogether; and, *provida omnium deliberatione; & unanimi consensu*, rose up in Arms against him, and would acknowledg him no longer their Soveraign, but *deprived him of all Kingly Authority*. He thereupon, being by Nature as fearful, as he was audacious unto Vice, fled into the Woods as his only safeguard, where wandring in the day like a person forlorn, and hiding himself in Caves of Wild Beasts in the Night, he was slain by a *Swineherd* that was Servant to *Cumbra*, and of him known to be *Sigebert*, in revenge of his Master's death, in the Wood that was then called *Andreads-Wald*; and *Kenulph* was made King in his stead, *An. Dom.* 757. *Speed* 's Hist. *fol.* 229. *Col.* 2. *Stow*'s Chronicle, *fol.* 77. *Col.* 1.

Daniel says, That *Ethelard, Sigebert, Kenulph*, and *Britric*, were rather Kings by *Election*, and their *own Power*, than by *Right of Descent, fol.* 9. 10.

Henry of Huntingdon's words are these; [Hen. Hunt. lib. 4. fol. 196. a. lin. 18. vid. Mat. Westm. fo. 14. lin. 53

Hollinshead tells us the same Story in these words:

Sigebert began his Reign in the year of our Lord 755. very near ended. He intreated his Subjects very evil, setting Law and Reason at nought: he could not abide to hear his faults told him, and therefore he cruelly put to death an Earl, named *Cumbra*, which was of his Council, and faithfully admonished him to reform his evil doings; whereupon the rest of his *Nobles* assembled themselves together, with a *great multitude of People, and expelled him out of his Estate* in the beginning of the second, or (as *Harrison* hath) the first year of his Reign. Then *Sigebert*, as he was fearful[23] of nature, fearing to be apprehended, got him into the Wood, called as then *Andredeswalde*, and there hid himself; but by chance a Swineherd that belonged to the late Earl *Cumbra* at *Privetsfloud*, found him out, and percieving what he was, slew him in revenge of his Master's death. *Hollinsh. fo.* 193, 194.

I find in a very ancient President in the Kingdom of the *West-Saxons*, That *Cudred* King of *West-Saxons* being dead, *Sigebert* his Kinsman succeeded him in that Kingdom, and held it but a small time; for being puft up with pride by the Successes of King *Cudred*, his Predecessor, he grew insolent, and became intolerable to his People. And when he evil intreated them, all manner of ways, and either wrested the Laws for his own ends, or eluded them for this own advantage; *Cumbra*, one of his Chief Officers, at the request of the whole People, intimated their Complaints to the Savage King; and because he persuaded the King to govern his People more mildly; and that laying aside his Barbarity, he would indeavour to appear amiable both to God and Man; the King immediately commanded him to be put to death; and increased his Tyranny, became more cruel and intolerable than before; ...... whereupon in the beginning of the second year of his Reign, because he was arrived to an incorrigible pitch of pride and wickedness, the *Nobles*, and *the People of the whole Kingdom, assembled together, and upon mature deliberation did by unanimous Consent of them all drive him out of the Kingdom.* In whose stead they chose *Kenwolph*, an Excellent Youth, and of the Royal Blood, to be King over the People and Kingdom of the *West-Saxons. Vid. Chronicon Johannis Brompton. fol.* 769, 770 & 795, 796.

(o) The People of the Kingdom of *Mercia* rose up against *Beornred* their King, because he *governed them not by just Laws, but Tyranny*; and assembling all together, as well Nobles as Ignoble, *Offa*, a most Valiant Young Man being their Captain, they expelled him from the Kingdom; which done, by the *unanimous Consent* of all Parties, as well *Clergy as People*, they Crowned *Offa* King....... Matt. Westminster. fol. 142. lin. 15.

(p) *Alured*, (who, as some affirm, slew his Predecessor *Edilwald*, or *Mollo*, and so by this means got to the Royal Dignity in *Northumberland*, in the Year of *Christ*'s Incarnation, 765) ruled over them with much Rigor, Cruelty and Oppression, that his People could no longer bear with his Misgovernment; and therefore after Eleven years groaning under his Tyranny, he was at last *expelled* out of the Province by his own Subjects, and enforced to abandon the same, as you [24] may read in *Speed*'s and *Stow*'s Chronicles.

(q) *Edwin*, King of *Mercia* and *Northumberland*, for his Mis-government, Tyranny and Oppression, following vain, base and wicked Councellors, rejecting the Advice of the wisest and Noblest Persons, was by the *unanimous Consent* of all his *Subjects, removed* from all Kingly Dignity and *deposed*; in whose place *Edgar* was *elected* King, *An.* 957. His Deposition grieved him so much, that *Grafton* says, he died soon after for sorrow.[1] *Vid. Hollinshead fo.* 23, 231.

Mat. Westminst. ......fol. 196. lin. 21.

Says *Rastell* in his old Chronicle, '*Edwyn*, the eldest Son of *Edmond*, Broder to *Ethelstone*, was next Kyng of *England*, the yere of Chryst ixclxi. He banyshyd Seynt *Donstone* for a Season, and toke Goodis and Jewelis from *Relygyus* Houss, and gaff them to *Alyantis* and Strangers. He was a vycyus Man of lyvyng, and also a Tyrrant to his Subjectis; that in Conclusions they depryvyd him from all Kyngly Dygnyte and Honoure.' This Book has not any Numbers of Pages, and therefore cannot particularly be referred to. *Vid. Fabian's Chronicle, chap.* 192. *fol.* 116 a. b. & *Grafton. P.* 153, 154. *Stow fol.* 83. *Col.* 1. *lin.* 44.

(r) *Grafton* writes thus of *William Rufus*, That he being in *Normandy* at his Father's death, departed thence before his Funeral Obsequies were finished and done, and in all haste adressed him into *England*; and being come into the Realm, he by and by made *Lanfrank*, then Archbishop of *Canterbury* (in whose friendship and faithfulness he had reposed no small trust and confidence) privy to all his Councel, praying him withal to put to his helping-hand, that he might be crowned King as shortly as might be, according to his *Father's Will and Testament*, the which was at the last brought to pass by the importune labour and suit of the said *Lanfrank*, promising all things in his name, that might by any means purchase him credit or favour with the People, that in all manners assented unto his Coronation, and so was he by him the said *Lanfrank*, with the Assistance of divers other Bishops, Anointed and Crowned King at *Westminster*, the first day of *October*, 1087. *Graft. Chron. Vol.* 2, *fol.* 21.

Malmsbury[2] says, *Robert* his Elder Brother, being in actual Rebellion against his

[1] *An Abridgment of the Chronicles of England* (London: R. Totyll, 1563).

[2] Will. Malmesbury (1090?–1143?) *Gesta Rerum Anglicarum*, 5 books, continued by *Historia Novella.*

Father, was *abdicated*; and *William* being very obedient in all things to him, a little before his death was adopted by him for his Successor, by his last Will: his words are, ... Will. Malmesbur. lib. 4. Fol. 67 b. lin. 22.

Brompton, says, that...... *William* the First gave and bequeathed the Kingdom of *England* to [25] *William* his Second Son. *Vid*. Brompt. fo. 980. lin. 40.

Simon of *Durham* says, *Rex* Willielmus V. Id. Sept. 1078. *moriens*, Willielmo *filio reliquit Imperium*. Simon Dunhelm. *fol*. 53. *lin*. 58. *Mat. Paris*'s words are, *Angliam, possessiones maternas cum Thesauris*, Willielmo Rufo *legavit, fo* .13. *lin*. 53.

Mat. Westm. says, *Rex* Guilihelmus *mirabiliter terram suam sic divisit*. Roberto *primogenito suo invitus & coactus* Normanniam, Gulihelm *secundo filio suo* Angliae *Monarchiam*, & Henrico *possessiones maternas & thesauri copiam delegavit*. fo. 230 lin. 45.

Oldenburgher indeed, in the 2d part of his *Thesaurus rerum publicarum*, makes no mention of King *William*'s leaving the Kingdom to his Son *Rufus* by Will, but rather asserts the contrary; quoting out of an old Book, called *Liber Cadomensis*, or the Book of *Caen* in *Normandy*, these very words of the *Norman*'s own saying: *Neminem Regni Angliae constituo haeredem, non enim tantum Decus* Haereditario Jure *possedi*. I appoint no Heir to the Kingdom of England, for I did not enjoy so great an honour by right of inheritance; and therefore he only recommended his Son *William* to the Peers of the Nation, who was there elected by the People, *Volentibus animis Provincialium*, as it said before.

But *Ingulphus*, who lived at his time, owns that *William Rufus* had the Kingdom of England bequeathed to him by his Father's Will, and that he was gladly received by Archbishop *Lanfrank*, and the rest of the Great Men of the whole Kingdom, and thereupon solemnly crowned at *Westminster*. His words are, ... Ingulph. Hist. in To. I. Rerum Anglicar. Scriptor Veterum, fol. 106. [1]

But whether he had it left to him by Will, or not, 'tis not worth while to dispute; if he had, he thought it not of force and virtue enough to secure the Title to him; for he wisely betook himself to another way, which he knew would be sure, without exception, to settle him fast in the Throne of his Father, and summon'd the great Council, or Parliament, composed of the Nobility, and Wisemen of the Kingdom; [Brompton, fol. 983. lin. 10; Polid. Virgil lib. 10, f. 164] And when he had told them in full Council what his Business was with them, they after a long and full debate of the matter, *unanimously* agreeed to *make him King*, and thereupon set the Crown upon his Head in *Festo Sanctorum Cosma & Damiani*.

(s) *Rufus* being dead, and *Robert* his Eldest Brother (who was Duke of *Normandy*) having been absent for five Years in a Voyage to the *Holy Land*, *Henry* the youngest Brother, *Frater Ultimus*, and a very Wise-Man for his Age, ...that the Great Men thought it by no means safe to be so long without a King, ... all the Clergy and People of *England*, being assembled in *London*, he promised [26] an amendment of those Laws wherewith *England* had been so much oppressed in his Father's and Brother's time, if they would be pleased too receive him for their King; to this it was universally answered, That if he with a willing mind would grant, and by his Charter confirm to them those Ancient Liberties and Customs, which their

[1] *Ingulfi Croylandensis historia*, ed. Sir H. Savile, 1601- *Rerum Anglicarum Scriptor*.... ed. W. Fulman, 1684.

Ancestors enjoyed in the time of *Edward* the Confessor, they would unanimously chuse him, and consecrate him for their King: *Henry* voluntarily and readily granting this, and taking an oath to perform what he had promised, they with One consent made him King. ...... Mat. Par. fo. 55, lin. 28].

Henry de *Knyghton*, the *Canon* of *Leicester*,[1] writes thus ...... Knyghton *de Eventibus Angliae, lib.* 11 *cap.* 8. *Col.* 2374. *lin.* 14 the sense of which is, That *Robert* being at his Brother *William*'s death in actual war with his enemies in *Normandy*, and the Barons of this Kingdom knowing him to be Cruel in his Nature, and a Hater of the *English* Nation, by the full Consent of the whole Community of the Realm, declared him illegitimate, because he was not lawfully begotten by *William* the Conqueror; whereupon by their unanimous Assent, they in a Parliamentary way refused him for their King, and set up *Henry* his Brother in his stead. And *Henry* prudently acknowledges this title in his Charter, whereby he confirms the Liberties which he had before promised to his People; ...... Know ye, that I, by the Grace of God, and the Common Council and Assent of the Barons of the Kingdom of England, am Crowned King of the said Kingdom. *Lambert de Prisc. Anglor. Legibus*, fol. 175. *Ric. de Hagulst.* 310. lin. 48.[2] And at his Coronation those Laws were made *de Communi Concilio Baronum Regni Angliae*, Mat. Par. ut sup.

Mat. Westm. says, *post mortem Regis* Gulihelmi Rufi, *in Regem est electus Frater ejus ille* Henricus, *fol.* 235. and so says *Brompton*, *fol.* 997, *lin.* 46.

The sense this King had of the Power of the Great Council of the Kingdom, made him take the same Course to secure the Crown to his Son *William*: For, says the Historian, in the 13th Year of his Son's Age, having called a General Council, and there caused all the Chief and Powerful Men of the Kingdom to swear that his Son *William* should succeed him in the Throne and Dominions; ... [27] Chronica Gervasii, Col. 1338, lin. 57.[3]

But this *William* some years afterwards was drowned, and so left his Father without any Issue-male legitimate. But he had a Daughter, married then to the Emperor, *Henry* IV. and therefore he summoned another great Council in the 27th Year of his Reign, to get the Kingdom setled upon her, and to receive her for their Queen after his decease, as *Malmesbury* relates the Story.... In which Council, all the Chief Men of the Nation bound themselves by an Oath, together with the Bishops and Abbots, That if King *Henry* should dye without Issue-Male, they would receive *Maud* his Daughter for their Liege Lady, immediately, without any hesitation. *Malmesb. Hist. Novellae, lib.* I. *fol.* 99, *lin.* 34 & i. And in the 31st year of his Reign, returning with his Daughter into *England*, he called another General Council of the Great Men at *Northampton*, and there again he got those that had before sworn Fealty to her, to renew their Oaths, and those that had not sworn as yet, to take the Oath of Fidelity to her; it is the same Historian, whose words are, ... Id. fol. 100. lin. 43. After all this Care, (which was the best he could take) to make his Daughter his Successor to the Throne of his Kingdom; yet no sooner was he dead, but another steps up, and defeats her of her

[1] *Eventibus Angliæ a tempore regis Edgari usque mortem regis Ricardi Secundi*, 1652, fol.

[2] Richard of Hagustade: *Historiæ anglicanæ scriptores X.* Simeon monachus Dunelmsensis. Johannes prior Hagustaldensis. Ricardus prior Hagustaldensis. [seemingly edited by Sir Roger Twysden 1597–1672]. Londoni, 1652.

[3] *Historical Works of Gervase of Canterbury*, ed. W. Stubbs, 2 vols (1879–80, Rolls series.)

Pretensions; and how he possess'd himself of the Crown, is now to our next Consideration.

(t) As the main Line of *Normandy* failed in this *Henry* I. who was but the Third Inheritor; so, says my Author, the Succession ever since proved so brittle, that it never held to the Third Heir in a right Descent, without being put by, or receiving some alteration by Usurpation, or Extinction of the Male-blood. *Sir Winston Churchill's Divi Britannici, fol.* 207.

Stephen, Earl of *Mortain* and *Boleine*, was the Son of *Adela*, or *Adelicia*, alias *Alice*, one of *William* the First's Daughters; and says *Daniel* in his History of him, He having no Title at all, but one of the Blood, by mere Election of the State, was advanced to the Crown, notwithstanding the former Oaths taken to *Maud*. Some imagine upon these Reasons of Council, the State refused *Maud*, for it not being then the Custom of any other Christian Kingdom (whose Kings are anointed) to admit Women to inherit the Crown, therefore they might pretend to be free from their Oath, as being unlawful. But *Roger*, Bishop of *Salisbury*, one of the Principal Men then in Council, yielded another Reason for the discharge of their Oath, which was, That seeing the Late King had married his Daughter out of the realm, and without the Consent thereof, they might lawfully refuse her. *Daniel, fol.* 58.

Sir *Winston* owns it an *Election*, tho he softens it in this manner, to say truth, The People did not so much elect him, as reject her. *Divi. Brit. fol.* 209. and gives divers Reasons for it, as may there be seen.

But the Clergy, says *Daniel*, would not admit him for their King but [28] upon Terms; nor durst they trust to his Word; nor Oath indeed, without the Voucher of his Brother for their greater, and more full Security. His words are, and to be the more secured of their Liberties, before his admittance to the Crown, he took a private Oath before the Bishop of Canterbury, to confirm the Ancient Liberties of the Church, and had his elder Brother *Theobald*, Earl of *Blois*, to undertake betwixt God and Him, for the performance thereof. *Daniel. ibid.*

Matthew Paris says, ...the Great Men of the Kingdom being assembled at *London*, King *Stephen* promised to amend their Laws, so as all should be pleased;... and thereupon the Archbishop of *Canterbury*, who was the first of them all that had taken the aforesaid Oath to the Empress, crowned him King, all consenting to it ... Mat. Paris, fol. 74. lin. 25. *Vid. etiam Gesta* Stephani *Regis*, fol. 927, & 928.

Johannes Prior Hagulstadensis writes after the same manner; That *Stephen* got the Crown by the general Consent of both Clergy and Laity. ...John. Hag. col 258. lin. 24.

Richard, Prior of *Hagulstade*, agrees with im in substance, though in different words... Ric. Hagulst. Col. 312. lin. 15.

Gervasius gives another Reason of *Stephen 's Accession* to the Crown, which is this; When in the Great Convention of Estates there were warm Debates about the Succession, one of the Chiefest Peers of *England* took a solemn Oath, That King Henry had in his presence, a little before he died, voluntarily, and of his own accord, discharged them from the Oath that had been taken to his Daughter *Maud*, upon some offence supposed she had given him; wherefore *Stephen* was almost *Nemine contradicente* chosen to be King.[...] Chron. Gervas. Col. 1340. lin. 13.

Ralph. de Diceto, Dean of *London*, tells us, That this Great Man was *Hugh Bigod*, the King's Steward ... Rad. de Diceto, Col. 505. Lin. 49.[1]

In the Charter which he soon after passed under his Seal at *Oxford*, he owned in the preamble of it, that he attained the Crown by Election only;...[29] Ric. Hagulst. Col. 314; lin. 15.

And the Pope, in his Charter of Confirmation sent to him, puts him in mind of it likewise in these words: *Communi Voto & unanimi Assensu* ... Id. Col. 313. lin. 63.

His Reign was indeed full of Disturbances, being almost continually in War to keep the possession of it, both with[a] *Maud* the Empress, and her Son *Henry* by her[b] Second Husband the Duke of *Anjou*; but at last[c] a Mediation was concluded on in a Parliament at [d] *Winchester*, and the Historians inform us it was upon these Terms; [e] That *Stephen*, during his natural life, should remain King of *England*, and Henry enjoy his Dukedom of *Normandy*, as descended to him from his Mother, and be proclaimed Heir Apparent, and his Successor, as the Adopted Son of King *Stephen*; and thereupon the *English* Earls, Barons, and Great Men by the King's Command, swore Fealty to Duke *Henry* saving that Honour they were to pay the King whilst he lived. Duke *Henry* ever after gives *Stephen* the name of Father, and the King him the name of Son, who was without any opposition to have the Crown in case of Survival. I shall only name my own Authorities, because I have been so large upon this Reign already, and direct to the Pages. [a Guliel. Neubrig. Rer. Anglic. l. 1 c.8. p. 303. lin. 23. [b Id. c. 29. p. 378. lin. 37. printed at Heidelburg.. [c Id. c.30. p. 379. lin. 40 [d Gervas. Chron. Col. 1375. lin. 6 [e Mat. Westm. fo. 246. lin. 15. Joh. Hagulstad. Col. 282. lin. 27. Hen. Hunting. lib. 8. fol. 228. lin. 6. The Agreement is at large set forth in a large Charter of King *Stephen*'s, where you may read the whole matter. *Vide Brompton, Col.* 1037, 1038 *&c.*

I shall only insert here three lines of it, to shew the Reader how *jus hereditarium* was understood then *Stephanus, &c Sciatis quod ego Rex* Stephanus Henricum *Ducem* Normanniae post *me Successorem Regni* Angliae, *&c haeredem meum* jure hereditario *constitui. Ib. ibid.*

(u) Upon the death of King *Stephen, Henry* the Second succeeded to the Kingdom according to the above-said Parliamentary Agreement in that Right which had been conferred on him *with universal Consent*, and he was one of the greatest Kings this Nation ever knew; for he was in right of his Father Earl of *Anjou*, in right of his Mother Duke of *Normandy* and *Britany*, in the right of his Wife, Duke of *Guien and Aquitaine*, Earl of *Touraine, Tholosse* and *Poictou*, and in his own Right, King of *England*; and not long after (by right of Conquest) Lord of *Ireland. Divi Britan. fo.* 212.

Radulphus de Diceto says, That King *Henry* being at the time of *Stephen*'s death out of the Land, as soon as ever the News of it came to him,...... Ymagines Historiarum. Col. 529. Lin. 13. Ypodigma Neustriae. fol.446. uses almost the very same words. *Mat. Westm.* 246. lin. 40.

William of Newburgh declares it thus ...... the King was received as Sovereign with [30] an Universal Rejoicing and Acclamation of the People. *Guliel.*

[1] *Opera historica*, ed. W. Stubbs, 2 vols. (London: Longman & C°, 1876).

Neubrig.Rerum Angl. lib. 2. c. 1. fo. 381.[1] Matthew Paris says, ... fol. 92. lin. 29.

Brompton says, He received this Hereditary Kingdom without any diminution, to the general joy and satisfaction of all; Col. 1043. lin. 47.

Polidore Virgil relates it thus ...... fol. 210. lin. 41.

(w) *Henry* being dead, *Richard* Earl of *Poictou*, going to *Roan* in *Normandy*, was there by *Walter* the Archbishop, girt with the Sword of the Dutchy of *Normandy*, and having settled the state of that Province, he came from thence to *England*, and so to *London*, and summoning there *all the Clergy and Layety, he was by them solemnmy and duly elected*; and after he had taken his coronation Oath, and swore to three things, viz. 1. That all the days of his life he would bear Peace, honour and reverence to the Holy Church, and the Ordinances thereof. 2. That in the People unto him committed, he would exercise Right, Justice and Equity. 3. That he would blot forth naughty Laws, and perverse Customs, if any were brought upon his Kingdom, and would enact good Laws, and the same in good faith keep, and without Mal-Engyn. *Speed. Chron. fol.* 514. *Col.* 2. *Brompt. Col.* 1158. *lin.* 60. He was *with their Advice and Assent* consecrated and Crowned.

Ralph de Diceto, then Dean of St *Paul*'s, who in the Vacancy of that Church and Bishoprick, supplied the Office of the Bishop at Earl Richard's Coronation, writes thus ...Col. 647. lin. 45. Roger de Hoveden gives it us in these words; ...... fo. 374. lin. 10.

Polidore Virgil is short; but yet owns that a Parliament was summoned to make him King...fol. 242. lin. 36.

The manner of this King's Coronation is delivered to us by *Hoveden* in the plenitude of all its Circumstances and Solemnities, to which I shall refer, that I may not be over-tedious; only observe that the Archbishop, (after the King had so solemnly taken the Oath, before the Clergy and Laity, *co-*[31] *ram Clero & Populo*) forbad him on the behalf of Almighty God, to presume to take upon that Dignity, unless he resolved faithfully to perform those things he had then at the Altar so religouslu sworn to; to which the King answered, That by God's Grace he was resolved to do so. R. Hoved ut supra. 374. b. lin. 9. Vid. Brompt. fo. 1159. Mat. Par. fo. 153. lin. 48.

(x) King *Richard* dying without Issue lawfully begotten, the Hereditary Right of Succession was in Earl, or Duke *Arthur* (for he is called by both Titles) of *Britain*, the Posthumous Son of *Geoffrey Plantagenet*, Elder Brother to *John* Earl of *Moreton*; besides, Arthur's Sister, *Eleanor*, was then living, who had a nearer Right to the Crown of *England*, than her Uncle *John* could as then pretend to: But however, he thought himself of propinquity of blood near enough (being the Son of a King, and Brother to a King, and the only Son of *Henry* the Second then surviving) to get the Crown, if he could *win over the State* to his Interest and Side, that being in his Opnion the surest way of establishing him in the Throne; and therefore he got first *their Allegiance sworn to him against all men*, before he came into *England*, and next by their *Humane Consent*, and way of *Election*, received the Crown upon the *Ascenscion-day*, at the hands of Hubert Archbishop of Canterbury; and afterwards by his Charter he declared to the World that he was Crowned King...

[1] Wm of Neuburgh or Newbury (1136–1198?) *Historia de rerum Anglicarum*, criticised the fables of Geoffrey of Monmouth.

by the Election and Favour of both Clergy and Laity. *Ex Vet. Registr. in Archiv. Cant. Archiepis.*

Hoveden says......pars posterior, f. 450. b, l. 42.[1]

Brompton 's words are ......Col. 1281.lin. 47.

Matthew Paris gives us the Speech that Archbishop *Hubert* made at his Coronation,... And tells the Assembly, (after he had demanded silence) ' Be it known to your discretions, that no Man hath right to succeed another in the Kingdom, unless (after seeking the Grace of God's Holy Spirit) he be *unanimously chosen by the University of this Kingdom.* And then he goes on a little after, and says, ...But if any of the off-spring of the deceased King was more deserving than others, as this John was, they ought more readily to consent to this Election. - And then concludes, ' We having [32] considered the Valour and Prowess of this Noble Person here present,... have all of us unanimously chosen him, as well in regard of his Merits, as of his Royal Blood,' Mat. Par. fol. 197.

But King *John* soon shewed what Spirit he was of; and contrary to his Coronation-Oath, *without the Council or Assent of his Baronage,* he subjugated as much as in him lay, the Kingdom (which was always *free*) and made tributary to the Pope, subverting the good Customs, and introducing evil Ones, whereby he laboured to enslave both Church and Nation with many grievous Oppressions, *&c.* for which after many Applications and Addresses made to him, the Barons were forced to begin a War with him; and at last, amongst other things, by his own express consent was agreed, that if He returned again to his former excess of misgovernment, the Barons should recede from their Fealty and Allegiance; but yet in a little while disregarding this *Contract,* he fell into new and almost insupportable Oppressions, led on by his wicked Councellors, who knew how to make their own advantages by his irregularities; and with all (as *Daniel,* fol. 121 observes) 'so harsh a thing is it to a Power that hath once gotten out into the wide Liberty of his Will, to hear again of any reducing within his Circle; not considering how they who inherit Offices succeed in the obligation of them, and that the most certain means to preserve unto a King his Kingdoms, is to possess them with the same conditions that he hath inherited them

For his Evil Oppressions, as well as Councellors to them, *vid. Mat. Westm.* fol. 268-70.... They observed (as *Daniel*'s words are)' which way his will bent, *and so did what they could* to turn him more violently on that side. Wicked Councellors, as if it were not enough to be above Men, but to be above Mankind, *as those Princes would be, that would not be under the Law*; considering the preservation of Kings and Kingdoms, is to have the Ballance of Satisfaction, both of the one and other, equal. - And worthily that Prince deserves to be deceived in his Executions, who understands not as well the Concellors as the Councel. *Daniel,* fo. 12.

Their Oppressions at last became so universal, that they were insupportable to the whole Nation, Nobility, Clergy, and People; whereupon *Chronica* W. Thorn. *In Decem Scriptor. Col.* 1869. lin. 54) ...... by the General Councel and Approbation of them all, they judged him unworthy of the Kingdom. Abjudicatus est à Regno, as Mat. Westm. words are, He was by judgment deprived of the Kingdom. ......(Knighton, Col. 2423) it was thought absolutely necessary to depose him

[1] Roger de Hoveden or Howden, d. 1201?, *Chronica*, and *de Gesta Regni Henrici.*

from the Throne of the Kingdom; for they would not any longer suffer him to Reign over them. And then, communicato consilio, after the Council had fully debated on the matter,.... (Matt. Paris fol. 279) they decreed to chuse some puissant person for their King, by whose assistance they might be enabled to recover their Ancient Possessions, all steafastly believing this, that no body could rule more Arbitrarily and Tyrannically than King John had done; and so after some time, ballancing upon whom their [33] free Election should fall ... all unanimously consentend, That *Lewis* the *French* King's Son, should have the Crown of *England* ; upon which they sent some of their own Body (... M. West. 274) both Lords and Commons, beyond Sea to the said *Lewis*, whom they had so chosen for their King, desiring him with all speed to come over into England, promising immediately upon his Advent, to deliver the City of London into his Hands, and to do him Homage and Fealty. Knyghton, ut sup. ...... Jo. Leslaeus *Episcopus Rossensis de Successionis Jure Regnorum Angliae & Hiberniae, &c.* p. 29 a.

Lewis coming to *London*, was joyfully received, and upon his Oath first taken to restore the peoples Laws, and recover their Rights, they *Elected* and made him King, and had Homage and Fealty done him, as the Soveraign Lord. Vid. *Daniel*, fol.123,124. *Lewis* himself, in his Epistle to *Alexander*, the Augustin Abbot of *Cant* owns his Election in these words, *De Communi Regi Concilio & approbatione, Nos in Regem & Dominum elegerunt, Chron.* W. Thorn. Col. 1869. lin. 56. But He, being a *Frenchman*, soon forget what he had bound himself to observe by his Coronation Oath, and was endeavouring all he could to make his Government here Arbitrary, and dependent upon his own Will and Pleasure, despising both the Councils and the Persons of the *English*; (as you may read in *Knyghton*, Col. 2424). Upon which they began to repent of their new choice; and their late King *John* happening most opportunely to take his leave both of them and of the World, they presently withdrew their Fealty from the *Monsieur* ; and we shall see how they came to place the Crown upon the next Successor's Head.

I shall only 1*st* give an account of K. *John*'s Murthering of *Arthur* of *Britain*, the Rightful Heir, (as the late Reverend Dr. *Tho. Pierce*, Dean of *Sarum*'s words are, in his Vindication of the King's Soveraign Right, *fol.* 2) from an Ancient Historical Manuscript in that famous Library of Mr. *Smith* late deceased, the Author of which, stiles it, *Chronica abbreviata de Tempore* Edwardi *Regis ultimi, &c, de progenio* Anglorum *Membr.* That is, he begins with *Edward* the *Confessor*, being the last of that name before the pretended Conquest, and continues his History down to the beginning of *Henry* the Third's time, wherein it was writ; (for the Hand of the manuscript, is a Hand of that very time). He tells us this story ...... [34] He kept his Nephew *Arthur* for some time alive in Prison in the Castle at *Roan*, but one Day in a Drunken fit, being fill'd with a Devilish Malice, he went and killed him with his own hand, and tying a great Stone about his Body cast it into the *Seine*, which was dragged to shore by a Fisherman's Net, was known, and secretly buried in the Priory of Beck, called *St. Mary in the Fields*, for Fear of the Tyrant. But as soon as the K of *France* was certain of this Murther, He summoned the Murtherer *John* to come and Answer it at his Court; for *Arthur* was the Legitimate Heir of *England*, Earl of *Britain*, and the K. of *France* his Son in Law. But he being conscious of his guilt, never durst appear there, but fled into *England*, where he committed most grievous Tyranny upon his Subjects to his dying day. The Court of *France*, for his contempt, adjudged and disinherited him (with all his issue) of all the Lands and Honours he held from that Crown.

Matt. Westm. says, that this *John*, a long time before, endeavoured unjustly to deprive his Brother *Richard*, from the Kingdom of *England*, and thereupon was accused and Convicted of Treason, and Condemned too in open Court, which Sentence was pronounced by *Hugh Pudsey*, Bp. of *Durham*, and E. of *Northumberland*, and so was never true King. But if he had been King for some time, and also a true (that is, Lawful) King, yet afterwards he had *forfeited* the Kingdom by the Murther of *Arthur*, for which he was Condemned in the Court of *France*; And he said also, That no King or Prince could give away his Kingdom, *without the consent of his Barons*, who were bound to defend the Kingdom. *Vid. Mat. Westm.* fol. 275. l. 45.

(y) Upon the Death of K. *John* the Kingdom being miserably harassed and abused by *Lewis*, the Great Marshall, *William* E. of *Pembroke*, sending for as many of the Nobility, Gentry and Commons as he could get to him in *Gloucester*, where *Henry*, K. *John*'s Eldest Son was, not then being full Nine Years of Age; set this young Prince before them all, and as he was a Man *magnae auctoritatis & sani consilii*, speaks to this effect to them,' Tho we have prosecuted the Father, *propter mala ejus opera*, and that justly, yet this young Infant is pure and innocent from those his doings; you know what the Scripture saith, The Child shall not bear the iniquity of his Father ...... Come, let us pity his tender years, and make and consitute him to be our King, & *ejiciamus e terra nostra*, this *French* King's Son, and his People, and ...... throw off this yoke of vile Slavery from us. At last the whole Council, ..., as if they had been inspired by Heaven, cried out with one voice, ... be it so, he shall be our King [An. Dom. 1216]; so the day was appointed for his Coronation, which was that of the Apostles, *Simon* and *Jude*. *Knyghton de Event. Angliae*, Col. 2426, 2427. and *Vid. Mat. Par. f.* 289 & 309. [35] lin. 39. Vid. *Mat. Westm.* f. 227 lin. 4. and 279. lin. 59.

This was manifestly against the Right of *Eleanor*, Prince *Arthur* 's Sister, who was then living and kept close Prisoner by the Tyrannical commands of her late deceased inhuman Uncle, She was the next immediate Heir to her Murthered Brother, and rightful Successor, and the *futura Domina*, and this *Henry*, tho he was *filius regis*, yet was he likewise the Son of a Murtherer (as is plain by the foregoing relation) and of an Usurper of another's Right all his days; and till the 25 year of this *Henry*'s Reign [An. 1241] (in which he died) he had no better a Title to the Crown, than what was given him by the said *Election*. Vid. *Mat. Par.* fol. 574. lin. 40.

(z) After the long and uneasy Reign of *Henry* III he dying, and his Son *Edward* being in the *Holy Land* at *Palestine*, the States assembled at the New *Temple*, and proclaims this Son *Edward* King, tho they knew not whether he were living, swears Fealty unto him: causes a New Seal to be made, and appoints fit Ministers for the Custody of his Treasure and his Peace. *Daniel f.* 157. ...... Annales Waverleienses. fol. 227.

(aa) In the 39th Year of *Henry* VI. *Richard*, Duke of *York*, lays his claim to the Crown in Parliament; and after long Arguments made, and deliberate Consultation had among the *Peers, Prelates, and Commons of the Realm*; says *Grafton*, it was *condescended and agreed by the Three Estates*, for so much as King *Henry* had been taken King by the space of 38 years and more, that he should enjoy the

Name and Title of King, and have possession of the Realm during his Life natural: and if he died or resigned, or forfeited the same, for infringing any point of this Concord, then the said Crown and Authority Royal, should immediately descend to the Duke of *York*, if he then lived, or else to the next Heir of his Line or Linage, and that the Duke from henceforth should be Protector and Regent of the Land. Provided alway, That if the King did closely or apertly study, or go about to break or alter this Agreement; or to compass or imagine the death or destruction of the said D. or his Blood, then he to *forfeit* the Crown, and the D. of *York* to take it. These Articles, with many others, were not only *written, sealed, and sworn by the two Parties*; but also were *Enacted in the High-Court of Parliament.* Grafton's Chron. fol.647. vid. Cott. Records, 39 H. 6., *from* n° 10 *to* n° 33.

But D. *Richard* being slain in the Battle of *Wakefield*, his Son *Edward* called a Council of Lords Spiritual and Temporal, and laid open his Title to the Realm to them, with the Articles of Agreement. After the Lords had considered and weighed his Title and Declaration, they determined by *Authority of the said Council*, Forasmuch as King *Henry*, contrary to his Oath, Honour and Agreement, had violated and infringed the Order taken and *Enacted in the last Parliament*; and also because he was insufficient to rule the Realms, and unprofitable to the Commonwealth; he was therefore by the aforesaid Authority, *deprived and dejected* [36] *of all Kingly Honour and Regal Soveraignty,* and Incontinent *Edward*, Earl of *Marche*, was by the Lords in the said Council assembled, *named, elected, and admitted*, for King and Governour of the Realm. And the People being together in St. *John* 's Fields to behold the Muster that was there that day, the Lord *Fawconbridge*, who took the Musters, wisely declared to the Multitude, the Offences and Breaches of the late Agreement done by King *Henry* 6. and demanded whether they would have the said King *Henry* to reign any longer over them; to whom they with a whole voice answered, *Nay, nay*; then asking them if they would serve and obey the Earl of *Marche* as their Sovereign Lord, they anwered, *Yea, yea,* cryng King *Edward*, with many great shouts, and clapping of hands. The Lords being advertised of the *Loving Consent*, which the *Commons* frankly and freely of their free will had given; they all presently with several of the *most substantial Commons* went to *Baynard* 's Castle, and acquainted the said Earl with their *Election*, and *Admission*, and the *Loving Assent* of the *Faithful Commons*. And the next day being conveyed to *Westminster, his Title and Claim to the Crown was declared*, 1. As *Son and Heir to* Richard *his Father, right Inheritor to the same: 2. By Authority of Parliament, and Forfeiture committed by K.* Henry. And the *Commons* being again demanded, if they would *admit* and *take* the said Earl as their Sovereign Lord, all with one voice cried, *Yea, yea*; which Agreement was concluded, He was then again proclaimed, and the 29th of *June* following he was at *Westminster* crowned King by the name of K. *Edward the Fourth.* Graft. Chron. f. 652, 653, 658. Vid. *Speed*'s Hist. fol. 851. Col. 1,2, Stow. Fo. 414. Col. 2. 415. Col.1.

Richard the Third being intreated (by a Petition delivered in a Roll of Parchment in the Name of the *Three Estates out of Parliament,*) to accept the Crown, at first modestly refused, but afterwards he said, 'Sith we well perceive that all the Realm is so set, whereof we be very sorry, that they will not suffer in any wise K. *Edward*'s Line to govern them, *whom no earthly will can govern against their wills*; and well we also perceive, that no man there is to whom the Crown can by just Title appertain, as to our self, as very right Heir lawfully begotten of our most dear

Father, *Richard*, late D. of *York*, to which Title is now joined *Your Election, the Nobles and Commons of this Realm, which we of all Title possible take for the most effectual,* We be content.' *Speed, fol.* 908. n° 63.

And then an Act of Parliament passed to establish K. *Richard*'s lawful Election. *Id. fo.* 709, to 714. And it was therefore ordained, provided and established, That the Tenor of that Roll, with all the Contents of the same presented and delivered to the King, *in the name, and in the behalf of the said* * *Three Estates assembled in Parliament, and by Authority of the same, he ratified, inrolled, and authorized, to the removing of the Occasions of Doubts, and Amibguities, and to all other Lawful Effects, &c.*

* In the Margin is this Note. The Three Estates must concur to make a Parliament, else his Title would neither be valid, nor satisfactory, but ambiguous, as before. No one or two of them being a full or real Parliament, but all conjoined.

And it declares towards the end, That 'the High Court of Parliament is of such Authority, and the People of this Land of such a nature and disposition, as Experience teacheth, that manifestation and declaration of any *Truth or Right made by the Three Estates of this Realm assembled in Parliament, and by Authority of the same*, maketh before all things, most faith, and certain quieting of Mens minds, and removeth the occasion of Doubts, and seditious Language', *Cotton, ut supra.*

FINIS

A Charge by the Chairman to the Grand-Jury, General Quarter-Sessions of the Peace for the County of ESSEX at **CHELMSFORD,** July 10 1705. By Nicholas Corsellis, Esq; one of Her Majesty's Justices of the Peace for the said County. Published at the Request of the Grand-Jury, &c. LONDON Printed in the Year MDCCV.

A 2- 1

A CHARGE by the Chairman to the Grand-Jury, at the General Quarter-Sessions, &c.

Being desired by the Grand-Jury, several of the Justices of the Peace and Gentlemen of the County of *Essex*, to print the Charge I delivered at the General Quarter-Sessions of the Peace, held at *Chelmsford* the 10th of *July* 1705, I rather chose to expose my self to the Censure of some People than refuse their Request, and have accordingly printed the same, and set my Name to it; which is as follows.

Gentlemen

Justices of the Peace have Power at their Sessions to examine, but not to try Treason, and several other Felonies; and where they have (in discretion) they do forbear to determine great ones.

What was Treason in some other Reigns will be so in this, whether it come from the North or the South; 'tis easier for a Moth to sindge its Wings than extinguish a dazling light. We have the happiness to live under a Queen who is a Native of our own Country,[1] acquainted with her People and Constitution, whom every body may heartily and without grumbling obey; who had by our Law the undoubted Right, all other Pretensions being well excluded by Parliament; who is of our own Religion and Church, and has by her Royal Word so declar'd her self, in her Speech on Wednesday the 11th of *March* 1701. Her Majesty taking notice of her succeeding to the Crown, says: "I am extremely Sensible of the Weight and Difficulty it brings upon Me. But the true Concern I have of our Religion, for the Laws and Liberties of *England*, for the Maintaning the Succession to the Crown in the Protestant Line, and the Government in [2] Church and State, as by Law Established, Encourages Me in this Great Undertaking," and concludes, "As I know My Own Heart to be Entirely *English*, I can very Sincerely Assure you, There is not any Thing you can expect or Desire from Me, which I shall not be ready to for for the Happiness and Prosperity of *England*: And you shall always Find Me a Strict and Religious Observer of My Word."

In another Speech, on Monday the 25th of *May*, 1702 her Majesty says, "My own Principles must always Keep Me Intirely Firm to the

[1] This, in opposition to the previous monarch, William III, of Orange, of Dutch origin.

Interests and Religion of the Church of *England*, and will Incline Me to Countenance those who have the truest Zeal to support it."

In a third Speech, on Saturday the 27th of *Feb.* 1702 her Majesty says, "That all those who have the Happiness and Advantage to be of Our Church, will Consider, That I have had My Education in it, and that I have been willing to run great Hazards for its Preservation, and therefore they may be very Sure, I shall always make it My own particular Care to Encourage and Maintain this Church as by Law Established, and every the least Member of it, in all their Just Rights and Privileges; and upon all Occasions of Promotions to any Ecclesiastical Dignity, I shall have a very Just Regard to such, as are Eminent and Remarkable for their Piety, Learning, and Constant Zeal for the Church; that by this and all other Methods which shall be thought proper, I may Transmit it Securely Settled to Posterity."

A Queen that has Wisdom and Prudence enough to see thro', and in due time put a stop to any little Arts and Contrivances laid against This Church, by designing Persons to skreen themselves; after all these Assurances, which in Honour she cannot, in Justice she will not in the least deviate from; Who can imagine otherwise without the highest Indignity and Affront possibly put upon their Sovereign? I say, living under such Blessings as these, it may be impertinent so much as to name High-Treason.

Gentlemen

You can't but know how necessary it is to Present, and as much as in you lies, Prevent the Writing and dispersing of false News, and Libels; I fear there are those that frequently find fault with the four late Reigns,[1] and seem plainly to begin at the uniting of *Great Britain*,[2] and reflect on the illustrious House of the *Stuarts*, upbraid One with Kingcraft, Falshood and Cowardice (as much [3] as in them lies) justifie the most barbarous, and villainous Treason and Murther[3] that ever was committed; another they call lazie,[4] and despite the eighteen Years Peace when they were glutted with Plenty, and to shew their extraordinary Kindness to the Family, reflect on the Father of her Majesty, which, one would think, might be reason enough to bury in silence all faults in him. Death it self can't secure against these base practises; they can't permit the very Ashes of a great Prelate of our Church to liet quiet in his Grave, without the ill name of a Papist, whose Death, had it been thought legal (without doubt) the Judgment had been revers'd by Act of Parliament, as a noble

[1] The last four reigns: those of Charles I, Charles II, James II, William III.

[2] The uniting of Great Britain: it was effective for the first time when James VI of Scotland came to the throne of England; but in 1705 the Union was on the way.

[3] Murther: that of Charles I.

[4] Lazie: Charles II.

Earls was, whereas his Enemies *Moderation* is sufficiently set forth. Of what dangerous Consequences may it not be, to have the Proceedings and Votes in either, or both Houses of Parliament, or their Members, or but one single Vote of them made publick without Authority, where the Writer puts in, or omits what he pleases; to have whole Lists, and those false too, of Persons that voted one way or other? And as if the first Grant from the Throne (as I take it of course) were only to indemnify against the Crown, but every privy Scribbler could (as he may fancy to call it) do himself right, and by characterizing Men of the strictest Honour and Worth, let loose the Mob upon them; these things make Men look back upon the late Times with horrid Amazement, these unnatural Divisions look as if we did not indeed desire that Peace we daily pray for; we must be in earnest if we hope to beat the mighty Monarch of *France*, who, we find, is easier conquered in a Coffee-house than the Field (notwithstanding our early Campaigns.) How pleasant so ever the clear 4 s. in the Pound[1] out of the Rack-rent, without any deductions for Repairs, Tenants breaking, Lands in the Owners Hands, and other accidents; several other Taxes and Excises, dearness of all Foreign Commodities, some twice or thrice shipt, and the cheapness of our own Product, plenty of Melancholy, or Vapours, and Paper credit, but pinching want of Money and Trade, and that hazardous too may be to the Courtier and those that fleece (I had almost said) flea the People. The consumption of Timber may easily shew what huge Sacrifices have been made to preserve the Soil; yet if the dark Secret of Families were look'd into, there would a number of Mortgages, and Arrears of Interest found, that has eat into the Bowels of the Ground, and almost devoured the poor ancient Country Gentlemen; not to say any thing of the sad case [4] of younger Children, and how young Ladies shall get Husbands, this should provoke us to Peace among our selves, as we would get rid of this grievous burthen; and nothing keeps Men more from Unity than the dispersing of false Reports.

It may be esteemed a critical time to declare a Man's Thoughts in freely; but this, ever since I was capable of judging, was, is, and I hope will be my Opinion, not being a hasty one, but grounded upon a long Consideration, and the prejudice of Education to the contrary; the more hazardous, the more it becomes every honest Man to publish of what Church he is and will stand by, especially where a Person appears in a publick Quality, and under an Oath to discharge an Office to the best of his Understanding and Judgment, which I shall endavour, without keeping silent for fear, if the Churches Enemies were more numerous and wealthy, as is by some boldly, but without good reason asserted, or warping for favour; I shall look on it as an Honour to be misrepresented,

[1] The land tax levied to finance the war of Spanish Succession.

and as some People may foolishly call it, lessened, for doing what I take to be my Duty. I too well know my own Incapacities and Inabilities to be fond of an honorary Trust; where a Man may have an Information against him, and yet never think himself to blame; a Trust which is easily Accepted, but troublesome and difficult in the Execution; where a Man spends his time and Money, and therefore ought in reason to be protected tho' he mistakes the Law, unless it be done corruptly. It would be thought hard in *Westminster-hall*, for a Judge that enjoys a Place of Ease and Profit, and never forc'd to accept it, to be punished for barely acting as such, tho' his Judgment be erroneous and afterwards reversed. There can be no such Monster as a Low Church, every Person must be zealous for maintaining her in all her just Rights, or whilst he pretends only to her, and is not hearty for her, he shews to the World he's of no Church at all; whoever lives not up to the glorious Principles of the Church of *England*, ought to take the shame to himself; but the practice of the particular Members is no just reflection upon her, who dispenses no Pardons for wilful Sins, or what she judges unjust in her Professors, or permits them hypocritically to comply upon OCCASION.[1]

The first of *Elizabeth* takes notice that the repeal of the Statute of the 5th and 6th of *Edward* VI. for an uniform Order of Common Prayer and administration of Sacraments, Rights and Ceremonies, in the Church of *England*, by the first of Queen *Mary*, [5] was to the great decay of the Honour of God and discomfort of the Professors of the truth of Christs Religion, repeals that repeal, confirms the Statute of *Edward* VI. enacts, That *if any Beneficed Person shall declare against the said Book of Common-Prayer, shall be for the first Offence suspended for one year, be imprisoned six Months; for the second deprived; offending again, imprisoned a Year; offending a fourth time, imprisoned during life. That if any Beneficed Person shall declare against the said Book of Common-Prayer, shall be for the first Offence suspended for one year, be imprisoned six Months; for the second deprived; offending again, imprisoned a Year; offending a fourth time, imprisoned during life. That if any other Person, or Persons, shall in any Plays, Rhimes, &c. speak any thing in derogation, depraving, or despising the same, or any part thereof, shall pay for the first Offence one hundred Marks, be imprisoned six Months; the second four hundred Marks, be imprisoned one Year. And enacts, That every Person within this Realm, shall diligently and faithfully, having no lawful excuse to the contrary, resort to their Parish-Church, where Common-Prayers, &c. shall be used, on every Sunday and Holiday, and there abide orderly and soberly, during the whole time, upon pain of Twelve Pence a Sunday, and enacts the retaining the same Ornaments as before.*

By the 22d of *Charles* II "For providing further and more speedy

[1] The problem of occasional conformity (the communion according to the rites of the Church of England), which so much irritated the members of the High Church fraction of the Church; again, the last five lines of p. 5, on the subject.

Remedies against the growing and dangerous Practises of Seditious Sectaries, and other disloyal Persons, who under Pretence of tender Consciences have, or may at their Meetings contrive Insurrections (as late Experience has shewn;) " these are the very Words of the Preamble of the Statute, it enacts, *That if any above sixteen be present at any Assembly, under pretence of exercise of Religion, where there are five or more besides those of the Houshold, it shall be lawful for one Justice to make a Record of the same, which is declared a Conviction; the Penalty of the first Offence five Shillings, the second ten shillings on every Offender; and in case of Poverty, the Fines to be levied on those able under ten Pounds, upon the Preacher twenty Pounds the first time, forty the next; and this upon the Penalty of one hundred Pounds upon the Justice.*

Yet notwithstanding the Church of *England* was armed with these and larger Powers, such has been her lenity, to agree to a Law that indulges all Dissenters, that do but call themselves Protestants, in effect to set up a Religion of their own; so their Preacher takes a Licence, signs thirty five, and part of another, of the nine and thirty Articles of the Church of *England*, and leaves the Doors unbarred and unbolted; which small Compliances if they refuse, Stubbornness, not Religion, must be the Cause, and they incurr the Penalty of these two, and other Acts dispensed with, and ought to presented by you. [6]

If any one takes up a Land-man, and don't carry him before a Justice, and pursue the late Act of Parliament (tho' with a Warrant) I take it to be a Misdemeanour and breach of the Peace and presentable by you; if it was lawful before, this Act was vain. The Parliament were so tender in this Point as to make it probationary, and that too but for a short time; it is the taking away that which is much dearer to a Man than his Goods, and next to this Life, his Liberty, and perhaps carrying him where the Queen's Writ can't be executed; and if he have an Action when he can, if ever he comes home, it is such a Remedy a poor Man had as good be without. I have already spent so much of your Time, that should I begin with the Statute of *Winchester,* and *Labourers*, which gives the first Power to Justices of the Peace, and but give an Abstract of all the Laws which give them a Jurisdiction, the Acts are so many, their Authority so large, and Office so extensive, I should tire your Patience. As the Trust increases daily, and requires greater Judgment, Honour and Justice, so do their numbers too; I wish its Reputation may not sink, but their Qualifications may be answerable.

Gentlemen

You look like Persons that have served here before, and understand your Business and Duty; it would be to no purpose to say more. If any Doubt arises the Court will be ready to give you further Information.

FINIS.

[1]
Norfolk Record Office: WKC 7 / 101; 404 / 5.[1]

Gentlemen of ye Grand Inquest

The Court of Sessions of ye peace is appointed by our Constitution for ye better Securing of ye persons & property of ye Subjects from Violence & Wrong, & for ye maintaining of publick order within ye Compass of its Juridiction. It is ye happiness of this Nation to have Justice as it were brought to our doors by ye many Settled Courts yt are all over ye Kingdom & by ye Itinerant Jurisdiction of ye Judges in their Circuits. That Justice is near at hand to us & ye Course of it cannot be obstructed even by our Princes, for if ye Sovereign should send any illegal message to ye Judges to stop their proceedings, it is their duty to go on in their business without having regard to ye same. In this manner has our wise & Excellent Government secured ye Subjects from abuses from one another & from Tyranny in ye Prince. But for an age past this happy State of things amongst us has been attempted to be overturned by too many persons racking their brains for inventions to discharge our princes from all humane obligations of doing right to their people. And tho ye notions for this purpose have been chiefly advanced by such as have had their particular View in making their Court to their prince in this manner, yet many well meaning persons have given into them & been so far imposed upon therein, as to make it a point of Conscience to be slaves, when God & ye Laws of ye Land Suffer them to be free. Upon this account it may be a piece of good Service to our dear Country to endeavour to rectifie these mistakes about Civil Government wch are so dangerous to ye publick liberty. And this it may be no hard matter to do, if we consider ye Original & End of Government. As to ye Original of it, since by nature men are equal, Sovereignty could not be introduced, but by ye appointment of God, or ye Consent of Men Express or Implied. (For as to Conquest, in Such a case ye people may be called prisoners or slaves, but not properly Subjects till their wills be brought to Submit to ye Government. So ye Conquest may make way for a Governmt but cannot institute it.) Now we do not find yt God ever appointed a Governmt for any nation that of ye Jews only excepted, & in their case it may be observed, yt tho Saul & David were of Divine Designation yet ye people assembled & freely chose them, wch intimates yt there can be

[1] Although this first text is not dated, it was most likely written in 1709. The three documents are 33 × 21 cm.

no orderly & lasting Governmt without ye Consent of ye people & God himself would not put men under a Government without their consent. But this is not to be understood, as if where ye Sovereignty is fixed in a line or a family, upon ye death of a Governour ye people may place [2] a Ruler over them without regard to ye settled form of Succession. No, men may bind their posterity for their good, & ye fundamentals of a Constitution are not to be departed from, unless in Extraordinary Cases where it may be presumed ye Framers of ye same never intended to bind them yt come after them & where necessity requires a variation. The most Adequate Notion then of Civil Governmt is, yt it is a Compromise made by such a Body of Men, by which they resign up ye right of demanding reparations either in ye way of Justice against one another, or in ye way of war agst their Neighbours to such a single Person, or to such a Body of men as they think fit to trust therewith. And in this account of Government ye End of it is intimated, namely ye protection of ye Community under it. Nor has ye Gospel made any alteration in this matter, for tho there be commands therein of being Subject to ye higher powers, yet what ye Extent of such power is, is not there express'd; but that must be learnt from ye respective Laws of each Nation. So that ye Christian Religion does not enlarge Civil Authority, but only Strengthens it by laying a further Obligation to that Subjection which ye Laws of any nation exact without requiring an obedience contrary to such Laws. By ye Constitution of this Nation our Sovereigns are limited in their Authority, & therefore to talk of unlimited obedience under a limited Monarchy is to betray ye freedom of our Country & to talk nonsense. The History of this Kingdom, its Laws, ye practice of our princes taking an oath at their Coronation to govern ye people according to ye Laws, do all demonstrate yt ye Royal dignity of this nation is so far from being a despotick kind of Governmt yt it carries along with it in its very essence, a mixture of interests betwixt prince & people, & lays an obligation upon ye prince to govern not by Arbitrary will but according to Law. Seeing then yt by ye Laws of ye Land we are free, & yt ye Laws of God do not prohibit us in ye enjoyment of this freedom, & yt ye End & intention of Civil Governmt was for ye protecting ye rights of Mankind, such doctrines as render this security precarious are agst Law & reason & ye publick wellfare & ought to be discountenanced as much as possible. Let us be content to make a conscience of paying that obedience to ye Queen, wch is due to her by ye Laws of ye Land wth Reverence & heartiness. But let us not make an oblation of ye Liberty of our Country, That would be foolish & unjust, & a Sacrifice, yt we have no reason to think would be acceptable to her, Since from her happy [3] Exaltation to ye Throne, she has always made ye Laws ye measure of her Governmt & before she ascended ye same exposed her self to ye utmost danger to preserve this Church & Nation when in a Sinking Condition.

Gentlemen, I need not trouble you wth all ye particulars Subject of yr Inquiry, wch are in General from felonies down to trespasses & misdemeanours, but shall confine my self to such instances as you may need a particular direction in or whereby ye publick is most Grieved. Something has lately happen'd in ye Town wch has made ye noise of a Riot & therefore I shall give ye doctrine of Riots in ye Law yt you may apply ye same as there shall be occasion. Now a Riot is where three persons or more meet to do an unlawful act or Lawful in an unlawfull manner to ye terror of ye people & do ye same. So that ye unlawfulness of ye act does not always accuse of this offence nor ye Lawfulness excuse. For if I claim right to a piece of Timber & employ three or more to remove it & they be no more yn are necessary upon such an occasion & I have no right to ye same, tho this be unlawfull & a Trespass, yet if it be done without a publick Terror, this is no Riot. On ye other Side, if three or more come together to ye Sessions or Market wch is a lawful act, yet if they come wth arms &c or in a Terrifying manner, this is a Riot. So if three or threescore persons go together to a publick house to refresh themselves but without menacing or giving any such cause of Terrour to any Body, this is no Riot (tho it is not prudent for people to go together in great numbers even upon an innocent occasion. Especially in ye night). Indeed if they stay there too long, they may subject themselves to ye penalty agst Tipling, these places being originally designed by ye Law for ye accomodation of Travellers & such poor inhabitants as could not lay in beer for themselves. But if ye Laws in this respect should be rigorously put in Execution it would spoil ye brewing trade & be no small diminution to ye queens Revenue. And therefore since a great deal of business is transacted in these places & trade & ye publick revenue are promoted by them, ye Magistrates by an alteration of Circumstances since their institution don't think it necessary to put ye Laws in Execution upon this Occasion, unless for ye restraint of drunkenness or to hinder ye profanation of ye Lords day, tho it were they would take care ye number of these places should not be excessive. And that these places be regular depends in a great measure upon you, it being your duty to present such of them, where Lewdness, gaming, drunkenness or any other disorders are suffer'd to be committed [4] to ye disturbance of ye neighbourhood & ye Encouragement of vice. And since you observe how desirous her Majesty is by her proclamation wch has been read to ye, yt piety & virtue may be encouraged among her people, I cannnot recommend any thing to you more effectual for this good purpose, than ye reforming these places. Now to resume ye Subject of Riots, ye Essence of this Offence seems to be in the matter of publick Terror, & is distinguished in its punishment from common Trespasses, by ye greatness of ye fine. Gentlemen, there are great complaints yt the Highways about ye Town are in a very bad Condition. It is for ye

Honour & interest of ye publick, yt an easie communication should be maintained between one place & another by ye Commodiousness of ye ways & therefore I desire you to present such Towns as shall be deficient in this respect, as likewise all inconveniences in the streets either for want of repair or by reason of annoyances. You are also to present all practices agst ye publick plenty by such as for their private gain make an artifical Scarcity by forestalling, ingrossing or regrating, & all abuses in dealings whether by false weights or measures or any other deceipt. The Buying & Receiving of stolen goods is a flagrant offence in this Town & you are too sensible of ye mischief of it, to be wanting in doing your utmost for ye suppressing so vile a practice. You are further to present ye neglect of Constables, Overseers of ye Poor & Surveyors of ye highways in their office & extortion & oppression in ministers of Justice, as likewise Idle wenchs yt live at their own hands, who serve to no purpose but ye debauching of ye youth & ye bringing charge to parishes & in a word whatever is amiss amongst us & proper for this Court to reform. Gentlemen, I need not put persons of your Character in mind of your oath upon this occasion wch obliges you to spare none for favour nor to present any Body out of hatred or ill will. I doubt not of your upright & impartial discharge of your office. And altho party humour dos too much disturb ye repose of ye Town, yet I hope it shall never enter into this place to pollute ye streams of Justice, but that here we shall always respect mens cases only & not their persons. In Confidence of finding from you all yt may be expected from persons yt love their Country & good order. The Court, Gentlemen, for ye present dos dismiss you.

(WKC 7/101/ 3)
Norfolk Record Office, WKC 7/ 101 - 405 x 5 / 4

Gentlemen of the Grand Inquest July. 24. 1710.

We are assembled here for ye dispensing of Justice & ye preservation of ye publick peace within ye Compass of this Jurisdiction. The Civil œconomy of this Nation is admirable for ye Security of publick & private Right. 'Tis our happiness to live under a Government where ye Laws are ye rules of ye prince's power, as well as the measure of ye Subjects obedience. Who ever knows any thing to purpose of our Constitution must know yt it is a mixed limited Monarchy. The Supreme Legislative power is in ye Queen, Lords & Commons in Parliament, but ye Executive part is solely in ye Queen, & From so great a share of ye Exercise of, ye Government being in ye Sovereign, it may well be called a Monarchy. The true End of all forms of Civil Government is ye protection & benefit of ye Society yt live under ye Same, & mankind can never be supposed to submit themselves willingly to one person or more, who by nature are their Equals, but for their common preservation. There is a Treason against ones Country, as well as ye Governour of it, & all wise & good men will be equally Conscientious in preserving ye Fences of publick Liberty as of ye prerogatives of princes. Therefore ye advancing wth so much warmth the doctrine of passive obedience & non resistance without any limitation amongst a people, who by means opposite thereunto have been so lately restored to ye free & secure Enjoyment of their Religion, Laws & Liberties, & at a time when we are Governed by a queen who pretends to no power, but what ye Laws allow, & to whom her Subjects pay ye most willing & cheerful obedience seems not to be accounted for, unless it is designed thereby to raise scruples in ye minds of ye good people of this land about ye lawfulness of ye present Governmt to dispose them ye better for ye reception of ye pretender. The authority of our Kings has no other foundation yn ye Rights of ye People have, I mean ye Laws of ye Land, for 'tis a rule yt ye Law makes ye King & there is nothing in ye Gospel nor in ye reason of ye thing, yt debars a nation from defending it self against ye Tyranny of its Governours, any more yn from ye invasions of a foreign Enemy. The Scripture I presume was never intended as a rule for ye Conduct of our Civil affairs, any otherwise yn by directing us to ye Exercise of prudence Justice Equity & Humanity in our transactions wth one another, nor are its Commands in relation to obedience to Magistrates delivered any [2] otherwise yn in General terms & upon of a supposal of ye Magistrate's acting for ye publick good; so that ye degree of obedience due to them must be learn'd from ye respective Laws of each country, & ye Scripture can't wth any good sense be construed to lay any obligation upon us in that respect farther yn ye Laws of ye Constitution do require. Of this Opinion was ye Nation in general at ye late happy Revolution, & I think ye Nobility Gentry & Commonalty assembled at Nottingham to assist ye prince of Orange in their declaration upon that occasion express'd themselves very properly. We hope (say they) all good protestant subjects will wth their lives & fortunes be assistant to us, & not be bugbear'd wth ye opprobrious terms of Rebells, by wch they (yt is ye Enemies of our Country's Liberty) would fright us, to become perfect Slaves to their Tyrannical Insolences & usurpations. For we assure our selves, yt no rational & unbiassed person will judge it Rebellion to defend our Laws & Religion wch all our Princes have sworn to at their Coronation. We own it Rebellion to resist a King yt governs by Law; but he was always accounted a Tyrant, yt made his will a Law, & to resist such a one we justly esteem no Rebellion, but a necessary defence. 'Twas to ye Lords assembled in these parts yt our Glorious queen to her immortal Honour took a dangerous journey to encourage by her presence ye measures concerting for ye preservation of a sinking Church & Nation. What this Kingdom did in its late Extremity is warranted by ye practice of our ancestors in ye like cases, & our History furnishes us wth many instances of ye Nation's demanding its Laws of our Princes, & making use of ye necessary means in ye defence of ye same. Our very Laws them selves seem to allow of this right, if our ancient Lawyers may be suffer'd to testifie upon this occasion. Bracton says, yt ye King dos no wrong, in as much as he dos nothing but by Law. The power of ye King is ye power of ye Law, a power of right, not of wrong. If ye King does injustice, He is not King. And in ye Laws of Edward ye Confessor it is said, yt unless ye King performs his duty, & answer ye End for wch he was constituted, not So much as ye name of a King shall remain in him. Much more may be found to this purpose in the before mentioned Bracton & in other ancient Lawyers of England, as Glanvil, Fleta & Fortescue. If it be objected hereunto, yt by a Statute made soon after ye restauration of K. C. ye 2d an oath was enjoyned upon some persons & a declaration upon others, yt it was [3] unlawful upon any pretence whatsoever to take up arms against ye King or any Commissioned under him. It may be answer'd, that this obligation is taken away by an act of ye 1st of Wm & Mary. And whilst this Law was in being, ye Forte of it might have some abatement, if ye Circumstances, when it was obtained, be considered. In ye precedent Confusions, ye pretended Reformers of ye publick abuses had gone so far as not only to murder ye King, but also to destroy ye very Constitution of ye Government both in Church & State. And therefore upon our recovery out of these miseries by ye restauration when ye nation was heated wth indignation at ye late proceedings, & it being so usual for people to run from one extream to another, it is not to be wondered if ye Regal power was carried too high in atonement, For its having been depress'd so low. But ye Revolution & ye act abovementioned have brought us back to our ancient Constitution, wherein there is sufficient provision, yt neither prince nor people can hurt ye other, but be reciprocally extremely beneficial.

I would not be understood by any thing I have here advanced to encourage any wantonness in ye people, to distress their Governours. Far be that from me, private persons must bear ye Injustice of their princes & nothing but ye prospect of ye entire destruction of a Constitution can justifie a nation doing what we did at ye Revolution. No danger can arise to her Majesty from a vindication of ye publick liberty. This is consistent wth our duty to her & I am sure none of her Subjects have express'd a greater veneration for her, nor will upon all occasions give more real instances of ye same yn ye Friends of ye Revolution. I would endeavour to inspire you wth a love of ye Liberty of yr Country & I hope we shall calmly consider things & fall into such measures as shall secure her Majesty & her people in a Safe & easie Condition & give no advantage to ye Common Enemy in his designs upon us, wch we trust in God he will never be able to effect unless by our divisions.

The returns of holding of this Court are so frequent, & by that means ye Business of it so familiar to you, yt I need not trouble you wth

Enumerating all ye Offences yt are presentable by you, wch in general are from petit Treason down to trespasses against ye peace nusances & misdemeanours.

[4] It may suffice to take notice to ye of such offences as are most flagrant amongst us. And here I cannot omit ye great Injustice practised in publick Elections, where persons not qualified by Law, or by an abusive repetition of their votes presume to intermeddle upon those Occasions. This is a fraud upon ye publick rights & may have a fatal effect upon our Constitution, & therefore is worthy yr Consideration to give a check to, by presenting such persons who take so shameful a Liberty, wch tends to disappoint ye intention of ye Law in determining upon such occasion by a fair majority.

You may observe by her Majesties proclamation agst immorality & prophaneness wch has been now read to you, how sollicitous she is yt piety & vertue may be encouraged. You ought to second her Majesties pious Intentions by discountenancing vice & prophaneness in presenting such publick houses, as suffer debauchery & disorderliness, as also all Common Swearers & such persons as do not go to Church or to some other place of divine Worship permitted by Law. There has bin a Complaint yt some of ye Overseers in this City have diverted ye mony raised for ye poor to their private use. This is a great wrong to ye poor & a hardship upon ye parishes in this dead time of trade & deserves ye severest animadversion. I recommend to ye to present all abuses upon ye publick, by forestalling, ingrossing or regrating, false weights & measures & ye wicked tho I fear too common practise of buying stolen goods, as also all incommodiousness in ye Highways & Streets either thro want of reparation or by reason of nusances & in a word every grievance to ye publick yt can be redressed by this Court. Gentlemen, being perswaded you will discharge yr selves suitably to ye service you are upon. I do for ye present dismiss you.

N.R.O. WKC 7 / 101 / 404 x 5 / 5

Gentlemen of ye Grand Inquest July 17 1711

We are assembled here upon a solemn account, having ye Administration of Justice. It is incumbent upon all of us, who have a share in that Important affair to discharge our selves Impartially. None are to be spared for favour, nor any one to be pursued out of hatred or Malice; but all yt we are to have in our View, is ye Suppressing of Offences, ye preserving ye persons & ye properties of ye Subjects & ye maintaining ye publick peace & good order as far as ye Jurisdiction of this Court can reach for that purpose. It is not unsuitable to this occasion to reflect upon our happiness in living under a wise & just Constitution of Government. No Kingdom in Europe has liberty in that perfection, as that we belong to. France, Denmark & Sweden were once as happy, as we are in that respect & ye consideration of what they have lost can only add to their present unhappy Circumstances. But if we be wise, we may profit by others misfortunes & be prompted to value & preserve that freedom wch once was their right & portion, & still is ours in both respects. Nay we need not go so far to learn our Interest; it is but bringing to remembrance ye Fears we were in of being in their sad Condition, when providence raised up our Great Deliverer to restore ye Freedom of our Government; & if we do not forget that happy transaction, wch rescued us from Slavery, & reinstated us in our ancient rights, we shall be cautious of such measures as tend to bring us into ye like peril. No doctrines should be advanced wch insinuate yt we have no rights but at ye pleasure of the prince. The Contrary of which is certainly true, for ye Subjects of this Kingdom have as good a title, nay ye same to their Liberty & property as our prince to ye Sovereignty, to wit by ye Laws of ye Land. [2] Such therefore are unjust foolish & dangerous Complements to Princes, & particularly can never be acceptable to our Glorious Queen, for she asserted ye Subjects Rights in her Early & hearty appearing for ye recovery thereof. She was contented to be postponed in the ordinary course of her Succession for ye rewarding of him yt restored ye Nations rights, has declared she should look upon them as her truest Friends who were most zealous for ye Revolution, & has lately assured us from ye throne, yt none of her predecessors ever had ye welfare of ye Subjects more at their heart, yn she has, nor do I believe they had. By ye ancient Laws of our Country tis Equally an offence against ye Crown to make ye prince have an ill opinion of ye people, as ye people of the prince, because ye one as well as ye other tends to ye destroying that confidence between them which is ye great support of both. And therefore I must leave it to your Consideration whether some of ye publick news writers have not taken a Criminal Liberty in this respect by blackening great numbers of persons as rebels or factious because they have shewed more concern yn some others for ye freedom of their Country but who at ye same time had given undeniable Evidence of their affection for her Majesties person and Government. For shame let these practises be discouraged, & let not one part of ye Nation trample upon ye other. The benefit of protection is equally designed by ye Government to be extended to all ye Subjects, & there is to be no discrimination in that respect but where any have forfeited that priviledge by their offences & this ought to be by legal adjudication & not by libels & mobbing. There have bin great heats in ye nation & to our reproach we have fallen foul upon one another [3] but I hope we are cooling & shall settle upon ye Common Interest of our prince & Country. In order to ye Establishmt of peace at home & ye recovery of it from abroad let us reform our manners. The Scripture says, from whence come wars & fightings among ye; come they not hence, even of yr lusts? Our Vices have a natural &

judicial Causality to introduce disquiet. Our Conceitedness our Ambition & our Selfish designs distract our affairs at home. And these & our other wickednesses bring Gods judgment of war upon us from abroad. Let us remove ye cause & ye Effect will vanish. Her Majesty by her pious proclamation wch has bin read to you recommends to all in authority ye incouraging religion & vertue & ye suppressing of irreligion profaness [sic] & immorality. But this may be read to ye end of the world without much effect, if nothing more be done. You are to consider yt this is not a thing of form. So far from it, yt you are obliged from ye Law of God & ye land to do your utmost to render her Majesties desires in this respect effectual. And therefore I give you in charge to present all publick houses yt suffer Lewdness & disorders to be committed therein, Common Swearers & prophane persons & such as do not worship God either in ye Church or in some other publick place of divine worship permitted by ye Law. I do with pleasure contemplate upon ye project on foot in this City to erect a workhouse for ye preventing of idleness ye mother of wickedness. ['Tis as?] Gods appointmt to ye only Nation yt he ever interposed as a Civil Governour, yt there should not be a beggar in ye Land. The suffering such in a publick manner is either a reflection upon our humanity in not providing for those yt cannot help themselves, or an instance of our negligence in not compelling those yt can, to do so. [4] I heartily wish ye good design I mentioned may take effect. Gentlemen I need not trouble you wth running over all ye offences wch this Court has a power to punish, wch in general are from felonies down to trespasses agst ye peace & misdemeanours & whatsoever of this nature comes down to your knowledge you are to present particularly. I recommend to you to obviate all mischiefs yt may arise to ye publick by enhansing of Commodities & Especially Victuals, as by forestalling ingrossing or regrating, or by false weights & measures. The Buying & receiving of stolen Goods is a wicked practice yt I am afraid this City suffers much by & I believe you are so sensible of it yt I need not press you to discourage this abuse. You are likewise to present all inconveniences in ye Highways & Streets whether from obstructions, annoyances or want of repair & in a word every thing yt is amiss amongst us & proper for you to present. Gentlemen the Consideration of your oath & of ye duty you owe to ye publick will engage you to a careful & faithful discharge of ye service you are upon & in confidence thereof ye Court dos for ye present dismiss you.

Mr. Baron *Lovell's* **CHARGE** to the **GRAND JURY** for the **County of Devon**, The 5*th* of *April*, 1710. **At the Castle of EXON.** *LONDON*, Printed for *A. Baldwin* in *Warwick-Lane* 1710

[3-A 2]

Mr. Baron* LOVELL's *Charge to the Grand Jury for the County of Devon, &c.[1]

Gentlemen of the Grand Inquest;

Her Majesty having been pleased to appoint us Judges for this Circuit, to put the Laws of this Nation in Execution, and being ready to proceed thereon, I cannot omit laying before you the Excellency of our Laws, compared with those Abroad. Laws, which do not authorize, but check and oppose Sword, Fire, Persecution, Oppression, and Inquisition. They preserve every Man's Liberty and Property, and are made for the Support of the good Government, as establish'd and settled by them. Her Majesty knowing that the best Foundation is in Religion, builds on that Rock, and I can assure you, [4] has taken an unalterable Resolution, to prefer none to any Dignities in Church or State (which are in her Donation) but such as are Men of conspicuous Virtue, Piety, Morality, and Temper.

A Wild Fire is running about, to the great Disturbance of the Peace. And whence comes it? From Priests and Jesuits.

You have in this City an Inflamed Preacher, who after having been toss'd from Place to Place, at last vents his turbulent Doctrine here[2]. Such doth not become the Pulpit, and nothing else is to be done there, but to preach up Vertue and Piety, as we do now earnestly recommend to you from this Place, and charge you to do it, as you must answer it before God and Man.

You have a Diocesan (whom I do not personally know, but am inform'd credibly is) a Man of Vertue, Piety, and Temper: All under him should

[1] Sir Salathiel Lovell, 1619–1713. Called to the bar at Gray's Inn, 1656; June 1688, Serjeant-at-Law, 1692 Recorder of London, 1695, King's Serjeant-at-Law, 1696, a judge on the Welsh circuit, 1708 appointed a baron of the Exchequer.

[2] Not identified.

follow his Example. They cannot adorn themselves better, than with such Qualities: And I hope he will countenance none (I am sure Her Majesty will not) but Men of those Principles.[1]

I have been present at the great Trial of a Turbulent and inflamed Preacher in *London*, who on a Day of rejoicing, [5] turned the Solemnity of it into Railing against the Government, and the Parliament, crying out, the Danger of the Church, contrary to Her Majesty's Word, and the Votes of Both Houses of Parliament.[2] And then caus'd a Book to be printed, which was dispersed abroad. The Text was good, but the Discourse had little of Piety, but much of venemous Aspersion, and virulent Reflections. It was high time to put a stop to such Inflammation; which could not be done, but by the House of Commons, taking notice thereof; and the Man was tried before the highest Court of Judicature (do not mistake me; by the Man, I understand his Principles) where all manner of Liberty of Speech was allow'd, and a moderate Punishment put on the Person, who at best is but an inconsiderable Fellow. Upon this I find the Country in a Ferment: And for what? Men may differ in Opinions; but must this create Disunion? No more Reason can be given for it, than for differing about our Shapes. You ought to live in Peace for your own sake, and for Her Majesty's sake (who is so highly affronted by these Disturbances, whilst she has nothing more at Heart, than the Welfare and Quiet of her People) and [6] also for the Honour of your Religion.

I would ask you of all those, that cry up the Doctrine of Passive Obedience what they mean; or what Necessity there is for trumping up that damnable Doctrine?

Many may say I am hot; I am fervent as the Subject on which I am requires. I doubt not, but some may still remember the dismal Consequences of it some 60 Years ago and upwards. Or at least most of you have heard the deplorable Calamities it drew upon this Nation.

Whatever Cloak the Assertors of the Dangers of the Church may put upon their Expressions, and whatever Pretensions they may make of having taken the Oaths, and sworn Allegiance; I say they are the Men that would overturn our excellent Laws: For that I find the greatest part of them, either never go to Church or it's much if ever they partake of Her Ordinances. If these Men were obliged to speak plain, it might soon appear that they aim at supplanting Her Majesty, and setting up a

[1] The bishop of Exeter would be Dr Offspring Blackall, rector of St. Mary Aldermanry, London, translated to the see of Exeter in order to keep the balance between Whig and Tory bishops in the days of a minor crisis in the Church.

[2] The preacher quoted here was the famous Dr. Sacheverell who preached a sermon *On the Perils of False Brethren*, before the Lord Mayor of London, 5 Nov. 1709, the anniversary both of Guy Fawkes' plot, and of William's landing in England. He was impeached and tried early in 1710 (27 Feb.–23 March).

Pretender (I must express my self in plain Terms) or at least preventing the Succession of the Crown as by Law established. [7][1]

What means these tumultuous Meetings (of which I have been informed) breaking of Windows, and insulting of Persons ? These are Breaches of the Publick Peace. I must tell you, Gentlemen, that as you are the Inquisitors of this County, you ought to present all such, who are Actors in it, and whoever incourages or countenances the Mob (I use the Word unwillingly; but must for Distinction sake) in such Actions. It's a Riot and Rout by the Law. It's your Duty to present them. I understand some Magistrates and Justices have endeavour'd to present and suppress such Meetings, and I hope many more will. I am certain, none but such can expect Her Majesty's Favour.

I must on this occasion tell you, that formerly some mistaken zealous Men for pulling down Bawdy-Houses behind *Lincolns-Inn Fields*, were prosecuted for High Treason, and some of them hanged, drawn and quarter'd.

At the Judges setting out from *London* for their Circuits, they had a particular Charge of Her Majesty to recommend Peace to you, and to observe the Transactions in the Country; and I doubt not but on return of all the Judges to Court, you shall hear further about that Matter. [8]

I must again recommend to you, to follow your Bishop's Example, who is a Man of Temper; preach up Piety and live in Unity. Bind your selves together with that Bond and let us not frustrate Her Majesty's Endeavours, to settle a lasting Peace Abroad, by creating a War at Home.[2]

Then proceeded on the common Matters of the Law; and concluded,

Once more I earnestly desire, and charge you to live in and promote Peace amongst your selves; if you have any Regard to the Welfare of the Church and State, and the Honour of Her Majesty; and if you expect that your late Posterity shall bless your Memory, after you have long enjoy'd the agreeable Fruits of a peaceable Temper.

FINIS.

[1] The Act of Settlement had settled the succession to the throne, in case William did not marry again and Princess Anne died without posterity. Her last surviving child, the Duke of Gloucester, died 30 July 1700.

[2] The efforts of the Tory government (Harley, Bolingbroke) to procure peace with France.

Sir *RICHARD COCKS* HIS **CHARGE** TO THE GRAND-JURY Of the County of *GLOUCESTER,* At the GENERAL QUARTER-SESSIONS Held for that COUNTY, *April* the 30*th* 1717. *LONDON,* Printed by *Samuel Palmer,* and Sold by J. Roberts at the *Oxford-Arms* in *Warwick-lane.* MDCCXVII (Price 3d.)

[3-A 2]
Sir *RICHARD COCKS*
His
CHARGE, &c.

Gentlemen,

I AM commanded by the *King'* s Proclamation, to enforce and recommend to you the indispensable Obligations you lye under, of becoming a sober and religious People. It is the Interest of Princes, to make their Subjects virtuous; for by the means the End of all Laws may be answer'd, with- [A 2-4] out having recourse to severities. The Design of all human Laws is, To secure Property, to oblige Men out of fear of Penalties, to live honestly and justly, and to honour and obey their Superiors. But these can restrain no further, than the Fear and Danger of being discovered can make Impressions upon us; whereas if Men were really virtuous and good, there would be no occasion for Penalties to awe them; for no Privacy or Security whatsoever can tempt a good Man to do the least Injustice to any one, much less Acts of Violence and Oppression. As for what concerns a future State, that being properly the business of the *Clergy,* I will not invade their Province. But since so many of them are graciously pleased to honour this Court, and are ready upon all occasions to assist us; I will beg leave for once to take a Text out of the Bible, to be the Foundation of my following Discourse. *When thou takest any matter in hand, consider the End thereof, and thou shalt never do amiss.*[1] Though upon Second Thoughts I find I had no Occasion to ask this Favour, since we have the Remark of an old Lawyer much to the same Purpose: *That a wise Man begins all his Actions from the End.* To illustrate this by Example. Did but Men consider the unhealthfulness, Poverty, and other ill Consequences that necessarily attend Drunkenness, they wou'd [5] not so often put their Hands with full Glasses to their Mouths. The *Stat.* of *King James the First* against this detestable Sin of Drunkenness, is very properly for your Perusal[2]. Did but Men consider the Scandal and Ignominy, that they bring upon themselves, by profane Cursing and Swearing besides the Folly of offending God thereby, and rendring themselves liable to

[1] This looks like a gloss on Luke 14: 28.

[2] 4 Jac. 5.

Temporal Penalties, without the least Profit or Pleasure; they would certainly unanimously agree, to leave off this ridiculous Vice. In short, if Men wou'd but seriously reflect upon the easy and happy Circumstances, the Credit and Reputation of Good Men on the one Hand, and on the other upon the Poverty, the Shame, the Fears and the Punishments that are the constant Companions of the Wicked, they would soon determine which to chuse. But the want of this great Lesson of Consideration has too often involv'd us in many publick, as well as private Calamities, and plunged us into almost insuperable Difficulties. We have seemed of late and do still in some measure, to be one of those Inchanted Islands, that the Poets so much talk of. We have seen Men of no Religion, Immoral, Profane, Atheistical Wretches pretend to be exceedingly zealous for the *Church*; and these have so infatuated many others amongst us, with the Fears and Apprehensions of the *Church*'s Danger; That under pretence of preserving that *Church*, [6] which is the Bulwark of the *Protestant* Religion (for so I may truly call the *National Established Church*) they have prevail'd upon their Followers, to expose their Lives and Fortunes, in order to Depose and Murther a Just, Good, and Gracious Protestant Prince, Zealously affected to that Church; and to set in his Place a *Popish Pretender*, educated in arbitrary *French* Principles, instructed in all the cruel Arts of *Popery*, and supported at that very time by a Pension from the *Pope* : And under pretence of restoring to you your Liberties and Properties (which you never enjoy'd in a more ample manner, and which by the Blessing of God were never more safe and secure to you than under the present just Possessor of the Crown) they have invited over a desperate Tyrant, and a poor starv'd beggarly People, to join with these *Well-wishers* to their Country. Good God! that any Men should be so bewitched, as to swallow such Absurdities as these are. *Gentlemen* , our All is at stake, I will speak plain Truths to you, and leave them for you to reflect on. If we do not put a stop to these Proceedings, we are in the worst Circumstances imaginable: 'Tis better to dye once, than to live always in Fear, and under the Burthen of heavy Taxes, occasion'd by the Plots and Villanies of these Men. You find that the Examples which have been made of some few of them, [7] have by no means awed or terrified the rest; nor has the Clemency shewn to the much greater part of them, in the least softened or obliged this wicked restless Faction. The best of Princes is not safe on his Throne; nor can we hope to be quiet in our Possessions, till this Party is entirely crushed. This last Design of theirs in inviting over the *King of Sweden*,[1] is a

[1] Charles XII of Sweden was the ally of England and Holland in 1700; but after the war broke out in 1702, he tried to stop the Anglo-Dutch trade with the Baltic provinces which Russia had occupied. George I, desirous to add the duchies of Bremen and Verden, to his electorate of Hanover, seized them and stood against Sweden. In 1716 Ch. XII threatened to support the Jacobites against George. The Swedish amabassador, Count Gyllenborg,

Demonstration of the unaccountable Temper, and the implacable Malice of these Men. For if that *wise Scheme* had succeeded, not only the Nation must have been inevitably ruined, but even they themselves who projected it, would have most certainly been involved in the general Desolation. It would not I think be altogether foreign, nor I hope ungrateful to you, since you heard so much of the *Swedes*, to give you a short Account of them. Every one will tell you that the *King of Sweden* is a most extravagant arbitrary Prince, and almost distracted with his Ambitions, and Disappointments; That his Ambition hath entirely ruined his Country, and that his People are poor beggarly Slaves. But I will carry you a little further back. In the Year 1587. They had a *Protestant King*, called *John* III. But his Queen *Catherine* was a Papist; and she by the King's Negligence, or perhaps Connivance, for some politick Ends, bred up their eldest Son, *Sigismund*, a Papist. *Stephen Bathor* the [8] then *King of Poland* dyes, and *Sigismund,* as a Papist, being qualified to be chosen, was elected *King of Poland. King John* dyed in 1592. and to oblige his Subjects, and to shew them, that he took more care of their Religion than his Sons; He by his Will appoints his Brother, *Charles Duke of Finland,* who was a zealous Protestant, to be Regent of *Sweden* in his Son's Absence. But *Sigismund* did not approve of *Charles* or his Regency; he therefore goes himself into *Sweden*, takes away the *Churches* from the *Protestants*, and gives them to the *Papists*; and committed many other Acts of Violence and Injustice, in order to establish *Popery.* These Proceedings of *Sigismund* obliged *Charles* and the *Swedes,* to have recourse to Arms to defend their Religion and Laws: and such was their Success, that in 1595 they brought *Charles* [sic; read Sigismund] to Terms, prevailed on him to take the Coronation Oath, and to swear to govern that Kingdom according to the Laws thereof, and to do nothing without the Advice of his uncle *Charles*, and the *Parliament.* After this he returns into *Poland*, soon repents him of his Contract, and by the Assistance of the *Poles*, enters *Sweden* again in an hostile Manner, turns the *Protestants* out of more Churches, and gives them to the *Papists* as before; plunders their Towns, storms their Castles, and commits great Ravage and [B-9] Devastation. His Souldiers without Check or Controul, ravished Young Women in the Sight of their Parents, and tyed married Women to Stakes, and forced them before their Husbands Faces. The *Swedes* provoked by such Usage, take up Arms again in their own Defence, and beat *Sigismund* back into *Poland.* To which Success their own Valour or Conduct did not do much contribute, as *Sigismund*'s having exasperated the People against him, by his Breach of Oaths and Publick Faith, and by his intolerable Cruelties

---

was so active in plotting against England that he was arrested, in spite of diplomatic usage, his papers were seized and they proved him so thoroughly guilty that no nation said a word in his defense.

and Barbarities; all which were demonstrably the Effects of his Religion, and his Education under the Discipline of Popish Priests. For *Sigismund* was not of a more cruel Disposition than other Princes his Co-temporaries, for he and the *Poles* agreed as well as their Kings and they used to do. But his Religion commanded him to govern Protestants with a Rod of Iron, and he thought his Duty to scourge them with Scorpions.[1] It was not only an unusual Saying, but a fundamental Law amongst the *Goths* and *Vandals*, *That Kings were made for the People and not the People for Kings*; and accordingly whenever a *King* degenerated into a *Tyrant*, they deposed him and elected a new One into his Place. According to this Rule, The *Swedes* had deposed *Errick* who was elder Brother to *John*, for his Cruelty and ill Government, and [10] made *John* King in his Stead. And in the same manner now, being quite tired out with the arbitrary Government of *Sigismund* , and perceiving no Hopes of his Amendment, they took up a Resolution to Dethrone him; and pursuant thereto, in the Year 1604, The *Swedish Parliament* abrogated his Regal Power, because, contrary to the Laws of his Country, he endeavoured to alter their Religion, usurp'd upon their Rights and Liberties, and attempted to govern by a Standing-Army. *Sigismund* had a Brother whose Name was *John*, a Protestant and an Enemy to *Sigismund* 's Proceedings; but being young, and thinking himself unable to contend with the Difficulties of the Time, he waved his Pretensions to the Crown. Therefore in April 1604 *Charles* was elected King, and the Senate, the Bishops, the Nobles, the Clergy, the Heads of the University, and the Heads of all the great Cities ratified and confirmed the same in spight of all the whimsical, nonsensical Notions of an *unalienable, indefeasible hereditary right*. And for their future Preservation, they made these Laws, first, *That no Papist should be capable of inheriting the Crown*; next, *That no King should marry a Papist*; and then *they intailed the Crown* on Charles *and his Issue, being Protestants*; and for want of such Issue, on the Protestant Issue of *Gustavus* the Father of *John*, and excluded only *Sigismund* and [B 2-11] his Issue; and under this Settlement the present *King of Sweden* now claims the Crown. From whence I cannot but observe, to what a pitch of Impudence the *Swedish Ministers* are arrived, who mentioning the *Pretender* in their Printed Letters, say, that their *King* believes him to have a Right to the *British* Throne: If he thinks so, it is demonstrable, that he has no Right to the *Crown of Sweden*, for he is descended from that very *Charles* whom the Parliament put in the place of *Sigismund*. Never were two Titles more alike, only King GEORGE's stands up on the much better foot; for in *Sweden* there are *Protestants* now in being before the Family of the present *King*, and besides the *King of Sweden*'s Grandfather had an hand in deposing *Sigismund*. Whereas neither King GEORGE, nor any of his Family were

[1] An allusion to 1 Ki 12: 11, and 2 Chro 10: 11, 14.

concerned at all in deposing *King James*, nor in making themselves his Successors; and King GEORGE is the next Protestant Heir. Happy had it been for this Nation had we excluded the *Duke* of *York*, which many of our bravest Patriots attempted, and for which Attempt too much of our best British Blood has been shed by pack'd Juries, and other Violence, under Colour of Law. There is no doubt but a Popish Heir may be as well and as lawfully excluded as a Popish Prince deposed, and certainly it is better to prevent a Distemper, than to run the Hazard of curing it. But the then King was too much under the Influence of his Popish Mother, and too much addicted to that Religion, to let such a Bill pass: The throwing out of which, (as we cannot but be now sensible) has brought so many Calamities upon this Nation. The Experience of all Ages may convince us, that Papists know no Obligations of Gratitude, and are to be bound by no Oaths. The fiery persecuting Reign of Queen Mary, is a dismal Example of this sort[1]; who made those very Persons the first Objects of her Fury, who were most instrumental in bringing her to the Throne, and to whom she had made the most solemn Promises. We may guess at their good Nature by the repeated Plots and Designs against the Life of Queen Elizabeth, tho' one of the best of Queens, and in whom even they could not find a Fault but that of being a Protestant. Their Gun-Powder Treason Plot in the Reign of *King James I*[2]. their *Irish Massacre* in *King Charles I.* Time, and their Hellish Plots and Designs in the Time of *King Charles II*[3]. (who tho' their Friend would not run their Lengths) are so many remarkable Instances, of what we must expect from these Men, whenever they get uppermost. We all remember, or have heard at least of the Attempts that *King James* II. made not only to change our Religion, [13] but to overturn our Laws and Constitution, in defiance of the most solemn Oaths and Protestations [4]: tho' he was famed for a strict Observer of his Word. Every one owns our to be a *limited Monarchy*, and I would be glad to hear any Rational Man give me any fair Distinction betwixt absolute and limited Monarchy; If in the latter the Prince may dispense with the Laws, and govern by a standing Force, and yet the oppressed People are obliged calmly to submit to him, and must make use of no Remedy but Patience. The Safety and Preservation of the Community, was the End and Design of Government,

[1] Mary Tudor revived the heresy laws and persecuted English Protestants; from 1555 to 1558 she sent 300 persons to the stake.

[2] The attempt made by Guy Fawkes and a group of Catholics to blow up Parliament and the King on 5 Nov. 1605.

[3] There were a number of plots, real or imaginary or contrived to fit the necessities of politics, against Ch. II, among which the plot revealed by Titus Oates.

[4] James II recalled the ancient charters to replace them by new ones, that were intended to make corporations more docile; he tried to pack parliaments, and extended his prerogative to appointing Roman Catholic officers in the army, Catholic divines in the universities, in defiance of all the laws of the realm.

and consequently if it happens to fall into such hands, as make use of their Power in such a manner as inevitably tends to the Destruction of the Community, they have no doubt a Right to defend themselves against such illegal Governors. As for Example, When a Prince is Lunatick or Defective in his Understanding, and thereby incapacitated to govern he may not only be deprived of his Power, but may, and ought to be governed himself. And if there is a stronger and more pernicious Incapacity than Madness or Folly, surely there is in such Case more Reason to remove a Prince from his Regal Office; and such a Incapacity is *Popery*, where the Subjects are *Protestants*. A Madman may possibly destroy himself, or wound, or kill this or [14] that Man, as his frantick Humour directs him. But a *Papist* is by his Religion obliged to destroy and root out *all Protestants*; and that the Practice of all *Popish Princes* has been agreeable to this Principle, any one that is skilled in History will perceive. Since the *Reformation*, more *Christians* have been butcher'd by Massacres, Inquisitions, and other Barbarous and inhumane Executions of *Papists*, than were destroyed by the whole *Pagan* Persecutions. All *Papists* not only hold it justifiable, but highly meritorious to destroy *Hereticks*, and that all Oaths and Promises (which the *Pope* according to them may dispense with as he pleases) made to such are of no force, and they account all *Protestants* to be *Hereticks*. It was therefore absolutely necessary for our Preservation to fill the vacant Throne, upon the Abdication of *King James*, with *King William* and *Queen Mary*, and to intail it on the Protestant Line; and such proceeding was not only expedient, but agreeable to our Laws, to Reason and Religion, and justifiable before God and Man: And there is no Prince upon Earth that has a better Title to his Crown than *King* GEORGE has to his. All the Allegations and religious Motives that the *High-Church* make use of, are only Delusions, Shams and Pretences to disguise their Zeal for *Popery*. For I can demonstrate that the Word of God is point blank against them, and com- [15] mands a legal Obedience to *King* GEORGE. Let us fairly consider the places they quote of Holy Writ, and let even they themselves be Judges. In the *Gospels* we find that our *Blessed Saviour* commands *the Jews to give* Cesar *his due*. And the *Apostles* in other places command us to *be obedient to the higher Powers*. We all own, that we ought to have more Regard for Religion and the Word of God, than any worldly Interest whatsoever. Let us then, to enable us to judge of these Matters, inquire into *Cesar*'s Title, *the Power* that was then in being. The *first* Cesar usurped upon the Rights and Liberties of the freest and the bravest People in the World, and thro' a scene of Villany, and a Sea of Blood, became at last their Master. But the *Romans* not us'd to Slavery, and so not easily brooking it, Stabbed this *Cesar* in the Senate-House; and were in some hopes that they should have recovered their expiring Liberties thereby. But *Cesar* had before his Death, by his Will adopted his Nephew *Augustus*; who at a vast Expence of the best Blood, not only of the *Romans*, but of the World, established Tyranny in *Rome*. *Augustus* adopted *Tiberius*, no ways related to him. *Augustus* dies, *Tiberius* succeeds: Our Saviour was Born in the Time of *Augustus*, and Suffered in the Reign of *Tiberius*. And this is the Title of the *Cesars* [16] to whom our *Saviour* commands the *Jews* to pay Tribute; and these the Powers to whom the *Apostles* enjoyned a strict Obedience and Submission. Now let us examine *King* GEORGE's Title. King *James* usurped upon our Rights, would have altered our *Established Church*, in order thereto dispensed with our Laws, and govern'd by a Standing Army; and plainly discovered by all his Actions, that he had a Design to entail Thraldom and Slavery upon us, and our latest Posterity. Besides every one was satisfied, that he had palmed more than one Suppositious Child upon the Nation,[1] to defeat the Hopes of the next *Protestant* Heirs. The Nation groaned under these Oppressions, and the Prince of *Orange*, who was not remote from the Crown in his own Right, and next of Kin in Right of his Wife, came over with an Army to demand Justice, and to have these Grievances enquired into. *King James* 's Evil Conscience disarmed him and his great Army, and forced him to confess himself Guilty, by leaving the Kingdom. The Representatives of the Nation, and all the Legislative Orders, met and declared the Throne vacant, and filled it with the Injur'd Prince, who had exposed himself to restore us our Laws, Religion, and Liberties for which, his Name will be deservedly for [C-17] ever Glorious: And then they entailed the Crown on *Queen Mary*, *Queen Anne*, and their Issue respectively, and on the Issue of *King William*, being *Protestants*; and made a *Papist*, or any on that married a *Papist*, incapable to Inherit or Enjoy the Crown. *Queen Mary* dyed in the Life-time of *King William*, without Issue; the Issue of *Queen Anne* dyed also; That good *King* therefore, together with his *Parliament*, in order to prevent Confusion, wisely settled the Crown not on a Stranger, or an adopted Son, but on the *Princess Sophia*, the next *Protestant Heir*, and the Heirs of her Body being *Protestants*. King *William* dyes, and *Queen Anne* and her *Parliament* confirm these Acts of Settlement. The Princess *Sophia* dyed in the Life-time of Queen *Anne*; and King *GEORGE*, after so many Successions, and so many Acts of *Parliament*, to which we had solemnly sworn, peaceably ascends the Throne.

And now having fairly stated the Titles, I defy any Man to give so much as a tolerable Reason, why King *GEORGE* 's Title is not better than the *Cesars*; and if that cannot be denied, I defy any one to prove, that we are not as much obliged to be faithful and obedient to King *GEORGE*, by the Word of God, as the Primitive Christians were to be

[1] The son born to James II by his second wife, Mary of Modena; he was to be the Old Pretender, or the Chevalier de Saint-George. Rumour ran that he was a changeling, in order to accredit the legend that the child was not legitimate.

Slaves to the *Cesars*. And thus you see, that not only [18] by the great Law of Self-Preservation, but by the Laws of God, and the Laws of the Land King *GEORGE* is our Lawful and Rightful King; and as such we ought to Defend and Obey him. And it is evident past all Contradiction, that the pretended Danger of the *Church* and the other religious Arguments of *High-Church*, are but mere Pretences and Inventions which savour of nothing but *Arbitrary Power, Popery, Self-Interest, Revenge*, and *Disappointment*. Having given you already such convincing Arguments, I am almost ashamed to offer others, that I own are not of so much weight. But Experience teaches us, that Arguments drawn from Interest have generally the most Influence. Now all of you have both seen and felt the great Charge and Expence these restless *High-Church* Plotters put us to this last Year by inviting over the *Pretender*. We paid two Shillings in the Pound extraordinary upon Land on that Account: And your Pockets must of Necessity suffer again this Year, by their inviting over the *Swedes*. This restless Faction is marvellously Fanciful; and, if you are but tolerably civil to them, they conclude that they have caught and inveagled you, and that you will join with them to ruine your *King*, your *Country*, and your *Religion*. Thus you may see by the *Swedish* Letters, that they [19] concluded the *Czar* would assist the *Swedes*, Because some Years ago, He took a Scotchman into his Family, of the same Name, as one of the *Scotch* Rebels. And for as wise Reasons they fancied, there were amongst Us Nine out of their Sense, for one considering Person; *that is*, Nine *Protestants* to One, for the *Pretender* against *King GEORGE*. In order therefore to convince them to the Contrary, you ought on all Occasions, to shew your Dislike both of them, and of their Practices; and to oppose them in every thing Privately and Publickly. *Gentlemen*, If you desire to live Long, and see good Days; If you would be happy and secure in the peaceable and quiet Enjoyment of your Liberties, Properties, and Religion, and freed from the heavy Burthen of Taxes; 'Tis in your own power to obtain these Blessings. And in order thereto, You have nothing now to do, but to become a sober and a religious People, grateful to Heaven for your wonderful Deliverances, and the greatest Felicity that can be conferred on any Nation; *a Wise and just Prince, and a hopeful Prospect, that future Ages will be happy in this Posterity*. I shall conclude with a Sentence which you all know, and which I wish you would heartily observe.

Fear God, and Honour the King, and meddle not with them that are given to change.

FINIS.

The Charge of Whitlocke Bulstrode, Esq; to the *Grand-Jury*, and other Juries, of the County of *Middlesex*. At the General Quarter-Sessions of the Peace, Held, April 21st, 1718. at Westminster-Hall. Printed at the Desire of the Justices of the Peace, for the County, and of the Grand-Jury, and other Juries. London: Printed for J. Brown at the Black Swan without Temple-Bar. 1718. Middlessex.

A*d General' Quarterial' Session' Pacis Domini Regis, tent' pro Com' Middlesex' prædict' Die Lunæ in Septimano proximo post clausum Paschæ scil' vicesimo primo Die* Aprilis, *quarto Anno Regni Domini* Georgij *nunc Regis* Magn' Britan'. *&c.*

HIS Majesty's Justices of the Peace for the County of *Middlesex*, Assembled at this present General Quarter-Sessions, being of Opinion, that the Charge this Day given, by *Whitlocke Bulstrode*, Esq; the Chair-Man, to the several *Juries* now Assembled, is *a very Learned and Useful Charge, and highly tending to the Service of His Majesty and His Government*; do, on their Behalfs, and also at the Request of the said *several Juries*, desire, that the said Mr. *Busltrode* would be pleased to cause his said CHARGE to be Printed.

Per Cur'

Harcourt.

TO

Whitlocke Bulstrode, Esq;

CHAIRMAN Of this Present **SESSIONS.**

WE the Grand-Jury, *Sworn to serve on the Behalf of our Sovereign Lord the King, for the Body of this County, for this present* Sessions; *Do return You our most Humble Thanks* for your Learned and Excellent Charge *given to Us, and the other Juries, on the First Day of this present* Sessions, and desire You will be [ii] pleased to cause the same to be Printed, for the *better Information* and *Instruction to Jurors* and *Constables* in the better Discharge of their Duties. And we shall Pray, &c.

Dated this 25th Day of *April*, *Anno Domini*, 1718.

John Hurst,	Thomas Milles,
Will. Brownejohn,	Henry Summers,
Andrew Davis,	Joshua Saunders,
John Smith,	David Tarrant,

Edward Kempton,
John Hide,
Joseph Esson,
Richard Marsh,
Joseph Colson,
Nicholas Barret,
Solomon Williams,
John Hunter,
James Peade,
William Clifton,
Thomas Lane,
Simon Appleby,
Samuel Pullin,
Richard Ordway,
John Knight,

[iii]
DEDICATION
TO THE
Right HONOURABLE
Sir *James Mountague*, Knight,

One of the Lords Commissioners of the *Great-Seal*; and One of the Honourable Barons of the Court of *Exchequer.*

MY LORD,

THE Honour of Your Lordship's *Acquaintance*, for above twenty Years past, gives Me a pleasing Reflection, when I think thereof. [iv]

Surely there is some *Analogy* between our Conversation on Earth, and what we shall have in the *Kingdom of Heaven*; but with this Difference, that here we are upon our Guard, and *with Reserve*, because we know not Mankind thoroughly; but there we shall be *open and free*; there we shall have an *Intuitive Knowledge* of those *with whom we converse*; we shall see into their very *Hearts*, and be assured they speak from *the Bottom* thereof; we shall God in his Glory, and one another in the Excellency of Perfection.

A Knowledge in this Life of a particular Science in an eminent Degree, is *for the Honour* [a- v] *and Advantage* of its Possessors; but where an *eminent Degree of Knowledge in one's Profession*, is accompanied with a *good Stock of polite Learning*, and a *great Integrity* and *Probity of Mind*, with a *proper Courage* to exert the same *on due Occasion*; These are Qualities not often found, even in Men of *Eminent Parts and Learning.*

I may justly say, from the *strictest Observation of your Lordship*, since I have had the *Honour of being known to You*, that this is *truly and properly without the least Shadow of Flattery, Your just Character.* [vi

'Tis some Pleasure to me to think, that the *Government* hath done itself *that Right*, in *placing your Lordship upon the Bench*, where you are an *Ornament, and a shining Example of Learning, Virtue and Courage* ; Conduct and Courage being as necessary to a Judge, as a General; It's one of the best *Means* to secure any *Government*, from *Contempt*, and to give it a *Duration*; to have *such persons in Courts of Judicature.*

The Want of which, in the Reign of King *James* II. went a great Way tow'rds the *overthrowing* that Prince. I can with more Pleasure look [a 2-

vii] *on a Government acting with Honour and Prudence*, than on a *Private Family* that exercises it self with a *good Oeconomy*. And as I can easily foresee, that a *Rake*, who has a great Estate left to him, will soon squander it away, and be undone; so may one judge of a *Government* (which is but a Multiplication of many Families living under one Head) that acts not by the Rules of its Constitutions and Justice.

Par Justice est affirme Royaume;

Is a good Motto in a Court of Law.

I should not have let the *following Charge have come abroad*, had I not been press'd to [viii] it, *by Gentlemen of great Worth and Honour*, whose *Request to me, were a Command*; *Your Goodness*, I hope, will over look its *Faults*; And if it may be of any Use to those Gentlemen in the *Commission of the Peace*, whose *Education had not led them* to the *Knowledge of the Law*; And to the Ministerial Officers, who are to put the Laws in *Execution, against Immorality and Prophaneness*; I shall greatly rejoice; especially to see this Government settled and continued, without any Fear of Change, on a *Protestant Basis and Virtue*, which all Men, [ix] that have taken Oaths to this Government, and all *Protestants*, will find it their *Interest*, as *well as*[1] *Duty*, so to *desire*, and *act accordingly*.

Before the *Elector of Saxony* became a *Papist*, *and King thereby of Poland*: I think, there were not above 120 *Popish Families*, in and near *Dresden*, his Metropolis: But since his Change of Religion, 'tis said there are now there, near *ten thousand*: The [x] like Defection has been in the *Palatinate*, where there is a *Popish Prince* and *Protestant Subjects*. So *vile is Mankind*, to Conform to the *Court for Advantage, even against their Consciences*. I doubt the Case would be *worse* with us, *here in* England, had we a *Popish Prince*; for I must confess, that *that true* English *Spirit*, that *English Integrity and Probity*, for which this *Nation* was heretofore *famous, is now quite lost and gone*. Men live luxuriously, *above their Fortunes, and then they do base and unworthy Actions, to keep up their Port, which may last for a Time, but not long*. Who [xi] ever reads the Book, intitled Monsieur *Mesnager's Memoirs*,[2] must have a very *mean Idea* of *British Honesty and Integrity*, not to mention its *Capacity*. *Its easier* to be a *Knave*, and *act vilely*, than to resist a Temptation, and *act up* to the *Height of Virtue and Honour*: There is scarce *Virtue enough* left us, even to keep out *Popery*, *the very Dregs of the Christian Religion: May the few, the very*

[1] See the Arguments against the *Pretender's* Title, in a Letter touching the late *Rebellion*; wherein is Treated, Of *English* Liberties; Of the Power of Princes; Of the Measures of Obedienbce of Subjects; and, Of Change of Governments. [This text was written by W. Bulstrode. The late rebellion is that of 1715.]

[2] Nicolas Menasger, *The History of the Peace from the Arrival of M.M. (18 Sept. 1711 to the Return of the Earl of Strafford from Utrecht (16 May 1712)*: see Somers Tracts, vol. IV. - *Minutes of the negociations at the Court of England, towards the close of the last Reign, wherein…* London: S. Baker, 1717. Mesnager was the French envoy to London, to discuss the terms of the peace of Utrecht.

few good Men, stand in the Breach, and divert the impending Evil! *For a total Defection, of Morals*, is a certain Sign of *Ruin, to any People*. [xii

I beg your Lordship will Pardon me, this Interruption from your weighty Affairs, and that You will believe me to be with great Truth and Deference.

MY LORD,

Your Lordship's, Most Faithful and Most Obedient, Humble Servant.

April *the 30th*, 1718.

Whitlocke Bulstrode.

[B-1]
THE
CHARGE
of
Whitlocke Bulstrode, Esq;
to the
GRAND-JURY
And the other Juries.

Gentlemen of the Grand-Jury

WE are call'd together to this Place, *by the Wisdom of our Laws*, from the several Parts of this County, to present to Us, *what Violations* have been made, of the Laws of the Land, by any Persons whatsoever, within the County of *Middlesex*. [2]

I hope that You, who are to be *the Instruments* of punishing Malefactors, will be careful to keep the Oath you have taken, viz. *In not omitting your Duty by not presenting Offenders, through Favour, Affection, or Fear*. And that you will not present any Persons for any Faults you think them innocent of, thro' Hatred or Malice.

As he that takes an Oath to give Evidence, swears that he will speak the Truth, the whole Truth, and nothing but the Truth, is guilty of Perjury before God, if he *wilfully conceals any Part of the Truth*; So, Gentlemen, if you know of any Offences, that I shall give you in Charge, and *do no present them*, you will be *equally Guilty of Perjury before God.*

The Oath you have taken to present *such Matters as I shall give you in Charge*; does more than Hint to me my Duty, not to omit acquainting you with a *full Accompt* of what Offences you are to Inquire and Present; so that if *Offences committed are not punished*, for want of Presentments, the Fault will lye at your Door, and not at mine.

The Trumpeter that blows the Trumpet, and gives warning, is free from the Blood of Him that is slain: Justice is painted blind; a good Emblem to shew us, that in Judgment [B 2- 3] we are neither to pity the Poor, nor favour the Rich; not to shew Love to our Friends, or Hatred to our Enemies; *to know no Man, in Judgment, not to fear the face of any Man, that is an Offender, be he never so great.*

When you do your Duty on a *Principle of Obedience to God*, you are sure of *the Divine Protection*: But when you positively transgress, or negatively omit it, for Fear or Love of Man; you put your selves out of *the Divine Protection, which is Almighty*, and trust to Man, who is no better than *a broken Reed.*

I shall divide my Charge to you, for your better Remembrance, into three General Heads: And then subdivide them into proper Particulars, with as much Brevity, as the Matter will admit.

And to avoid Prolixity, I shall wave the[1] Definition of some Terms of Art, (which I must necessarily make use of) presuming you understand them by your frequent Service in this Place.

The First Part of your Duty, and what you are to inquire of, is relating to the *Divine Majesty.*

The Second, relates to his Viceregent the *King.* [4]

The Third, to your *Fellow Subjects.*

As to the First, you are to Inquire and Present all Persons, that are guilty of *Blaspheming the Name of God.*

Blasphemy defin'd. *Blasphemy is in its general Sense, an Evil-speaking of any one; Maledicentia*: But by Use and Custom (*the Governour of the Sense of Words*) it is appropriated to an *Evil-speaking of God*; and sometimes it is taken *for prophane Cursing and Swearing.*

By the Law of *Moses*, he that *cursed* his Father or Mother, was put to Death, that is, *spoke Evil of, or wish'd Evil to his Father or Mother.*

God himself pronounced Judgment against the *Blasphemer*, and bid *Moses* bring forth him *that cursed*, that he might be stoned to Death, which was accordingly done.

Under this Head, I think prophane *Cursing* and *Swearing*, by the Name of God, may be well comprehended; For the *Divine* [5] [*Prophane Cursing and Swearing*] *Majesty has so adjudg'd it. Blasphemer and Curser, are synonymous Terms in the Language of Holy Writ.*

Had not God forbid this Sin by the *Third Commandment*, the Light of Nature would have told us it were a great Crime: For Reason tells us, that Mankind should have such a *Veneration of the Divine Majesty, our Creator*, as not to use that Word, which forms *an Idea of God* in our Minds, but on *solemn Occasions*,

Jews. The *Jews* were forbid, on Pain of Death, to pronounce the Great and Tremendous Name of God, *Jehovah*; it was lawful for the High-Priest only to use it, and but *once a Year*, at the solemn Benediction of the People, at the Feast of Expiation.

Turks. The *Turks*, when they pronounce the Name of *God*, they put their Hands to their Foreheads, and bow in Reverence to the *Divine Majesty*; they are so tender in this Point, that if they find a Piece of Paper on the Ground, on which the Name *of God is writ*, they take it up and lay it by carefully, that it may not applied *to an indecent Use.*

Heathens. The *Heathens* never did, nor now do imprecate Damnation to themselves; or in their common Conversation curse them-[6] selves or others, by the Name of the true or false Gods, unless it be in some Parts of the Coast of *Africa*, where our Ships passing to the *Indies*, put in for fresh Provisions: *Our naughty Mariners* have taught the Natives, with a little *English, much Prophane Cursing and Swearing*, which poor Creatures are

[1] 'your' crossed out, 'the' in the margin.

taught to think, that such Oaths are *an Embelishment to our Language*; such is the Vileness of a bad Example.

Christians. Our Saviour has forbid in our common Conversation, *all manner of Oaths*, and has permitted us, in our Asseverations to gain Belief, only a double Affirmative, or a double Negative, and to carry it no farther: If a Man can't be believ'd upon his Word, I am sure he ought not to gain Credit by breaking the Laws of God to attain it.

Influence of Religion. He that has *no Awe of the Divine Law*, can have no Check *or Restraint to keep him* within the Bonds of Truth: No Principle *of Honour* can be of equal Tye or Force to keep Mankind within the Laws of Virtue and Truth, like that of Religion, *viz. the Fear and Love of God*: For as *for Honour*, alas! when the *Candles are out, or in Masquerade*, Honour is gone; but Virtue flowing from Religion, *is chast in the Dark. Such is the Difference between Religion and Honour.* [7] Is it not an *Astonishment*, that the People of *Great-Britain*, who yet call themselves Christians, *Curse and Damn themselves and others*, by the *Name of God*, in *a Morning fasting, in cool Blood, without any Provocation*?

The Jew that was *ston'd to Death* by the Command *of God* for *prophane Cursing*, was in a great *Passion*, was contending with another Person, and might have had some Provocation to Curse, *which tho' not excusable, yet might mittigate somewhat the Fault*, in respect of humane Frailties.

But many *Christians* in their common and ordinary Conversation, invoke God to *damn them*, when they ask what *o' th' Clock 'tis*, or even one how the other does.

The most senseless Practice in the World, and which nothing but the *Excess of Folly and Wickedness* cou'd make *Mankind ever be guilty of.*

O! that the Christian Religion, which is the best Religion in the *World*; and that this Nation, which is the purest Part of the *Christian Church*, shou'd have such *Miscreants* for its Possessors!

The Sin of *prophane Cursing and Swearing* is so very great, and become so general [8] *amongst the common People*, the Soldiery and Mariners, Hackney-Coachmen and Carmen especially, that 'tis much to be fear'd, if there is not some stop put to it, it will draw down *Vengeance from Heav'n upon us*: No wonder that *our Ships* so often miscarry, when *our Mariners curse and damn* themselves *through the Sea to Hell.*

When the *moral World* is so much out of *Order*, why should we expect a *Calm* in the *Material*? The *Storm arose* for *Jonah's sake*, and even the Heathen idolatrous Mariners, (who do not Curse and Swear as ours do in a Storm, but call'd upon their several Gods) by the Light of Nature found out the Cause by the Effect, and adjudg'd *Jonah's Crime to be the Cause*, before God's Providence had confirm'd it.

Why should not the *Elements* made *to serve us, oppose and resist our Designs*, turn their Point and Edge against us, when *we rebel* against their *Creator* in so vile a Manner, as by *blasphemous Oaths and Curses, even affront the Divine Majesty to his Face*?

An *habitual Swearer* is a common *Nuisance* to the Place where he lives, worse than a Dunghill before one's Door.

He has *no right* to Credit, in whatever he says or Swears: This Sin comes not [C-9] alone, for these People let themselves loose to *Lewdness and other Vices* in the highest Degree.

They breath *Contagion* where-ever they come, they defile Humane Bodies by their corrupt and filthy *Emanations*, and they taint humane Souls by their execrable Oaths and Curses, which is the worst Sort of *Plague*.

For the *common Plague* infects only the Body, which is only the Case or Instrument *of the Soul*; but these Miscreants taint *even the Soul*, the very Man himself, for the *Soul is the very Man himself*; they teach by their vile Example, even Women and Children to Curse and Swear.

Penalty on prophane Swearing and Cursing. There are particular Laws provided against this great and crying Sin. [*21 Jac. c. 20*] *This Statute* gives a Shilling for every prophane Oath or Curse.

[6 & 7 W. 3.] This Statute confines the Penalty of 1 s. to Day-Labourers, Servants, common Soldiers and Seamen; and every other Person is to pay Two Shillings for the first Offence, for the Second double, for the Third treble; the Prosecution of which, is to be within Ten Days after the Offence committed: You see what Penalty the Law hath [10] put upon these Offenders; if you have *any regard for your Country, for the honour of God, or for your own Souls, set your Faces against this Sin.*

You ought to complain of these vile Wretches to the Magistrates, that they may be brought to condign Punishment; so that *where the love of Virtue cannot restrain them, the fear of Punishment may.*

Church Defaulters. You are to present Persons that do not come to Church, or to some religious Meeting allowed by Law, *every Lord's Day*; for the Act of *primo Elizabethæ*, which gives one Shilling a Sunday for absenting from the Church, is not taken away by the Toleration Act of 1 *W. & M.*

Trade on Sundays. Present all that follow their Trades on the Lords Day, except in cases of *Necessity or Mercy*; for God hath reserved to himself a *seventh part* of Time for his peculiar *Service*, and *publick Adoration*; and in infinite Goodness, hath indulged us *six Parts in seven* for our honest secular Affairs: Remember that God himself gave Judgment to stone the Man to Death, that gather'd Sticks on the *Sabbath Day*: Now tho' our Saviour both by his Example and Doctrine, has abated *the rigour of that Law*, and justly exposed the folly of *the Jews* in their *superstitious observance of that day*, so as to deny [C 2-11] *Mercy* to a *Man* on that Day, and at the same time to exercise it to a Beast; and tho' the seventh Day is transferr'd to the first Day of the Week, yet the Morality of that Law is *Eternal*, and binds not only Christians, but the whole Race of Mankind *duly inform'd*, to set apart a seventh Portion of Time for the more solemn Service of God: And they who exercise their Trades, or Employments, on that Day, except in Acts of Necessity or Mercy; or spend their Time that Day in Sports and Games, (gaming Assemblies especially) or in vain Diversions, may justly be said to be guilty of *Sacriledge, in robbing God of the publick Honour*, more particularly due to his Majesty *that Day*.

The *World* sticks too close to us, by our six Days Conversation with it, and 'tis well if we can divest our selves of it, if with Sincerity we apply our selves more intensely to the Business of our eternal Welfare on *the seventh Day*.

That great Man, the Lord Chief *Justice Hale*, made it this Observation, that the more strictly he kept that Day, the *better Success* he had the *Week following*.

Try the Experiment of it in your own Families, and you will find the same Effect as he did; for God is *no Respecter of Persons*, [12] but exercises the same providential Goodness, to all *that equally love and obey him*.

Heathens keep the 5th Day holy. The *Heathens in Malemba*, on the Coast of *Africa*, keep every *fifth Day holy*; And cannot we Christians afford to keep the seventh Day so?

Immorality. You are to take care, that the Laws be put in execution against Immorality and Profaneness, as the Proclamation directs.

Religion. Take care of *Religion*, and *suppress Vice*: Present the Authors of Books writ against Religion; As for Atheism, such as that of *Spinosa*, and other detestable Authors, or that are *contra bonos Mores*, or that revile the *Scriptures*; Authors that deny their *Creator*, and yet *swear by him*; Or if they acknowledge a God, they confine his Majesty to Heav'n, and exclude a Providence, or that God governs the World, or presides over *Humane Affairs*.

Whereas the *Scriptures assert*, and good Sense, attests, that not a Sparrow (one of the lowest in value of the Animal Creation) falls to the Ground, without a *permissive or directive Providence*.

For what can be difficult to an Almighty Power, or what too low for infinite Goodness? [13] If you can't find the Authors, present the Publishers or Printers of them.

Zeal in these Matters, will never *sink* or *deprave* it self into *Superstition*: A Lukewarmness herein is a very *great Sin*; a sort of Indifferency for the Honour of God, for which there can be no excess *of zeal*.

Gentlemen,

You will not act so in your own Affairs; Have but the same *zeal* for the *Creator of the World*, as you have for the World, and you will not act amiss; tho' the Ballance ought to turn on the *Creators Side*.

Perjury. *Perjury* is to be inquir'd into, which is a very heinous Crime, both with respect to God and Man.

To God. For he that takes an Oath Judicially, calls God to attest or witness, that what he says is Truth. Now to invoke the God of Truth to attest or witness a Lye, is the greatest *Affront both to the Purity and Truth of the Divine Majesty imaginable.*

To Man. For *Perjury* tends to *pervert Justice*, by which every Kingdom is establish'd, nor can any subsist without it. [14]

Subornation. Subornation of *Perjury*, is a great Crime, for he that suborns a Man to commit *Perjury*, acts the Part of the *Devil*, in tempting one to commit a great Sin - Present such Offenders.

Forgery. Forgery is to be inquir'd into, (which is generally a *Concomitant with Perjury*) punishable both at common Law, and by the Statute of 5 Eliz.[5 Eliz. c. 14] and has two Divisions. First, its the *falsly forging* or making, or attempting to the forging or making of any intire Deed, Court-Roll, or Will of any Person; to the intent the Free or Copy-hold Estate of any Person may be molested. *Secondly*, the *razing or altering a Deed* after it is executed, in a material Point, is within the Statute.

The publishing such a Deed, or Will, as true, knowing the same either of his own Knowledge or Relation of another, to be *false and forged*, is by another Branch within this Statute. If A aliens an Estate to B, and afterwards aliens the same Estate to C, with an antedate to the Deed of B, he is a forger within the Statute.

Punishment. The Punishment is *Pillory*, cutting off his Ears, slitting his Nostrils, searing them [15] with an hot Iron; forfeiture of Lands for Life, and Imprisonment for Life for the first Offence, and Felony for the second, after Conviction for the first.

These Faults are the more heinous, and consequently deserve the greater Punishment, because they are committed with *great Deliberation*, and are always Sins of *Wilfulness and Presumption*, therefore the more carefully to be presented.

Reason of the Act. This Crime was frequent before *5 Eliz.* but the Punishment being so Remarkable, has deterr'd Men from the frequency of its guilt.

Thus wise Laws duly executed, prevent much Evil.

Witchcraft, Sorcery and Inchantment. As for Witchcraft, Sorcery or Inchantments, which were anciently the common Topicks under this Head of Offences against God, by the Learned of old: I Shall not trouble you with them, there being no such Practice now, blessed be God within this Kingdom.[1]

And so much for my first general Head of Offences against God.

The Second General head relates to *the King.* [16]

[1] On the subject, see H.R. Trevor-Roper, *The European Witch-craze of the 16th and 17th centuries.* Penguin Books, 1978, repr. 1988.

And under this Head you are to inquire *High Treason, and the* several parts of it.

[25 Edw. 3.] Before the 25th of *Ed.* 3. what was *High Treason* by the Common Law, was very uncertain; but that Statute hath reduc'd the several Species of *High Treason* to a Certainty.

They are of four Kinds.

Viz. First, *What concerns the King and his Royal Family.*

Secondly, *What concerns his Officers in the Administration of Justice.*

Thirdly, *What concerns his Seal.*

Fourthly, *What concerns his Coin.*

1. *As to his* Majesty and Royal Family.

Compassing the Death of the King. To compass, or *even imagine* the Death of the King, Queen or Prince, and declaring the same by some Overt-Act, is High Treason.

This Law comes the nighest to the *Divine Law,* or any of our Laws; for the *Divine Law* punishes the *Evil Thoughts,* and *Evil Intentions of the Heart*: For from thence is the *Spring* of all our Actions, and *God* [D-17] sees them as plainly before they break out into Over-Acts, as Men see them when they do. The *Overt-Act* is but the *Means* whereby the *Wickedness of the Heart* is known and discover'd by the short Capacity of Man; but the Sin is in the Thought or Intention of the Heart, to contrive the Death of the King.

The King is the Life and Soul of the Kingdom, therefore the utmost Care is to be taken for the Preservation of his Royal Person; and especially at this time, when *Apprentice Boys* pretend to determine the Title and Right *of Kings,* and are blown up *by the Disturbers of our Peace,* into such an height *of Enthusiasm and Madness,* into such *desperate Wickedness,* as to think it lawful to *murder his Majesty,* whom *God's Providence,* and the *Laws of the Land* hath *blest* us with being our *King*:

A King, who has made the Laws of the Kingdom the Rule of his Government, and done no Act of Violence to the meanest of his Subjects.

Is it not an unaccountable Thing, that Men who pretend to be Protestants; To love our Religion, Laws and Liberties, should yet be so for a *popish King*? Whom, whenever *for our Sins, God suffers* such a Prince to rule over us, with him will come in- *Superstition and Idolatry, Slavery, Oppression and Tyranny,* and I shall be contented when I am dead to have that Sentence writ on my [18] Tomb - with a - *Hic jacet Author hujus sentenciæ.* [1]

Have a care of the *Lives of the Prince and Princess,* in *whose Preservation, next to that of the King,* the Safety and Joy of the Nation, *under God,* consists.

What Overt-Acts. Declaring by an open Act, *a design to Depose or Imprison*

[1] = Here lies the author of this sentence.

the King, is an Overt-Act to manifest a compassing of his Death; *For the Prison and Graves of Princes, lie close to one another.*

Conspiring the Death of the King, and providing Weapons to effect it; or sending Letters to second it; assembling People to take the King into his Power, writing Letters to a foreign Prince, inviting to an Invasion, are *Overt-Acts.* Words put *into Writing,* [3 Inst.14.] are an Overt-Act of *Compassing, but bare Words are not.*

2d *Part of* 1 *Branch levy War.* To *levy War* against the King, is another *Species of* High Treason, but what is a *levying of War,* needs some Explication.

What. A raising a *Force* to burn, or thrown down a particular Inclosure, is only *a Riot*; but if it is to *go from Town to Town, and cast in all Inclosures*; Or to *change Religion*; Or to inhance the *Sallaries of Labourers*; These are respectively by *construction of Law, A levying of War,* because the Design is *General.* [D 2-19]

Keyl. 72. 1 Vent 251. So the *London* Apprentices breaking prison, was adjudged a *levying of War.*

3d Part of 1st Branch. Adhering to the King's Enemies what.. Holding a Fort or Castle against the King's Forces, is a *levying of War.*

The third Species of Treason under the first Head, is *adhering* to the King's Enemies, which is explain'd by the Statute it self; and that is – A giving them *Aid,* within the Land or without.

The Word *Adhering,* needs some farther Explication; the *writing and sending* the Secrets of the *King* to the *Enemy,* is adjudg'd and adhering to the King's Enemies; tho' delivery not proved, if put into the *Post-Office; to be sent beyond Sea,* as was lately adjudged in *Gregs Case.* [6 Anne]

Surrendring the King's Castle or Fortress for a Reward to an Enemy, is likewise an *Adhering.*

But who an Enemy?

The King's *Subject* becoming a *Rebel,* is an Enemy; but he that Succours him out of the Realm, is not an Adhering within this Clause.[20]

There are some other Species of *High Treason* relating to the Royal Family, within 25 *E.* 3; which because you'll have no occasion to inquire into, I need not trouble you with the Particulars; and therefore I shall apply my self to the other Branches of High Treason mentioned before, which are Treason by *Interpretation only.*

2d General. As killing the *Chancellor, Treasurer, Justices of either Bench, Justices in Eyre, Assize,* or of *Oyer and Terminer,* in their Places doing their *Office.*

3d General. That which concerns the Great Seal.

The *Counterfeiting* the *Great Seal* or *Privy Seal,* is *High Treason.*

Aiders and Consenters to such Treason, are within this Act.

4th *General.* The fourth and last kind of High Treason by this Statute, concerns *the Coin* of his Majesty.

Counterfeiting Coin. The Counterfeiting of which was *Treason* by the *Common Law*; so this Statute, as to this some other Points, is but in *affirmance* of the *Common Law*, [21]

5 Eliz. But the *Clipping, Washing, and Filing* of the Money of the Realm, or of other Realms allowed to be current here by Proclamation, for Lucre or Gain, tho' it is not within 25 *E.* 3. yet its made High Treason by 5 *Eliz.* [18 Eliz.] And so is the *Impairing, Diminishing, Falsifying, Scaling, or Lightning such Money, by* 18 Eliz. 1 Mar. 1. And by the first of Queen *Mary, the forging and counterfeiting Money*, made currant by *Proclamation*, is *High Treason.*

1 & 2 P. & M. By this Statute the *bringing into* this Realm *from foreign Parts*, beyond the Seas, any false or counterfeit Coin, knowing the same to be false and counterfeit, to the intent to pay the same; and their Procurers, Aiders and Abettors, are guilty of *High Treason.*

6 H. 7. The *bare forging* the King's Coin, *without uttering*, was declared High Treason by the Judges, 6 *H.* 7.

8 W. 3. c. 26. As to *Mill-money*, its High Treason to make or assist in making *Puncheons, Edgers*, or other *Tools*, for the coyning of Mill'd-Money. *And so much for the Coin.* [22]

There are some other Offences of another Nature made High Treason, by preceding and subsequent Statutes.

5 Eliz. c. 1. By this Statute, they that maintain the *Authority of the Bishop of Rome* by *Writing or Printing* in the King's *Dominions*; for the First Offence incur a *Præmunire*, and for the Second Offence (a Conviction being had of the first) if they do it only by *Words, its High Treason.*

13 Eliz. c. 2. The bringing in *of Bulls*, or putting them in Execution, or *reconciling any to the Sea of* Rome, is *High Treason* by 13 *Eliz.*

The Aidors or Maintainers of such Offenders, or that maintain the Authority of the See of *Rome* within this Realm, incur a *Præmunire* by the same Law. And so do they who *conceal an offer of Absolution from*, or *Reconciliation to the Church* of *Rome.*

Agnus-Dei *Beeds &c.* They who bring into this Realm a Thing called an *Agnus Dei, or any Crosses, Pictures or Beeds*, from the Bishop of *Rome*, or from any *Persons* having *Authority derived* from the See of *Rome*, and shall deliver them to any Subject of this Realm, incur a *Præmunire.* [23]

This Statute wisely calls these Things *Vain and Superstitious*, and takes notice that the *Pope himself* used to consecrate the *Agnus Dei*, and that the other Things were hallowed by Bishops, and Substitutes from the Pope; and that the Pope granted divers *Pardons, Immunities and Exemptions*, to such as should *receive and use them.*

In the Days of *popish Ignorance*, the *foolish People* were made to *believe*, that these *Things wore by them*, would fright away the *Devil* and *other Evil Spirits*; but the true *use of them* was for the *crafty Priests*, to *gull* the People out of their *Money for them.*

So the *crafty Spaniards* for broken Glass, Beeds and other Trinkets, got Silver and Gold in exchange from the *foolish Indians.*

23 Eliz. c. 1. By this Statute of the 23 *Eliz.* the *absolving the King*'s Subjects from their Obedience to his Majesty, or Reconciling them to the Obedience of the Pope, its High Treason in the *Reconciler*, and *Reconciled.*

27 Eliz. *Popish Priests. A Popish Priest* that is a Native of the *King's Dominions*, coming into this Realm, and not submitting to his Majesty, by taking the Oaths appointed within *two Days* after his arrival, incurs the Penalty of *High Treason*, by 27 *Eliz.* [24]

3 Inst. 101. By the same Statute its Felony without Clergy, to Receive, Retain, or Maintain him knowingly. *These Law*s may look severe to those who are not acquainted with *the History of those Times.*

Reasons of these Laws. To vindicate therefore the Honour of the glorious Queen *Elizabeth*, and the Justice of the Nation: I will inform you of the Reason for making these Laws.

Pope Pius *the* 5th, *Excommunicated Queen* Elizabeth by a Bull dated in the Year 1569. whereby he *deposed the Queen, absolved her Subjects* from their Oaths of Allegiance, and *Anathemathised*, i. e. *cursed* these who continued in Obedience *to her Majesty*: This Bull of Excommunication was publish'd in *London*; and as for the *Agnus Dei*, Pictures, Beeds and such *Roman* Trinkets, they were used likewise to withdraw the Affections of those who *were attach'd to* Rome *from their Allegiance to the Queen.*

This that great Man Dr. *Burnet*, late *Bishop of Salisbury*, has made manifest by a Letter of Secretary *Walsingham's*, which he has perpetuated in his *excellent History* of the *Reformation*, and by a Copy of the Bull it self. [E - 25]

And my Lord *Coke* in his Treatise of *Ecclesiastical Laws*, hath confirm'd the same; where he shews, that in *Edward the First's Reign*, the bringing a Bull of Excommunication from *Rome* into this Kingdom by one Subject against another, was adjudged *High Treason* by the Common Law.

Thus Pope *Pius the* Vth, was that *wicked Author* of the *Schism in* England; for the Christians of all Perswasions here, came to the publick Service of the Church, *till the* 11th Year of the Reign of Queen *Elizabeth*; but when that *Bull* of his came forth that deposed *the Queen*, those who *obey'd the Pope*, declin'd coming to our publick Devotions, and ever since the Schism has continued.

Were it not common for the *Bishops of* Rome thus to do to *Protestant Princes*, whom they call *Hereticks*, it were *an Impudence* in this *Pope* never to be forgiven: *That the Crown of* England, *which is an Imperial Crown*, Subject to none but the Divine Majesty; the *Bishop of* Rome, that hath no *Jurisdiction here*, should pretend to take away from the Queen, *absolve all her Subjects* from their Allegiance, and curse them that paid their Duty of Obedience to her; which besides the Law of Nature, the express Law of

God, the Law of the Land, and the Sanction of [26] an Oath solemnly taken in the Presence of God, they were oblig'd to perform; *Is an Astonishment*: If these Things are not the doings of *Antechrist*, there never was an *Antechrist*.

Had the People of *England* been as *wicked* as the *Bishop of* Rome, to have obey'd his Decrees, what Bloodshed and Confusion would this Nation have been brought to? There were some Plots and Rebellions occasion'd thereby.

But God preserv'd *the Queen* against all the *Plots* and Attempts of *Popish Princes*, the *Pope*, the *Jesuits*, and *all the rest of their black Crew*, through a Course of 44 *Years glorious Reign*, she having continued *stedfast* in the *Protestant reform'd Religion*, and *trusted in her God*:

While at the same Time, God suffer'd *Henry the* IIId, and *Henry the* IVth. of France, *her Contemporaries*, both to be Assassin'd, who were Protestants in their Hearts; but vilely (*Henry* the IV*th* at least) turned Papist, *in hopes to enjoy* the Crown of *France more safely*; the one being murder'd by *Clement a Fryar*, the other by *Ravilliac*.

Thus you see how much *wiser* and better it is to trust in the *Arm of God*, than in the *Arm of Men. Excuse this Digression.* [E 2-27]

3 Jac. 1. c. 4. Sect.22, 23. Putting into Practice to perswade any *Person*, or to absolve him from his *Obedience to the King*, or to *reconcile a Person to the See of* Rome, is *High Treason in both*; and so it is in all Aiders and Procurers. This Act was made soon after the Discovery of the *Gunpowder-Treason Plot*.

6 Anne. By this Act, it is High Treason to maintain, that the King and Parliament cannot bind the Descent of the Crown.

Pretender. And so it is, if any Person by Writing or Printing, maintains that the Pretender hath Right to the Crown; and if by Words, the Party incurs a *Præmunire*. *And so much* for High Treason.

Misprision of Treason. You are to inquire of *Misprision of Treason*, that is, a Knowledge and Concealing of Treason, and not discovering it; but when the *Knowledge and Consent concur, its High-Treason*. As when one receives and comforts a Traitor knowingly, let him be a Counterfeiter of Coins, or any other Species of High Treason, such a one is a Principal; for there are *no Accessaries* in the *highest and lowest Offences*, as in *Treason*, nor in *Trespass*, Riots, Routs, and forcible Entries. [28]

14 Eliz. The counterfeiting of any foreign Coin of Gold or Silver, which is not permitted to be current in this Kingdom, is *Misprision of Treason* by 14 Eliz.

3d *General Head*. *My third General Head relates to your* fellow-Subjects.

25 E. 3. *Petty Treason*. And first for Petty-Treason, by 25 *E*. 3. its Petty-Treason in a *Servant to kill his Master*, or a *Wife her Husband*.

This Law extends to *Similar Cases*; as when a Servant kills his *Mistress*, that is a single Woman, or his Masters Wife: And where a *Servant* upon

Malice taken during his Service, *kills his Master* after departure from his Service; these are Petty-Treason.

So *if a Son* that receives Meat, Drink, or Wages, from his Father or Mother, kills either of them, its Petty-Treason; for in these Respects, when of *adult Age*, he is look'd upon as a Servant.

Felonies. You are to present all Persons guilty of *Felonies, as Murderers, Burglers, Robbers on the Highway, Slitters of Noses, cutters out of Tongues or Eyes, Poysoners, Pick-Pockets, Cut-purses, Ravishers of Women, burners of Houses, Barns with Corn, Sodomites*, and all other sorts of Felonies. [29]

Accessaries. And *all accessaries* to these Crimes, before and after the Facts.

Principals who. But whoever are *present and abetting* are Principals; if two or more come to do an unlawful Act, and are present at a Felony committed, tho'*one* of them *only* doth it, they are all *Principals* in Law.

Poyson. In some Cases a Person absent may be Principal; as he that puts *Poyson* into a Thing to *poyson another*, and leaves it, and is absent when taken, he is a *Principal* in Law.

Accessaries who. Before. Accessaries *before a Felony*, are those who command or advise a Felony to be done, which accordingly is done in *their absence.*

After. Accessaries after, are those who *know a Felony* to be committed, and not only not *discover it*, (for that is only a Misprision) but *conceal and help the Felony*, either to make his escape, or otherwise assist him. [1]

A Felon fled to his Brothers House, who receiv'd him, and shut the Doors against the Pursuers, adjudged an *Accessary.*

7 R. 9. *Dyer* 186. An *Adulterer* advised a Woman to murder an Infant when born; The Adulterer is *accessary*, tho' at the time of the Advice, the Infant was not in being. [30]

One may be *Accessary before* the Fact, that commands one Evil to be done, and the Principal does another, *E. G.* If *A.* commands to *rob such a Person*, and he attempts to rob him, the Party resists, and they two fight, the Thief kills the other; *A* shall be *accessary* to the *Murther*, because in attempting to rob the other, the Thief pursued the *command* of *A.* and in *execution* of it, another thing ensues, *A.* shall be adjudg'd partaker of it, because his *Command* was the occasion.

5 Anne c. 31. [*Receiver of Stolen Goods*] By this Statute, if any *Person* shall receive, or *buy stoln Goods* knowingly, or shall *harbour or conceal* a Felon, knowing him to be such, shall be taken as *Accessary* to the Fact, and suffer Death as a Felon.

1 Anne. Tho' the *Accessaries* are not to be tried till the *Principal* is *convicted* by Verdict or Outlawry; yet all Receivers of stoln Goods by *primo Annæ* knowing them to be stoln, may be prosecuted for a *Misdemeanor*, before the Principal is convicted.

[1] The text should obviously read: "help the Felon, either...".

Forcible Entries, &c. You are to present all forcible Entries, Riots, and Breaches of the Peace.

Libels, &c. The speaking of *ill Words of his Majesty*, for they are punishable at *Common Law.* [31]

The King not being within the Statute of *Scandalum Magnatum.*

Libels that are made publick against *the Ministry* or other *great Men* ; Present the Printers and Publishers as well as the Authors.

Nusances. Present *Nusances* ; for a Nusance is an Offence of a publick Nature against the common Good.

Bridges. If publick *Bridges* are out of Repair, the County must repair them, unless by Prescription private Persons do it; You may present the County.

Highways. So of *High-Ways*, the County of common Right are to Repair them; You *may present the Parishes* in which they lie, if they are not kept in due Repair.

Ditches. The *scouring of Ditches* must be taken care of:

Nusances in Thames. All *Nusances* in the *River of Thames*, are presentable; For all publick Rivers, are as the King's High-way, throwing Filth, or any Thing else that may annoy Vessels passing to or fro there, are *Nusances.* [32]

Extortion. Inquire whether any Officers are guilty of *Extortion*, by taking *more* than *their due* and allowed *Fees.*

Clerk of the Market. Whether *the Clerk of the Market* does his Duty; He ought *twice a Year*, to summon in all *Weights and Measures*, and break them that are less than they ought to be, according to the Standard. Holy Writ tells us, *that false Measures, and false Weights are an abomination to the Lord.*

Undersheriff. Inquire whether the *Under-Sheriff* performs his Duty, whether he takes more than he ought to do, or *returns Jurors* at the instance of either Party.

Bayliffs. How his *Bailiffs* Act, whether they *Extort.*

Coroners. Whether the *Coroners* perform their Duty.

Constables. Whether *Constables* do theirs: If they neglect to make Presentments, Hue and Cry after Felons; Whether they omit to execute Warrants deliv er'd to them, or Watch and Ward.

Gaolers. Whether Gaolers extort from those unhappy Wretches their Prisoners, or hinder their *Ordinaries* from coming to *Malefactors* to prepare them for another Life. [F-33]

Forestallers, Ingrators,[1] *Ingrossers.* You are to present all *Forestallers, Regrators*, and *Ingrossers,* for these inhance the Price of Victuals.

Cellar-Stairs in Street. I hope you will not think it too Minute to mention to you, that there are divers People that make their *Cellar-Stairs come so far into the Street*, that Passengers in dark Evenings are in danger of falling

[1] There we should read: Regrators.

in, and breaking their Legs and Arms, and even *their Necks*. These are publick *Nusances*, an Incroachment in the King's *High-way*, which ought not to be obstructed by any one.

Forms in the Streets. And so is the setting of *Forms* or Benches in the Street, made used of to lay Goods on exposed to Sale.

This is a *narrowing and straitning* of the King's High-way, whereby the King's Subjects that pass along the Street are often in Danger, and sometimes thrown down by *Hackney Coachmen*, who drive furiously for a Fair, and loose their Lives thereby.

Gentlemen,

It is *your duty* to present *these Offenders*, and ours to punish them for what is past, and thereby to prevent the Evils for the time to come. [34]

Bawdy-houses, Ale-houses, &c. You are to present all *Bawdy Houses* and all Ale-houses, Brandy-Shops, and other Sellers of Drink that have no Licences, and those that have, who keep Shovelboard-Tables, Bowling-Alleys, and Nine-Pins; for these Allurements keep Gentlemens Servants and Apprentices too long from their Master's Service: Here they learn Gaming; loose their Money, then rob and pilfer from their Masters or Parents to Recruit; and by quick Progressions, at last come to the Gallows; nip this Vice in the Bud.

Night-Walker. Present all *Night-Walkers, Men and Women*, that *walk the* Streets *to pick up one another* to commit Lewdness *on Sight*; a Sin, little less than that of Sodom.

Play Houses 39 Eliz. Present all *Play-houses* not duly Licens'd by the 39 *Eliz*. all common *Players of Interludes, are adjudged Rogues*, and to be punish'd as such; By that Statute there was a Priviledge given to all the Barons of the Realm, and to all other Persons of a greater Quality, to Authorize or License Players of Interludes, under their Hands and Seals by way of Exception; but the Parliament of *England* found that so very inconvenient to the Nation, that that Liberty continued but six Years.

I Jac. 1. c. 7. For in the first Year of King *James* the First, that Priviledge was taken away by [F 2- 35] Act of Parliament, and th shew the Sense of the Nation, continued the same. The Act *of* 12 Ann. *which reduces all the Acts touching Rogues, Vagabonds and Vagrants into one*: In the Enumerating the several Sorts of Persons called Rogues by the Statutes, common Players of Interludes and Juglers, are reckon'd amongst such, and to be punished accordingly.

So that for 120 Years past, and to this Day, the Parliament of *England* have, and do call and esteem these *Common Players - Rogues*.

'Tis for the Honour of some Gentlemen that sit here, to have suppress'd some of them.

Men should not make themselves Monkeys to get Money; Or taint the Morals of those who see or hear them: Its below the Dignity of Humane Nature; Revere your self is a good Rule.

One Play-House ruins more Souls, than fifty Churches are able to save. [36]

Gaming Houses. Common Gamesters. All *Gaming-Houses* and other *disorderly Houses*, Take care to Present; and all common Gamesters that draw in young Gentlemen of Fortune; They ruin may worthy Families; They are *common Nusances*, and *a Pest to the Nation*: When *the young Heir*, who *has a great Estate*, and *an unequal Wit*, has the Misfortune to fall in amongst them, they are so many Horse-Leeches, that suck out the Blood and Vitals of the young Squire or Lord; who loose as much Money *in one Night, nay, at one Throw, as the industrious Ancestor had been gathering together in many Years.*

Drury-Lane. Have an eye to the *Drury-Lane Houses*, that receive young Women and Gentlemen to commit Lewdness therein; who being too near the *Play-House*, have their Minds there tainted by hearing lewd Plays; *when the Mind is once tainted, the Body is soon prostituted*: We have punish'd some of these naughty Houses lately by Fine and Imprisonment, and if the rest will not take warning by them, to reform and amend, they ought to be Extirpated. [1]

I cannot in this Place, but commend those High-Constables who, with the Assistance of other virtuous Men, and good Subjects, have been very instrumental in presenting some of these naughty Houses; I hope they will go on, and finish what they have so well [37] begun? They may be sure of due Encouragement from this Court; for *all good Men should set their Faces against all Manner of Wickedness, and zealously encourage the promoting Virtue and Piety*, which so many excellent Persons, to the Honour of this Nation, have so worthily, and successfully applied themselves to.

Masquerades. There are *Masquerades* lately set up, *even in* Lent, *near these Houses; they are a Scene of Lewdness, A Congress to an unclean End: The Debauchery is here begun, and finish'd in the Neighbourhood.*

Drunkards. 4 Jac. 1. There is a Law against *Drunkards* ; five Shillings for the first Offence, and on conviction a second Time, the Party is to be bound to his good Behaviour for 6 Months.

The *Drunkard debases himself*, and sinks below even the *brutal Nature*, for *Brutes won't be drunk* ; *Man, foolish Man*, only by painful Practices arrives at that *Priviledge* ; ill Men take more Pains to be excessively bad, than Men of good Dispositions do to attain to exalted Virtue : The Industry of the one, will even shame the Sloathfulness of the other at the last Day; the *sloathful Servant* was called *Wicked.* [2]

Tipling in Ale-houses. There is a Penalty on the Alehouse-keeper, Inn-keepers and Vitlers, that suffer [38] People to continue Tipling in their Houses; These Houses were never intended to entertain loose and idle People, to squander away their Time and Money, by sitting guzling there

[1] See D. George, *London Life in the 18th Century*, Peregrine Books, 1966. Ch. 2, 92-93.

[2] Matt. 25: 26.

for many Hours: But for poor People, that are labouring Men, to refresh themselves after their Work, that cannot lay in Stock of their own, and to entertain Travellers in their Passage on their lawful Occasions.

Stocks. You are to present all Parishes that have not Stocks, Whipping Posts and Cages in them: The want of this last, occasions very great Expences to Parishes remote from hence, and sometimes the escape of Criminals, while the Facts are under Examination.

Generals. And if there are any things else of a publick Nature, that are mischievous to Mankind, that I have omitted you are to Present them also from the highest to the lowest Offences, from Treason to Trespass.

Exhortation. You see now Gentlemen, how the Common and Statute Law have provided against all manner of Wickedness.

No Nation under Heaven has better Laws than we have; besides, we have every Sessions of Parliament, (which sits annually) new Laws made to redress emergent [39] Evils; but yet the Nation is but little amended by them.

What is the Reason of it? 'Tis becaüse the *Laws are* not duly put *in Execution*; Foreigners may justly complain, that *our Laws* are *very numerous, and ill executed*, which is a Reproach to the Nation.

If you Gentlemen of the *grand Inquest*, would be industrious in presenting the *Enormities* you know of; What with the excellent *Discourses, and virtuous Lives of our Learned Divines of the Church of* England: What with your Presentments of *Immoralities and Profaneness*; and the *Justices of the Peace of the Kingdom*, executed speedily *Justice against all such Offenders, and giving a good Example.*

It may still be hoped, that the Nation may be somewhat amended and Reform'd.

Atheism and *Irreligion* quite Discountenanc'd; *Virtue and Piety encourag'd*, and thereby the Honour of God promoted, which will bring down Blessings from Heaven upon the Nation; for holy Writ tells us, *They that Honour God, God will Honour, but they that despise him shall be lighlty esteem'd.* [1]

I pray God direct you in your Presentments.

FINIS.

[1] 1 Sam 2: 30.

THE SECOND **CHARGE** OF *Whitlocke Bulstrode*, Esq; TO THE GRAND JURY AND Other JURIES OF THE County of *Middlesex*, AT THE General Quarter-Sessions of the Peace, held the Ninth Day of *October*, 1718. at *Westminster-Hall*.

Printed at the Desire of the Justices of the Peace for the County, and of the Grand Jury.

In the *SAVOY*.

Printed by Eliz. Nutt and R. Gosling, (Assigns of *Edward Sayer*, Esq;) for R. Gosling at the *Mitre* and *Crown* in *Fleetstreet*, 1718.

A 2- i

To the Right Honourable *Thomas* Lord *Parker*, Baron of *Macclesfield*, Lord High Chancellor of *Great Britain*, &c.

My Lord,

THE great *Humanity*, with which your Lordship *treats all Mankind*, and the great *Goodness* with which your Lordship *receives Men of Distinction*, cannot but render you dear to the *whole Nation*.

How much more *lovely* is such a *Conduct than Learning* cloath'd with the *morose and sour Temper of the Cynick*! And yet how much is such *a Loveliness increas'd*, when such a Treatment proceeds from a *sincere Heart*, and not like that of a Courtier who *never thinks as he speaks*, or intends to *perform* what he solemny *promises*!

Your Lordship succeeded that Great and Excellent Lawyer, *that Stout and Honest Judge, my Lord Chief Justice* HOLT, in the Court of *King's Bench*; whose exquisite Skill in the most abstruse Part of the Law, *that of special Pleading*, will render his *Memory immortal*.

And yet the *Brightness* which shines in that Court, by his *Presence*, rather receiv'd [ii] *an Increase* than *Diminution of Light* by your Lordship's *Accession to his Seat*.

Your Predecessor my Lord *Cowper*, late *Lord Chancellor of Great Britain*, twice voluntarily *gave up the Great Seal* with as much Honour as any of his Predecessors ever retain'd it; whose *Penetration, Integrity, and natural Modesty* caused him to be belov'd of all Men; the *latter* giving a *Lustre* even to his Face. Your Lordship is come into a new scene of Action: A Court of a quite different Nature from that, from which his Maejsty has rais'd you. But what can be difficult, tho' new, to a Person endowed *with general Learning, a quick Apprehension, sedate Judgment, and of an exalted Genius*?

I may say of your Lordship as the Queen *of Sheba did of Solomon*, who having *tasted of his Knowledge and great Abilities*, and seen the *excellent Conduct of his Family*, cry'd out in Rapture; *Happy are thy Men: Happy are these thy Servants, which stand continually before thee, and that hear thy Wisdom.* [1]

[1] 1 King 10: 8; 2 Chr. 12: 7.

Princes are so much *rais'd above the rest of Mankind*, that few have an Opportunity of knowing them.

The best Way therefore for a Person to make a *Judgment of his Prince*, who has not Access to him, is to consider *the Qualifications* of those, he advances to *Great Places*.

The mean Abilities of the Minister of State, shews the short Capacity of the Master: But [iii] *the great Endowments of the Minister, proclaim the Master a wise Prince.*

If this Rule I have laid down be true, *our King may reckon'd a* Solomon, *for the Choice of your Lordship.*

I know nothing tends more to the Support of a Government, than the placing Good and Wise Men in the highest Stations; especially in Courts of Judicature, from whence the unsuccessful go away satisfied, though not pleased.

But then the Honour of such Great Men, ought to be carefully preserved and maintain'd; *their delicate and nice Understanding can't bear the least Ruffle, much less a rude Touch.*

The bold and ignorant, tho' favour'd at Court, should not come near them; it should be told them, as the Heralds used at the Pagan Sacrifices,

Procul, ô procul este Prophani!

Their Province ought not to be invaded by any Great or Whiffling Courtier. No Man of *Learning, Estate, and Spirit*, can or ought to bear such an *Indignity* or *Affront*: And *whenever such Great Men are sour'd by such a Treatment*, which causes them to *resign*; the Government has lost an Arm, or a Leg, that should support it.

The principal Rafters of the Building are withdrawn. [iv]

Moses his Hand is then let down, and *Amalek* is likely to prevail.

The Arms of the Crown are supported by tw of the bravest and strongest Creatures; a *Lion*, and an *Unicorn*; which intimate, That the Wisest and Strongest Heads, and the Best of Men, are most fit to support the Throne and Royal Dignity.

When the contrary to such are chose, the Government becomes lame and infirm, subject to Changes not easily to be foreseen, and falls into Contempt.

May your Lordship continue the Support of the Crown; and may no Indignity be offered to your Person; or any Invasion of your Province, to make your Mind uneasy. May all Mankind approach your Lordship with a due Regard: And may you many Years continue the Safety, Ornament, and Glory of the Nation: Which (with your Acceptance of the following Charge) will be an infinite Pleasure to

Your Lordship's

Most Faithful and

Most Obedient

Humble Servant,

Whitelocke Bulstrode. [v]

Midd. ss. Ad Generalem Quarterialem Sessionem Pacis Domini Regis tentam pro

Comitatu Middlesexiæ, *apud* Hick's-Hall *in* St. John-Street, *in Comitatu prædicto per Adjornamentum Die Veneris scilicet Decimo Die* Octobris *Anno Regni Domini* Georgii *nunc Regis* Magnæ Britanniæ, &c. *Quinto.*

THIS Court being of Opinion, that the Charge given by *Whitelocke Bulstrode*, Esq; the Chairman, on the Ninth of *October* Instant, being the first Day of this present Quarter-Sessions, *is a Pious and Learned Charge, tending to suppress the Vices of this Age, to promote Virtue and Religion, the Honour of God, and Welfare of the Nation*: Doth as well on their own Behalfs, as also at the Request of the Grand Jury, now assembled, desire that the said Mr. *Bulstrode* will be pleased to cause his said Charge to be Printed.

Per Cur'. Harcourt. [vi]

To Whitelocke Bulstrode, *Esq; Chairman of this present Sessions.*

We the Grand Jury for the County of *Middlesex* return you our hearty thanks for your Excellent Charge to us: And humbly desire for the better Information and Encouragement of Constables and other Officers, that you will cause the same to be printed and published,

October 16, 1718.

Joseph Earl	Jonathan Parsons
Thomas Repass	Abraham Clarke
Peter Triquet	Peter Bluzee
Auther Farley	Caleb Williams
Abraham Doleal	William Hage.
George Speere	Nicholas Cooke
Richard Sturley	Ralph Maxeg
Samuel Reed	John Thomas
Paul Batchelor	John Deane
David Malley	Jonh Paine
Jon Cookson	Peter Ferry
Phillip Nutt.	

[B -1]

THE SECOND

CHARGE

OF

Whitelocke Bulstrode, Esq;

TO THE

GRAND JURY,

And the other Juries.

Gentlemen of the Grand Jury

YOU have taken upon you a very *great Duty*; *Great*, with Respect to the Subject Matter, which falls under your Cognizance; and *Great* with Respect to the Dignity and Antiquity of the Office.

As to the first, the subject Matter is, as to *Offences general*; but confin'd to Place; for you are [2] to enquire of *all Offences* which are committed (within this County, either *against the Laws of God, or Man, by any Subject whatsoever*).

Dignity of the Office. As to the second, the Dignity of your Office appears, even *ex Vi termini, Grand Jury*; which distinguishes you from the *Petty Jury* as Men of *greater Consideration.*

The Sheriff usually returns (as he ought to do) Gentlemen of the *best Quality, Estate, and Understanding,* in the County, to serve in *this Office*; unless they are exempted by particular Employments, as *Divines, Lawyers, Physicians, and some few others.* You are a *Court of Record*; *your Presentments* are affiled, as *Matters of Record,* which are to endure as long as our happy Constitution lasts. You differ only in this from other *Courts of Record,* that your Presentments are *traversable,* wich the Records of other Courts are not.

Antiquity. As for the Antiquity of this office; it is co-evous with the Common Law it self, which is *Time immemorial*; and this Law is *mostly* drawn from the *Laws of God.*

The *Laws* of this Kingdom may be consider'd under *three general Heads, (viz.)*

First; The *Common Law,* or *general Custom of the Kingdom*; which had *its Ground from Acts of Parliaments,* worn out by Length of Time.

Secondly; *Particular Customs in particular Places,* which differ from the Common Law, introduc'd by the several Nations that have been *Victors here*: These may be properly styled, *Leges Loci* [1]; which are strictly to be taken.

Thirdly; The *Statute Laws,* which when they are *negative* toll the *Common Law,* but when they are *affirmative,* do not: They are then only *accumulative.* This Kingdom is di-[B 2- 3] vided into Shires and Counties; and some of these have in them particular Corporations, for their better and more orderly Government.

Four Times a Year the *Grand Juries* appear, at the *Four General Quarter*-Sessions of each County and Shire, for the Keeping of *the Peace and Tranquillity* of the *Nation.*

Twice a Year generally, the Judges hold their *Assizes* in every Shire and County where the *Grand Juries* likewise *meet.*

And the Corporations have their Sessions, and Grand and Petty Juries: And these being drawn by our *excellent Constitution,* from the several parts of *each County and Shire*; there can be no Breach of the Law, *morally speaking,* committed within this Kingdom, that can escape their Knowledge.

Gentlemen of the Grand Jury,

The Laws of the Land have set you, as *Watchmen upon an high Tower,* to

[1] = local rules.

give Notice to the *Government* of the *Transgressors of the Law*, of the *Sinners against the Kingdom*, which are the greatest Enemies thereof; for they draw down God's Vengeance upon us: *National Judgments always, at least generally, follow national Sins.*

God is the most powerful Being to hurt is, more than any foreign Enemy can do, (but does us always more *Good* than the best of our Friends) whom we ought to serve, and obey with a Filial Reverence and Love. And as the *Watchmen* that give no Notice of the *Approach of an Enemy*, commit a *Capital Crime* against the Government that has appointed them: So, Gentlemen, if you know, or are inform'd of any Persons that are Violators of the Laws of [4] the Land, and do not give Notice thereof, by your Presentments, you will be equally guilty of the like Crime.

'Tis a *Maxim in Divinity*, and even in our Law, *Qui non vetat peccare, cum potest, jubet*; that is, He that does not prevent Evils, when 'tis in his Power, does, in effect, commands them to be done; is even a Principal in the Evil.

Have a Care of being Partakers in other Mens Sins; by suffering them to go on through your Default; when by your *Presentments*, and *our Punishments* of the *Offenders*, they may be reclaim'd and become good Men.

Constables Jury. Let this stick with you, *Gentlemen of the Constables Jury*, whose Neglect of Presenting Persons for not coming to Church, or some religious Meeting, allow'd by Law, on every Lord's Day, may be the Occasion of the Ruin of many Souls. For tho' *Men* should not come to *Church* for *Fear of the Penalty* of being *absent*; [Church Defaulters] but on a nobler *Principle of Love* and *Gratitude to our great Creator*, and *most munificent Benefactor*; yet when Men are there present, the *Scripture*, which, like a *two-edged Sword, divides* between the *Joints* and *Marrow*, may strike so powerfully as to work the Reformation of Mind, and thereby cause them to become *good Men* in *this World, useful Members in the Common Wealth*, and *eternally happy in the World to come.*

Consider therefore, gentlemen, what Good you may do, by such Presentments.

Compel them to come in — I think may literally and justly be applied in this Case: Wherein you obey our Saviour's Commands, and may do much good thereby to Mankind. For in this Case, *you force not the Conscience*, but [5] *compel* Men to *serve God, even in their own Way*, by coming to Church or to Meetings of their own Perswation.

Trades on *Sundays*. Take Care to present Persons that follow their Trades on the Lord's Day, except in Cases of Necessity, or Mercy: God has given us six Parts of Time in seven to follow our honest Employments; and surely we may well afford to dedicate the seventh part to the more solemn Service of our Creator.

I am credibly inform'd, That the Butchers in *Westminster* Market, St. *James*'s Market, St. *Anne*'s Market, *Newport* Market, *Clare* Market,

Hungerford Market, *Brooke*'s Market, and the Butchers of *Whitechapel*, do kill their Sheep and Calves on a *Sunday*, and hang the Meat out at their Stalls on a *Sunday* Morning, all the Time of Divine Service, as much as on a *Saturday*.

These are great Prophanations of the Lord's Day; therefore be sure to present the Persons that are guilty thereof.

Gentlemen of the Grand Enquest,

From the frequent Meetings of the Grand Juries of the Kingdom, that are drawn from the several Parts of each County and Shire, and from the Consideration of the Duty incumbent upon them, increas'd by an Oath to present all Crimes, I may well conclude, that if the *Grand Juries* of this Nation would keep *their Oaths*, and do their Duty, *as honest Men, and good Subjects should do*; (which I promise my self that you will do) and if the Justices of the Peace of this Nation would be zealous in Promoting the Peace and Welfare of their Country, being powerfully assisted by the Judges in their Circuits, there would be no [6] Danger of Enemies from Abroad, while we were all at Peace and Quiet at Home. And if *Frugality, Sobriety*, and *Industry*, were practis'd and encourag'd by the *Gentlemen, Freeholders*, and *Traders* of this Kingdom, there would be fewer Temptations to do Evil for the sake of Money.

Men that do not run out of *their Fortunes*, but live *within Compass*, have but little Temptation, by *Offices*, or *Money*, to play the *Knave, to betray their Country*, sell *their Votes*, or do any base or mean Action: But when a *Gentleman* has ruin'd his Fortune by *excessive Living, Debauchery, Gaming*, or *Parliamenteering*, the Temptation to do what he *is bid*, tho' ever *so wrong*, for a *great Rewards* is *too powerful* to be resisted by an *ordinary Degree of Virtue*.

Necessitas cogit ad turpia.

Foreigners that see *our Gazettes*, weekly *stuff'd with* a vast Number of *Bankrupts*, may be apt to conclude that the *Trading Part of the Nation are a Parcel of Beggars*. But he that sees *the Finery of their Houses, their rich Furniture, and elegant Paintings; their Profeness and Delicacies in their Entertanments; their costly Wines; their three Courses*[1]; *their Services in Plate; the Splendor* of their *Wives and Daughters* within Doors; and their *Equipages* of *Coaches* and *six Horses, Footmen*, and *Horsemen*, to attend them to their *Country Seats*; would think, he rather met a *foreign Prince of a Younger House*, or some *English Nobleman*, or a *Gentleman of the first Quality*, than a *Trader on the Exchange*. [7]

No Wonder, after such a *Way of living*, so many Traders become *Bankrupts*; and thereby *rob Widows and Orphans* of all their *Substance*. He that *picks a Pocket*, or *robs a House*, is the less *Criminal* of the two: These make a Prey often but of *Twenty or Thirty Shillings Value*: But the *Bankrupt* often breaks for an *Hundred Thousand Pounds*, and *ruins many Honest credulous Families thereby*.

[1] Hi sunt qui comedant uni Patrimonia Mensa.

If we had a Law that made it *Felony without Clergy* for any *Person* that *broke through extravagant* and *luxurious Living*; it would stop those *profuse Livers* in the *Career of their Luxury*, when *they consider'd that they were Riding Post to the Gallows.*

Hadrian, the *Roman* Emperor, made a Law, That they who *ran* out of their *Estates*, should *be exposed* to a publick *Shame* in the *Amphitheatre*, and then *banish'd Rome.*

The *Romans* were a glorious People while they lived *frugally, soberly*, and *virtuously*; and loved and preferr'd the *publick Welfare* to their *private unjust Gain*; *God* blessed them with *Victory*; They became Conquerors of the World. But when *Offices* and *Employments* were set *to Sale*; when the *Romans* parted with their *Morals to acquire Offices*, and had no Regard for the *Good of their Country*;'twas well and *justly said of them*; '*Vale, venalis* Roma, *mox venditura teipsam, si emptorem inveneris.* Go, naughty saleable Rome, quickly to be sold, if a Buyer can be found. 'They soon after *dwindled away*, and became *a Prey even to the Barbarians.*

No *Nobleman* or *Gentleman takes Money* himself, or suffers any other Person to do so, of any one, to put him into his *Steward's Place*; well knowing, that such *Steward* will make himself *whole* out of *his Master's Estate.* [8]

Vendit Alexander *claves, altaria sacra;*
Vendere jure potest; emerat ille prius.

The Case is *worse*, when a *Nation suffers such Practices*, inasmuch as *private Men* have *more Opportunities*, and are generally *more jealous* in looking after their *Servants, than a Government well can.* The Virtue even of this *Nation* is so far *lost*, *(for I spoke before of the* Roman) that few Men are just and honest in their Employments, on any other Principles than the Fear of losing their Places; so, that when they can play the *Knave, without Discovery*, they are *sure to lay of hold to the Opportunity*: For to cheat the Publick, they think is *no Wrong*: Few, very few, serve the *Government* in any *Offices* or *Employments*, but purely in Order to *serve themselves.*

Therefore, Gentlemen, if you know of any *Wrong* or *Fraud*, done to the *Government*, by *any Person whatsoever*; be sure to *present such*; and we will make Examples of them.

Most Nations, in the inflicting *Punishments* for *Offences*, do rather respect, in the Punishing Part, what *Mischiefs such Offences* do to the *Publick*, than the *Malignity* or *Turpitude of the Fault*, with Respect to the *Divine Law*, or *Judgment of God.* Thus *Theft*, which by the *Divine Law* was punish'd only with a *four-fold Restitution, and in some Cases five*, is by our Law *punish'd with Death.* And thus *Adultery*, which by the Divine Law was punished with *Death*, by the *Common Law, Damages* only are given to the *Husband* in an *Action on the Case*: And by the Ecclesiastical Laws, the Offender is to do Penance in a *white Sheet*; the Common Law [C-9] not directly intermedling therewith: How well or ill these Things are, belongs to our Legislators to judge. But I shall begin my Charge to you,

1st; *With Offences against God.*

2dly; *With Offences against the King.*

3dly *; With Offences against your Fellow-Subjects.*

Some Offences are *so heinous in their* Nature, so *foreign to the Lusts, and Passions, and even Wickedness of Mens Hearts*; that neither the *Divine Majesty*, nor his *Creature Man*, made any *Laws* against *them*, 'till both were necessitated so to do, when those *Crimes were committed by some Monsters in Nature. The Wisdom both of God* and Man herein being to *be admir'd*, that on the Enacting of Punishments against Offences, neither *would suppose Mankind* would ever be *guitly thereof*. For, to *forbid a Crime*, to a *superlative Wicked Heart, possess'd* by Satan, is *to put him in Mind of doing it*: Whereas otherwise, he would not, peradventure, ever think of it. Thus there was *no Law* made by the *Divine Majesty*, or his Servant *Moses against Cursing or Blaspheming (the Name of) God*: until the Son of an *Israelitish Woman whose Father was an Egyptian*, quarelling *with a Jew, blasphemed the Name of God, and curs'd*; [Lev. ch. 24, v. 10-16] For this unheard-of *Crime and Wickedness*, the Standers by *seiz'd him*, and carried him *before Moses*, the *Chief Justice of Israel.* He was *surprized* at this *heinous unheard-of Crime*, and *committed him to Custody*, till the next Day; that (as the Text says) *the Mind of the Lord might be shewn them. And God spoke to* Moses *to bring forth him that cursed, and bid all the Congregation stone him.* And after this Sen-[10] tence was passed and executed on this wicked Wretch; then it pleased God *to make a general Law*, that *Whoever cursed God, or blasphem'd his holy Name*, (i.e.) *Spoke Evil of God, should surely be put to Death*; which was afterwards *a standing Law among the Jews*; And this *is remarkable*, that the *Mother's Name of this wicked Wretch is mention'd in Holy Writ*, and the Tribe he was of; to remain as *an eternal Blot and Reproach on that Family and Tribe, for producing both a Monster*, as *should speak Evil of God*, for being *an Original* in that Sin: And, by the Way, let our prophane *Cursers and Blasphemers take* Notice hereof, at their Peril: lest when the Books of *Remembrance* are open'd at *the last Day*, their *Names* should be found *written* there, as *Blasphemers*; to remain there as an *eternal Monument of Infamy to them, and to stare them in the face, to their eternal Shame and Confusion, to their endless Misery and Pain,* which may render them *a Shame* and *Reproach,* even *to Hell it self,* and *thereby* increase their *Anguish.*

The Romans are said to have made no *Law* against *Parricide* ; for they did not suppose, that any Man would be so monstrous as to take away the Life of that Person that gave him a Being; tho' *Nero*, and some few other *Monsters in Nature, did so.* We had no Law against *prophane Cursing and Swearing*, 'till 21 Jac. I when *that vile sin* became *too fashionable in this Nation*; which went a great *Way towards bringing* upon this *Nation, God's Judgment of a Civil War*; for *National Sins* are generally pursued with *National Judgments*; which is a Proof among many others of God's *Government* of the World, and that nothing *happens* by (a foolish Word call'd) *Chance.* [C 2-11]

You are above all Things, Gentlemen, to *demonstrate your Zeal* for *the Honour and Glory of God*; which you cannot do better in your Station, than by your *Presentments of all persons guilty of Immorality and Prophaneness, as the Proclamation now read to you directs*; which I desire you will take along with you, and seriously consider of.

One cannot walk *the Streets*, or ride *the Roads*, but if *one hears* two or three *ordinary Fellows talk together*, but every other Sentence they *curse or damn themselves, or others*, by the *Name of the Almighty God*, in their *common and ordinary Conversation* ; not *in Heat, or the Bitterness of Passion*, but *calmly and sedately*, as *the natural Dialect of the Beast.* They use the *most reverend and tremendous Name of God*, with as much *Familiarity, Sauciness*, and *Impudence*, as they do their Dick or Tom. Oh! transcendent Wickedness! Oh! Impudence never to be forgiven! *God* has said, He will not hold *him guiltless* that takes *his Name in vain*: As if *his Majesty* had been pleas'd *to declare*, That no *Sacrifice*, no *Expiation*, should *atone* for such *impudent Sins*, to which *Human Nature* has not so much as *any Temptation*: But that the *Guilt of* such *Crimes* should always remain *upon the Head of the Offenders*, to *their eternal Shame and Confusion.*

God who, by *his own Law*, has *so well secur'd human Properties*, as not only to forbid Theft, but even *coveting what is another's*, knowing that such Coveting is a Step and an Approach to Stealing, is *so jealous of his own Glory*, that he has forbid us to make any *Image* or *Figure*, or any *Representation* of his *Majesty*; because all such Actions, would fall *infinitely short* of the Glory of the *Divine Majesty*; and *lessen* and *bring* [12] *down in our Minds the glorious Idea*, which we *ought to conceive of the infinite Power, Wisdom*, and *other Attributes of the Almighty*: *How then* will his *Divine Majesty resent the perpetual Dishonour of prophaning and despising his holy Name*, (that is, his *Person*) even in the best Reformed Christian Church in the World!

But we *have chose Darkness rather than Light. None of us, poor Mortals*, that are of a *few Inches long*, made of *Dust and Ashes*, and to be resolv'd into *Dust and Ashes again*; *here to Day, and gone to Morrow*; but would be very angry, and take it with Disdain: ——— If our *inconsiderable Names* were treated thus, with Scorn and Contempt, as to be in the *Mouth of every ordinary and profligate Wretch, to so vile and impertinent a Purpose.*

Whereas the *Name* or *Person of the Almighty God* (which in Scripture Language are all one, of the *same Import*) should never be so much *as thought on*; *much less, spoke*; but with the *most profound Reverence, with the utmost Love* and *Affection* to so *infinite a Bounty*; who gives us all the *Good we enjoy, and delivers us from* all the *Evil we avoid, both moral and natural.*

The *Jews* have a *Tradition*, that *Noah* and his Family govern'd themselves by *seven Precepts, as an Abstract of the Law of Nature*; one whereof was, *not to blaspheme the Name of God.* But that Law had not the Sanction of a Penalty, till God himself enacted it, on the Occasion before mention'd; which Penalty was Death.

We are taught by *our Saviour* to pray daily, that God's Name may be *hallowed*, or *sanctify'd* : (i.e.) To be esteem'd holy infinitely *above* all *other Names*: To be *admir'd, glorified*, and *praised*, even as the *Angels glorify it in Heaven.* [13]

But instead of that, we Christians *blaspheme his holy Name* an hundred Times a Day, by *prophane Cursing and Swearing* in *our common and ordinary Conversation.* A *dreadful Sin*! Our Legislators indeed have provided against it: But the Execution of this Law is not well attended; and the *coming* at it, not very easy.

When the *Laws of the Land* cannot keep *down a Sin*, but it becomes *spreading, rampant*, and *universal*, I know no *other Way*, when *human Means can't prevail*, but *that God* himself should *interpose by his Almighty Power*; and by *pouring down Vengeance from Heaven*, try to *reclaim that People* which *Human Laws can't reduce. Look to it*; for, I am afraid, it's coming upon us: The Plague, it's said, is already broke out in *France*; and we are very near Neighbours; our Weekly Bills increase[1]; Death's at our Doors: worse than *Hannibal ad Portas.*[2]

Our *Common Law* has condescended so low, as to punish by Indictment, or Information, a *common Scold, communis Rixatrix*: Now this *silly Woman* only makes a Noise amongst her Neighbours, and *claps her Hands* to *increase* the Sound of *impertinent Words*; which to the *Crowd*, is *even Musick, but to nicer Ears*, somewhat of Jargon or Caw-Jack. Now if this is an Offence against the Publick Peace and Quiet of the Nation, which only *grates* upon the Organ of *Hearing* on the *tender and distinguishing Ears of a wise Person, and sinks no deeper*; what must the *hearing perpetually* of *that Name (which*, above all Things in the World, *we ought to love, reverence, and adore) being daily and hourly prophan'd, and vilify'd, scorn'd, and contemn'd, what Impressions of Sorrow and Grief, and the utmost Concern*, must it make on all Mankind, that have the least *Sense* [14] *of Gratitude to God* for *his Favours to us*, or the *least Zeal for his Glory*?

I think a *common Swearer* is a *Nusance to the Place where he lives*; and though the Common Law has no Case adjudg'd in this Point, because this Sin was never so rife as it is now; yet since it is a *stronger Case* than that of a *Scold*, it hath infinitely *more mischievous Consequences*;

Ubi par Ratio, ibi idem Jus,

Is a good and true Rule of Law; Where the Reason is the same, the Law ought to be the same. If it be said, That divers Statutes have given Remedies *against prophane Swearing and Cursing*; I answer, That it's plain *those Remedies*, or *Means*, do not *attain the End* for which they were *made*:

[1] = Mortality Bills, the lists of persons deceased in a week.

[2] = Hannibal at the Gates [Hannibal at the gates of Rome], an imminent danger.

Besides, these Acts of *Parliament* being only in the *Affirmative*; do not take away any other *Remedy*: And as for *Precedents, every Precedent* had a Beginning; and there can never be a better Precedent, than to make an *Example* of a Common *Swearer*, by *Indicting* or *Presenting him as a common Nusance.*

Gentlemen,

Set your Faces against this loud and crying Sin; let your *Exclamations* against it, wherever you come, *stifle and suppress* it, that the Cry thereof may not go up tp heaven.

Consider what *Honour God* bestow'd on *Phinehas*, who was zealous for his *Majesty*, in the Matter of *Ximri* and *Cozbi*: How by that one Act he stopt the *Plague, averted God's Wrath*, and saved *many Thousands*; and obtain'd for himself and Posterity the *Honour of the everlasting Priesthood.* [15]

God is the best *Master* to *reward* his *Servants*, and the best *Friend* to do us good. As for *Kings*; alas! they *see with other Men's Eyes*, and *hear with other Men's Ears*; they often *do Injuries to their Friends, and confer Benefits on their Enemies*; and it can't well be otherwise. But it is not so with *God*, who sees, and hears, and knows all Things, and determines with unerring Wisdom.

Therefore if you *love, and desire the Welfare* of your *native Country*, the *Welfare* of *your Wives and Children*, the *Welfare* of your *Souls, Bodies, and Estates*, shew your zeal in the suppressing of this crying Sin, and in every Thing else that tends to *lessen* or *diminish* the Divine *Honour and Glory*; and be certanily assured, you'll find your Accompt in so doing. The Scripture *has pronounc'd a Curse upon him* that doth the Work of the *Lord negligently*, and a mighty Blessing on them who are *zealous for the Divine Glory.*

Books against the Scriptures. Whatever *Books* or *Pamphlets are writ against the Scriptures*, or *that* are *contra bonos Mores*; or that *tend to the dishnouring of God*, or to *depreciate the Authority of the Apostles, by exposing their Infirmities*, (as if being Men, they should not be subject to human Frailties) which seems *to be level'd against all Reveal'd Religion*, and to send us back to *Paganism*, or that *tend to represent our Saviour* as a meer Man, which takes off *his meritorious Sufferings*, and *overbrows the whole System of Divine Goodness, in his superlative Mercy to Mankind*, in our *Redemption*, and *in his Oeconomy in the Christian Church*; which a late Author seems to drive at, (I mean Mr. Toland) whose pernicious Book, called *Nazarenus*, is incomparably well answer'd, and confuted by the learned and judicious Mr. Mangey.[1] Present [16] the Authors, the Printers, and Publishers of such Books. And so much for the Offences against God.

My second Head, is *touching Offences* against *the King.*

Under this Head, you are to enquire of *High Treason.* What was High Treason by the Common Law, was very uncertain till the famous *Statute*

[1] *Nazarenus: or Jewish, Gentile and Mahometan Christianity*, 1718. Because of its recent publication, a controversial book, answered by Mangey.

of 25 *E.* 3. reduced the *several Species of High Treason to a Certainy.* They may be reckon'd under *four general Heads*, viz.

1 *st*, What *concerns the King and his Family.*

2 *dly*, What *concerns his Officers in the Administration of Justice* .

3 *dly*, What *concerns his Seal.*

4 *thly*, What *concerns his Coin.*

Of which briefly.

As to the First.

Compassing, or *Imagining the Death of the King; Queen*, or *Prince*, and *Declaring* or *Manifesting* the same, by some *Overt Act*, though that Act take not Effect, is *High Treason*, by 25 *E.* 3. Declaring by an *open Act a Design to depose*, or *imprison the King*; is an *Overt Act, to manifest a Compassing of his Death.*

Cr. Car. 332. *Arthur Crohagam*, an *Irish* Man, and a *Dominican* Fryer, said at *Lisbon*, 7 C. 1. He *would kill the King*, (meaning *King Charles the First*) if he could come to him. And came afterwards into *England for the same Purpose*: It was adjudg'd High Treason within 25 *E.* 3; and he was accordingly executed. [D- 17]

2 Ventr. *Patrick Harding's Case. 1 W.* & *M.* Raising Men to joyn with a Prince that is at War with the King, is adjudged a Compassing the *Death* of the King, and an *Overt Act.* But the Levying of War, being a distinct Species of Treason within this Statute, a Conspiracy to levy War is no Overt Act, unless *levied.*

Francia the *Jew*'s Case. But the *solliciting Assistance from Abroad*, or *at Home*, and consulting and agreeing to an *Invasion to levy War*, are sufficient *Overt Acts* to prove a *Conspiracy*, a *Compassing*, and *Imagining the Death of the King*, within the first *Branch of this Act*; as was lately held in *Francia* the *Jew*'s Case.

7 *W.* 3. By the 7 *W.* 3. There must be *two Witnesses* to an Indictment of *High Treason*; (*i.e.*) to *the same Overt Act laid* in the *Indictment.* Or one to *one Overt Act*, and *another to another Act of the same Species of Treason.* For *where there are two Species of* Treason laid in an Indictment, one *Witness to one Overt Act*, and *another Witness to another Overt Act*, of a *different Species of Treason*, shall not be deem'd *two* Witnnesses *within that Statute.*

It is High Treason within this Statute to kill the Chancellor, Treasurer, Justices of either Bench, Justices in Eyre, Assise, or of Oyer and Terminer, in their Places, doing their Office.

The Counterfeiting the Great, or Privy Seal, is High Treason by this Statute.

And so is the Counterfeiting the Coin of this Kingdom.

The *Subdivision* of these *Heads*, and the other *Species of Treason*, by late Acts, *having spoken fully* to in my Charge lately given here, which *is in Print*, I refer you to, and shall omit *speaking to them now.*[1] [18]

[1] We should understand here: "*speaking of*". See the first Charge by Bulstrode.

And so much for my second Head of Offences agaisnt the King.

3d General. My third General head related to Offences against your Fellow-Subjects. of which some are Capital, and some not.

Of the *Capital*, they are of *three Kinds*.

1*st*; Such as are committed against *the Life of a Man.*

2*dly*; Such as *relate to his Goods.*

3*dly*; Such as are against his *Habitation.*

As to the First: You are to enquire of Murther.

Murther defin'd. Murther is when a Person kills another, of Malice, within any County in *England*, so that the Party dies of the Wound within a Year and a Day, after the Wound given.

Now though every Killing of a Man is Homicide, yet every Homicide is not Murther; the Terms are not convertible.

As the Laws of God have distinguished in the several Ways by which Men are killed, and of one Man's Killing another; so has our Law.

For if *two* Men quarrel, and *presently go out, and fight, and one kills the other*; this, *by our Law*, is call'd *Manslaughter*, and the Party hath his Clergy; in Consideration of *human Frailties*, and the Passions to which human *Nature is subject* .

But if they *sleep upon it*, and *fight next Day* (the *Passions having had Time to cool) it is Murther.*

There was a Case, lately adjudged *Murther*, that is fit for *all the Rakes of the Town to know.* Two Men, *Burdet* and *Winchurst*, went late at Night into *Drury-Lane*, and *quarrell'd with th*e [D 2-19] *Watch*; *after that*, they met with *Captain Falkner* with a *lewd Woman with him* ; he was Stranger to both of them; *they jostled him*; *Winchurst* had *no Sword*, but *bid Burdet draw*; *who drew* accordingly; *Falkner drew*, and *Burdet ran him through, whereof he instantly dyed.* It was adjudged *Murther* in them both, because they had Malice against all Mankind: And they were both executed.

There is a Death called *Chance-Medley*; which is, where a Man doing a lawful Act, *without Intent of Hurt to another*, yet *Death casually ensues.* And there is a *Homicide, Se defendo, which saves his Life.*

Yet in these Cases, such Regard hath the Law for the preservation of human Life, that a Forfeiture of Goods is incurr'd.

And where a Man is kill'd without the Default or Procurement of another Person; as by a Fall from an Horse or Cart, or Tree, the Thing *that* occasions *the Death is forfeited.* So it is, if *One is kill'd by any Beast; it is a Deodand.*

But where a Bill is brought to you *against any Persons* for the *Murther* of another, you are to find the Bill *Murther, as laid*; and not to distinguish, by finding the Bill, Manslaughter, *per Infortunium*, or *Se defendo.* For you being but in the *Nature of Accusers*, and your *Verdict not final*, but *traversable*, these Distinctions *lye* properly before the Petti Jury, and not you.

There is a *justifiable Homicide*, which induceth no Forfeiture. As, if one comes *to burn my House*, or to *rob me in the Highway*; or in *my House*; if I, or my Servant *kill him*, it is no Felony, nor Forfeiture of any Thing.

So if a Woman kills him, that *assaults to ravish her*, it is *no Felony*, or *Forfeiture of any Thing*. [20] And so much for my first Head.

As to the second Head, What relates to the Goods of a Man; which may be placed under the Title of *Felony, it may be thus defin'd*:

Felony defin'd. Felony is, where a Thing is taken with a felonious Intent; that is, So privately, that he who takes it, intends that he, from whom it is taken shall not know it. I speak not here of Robbing on the Highway; for that is a Felony of another Species.

The taking *Goods out of a Cart*, passing *on the Road adjudged Felony*; otherwise, if dropt off the Cart, and taken up in the Road.

21 *H*. 8. c.7. It is Felony, if a Servant *imbezils his Master's Goods, deliver'd to him to keep, of the Value of four Shillings*, or more. But this Act does not extend to *Apprentices, or other Persons under the Age of Eighteen*.

Cr. Eliz. 372. It is Felony to *steal Fish out of a Dam, or Pond, or Trunk*.

3 & 4 *W*. & *M*. By this Act, *if a Lodger* takes away any *Chattels, Bedding, or Furniture*, with an Intent to *steal, imbezil, or purloin them*; tho' he had them by *Contract, or Agreement*, to use them in *his Lodgings; it is Felony*.

1 Vent. 187. If one *cuts Corn, and lets it lye*, after it is cut; and *at another Time, he comes and steals it; it is Felony*.

Kelynge 931. One broke an House *in the Day-Time*, no Body being in the House, and *took Plate out of a Trunk there*, and laid it on the Floor; but *before he carried* it away, *was surprized*. 'Twas adjudged *Felony*. For *by taking the Plate* out of the Trunk, he had the Possession of it, and that is *Stealing, and Felony, and Clergy tolled by* 39 *Eliz*. [c.15] *being above five Shillings in Value*. [21]

Cr. Car 3. A Man may be guilty of Felony, *in Stealing his own Goods*. *E.g.* If a Person delivers his own Goods to one, to make use of, and *the Owner* afterwards *privately steals them, to the Intent* to charge the *Party to whom delivered*; it is Felony.

Kelynge 4. If Cattle are *distrain'd*, and put in a *Pound*, and one who hath a *Design to steal them*, goes to the *Sheriff* and gets a *Replevy* for them, and *by Colour thereof*, the Cattle are *deliver'd to him*, he drives *them away, and sells them, having no Colour of Title to them: This is Felony*.

And let this suffice for Felonies relating to Stealing. The common Thefts of Picking Pockets, cutting Purses, and Robberies on the Highway, are so well known to you, that I shall not so much as suspect your Knowledge and Understanding, as to think you stand in Need of any Detail of them, or Information concerning them.

My Third Head is of Offences against *a Man's Habitation*.

And first of *Burglary*.

Burglary defin'd. Burglary, by the Common Law, is where a Person, in the Night-time, breaketh, and entereth into the Mansion-House of another, to the Intent to commit some Felony there, tho' that Intent be not executed, and though casually, no Person be in it.

What Night. By *Night* is meant, *when it is do dark, or duskish,* that *by the Light of the Sun, you can't distinguish the Face of a one Man from another.*

The entring into a House, tho' the Doors are open, is *a Breaking of the House, in Construc-* [22] *tion* of Law, to maintain a *Trespass*, but not a Burglary.

What a Breaking. But if a Thief breaks the *Window, draws the Latch, unlocks the Door*, these *are a Breaking.*

A *Sash Window* was somewhat *up*; but *not so high* that the *Burgler could get in*; he *lifted up the Sash so high as to get in*, and then *went in, and was taken*: Adjudg'd Burglary, and the *Man executed for it.*

What an Entry. Setting the Foot over the *Threshold, putting a Hand*, or a *Hook, through the Window, or over a Door, to draw out Goods, is an Entry.* In some Cases, a *Burglary may be committed without a Breaking, or Entry.* Divers come to *commit Burglary*, and one *does it*, the rest *watch at the Lane's End* ; it is Burglary in all of them.

A Thief gets in by the Doors open in the Day-time, lies there *till Night*, then robs, and *breaks the Door in the Night, to get out*: 'Twas doubted, whether this was Burglary, or not: But 12 *Annæ* [c. 7.] has declared, and enacted it to be Burglary.

What a Mansion-House. A Church is a *Mansion-House* within this Law; for 'tis *Domus Mansionalis Dei.* Chambers in an *Inns of Court, or Chancery, are Mansion-Houses*: And so is *a Shop, whether Parcel* of a *Mansion-House, or by it self, in Construction of Law.*

Kelynge 42, 43, 44. Thives came to the House of *Le Mott*, with Intent to rob him, and finding the Doors lock'd, pretended they came to speak with him; whereupon a Servant open'd the Door; they came in, and robb'd him, this being in the Night. *Adjudg'd Burglary.*

For the Intention being to rob, and getting the Door open on a false Pretence, was in *Fraudem Legis*, and so *they were guilty of Burglary*; [23] tho' they did not actually *break the House.* For this was in Law an actual Breaking, being obtain'd by Fraud, to *have the Door open.* So if a Man pretend a Warrant to a Constable, and get *him along with him*, and, under that Pretence, gets the Doors *open'd to them*, and robs the House; if in the Night, *it is Burglary.*

So if an *Habere facias Possessionem* is obain'd *by Fraud, and Possession got, and Goods taken away* by *Night*; that is Burglary, being *in Fraudem Legis.*

5 *Ed.* 6 c. By this Act, if a Robbery is done in the Night, or in the Day, in a Booth, or Tent, the Owner being therein, *Sleeping or Waking, is Burglary.*

10 & 11. *W.* 3. Shop-lifting. If any Person steals *any Goods, Wares, or Merchandise, privately and feloniously, of the Value of five Shillings, or more*, in any *Shop, Warehouse, Coach-house, or Stable, by Night, or Day, though the Shop is ot*

broke open, or any Person put in *Fear, or shall assist, hire, or command any Person, to commit such Offence*, shall lose the Benefit of Clergy.

Kelynge 83. If any Inmate's Chamber-Door is broke open in the Night, it is Burglary: But the Indictment must be *Domum Mansionalem* of him that let him, and not of the Inmate; and Stealing the *Goods of the Inmate*.

He that *burns another* Man's *House maliciously and voluntarily*, is guilty of *Felony*.

And so much for Offences against a Man's Habitation.

As for Offences not Capital, I shall begin with Gaming Houses. [24]

Gaming Houses. These are of two Sorts: The one helps to undo *ordinary Men*, such as *Day-Labourers, Apprentices, Servants, and Handy-Craft Tradesmen*: The other to undo Gentlemen of Quality, and Fortune; not to *mention Noblemen*.

The first are such *Alehouses* that have *Shovelboard Tables, Nine-Pins, and Bowling-Alleys belonging to them*. Here the People I first mention'd, come at *Night, spend and lose that Money at one Sitting, which would keep their Families the Week following*.

When their Wives or Children come to call the Husband or Parent Home, they *deny* them, and use them *scurvily*.

Here they get a vicious *Habit of Gaming and Setting, Lewdness, and Swearing*, and *by Degrees*, give themselves up to all *Manner of Wickedness; and neglecting their Work, leave their Wives and Children a Burden to the Parish*.

'Tis for the Credit of the last *Grand Jury*, to whom I gave this Matter in Charge, that they have presented *several of them in the upper Part of Westminster*; and much for the Honour of those *Gentlemen* in the *Commission* of the *Peace*, that have *stood by them herein*.

The other Sort of Gaming-Houses help to undo Persons of the *first Quality*, and *Young Gentlemen of Estates*.

We sent to enquire lately about the Gaming-Room at *Hampstead*, and we had an Account brought us, That just before our Messenger came, there was a *Young Gentleman lost Sixty Guineas to a Sharper of this Town*; who went off as soon as he had got his Prey: It seems it was *the Young Gentleman's ALL*; *which put him upon such a Frenzy*, that he threw his *Hat one Way*, his *Peruque another* ; said, He was *ruin'd, and* [E-25] *undone in Body, Soul and Estate, by Gaming; and having one Guinea left*, threw that away also, and fell into a Fit of *Cursing and Swearing, and Blaspheming the Name of God*; Which, I believe, are the common Effects of *losing Gamesters*.

We had an Account that *the Shops and Tables for Gaming there*, had been *the Ruin of a great many young Gentlemen*. Were not *Men undone by Gaming*, yet if the *Losers generally* curse and blaspheme the *Name of God*; this, *this only*, is a sufficient *Motive to a worthy Man*, to set *his Face against these Gaming Houses, and present them*.

But alas! What is the Loss of Sixty Guineas? 'Tis said, that somewhere, in or near *Marybone*, there are Persons of Quality that set a *Thousand Pounds upon a Throw. A Sum* that would buy an *Annuity of One Hundred Pounds a Year for* Life, by which a *private Gentleman* might live *comfortably, and do much Good in the World*: Or, it would *buy an Estate in Fee-simple* to keep *an ordinary Man's Family, and Posterity, as long as it, or the World shall endure.*

What have these Persons to *answer* both to God and Man, for throwing away so much *Money in the sixtieth Part of a Minute* that would *provide a Family as long as the World endures*? It is charg'd upon *Nero*, as one of his *great Faults*, tho' he was Emperor of the greatest Part of the then known World, and had the Riches of the Universe in his Power, *that he usually plaid away ten Thousand Crowns at a Cast of Dice*; for whose *Extravagancy, Luxury*, and other Crimes he became so hated by his Subjects that he was his own *Executioner at Last.* [26]

It is *remarkable*, that even *sharping Gamesters*, tho' they win ever so much Money, at *some Times, they lose it afterwards, and generally dye Beggars.*

Of which we have two famous Instances of late, amongst many others; *That two Noblemen, one* of the greatest *Estate in the Kingdom; and the other had above Thirty Thousand Pounds a Year, and the most ancient of the Nobility*, that was *the Augustulus of his Family*, both *great Gamesters, and both gamed together*; *sometimes for Twenty Thousand Pounds*, at a Night's Sitting; *both dy'd Beggars, and* both their Families are *extinguished.*

Riches are a great *Blessing*; because they are the *Means* to furnish us with the *Necessaries and the Conveniences of Life*; not only to provide for our *Families and Relations*, but they give us the *happy Opportunity of doing Good to Mankind.*

God has furnish'd *the World* with every Thing necessary and convenient for all the *Inhabitants of the Earth* that are *alive at one Time*; which justifies the Divine Providence, as to *his Justice*, in the *Government of the World*; and whereas (Government being from God) it is *as necessary for Government*, as *there should be a Subordination of Men*; as that there should an *Inequality of Estates.*

Now God's Attributes of *Bounty and Mercy*, are both *herein manifest.* For that his Majesty hath commanded the *Full to feed the Hun-*[E 2-27] *gry; the Rich to help the Poor; the Powerful to assist the Weak; the Redundant, the Needy.*

If we have *over* and *above* what will make a due *Provision* for our selves, Families, and Relations, according to our *Circumstances of Life, wherein Discretion is to be Judge* ; and he that vainly squanders that away through Luxury or Gaming, or any other Vice, may be *justly said to rob the Poor.*

The Rich are but *Trustees for the Poor, in this Case, and let them look to it*, how they abuse their Trust, the mighty Talent of Riches bestow'd upon them.[1]

[1] See F. Bacon, *Essays or Counsels; Civill and Morall* (London: J. Haviland & R. Whitaker, 1625). Essay 34, 'Of Riches': "Of great Riches, there is no Reall Vse, except it be in the Distribution; The rest is but Conceit. So saith Salomon; Where much is, there are Many to consume it; And what hath the Owner, but the Sight of it, with his Eyes?"

What these *Gamesters* will have to *answer* for themselves, at the last Day, let *Dives*, and them think of it, and *tremble*[1].

It is a *greater Act of Charity*, and *Self-Denial*, to continue to do good to a Man, who is *ungrateful*, than to him that is *thankful*.

Thanks are a Sort of *Payment* to an ingenuous Mind; it being a Pleasure to receive Thanks, as well as to give them where due.

But 'tis *yet* a much greater *Act of Charity* to do Good to Mankind, without *their Desires*; and 'tis *superlative Goodness to do it against their Will*; In this *last Case, we imitate God himself*; who [*did*] *and would often have gathered the People of Jerusalem together, as a Hen gathers her Chickens under her Wing*; (*but* [28] *they would not be so gathered (that is saved) who compell'd some to come in.*

Gaming-Houses are to be *presented and suppress'd*, that they who *have the Itch of Gaming on their Fingers*, may want an *Opportunity and Means of undoing themselves*. Let us save them *without their Thanks, without their Desire, nay against their Will.*

Gamesters should be serv'd as *Norris* does *Madmen*: *He locks them up; puts Bars in their Windows; takes Knives from them*; that they may not cut their own Throats, or do themselves some other Mischief, which may save the Expence of a Commission of Lunacy.

Weights and Measures. Take Care of Weights and Measures, that the People may not be cheated in their Bread or Drink; and the Butchers *Weights be according to the Standard.*

And present all *Forestallers, Regrators, and Ingrossers*; for these inhance the Price of Victuals, and render the Poor less able to support their Families.

Seditious Pamphlets; Lying Newspapers. Present the *Authors, Printers, and Dispersers of seditious Pamphlets, and Lying News Papers*, that endeavour to *bring the Government into Contempt, and sour the People against the Administration.*

We are *grown wanton* with Liberty and Property, and so we are like to continue, [29] 'till Slavery comes upon us, which our Sins deserve.

When Blessings are long abus'd, God Almighty, in his Providence, does often remove them from Mankind.

The *Abusing of Liberties and Franchises*, even *by our Law*, in many Cases, incur a *Forfeiture.*

As for *Play-Houses, Bawdy-Houses, Masquerades, Gaming Assemblies, Night-Walkings*, and such *other Crimes*, with which *this Town abounds*; I have spoken so fully against them in my former Charge, which is *in Print*; that I shall not trouble you with them any *farther at this Time*; but refer you to that Charge.

And I pray God guide you in your Presentments.

F I N I S.

[1] Cf Luke, 16: 20 sq.

Civitas, Burgus, } ss. Ad general' quartial' Session' Pacis Dom' Regis ten' & Villa *Westm*' in} apud *Westm* ' pro Libert' Decani, & Capitul' Eccl',

Com' *Middl*' } Collegiat' Sancti Petri *Westm* ', Civit, Burgi, & Villæ *Westm*', in Com, Midd', & Sancti *Martini le Grand, London*', die Mercurij fcil' Septimo die Octobris, Anno Regni Dom' *Georgij* Dei Gratia nunc Regis *Magnæ Britanniæ*, &c. Sexto.

His Majesty's Justices of the Peace for this City and Liberty of Westminster, *assembled at this present General Quarter-Sessions, being unanimous of the Opinion, That the CHARGE this Day given, by* WILLIAM COWPER *Esq; the Chairman, to the* GRAND-JURY *now Sworn for our Sovereign Lord the King, for the Body of this City and Liberty, is a very Learned, Judicious, and Excellent Charge, highly tending to the Honour of Almighty God, the Suppression of Vice and Immorality, and to the Service of His Majesty and His Government, and will be of great Use and Information to Grand-Juries, and the Publick Officers of this City and Liberty, in the Discharge of their respective Duties; Do desire that the said Mr.* Cowper *will be pleased to cause his said Charge to be Printed and Published.*

Per Cur'

Middleton.

THE **CHARGE** OF **William Cowper** ***Esq*;** TO THE **GRAND-JURY** OF THE **CITY and LIBERTY of** *Westminster,* &c. At the General Quarter-Sessions of the Peace, held *October* the 7th, 1719. in *Westminster- Hall.*

LONDON: Printed for Charles King at the *Judge's-Head* in *Westminster-Hall.* 1719.

[5]

THE **CHARGE** OF **William COWPER,** ***Esq*;** TO THE *Grand-Jury* of the City and Liberty of *Westminster*, &c.

Gentlemen,

You that are Sworn to serve upon the *Grand Inquest*, for the Body of this City and Liberty!

The Laws of *England* are, undoubtedly, as the great Oracle of them, my Lord *Coke*, remarks, in the best, [6] most exquisite, and peculiar manner that could have been, framed and adapted for the Government of this Realm; and the frequent Occasions they give us, of Meeting, as now we do, are none of the least Proofs of the Excellency of them; the Reason thereof being for the quick and ready Distribution of Justice, which is the Soul of it, and without which it loses its very Nature.

WHOEVER observes too, the decent and good Appearance that there is at present, in, and about the Court, must reflect on it with great Satisfaction, as it argues a most commendable Zeal, in All concerned and a Disposition to attend, as they ought, the Duties of their several Stations; that while they receive Benefit, and Protection, from the Laws, they may not be wanting to do those Laws all possible Honour. [7]

Gentlemen of the Grand Jury,

THE Satisfaction I take in this very good Prospect, does, in some sort, alleviate the Difficulty which this Day produces, peculiar to my self, who sit here, after so many Grave and very learned Persons (most unworthy as I am so to do!) whose CHARGES from hence, are, for Fullness of Matter, Learning, and Accuracy, very hardly, if at all, to be equalled; the Confidence I have, That they cannot be forgot, and likewise, That All or Most of you are of very Good Experience, as *Grand-Jury* -Men; will give me a fair Liberty (without Injury, as I hope, to the Trust I have the Honour to receive from the Bench) to be more particular, with relation to such Points only as the Times we live in, and more frequent Occasions, call upon us to take Care of. [8]

Gentlemen

THAT the Honour of Almighty God, and our most Holy Religion, do's exceedingly suffer in These Days, by that open Disregard to both, apparent among us, in so many Instances is a Truth, Sad indeed! but to our Shame, too plain to be denied! His Majesty's Proclamation,[1] which was now just read, as it points out to us many of those Instances, – so it hints to us, in good part, the Remedies to be applied; – our Good and Gracious Prince, thereby also declaring, That his own Example shall not be wanting us, in the Discharge of those our great Duties. – Happy are we in that Example! but happier should we be, if we would make a right Use of it! I exhort you, Gentlemen, to enquire into, and Present, with that Steadiness and Impartiality becoming good Christians, all the Offences that Proclamation is level- [B - 9] led at, as they shall come to your Knowledge. – Some others I shall hint to you, which, before I mention, I shall premise this for Method's sake, that they might, and, perhaps, fitly enough, have been introduced under another Head, and

[1] There were two Proclamations: *By the King, a Proclamation... for putting in execution the laws against Unlawful Clubs & ...effectual Punishing Rioters.* John Baskett, 1717. -The other one: *a Proclamation, requiring the Laws to be put into Execution against all Persons concerned in the late Rebellion, who were excepted out of his Majesty's ...Pardon in Parliament.* J. Baskett, 1717.

recommended to your Enquiry, as Matters destructive of the Government and Constitution of this Realm, now most happily Established and Secured under His Majesty King *GEORGE*. So, indeed, they are: – But these Principles do not stop there; but are such, as (whatever they are, at this Time, more particularly levelled at) must, if they prevail, by their natural Tendency, extinguish and root out All Religion, Morality, and Government, and the very Memory of them, from amongst us, and dissolve the Bands of Human Society it self. [10]

Gentlemen

The Time is now upon us, when Common Swearing and Cursing, abominable as they are! are become (if I may say so) the lowest Instances in which the Sanctity of Oaths is trampled under foot; it is Unlawful, and Immoral, to break our Promise made to our private Neighbour;- 'tis exceeding Wicked to deceive him by an Oath:– But what shall I say it is,– when Oaths, most Solemn, and Particular, devised by the Legislature, as the Last Test of a Man's Duty to his King and Country, and appointed to be, and actually taken, for the greater Solemnity; in the face of the Publick Justice of the Kingdom, (a greater Security than which cannot be contrived, especially, when, as in many Cases, accompanied with the Holy Sacrament,) and treated publickly as Trifles, and of no Obligation? and ranked with Others which are so com-[B 2 -11] monly abused among us, that they are become even a Proverb ?

WHAT shall we say, when we see those, who have laid themselves under these High and Solemn Obligations, To be True and Faithful to His Majesty King *GEORGE*, by the whole Tenor of their Actions, Writings and Speeches favouring the detested Cause of Popery and Slavery? and to that End, reviling with the utmost, His Majesty's Person and Government, by mean and abject Forgeries, magnifying the Power of his Declared Enemies, and employing all Engines, to take, and alienate, from Him the Treasure, that of all others he most values, the Hearts of his People? thus secretly undermining, as many do, and as others, Openly and in Arms opposing his Rightful and Lawful Government (to which themselves have Sworn,) and by these Methods annulling (as much as in them [12] lies all Civil and Religious Tyes whatsoever; and by these Practices declaring to the World, That they hold themselves under no Obligations from Oaths taken to the King? That they allow, nay, approve, the taking them, with Intent, when thereby intrusted, the more effectually to betray Him and their Country? and that they deem this Habit, and outward Appearance of a Good Subject, (especially when sanctified by an Oath) a convenient and allowable Disguise, to conceal a far different Inclination? And some of their inferior Instructors (who are to keep the Common People, *Right*, as they call it) thus deceitfully teach 'em to compass, even their own Destruction, should they succeed in their

Attempts, by breaking thro' all Relations they stand in to God, the King, their Country, or one another; whose pestilent Works come out Weekly, or otherwise, to carry on the Superstructure rais'd on these [13] sandy Foundations, under the Titles of *Orphans, Scourges, Saturday's-Posts,* and the like Traiterous and Seditious Libels, which I hope you will Enquire of, and Present.

Gentlemen

I CANNOT, upon this Occasion, pass over in Silence, those Real Enemies, and Dangerous Ones too, to our most Excellent and Established Church, who are always suggesting it to be in Danger, except when it Really is so. – If, when they use the Term *Church,* they mean the True, and Pure, Church, as Established by Law, in *England,* and *Ireland,* at this Day; 'tis a strange Absurdity to say, That it is most Safe, when every Thing is most Visibly tending to let in a Popish *Pretender* and Religion upon it; and least so, (or what is the same thing, most in Danger) when its only Sworn Enemies, are, by God's Providence to it, at last (as we may justly [14] hope) put beyond any Possibility of Hurting it: We have the Word of God for it (which, I think, a Great Security to the Church,) That *the Gates of Hell shall not prevail against it* ; – and Common Sence (were it a little more in fashion) would tell any Well-disposed Man, that some other Church is meant, which we ought to wish always to be in Danger, or a Point beyond it; whether it be the Church of *Rome,* or that of a much Later Invention, *The Catholick Non-juring Church of* England; betwixt which there is so near an Alliance, That we should be equally guardful against both; and as this Cry serves them alike, I hope you will Present any Instance you know of promoting it: Not forgetting those Seditious Meetings of these New Churchmen, under Pretence of Religious Worship, (of which there are, I doubt, too many) where the *Pretender* to His Majesty's Crown is avowedly prayed [15] for, and which therefore are not Tolerated by Law, and where 'tis certain, Principles are instilled, as the Dictates of Religion, contrary not only to the Commands of God, but the very Order of Nature:- For Instance only,- Those who won't let some Men take up Arms against the King, upon any Pretence whatsoever, can teach their own Disciples to Assassinate Him in his Palace; Murder, and of a King too, is, it seems, Meritorious (in them only,) notwithstanding the *Sixth Commandment.* -- And from these Schools have proceeded, even Martyrs, (as they are stiled) for such Execrable Opinions.

Gentlemen

IN observing these Particulars, you will fulfil a great part of your Duty, to your Country, your King, and Rightful, and Lawful, Government, which will bear those Epithets, as long as Common Sence and Reason are to [16] be found anywhere in this World, and can never be born down by Patriarchal, and other Schemes, and Artful Terms, which are of meer Modern finding out, which the Inventors of them never *certainly* understood, nor could in any Sort make out; and of which I will say,– That the only clear Proposition possible to be deduced from them, is,- "That they tend to put Mankind under the deepest Slavery both Religious and Civil, without Warrant from, and contrary to, the Word of God, and his declared Purposes towards Men, in all Capacities and Relations."

IT is not His Majesty's Ambition or Desire to tyrannize over any Nation, by, or upon, such Principles as These: Would you be convinced of that? Remember, how his Exemplary Rule in his own Dominions Abroad, where there is no Law but his Will, was such, as made his Subjects there re-[C-17] sign him to our Wishes, with Floods of Tears.

SURELY, if the Voice of God, be in the Dispensations of his Providence, the Success, and Honour, he has mercifully poured out on the King, and his Interests, do loudly speak him the Care of Heaven! His Enemies have daily the Rewards of their impious Schemes, and Devices! Every Hour produces new Disappointments to them! The Anniversary Petition of our Church to God, on the Day appointed to give Thanks for the Restoration of the Royal Family and Government, seems fully granted in the Person of His Majesty. Those that are implacable, are cloathed with Confusion and Shame! but upon His Majesty's Head does the Crown flourish! and may it do so upon those of his Royal Progeny for Ever! [18]

Gentlemen

HIS Majesty's Cares for us are never intermitted, nor should our Vigilance for his Safety be less so, as our own likewise depends upon it; next to Almighty God, He is the proper Object of your Publick Duties: You are to Fear God, and Honour the King: To do our Duty in the first of these, at present, you are to Enquire of, and Present, All Blasphemy, Prophane Swearing and Cursing, People that make Default in coming to Church, or some Religious Meeting allowed by Law, those that follow their Trades on *Sundays*, unless in the two excepted Cases of Necessity or Mercy; all Perjury in Oaths judicially taken, all Subornation of Perjury and Forgery.

THESE, in their Nature, seem to be, more immediately, Offences against the Divine Majesty. [C 2- 19] FOR the King, To what I have already said, I shall add, You are to Enquire of High Treason in all its Parts.

THOSE now more immediately necessary to hint, are,

1. COMPASSING or Imagining the Death of the King, or his Eldest Son and Heir.

THESE, declared by Overt-Act, are High Treason.

AN Overt-Act, is something done designedly by the Party, tending to endanger the King's Life.- Bare Loose *Words* are not an Overt-Act; but if Treasonable Words are spoken, *Words of Intention*, an *Act done* thereon, tending to bring them to *Effect*, These coupled together are so. And in *Charnocke's Case* , 8° W. 3. Lord [20] Chief Justice *Holt*, delivers an Opinion, " That *Arguments*, and Words of *Perswasion* to engage in a Design, or *directing* or *proposing* the *best Way* for effecting it, are *Overt-Acts of High Treason*," as it was Resolved twice in K. C. 2. Time: And *Tong's Case*, 14 C. 2. was, Consulting to seize *White-hall*, [*Kelyng.* 15.17.- *Hawkins P.C.* 38, &c.] where the King was: And the Author of a late Approv'd Treatise on these Matters, among others, upon a full and learned Discussion of this Point, declares (and says, I believe, very truly) " That it has been often adjudged, that *deliberate Words*, which shew a direct Purpose against the King's Life, being spoken *maturely and advisedly*, do amount to an *Overt-Act of Compassing* and Imagining his Death."

2. LEVYING War against Him; under which is contained every Attempt with Force, to execute any Ge-[21] neral Design of Reforming and Altering any thing of a Publick Nature.

AS is also the Holding the King's Forts, Castles, or the like, against his Forces.

3. 'TIS a Species of High Treason, as declar'd by *Stat.* 25 *E.* 3. likewise, To adhere to the King's Enemies, Within, or Without the Realm.

AND the word (Adhering) is extended by Construction, to Cases, where any Person sends or Communicates his Secrets to the Enemy, if that be prov'd, tho' the Message or Letter be not actually delivered: As was held in the Time of the late Queen *Anne*, in the famous Case of Mr. *Gregg*, [1]

AND a Man is said to Adhere to the King's Enemies, That Surrenders his Forts, Castles, or the like, to them for Reward. [22]

4. 'TIS another Head of High Treason, To Kill the Lord Chancellor, Lord Treasurer, Judges of either Bench, Justices in *Eyre*, those of Assize, or of *Oyer* and *Terminer*, *Sitting in their Places, and doing their Offices*.

5. 'TIS likewise High Treason to Counterfeit the Great or Privy-Seal, or to Aid or Consent to it, *where it is actually done*.

6. AND at the Common Law, it is High Treason to Counterfeit *the Coin*; and by several Statutes, the Clipping, Washing, Filing, and the like, and the Making Tools for Coining Mill'd Money, is so too.

OTHER Statutes have made Offences Treason, which were not so by the Common Law, or by 25 *E.* 3. such as Maintaining [5. *El. c.* 1.] [23] the Authority of the See of *Rome*, is Treason for the Second Offence, and a Premunire for the First [13 *El. c.* 3.] putting in Ure *Bulls* from thence,

[1] Gregg was secretary to one of Anne's ministers, and was sentenced on a charge of high treason.

is High Treason; Aiders and Maintainers of those who do so, incur a Præmunire; and those who conceal an *Offer of Absolution* from, or *Reconciliation* to, the Church of *Rome*, are guilty of Misprision of Treason; And such as bring in *Agnus Dei* 's, and the like Vain and Superstitious Trinkets, and deliver them to any Subject of this Realm, are guilty of a Præmunire; It is High Treason to *Absolve the King's Subjects* from their Obedience, or reconcile them to that of *the Pope* , in both the Parties. [23 *El. c.* 1.]

SO it is for any *Popish Priest*, who is native of this Kingdom, to come into it, if he don't take the *Oaths* appointed, within Three Days after his Coming; and [24] it is Felony without Benefit of Clergy in any who Receives, Retains, or Maintains him *knowingly*: And other Laws there are of this Nature.

Gentlemen

BY a Statute made in the Sixth Year of the late Queen *Anne* 's Reign, for the Security of her Person and Government, and of the *Succession* to the Crown of *Great-Britain* in the *Protestant* Line, It is Enacted, " That any Person, *maliciously, advisedly*, and *directly*, by *Writing* or *Printing*, Maintaining and Affirming her said then Majesty, not to be Lawful and Rightful Queen of these Realms, or that the *Pretender* hath any Right or Title to the Crown, or any other Person, otherwise than according to the Act 1. *W. & M.* and 12.*W.* 3 and the Acts of *Union*, or that the Kings and Queens of this Realm are not able, by and with the Authority of Par- [D-25] liament, to make Laws of sufficient Force to bind the Descent of the Crown, &c shall be guilty of High Treason." And by the same Statute, the *maliciously* and *directly* maintaining these Points, by *Preaching, Teaching*, or *advised Speaking*, is a Præmunire.

Gentlemen,

I CANNOT omit to press your particular regard to this Law, among your other Enquiries; and that you would be diligent to Present any Offences against it that shall come to your Knowledge.

Gentlemen

YOU are to Present Misprision of Treason, at the Common Law; [26] which is, barely *concealing it*, without Evidencing *a Consent* to it, for that is High Treason.

And such Misprision, by Statute as *per Stat.* 14 *Eliz.* Counterfeiting any Foreign Coin, not Current here, is declared to be.

MISPRISION *of Felony*, is likewise Presentable by you, which is *Concealing* a Felony, or *Procuring the Concealment* of it, or *Compounding* it: This is an Offence at the Common Law.

SO you are to Present Petty Treason and Felonies of all Sorts, with all Accessaries thereto, both before and after: But you are to take Notice, [D 2-27] That in the Highest and Lowest Offences, as High Treason, and Trespasses, Riots, and the like, there are no Accessories, but all are Principals.

YOU are to Present all Receivers of Goods Stol'n, knowing them to be so; all Riots, Routs, and Unlawful Assemblies; and, in general, all Breaches of the Peace, Libels, and Nusances, in the River *Thames* and elsewhere; and all Bridges and Highways out of Repair, and who ought to Repair them; and Extortion in all Officers whatsoever; all Houses of Lewdness and Common Gaming, or Persons Guilty of either; and Common Tipplers in Ale-houses, and the like. [28]

Gentlemen

I FORBEAR at present, a more exact Disquisition of these, and the Mention of some lesser Particulars, the same having been lately, judiciously handled in this Place, by that Learned Gentleman, Mr. *Bulstrode*, the Late worthy Chairman of the Quarter-Sessions for the County of *Middlesex*, (of whom I desire, upon this Occasion, to make honourable mention) he has been so regardful of the Common Good, as to make his, Living Charges; and has given you, Gentlemen! and all others who attend these Services, an Opportunity, I earnestly wish, would be taken, of having those most useful Discourses, upon these Occasions, always in your Hands. [29] *Gentlemen of the Grand Jury!*

THERE is nothing more certain, than That no Government can subsist (any more than a Body Natural) where, besides a due Texture and Composition of the Parts, they do not act in such a just Subordination to each other, as to execute their several Functions, readily and duly, for the Sustentation of the Whole – To speak more plainly, The Administration must suffer in all its Parts, when Ministerial Officers, whose *Obedience* only is their *Justification*, will take the Part of Judges upon themselves, and will either not execute what they are enjoined, by a Competent Power, or do it in part only, as they think proper; by such Means, in effect, setting aside, or varying, those Orders at [30] their Pleasure. The Great Prudence of our Law, to prevent the Delay, and, indeed, the total Obstruction of Justice, and to keep up its due Honour, has provided, That Obedience to any Warrant, tho' it be *beyond* the Power of the Magistrate, as to the Point requir'd, yet if he has a Jurisdiction in the Thing, should Indemnify the Officer; and he is Punishable for his Disobeying even such a Warrant. Thus is their Duty most plainly chalked out to them; and it is of extreme ill Consequence, when they mistake it in these Points; they easily then take another Step, and treat the Persons, and Authority they refuse to Obey, with *Contempt* and *Rudeness*: Were this to run through the Constitution, nothing but Destruction could attend it; and, I doubt, it does prevail too much, in the inferior Parts of it: There are some, I am sure, who [31] hear me, that have seen prodigious Miscarriages of this Kind, nor need I say, that in my own very little Experience, I have had Cause to resent, in a legal Way, more than one Indignity of this Nature: I therefore, *Gentlemen*, most earnestly recommend to you (as the properest Means of stopping these Enormities) to Present any Contempts you shall know of in Constables, and other Officers, and *Persons by Law put under the Direction of Justices of the Peace, or other Magistrates*; that the regular Administration of Justice may be preserved, and the due Respect to it kept up; and, to the End, that those may be punished (as they shall be, if Convicted upon your Accusation, in the most Exemplary Sort) who shall so far throw off their Regard to their Duty, themselves, and by such ill Precedents, lead the Way to others to do so. [32]

Gentlemen

THERE is one Thing more, which is seldom mentioned in *Charges*, and, perhaps, for that Reason the less heeded; but it is (and more especially to you, who are upon your Oaths) of exceeding Consequence, and without attending rightly to it, I tell you plainly, you cannot keep the Oaths you have taken.

IT is almost an Universal Complaint, (and I had some Reason to take Notice of it,) That *Grand-Juries*, in considering of Bills before do them, demean themselves, as if they were Trying the Party, upon Issue joined; and do require the same Degree [E-33] of Evidence, that would go to Convict him before the Petty Jury, if a Bill had been found, and he had pleaded *Not Guilty*, and put himself thereby in his Defence.

Gentlemen

BY Law, You are no more than *Accusers*, you are not *Tryers* of the Fact; you are no where said to *Try* , but to make *Enquiry* and *Presentment*; You see the Law has not appointed the Party to come, or to join Issue by Pleading before you; but if you think fit to Accuse him, he is to have the Benefit of a Full Hearing and Defence, at a subsequent Tryal, if he will make any: If, therefore, from any thing that is Sworn before you, or Told you, by any under an Oath, tho' but a single Person, or from the Knowledge of [34] anyone amongst you, you have such a probable Suspicion given you, as makes it reasonable to put a Man on that Defence (which he is then to make at large) you are in such Cases, as I take it, by the Duty of your Oaths, to find the Bill.

JUST Cause of Suspicion given upon Oath, is your Rule; but Direct and Certain Evidence, is that of the Petty Jury, to whom the fuller Examination of the Fact, with its Incidents, Circumstances, and the like, seems to be Committed by the Law.

IF there be good Reason appearing, to Accuse a Man, he should no more be Acquitted, than Condemned, *unheard*; and no Defendant [E 2–35] is, or ought to be heard, before you.

ALL you have to do, is to put the Party in a Way of being fairly Tryed; and if you take upon you to Try him (in Effect) your selves, you do therein invade the Office of the other Jury; you render in a great Measure useless, that other Excellent Part of our Constitution, and prevent (perhaps, without intending it) many great Offenders from being justly Punished.

I AM most inclinable to hope, *Gentlemen!* That the Occasion given by *Grand Juries* for this Complaint, proceeds, from not perfectly knowing, or heeding, the Nature of their Employment, rather than from any Dis-[36] position to abuse it to sinister Purposes.

I CANNOT think Men so profligate (who must needs be of Figure in their Countries,) as one Hour to take a most Solemn Oath, *to Present no Man for Hatred, Malice, or Ill-will, and to leave nothing Unpresented for Fear, Favour, or Affection*; and so far to forget that Oath the next, as to give Way to the Influence of any, or perhaps, all these, in their Turn: Such Motives, must, and will always be inexcusable, before God and Man; and after what I have said on this Head, in the Discharge of my own Oath, and the Duty I owe to the Court, as I hope Ignorance cannot be hereafter pretended, there can be left no Excuse whatsoever. [37]

Gentlemen

UPON the whole Matter, I exhort you with all Earnestness, to set about, and to do, the Duty, you are now called to, with an Impartial Zeal, for the Honour and Service of Almighty God, and the Safety, the Happiness, and Prosperity of the King, and your dear Country; keep these Great Ends steadily in View: Think with *Coolness*, and *Temper*, and hear with *Patience*; and you cannot well fail of judging aright, in most Matters: So shall your Conduct become most Useful and Acceptable to this Great and Wealthy City, for which you are Entrusted; and your Behaviour, Exemplary, to All about you, who may in This, or any Other Place, be Summon'd upon the like Duty! [38] And I shall have, with the most Real Pleasure to my self, an Occasion given me, in the Name, and with the Concurrence of the whole Court, of Thanking you very heartily for your Services.

FINIS.

THE **CHARGE** OF *James Mountagu* Esq; TO THE GRAND JURY, and other JURYS of the County of *Wilts*: At the General QUARTER-SESSIONS of the Peace, held at the *Devizes*, *April* 26. 1720. *Printed at the Request of the* GRAND JURY

To love the Publick, to study Universal Good, and to promote the Interest of the whole World, as far as lies within our power; is surely the Height of Goodness, and makes that Temper which we call Divine. Ld *Shaftesbury*'s Characteristicks, *vol. I. p. 37.*[1]

LONDON: Printed for R. MOUNTAGU at the Bible in *Shear-Lane* near *Temple-Bar*, and sold by Mr. GRAVES in *St-James's Street*, Mr. BETTESWORTH in *Paternoster Row*, Mr. MEADOWS and Mr. BROTHERTON in *Cornhill*, and Mr. STAGG in *Westminster-Hall*. 1720. (Price One Shilling.)

[A 2 – 3]
TO
James Mountagu Esq;

CHAIRMAN of the Quarter-Sessions held at the *Devizes* the 26th Day of *April* A.D. 1720.

WE the Grand Jury, sworn to serve on the behalf of our Sovereign Lord the King for the Body of this County, for the present Sessions; do take the liberty to return our hearty Thanks, for your Excellent Charge: wherein you have so fully instructed [4] us, in our Duty to God, our King and Country.

It is unanimously our humble Request, That for the Publick Good you will order it to be printed; which will much oblige,

SIR,

Your Humble Servants,

Fran. Yerbury, Isaac Gale, Tho. Eyles, John Gaisford, Tho. Bush, John Weeks, Will. Smith, Joseph Ponting, W. Alexander, William Axford, Jos. Marsham, Isaac Aldridge, John Bedford, Jeff. Meriwether, John Browning, Will. Wayland, James Crew, William Smith, Samuel Cooke, William Nash, John Mortimer, John Wetherell, John Fry, Jonathan Scott, Robert Wilshier, John Hiscock. J. Nicholls, [5]

[1] 3 vols. published 1711; 2nd ed. Corr. 1714: Vol. I, p. 37=A letter concerning Enthusiasm.

TO THE *Gentlemen of the Grand Jury* Assembled at the County Quarter-Sessions held at the*Devizes, April* 26. 1720.

GENTLEMEN,

As I was never fond of appearing in Print, so nothing but your Request, amounting to a Command, should have prevailed with me to expose this to publick View. [6] I KNOW very well its Fate must be to run the Gantelope thro the censorious Band of Mankind, and perhaps receive the smartest Strokes from some who may think themselves pointed at, without describing their Dress.

HOWEVER, that gives me the least Concern, being fully convinced, that as long as it is my Duty, in the Station I am, to enforce the Execution of these Laws, calculated for the Preservation of our Holy Religion; I should have been much to blame, if I had not marked out that Rock, which, humanly speaking, without due Care and Caution our Excellent Constitution in Church and State may sooner or later split upon; especially since many of these proper Pilots, whose peculiar Duty it is to steer us right, at this time, for [7] the Support and Security of the former; seem at present to lie hoodwink'd in Harbour.

AS my worthy Brethren[1] have done me the Honour, for the better Part of twenty Years, to place me in the Chair, I do assure you, I have always made it my chiefest Care, punctually to pronounce their Orders; and have been ever cautions in that Station, to advance nothing, but what the Laws require should be inculcated for the service of our Sovereigns, and Benefit of our Countrymen, and for supporting the Dignity and Honour of the King's Commission: being fully convinced, whenever we suffer that to be lessened, the Administration of Justice will become lame and impotent.[8]

THE Zeal you Gentlemen of the Grand Jury have shewn, by your Presentment, for the Dignity and Independency of our Commission, ought to be thankfully acknowledged by every one, who is distinguished therewith: nor does the just Resentment of my worthy Brethren less deserve the Commendations of all, who truly love and honour its Author.

I AM so far from blaming the Inhabitants of *Marlborough* for exerting themselves in vindication of their Franchise, that I think they deserve all due Commendation.

AND surely, every impartial Man cannot but admit of the same, to those Worthy Justices of this County, who acted with Steddiness and Courage in [B -9] the Worst of Times; and who have used lawful Means only, to preserve the Dignity and Power of the Commission from being any ways exposed or lessened: Since 'twould be very hard, should they alone be blamed for doing an Act equally praise-worthy.

I MUST needs own, I have not been a little surprized at the *Mighty*

[1] Here, the term used by JPs to speak of themselves.

Pains there has been taken, to support the *Marlborough* Presentment: which, I, think, has been justly censured; and the more, since it appears to be, upon the strictest View, a Composition as full of Absurdity as it is of Words.

I SHALL forbear making any Remarks on this same celebrated Piece; it being beneath the Dignity of Magistrates to debate with those, whose Duty it is, to present all Encroach-[10]ments and Insults on their Authority, rather than arraign them as Malefactors.

ESPECIALLY in this Case; since if the Justices of the Peace have any Power called *Arbitrary* allowed them by the King's Commission, it is admitted on all hands, in the Instance of this Court of Quarter-Sessions being held in any Town in the County, where they shall judge it most proper.

NOTHING could please me more than your being present, when the *Sum and Substance* of the fore-mentioned Presentment was under our Consideration: and I dare say, you are all perfectly satisfied, tho we did not all agree in our Judgment, that every Gentleman gave his Opinion agree-[11] able to the best of his Understanding.

THE only Author I have borrowed from, is Mr. *Rushworth*; which may be easily discerned by those who have happily spent any time reading his valuable Collections.

GENTLEMEN,

'Tis with pleasure I submit what follows to your Patronage and Protection; and heartily wish it may be of that use for which I principally designed it, viz. For the Honour of God, the inculcating a due Obedience to our Great and Good King, and for the Advantage and Service of my Countrymen. If it may any Ways promote these desirable Ends, I am more than recompenced; especially since the Fa -[12] vour you did me, in proposing its Publication, is much above the Merit of,

GENTLEMEN,

Lackham, *Your most Faithful*
May 10. 1720 *Humble Servant,*
J. Mountagu.

C -13

THE
CHARGE
OF
James Mountagu Esq;
TO THE
GRAND JURY, and other Jurys.

Gentlemen of the Grand Jury,

THE chief End of our meeting here, is for the Publick Welfare; and by the King's Commission lately read to us, we are now impowered to put in [14] execution the Best Laws that were ever framed in the World.

A BODY of Laws wisely and justly calculated for the Good of ourselves and Fellow-Subjects, admirably well adapted to support and aggrandize the Dignity and Excellency of our Sovereigns, and above all, religiously intended for the Honour and Glory of God.

AS these great Ends cannot but raise in us all Emulations to do the best we can in our proper Stations, as the Execution of these Laws is the very Life and Essence of them; I hope it will not be deemed impertinent, if at this time I deliver myself to you in such a manner, I presume not improper on the present Occasion.

WE live in an Age when Cavil and Calumny never more abounded; and at a Time, when Men in publick Stations ought to have a special Regard to what they say or do; not as being conscious of any Ill, but as [C 2 -15] their Words and Actions expose and subject them to publick Censure, and too often to unjust Reflections and Reproaches.

THESE Considerations at present have put me upon this Method, that if hereafter it should be my misfortune to be unfairly represented, I may the better be able to vindicate myself, by producing what I now shall offer to you.

TO tell you, *Gentlemen*, that Laws are absolutely necessary for the Well-being of a People, is a truth which needs little Argument to prove it; since your own Observations and Experiences are sufficient to convince you, that without them there would be no Order, no Government, no Peace, Safety, or Quiet amongst us.

LAWS, says a Learned Gentlemen, (especially when instituted as ours are) put a difference between Good and Evil, Just and Unjust: If Laws were abolished, all things would fall [16] back into Confusion; which, considering the depraved Condition of Human Nature, would produce the greatest Enormities: Lust, would become a Law; Envy, Avarice, and Ambition, would become Laws; and what Dictates, what Decisions, such Laws would produce, any mean Capacity may easily apprehend. And therefore if the Force and Authority of Laws, to prevent, to restrain, and to repair Evils, were lost, all kind of Disquietude, Rapine, and Mischief, would break in upon the State.

ALLEGIANCE from the People to their Sovereigns, and the Prince's Protection to his Subjects, are reciprocally stipulated by Laws.

THEIR Abolition would cancel that Protection, and then would the Vigour and Chearfulness of Allegiance dwindle and moulder into Anarchy and Confusion.

FOR as by Law the Prerogative of the Prince, and the Peoples Li-[17] berty, are a Support and a Security to each other, when moving in their proper and stated Spheres; so would it happen, (should the Force and Authority of Laws chance to cease) that Nature would become rampant, and all things (without Omnipotent Interposition) would be huddled and hurried into a Chaos.

'TWAS excellently well said by King *Charles* I. in a Speech to his Parliament, speaking of our Laws, (and which I think we ought all to imprint in our Memorys) That the Law is the Inheritance of every Subject, and the only Security he can have for his Life, his Liberty and his Estate; and which, if neglected or disesteemed, under what specious Pretence soever, a great Measure of Infelicity, if not an irreparable Confusion, must without doubt fall upon them.

AND therefore as the Law is the Safeguard; and has as it were the [18] Custody of all private Interest; as our Lives, our Libertys, and our Estates, are all in the keeping of the Law, (without which, every Man would be apt to say he had a like Right to every thing)[1], I think beyond all contradiction, it is absolutely necessary, that we should be under the Government, Jurisdiction, and Controul of a well-framed Body of Laws.

IF Laws therefore in general are unavoidably requisite for the Peace and Quiet of Mankind, if no Nation or Community can long subsist without them, we surely have all the Reason imaginable to deem ourselves the happiest People in being, regarding the Excellency of our Law as instituted amongst us.

PERMIT me therefore to give you a short Description of this valuable Part of our Excellent Constitution. The Government of this Kingdom is that of a Limited Monarchy, and the People of this Nation are, [19] and always were accounted a Free People; and as an Evidence thereof, no Law made here has any Force of Authority, unless they by their Representatives in Parliament give their Consent thereto.

THE Legislative Authority is composed of the Three States, the King, The Lords, and the Commons. The latter represent the People of all Conditions, as well Clergy and Laity; the Peers are a distinct Body of themselves; and his Majesty (never in greater Splendour than when he appears in his Legislative Capacity) presides over the Whole; and by virtue of his Regal Power, gives Life and Sanction to every Law agreed to by the other Parts of the Legislature: not that he is obliged to pass any Bill into Law, provided he shall think it disagreeable to his Subjects or his own Interests. Nor, on the other hand, are the Lords or Commons constrained to give their Assent [20] to any Bill intended to be made a Law, if it appears to them likely to be detrimental to the Peace and Prosperity of those they represent.

SO that each Part of the Legislature has a negative Authority, when it shall think necessary to exert the same; and what is peculiarly a Happiness to us of this Nation, when a Law is thus made, every Branch

[1] This would be to return to the state of nature, as defined by Hobbes.

of the Legislative Authority is Subject to its Force and Power, nor is it to be dispensed withal, or repealed, but by the joint Consent of those who made it.

THESE Circumstances in the instituting of our Laws, are the Subjects of Admiration, and universally applauded. And now when many Nations in the known World groan under Tyranny, Oppression, and Arbitrary Power, we still possess what all just and impartial Authors allow to be an Original Right, and naturally due to all Human Societys. [D - 21]

THUS much I thought necessary to premise, with relation to the instituting of our Statute-Laws; and farther, think it proper to observe, That as the Common Law of the Land at first received its Energy and Force indisputably from common Consent, so has its prescriptive Operation given it the same Sanction and Power, with those Laws made and ordained by the Legislative Authority.

I WOULD not have any body mistake me, and imagine, that from hence I infer, That the Laws I have been speaking of, are calculated for the Good of the Governed only: No, Gentlemen, they are equally framed to support the Dignity, Authority, and Grandure of our Sovereigns, and all due Regard must be had for the Prerogative of the Crown; which, together with the Libertys of the People, are so well guarded by the Laws of the Land, that nothing but open [22] Force and Violence can injure the one or the other.

AND as our Happiness does not terminate here, I fancy 'twill not be unacceptable, if I describe to you with all the brevity that is possible, the great Advantages we enjoy, with regard to the admirable Order in the Administration of our Laws: and I think I may venture to affirm, that the Tryal of Causes, whether Civil or Criminal, by Jurys, (how much soever of late abused) is the darling Privilege of the Subject, and a peculiar Franchise, which no People, as I know of, enjoy, besides ourselves. It is a Liberty immemorially deliver'd down to us, and of so inestimable a Value, that[1] King *Alfred*, a *Saxon* King, put one of his Judges to death, for passing Sentence upon a Man, when three of the twelve [D 2 -23] disagreed in their Verdict from the rest: And the same King put another of his Judges to death, for passing Sentence of Death upon an *Ignoramus* returned by the Grand Jury: And a third, for condemning a Man upon his Inquest taken *ex Officio*, (as before the Coroner, or the like) when the Delinquent had not put himself upon his Country, that, to be tryed by a Jury.

I KNOW there are some who pretend to dispute this Piece of History, and urge, that this Way of Tryal by Juries was introduced by *William* the Conqueror, as a *Norman* Custom; and [2] others do as positively affirm the

[1] Nath. Bacon's *Historical Discourse of the Uniformity of the Government of* England.

[2] Whitlock's *Memoirs*, p. 460

Normans learnt this Method of us. HOWEVER, be that as it will, our Law-Makers in *Henry* III's Time, when they were reinforcing the Subjects Libertys by that famous Statute [24] called *Magna Charta*,[1] have therein declared, That no Freeman shall be taken and imprisoned, or be disseized of his Freehold, or Liberties, or Free Customs, or be outlawed, or exiled, or any other ways destroyed; nor will we pass upon him, *says the Law*, or condemn him, but by his Peers or Equals, or by the Law of the Land. And by an Act made 28 *Edw.* III. it is enacted, That no Man, of what State and Condition soever, shall be put out of his Lands or Tenements, nor taken, nor imprisoned, nor disinherited, nor put to death, without being brought to answer by duе Process of Law. Where, by the way, you must observe, that these words, *by the Law of the Land*, and *by due Process of Law*, have been always expounded to be by Presentment or Indictment of Good and Lawful Men, that is, Jurys.

THESE are but Specimens of those Excellent Laws mentioned to [25] you; and tho they are Statutes are but Recapitulations of the antient Liberties of the Subject; and indeed, generally speaking, the whole Body of our Statute Laws, together with the Petitions of Right, are but Declarations and Confirmations of the Common Laws of the Kingdom.

WITH us, tho a Man be most notoriously guilty of the greatest Offence, even Treason itself, they cannot be legally punished, till his Crime be first enquired of by the Grand Inquest, such as yourselves, Men of Substance, Probity and Integrity, indifferently chosen, and before whom the whole Circumstance of the Crime must be laid. And if after a full Inquisition made, there be Proof sufficient given, for them to charge the Criminal; yet that shall not throughly convict him, but there must be a farther Tryal by a Petit Jury, against every one of which he may object, for Causes lawfully assigned, nay, [26] against thirty-five he may challenge, without shewing any Cause at all.

HE has also the liberty to confront his Accuser, and shall have his Witnesses examined on their Oaths; a Privilege granted by Law in the late Queen's Reign, and of great advantage, since the Evidence given obtains greater Credit from the Jury.

HE shall have Counsel assigned him; and, as our Law directs, the Judge himself is to be so far of Counsel for the Delinquent, as to state the Law right, and to suffer no indirect Practice to be done to his injury.

IN all summary Proceedings, where the Matters are to be heard and determined by the Magistrate[2], upon the Oath of one or more Witnesses, if the Party shall think himself aggrieved by the first Adjudication, he has the liberty of appealing to a more supreme Judicature; where, if

[1] Reissued at Bristol, Nov. 1216.

[2] "the Matters are to be heard and determined"; this is the exact formula "Oyer and (De)terminer," of one of the five commissions.

the first Judgment shall appear to be irregularly obtained, it may be discharged, [27] and as the Case requires, Satisfaction awarded for the Injury done him.

'TWOULD be tedious to enumerate the multitude of Advantages the Subjects of this Kingdom enjoy, with regard to the Administration of our Laws.

I THINK from what I have hinted, you cannot but be convinced, that no People are so happy as ourselves, with respect to the good Œconomy and Order, in the Distribution of Justice.

THUS, *Gentlemen*, I have endeavoured, in as brief a manner as I was able, to shew you the Excellency of these Branches of our happy Constitution. And as I told you in the beginning of my Charge, that the chief Ends of our meeting here, were for the Honour and Glory of God, the supporting the Grandure of our Sovereign, with a due regard for his Happiness and Welfare, as well as for the Good of our-selves and Fellow-[28] Subjects; so do I now think it indispensibly your Dutys at this Time, to exert yourselves like good Christians, as well as good Subjects, and by making a right use of these Excellent Means, obtain those Great and Glorious Ends.

I HAVE often been considering with myself, what should be the reason, that, notwithstanding we have the best Constitution of the World, regarding the Excellency of our Laws as instituted amongst us, together with the admirable Order in their Administration and Execution, Offenders should daily increase, and our Legislators labour under a necessity of making new Laws to punish new-formed Offences: as if the implacable and restless Malice of Mankind had not scope enough to vent itself, but was daily finding out new Evils, that were not within the Verge of your Inquiry, or the Reach of our present Authority. [E -29]

I SAY, Sirs, this has been the frequent Subject of my Thoughts; and upon an impartial Inquiry I find these to be the Causes, *viz.* A daily barefaced Slight and Contempt of the Laws of God and our Country:

A HEEDLESS Regard of the subordinate Magistrates Authority: As well as

THE most daring and insulting Behaviour, both in Words and Actions, perhaps, that ever was heard of, towards our Great and Good King, who by the Providence of God is happily placed over us.

THE More I have considered hereof, the more I am convinced, that these are the Epidemical Maladies in the State: and as Medicines, when timely and properly applied, are Helps and Supports to the Body Natural, so (to prevent the Body Politick from falling into Ruin and Decay) it is necessary, that the Laws be forthwith vigorously put in execution. [30]

AND as you, *Gentlemen*, and other Grand Jurys, may not improperly be called the Physicians of the State, 'tis from you must proceed the necessary Prescriptions relating to this Country; whereby we may be enabled effectually to purge it of the present Malignancys it labours under.

IT is a certain Truth, never to be disallowed, That no Man can be a real good Subject, unless he is a good Christian; nor will that Man's Expressions of Duty and Loyalty be ever accounted sincere, unless he shews himself zealous for the Honour of God and Religion.

THE Laws of God are the Fountains and Sources from whence Obedience to the Magistrate is derived: and for any one to pretend to be Loyal without a due Regard to those Laws, it is like the beginning at the wrong end; and I think such a Loyalist may be very aptly compared to Seed sown in stony Ground. [E 2 - 31]

WHATSOEVER they may think of themselves, it can never enter into my Thoughts, that those who are guilty of Excessive Drinking, Blasphemy, Profane Cursing and Swearing, Lewdness, Profanation of the Lord's Day, and such Like, be of any Religion at all; but, on the other hand, are professed Enemys to our King and Constitution.

DOES not his Majesty declare it to be his Royal Purpose and Resolution, to discountenance and punish all manner of Vice, Profaneness, and Immorality, in all Persons, of what Degree or Quality soever, within his Realms? Yes, he does; and gives these Reasons for it:

THAT it is an indispensible Duty on him (and of course on all of us, who act under his Authority) to be careful above all things to preserve and advance the Honour and Service of Almighty God and to discourage and suppress those Vices, which are [32] so highly displeasing to God, and a Reproach to our Religion and Government. And as these Vices have a fatal Tendency to corrupt those Persons otherwise religiously disposed, they may, if not timely remedied, draw down Divine Vengeance on his Majesty and his Kingdoms.

HOW piously, and with what unfeigned Zeal, his Majesty expresses himself! How affectionate he appears for his Subjects Welfare, is evidently demonstrated, if you will but peruse the Proclamation lately read to us; in which you may observe, his Majesty commands us to give it in Charge.

AND therefore, as you have sworn diligently to inquire, and true Presentment make, of all such Matters and Things, as shall be given you in Charge; I dare hope, from a due Regard you have for his Majesty's Prosperity and Happiness, as well as [33] for your own Tranquillity and Welfare, that you will not stand indifferently by, and suffer Vice, Immorality and Profaneness, together with those other Offences described in the Proclamation, to exert themselves with Insolence and Impunity; whilst every thing that is good, virtuous, and praise-worthy, is reviled, scoffed at, and ridiculed.

IF we would but rightly consider, it must appear to us matter of great Shame and Scandal, when 'tis observed, that Swearing and Cursing (tho they are unprofitable Vices) are now-a-days become so fashionable, that there are too many, who think there is no Energy in their Discourse, unless each Sentence is graced with a full-mouth'd Oath.

IT is a common Observation, That the meaner sort of People affect the Air, Garb, and Dress of their Superiors; these soon grow out of fashion: I heartily wish this A-la-[34] mode Eloquence would meet with the same Period.

I AM sure there is the same reason for it; since it is too true, what that Great and Good Man Archbishop *Tillotson*[1] says, in a Sermon against Swearing, That a Man cannot now-a-days walk the Streets, without having his Ears grated with this hellish Noise.

GENTLEMEN, I will trouble you no longer in this Head, but refer you to the Directions in his Majesty's Proclamation; wherein he has expressed himself so pathetically, that That alone is a much better Rule for you to go by, than any I can prescribe.

I DARE hope there is nobody here present, but who is extremely sensible how happy we are, in being governed by the best of Kings; who makes the Laws only, the Rule of his Government, and who, as he is the Guardian of those Laws instituted for the Preservation of our Libertys, [35] ought to be most dear and valuable to us.

HIS chiefest Delight is in doing that, which will most conduce to his Peoples Happiness; and as he has nothing more at heart, than the making every one of his Subjects easy, it is undoubtedly incumbent on us all, to take the greatest Care imaginable of his Sacred Person, Welfare, and Government.

I SHALL therefore postpone what I have to say, with relation to the heedless Regard of the Subordinate Magistrates Authority, and endeavour to convince you, how necessary it is, (especially at this time) that you should exert yourselves for the Honour and Safety of our King and Governour. And now I am on this Head, I must beg the liberty to urge what I am about to say, with a more than common Concern, from the daily and bare-faced Practices, too too evident amongst us. [36]

SUCH is the Behaviour, such are the Expressions continually seen and heard, almost every where, towards the King, especially amongst the ignorant and meanest of the People, that to me it is very evident, there are those, of a more superior Degree in Knowledge and Circumstances, who inculcate and encourage these Practices, and whose Schemes not being yet perfect, and ripe for Execution, in the mean time they are sowing Sedition amongst the common People, who are to be made their immediate Tools, to work up the Projects into Faction and Rebellion.

BESIDES the Instructions given them, to bespatter their Sovereign with the lowest Degrees of Slander, such as would grate your Ears, were

[1] Archbishop Tillotson was promoted to Canterbury in 1691, and died 1694.

I to enumerate; nay, such as they dare not revile each other withal: They are taught to believe, that his Majesty has drained the Nation of vast Sums of Money; more perhaps [F-37] than the whole Species of the Kingdom amounts to, to make the Grievance appear of the first magnitude.

WHEN every body knows, who is not obstinately and wilfully ignorant, that besides the revenue allotted him, for the Support of his Royal Dignity, it is not in the power of his Majesty to meddle with one Penny of the Publick Moneys: it being not only by the Power of Parliament, but applied by the same Authority for the Publick Service; and every one is accountable to them, for the least Sum that passes thro his hands.

THEY have been likewise taught to believe, that the late War with *Spain* would be our Ruin, and that it put so total a Stop to Trade, that we must be undone; and then to make his Majesty odious, the King is to be blamed for the whole.[1]

WHEN Every one knows, that the two Houses of Parliament chearfully joined with the King, in declaring [38] and carrying on that necessary War; which, by the Blessing of God, is terminated to the Glory of our Sovereign, the Honour of the Nation, and to the Advantage of all its Inhabitants.

GENTLEMEN, there was a Necessity for the beginning of this War, since the cunning Cardinal, who lately ruled in *Spain*,[2] had (we have plainly seen) laid such Schemes, as, humanly speaking, had they succeeded, (and had not Providence interposed, they must have succeeded) would have made his Master Universal Monarch.

'TWOULD be tedious to describe all his Machinations; let it suffice, that he pushed very fair for the joining *France* and *Spain* under one Head, and if he had succeeded in that Attempt only, I will leave you all to judge what would have become of your Trade, together with your Religious and Civil Liberties. [F 2 - 39]

ARE these then the Rewards for a Prince, who under God has rescued us from Popery and Slavery? Are these the Returns for the Fatigues and Perils he has undergone, for perpetuating Peace and Happiness to his People? No, surely. Tho 'tis too plain, that these, amongst many others, are the malign Influences daily made use of, to sour the People against their Sovereign: the authors knowing very well, that when the common People can once be made to think ill of their Prince, 'tis an easy matter to put them upon committing the highest Acts of Treason.

IT is your Duty therefore, in the strictest manner, diligently to inquire of all Treasonable and Traitorous Acts or Conspiracys, which may be

[1] The war of Spanish succession, ended by the treaty of Utrecht, which the Whigs found far too favourable to France.

[2] Cardinal Portocarrero, the minister of Charles II of Spain.

done, perpetrated or designed, against his Majesty's Sacred Person and Government.

HIGH Treason, called in Law, *Crimen Læsæ Majestatis*, Mr. *Dalton*[1] [40] tells us, was always esteemed a grievous Offence, done or attempted against the Estate regal, *viz*. against the King, who is the Head, Life, and Ruler of the Commonwealth.

BEFORE the making of the statute de *Proditionibus*, in the 25th Year of *Edward* III. Treason at the Common Law was variously described; and according to the Temper of the Times, Facts were declared, or not declared to be Treason: which kept the Subjects in such continual Dread, and under such fearful Apprehensions, (the Punishment for this Offence being the most severe our Law does inflict) that in the 25th Year of that King's Reign, the Law which describes the Species of Treason, was made.

AND it was then thought of so great benefit to the Subject, that the Parliament who made it, as my Lord *Coke* tells us, obtained the Name of *Parliamentum Benedictum*. [41]

THIS Statute declares, That compassing or imagining the Death of The King or Prince, is Treason; so is levying War in the Realm, or adhering to the King's Enemies therein.

COUNTERFEITING the Great or Privy Seal, or Money, and foreign Coin made passable therein, are Treasons. Killing the Chancellor, Treasurer, Justices of either Bench, in Eyre, or of Assizes, and all other Justices assigned to hear and determine these Facts, are also Treasons.

THERE are some few other Species of Treasons declared in this Law, which are not to be presumed will be ever committed, so needless for me to repeat.

THUS it was, by that Law, that Treason stood then defined, and as it were circumscribed, with this Proviso, That if any like Cases of Treason might afterwards happen the Justices were to stay going to Judgment, till the Matter were considered [42] of in Parliament, whether it might be judged Treason or Felony.

FROM the making of that Statute, down to Queen *Elizabeth* 's days, I know not of any Law (except temporary ones, and some made with regard to counterfeiting, diminishing, and defacing the Coin) that was declaratory of any Treason, save that of 25 *Edw*. III.

THE Parliament in Queen *Mary* the First's days, was so careful to have that Matter clear, that in the first Year of her Reign it is enacted, That nothing shall be deemed Treason, but what is declared so by the 25 *Edw*. III.

IN Queen *Elizabeth*'s Reign, to strengthen the Reformation, some Facts were declared Treason, that were not so before.

[1] Thomas Dalton, English lawyer (1682–1730).

AS in the first Year of that Reign, the third Offence in maintaining foreign Authority, is Treason.

IN the fifth Year of the same Queen's Reign, the second Offence,[43] in maintaining the Authority of the See of *Rome*, or refusing the Oath of Supremacy, is Treason.

TO bring into the Realm, and put in execution the Pope's Bulls, is Treason by the 13 *Eliz.*

TO withdraw any from ours to the *Romish* Religion, or to be reconciled to that Religion, is Treason by the 23 *Eliz.* and 3 *Jac.*I.

JESUITS, or Seminary Priests, being Natives, and coming into the Realm, and they that are in Seminarys abroad, and not returning within six Months after Proclamation, nor submitting to take the Oaths, are guilty of High Treason, by 27 *Eliz.*

BY that Law which attaints the Pretender, made in the 13, 14, of *Will.* III it is declared High Treason, to hold any Correspondence with the Pretender: an Offence, I doubt, frequently committed now-a-days.

IN the first Year of the late Queen's Reign, it is declared Treason in any [44] Person endeavouring to deprive, or hinder, the next Successor in the Protestant Line, from succeeding to the Crown after her Death.

AND if any, by Writing or Printing, maintain and affirm, that his present Majesty is not Lawful and Rightful King of these Realms, or that the Pretender has any Right to the Crown; such Persons or Persons are guilty of Treason, by an Act made in the sixth Year of Q. *Anne*'s Reign.

I HAVE been somewhat the more particular in describing the several Species of Treason, as they now stand declared by Law; and the rather, since should any of them at this time be attempted, it not only endangers his Majesty's Life, but tends to the Overthrow and Destruction of our Government and Constitution both in Church and State.

MY relating to you those particular Statutes, made to secure us, and [G-45] our Holy religion, against the pernicious Consequences that must accrue by the Increase of its Opposite, would be needless, did I not say somewhat more to you on that Head.

I THINK it therefore my Duty to take notice, That of late Popery seems to have met with a more favourable Reception from some Folks than formerly: And indeed, from that Quarter, whence heretofore it was frequently and truly described, to fortify the common People against it, (for what Reason, I know not) there now remains a total Silence. Nay, what was worse, some time ago, instead of those noble Declamations exposing its baneful Influence, bitter Invectives were broached against our Protestant Dissenting Brethren.

But God be thanked, that Rancour is very much abated:

THO Popery still remains, in the Opinion of many amongst us, a good-natured easy Religion. [46] GENTLEMEN, Popery is Popery still;

and if any of you will but read the History of Queen *Mary* the First's Reign, there you will see many shining and bright Instances of its Good-Nature.

WHAT but the Principles of that Religion could prompt that Queen to break her Word with *Suffolk* -Men? who were so very instrumental in placing her on the Throne.

WHAT but the same Principles could persuade that unhappy Prince King *James* the Second, to break his Coronation-Oath, dispense with the Law, and use the Protestant Clergy as he did, when some of them had, in an extraordinary Manner, preached up that sweet-savoured Doctrine (so greedily relished by some Potentates) of unlimited Passive-Obedience and Non-Resistance?

TO pass by the prodigious Influences such Principles have upon too many of our own Countrymen, of [G 2 - 47] that Persuasion, tho they live so easy and happy amongst us:

WHAT but the same Principles can inflame the Zeal of some Popish Powers abroad, to break all the sacred Oaths, Treatys, and Assurances, with their Protestant Subjects? [1]

AND who, I pray, after all, next to the Hand of Providence, is more likely to save us and them from the cruel Effects of that sanguine Religion, than our Great and Good King?

HENRY the Eighth, Ancestor of our King, had the Title of *Defender of the Faith* given him by Pope *Leo* the Tenth, for entering the Lists against *Martin Luther*, in defence of this Religion, which declares, That no Faith is to be kept with Hereticks, that is, Protestants.

HOW much more then, does our Great Deliverer deserve that Title, and the utmost Thanks and Praises of all true Protestants, who so bravely exerts himself every where, in the De-[48] fence of the Faith once delivered to the Saints; and who, I dare say, by his invincible Steddiness, and powerful Influence abroad, will in a little time effectually blunt the Sword of Persecution?

THAT Good King, expressing his Sense and Zeal against Popish Recusants and Popery, says, That he was always careful, by proper Means, to fortify all Ways and Approaches, against their foreign Enemy.

AND surely if this Enemy was so formidable in that Age, how much more ought we to secure all Avenues and Approaches, when we have a Popish Pretender ready to be topp'd upon us on all occasions, and when there is great reason to fear, he has many more Devotees amongst us [49] than we are aware of, ready to assist him?

LET us not therefore flatter ourselves, that Popery is at that mighty distance, and that we are clear of all Danger from it.

IT compasses Sea and Land to make one Proselyte; and the Inhabi-

[1] A possible allusion, again, to the revocation of the Edict of Nantes, 1685.

tants of the remotest Parts of the Earth, have miserably smarted under its bloody Institution. INDEED there is great reason to believe, it will never retrieve its antient Dominion, until Protestantism is abolished in this Isle: which God forbid.

SINCE therefore extinguishing the Light of the Gospel amongst us, is the best Means that can be made use of, to regain that Kingdom of Darkness: it is doubtless your Dutys, by proper Inquirys, to prevent the Growth of that cruel Religion here.

I SHALL dismiss this Head, with the Words of Mr. *Pym*, a famous Man in the last Age. [50]

'TIS certain, *says he*, there can be no Security from Papists, but in their Disabilitys.

THEIR Principles are incompatible with any other Religion: Laws will not restrain them, nor Oaths; for the Pope dispenseth with both, and his Commands influence them against the Realm, both in Spirituals and Temporals, in *ordine ad Spiritualia*.

WHETHER this may be a Digression, 'tis submitted to your Judgments.

SURE I am, if we call to mind who were the chief Instruments in promoting and carrying on the *Preston* Rebellion, we shall soon be convinced that Papists, and those who are Popishly inclined, are the only People the Enemys of our Constitution, in Church and State, can throughly rely on.

GENTLEMEN, In the Station you now are, you may do great Services [51] to Yourselves and Fellow-Subjects; and by making a diligent Inquiry into those Offences I shall briefly enumerate, terminate this Session for the Publick Good.

IT is very true, that in Capital Crimes, and difficult Cases, which may arise before us, this Court does not proceed to hear and determine.

BUT with relation to any Offences committed within the County, I think you have full Power to inquire; and therefore, the greater the Offence, the more diligent ought you to be in your Inquiry.

WHAT I have said on the Head of High Treason, I hope is sufficient to animate your Zeal for the Safety of our King and Royal Family.

NOR ought you to be less diligent in your Inquiry, with regard to Misprisions of Treasons; which are, knowing and concealing of any Treasons. [52]

ALL Acts of what nature or kind soever, which tend to the depriving your Fellow-Subjects of their Lives or Propertys, are inquirable of by you.

AS are all Felonys whether declared so by Common or Statute Law.

TO enumerate them, would be tedious; and I the rather wave it, being well assured and satisfied of your Experiences and Abilitys.

BESIDES all manner of Felonys, which you are impowered to inquire of, by the express Words of our Commission; Forestalling, Regratings, Ingrossings, and Extortions, are within the compass of your Inquiry.

AS it that base Practice, of using false Weights and Measures; by which many are defrauded, especially the Poor, when they think at the same time, Justice is done them by the Turn of the Scale.

THE great Neglects of those Officers, in doing their Dutys, who are [H -53] more immediately under the Jurisdiction and Command of this Court; are inquirable of by you.

HE must be a great Stranger in these Affairs, who is ignorant hereof; so that I will waste no Time on this Head.

NOR are you limited here, since our Commission impowers you to inquire of all and singular other Misdeeds and Offences, by whomsoever, and howsoever, done or attempted in this County.

NUSANCES, whether by Inns, Alehouses, or on the Highways, and Bridges:

DESTROYERS of the Game, Cottages and Inmates; all Trespasses, with Force and Arms:

RIOTS, Routs, Affrays, Unlawful Assemblys, Batterys, Forcible Entrys, and Forcible Detainers, Breaches of the peace: all these are inquirable of by you;

As are all kinds of Misdemeanours, [54]

AMONGST which, there is one that stands in need of your more immediate Inquiry, and which leads me to that Head I proposed to speak to, *viz.* A heedless and contemptible Regard of the Subordinate Magistrates Authority.

WHICH is every where so obvious, not only amongst the common People, but even amongst some of the Better Sort, that one would almost imagine, they are taught to believe that our King is not the Lawful and Rightful Governour; and of course, those acting under him, have no legal Authority.

OR else, from the Lenity of the Government, they have suffered this Audaciousness to grow upon them.

I SHALL forbear mentioning some Facts, very remarkable; since 'twould be too plain a Description of the Actors, and since I hope, in a little time, they will be convinced, that the present Government is upon a good [H 2- 55] and lasting Foundation; and that Justice is now as legally and equitably administred, and in any former Reign.

'TIS become a common Practice (especially amongst some of those concerned in the Woollen Manufacture) to impose Laws and Rules upon the Poor they employ, and to erect Courts of Justice in every Shop and Wool-Lauft.[1]

[1] A Somerset and West-country word to mean, a loft. Apparently, M. here alludes to the rather unpleasant way in which clothiers were alledged to treat weavers in the way of

AS if the Magistrate, who in these Cases has full Power to hear and determine, was thought not fit to administer Justice.

SUCH are the Practices in many other Cases.

AND what is this, but insulting the Laws, and the Supreme Administration, under whom we act? overturning and tearing up the Government by the roots, to introduce the worst of Ills, Anarchy and Confusion?

GENTLEMEN, notwithstanding the many confused and slavish Notions of Indefeasable Hereditary Right, [56] King GEORGE is our Lawful and Rightful King; and every magistrate, who acts by his Commission, and under his Authority, is a visible Ray of his Executive Power: and if this Maxim, *Honorandus est sicut ille cujus vicem gerit,*[1] holds good, and a proportionable Deference is due, regarding the Person he represents; the Subordinate Magistrate is not so contemptible an Animal, but for your own Peace and Quietness very worthy of your Care.

I COULD heartily wish, there had been no reason for me to proceed any farther on this Head:

BUT I am forced to it, from the most insolent and unparallel'd Piece of Practice, that perhaps ever was heard of; no less than this Court's being in a manner libelled, in a Presentment by a Grand Jury, for exerting and supporting its own Dignity and Authority.[2] [57]

GENTLEMEN, If this Court has any Authority at all, it has an indisputable Power to assemble itself in any Town of this County, unless prohibited by express Words in its Charter.

AND if it has any prudence, it is very fit it should be shewn, in assigning the *Locus in quo,* [3] where those Justices, who compose it, may sit and act with Freedom and Safety; as well as for the benefit of those, who apply for Justice.

TO give you a full Account of this Affair, would at present take up

---

truck payments, stoppage of wages for damages, manipulation of weights and measures, etc. A pamphlet published in 1727, after the 1726 riots, quoted the very words of this Charge, accusing him (under the nickname of *Intimidate*, and making an allusion to his noble blood, since he was the grandson of the 1st earl of Manchester) of having sent a party of dragoons to stop a march of cloth weavers.

[1] = He must be honoured as he, whose power he is wielding.

[2] The episode alluded to is already mentioned in the introductory pages. The corporation of Marlborough was favourable to the Pretender, and they forbade the magistrates to hold their Q-S within the limits of the borough, making use of a clause of their charter that granted them a court of their own. This position was highly resented by some of the freeholders of the Marlborough division, who retorted with an inflamatory Presentment; at the following sessions, i.e. the one chaired by Montagu, this could not be left unmentioned, and M's attitude explains that the jury were so eager to see the text of the Charge through the press. See James Wayler's *History of Marlborough* (1854), pp. 362–68. The same book describes Montagu as favourable to the Hanoverian settlement. Thanks are due to Mr. K. H. Rogers, Wiltshire County Archivist and Diocesan Records Officer, for this information.

[3] *Spectator* n°125.

too much of your Time: Tho somewhat must be said, in Justice and Honour to the Court of Quarter-Sessions.

IT is very true, that the Michaelmas Quarter-Sessions has been held, till of late, at *Marlborough*; and no doubt had continued to assemble there at that Season of the Year, had not the Corporation opposed the Execution of our Authority therein, not only as Justices of the Peace, but as [58] a Court; of which many Instances can be given.

WHAT then could this Court do? To sit and act there, the *Non se intromittant* Clause in their Charter inhibits.

AND for so doing, subjects us to Actions; and perhaps stamps a Nullity on our Proceedings.

THE *Michaelmas* Quarter-Sessions must be held somewhere.

AND therefore, to prevent Clashings of Authority, and many great Inconveniencies; 'twas thought proper, and this Court did order, that the *Michaelmas* Sessions should held alternately at *Caln* and *Chippenham*; the former a very convenient Town, and nearest to the Division; the latter as commodious a Place, and where it has been often held without objection, when removed from *Marlborough*.

NOR had the Justices, in doing this, any other View, than supporting [59] the Dignity, Honour, and Independency of this Court, and its Commission.

AND for so doing forsooth! this Court has been told, and in the face thereof (for the Court is always the same, tho composed of different Persons)

'THAT it has greatly oppressed and grieved the Freeholders of the Division of *Marlborough*, and thereby has obstructed Justice.'

I CAN assure you, it is well known to many, that some of the most Learned Lawyers in this Kingdom have said, That we are prohibited by their Charter, entering and acting there.

AND to my own knowledge, some of the principal Men of that Learned Profession have commended the Proceeding, for which this Court stands thus calumniated on Record.

A GRAND Jury of Middlesex may, with the same reason, present the [60] Justices of the Peace for that County, for not sitting at *Brentford* instead of *Hickes's-Hall*.

NAY, the Gentlemen of this County, convened as Grand Jurors at *New Sarum* might as well present the Judges of Assize, for drawing them to the Confines thereof.

AND therefore they who imagine that this or that Town in the County of *Wilts* has a Right to this Court's sitting there, are in the Wrong; since it is *ex gratia Curiæ*, and not *ex debito Justitiæ*, that this Court of Quarter-Sessions assembles itself, in the several Quarters of the County.

GENTLEMEN, I hope before we part, you will resent this insolent

Usage; and, to use the Language of the Law, *secundum modum Delicti*, give it its due Reward.

I CANNOT help thinking, that when this Matter is hereafter related, (as doubtless, when ever, 'twill be with a *Mirabile Dictu*) nothing will [I-61] create greater Wonder, than how such a rude and saucy Invective could be midwifed into Court, without any Noise; when so many Worthy and Learned Gentlemen were there: unless they who introduced it, were presumptuous enough to imagine, the Begetter of it was present, and who on its first Squall would have owned his for its precious Offspring.

I HAVE, Sirs, now but two other Matters to mention; and I will be very short in both.

NOTHING has touch'd me more nearly, and that with the highest Concern imaginable, than the negligent and remiss Behaviour I have observed in former Sessions, amongst Jurors, assembled here to do their Dutys on their Oaths to the King and Country.

I AM afraid, too many of late have contracted a mean Opinion of that solemn Act, the taking of an Oath. [62]

OF you who are present I hope better things, and of such, which will much better suit the Ends of our meeting here.

AN Oath is the most sacred and solemn Appeal to God Almighty, who knows the Secrets and inmost Thoughts of our Hearts.

AND if we really believe the Omniscient Power of God, we must be convinced, he is already apprized, whether we are, or are not sincere.

AND therefore, to invoke him to be a Witness of our Assurances, when at the same time we have no Intention of performing them, is an Act of the greatest and most daring Impiety.

BESIDES, such Prevarications do in the strongest Terms imprecate this Divine Vengeance; which I think may be plainly deduce from the last Words of your Oath, *So help me God.* [I 2 - 63] THAT is, If you perform your Promise, which you have presumed to call on God to testify; you hope for, beg, and desire his Blessing: if not, the contrary is obvious, without a particular Relation; and indeed 'tis too melancholy to be described.

THE Heathens, who had but poor and earthly Notions of their Deities, had quite a different Opinion of the Sacredness of an Oath, and held it in much greater Veneration, than, I fear, many amongst us do, who would think themselves much abused, should they be told they were not Christians.

I VERY much suspect, there are some amongst us (not a few) who of late have been industriously labouring to weaken the Force of an Oath; and thereby sacrificing the Souls of very many poor deluded Wretches, for the accomplishing their base and devilish Ends. [64]

GENTLEMEN, As the Force and Efficacy of your Oaths will more or less prompt you to the doing your Duty, I could not help mentioning this; tho I hope, with regard to you who are present, an unnecessary Digression.

I SHOULD have now nothing else to say, but dismiss you;

DID not our unhappy Divisions, which too often interfere in our publick Actions, oblige me to say somewhat thereupon. And therefore, I hope you'll pardon me, if I bear upon your Patience, in troubling you with a word or two upon this Head.

I DARE believe, you are all very sensible, how unhappy we are, with respect to those malicious Distinctions and Animositys, which are industriously disseminated amongst us:

AND which cannot but convince you, since our Enemys, by open Force, are unable to destroy us, they are resolved on our Ruin, by dividing us. [65

TO that end, they have separated us into Partys, distinguished by the Names of Whig and Tory, High and Low Churchmen; Characters in themselves so odious and ridiculous, that there can be no other Ends in such Descriptions, but mere Aggravations.

SO that I beg of you, in your Proceedings, totally to disregard them; and have nothing else in view, but the Cause and its Circumstance, as it comes before you.

YOU may rest assured, these monstrous Denominations are purposely broached to divide and weaken us; and our Enemys have in a great measure gained their Ends, if we suffer ourselves to be irritated and inflamed by them.

'Tis with great Submission I beg leave to suggest, I know no other Distinction amongst us, who profess ourselves to be of the Established Church, but by being Good or Bad Churchmen: and without Reflection I'll take [66] the liberty to say, 'twould be better for us all, were we better Churchmen than we are.

I AM confident, our good Examples in this Particular would be the best Demonstration of our Sincerity, and the most effectual Means to obtain that desirable Felicity.

IT is a Misfortune indeed, and no small one, that some of our Fellow-Subjects do unhappily dissent from us, with regard to the Excellency of our Church-Œconomy, and Good Order; which I will be bold to say, are the best in the whole World.

BUT they are Christians and Fellow-Subjects, and have a Law dispensing with their Dissension; and the late Queen did declare, she would inviolably maintain it, and his present Majesty is bound to support it.

SO that I think, as long as they continue to live in obedience to the Law, it is only Christian, and highly [67] Praise-worthy, to use them with Brotherly Kindness.

BUT if this be a Misfortune, there is yet a much greater, and which in the end must prove fatal to us:

I MEAN, that Distinction of High and Low Churchmen.

DIVIDE *and Rule*, is a known Maxim in State-Politicks, and seldom fails, if rightly apply'd.

HOW far our Enemys have succeeded by it; I will leave you all to judge.

I THINK I may confidently aver, they are nearer their desired Ends, by this last Attempt, than ever.

THE Miserys that must ensue, should they succeed, are so emphatically described, in a SPECTATOR, that I think nothing comes up to it.

'THERE cannot, says the Author[1], a greater Judgment befall a Coun-[68]try, than such a dreadful Spirit of Division, as rends a Government into two distinct People, and makes them greater Strangers, and more averse to one another, than if they were actually two Different Nations.

THE Effect of such a Division, is very fatal, both to Men, Morals, and their Understandings: It sinks the Virtue of a Nation, and not only so, but destroys even Common Sense.

A FURIOUS Party-Spirit, when it rages in its full Violence, exerts itself into Civil War and Bloodshed; and when it is under its greatest Restraints, naturally breaks out into Falshood, Detraction, Calumny, and a partial Administration of Justice.

IN a Word, it fills a Nation with Spleen and Rancour, and extinguishes all the Seeds of a Good-nature, Compassion, and Humanity. [K- 69]

I THINK what I have repeated, is enough to convince you of the unspeakable Miserys that must accompany intestine Divisions.

AND therefore I will dismiss you with that never-to-be-forgotten Exhortation of our late Glorious Deliverer, King *WILLIAM* III. in his last Speech to his Parliament:

LET me conjure you, to disappoint the only Hopes of our Enemys, by your Unanimity. Lay aside Partys and Divisions: let there be no other Distinction heard of amongst us for the future, but of those, who are for the Protestant Religion, and the Present Establishment; and of those, who mean a Popish Prince, and a Papal Government.

GENTLEMEN, I have now done; and if I have detained you some-[70] what longer than usual, I hope you will pardon me, since what I have said, is designed for the Publick Good.

FINIS.

[1] *Spectator* n°125.

The Third **CHARGE** OF *Whitlocke Bulstrode,* Esq; TO THE GRAND - JURY, And other ***JURIES*** of the County of Middlesex, At the General QUARTER-SESSION of the Peace held the Fourth Day of *October*, 1722, at *Westminster-Hall.*

Printed at the Desire of the *Justices of the Peace* for the County, and the *High-Constables* and *Petty-Constables* JURIES.

——*Quid Demens manifestat negas? en Pectus inustæ*

Deformant maculæ; vitiisque indevit imago

——*Aduletra mens est.* Claud.

LONDON, Printed for D. BROWN at the *Black Swan and Bible* without *Temple-Bar*, and R. GOSLING at the *Midde-Temple-Gate, Fleet-Street.* 1723.

T O **Whitlocke Bulstrode**, Esq;

WE the High Constables and Petty Constables within the several Hundreds of the County of Middlesex, being duly sensible of the great growth of Immorality and Profafeness within our several Districts or Divisions; And knowing that, with the Divine Assistance, nothing can put a Stop to the further Progress thereof more, than the Zeal and Vigilance of the Worthy magistrates and other Inferiour Officers, in putting the Laws in execution agaisnt such Offenders; Do make it our humble Request to Your Worship, That you would be pleas'd to cause the Excellent CHARGE, given us this Day, to be Printed: Which [* 1] we hope may tend to the Encouragement of Inferiour Officers to do their Duty, and be a great Means to prevent growing Impiety. We are, with the greatest Respect,

Dat. *Oct.* 4

1722 Your Humble Servants,

Thomas Jones,	Thomas Pratt,
Jasper Clarke,	John Jefferies,
William Murden,	Samuel Hawkins,
O. Jones,	William Coleman,
Henry Clarke,	John May,
John Street,	Robert Lane,
Geroge White,	William Plummer,
Joseph Welch,	Andrew Kendall,
Thomas Heath,	Thomas Blaniard,
Benjamin Watts,	Joseph Wildman,

Thomas Cox,
Edward Hodson,
James Honey,
Samuel Bradley,
William Lovett,
James Nodes.

[ii]
THE
PREFACE.

WHEN I had writ the following Charge, *I did not intend it shou'd* ever come abroad; *having had more* Honour, *than was* due to me, *given before, in my* Two CHARGES *already* Printed *at the Desire of the* Gentlemen in the Commission of the Peace, *and the several* Grand-Juries.

Upon the Thanks of the Commission, *and their Desire, after this* Charge *given, to* Print it, *I begg'd of them, they would not insist upon it; but could not* prevail.

After that, the High and Petty Constables Juries *made* Application to me, in Writing, *to the same Purpose* ; which pass'd in the Negative.

I had a Doubt in my own Mind, at last, *how far I might be capable, in refusing what was so earnestly desired, in case any thing, I had said, might prove Useful to the Publick; or that* any one Person *might receive Benefit by it.*

And this Consideration stuck with me the more, I confess; forasmuch as there is late come to my knowledge, *that a very Learned Gentleman, Monsieur* James-Stanislaus Rivers, *a Native of* Maltha, *and bred a* Roman Catholick, *has declared* [iii] *under his Hand, to the* Commissioners for the Relief of Proselytes, *That the Book of Letters between Dr.* Wood *and Me, which he had read, was a* great Motive to his embracing *the* Protestant Religion, *as taught in the* Church of England, *and* renouncing Popery.

Another Motive to it, besides the Commands above, *is, to set in a* true Light, *the Practice of the* Jews, *in relation to their* Secondary Wives; *which our Old English translates* Concubines; *and our Modern* Sparks *of the Town call* Mistresses; *and the Ordinary People, by the* Gross Name. *But Words, in the* living Languages, *in time, lose their* primitive Signification, *and acquire, at last, a quite* different sence.

As to the Occasion, *or* Offence, *which Witty Men, who indulge to Uncleanness, by Principle, take hereby, (And who is more* deceived, *than he who deceives himself?) and which much* prevails, *ev'n amongst some who have been our* Legislators, *if not so now; I thought it proper to shew them their Errour. And if but one Man proves to be reformed, by my giving way to the Publishing this* CHARGE; *the* Satisfaction *I shall* receive thereby, *will* surmount the Dishonour or Tarnish my Character may receive, *by its* Publication, *or* Envy *from the Invidious.* [B-1]

The THIRD **CHARGE** OF *Whitlocke Bulstrode*, Esq; TO THE GRAND-JURY, &c.

Gentlemen of the Grand-Jury,

AND

You Gentlemen of the Constable Juries,

WE are Met here *for Excellent Purposes*; that is to say, *To Suppress and ev'n Root out Vice, Immorality, and Profaneness*; And, what is the Natural Consequence, To Plant *Vertue and Religion*, the *Fear* and *Love of God* in Mens *Hearts*, in the room thereof. [2] These are Noble Ends: These Views should inspire the *Coldest Heart*, and the most Dull and Phlegmatick Constitution, with *Ardour and Zeal*. The *Clergy* (it's hoped) are armed *with the Sword of the Spirit*; which, to *Mild and Tender Consciences*, is sufficient to *suppress Vice*, and *inculcate Vertue*: But we are armed with the *Temporal Sword*, which over *Naughty Minds*, has the greatest Influence; and we hope also, that we are not without the *former*.

If you would be *Blessed in this World*, and have your Names *inroll'd with Honour* in the *Kingdom of Heaven*, Exert your selves, in this *spiritual Warfare*, with your utmost Vigour, to the pulling down the *Kingdom of Satan* in this World, (which is become very Powerful) and the erecting the *Empire of God*, evn' here on Earth, instead thereof; which is your Daily Prayer.

You have a *Noble Example* before you, of many *Worthy Gentlemen*, in the Commission of the Peace, who have laid out their Time, and Money, and have frequently met in Numbers, not only to *Extirpate Vice and Wickedness* in General, but especially the flagrant reigning Sin of *Excessive Gaming*, (those Nests of *Gamesters*, that ruin young Gentlemen of Fortune;) and that have, by their *indefatigable Diligence, Prudence and Courage*, suppress'd many wicked *Gaming-Houses*, where Highway-Men, and the Worst of Mankind resort. They have Ordered their Warrants to be executed by *faithful and honest Men*, who have done it with such *Courage and Bravery*, that have caused [B 2-3] the Gamesters therein, to flie from them, and ev'n to creep over Houses, to avoid being Taken.

And in this Place, I Cannot, without Injustice, but take Notice, how *Pleasing* this Service has been to His MAJESTY, and His *Ministers*, signified by the Excellent Lord *Townshend*, in his Letter to Us; which has, I hope, *inspired* the whole Commission with Zeal in these Matters. Nor ought I here to forget, but mention with Honour, that *Worthy Gentleman, Mr. De la Fay*, one of our Number, who was very Instrumental therein.

Every Nation, or Common-wealth, may be compared to a *Ship*, that has many Persons on Board. Now, 'tis the Interest of every Man in the Vessel, not only to endeavour to keep the Pilot Sober and Diligent, but that all the Company should be Sober, that the Ship may be well steer'd, and avoid splitting on a Rock, or running a-Ground, to the Loss of all the Persons in the Ship.

Mankind, in their several Stations, should, in the first place, do what they think would most Promote the *Divine Glory*; (but that is generally postpon'd) and, in the next place, contribute all that is lies in their Power, that will tend to reserve *the Pilot*, the Publick Welfare, and their Own.

As the *Flagitious Wicked Lives* of Single Persons, do most certainly draw down God's Vengance upon them in this World; and if their Children continue in the Vices of their [4] Parents, their *Persons, Estates*, and *Families* become soon extinct: so when these *Wicked Persons* Multiply, and Encrease, a Nation of such Wretches, will be like that of the *Canaanites*, the measure of whose Iniquities being full, they became Ripe for *Destruction*.

National Sins are always punish'd, sooner or later, with *National Judgments*: For, in the next World, God will not *Judge Mankind as Nations*, but as *Individuals*; tho' the *Crimes* of particular Persons, will be more or less *aggravated* as they more or less contribute to the Corruption of the *Community*.

Who would ev'n be King of a *Vile People*, any more than he would be King of the *Hottentots*, who have human Shape, without Human Understanding?

Gentlemen of the Grand-Jury,

AND

You of the Constable Juries,

I have spoken so fully in my Two Last CHARGES from this Place, which are in Print, and which, I believe, some of you present did hear, touching Offences committed immediately against *God*, such as *Blasphemy, Prophane Cursing and Swearing*, and *Prophaning the Lord's Day*; And of the several Species of *High Treason*; and of Crimes committed against the *Life, Property, Habitation, and Welfare of Mankind*, of the *highest and the lowest Offences*; That I shall [5] refer you to them, without troubling you with a Repetition, which to me is grievous, or citing more Cases to the same Purposes.

Those Two making a short Compendium of the *Crown-Law*.

I shall now apply my self to speak to such Crimes, which I find most *flagrant* amongst us, and which have a great Tendency to Ruin the Morals, and the little Vertue that is left us still remaining in the Nation. I shall place these Crimes under the following Heads, and speak to them distinctly.

First, *Disorderly Houses*.

Secondly, *Bawdy Houses*.

Thirdly, *Play Houses*.

Fourthly, *Masquerades*, alias *Balls*.

Fifthly, *Gaming Houses*.

As for *Disorderly Houses*;

I mean such *Publick Houses*, as suffer Men to sit Drinking in them 'till *Late at Night*, or rather, *Early in the Morning*, be those *Taverns, Eating Houses*, or *Ale Houses*. Surely, these Houses, were first Instituted for Publick

Meetings, to do Business in, and for Friends to meet for Conversation, and Refreshment; and not to sit Drinking in them six or seven Hours, *toasting the Healths* of others, 'till they have lost *their own*, and ev'n their *Understandings* also. [6]

The dismal Consequences that I have observed to have attended these *Debauchees*, obliges me to make take Notice of them.

There is scarce a Session, but we find much Mischief done by these *Midnight Debauchees*. Ordinary Men, that get Drunk, in going Home in the Night, either Quarrel with Drunken Fellows like themselves, Break one of the others Heads, Lame a Limb; and often-times Death ensues: or are Pickt up by *Midnight Whores* in the Streets, who Pick their Pockets of the little Money that is left, and while so doing, in exchange, give them a *Disease*, which they carry Home as a Present to their *Wives*. When brought before us, for these Male-Feasances, they offer in Excuse, That they were *Drunk*. As if the Sin of *Drunkenness*, should palliate or excuse the *Evils* they do when Drunk: or, as if the committing one bad Sin, should atone for a second that is worse.

Gentlemen, and *Men of Quality*, that sit up Late, at Taverns, or Eating Houses, stay often 'till *Two or Three* o'th' Clock in a *Morning*, and sometimes Later; being *inflamed* with *Burgundy*, and inspired with Madness, coming *Red-hot* into the Streets, they resolve to do some *Outragious Wickedness*; for they are above committing *small Sins*: *They would fire some Ancient Church, if they could, or (*Nero *like) some Famous City*: But not being able to do so, they are contented to commit the *humble Sins* of Killing the next Man they meet, tho' he should prove to be their *dearest Friend*. [7]

We have had many Instances of this Sort: Not long since, a *certain Nobleman*, with three others with him, about Four of the Clock in the Morning, Ran a Gentleman Through, who was going a Journey, whom they never saw before: The Wound happened not to be Mortal, and they escaped: But soon after, one of these *Midnight Debauchees* Kill'd a Watch-Man, for which he was fairly Hange'd. *Winchurst* and *Burdet* were lately hang'd, for Killing Captain *Falkner* in the Street, whom they never saw before.

I shall not multiply Instances of this Sort: But let this suffice, to cause you to Present all *Publick Houses* that suffer Persons to continue so late a Drinking, the Consequences of which are *so dismal*. If you know of such Houses, and will not Present them, let me beg of you to consider the *mortal Sin of Perjury* you incur thereby.

There are some *other Houses*, that may not so strictly be call'd *Publick Houses*, and yet do a great deal of *Publick Mischief*. Tho' they have no *Signs*, yet are they sufficiently known by the *Rakes of the Town*; such are, the *Drury-Lane Houses*, and other Houses near the *Play-Houses*, and where *Balls and Masquerades* are set up; (those *godly Places* for the education of *Youth!*) The Keepers of these Houses are ready to open their Doors to any *Gentleman and a Lady* that come to them in a Coach, especially if in *Masquerade*; for then, they know the Business they come about, and all [8] is Ready for them. Present these *Naughty Houses*, as well as the former.

II. My next Head, is against *Bawdy Houses*: A Word so *Broad*, that the Name should not be so much as known, or mention'd in a *Christian Country*. It's a Reproach, I must confess, both to the *Ecclesiastical and Civil Magistrate*, that there are such Houses in Being; especially in a *Reformed Christian Country*, where by the Principles of our Religion, the Habit of *Fornication*, as well as *Adultery*, exclude *Christians* from the *Kingdom of Heaven*.

St. *Paul*, writing to the *Ephesians*, tells them, That no *Unclean Person* has any Inheritance in the Kingdom of *Christ*; and that *Fornication* shou'd not be so much as *named* amongst them: Neither should they accustom themselves to *Smutty Conversation*, which mix't with Wit, very much Defiles the Mind.

St. *Peter*, with great Earnestness, dehorts those he writes to, from *Uncleanness*; as if it were the particular, specifick Sin, that destroys Human Souls; saying, *I Beseech you, abstain from Fleshly Lusts, which war against the Soul.*

I have observed, that most of the *Malefactors* that die an *Ignominious Death*, date their Ruin, from their Conversation with *Lewd Women.* [1]

I believe there are few *Noblemen*, or *Gentlemen*, that have run out of their Estates, and are reduced to Want, but the *Causa Causans* [2] thereof has been *Whoring*, and *Gaming*; and sometimes, one of them alone has done it. [C-9]

The *Sodomites*, and five Cities adjacent, *Pentapolis*, that burnt with *raging Lusts*; that Sin, which our Common Law justly calls, *Crimen Detestabile, inter Christianos non Nominandum*,[3] provoked the *Divine Majesty* to so high a Degree, as to pour down Fire from Heaven to Consume them: a Monument of the *Divine Vengeance* remaining to this Day in the Place where those Cities stood, being a filthy Lake, call'd the *Dead-Sea.*

Solomon, who had too-much Experience in the Matters of Uncleanness, *wherein his Wisdom was superseded*, had but one Son, of many Hundred Wives, and he was a *Fool*: He tells us, that *a Whore is a deep Ditch*; intimating, That a Man that falls into it, cann't easily get out of it; and that she will *reduce a Man to a morsel of Bread.* Which we find, by daily experience, to be true, in the *Rakes* of the Town.

In *Popish Countries*, where *Fornication*, by the Principles of *their Religion*

[1] This is to be found as a leit-motiv in criminal biographies, so numerous at the time; cf, e.g., Defoe's *A Narrative of all the Robberies, &c. of J. Sheppard*, 1724, ed. G. Lamoine (Plan de la Tour: Editions d'Aujourd'hui, 1980), p. 6, where he mentions his "frequenting of this wicked house [in Drury-Lane] brought me acquainted with *Elizabeth Lyons*, and with a Train of Vices..."

[2] = the real cause.

[3] = The detestable crime which is to remain unnamed among Christians nations.

corrupted, and the Doctrine of their *Priests*, is a Venial Sin; the *Reproach* is not so great, if any, to the *Magistrate*; 'tis said, they are there *tolerated*, (as it was with us in *England*, 'till the *Reformation*) and a Tax set on them: Which is an Open Allowance of them, but a great Scandal to Christianity, to that Religion which has enjoyn'd the *Purity of the Mind*, Cleanness of Thought, and such a Chastity to the *Eye*, as to forbids an *Unchast Look*.

As St. *Paul* says, that *He, and the other* [10] *Apostles, were Workers together with our Saviour, for the Salvation of Mankind*: so I may say, That the People who keep *Bawdy Houses*, are Workers together with *Satan their Master*, (and do him *supereminent* Service) for the *Destruction* of Mankind, *in Body, Soul, and Estate*.

Blessed Employment! These are Ministers of State to *Belzebub* in this World, and will doubtless be exalted to the *highest* Degree of Infamy and Pain in the next.

Inst. 488. Inst. 206. *Fornication* and *Adultery* were Anciently punish'd at *Common* Law, by *Fine, and Imprisonment*, and Inquirable in *Turns and Leets*, by the Name of *Lecherwite*: But Now, indeed, my Lord *Coke* tells us, those Offences belong to the *Ecclesiastical Court*. Yet the Keepers of *Bawdy-Houses* are Punishable still, by *Indictment* at *Common Law*, by Fine and Imprisonment, being, as it were, a *Common Nusance*.

From whence I infer, That if the *Procurers* of *Fornication and Adultery* are Punishable at *Common Law*, as a *Nusance*, the *Actors* themselves should be equally Punish'd by the same Law.

But in the Days of *Popery*, when the *Power* of the *Church* ran *high*, and the *Laity* were *stupidly Ignorant*, and the *Priests* of the *Roman* Church had intirely the Ascendant over them, and *lock'd up* the Scriptures from them, in the Learned Languages, and Retail'd only to them the *Pater Noster*, and *Ave Maria*, and that in Latin, which the People did not understand; [C 2-11] I say, these *Priests* being *prohibited Marriage*, and subject, as other Men, to *Fornication and Adultery*, they *usurp'd* the *cognisance* of these two Sins to themselves; that they might Pardon one the other with the more *slight Penance and Punishement*, and that privately, that the Laity might not know it; And this they termed, *pro Salute Animaæ*.

'Tis to be wished the Parliament wou'd Restore the *Common Law* to its Ancient Jurisdiction; and then, the scandalous Keeping of Women, and the Open and Bare-faced Commission of the Sin of *Uncleanness*, in the Face of the Sun, would, or might be soon suppressed: Without which, I believe, this Kingdom will never be Happy: For the *Ecclesiastical Courts*, I perceive, take little or no Care to Punish these Offences; and when they do punish them, the Punishment is in no sort *adequate* to the Crime.

Having mention'd, that *Fornication*, in the Church of *Rome*, is held as a Slight and Venial Sin; and believing that many *Persons of Quality*, and the *Richer sort of Traders, and Men in Business*, that are not abandon'd to all manner of Wickedness, have some Shiness of being guilty of *Adultery*, believing it a *Capital Crime*, and expressly forbid by *God*, in the *Seventh Commandment* ; yet give themselves a Loose to *Fornication*, and keeping of Women; as if that Sin was not forbid in that Command: lest, I say, by the Expression above, I should seem to give some *Encouragement* to young Gentlemen, and Others, to indulge therein, who are too apt of [12] themselves to run into that Vice of *Fornication*, and that upon *Principle*; give me leave to say a few Words thereon, it falling very naturally under the Head of *Bawdy-Houses*, those being the Scenes where those Sins are committed; And I'll endeavour to set this Matter before you in *a true Light*.

First, That tho' our Translation renders the Seventh Commandment, *Thou shalt not commit Adultery*; and that *Castalio*,[1] in his *Elegant Version* of the *Bible* into Latin, uses the Verb *Adultero*, which, in the common acceptation of the Word, signifies, *Lying with another Man's Wife* ;

ad alterius Toram ascendere: yet in St. *Jerom*'s Translation, printed at *Paris* in 1534, and in the *Antwerp* Edition, Printed in 1565, the Word *Mœchor* is used, which signifies any Act of *Whoring; Fornication, as well as Adultery.*[2]

I have look'd into two Latin Manuscript *Bibles* of St. *Jerom*'s, which I have by me; one, which is supposed to tbe about One Thousand Years old, and the other somewhat later, both which use the Verb *Mœchor*. And *Junius* and *Tremellius*, in their Version of the *Bible* into Latin, which the Learned Chief Justice *Vaughan*[3] commends, as done with great Care, use the Verb *Scortor*, in the Seventh Commandment, which is of the same signification with the Verb Mœchor, which comprehends Fornication, as well as Adultery; and in their Marginal Notes on this Text, say thus: *Qui vertunt, Nec Committas Adulterium, Præceptum, nimis* [13] *restrigunt, significat enim vox, Omne Genus Scotationis: Et summa inter Hebræos Doctores Autoritatis; Aben Hezra ita interpretatur*. Which, because some of you, *Gentlemen*, may possibly have forgot your Latin, by disuage, I'll tell you in English; "They who translate the Command, *Thou shalt not commit Adultery*, do too narrowly and strictly restrain the Command"; for the Hebrew word signifies, *Every sort of Whoring and Uncleanness*; And the famous Rabbi, *Abben Ezra*, who is of great Authority among the Hebrew Doctors, so interprets the Command. "This Rabbi, *Abben Hezra*, was a *Spanish* Jew, a Man of great Learning, and of exquisite Skill in the Hebrew Language."[4]

[1] Castalio or Sébastien Chateillon (1515–63), *Biblia sacra ex Sebastiani Castellionis interpretatione*...-1st ed., 1551, the best ed., 1573.

[2] The two ed. could be: *Biblia sacra integrum utriusque testamenti corpus complectens*. Parisiis: ex edibus Yolande Bonhomme, 1534; *Biblia ad vetustissima castigate*... Antverpiæ: Chr. Plantini, 1567. on the text of the Louvain ed., B. Gravius, 1547, by Johannes Hentensius.

[3] Sir John Vaughan, 1603–74, C.J. of the Common Pleas, 1668.

[4] Most likely Abraham Ibn Esra, whose first printed work is given as: Lyons, 1496. See *Catal. ouvrages imprimés de la Biblioth. nationale*.

The Learned and great Critick Mr. Poole[1], in his *Annotations on the Bible*, on this Command, says "That tho' under this Command, there is mention'd only one kind of Uncleanness, being eminently Sinful, Unjust, and Pernicious to Human Society; yet, under this Command, are comprehended and forbidden all other Kinds of Filthiness, as *Bestiality, Sodomy, Whoredom, Fornication*, &c."

The *French* Nation translate this Seventh Command, by the Verb *Pailliarder*; which signifies, to *Haunt Bawdy-Houses*, or, to *Lie with any Single or Marry'd Woman*. Now the Substantive *Pailliard*, from whence the Verb *Pailliarder* is derived, signifies a *Whoremaster*. The Words in the Command are these, *Tu ne Pailliarderai point*:[2] which truly translated, is, *Thou* [14] *shalt not commit Whoredom*. - *Theodor. Beza*, in his Translation of the *Old Testament*, uses the Verb *Scortor*, - *Ne Scortator*, and in the *New Testament*, the Verb *Mœchor*; both which Words signify, not only the two eminent Species of Uncleanness, *Fornication* and *Adultery*, but all other Species of Uncleanness.The Words of our *Saviour*, as he translates them, are these: *Audistis doctum fuisse à veteribus, Non Mœchebaris: Ego verò dico vobis, Quicumque aspicit Mulierem, ut eam concupiscat, jam adulterabit cum ea in core*. The English of which, in our Translation, runs thus; - *You have heard that it was said by them of old, Thou shalt not commit Adultery: But I say to you*, says our Saviour, *that whosoever looketh on a Woman, to lust after her, hath committed Adultery with her already in his Heart*. By which Place 'tis plain, our Saviour forbids *Unchast Looks* on *Single Women*, as well as *Married*, and uses the Word in the extensive sence.

The Annotations on this Verse by *Beza* are very excellent; give me leave to cite them: *Scortator censetur coram Deo, quisquis mulierem concupiscit, ac proinde oculi continendi sunt, & membra omnia, omnesque adeo occasiones, quibus a malè agendum commovere possumus, vel maximis cum damnis sunt vitandæ*. In English thus: " He is a Whoremaster before God, who lusts after any Woman; and therefore we are to lay a Restraint on our very Eyes, and all the Parts of our Body: so that we are to avoid all Occasions by which we may be [15] moved to do Evil, as we would avoid the greatest Danger."[3]

Dr. *Hammond* tells us on this Place, That *ev'n The Incontinence of the Eye, is forbidden by our Saviour; much more is Fornication*.[4]

[1] Matthew Poole, 1624–79, *D. N. B.*

[2] Whitlocke's Latin is obviously better than his French. 'Paillard' is originally one whose only bedding was straw; the imperative should be, in the 2nd person singular, • tu ne paillarderas point".

[3] *Erasmus*, indeed, has render'd GUNH, *Uxor; Quiculque aspexerit Uxorem alterius ad concupiscendam eam, &c.* But the Annotator on the Old and New Version prefers *Mulier* to *Uxor*; *Sic Rectius (inquit) Vetus Interpres quam Erasmus, Qui Uxorem Interpretatur, &c. Neque duntaxat dictum velit Christus, adulterim etiam Oculis committi, sed aliquid amplius; Nempe omnem libidinosum, asectul cocuspicentis Mulierem, sive nuptam, sive inuptam, hoc præcepto prohibere, &c.*

[4] Henry Hammond, D. D., 1605-60 See *D. N. B.*

Our present *Learned and Excellent Archbishop of Canterbury*, in his Exposition of the Principles of the Christian Religion, Explain'd; on the Seventh Command, tells us, *That all, ev'n distant approaches to uncleanness of evry sort, are forbid by our Saviour*, in the 5th of St. *Matthew.*[1]

And the*Learned Burkitt*, on the same Text, tells us, that our Saviour, in the Explanation of the Seventh Command, not only forbids the *gross Act* of Uncleanness, and the *Carnal Lying* with a Woman, which the *Pharisees* understood was the only thing prohibited; but that he condemns *Speculative Wantonness*, no less than *Practical Uncleanness*; and forbids ont only the Outward Action, but the *Secret* Purposes and Intentions - the very first Out-goings of the Soul after Unlawful Objects.

And Dr. *Whitby*, on the Place, is of the same Opinion. [16][2]

Levit. 20.10. Now, as *Adultery*, *Incest*, and *Sodomy*, by the Levitical Law, were punished with Death; so, by the same Law, *If the Daughter of a Priest play'd the Whore*, she was to be *burnt alive.* The *Jews* were strictly forbid prostituting their Daughters, to cause them to be Whores; *lest*, says the Text, *the Land fall to Whoredom, and it become full of Wickedness.*[3] God himself was pleas'd to *destroy* no less than *four and twenty thousand of his own People* at one time by a *Plague*, for committing *Whoredom with the Daughters of Moab.*[4]

Numb. 25: 9. *Judah* commanded his Daughter-in-Law *Tamar* to be *burnt*, for playing the *Whore*, whilst she was a *Widow*: Which had been executed, had not the Fact, by Mistake, been done by *himself*; she being then *Veiled*, or in *Masquerade*, and he not seeing her Face.

It may be Objected, That the *Patriarchs* had many *Concubines*; which, in our English Language, we repute as *Whores*, for the which no Reproach, in Holy Writ, is laid on them; ev'n *Abraham himself* had *Concubines.*

Our witty *Debauchees* of this Age, that have some pretence to Learning, indulge and shelter themselves under this Example, and pretend to *justify their Practice.*

Which Matter being generally misunderstood, give me leave to explain the same: - The *Jews* had *two sorts of Wives*; the one they called *Uxores Majoris Gradus*, or, *Primary Wives*, of the Upper Form, tho whose Issue the Real Estates of the Fathers was allotted. [D 17] The other *Wives* were, *Minoris Gradus*, or *Secondary Wives*, called, by our Translation, *Concubines*; which, in truth, signifies no more than a *Bedfellow*: The Children of these Women had the Personal Estate divided amongst them. These Women were not *Whores*, not *Infamous*, nor their Children *Bastards*, but *Legitimate*;

[1] Matt. 5: 28, 32.
[2] 1638–1726. See *D. N. B.*
[3] Lev. 19: 29.
[4] Num. 25: 1.

Had they been esteemd *Whores*, their Children would have been *Bastards*, and by the *Law of God* [Deut. 23.2.]they would have been prohibited entring into the *Congregation of the Lord*, ev'n to the *Tenth Generation*, which to these Children was never done.

But thus *Infamous*, we may see, was a *Lewd Woman, and her Issue*, ev'n in that low and vey imperfect state of the *Jews*, that the Guilt of the Parents reflected a *Dishonour* to the Issue, not to be purged out in less than *Ten Generations*, which may take in some *Hundreds* of years: But yet in the *Roman* Church, a *Bastard* may be a *Prior of France*.

[Judg. 19.2.] If any of these *Concubines* played the *Whore*, they were to be put to *Death*. The *Jewish* Law look'd upon them as *Wives*, tho' of Lower Dignity than those of the Primary Sort I have mention'd. The other difference between them, was this: The *Chief* or *Primary Wives* had the *Government* of the *Family* put under them Management; this Wife was as a *Mistress*, the other as a *Servant*; yet she had *Jus Tori*, as True and Lawful Right to the Marriage-Bed, as the *Chief* Wife had, but in other respects she was a Servant. [18]

I hope I have now clear'd this Point, That *Fornication*, and *all other Acts of Uncleanness*, are equally forbid by the Seventh Command, as *Adultery*; with which I Conclude my *Second* Head, touching *Bawdy-Houses*: My Length of which, I hope you 'll excuse, and I Charge you to present all such.

My *Third* Head relates to *Play-Houses*.

III. 'Tis to be wish'd there were none in the Kingdom, because of the great Evil they do to Mankind. If the *Poets* that write for the *Play-Houses*, would but consider the *Patent* the *Players* Act by, they wou'd find, that the Ground and Foundation, the very Reason and Intention of such Permissions, are to Represent *Vice* in its proper *Odious Colours*, in Comedy; and in Tragedy; To bring off the *Injur'd, Virtuous Hero*, at last, through many amazing Scenes of Oppression and Difficulty, through infinite Hazards and Dangers, to an *Exitus of great Honour*. In a word, the *Promoting of Vertue*, and *Suppressing of Vice*, in a Theatrical Manner, was the Original Intention of *Plays*; which is more apt to work on the *Passions*, and move the *Affections*, than dry Moral Discourses generally do: Because, the *Passions* and *Affections* being well wrought on, come at last to the *Heart*, and sometimes stick there. This would be a *Noble Undertaking* in the *Poets*, and would do *infinite* [D 2-19] *Good* to the *Light Part* (which is the *greatest*) of Mankind.

But alas! instead hereof, they endeavour to Represent *the Vice of Lewdness and Debauchery* with delicious Colours, and mingled with Wit, make the *Debauchee* the *Fine Gentleman*; and laugh *Chastity* in particular, and *Vertue* in general, out of doors: which is a pleasing Jest to the *Rakes* and *Lewd Women of the Town*, (which I believe, are generally the greatest part of the *Audience*) and confirms them in their *Vices*.

But the Evil rests not here; for these Representations leave an *ill Impression* on the Minds of some *Innocent Vertuous Gentlemen and Ladies* that sometimes come there, which are not entirely effaced.

Let such *Poets* consider, and the *Actors* too, if they ever think, what Offence they give to the *Audience*; how many *Young Noblemen and Gentlemen of Fortune*, how many *Young Ladies*, may date their *Ruin* from the Time they *heard* and *saw* the *Lascivious Plays*, and from the Unclean Idea's impress'd on their Minds at *Play-Houses*, which inflamed them with Unlawful Desires, and subjected them to Ruin, the very first Opportunity that offered. For when the *Mind* is once *tainted*, the Body is soon *prostituted*.

These *Poets*, ev'n after they are dead, if their *Plays* survive them, by their *vitious Plays*, help *Satan* to ruin Mankind in this World, and utterly to destroy them in the next. [20] What Reckoning, what Accompt, will those Witty, unthinking *Poets* have to make for these great Evils, at the *Dreadful Day of Judgment*! Let them remember the *direful Wo* our Saviour pronounces against them which *give Offence*, that is, occasion Mankind to Sin.

These Plays being *contra Bonos Mores*, both the *Poets* and *Actors* are Presentable; the *Patent* they have, not warranting them herein; and the *King's Proclamation* for Suppressing of *Vice, Immorality and Profaneness*, being directly against such Doings. These *Plays* are a Nusance to the *Vertuous* part of Mankind who happen to see them, and sink the *Vitious* deeper in the Mire of Destruction.

They who Act by *Patent* or *Grant* from the Crown, as His Present Majesty's Servants, I think, fall not under the Denomination given to *Common Players of Interludes*, by 39 *Eliz.* and 12 *Annæ*, made against *Rogues and Vagabonds*, for that the *King's Servants* cann't decently be call'd such: But all other Common Players of Interludes, are, by those two Statutes, denominated *Rogues and Vagabonds*, and may be Taken up, and Punish'd as such. And I think, all Magistrates should issue out their Warrants against all *Stroling Actors* who go about the Country, defiling the Minds of all that hear them, and calling Persons off their Trade and Business. And *Constables* may Disperse such Meetings, and Take up Offenders as being an Assembly congregated without Authority, and ev'n agains Law, and bring them before [21] the Magistrate, to be *Bound over* and *Indicted* for the same.

Fourthly, My next Head is touching *Masquerades*, alias *Balls*.

IV. I cann't help repeating, That these are a *Scene of Lewdness*; a *Congress* entirely to an *Unclean End*: The *Debauchery* is There begun, and finish'd in the Neighbourhood. A Dangerous, *a very Dangerous Step* those *Vertuous Ladies* take, who out of an *Impertinent Curiosity* go There! *There*, where Women, *Lewd Women*, Dress in Mens Habits, that they may vent their *Obscenity* more freely, and that to their own *Sex*; And where Men Dress in the Female Habit to give and receive a flood of *Unclean*, and, to them, *Luscious* Conversation.

Had *Masquerades* been in Use at the Time of the *Apostles*, it would have been impossible *Christianity* could have had any Success; cou'd have gain'd any Ground, where those had been practis'd. One *Masquerade* wou'd have carry'd off more Christians from the Christian Faith and the Purity of a Christian Life, than the *Raising Ten Men from the Dead* would have kept in it.

When Mens Minds are upon the *flutter*, when Men form to themselves *ten thousand foolish Idea's* of (I know not what) Imaginary Pleasures; when their Fancies run all that way, and their Souls are ting'd, or rather, stain'd through [22] with the Images of Whimsical Raptures: our great Enemy the Devil improves these Imaginations to our Ruin and Destruction; and the Person becomes *more and more* Defiled, by Indulging to Impure Thoughts.

The Devil never had a better and surer Friend, to help forward with his *pernicious Designs*, than the Inventor of *Masquerades*, which of late Years was brought over from France, that *Godly Country*: But this Naughty Practice has lately been Discountenanced *by the Court*; And it is to be hoped, will never be Revived.

Wherefore, I shall only add this; *That Company meeting together in Numbers in the Night*, is contrary to the Laws of the Kingdom: Meeting in *Masks*, makes it more Unlawful: *Gaming* There, *adds* to the Crime: And the End of most that come There, being *Debauchery*, still makes it Worse.

Gentlemen of the Grand-Jury,

AND

You of the Constable Juries,

'Tis my *Duty*, To put you in mind of these *Offences* against the *Law*, to the End you may do Yours, in *Presenting the Offenders*, whensoever this *Naughty Practice* shall be set up again; And it will then be our Duty to Punish them, as the Law directs. [23]

Fifthly, My Last Head that I am to speak to, is, touching *Gaming-Houses*.

33 *H*. 8.c.9. *Gaming-Houses* are Prohibited by 33 *H*. 8. By that *Act*, there is a Penalty on the Person that *keeps* such House, and so there is on the Person that *uses* it: And *Dice-Tables, Card-Tables, Bowling-Allies* and *Places of Bowling*, are particularly prohibited by it; And so are *Unlawful* new Games then invented, or which should then after be invented and found out. The Penalty is Forty Shillings, *for having, keeping, or suffering any such Game* within any *such House, Garden, Alley or other Place*; And Six Shillings and Eight Pence a time for *every Person that uses such House.*

By this *Act*, every *Justice of the Peace*, and every *Mayor, Sheriff, Bayliff*, and other Head-Officer, within every *City, Town, or Borough*, may enter into all Houses and Places where such Games shall be suspected to be used; And to *Arrest and Imprison* as well the *Keepers of such Gaming-Houses*, as *the*

Persons that come to them, and to *Detain* in *Prison* both the said *Offenders*, 'till the one has given *Security*, no longer to *keep* any *such Gaming-House*, or *Place*; And the other, *no more to Play* There.

There's a Penalty in the *Act*, of *Forty Shillings a Month* on the *Magistrates* above, *for every Monthly Neglect* to Search; And a *Prohibition* on all *Artificers, Journey-Men, Husbandmen, Servants, and some others, not to Game* at [24] any of the *Games* above, in any Place whatsoever, or at any Time, but at *Christmas*, on the Penalty of Twenty Shillings.

2 & 3 *Ph.* & *M.* c. 9. By the 2 & 3 *Ph. & M.* the *Mischiefs* are recited that did arise by *Granting Licenses* to some Persons, for *keeping Houses and Places for Gaming*; and by that *Act*, all such *Licenses* are Declared *Void*.

16 *Car.* 2. c. 5. By 16 *Car.* 2. He that Wins any Money by *Fraud, or Deceit, by Cards, Dice, Tables, Cock-fighting, Horse-racing*, and *other Games* mention'd in the Act, forfeits *Treble the Value* of the *Money so fraudently Won*. It provides likewise, That whoever Loses above an Hundred Pounds at Play *upon Tick, the Winner shall have no way to Recover it* .

But the Wisest and Best Law that has been made against *Gaming*, is what I am now going to mention, and is to the *eternal Honour* of the Gentleman who fram'd it; I think it was Mr. Hungerford:

9 *Annæ* c. 14. By 9 *Annæ*, which is made to Prevent *Excessive and Deceitful Gaming*, all *Securities* given, for Money *won at Play*, or by *Betting*, are Void; And if *Land Security* is given for such, such Land shall go to the next Person that should succeed, as if the *Mortgager* were Dead.

And, by the same *Act*, it Provides, That whoever Loses *Ten Pounds* at Play, he may bring an Action, and Recover the Money so Won at Play, against the Winner, and have Costs of Suits. And if such Loser shall not bring his Action within Three Months after his Loss at [E-25] Play, *any other Person* may sue for the same, and recover it, and Treble the Value, with Costs of Suit against the Winner; where of a Moiety is to go to himself, and a Moiety to the Poor of the Parish where the Offence was committed.

So that if this *Wise Law* were but put in execution, the *Winner*, in every Case above, would be the *Loser*, and all *Sharping Gamesters* would be blown up at once.

This *Act* further Provides, That any Person that by *Fraud* or *Ill Practice* gets or wins, at one time at Play, above *Ten Pounds*, may be *Indicted*, or *Inform'd* against for it; And shall forfeit *five times* the Value, and suffer *Corporal Punishment*, as in Perjury, and be deemed *Infamous*.

By this Excellent Law, Two Justices of the Peace may cause any Suspected Person, that has no visible Estate, Profession, or Calling to support himself by, to be brought before them; And if such Person shall not make it appear, that the principal part of his Maintainance is got otherwise than by *Gaming*, they may *bind him to his good Behaviour*, with Sureties, for a Year; and if he cannot find Sureties, they may commit 'till he can. And if such Person do find Sureties, and shall afterwards, at any one time, Play, or Bett, for more than Twenty Shillings, it is a breach of his good Behaviour, and a forfeiture of his Recognizance.

And that the *Bullying Gamesters* may be Deterr'd from *Challenging* their Easy Cullies, for Non-payment of the Money won of them [26] at Play; It is further Provided, That if any Person *Assaults*, or *Challenges* another to *Fight for Money won at Play, on Conviction*, on an Indictment, or Information, for this Offence; *he forfeits all his Goods, and Personal Estate*, and is to be *Committed* to the County Jayl, *without Bail, for two Years.*

The Wit of Man could not have contrived a better Law than this, against the Mischiefs that arise by *Gaming*; unless they would have made it *Felony, without Clergy*, for any Man to *Game at all.*

But what do all these excellent Laws signify, unless there was so much *Honesty* in the Subject as to *Obey* them?

We see, by these Laws, the sense of the Nation, for about Two Hundred Years past, of the Mischiefs of *Excessive Gaming*. The *Magistrates* in this County, to their *eternal Honour*, have not been wanting, on their parts, to put the Laws in execution.

But if the *Government* make ever so many Laws, That *Felo de se*, that is *Sanæ Memoriæ*, shall forfeit his Goods and Estate, so that he makes his Posterity Beggars; yet if such a One will shoot himself through the Head, who can help it? *Gentlemen and Ladies, and ev'n Men in Trade, Shopkeepers, will Game publickly, and that for Excessive Sums, in spite of all Laws.*

I am inform'd, That at *Richmond*, a Trader sets an Hundred Guineas a Main, and makes nothing to Lose Five Hundred Guinea's at a Night's sitting. [27]

There is a strange *Spirit of Gaming* run through the whole World: We hear of the Excess of it in *France*, in *Spain*, in the *West* and *East Indies*: I am told, that the Super-Cargo's that Trade from *India* to *China*, will play there, at one sitting, the very Cloaths off their Backs. Where will this end, God only knows.

The Sin is great; for the vast Sums so Lost at Play, ought, in some proportion, to be employ'd in Charitable Uses. God has not given any Man many Thousands, to be thrown away in *Gaming*. But besides, such Men Beggar their Families thereby; and he that does so, *Holy Writ* tells us, *is worse than an Infidel.* [1]

'Tis to be hoped, our Afflictions, in time, will make us Wise and Considerative, to the *Amendment of our Lives*, and thereby to obtain the Almighty's Favour: For the Method of *God's Governing the Moral World*, is this; His *Majesty* first would draw a Nation to *Himself*, and to give Obedience to *his Laws*, (wherein its own Happiness consists) by the *soft, gracious, and Beneficient Acts of Bounty and Goodness* to it; which should prevail,

[1] 1 Tim. 5: 8.

and has in truth a Natural Tendency to work on all good Dispositions, Not to Displease *that Being* who is so Kind to Us; but to do every thing that a People can think will be most acceptable to *his* Goodness.

But if this Method of *Gentleness and Tenderness*, of *Bounty and Munificence*, by a *Gracious God* to a Nation, will not prevail; then *God* takes what his *Goodness* calls, *his strange Work*, [28] in hand, (as being foreign to his Mind to afflict his Creatures) and tries to reduce that People, by Methods of Vindictive Justice, *whom Goodness had no Power over, to perswade.*

Gentlemen,

I shall not Recapitulate what I have said to you; but am throughly perswaded That if You, and the other *Grand Juries of the Nation*, would do their Duties in Presenting *Disorderly Houses, Bawdy-Houses, Play-Houses*, that Act not by *Grant of the Crown*, (of which, I think there is but one, and that too much) *Masquerades*, and *Gaming-Houses*, where the Seeds of Iniquity are plentifully sown; which being Presented, will be suppress'd: Then the Nation will be, at least, *negatively Vertuous*, which is one good step towards being *positively so.*

I shall trouble you no further, but leave what I have said to your Consideration, and hope God will guide you in doing your Duty: Which if you shall neglect to do, as most of you have hitherto, I shall, however, have *deliver'd my own Soul.*

But such Neglect will be severely Answer'd for at the Last Day; which tho' Men in Health may think is far off, yet to every Man, at the *approach of Death*, that has led an *Ill Life*, will be thought too near at hand.

FINIS.

A CHARGE Given to the GRAND-JURY Of the COUNTY OF *GLOUCESTER*, AT THE Midsummer-Sessions, 1723. By **Sir RICHARD COCKS**, Bart The Second Edition.

LONDON, Printed for John *and* Barham Clark, *at the* Bible *and* Crown *in the* Poultry, *near* Cheapside. M.DCC.XXIII. (Price 4*d.*)

[A 2 -p. 3]
SIR RICHARD COCKS
HIS
CHARGE, &c.

Gentlemen,

The great Infirmities of my Body forced me for some Years last past to decline all Publick Business: and tho' I am now very little better, nor indeed will my Age give me leave to expect much Amendment; yet the Desires, or rather the Commands of the Gentlemen and Freeholders, to whom I am so much in-[4] debted, are of more force than, and superiour to, my own Inclinations, and just Excuses. I am therefore once more come amongst you, and I cannot but think it probable, that in this Juncture of Affairs, you will expect and require from me some account of our present Circumstances. Give me leave therefore to look a little back: And from that Reflection I must observe to you, that out of Gratitude as well as Duty, we ought to be the most sober and religious People in the World; for there is no Nation under Heaven, that can shew so many signal, wonderful, and miraculous Preservations from the visible and immediate Hand of Providence.

Some of you remember the first landing of King *William,* and the disarming of King *James*, and his Flight, I may say, without Bloodshed, or Devastation, and the seasonable Deliverance from Popery and Slavery, two very dear and inseparable Companions; and after that, you cannot forget the Attempts and Conspiracies form'd against the Life of that Instrument of Heaven, nor their ruinous [5] and destructive Schemes to the Protestant Interest in Queen *Anne*'s time; and the Invasions since his Majesty's Accession to the Throne, are fresh in every one's Memory. From all these, God has in a wonderful manner preserved us: But neither these Miracles, nor Time, their Oaths, nor the King's Clemency, nor any Tie, Gratitude, or Obligation, can extirpate the Malice, or extinguish the Ambition of a restless Party amongst us, who cloak all their Villanies, under the Pretence of Religion, and a feigned Zeal to restore the Injured and Oppressed to their Right.[1] They have therefore, in despight of all that is sacred amongst Mankind, in violation of their Oaths, notwithstanding all the Discouragements and Disappointments they have met with, endeavoured to destroy the present Protestant Possessor of the Throne, and his Royal Family, and to set up in his and their places, a bigotted Popish Pretender. They have in the most solemn manner sworn to support and defend the Protestant, and they have in as solemn a manner renounced and abjured the Papist: But to palliate these Matters, and to excuse these [6] unheard of Villanies, as I before observ'd, they pretend a Concern for the Church, and a Zeal to restore an Injured Prince to his Right. The honest Heathens accommodated their Conveniences to their Oaths; these Men violate their Oaths, I will not say to serve their Conveniences, but what is very far from it, to ruin both Us and themselves. If Oaths shall once be esteemed insignificant, what must become of Property, and even in Civil Contests, what can be relied on as Evidence to determine our Rights? What Obligation can Art or Invention imagine, or find out, to supply the Place of Oaths? What Security can a Prince possibly have from his Subjects for their Allegiance, or what Assurance can the Subjects ever have from their Princes, of their good Government and Protection, if Oaths may be dispensed with at the pleasure of the Taker[2]? There can be no Confidence, no Assurance possibly given on either side, but the World must be filled with Mistrusts, Bloodshed, and Ruin. Farewel mutual Peace, Sincerity, and Tranquillity! [7] As to the Obligation due to Princes, from the Scripture, and the Judgments pronounced against the Blasphemers of God's Holy Name; which must in the highest degree attend Perjury; I will leave those things to the Clergy to instruct you in. For tho' there has been one of the Highest Order guilty of that Abomination, and I fear more than one of the Inferiour; yet I hope and believe, that there are many good Men of that Order, that have not bowed their Knees to *Baal*, and that they will therefore the more earnestly inculcate into you this so necessary a Duty of religiously observing Oaths.

I told you that these Violaters of Oaths amused themselves, and endeavoured to seduce others, and became bewildred by an *Ignis Fatuus*, by a foolish Notion of a Right in the Pretender: What Right, what Pretence of any Right can there be? Every one that knows anything of our Excellent Constitution, knows that long before these Days, it was highly Criminal to say, That the Parliament could not dispose of [8] the Crown: And I pray you now, let us consider and examine King *George*'s

[1] This speech is an evident condemnation of Jacobite attempts against George I.

[2] The problem of oath-taking was an important one, since one person on his oath could charge anybody with a crime or felony, and bear (false) witness in a trial.

Title; and if we find it a good one, we may fairly conclude, no other Person can have any. Did he come to the Throne by Force, Bribery, or by artful Sollicitation, or by your voluntarily Invitation, by Act of Parliament made upon the justest and most justifiable Reasons imaginable, for the easy, happy, and Good Government, of the present Generation, and of future Posterity, for the End and true Design of Government itself? People were not made for the Service and Pleasure of their Governours; but the very End and Design of Governours and Government, was for the Advantage and Security of the People.[1]

The Wise and Great Prince that then filled the Throne, Good as well as Wise and Great, and his judicious Council, met in Parliament; and perceiving and foreseeing the Misfortunes that were like to befall the Nation upon the Death of the duke of *Gloucester*, who was the last Protestant Prince on whom the [B-9] Crown was intail'd;[2] and having learned by so late an Example the Miseries that must unavoidably overwhelm the then flourishing Nation, if a Papist should ever be again placed on the Throne: To prevent those Absurdities, those just Fears and dismal Views, they settled the Succession to the Crown not upon the Lineal Heir, that might or should be a Protestant; for that might, and probably would, have bred vast Confusion and Disorder, and would not have answered the Ends of securing the Peace and Tranquillity of the Kingdom: For what Papist could not have been dispensed with by the politick and irreligious Church of *Rome*, in order to have capacitated him to have taken possession of the *British* Throne, to have served their wicked Purposes? There was therefore in the second Entail no incapacitating Clause, to bar the Right of any other Papist, but the Pretender's empty Claim: and that not because was any Right in it, or any Pretence or Colour of Right, but because then some Princes (Enemies to our Religion and Nation) the better to colour their Ma-[10] lice and Ill-will towards us, and to seduce the turbulent Spirits amongst us, and the more to encourage those whom that horrid Religion of Popery had forced on all occasions to disturb our publick Peace, endeavoured to make the World believe that they assisted the Pretender, and espoused his Quarrel, only to recover a Right inherent in him. To remove all Difficulties therefore out of the Minds of rational Men, not bigotted by Popery, or distracted by Poverty; or blinded with vain imaginary Hopes of Places and Preferments from the Ruins of the Publick; which Ambitions and vain imaginary Hopes too much influence many, for which we suffer: To remove all Difficulties, all Uneasinesses out of the Minds of honest and rational Men, this absolute, supreme, governing Power renounced and abjured the Pretender, and set a Price upon his

[1] This will be found like a leit-motiv all through the XVIIth century and later on again.
[2] The Duke of Gloucester, the latest surviving child of Queen Anne, died July 1700.

Head, to reward any that would destroy him, or take him alive, in order to have him receive condign Punishment for his impudent and impertinent Pretences: And this Dictatorial Power then settled the Reversion of the Crown on a [B 2-11] remoter Branch of the Royal Family, that had long been, and were then Protestants. They did not leave the Succession at random, but settled it upon deep and wise Thought, upon mature and deliberate Consultation, upon Foresight, not Compliment; that is, upon the true Rules, and Foundation of Governement, so long as probably they should be capable of well-governing the People: that is, so long as those of that Family should be Protestant Princes, they should by an Hereditary Right succeed one the other.

These are the *Pacta Conventa* founded upon the best Reason, agreeable to the very fundamental Rules of Government between the People of *Great Britain,* and the*Hannoverian* Family: To this Settlement we swore in Queen *Anne*'s time, and have done the same very often since. This Settlement appeared so just and reasonable, that at the General Peace[1] those that were the Pretender's Friends, and the Popish Princes and Potentates, as well as Protestants, swore to support it or to be Guarantees [12] for it. What Prince in the World has a better Title than King *George*, or what Pretender a worse Title than the Chevalier of St *George*? Of which I could tell you more, were it worth time, or any way necessary.

To set all this in a clear Light suitable to your Capacities, let me ask you this Question; If any Neighbour of yours should tell you that he had an honest good Landlord, and a good Bargain, but that a meddling Fellow had told somebody that his Landlord had no good Title to the Estate he had lett him, but that the Right was vested in one unknown to him; that he had the Character of being a very hard cruel Man that would ruin his Tenants; and if this Neighbour should tell you, that because this Busy Body had told somebody that his kind honest Landlord had not a good Title, and because he could not rent that Estate of the cruel hard Landlord, he resolved to leave his good Bargain, and his good Landlord: Would you take this nice conscientious Man to be very wise? And if you please to consider of it, this [13] will appear to be the very Case of all our Protestant Discontents: I think all we ought to aim at, is to be well governed; and then if that happens, I am sure, for my part, I will neither at present, or hereafter, ever be troublesomely inquisitive, about my Prince's Title. I never had any particular Favour, more than an Opportunity of spending my own Money in the publick Business, from any Prince; I never so much as saw King *George*, or any of the Royal Family, nor the Prentender, or his Progeny: I have, it is true, sworn to

[1] The general peace: that of Utrecht, signed in April 1713. Anne was recognised ipso facto as Queen of Great-Britain, whereas in 1701 Louis XIV had violated his former promise in recognising the son of James II as James III.

King *George*, and abjured the Pretender; but if it were possible for me to believe, that King *George* and his Family were Papists, and the Pretender and his Family were Protestants, I believe I should be sooner for the Pretender, than for King *George*; and this I may lawfully say, for all my Oaths. For a Papist is, as I have demonstrated to you before, uncapable of inheriting or possessing the Throne by our Laws, made upon the truest Reason and consummate Wisdom of the Nation. [14]

Had I lived in the Times of *York* and *Lancaster*, I believe I should have been a Neuter[1]; our Laws, and Liberties, and Religion, were no ways concerned in this Quarrel; which-ever Side prevailed, they remained unshaken, and equally secure. In our modern Contests, Men generally mistake the Question; when they say, such a one is for King *George*, and such a one is for the Pretender, the true State of the Case is, Whether Men are for or against themselves? And to speak plainly, I am for myself, and for that reason I am chiefly for the present Establishment. Those that are Protestants, if they are for King *George*, are for themselves; if they are for the Pretender, they are against themselves, tho it may be there are some Men that do not look so far. If a private Man should prove lunatick, if he were Master of a Family, the Law would appoint him a Guardian, and not leave his Family and Estate to be managed by his Care, who was uncapable of taking care of either: If the eldest Son, on whom the Estate and Honour was intailed, [15] should lose his Senses, the Father, in order to preserve the Honour an Estate in his Family, would procure an Act of Parliament to disinherit him, which is visible in the late Act passed for the Service of my Lord *Digby* and his Family; in which Case, had we time, I could tell you some Things worth your Observation: But this I will take notice of to you, that we ought most certainly to be more concerned for the Prosperity and Welfare of the People of these united Kingdoms, than for any private Family, tho' the greatest in the Kingdom. To exemplify this; Was a King mad, would you let him go at large, to kill whom he pleased, and to commit any Outrage his Frenzy and Wild Fancy suggested to him? And how much sooner ought you to tie the Hands of a Papist, were he King, and to exclude those from the Hopes of Succession to the Crown, that were bred up with those ruinous and destructive Principles to a Protestant People, which they call Religion, obliging them to keep no Faith with Hereticks, nor observe any Oaths made to them, but to extirpate them [16] and their Religion, Root, and Branch[2]? All which is proved too evidently, not only by their Books and Tenets, but by their Practices and Attempts, too many to enumerate. There are some Wise Men in their

[1] The Wars of the Roses.

[2] A possible allusion to the Root and Branch Petition of 11 December 1640, against episcopacy.

own Opinions, who are pleased to tell us, That a Popish Prince may be safely trusted with the Charge of a Protestant People: But these Men do rather want a Keeper to look after them, than an Argument to convince them.

The Disturbers of the Peace of the Protestant Establishment, make a great Outcry against the Governement, on account of the many unfortunate Sufferers by the *South-Sea* Scheme[1]: And what is more in this than mere Calumny? Did the Government force them to engage in that unhappy Project, or their own Covetousness and Pride? And what has the Government to answer for that? Is the Government to be blamed for our irregular and unaccountable Passions? [C-17]

Gentlemen,

Could we but look into the Secrets of these Men that would, and do delude us, under a colour of Zeal for Right and Religion; we should then find all their Aims and Intentions to be only a strong Desire to set the World in an uproar, out of hopes, that in the scramble they may possibly get something to gratify their Ambition, or to supply their Necessities? You may depend upon it, that those Men who value no Oaths, have no Religion; and yet, as I observed before, they seduce others, sometimes by their pretended Concern for the Danger of the Church, sometimes by a pretended Zeal for Right. Would they but speak plainly, and tell us the Truth, which is this; That if they could breed Discord amongst us, and by the help of our Follies, and their own Arts, they could set the Pretender on the Throne, that then they expected to share and divide amongst themselves, all the Places of Honour and Trust in the Kingdom: Would they discover this visible [18] Matter of Fact to you, and tell you in intelligible Words, that they desired your Assistance to bring in Popery, and to change our admirable Constitution, only to make them great and rich, in my Conscience you would sooner consent to hang them, than to give them an Helping-hand for such a purpose. And this seems to be an irresistible Truth past all Contradiction; for we have seen the most Distinguished, because the worst Opposer of our Peace and happy Establishment, change his Side intirely, the first Opportunity he had of changing his vain imaginary Hopes for certain Honours and Advantages. I give these Instances, not only to convince you that the sole Prospect of these uneasy religious Deluders is no more in reality but a strong Intention to advance themselves; which if they can by any means accomplish, they will then leave their blind deluded Followers and Party to shift for themselves: But I mean from these Instances to persuade all those that have been [19] deluded, to forsake such worthless and dangerous Leaders, and to throw themselves into the Arms of a

[1] The unfortunate and famous South-Sea Bubble, in 1720.

merciful and gracious Prince, whose Favours to such branded Offenders may give them sufficient Assurance, that those who have only been deluded, need never fear Forgiveness, but may expect any Favour they can in reason desire. Had I Time and Leisure, I would expose all their Cheats and Artifices to your View.

They tell us, and I think deservedly, that if there was a Plot and Conspiracy, why were not more of the detected Criminals executed? If there was no Plot, why were so many confined and punished? As for the Plot, I believe all the Particulars I mentioned are so plain and visible, that no one will deny them, but those that are acquaintanced with them; and why they have not been punished according to their Merit, is to me unaccountable: but this I dare affirm, that they who receive Advantages to themselves or Friends from Cle-[20] mency, have very small reason to make Reflections on it: But this is like the Party.

Gentlemen,

You have heard the Proclamation against Vice and Immorality read, and you find by it, that I am obliged to inforce it to you: You all remember the Book that tells us, *Because Judgement is not speedily executed, therefore do the Sons of Men give themselves over to work Wickedness.*[1] The old Heathens observed, that so long as they lived virtuously, according to the Rules of Reason and Religion, every thing they undertook went well with them, and succeeded at home and abroad; but when they gave themselves up to Luxury and Debauchery, and neglected their religious Duties, every thing went contrary; they became poor at home, and contemptible every where; they were divided in their Opinions, subject to the Insults of pitiful Enemies, and molested with intestine Discords and Civil Wars. [21]

Consider with yourselves, amongst your own Acquaintance, and you will easily perceive, that those Families who live in the Fear of God, live in his Favour, in Health, Prosperity, and Plenty; when the Dissolute and Immoral not only beggar their Estates, and become necessitous, but often shorten their Days, and come to untimely Ends, the just Reward of their Wickedness and Follies. A Kingdom is but one great Family, composed of many little ones, and it fares with the great united one, as it does with every divided single one: Dominion and Power are translated and conveyed from the Vicious and Wicked, to the Virtuous and More Good. From whence proceed our Perjuries and Conspiracies, but from the Contempt of God, and the Neglect of Religion? Would you live in Peace and Plenty at Home, would you become great and esteemed Abroad, I may say these great Blessings are in your own reach and power, there is no more to do, than to become a sober and reli-[22]

[1] The quotation is not accurate; Eccles. 8:11.

gious People; and in order to accomplish so great an End, and to perform so necessary a Work, we must punish Vice, and discountenance Immoralities. Punishments and Fear of Penalties make Men considerative, and Consideration makes Men wise, and Wisdom makes Men religious. I can't part with you, without putting you in Mind of the particular Obligation that is incumbent on Us and You, to be very circumspect in our Lives and Conversations, for these Reasons: for with what Assurance can a debauched immoral Justice recommend Virtue and Piety to you? And with what Confidence can a profane Juryman present those Irregularities, which, it may be, his own unthinking Self, by his ill Example, has occasioned. Let us at last grow wise; let us become a sober and religious People; let us leave off Faction, and let us unite for our common Safety and Preservation: "Let there be no other Distinction heard of amongst us, but of those that are for a *Protestant Prince, and the pre-*[23] *sent Establishment*: and of those that are for *a Popish Prince*, and *a* French *Government*." These were some of the last Words King *William*, of Glorious Memory, spoke to us; and with these I chuse to conclude, hoping that, for his sake, they will make the more lasting and deeper Impression on you.

FINIS.

THE **CHARGE** TO THE **GRAND-JURY** of the **CITY and LIBERTY** of ***WESTMINSTER***

At the General Quarter-Session of the Peace, held in *Westminster-Hall*, *October* 6. 1725.
By SAMUEL RYDER *Esq*, Printed for J. ROBERTS, near the *Oxford-Arms* in *Warwick-Lane*. M.DCC.XXVI.
(Price Six Pence.)

[A 3 - 5]

Gentlemen of the Grand Enquest,

THE short notice I had of the Honour designed me on this Occasion, together with the Misfortune of a Mind weakened and impaired by a long Infirmity of Body, might in reason have excused me from the Task I am now undertaking: But when I consider the Oath ye have taken, to present all such Matters as shall be given ye in Charge; it seems to me to imply an Obligation on the Court to give ye matters in Charge: and therefore I shall endeavour to [6] acquit my self of that Duty in the best manner that, under such disadvantages, I am able: And that ye may the better retain what I deliver, will (by way of Method) reduced the Matters which I shall recommend to your Enquiry, to three heads.

I. *Such Offences as concern GOD, and his holy Religion established amongst us.*

II. *The* KING. And, lastly,

III. *Our Neighbour, or Fellow-Subject.*

I. For the First, The time would fail me to enumerate particularly the various Methods by which God, and his holy Religion, are dishonoured in these our days. The Proclamation just now read, has in a pious and lively manner, laid the principal grievances of this sort before ye, and thereby rendred unnecessary any Observations of mine. [7]

Let it suffice at present, that I mention such Offences, as abounding in this Liberty, and tending in their natures, universally to corrupt the Manners of the Inhabitants, are the great Causes of the Decay of Piety amongst us, and require our united and most serious endeavours to suppress. These are keeping of Gaming-Houses, Bawdy-Houses, (such as experience teaches us differ from them in Name only) Retailing Strong-Water Shops, and the printing and publishing of Books and Pamphlets of an obscene and immoral tendency.

When we consider how many unfortunate Persons, who might otherwise have lived comfortably in their Families, are driven by haunting Gaming-Houses to Necessity, and put thereby on repairing their broken Fortunes, by the most capital violations of their Neighbour's Proper-[8] ty, and how they are concealed there from the publick Justice, while those Spoils enable them to ruin others as unwary as themselves, and thus live on a perpetual Round of Rapine and Fraud. How many on the other hand, of mean Originals, have in a few Years raised uncommon Fortunes upon the Ruin of their Betters. How they are form'd into regular Societies and are so hardy as to presume to defend their Settlements even with Force.

How many Men taken out of Bawdy-Houses appear here at every Session upon Recognizances taken for their good Behaviour; and how many detestable Prostitutes, found with them, appear by the Calendar of the House of Correction, to have received there the Reward of their Misdoings. When we reflect, [B - 9]

How that Degree of People especially on whose Labour and Industry the Support of the Community principally depends, are disabled by the immoderate use of strong Liquors to serve either themselves or their Country; and render themselves an insupportable Burden to the Parishes to which they belong: together with the execrable Cursing and Swearing, and odious Drunkenness that abounds in all those Places respectively.

When we find in Shops, *A Defence of publick Stews*, *The publick Benefits of private Vices*,[1] with a multitude of others too gross in their Titles for modest Ears to hear mentioned, exposed to view in the most publick manner, it must needs shock every good Christian to consider what must be the unavoidable Consequence of such glaring Impiety. I exhort and charge ye, [10] therefore, as Christians, for God's sake, diligently to enquire, and true Presentment make of all such Offenders; and as *English* Men for your Country's sake; for it is undoubtedly true, that *Righteousness exalteth a Nation, but Sin is a Reproach to any People*, Prov. xiv. 34.

Gentlemen,

The established Religion of our Country, in particular, is fenced against its implacable Enemies the Papists, by the following among other wholesome Laws: All such as extol the Pope's Power a second time (5 *Eliz.*I) Put in ure Popish Bulls, (13 *Eliz.* 2. sect.2, 3.) Refuse a second Tender of the Oaths, (5 *Eliz.* I. sect. 11.) Pervert, or are perverted to Popery, (23 *Eliz.*1) Receive Popish Orders or Education, (27 *Eliz.* 2 sect. 3.) Are guilty of High-Treason. All such as make use of Papal-Bulls to disturb such [B 2- 11] Presentations as others ought to make (25 *Eliz.* 3. Sta. 6. sect. 4) Pursue, or cause to be pursued, in the Court of *Rome*, any

[1] Two books by Bernard Mandeville, the former published 1724, the latter, Part I, 1714.

Processess, or Instruments, or bring, receive, notify or execute them, (*Statutes of Provisors*, and 16 *R*. 2. 5.) Appeal to *Rome* from any of the King's Courts, (24 *H*. 8. 12 and 25 *H*. 8. 19) Exercise the Jurisdiction of a Suffragan without the Appointment of the Bishop of the Diocese, (26. *H*.8. 14) Refuse to elect or consecrate the Person nominated by the King to a Bishoprick, (25 *H*. 8. 28) Maintain the *Pope*'s Power the first time, (5 *Eliz*. 1) Bring in *Agnus Dei* 's, or such like superstitious things, (13 *Eliz*. 2) Contribute to the Maintenance of a Popish Seminary, (27 *Eliz*. 2) Refuse the Oaths, (13 & 14 W.III. 6 and 1. G. 13.) are guilty of a *Præmunire*: And all are presentable by ye; as are those who relieve a Popish [12] Priest knowingly, being Felons by Law (27 *Eliz*.2) The unparallel'd Cruelty of these Bigots towards our innocent Brethren in the North, and the wicked Obstinacy most of them persist in to hazard their Lives, and all that thro' a misguided Zeal they account dear to them, rather than give Satisfaction to the Injured, (tho' outwardly they profess Christianity) shows how little they are endued with that *Wisdom from above, which is first pure, then peaceable, gentle, and easy to be entreated, full of Mercy, and good Fruits*, Jam. iii. 17. And must kindle in the Breast of every true *Briton* a Zeal for the Security of his faith, by enforcing as much as in him lies, the Execution of Laws made against those who esteem it damnable, and watch all Opportunities to root it out of the World. But above all, under God our Religion is secured by the Settlement of the Crown upon his present Majesty [13] and his Royal Family: A King in reality as well as title, A *Defender of our Faith*, strengthened with a numerous Issue, (and may they still increase!) the solid Foundation of our present and future Happiness. Blessed be the glorious and immortal Memory of the Prince who left us this invaluable Legacy! And be it our Care to secure the Benefits of it to our latest Posterity. Which, (after pressing ye particularly to present all such as maliciously, advisedly, and directly, by writing or printing, maintain and affirm, That the Pretender hath any Right or Title to the Crown, or any other Person, otherwise than according to the Protestant Settlement; or that the Kings and Queens of this Realm are not able, by and with the Authority of Parliament, to make Laws of sufficient Force to bind the Descent of the Crown; who are, by Law, Traitors: And also all such [14] as are guilty of a *Præmunire* by maliciously and directly affirming the same by preaching, teaching, or advised speaking (6 *Ann*. cap. 7) naturally leads me to consider such Offences as concern,

II. The KING. And under this head ye are to enquire of Treason against him, by compassing, or imagining his Death, the Death of his eldest Son and Heir, levying War against him; adhering to his Enemies, giving them Aid or Comfort in the Realm, or elsewhere; counterfeiting his Great or Privy Seal; counterfeiting his Money, or bringing false into the Realm; slaying his Chancellor, Treasurer, Justices of the one *Bench* or the other, Justices in *Eyre* or of *Assize*, and all Justices assigned to hear and determine, being in their Places, doing their Offices, (25 *E* . 3. Stat. 5 cap. 2) [15]

All Felonies against him by debasing his Coin, (8 & 9 *W.* 3. c. 26) Unlawfully diminishing it, (6 & 7 *W.* 3. 17) Attempting to kill, assault, strike or wound any Privy Counsellor in the execution of his Office, (9 *Ann.* 16.) Passing beyond Sea to serve a foreign Prince, (3 *Jac.* 4) Embezelling his Armour, (31 *Eliz.* 4) Stealing his Naval Stores, (22 *Car.* 2.5.) Counterfeiting his Stamps, or uttering, vending, or selling any Vellum, Parchment, or Paper with counterfeit Marks, knowing them to be so, (9 & 10 *W.* 3. 25.) or privately and fraudulently using any Stamps to defraud him of his Duties, (10 *Ann.* 19, 26. 12 *Ann.* 9, 19.)

All Misprisions of Treason, which consist in the bare knowledge and concealment of High Treason, (2 & 3 *Mar.* 10) And such an Offence the forging foreign Coin not current [16] here is declared to be, (14 *Eliz.* 3.)

All Contempts against his Courts of Justice, by striking therein, rescuing a Prisoner from them, making an affray near them, disturbing them by threatning, or reproachful Words to any Judge sitting in them; reflecting on the Justice, or Honour of them; injuriously treating those Persons who are under the more immediate Protection of them.

All Contempts against his Prerogative, by refusing to assist him for the Good of the Publick; preferring the Interests of a foreign Prince, or disobeying his Majesty's lawful Commands, or Prohibitions.

All Contempts against his Person, or Government. To enumerate particulars under this last head, were as endless as I hope it is at this time [C-17] unnecessary; when we have on the Throne a Prince adorned with all the Characters even of a fine Gentleman; whose religious Regard to his Royal Promise, often given us, to preserve our Constitution both in Church and State, and his unbounded Clemency towards such of his Enemies as have given Signs of their Repentance, entitle him to be the Love of a Loyal and Obedient People, as he is the Care of Heaven; if any Argument for such a Thought can be drawn from the visible interposition of Providence, to protect him from all his open, and secret Enemies. In his Reign, our Rights, Religious and Civil, are secured by the free and uninterrupted Course of Laws (made by Representatives of our own chusing) in our Courts of Justice: At the head of them, a Noble Lord sworn truly to Counsel the King, whose [18] consummate Knowledge in, and remarkably impartial Administration of those Laws, had long since advanced him in the Wishes of all People, (however in other things they might differ in Opinion) to that high Station which at present he adorns. If these are Causes of Discontent, let such as think them so, depart, or be sent, to Governments more agreeable; while we at home, *Fear God, honour the King; and meddle not with them that are given to change* . Prov. xxiv. 21. 1 Pet. ii. 17.

III. I come in the last Place to charge ye with such Offences as concern your Neighbour, or Fellow-Subject. Of these, some are Capital; as,

1. Such as are committed against his Life, without Malice, as Man-[C 2-19] slaughter, or killing upon a sudden Quarrel; or sometimes Chance-Medley, as doing a lawful Act without an intent to hurt, and Death ensues. With Malice, as Murder; and Petit-Treason, where a Servant kills his Master or Mistress, a Wife her Husband, or an Ecclesiastical Man his Prelate.

2. Such as concern his Goods; as Grand Larceny, or a felonious and fraudulent taking and carrying away, not from his person, nor out of his House, above the value of twelve Pence. Petit Larceny, if of or under that Value. If any Person take away with an intent to steal any Goods to the value of forty Shillings, which they are to use in their Lodgings, this is Felony, (3 & 4 *W. & M.* 9) As it is if a Servant of the Age of Eighteen Years, and not an Apprentice, withdraw himself with Goods of his Master or Mistress, [20] to the intent to steal the same, or without their assent or commandment, imbezil their Goods with the same intent to the value of forty Shillings, (21 *H.* 8. 7.) Robbery, or a felonious and violent taking from his Person, putting him in fear. Larceny from his Person without putting him in fear, either privily, by picking his Pocket, or cutting his Purse, (8 *Eliz.* 4.) or openly; Horse stealing, (2 & 3 *E.* 6. 3.) Stealing out of his Shop, Coach-House, or Stable, to the value of five Shillings, (10 &11 *W.* 3. 23.) Stealing to the value of forty Shillings or more, out of a Dwelling-House, (12 *Ann.* cap. 7) All Buyers or Receivers of stolen Goods, knowing them to be stolen, (3 & 4 *W. & M..* 9.) Counterfeiting Bank Notes, (8 & 9 *W.* 3. 20) Exchequer Bills, (7 & 8 *W.* 3. 31. - 8 & 9 *W.* 3. 24. - 5 *Ann.* 13. 7 *Ann.* 7 9 *Ann.* 7. I *Geo* 12.) South-Sea Bonds, (9 *Ann.* 21,) or Lottery Orders, (12 *Ann.* 2.)

3. Such as concern his Habitation, as Burglary, or breaking and entering the Mansion-house of an other in the Night-time, to the intent to commit some Felony within the same, whether the felonious Intent be executed or not. Arson, which consists in maliciously and wilfully burning the House of another by day or night.

Ye are likewise to present Offences against Women, as Rapes, forcibly marrying of Women of substance against their Will, (3 *H.* 7. 2.) All Persons who being married, do marry any Person or Persons, the former Husband or Wife being alive, (1 *Jac.* 11.) All such as on purpose, and of Malice fore-thought, [22] and by lying in wait, unlawfully cut out, or disable the Tongue, put out an Eye, slit the Nose, cut off a Nose, or cut off and disable any Limb, with an intent to disfigure any Person, (22 & 23 *Car.* 2. 1.)

Of Offences not Capital presentable likewise by ye, there are great Numbers; such as Misprisions of Felony, which is a concealment or procuring the concealment thereof, (3 *E.* 1. 9. 3 *H.* 7. 1.) Theft-bote, where one not only knows of a Felony, but takes his Goods again, or other amends not to prosecute. All Assaults and Batteries, Affrays, forcible Entries and Detainers, (5 *R.* 2.7. -15 *R.* 2.2. -8 *H.* 6.9. -31 *Eliz.* 11 -21 *Jac.*1. 15.) Riots, Routs, unlawful Assemblies, (34 *E.* 3.1. -17 *R.* 2.8. -13 *H.* 4. 7. -19 *H.* 7.13.) Neglect or Breach of Duty in Officers, Bribery, [23] (12 *R.* 2.2. -4 *H.* 5. -5 & 6 *E.* 6. 16) Extortion, (3 E. 1. 26.) tho' disguised under the plausible Name of Charity for poor House-keepers, or any other Name. Perjury and Subornation thereof, (5 *Eliz.* 9) Forgery, (5 *Eliz.* 14.) Cheats, (33 *H.*8 1.) Conspiracies, Libels, common Nusances in the High-ways, (13 *E.* 1. 5 - 5 *Eliz.* 13.- 18 *Eliz.* 10.- 2 & 3 *Ph. & M.* 8.- 22 *Car.* 2. 12. - 3 & 4 *W. & M.* 12- 7 & 8 *W.* 3. 29.- 8 & 9 *W.* 3. 15.- 6 *Ann.* 29.- 9 *Ann.* 18. -1 *Geo.* 11) by doing any Act to render them less commodious to the King's People; in Bridges, by suffering them to be out of repair; in Publick-houses, (12 *E.* 2.6. - 6 *R.* 2.9.- 3 *H.* 8.8.- 5 & 6 *E.* 6. 25- 1 *Jac.* 1.9. - 4 *Jac.* 1. 15.- 21 *Jac.* 1.7, 21.-1 *Car.* 1. 4. - 3 *Car.* 1.3.) by usually harbouring Thieves, or Persons of scandalous Reputation, or suffering Disorders therein; setting up a [24] new one where there is no need, or in a Place otherwise unfit in respect of its situation. Monopolies, (21*Jac.* 1.3.- 16 *Car.* 1. 21.) Forestalling, Ingrossing, and Regrating, (5 & 6 *E.* 6. 14.) False Weights and Measures,(9 *H.* 3.25.-51 *H.* 3.Stat. 6.- 31 *E.* 1.-14 *E.* 3.12.- 25 *E.* 3. Stat.5.9.- 27 *E.* 3.10.- 13 *R.* 2.9.- 15 *R.* 2.4.- 16 *R.* 2.3.- 1 *H.* 5. 10.- 2 *H.*6. 11.- 8 *H.* 6.5.- 11 *H.* 6.8.- 7 *H.* 7.4.- 12 *H.* 7.5.- 22 *Car* 2.8.- 11 & 12 *W.* 3.15.) Barratry, Usury, (12 *Ann.* 16.) Maintenance, (1. *E.* 3.14-20 *E.* 3.4.- 1 *R.* 2. 4.) or the upholding of Quarrels or Sides, either in the Country, or in Courts of Justice, by maintaining one Side to have part of the thing in suit, which is called Champerty, (3 *E.* 1. 25.- 13 *E.* 1.49.- 28 *E.* 1. 11.) or labouring the Jury, which is called Embracery, (5 *E.* 3.10.- 34 *E.* 3. 8.- 38 *E.* 3.12.) [D - 25] Lastly, buying or selling pretended Titles, (1. *R* .2.9.- 32 *H.*.8. 9.) And every other Offence omitted by me, which your Experience can suggest to ye.

Gentlemen,

Having thus mentioned to ye in general, the Offences which ye are to enquire of, and present, I forbear an exact Disquisition of the particular Acts which may make any Persons guilty of any of them; both because it is scarce possible that your Memories should retain them sufficiently to be of any use to ye in your Enquiries, and because Precedents allow ye the liberty of desiring the Assistance of the Court, by examining the Witnesses in your Presence, and giving their Opinion and Di-[26] rection therein, in case of any Doubt amongst ye. But I cannot conclude, without making one Observation useful for your Conduct, which I the rather do, because I do not remember it ever to have been touch'd upon in this Place.

Gentlemen,

Ye have bound yourselves by your Oath, not only to present such Matters as shall be given ye in Charge, but all other Matters and Things as come to your Knowledge touching this present Service. Ye are sworn for the body of this City and Liberty, and are, or ought to be returned out of different Quarters of it, that no Offence in your several Neighbourhoods, nor probably throughout the Liberty, may [D 2 -27] escape the Knowledge of one or the other of ye. I cannot impute it to a wilful Breach of, but to want of Attention to, the Oath in those who have gone before ye; that scarce any thing has been presented but what comes from particular Prosecutors.

The few, scandalously few Presentments of the Constables, whose almost daily walking through, and acquaintance with all the parts of the Liberty, cannot fail of conveying to their Knowledge that infinite number of Annoyances, which every body takes notice of but themselves, add but to the Necessity of this Remark; [28] To press the Obligation of your Oath, of which ye cannot be insensible, too much upon ye, would shew an unbecoming Distrust of ye thus informed. In a word,

Imitate therefore (but upon nobler Motives than theirs) the Behaviour of that other Jury of this Liberty, through whose diligent Enquiry, scarce any the least Annoyance escapes unpresented.

For the rest, – If ye present no Person for Hatred, Malice, or Ill-will, nor leave any unpresented for Love, Favour, or Affection, Gain, Reward, or Hopes thereof, ye have fulfilled your Duty: And besides [29] meriting the Thanks of the Court in a particular manner, ye will have the Comfort, by *Converting many from the Error of their ways; of saving Souls from death, and hiding a multitude of Sins.* James v. 20.

FINIS.

THE **CHARGE** OF **Sr**. *Daniel Dolins*, **Kt**. TO THE **Grand-Jury, And other Juries** OF THE County of *Middlesex*; At the General Quarter-Sessions of the Peace, Held the Seventh Day of October, 1725 at *WESTMINSTER - HALL. Printed at the Desire of the* Justices *of the Peace for the County, and the Jury of High-Constables and Constables. LONDON*

Printed for SAMUEL CHANDLER, at the *Cross-Keys* in the *Poultry*, M.DCC.XXV.

Missdx. Ss *Ad General' Quarterial' Session' Pacis Domini Regis tent' pro Com.* Middlesex' *apud* Hick'*s*-Hall *in St* John-Street, *in Com. praedict. per. adjorn. Die Mercur. scilicet decimi terita Die* Octobris, *Anno Regni Domini* Georgii *nunc Regis* Magnae Britanniae, *&c dudecimo.*

THIS Court being sensible that the Charge, Given by Sir *Daniel Dolins*, Kt. Chairman of this present Sessions, on *Thursday* last, being the first Day of this Sessions then begun and holden for this County at *Westminster-Hall*, to the Grand-Jury, and other Juries, then and there assembled, *Is a Pious, Loyal, and Learned Charge, very much tending to promote a Dutiful Zeal and Affection for His Majesties Person, Royal Family, Administration, and Government: The Suppression of Vice, and all Kinds of Corruption; and well suited and fitted for the Encouragement, Encrease, and Propagation of Virtue; and a Faithful, Diligent Discharge of every Office and Trust* : Doth Order, that the Thanks of this Court be, and they are thereby Given to the said Sir *Daniel Dolins* for His said Charge; And this Court doth Desire, that for the Benefit of the Publick, the said Sir *Daniel Dolins* will be pleased to Cause his said Charge to be printed.

per Cur'

WALTER

[A]

The DEDICATION
To the Worshipful
Sir *Daniel Dolins*, Kt.

Chairman at this present General Quarter Sessions of the Peace, now holden for the County of *Midlesex*,

WE the Jury of Constables, whose Names are hereunder written, do give you our Humble Thanks for your Excellent Charge, and desire you will be pleased, for the Good of the Publick, to cause the same to be printed. Witness our Hands the Seventeenth Day of *October* 1725.

Clifford William Phillipps, High Constable of the Tower-Division.

Joseph Sutton, High Constable of the Hundred of Gore.

Joseph Cooper. Joshua Gilbert. Gilbert Roddy. Walter Husbands. John Townsen. James Bolton. William Stretton. William Biddel. Walter With. John Sparks. Thomas Pond. Richard Andrews. John Hunt. Richard Hatt. Lindsey Marsingale. Thomas Anderson. Solomon Ware. Richard Gapper. Thomas Bell. John Reddell. Richard Prentis.

[A -ii]

TO THE Right Worshipful **His Majesty's Justices of the Peace for the County of** ***Middlesex*****.**

Permit me, Gentlemen, in the Beginning of this Dedication, and Address, to express my Gratitude for the Honour you have done me, in desiring me to publish in Print the following Charge to the several Juries for the County of *Middlesex*, composed and delivered by me, at the Request of your Worthy Chairman, the Ingenious, [iii] Learned, Judicious, and Excellent Mr. *Abney.*[1] The many Favours and Civilities I have received from you; and your uncommon kind Acceptance of my sincere, well-meant Services to you and the Publick, cannot be pass'd over in Silence: Your Repeated Applications, and Obliging Expressions of Desires to Advance me to the Honourable Chair, deserve and merit a particular Notice, and becoming grateful Acknowledgments from me. Could I have found in my self Abilities and Qualifications answerable to your Favourable Apprehensions, and Equal to the important Trust, I should not have waved, or denied, what was desired; especially by Gentlemen, for whom I have so Great and Just a Value and Esteem, and in a Matter relating to the Service of my King and my Country: The Experience I have since had, *as it were of Necessity, upon the Request, as I said, of my Honoured Friend*, of the Nature of the Office, and Duty of the Chairman, hath convinced me, and I believe *you likewise*, what Occasion I have had, and how much I have been obliged to you, Gentlemen, *especially of the Long Robe*, for your seasonable Interpositions and Directions, in Matters of Difficulty, and considerable Moment and Importance: If I have learnt any thing by these occasional Services, that may any ways qualify me to discharge the like Dutiful Assistant Offices for the future,

[1] Mr. Abney: probably Thomas Abney, later Sir Thomas, a baron of the Exchequer 1740, a Justice of the Common Pleas, 1743. Died of the gaol-fever at the Black Sessions of May 1750 at the Old Bailey. He may have been Chairman of the Bench until 1725.

I shall readily employ the same, for the [iv] Ease and Accommodation of any Gentleman that shall be chosen, and consent to undertake this Honourable, Laborious Trust: The Inconveniencies attending the constant, continued Discharge of the Chairman's Duty, may, I am sensible, be so considerable, with respect to Gentlemens particular, or rather Publick Affairs, as to make the Office, if not Burdensome, yet at least Uneasy in some Degree, even to those, who, for the General Common Good, have been willing readily and and chearfully to take it upon them, and already have discharged it with so much Honour to the Commission, and themselves, and Extensive Benefit to the Publick. The Recess some Gentlemen have had for a Time from the Chair; and the Reasonable Prospect they have of Success, in the Delightful Service of their Soveraign and Fellow-Subjects; will (I encourage my self) upon proper Application, excite and engage them to renew their Pleasant Toil and Labour, in so *Respectful* and *Commendable* an *Office*; in a *Service so necessary and beneficial to the Publick.*

As to the Charge it self, Gentlemen, I Cannot be so vain, as to think it perfect in its Kind, or free from considerable Defects and Imperfections, easily to be discovered by Quicker Sights, more Penetrating, Piercing Eyes, and Impartial Judgments than my own. All *known, wilful Errors and Mistakes*, [v] after a careful Perusal and Review of it, I may venture to purge and clear of it: And for unvoluntary ones, I am assured of your candid Construction, and equitable Interpretation, or Forgiveness for them: Such as it is, at your Request, and in Pursuance and Obedience to your Order, I submit it to the Publick. The favourable or good Character you have been pleased to give the World of it, tho' it very much exceeds the Deserts of the Performance, yet it very Truly Represents, and exactly Expresseth the *Aim and Design* of the Author: The concurrent unanimous Recommendation of the Court, gives me some good Liking of it, and more Promising Hopes than otherwise I could have had, that it may in some Degree *Answer or Further* those Great and Glorious Ends and Purposes (*or at least some of them*) mention'd in your Order of Court.

The Promoting a Hearty Zeal and Affection for His Majesty, and the Royal Family, and a grateful Sense of the Happy Administration and Government of our Publick Affairs, are Ends worth *Designing and Striving for*, by every True *British* Protestant: The using all Lawful Means and Endeavours, for the Advancement of Piety towards God, the Suppression of Vice, and the Incouragement and Increase of Virtue; are such Noble, Generous, Kind, Beneficent Attempts, for the Good of Mankind in general; that not the [vi] Men who Profess the Christian Religion *singly*, but the Men that Depend only on Reason; the Men of good Sense and Judgment, and of Moral Honesty and Probity, *must if they will act Conformable to the Principles they pretend, or profess to be Influenced and Governed by; Heartily Espouse, Diligently Prosecute, and Delighfully Glory in, and Please themselves withal.* The Attainment of these Great and Good Things; And the Exciting a Due Care, Diligence, Integrity, Incorruption, and Circumspect Behaviour in *All Ministerial Officers and others*, in their several respective Trusts, Relations, and Capacities, for the Glory of God, the Honour and Safety of his Majesty; and the Peace, Benefits, and Prosperity of that Publick Administration, and Government, which every *True Britton*, with so much Comfort and Pleasure lives under; is, I perswade my self, the Great Aim, and End of your Order; and my Obedient Concurrence therewith: If therefore these, or any Number of them, or any other valuable Ends, be attainted by the *Publication* of this Charge, I shall then, Gentlemen, have inexpressible Cause, and Reason, to return the unmerited Thanks the Court has pleased to Order to be given me, back again, with Vast, Additional Degrees of Gratitude and Obligation to the Court: But if the Event should be otherwise, and the Success [vii] not Answer your Kind and Honourable Intentions, yet I shall always think my self bound Thankfully to Acknowledge the Honour you have conferred on me, beyond the Deserts of,

GENTLEMEN,

Your very much Obliged, most Obedient, and most humble Servant,

Hackney, Octob.

21. 1725 **Dan. Dolins.**

[B - 1]

The **CHARGE** of Sir *Daniel Dolins*, Kt.

Gentlemen of the Grand-Jury, and you Gentlemen of the Juries of High-Constables and Constables[1],

THE Excellency of our Constitution, and Admirable Frame of Government; The Wisdom, Justice, and Goodness of our Laws; The Peculiar Happiness of the Blessed Isle of *Great-Britain*, under the Mild, Auspicious, and Extensively Glorious Reign of our Most Gracious Sovereign Lord King *GEORGE* ; The present Prudent, Peaceful, and Prosperous Administration of all our [2] Publick Affairs, in his Majesty's Absence,[2] so much to his Majesty's Honour; and the Ease, Quiet, Profit and Advantage of all his Subjects; And lastly, The Secure Enjoyment, and Free Use of our Properties and Estates, with all those valuable Religious, and Civil Rights, Liberties and Privileges, possess'd by us, without unreasonable or unnecessary Restraints; so that every Man may be as good and virtuous, as righteous and just, as beneficent and kind, as charitable and merciful as he pleaseth; tho' not so bad and injurious,

[1] The notes given in the margin in the text are quoted here between [ ].

[2] When the king was away in Hanover.

so oppressive and cruel, as some Mens evil Inclinations and Dispositions, excite and prompt them to be.

These, GENTLEMEN, are all of them Subjects of a very pleasant Sound to an *English* Ear; and might, if I had Time, very delightfully and usefully be enlarg'd upon before this Audience. Every one of you, that thinks for himself, and judgeth coolly and calmly as he ought, must, I perswade my self, be sensible of his great Happiness, in living under such a Soveraign, such an Administration of the Government, and such Laws, as we at present are blest with; But yet, I must beg Leave to tell you, that notwithstanding so large a Stock, such vast Materials of Happiness, we shall be far, very far, from being compeatly happy, unless we rightly use, and put them well together: Unless all of us, according to the Duty of [3] our several Stations and Relations, our respective Offices, Trusts, and Capacities, do our Best to promote and further the Execution of those good Laws and Statutes, that have been made for the Publick Safety and Benefit. The best framed Laws, GENTLEMEN, must be useless, insignificant, dead Letters and Things, if either they influence not the Practice, or correct not Disobedience: And how can this be done, and Obedience be thereby secured, but by their Execution? Far be it from us of this Nation, to have it said of us, either at Home, or Abroad, that we have the best Body of Laws, but the least observ'd, or the worst executed, of any Kingdom or People in the Universe. It is very much, GENTLEMEN, in your Power, and will be in the Power of others, who shall be in the same Capacity of Grand and other Jury-Men, in this County, or elsewhere, either to prevent, or wipe away this very shameful and ignominious Reproach: You are summon'd from the several Parts of this County, and therefore, from your several Stations and Situations, are suppos'd to be acquainted with most, at least, of the open and notorious Breaches and Violations of the Laws, presentable in this Court: And when you are come hither, you, each of you, take a very solemn Oath, in the Presence of the Great, All-seeing GOD, and in the Face of this Court; That you will *diligently* inquire, and true Presentment make of all such [4] Matters and Things, as shall be given you in Charge. The very Name of *Grand* -Jury Man, is a Title of Respect; the great Antiquity of this Institution, adds to the Former Respect, a Degree of Reverence; and makes it in some Sense Venerable; But the Greatest, the Truest, nay, I was about to say, and may Venture to speak out, the only Real Honour that attends this high and important Trust, is derived from the great Powers the Law invests you with; and the mighty extensive Benefits and Advantages, which will accrue to our Soveraign Lord the King, and his Subjects, from a faithful, diligent, judicious, and impartial Discharge of this great Trust committed to you; If, GENTLEMEN, you are neither influenced by Envy, Hatred, or Malice, on the one Hand, nor biass'd by Fear, Favour, Affection, Reward, Gain, or Hope, on the other; but in all Things, according to the Best of your Knowledge, Skill, and Judgment, after an honest and impartial Search and Examination, you Present the Truth, the whole Truth, and nothing but the Truth; Then will you be truly honourable; Honour will become, and set well and gracefully on those that act thus according to their Oaths. But if these Things be wanting, the Honour vanisheth; the Name of Grand-Jury Man is a vain, empty, insignificant Name and Title; and the Man that thus betrays his Trust, will be treated with Contempt, Ignominy, [5] and Reproach, by those that love their King and Country best.

The Court, GENTLEMEN, depend therefore upon *your due Discharge* of the Trust reposed in you. The Solemnity and becoming Manner in which your Foremen, and the rest of you their Fellows, have generally taken the Oath appointed by Law, gives us promising Hopes, that you will observe and keep it, now you have taken it. I shall proceed therefore immediately to lay before you those Matters and Things, which the Court by me do earnestly require intreat and perswade, and authoritatively direct and charge you, diligently to enquire, and make true Presentment of.

It will hardly be possible to specify, much less to enlarge upon every Matter or thing, that is Presentable by you: For Order and Method-sake, and likewise to help your Apprehensions and Memories a little, I shall distinguish them into Matters and Things, relating to God and Man; to the King, and all his People and Subjects; to the Bodies, to the Estates and Properties, to the Safety and Peace, to the good Name and Character, to the Comforts and Conveniencies of Men; to their Houses and Habitations, for their secure and quiet Enjoyment of Themselves, Families, and Goods. And these may again be subdivided into almost [6] innumerable Branches: but as this would rather perplex and confound, or at least load your Memories, rather than help you really to distinguish and discern between Offence and Offence; I shall give you no Trouble with those minute Matters: There is another Division of Offences Presentable by you, that is not to be omitted by me; namely, into Offences Capital, or not Capital; that is, those Offences that are to be punished with Death, and those that are not to be punished with Death, but some lighter Punishment; as Fine, Imprisonment, corporal Punishment, Transportation, and the like.

As to Offences against the Divine Majesty; as far as they lie within the Reach of human Knowledge, are cognizable by a Civil Jurisdiction, and are subject to temporal Punishments; they are to be taken Notice of, and Presented by you in the first Place. I would feign hope every one of you, GENTLEMEN, have that Awe and Dread, that becoming Fear and Reverence, nay that Love and Affection, that Grateful, Ingenuous Disposition towards your Great Creator, Preserver and Benefactor; towards the King of Kings, and Lord of Lords, (*your Soveraign supream Lord and*

King) as not to suffer any Blasphemy and Profaneness; any vile, detestable, ludicrous, impious Treatment of the Divine Name, Nature and Attributes, that come to your Knowledge upon Inquiry, to pass [7] unrepresented: It is justly said, that the Name and Character of good Kings and Princes is so far Sacred, as to be treated with Decency and Respect; but this is absolutely, unlimitedly true of the Great Majesty of Heaven and Earth; He is infinitely Holy, and Perfect; and therefore His Name ought to be Sacred in the Highest, and most Exalted Sense. As to the Particular, Specifick Offences against the Divine Majesty, to be given you in Charge, I shall rather refer the Notice of them till we come to consider his Majesty's Royal Proclamation read to you; A very Moving, Pressing, Powerful, and most Authoritative Charge given to us, and you, and the whole Kingdom.

The next important Article of Inquiry, that I am to lay before you, is High-Treason; that is, the highest, most fatal, and most flagitious, capital Offence, that can be committed in any Community, that is called a Kingdom, or under Monarchical Government; as being against the King, the supream Had of Honour, Influence, and Government. And you consider how great and gracious a Soveraign is now setting on the Throne of *Great-Britain*, His Sacred Majesty King *GEORGE*; ever securing, and inviolably maintaining all Legal Rights, Liberties, and Privileges, to all his Subjects; ever dispensing unspeakable Blessings and Benefits amongst [8] all his People: And what an Illustrious, Excellent Royal Progeny we are now Blest with, Eminent for Princely Virtues and Endowments, Their Royal Highnesses the Prince and Princess of *Wales*, and their numerous Royal Issue, promising Happiness to our Prosperity at far distant Years, or Ages: How must this abominable Crime, in these Lights and Views, be aggravated, and made more odious and detestable; as being against such a Soveraign, and destructive to such a Royal Family.

Consider, GENTLEMEN, a little further; His sacred Majesty at this Time, with the joint wise Counsels, Advice, and powerful Assistance of the Mighty, Magnanimous, and truly Protestant Prince and Soveraign, the King of *Prussia*, his Majesty's Royal Son-in-Law[1]; strenuously, incessantly, and gloriously, making the noblest Efforts, to recover the just Rights, and Religious Privileges of our Brethren, of the same Holy Religion Abroad.

Their melancholy and miserable Condition ought, methinks, to affect every true *British* Protestant, as with a Christian Sympathy, and sincere Concern and Grief for the unhappy Sufferers; so with a proportionable Degree of Honour, Love and tender Care, of our Gracious and Compassionate Soveraign, so readily and cheerfully offering them his best [9]

[1] Friedrich Wilhelm I, who married Sophia Dorothea in Berlin, Nov. 1706.

Help and Assistance: Nor ought we to forget to be in a particular Manner thankful our selves, for our happy Situation and Circumstances, so vastly different, and so much better than theirs.

The serious Consideration and Reflection on these Things put together, the Court depends upon it, will animate and quicken you, GENTLEMEN, in your Enquiries into all Sorts of Treasons against his Most Excellent Majesty King *GEORGE*, and his Royal Highness *George* Prince of *Wales*. Here, if any where, and above all, we expect it from you, that you will be, as we say, quick and sharp-sighted: To find out all latent, lurking Treasons, you are *most diligently* to enquire, and make true Presentment, of any Sort or Kind of this heinous Offence, whenever you have found it. And this leads me to inform you, That High-Treason is of Four Sorts or Kinds.

That which immediately belongs to the King, and the Royal Family.

That which concerns His Officers in the Administration of Justice.

That which related to His *Seal*.

And that which regards His *Coin*.

As to the *First*, Compassing the Death of the King, or his Royal Highness the Prince of Wales that is, declaring by an Open Act, a Design to Depose, Imprison, or Murther the King *&c.* [25 Edw. III] is [C -10] High-Treason within this Branch. So that you see the Thought of the Heart must be expressed by some open known Act and Deed; otherwise indeed, it cannot be of humane Cognizance; such as Words put down in Writing; providing Weapons to kill the King, *&c.* sending Letters to second and further His Death: Assembling People to take the King into their Power: Writing Letters to a Foreign Prince[1]; inciting to an Invasion; and the like: Actual Levying War against the King, is likewise contain'd in this First Kind of High-Treason: Persons consulting and conspiring together for this Purpose; especially if a War be levied, the Conspirators, as well as the actors, are Traitors; So is raising a Force, to burn or throw down Inclosures in general, from Place to Place, or Town to Town: Or to change Religion; Or to augment the Wages of Labourers: Holding a Castle, or Fort, against the King's Forces, is a levying War: Adhering to the King's Enemies, either by giving them Aid, Assistance, or Comfort: Or by surrending the King's Castle to such a one for Reward; this is likewise a Part of the First Kind of High-Treason above-mentioned.

The Second *Sort* of High-Treason, I told you related to His Majesty's Officers in the Administration of Justice; as killing the Lord Chancellor; Treasurer; Justice of either Bench; Justice in Eyre; or of Assize; [C 2-11] or Oyer and Terminer; But then you are to take Notice, that it is confin'd

[1] This recalls the letter of invitation sent to William of Orange by the Immortal Seven.

to these Officers only, and to them only doing their several Offices, in their Places, or Seats of Justice.

The next Species of High-Treason I mention'd to you is, the Counterfeiting the Great, or Privy Seal: This must be taken strictly: For Compassing, Contriving, or Designing to Do this only, is not High-Treason: Nor Affixing the Great Seal by the Chancellor without Warrant; nor fixing a true Great Seal to another Patent; but a Great Misprision. All Aiders and Assisters to the Counterfeiting the Great and Privy-Seal, are also guilty of High-Treason by the same Act: And so likewise as to the Privy Signet, or Sign Manual, by another Statute. [1 & 2 of P. & M. c. 11

The Last Sort of High-Treason, I said related to the Coin: To forge the King's Coin was High-Treason, tho' the Offender did not utter it: And the Counterfeiting it is affirmed to be so by Statute; Clipping, Filing, washing it, *&c.* is now made High-Treason, by another Statute. Forging and Counterfeiting of Foreign Money made Currency by Proclamation, is also High-Treason; Bringing Counterfeit Money from Abroad, is likewise High-Treason; provided [25 Edw. III; 5 Eliz. c. 11; 1 Ma. 1; 1 & 2 Ph. & M] it be made after the Likeness of English Money; be brought from a Country belonging to some Foreign Prince; and brought in knowingly; and uttered by the same Person, either in Trade or Merchandize; or Payment made thereof; By a Statute made the *8th* and *9th* of *W.* III. c. 26. made perpetual by 7 *A.* c. 24. Any Person mending a Puncheon, Matrix, Stamp, &c. or Conveying any of the Instruments out of the Mint; or edging any diminished, or counterfeit Coin, like Edges made at the Mint; shall be guilty of High-Treason: So likewise they that colour, or gild Coin, resembling the current Coin, *&c.* as also their Aiders and Abetters.

Thus, GENTLEMEN, I have laid before you the most material Instances of High-Treason, under those Four Sorts and Kinds I at first divided it into; Some I have purposedly omitted, as not properly falling within your present Enquiry; and therefore not necessary or useful to be given you in Charge.

Before I proceed to other Things, made High-Treason by Statute, of a different Nature from the former, I think proper to put you in Mind of that Excellent Statute of the *6th* of Queen *Anne*, Entituled, "An Act for the Better Security of Her Majesty's Person and Government, and of the Succession to the Crown of *Great-Britain* in the Protestant Line; – Which [13] makes it High-Treason in any Person, who maliciously, advisedly, and directly, by Writing, or Printing, maintain and affirm, That Her then Majesty was not Lawful Queen; or that the pretended Prince of *Wales* hath any Right to the Crown; or any other, but by the Acts of Settlement Or that the King and Parliament cannot bind the Succession.

The High-Treasons by other Statutes are these: Refusing the Oath of Supremacy, upon the second Tender [5 Eliz. c.1]: Bringing in Bulls, or executing them, or reconciling thereby to the Church of Rome [13 Eliz. c.2]; Absolving Subjects from Obedience to His Majesty, or reconciling them, as they call it, to Rome [23 Eliz. c. 1]; both in the Person that Reconciles, and is Reconciled: The same, if a Priest, or any Englishman in Foreign Seminaries, come into this Realm, and submits not himself in two Days [27 Eliz. c. 2]. By the Statute of King *James* I. not only the Absolvers and Reconcilers, but their Aiders, Abetters, Procurers, *&c.* are guilty of High-Treason [Anno Tertio c. 4].

Misprision of Treason, is a bare Knowledge of a Treason without Assent: Every Man therefore that knows a Treason, and would keep himself from Danger of [14] Treason, or Misprision, ought to shew his Abhorrence of the Treason; and that He is no ways Partaker of the Crime by immediately discovering it, as soon as known, to His Majesty, Privy-Coucil, Secretaries of State, or other Magistrates.

You are also to Present All Petty-Treasons; that is, when a Servant kills his Master, or Mistress, or Master's Wife, during his Service: Or even after his Departure, if upon Malice contracted during his Service: Or when a Wife kills her Husband; whether alone, or with a Stranger; but if by a Servant, then Petty-Treason in both: If a Son at Age, receiving Meat, Drink, and Wages, kill Father or Mother, it is Petty-Treason; because he is thereby Treated, and so shall be reckon'd and esteem'd as a Servant: All Aiders, Abetters, Procurers in Petty-Treason, are within the Statute of the *25th* of King *Edward* III.

The next General Head of Enquiry that I am to recommend to you, GENTLEMEN, is, concerning Felonies; which are such either by Common Law, or by Statutes; The former, that is, Felonies by common Law, are divided into these four Sorts: (1). Such as are committed against the Life; or (2.) Against the Goods; or, (3.) Against the Dwelling of a Man; or (4.) Against the Protection of Publick Justice. [15

Under the First Head, You must take into your Consideration, the Case of a Man that kills himself; or, as our Law terms it, is *Felo de se* ; and also of those that kill other Men: And this may be done sometimes *unvoluntarily*, as by Misfortune; *per infortunium*, our Law calls it; or *per necessitatem*; either in the necessary Defence of Justice, or of one's self; or *voluntarily*, without Malice, as in Manslaughter; or with Malice, and then it is Murder. No Man can be said to be *Felo de se*, who is not at the Age of Discretion, or *Compos Mentis*; And therefore a Lunatick during Lunacy, or *non Compos*, by a Disease, or otherwise, killing himself, is not guilty of Felony: Here I Would observe, as in other Felonies in which Death is contained, it must ensue within a Year and a Day after the Stroke: *Chance Medley*, or Death *per infortunium*, supposeth the Man that kills the other, to be have been doing a lawful Act: If the Death happened otherwise, the killing would have been either Murder, or Manslaughter: There is another kind of Death by Misfortune, which is not only without the Fault, but without the Agency, or Procurement of any other: As a Man falling from a Tree, a Horse, or Cart, and the like. If the Death that hath happen'd, be really *ex necessitate* ; it must have been either in the Execution of Justice, by a Person that hath proper Jurisdiction in that [16] Cause; and perform'd and done by a proper Legal Officer; and pursuant to the Judgment given; Or in advancement of Justice; If a Bailiff, or Sheriff, having a Warrant to Arrest a Person Indicted of Felony, and he will not surrender himself to be Arrested: Or the Bailiff, or Sheriff, opposed and Resisted in the Execution of a Civil Process, kills the Person thus resisting his Authority, it is no Felony; but Death *ex necessitate*: But in all of these, and the like Cases, Care must be taken, that Malice does not screen, or lurk under a pretended Necessity; for then it will be Murder, and not *ex necessitate*, of Necessity. It is just likewise Homicide if Necessity, and justifiable, if it be done in Defence of my House, that Rogues come to Rob or Burn; Or of my Person: When Assaulted in the House, or High-way, by High-way-men or House-breakers; If I or my Servant kill them, 'tis no Felony; the same if a Woman kills the Person that Assaults her to Ravish her.

If the Necessity pleaded be *se defendendo*, it must be in the necessary Defence of Life, and there must be a giving back; Unless the doing that, as the Circumstances are, must manifestly hazard and endanger the Life of the Person Assaulted.

All voluntary Homicide, is either with, or without Malice; If with Malice Forethought, then it is Murther: If without, then Manslaughter. This Malice may either be [D-17] implied, or expressed; if the Manner in which it is done, shews a Design and Intention to do it, Malice is imply'd: So likewise if the Person kill'd be a lawful Office, or his awful Assistant, unless he do what is not warrantable; for then it is only Manslaughter: if a Person Assaults another with a Design to Rob him; the Assaulted resists, and is killed; Malice is implied, tho' there may be some Variety in this, as to Principals of the First and Second Degree, and Accessories before the Fact; with the Distinctions of which I shall not trouble you: Yet in every Instance of this Sort of Murder, Malice is suppos'd to be a necessary Ingredient; the Spring and Cause continuing to operate till the Stroke, or other Act, be perform'd, which produceth the Effect, *viz.* the Death of the Person.

As Murther supposeth Malice an Ingredient, so Manslaughter supposeth the killing to have been without Malice Forethought, either imply'd or express: A sudden Quarrel, or a sudden Provocation, or an unlawful Act without Deliberation, or Intention of Personal Hurt: One or more of these precede or accompany that which occasions the killing in what we call Manslaughter; and all of them are inconsistent with Malice Forethought.

You are likewise, GENTLEMEN, to enquire into, and Present Felonies relating to the Goods of any Person, which is term'd in Law *Larceny*; and that is either Simple or Mixt: The First is, again divided into Grand Larceny, when the Value of the Goods is above Twelve-pence; and Petty Larceny, when it is of or under the Value of Twelve-pence. The Things taken must be purely personal Things, but not from the Person, or out of the House of him who hath a Right to them; for then it will be an Offence of another Nature and Denomination: It must appear to you likewise, that the Taking away was Felonious, or with a Design to steal the Thing taken away: But there is no Difference to make the taking Grand or Petty Larceny, whether one or more were concern'd, or the Goods amounting together to above Twelve-pence were taken at one and the same Time or not.

If the Felonious taking away be of Money or Goods, of any Value, from the Person, and at the same Time with Violence, or putting him in Fear, then it is Robbery; but if it be done without Force or Violence, *Clam & Secrete, Privately and Secretely,* as in Picking of Pockets, Cutting a Purse, and the Like; then it is called Larceny from the Person; If this Felonious taking away of Money or Goods, be out of the House of a Person that lives in it with his Family; this [D 2-19] is Robbery, with an additional Aggravation.

I now proceed to lay before you, to be enquired into and Presented, the Felonies relating to the House, Dwelling, and Habitation of a Person; And they are generally known to be the Two: Either Breaking and Entring into the Mansion House of another in the Night Time, which is commonly called Burglary: Or Burning of a House and Habitation. Breaking a Window, drawing a Latch, Unlocking a Door, Breaking a Hole in the Wall, and the like are to be esteem'd a Breaking within the Law: Tho' an Actual Breaking, or Entry, is not always necessary; that is, there are some Cases that are Burglary without them; which it is not needful to recite: if this be done when it is Dark, it is done in the Night, in the Construction of the Law; A House that a Man commonly dwells in, or by Course and Turn, if He hath Two Dwelling Houses, tho' occasionally it may be empty, shall be reckon'd his Mansion House, and all the Out-Houses and Buildings belonging to it. So a Chamber in one of our Inns of Court, where a Person commonly resides and lodges, shall be called a Mansion House: If this Breaking and Entring the Mansion House in [20] the Night Time, be with an Intent to commit a Felony, then it is Burglary; but otherwise, if only to commit a Trespass, or make an Assault upon the Owner of the House.

Voluntarily and Maliciously Burning the House, Out-house, Stabling, or Barn, with Corn in it, is likewise Felony, and Presentable by you;

whether he begins with his own House, Designedly and Maliciously to Burn the House of another, and accomplisheth it in whole or in Part; or whether he Maliciously and Designedly Burns one, which Burns another's against whom he had not Malice; It is however Felony with respect to the Last as well as the First.

The last Sort of Felonies at Common Law, I shall *now* mention, and relates to the Hindrance and Obstruction of Publick Justice, by Preventing the Felon's being brought to his Trial, and attending the Issue of the Law: This may be done by the Prisoner himself, by Breaking Prison, or Escape: By the Officer that hath the Felon in Custody; either *voluntarily*, or *unvoluntarily*; if voluntarily, then a Felony having been really committed, and the Felon committed by a lawful Warrant, the immediate Officer that voluntarily permits the Felon to escape, is himself chargeable with Felony: If *unvoluntarily*, but thro' Negligence, then the Officer who thus permits it, is liable to [21] be punished with Fine, according to the Crime of the Person Escaping.

As to the Felonies by Statutes, GENTLEMEN, they are so many, that the Time will not permit me to enter into the Detail or particular Enumeration of them; Nor is it necessary, there being no such Disputes or Difficulties about them, as should obstruct your Enquiry, or prevent your Presenting them, as they shall come to your Knowledge.

The next Sort of Offences that you are to make diligent Enquiry into, and truly to Present, are those which we before called, *not Capital*; such is Forgery,[1] Perjury, and Subornation of Perjury: These are Detestable Crimes, and therefore I hope will be narrowly look'd into, in your Enquiries, that they may be vigorously Prosecuted, and receive the just Sentence and Punishment they deserve.

You are likewise to Present all forcible Entries; All Riots and Tumults, in pursuance of the seasonable Act read to you before the Charge; and All Kinds of Breaches of the Peace: Also all Fore-stallers, Regraters, and Ingrossers; These are Pernicious Sorts of People; who Plot and Conspire together to Advance unreasonably, or without any Real, Just Occasion the Price of Victuals, to the great Oppression, and Breeding of Murmuring and Discontent, especially amongst the lower and meaner Sort of People: [22] You are also to Present all Nusances; the Decays of Publick Bridges; and common High-ways ruinous, and much out of Repair.

You do not, GENTLEMEN, I presume, expect that the Court should specify in their Charge, every Offence of the lower Kinds, which come within your Sphere, or the Duty of your present Trust to Present. The

[1] What was true when this was written, was no longer valid years later: see f. ex. the case of Dr. Dodd, one of George III's own chaplains who was hanged for forging a bill of exchange in the name of Lord Chesterfield, 1777.

allowed Time would not permit it; and many of you may be supposed not to want the Information after you have received so many *Excellent Charges* of the like Nature in this Court, from Gentlemen of the Best Capacities, Abilities, Qualifications, and Endowments: But there are two or three Things that I must beg Leave to insist upon, and earnestly press you very diligently to enquire into, and truly to Present.

All Treasonable Books and Papers printed; and Treasonable Words spoken, against His Majesty: All Libels against his Principal Ministers of State, and Officers of Justice, in Higher or Lower Order and Degrees. We are so happy indeed, as to have lived to see this Wicked Spirit in a good Measure tamed, and the foul Mouth of Malice, Scandal, and Falshood, with Respect to His Majesty, and His Prime Ministers,[1] at least, if not quite shut, yet much closed, or more silent than formerly: A Wise Government; A Cool and Calm Administration; A due Mixture of Pains, Penalties, and wholesome [23] Severities, with Connivance, Forbearance, Indulgence, and Pardon, will be happy Effects in this Respect, and make subside that sharp or bitter Ferment, that frets and vexes the Publick Body: But then, GENTLEMEN, you will remember, that strict Vigilance, An open, watchful Eye; and an attentive, listening Ear, are necessary to guard us against these Attacks. The Greatest Personages among us, as well as those in Inferior Stations of Office and Government, are liable to undergo a long Course of the vilest, ill-grounded, far distant Scandal and Reflection, without almost a Possibility of discovering *themselves* the Authors and Publishers of the Base Falshoods, or even the Libels that contain them: Professed Friends to the Publick, too often deny their proper Assistance, and, if they do not please and gratify themselves with the vile, lurking Scandal, creeping from Hand to Hand, in a mean, clandestine Manner; yet are weakly credulous, and too far Conspiring with *Avowed Enemies*, to shroud and shelter the Wicked Instruments of the False and Lying Accusations: But you, GENTLEMEN, who are upon your Oaths, in Duty Bound, and perhaps the Best Situated, the Best Qualified, to make the Discovery, and bring the Offenders under Just Prosecution; will not, I hope, think your Discharge your Duty, now laid before you, *as you ought*, with Presenting all such Offences and Offenders, as [24] upon your Enquiry shall come to your Knowledge.

The Second Thing I would recommend to you, in a very particular Manner, to Present, is, The Neglect, that is, the wilful Neglect of Duty in Ministerial Officers, punishable by our Laws: This, I am persuaded, appears to you, and all Mankind, so great, so shameful, and so mischievous to the Publick; that every Body will say, It is High Time to

[1] Note the interesting early use of the expression "his prime ministers'", even if it is in the plural.

Redress it; Or the ill Consequences of it must, in a great measure, be fatal and Destructive to the Publick; It is this that obligeth the few, comparatively few, Good, Faithful Officers we have, to call into their Aid and Help, other Honest, Sincere, Couragious Persons, in Order to the Discovery, and bringing to Justice, some of the Vilest, most Flagicious, and Wicked Offenders.

If you, GENTLEMEN of the Juries sworn, and those that shall succeed you from Time to Time, would but Present, and Bring to Punishment as far as the Law will Allow you, all Officers for the Careless Performance, and shameful Neglect of their Respective Duty; then there might be some Hopes, that the Assistance of others might be spared; but till then, whatever Shame it may reflect upon Bad Officers, the few Good Officers, comparatively I mean, that there are; and even the Magistrates themselves, as they have not, so they will not for the future suffer their good Designs and Endeavours for the [E-25] Publick Service, to be much frustrated, nay, almost entirely, if not altogether, *Defeated*; for Want of using the Service and Assistance of those Persons they can Confide in, and Depend upon; and may Legally employ as Legal Assistants to the proper Officers: How little could have been done without such Assistants, in that Glorious Enterprize of Suppressing the Publick Gaming-Houses; which were become, in many Respects, a Nusance to the vast and populous Cities of *London* and *Westminster*, and Parts adjacent; I leave to those Worthy Gentlemen to tell you; who were so Generously employed in that Honourable Work, with the good Wishes, and Joy of their Brethren in their Happy Success, for the Common Good and Benefit of the Publick in general, and of the County of *Middlesex* in particular.

The last Thing, GENTLEMEN, that I lay a very great Stress upon, and recommend with a good deal of Earnestness, and Importunity to you, is to Enquire into *All Breach of Duty in Officers*; that I mean *especially*, which is plainly voluntary and wilful: The Acting Contrary to the Duty of their Offices: or Acting Corruptly in the Administration of them: And Here I wish there was less Occasion for Complaint and Mourning, than for what was mentioned under the former Head: Extortion, Bribery, and all Sort of Corruption in Officers, either to excuse from Duty and Legal Service: Or to screen and [26] save from Justice and Punishment; are Offences to be punish'd very severely; as having some of the worst and most pernicious Influences on all Justice, Order, and Government.

Let me therefore, GENTLEMEN, again Beg and Entreat, as well as Enjoyn and Charge you, strictly to Enquire into these notorious, abominable Corruptions and Abuses, under Pretence and Colour, and as it were, under the Protection of Justice; and in particular, if any Peace-Officers, or their Assistants, unlawfully Apprehend, and Take up Persons no ways mis-behaving themselves; but employ'd, or going only about their Lawful, necessary Business and Affairs, and afterwards Discharge them for a Bribe, Fee, or Reward: There is an Absolute Necessity, GENTLEMEN, from the Outcry, Noise, Clamour, and undistinguishing Complaint made, of taking some effectual Measures, of making a Difference and Distinction between the Good and the Bad; some that may Act for Base and Wicked Ends; and others from Noble, Generous, Humane and Kind Principles; between the Precious (as I may say) and the Vile: That the one may in Justice, for the Common Good, receive their due Praise and Commendations; and the other condign Punishments, suitable to their Deserts. If Officers and their Assistants, employed even in Suppressing and Punishing Vice, Immorality, and Prophaneness, should upon a [E 2-27] Fair, Candid Hearing, and Examination, be Duly prov'd, and found to have taken any Sum, or Sums of Money, of any Person Apprehended, *Whether he be brought before a Magistrate or not*; The more Holy, the more Righteous, or Better the Work in which They are engaged, The more Rigorous, and more Exemplary in several Respects ought to be the Punishment to be Inflicted on Them. And every Sincere, Honest Peace-Officer, and his Assistants, especially those that employ themselves in the Discovery and Prosecution of Vice, Immorality, and Prophaneness, must, I am confidently persuaded, say to this, *Heartily*, *Willingly*, and *Truly*, Let it be so; We cheerfully submit our selves to this Trial and Examination, and the worst Sentence and Punishment, if upon Due Proof found to be Guilty.

The Best Things are liable to be Counterfeited, in order to be made the Instruments of Worldly Gain, and Secular Advantage. The Reputation and Recommendation these Things give Men with Persons of Credit and Character, shews their Internal Real Excellency and Goodness, and *may* make *some* be at the Pains and Trouble to Counterfeit them; For to Play the Hypocrite, is to Act against Nature, which must be uneasy as being unnatural: What Pity is it then, that Any should be at all this Toil and Labour, barely to Resemble, or Dissemble, what they have not; and at the last miss or lose the truly [28] Valuable End and Reward; which in the *Best*, and *most Worthy* Designs and Undertakings, can only attend *Sincerity*? And how Wicked and Abominable must it be, to depreciate and sully Things of the Greatest, Highest Value, and Brightest Lustre, by Prostituting, and Using, *or Abusing them rather*, for Base, Vile, and Evil Purposes?

This Kind of Scandalous, and I would hope (*except in very Few Instances that can be duly Proved*) Unjust Reflection, is, however, pretty commonly and liberally flung upon those Gentlemen, that have the Honour to serve His Majesty, and the Government, as Peace-Officers: Their Offices are very useful, advantageous, and necessary Offices for the Publick Good; but are never design'd as Offices for Corrupt Gain and Profit: I must recommend it therefore to you GENTLEMEN of the Juries of High-Constables, and Constables, in a particular Manner, not only to be extreamly Cautious and Circumspect in this Respect, in the Execution of your Offices *your selves* ; to take away Occasion from them that may seek an Occasion, to censure and Accuse you: But especially strictly to Enquire, into, and Present such Peace-Officers, as may have been Guilty of these and the like Vile and Wicked Practices. By this Means, GENTLEMEN, you will most effectually either clear your Order, or Body, of the Imputation; Or best satisfy your own Minds, that you have done your utmost, to [29] Cure and Prevent, for the future, the Evils and Mischiefs complain'd of:

I shall now, GENTLEMEN, proceed to lay before you His Majesty's Royal Proclamation *for the Encouragement of Piety and Virtue, and for the Preventing and Punishing of Vice, Prophaneness, and Immorality*; the Impressions of which I would leave with you in this Order, promising my self that they will, as they ought, be the Deepest, most Lasting, and Influential. His Majesty, as you have heard in this His Royal Proclamation, doth direct and command His Justices of the Peace, as well as Judges of Assize; not only to Cause the same Publickly to read in Open Court; but also to give strict Charges at their respective Assizes and Sessions, for the Due Prosecution and Punishment of all such Persons, as shall presume to offend in any of the Kinds mention'd therein; and also of All Persons, that, contrary to their Duty, shall be *Remiss or Negligent* in Putting the Laws against those Offences in Execution; These Offences are either more particularly or generally mention'd and express'd; Of the First Sort are, Excessive Drinking, Blasphemy, Prophane Swearing and Cursing, Lewdness, and Prophanation of the Lord's Day, All Publick Gaming and Gaming-Houses, especially on the Lord's Day; and other Lewd and Disorderly Houses. The Second Sort are express'd by these general Words; Or other Dissolute, Immoral, or Disorderly Prac-[30] ctices: These are all of them Direct Violations of the Laws, both of God and Man, highly Affronting to the Divine Majesty; shameful and scandalous, if allowed of, to the Kingdom; and destructive and pernicious to the Peace, good Government, and Happiness of the Publick; and therefore as His Majesty is pleased to Direct and Command, *to be Effectually Suppress'd, Prosecuted, and Proceeded against with the Utmost Rigour that may be by Law.* For this Great End and Purpose, His Majesty is pleased strictly to Charge and Command, not only All his Officers and Ministers, Ecclesiastical and Civil; but also all other His Subjects whom it may concern, to be very vigilant and Strict in the Discovery, and the Effectual Prosecution and Punishment of all Persons, who shall be guilty of one or more of the Offences above mentioned. After this *Awakening, Pressing Charge* from His Majesty, once more deliver'd to us, according to *His strict Injunctions* ; I hope no one will excuse himself from this Honourable Service; the Encouragement of Piety and Virtue, and the Preventing and Punishing of Vice, Prophaneness, and Immorality: From this Time forward, GENTLEMEN, I would feign hope, that senseless, stupid, bold Blasphemers; prophane Cursers and Swearers, open Prophaners of the Lord's Day, especially in Time of Divine Worship and Service; and Beastly Drunkards, that contrive to drown and confound their Reason and [31] Senses with Liquor, and the Venders of Gin and other strong Waters[1]; who against the Law not only frequently suffer Tipling, but dead-Drunkenness, in their Shops and Houses; shall not escape your Prosecution, when they do not escape your Knowledge. The Cry of the last mention'd Wickedness, I mean Excessive drinking Gin, and other pernicious Spirits; is become so great, so loud, so importunate; and the growing Mischiefs from it so many, so great, so destructive to the Lives, Families, Trades and Business of such Multitudes, *especially to the lower, poorer Sort of People*; that I can no longer doubt, but it must soon reach the Ears of our Legislators in Parliament assembled; and there meet with a suitable, proportionable, and effectual Redress or Punishment. But to proceed: the Keepers of Publick Gaming-Houses, Bawdy-Houses, and other Lewd and Disorderly Houses; those Nests and Scenes of vile and infamous Practices, with all the Retainers and Harbourers; who there lay in wait to ensnare and entangle the innocent, the ignorant, the unthinking, unwary, and unexperienced, till they become as scar'd and hardned, as impudent and shameless, as wretched and miserable as themselves; All detestable, unnatural Sodomites; and those guilty of Sodomitical Practices: All Ravishers and Assaulters, in order to Ravish Women and Infants: All Violaters of Womens Chastity; and common, abominable Prostitutes for filthy Lucre, Gain, and Hire; [32] These are all of them, in their several Ranks and Orders, common Nusances, Enemies to Mankind, and human Society in general; Offenders in a very high and notorious Sense against God, the King and the Subject, at the same Time, and in the same Instances; and therefore ought to be proceeded against, according to His Majesty's Commands, with a proportionable Vigour and Alacrity; with the utmost Severity and Rigour as may be by Law.[2]

And now to conclude, in order to Encourage you, GENTLEMEN, to bring such notorious Offenders; and all other Offenders, against our excellent Constitution and Laws, and in particular all *Traytors* to the Sacred Person, Family, and Government of our Great and Gracious Sovereign Lord King *GEORGE*, and the Happy Settlement of the Succession in the Protestant Line; to Condign Punishment; (and that either in or out of Sessions, as the Case shall be and require;) I do, in the Name of the Court, and my Brethren, now Promise and Assure you, of all the

[1] Note that JPs are already complaining of gin.

[2] This is a moral condemnation of prostitution, but one may note a total absence of reflection on the origins and reasons for the continuation of this activity.

reasonable, lawful, fitting Encouragement and Assistance of this Court, and of the Members that compose it, as Justices of the Peace for the County of *Middlesex*.

FINIS.

THE **CHARGE** OF Sir *John Gonson*, Kt TO THE **Grand Jury** OF THE CITY AND LIBERTY OF *Westminster*, &c. At the General Quarter-Sessions of the Peace, Held the Twenty fourth Day of *April* 1728 in WESTMINSTER-HALL. Printed at the Desire of the Justices of the peace for the said City and Liberty; and of the Grand Jury. The Second Edition. *LONDON:* Printed and Sold by Joseph Downing, in *Bartholomew-Close* near *West-Smithfield*, 1728.

Civitas, Burgus & Villa Westm. *in Com.* Middx. { ss. *Ad Generalem Quarterialem Sessionem Pacis Domini Regis ten' apud* Westm. *pro Libertate' Decani & Capituli Ecclesiae Collegiat. beati* Petri Westm. *Civit. Burgi. & Villae* Westm. *in Comitat.* Middlesexiae, *& sancti* Martini le Grand, London' *Die Mercur. scilicet vicesimo quarto Die* Aprilis, *Anno Regni Domini* Georgii *Secundi, Dei Gratia, nunc Regis* Magnae Britanniae, *&c. primo.*

HIS Majesty's Justices of the Peace for this City and Liberty of *Westminster*, now assembled at this General Quarter Sessions of the Peace held for the said City and Liberty, being of the Opinion that the Charge this Day given by Sir *John Gonson* the Chairman, (in the Absence of the Right Honourable *John* Lord *Delawar*, the present Chairman of this Session) to the Grand Jury, sworn to enquire for our Soveraign Lord the King, for the Body of this City and Liberty; and to the High and Petty Constables of the same, is *a very Loyal, Learned, Ingenious, Excellent, and Useful Charge, highly tending to the Service of His Majesty, and his Administration and Government*: Have unanimously agreed and resolved, That the Thanks of this Court be, and the same are hereby given, to the said Sir *John Gonson*, for his said Charge; And desire that he will be pleased to cause the same to be Printed and Published, for the better Information of the Inhabitants, and publick Officers of this City and Liberty, in the Performance of their respective Duties.

per Curiam
MIDDLETON.

To the Worshipful
Sir John Gonson, Kt.

Chairman of the Quarter-Sessions, *&c.* held for the City and Liberty of *Westminster*, the 24th of *April*, 1728.

WE the Grand Jury, sworn to enquire for the Body of the City and Liberty of *Westminster*, having received a most Learned and Excellent Charge from the Chair given by your Worship, do hereby return you our most sincere Thanks for the same; And pray you will be pleased, for the publick Good, to cause the same to be Printed.

William Atkinson. John Jones. John Ismonger. E. Salisbury. William House. Gray Sambach. John Henshaw. Stephen Saugé. John Clayton. Thomas Turner. John Ferguson. Philip Gardiner. Jonathan Healey. William Taylor. Hem. Lockton. Th. Cleaver. John Andrews. Jos. Morris. Nathaniel Lee.

[B -1]

THE

CHARGE

OF

Sir *John Gonson*, Kt.

Gentlemen of the Grand-Jury;

Civil Government was instituted for the Preservation and Advancement of Men's Civil Interests, for the better Security of their Lives, Liberties, and Properties.

Men soon became sensible of the Necessity of Civil Government for [2] these Ends, from the Inconveniencies they suffer'd by a private Life, independant on each other: For in such a State, unless every Man would keep strictly to the Rules of Justice and Equity, which the Pravity of humane Nature and long Experience forbid us ever to hope for, the Weak would become a Prey to the Strong; every one would be at the Mercy of him that was mightier than himself, and the World would be full of Fraud and Injustice, Cruelty and Oppression.

No sooner did Mankind begin to multiply, and to contract new Relations and new Duties, but their Interest interfered with one another, and gave rise to those Wrongs and Injuries, which daily encreas'd in the World, and quickly moved Men to enter into Societies, and form themselves into regular Governments, for the mutual Security and Defence of their Persons and Properties, both against Violence from Abroad, and Rapine and Fraud at Home. [B 2 -3]

For these Ends and Purposes Societies were at first Erected, and grounded upon the mutual Compact and Agreement of those who entered into them, to stand by, an assist each other, both against Foreign Violence, and Domestick Wrongs. To repel the first of these, there must be external Force and Strength, which consist in Arms, Riches, and Multitude of Hands; the Remedy of the other lies in wise and wholesome Laws, agreed upon by the Society; and the Care of both is, by common Consent, committed to the Civil Magistrate, who is moreover arm'd with the Force and Strength of all his Subjects, in order to put those Laws in Execution.

From this brief Account of the Nature and Design of Civil Government, it is obvious, That if ever the true Ends of Government are answered, it is under our most happy Constitution, which is a Mixt Limitted Monarchy, where the Prerogatives of the Crown, and the Liberties of the People, are so [4] interwoven, that the Rights reserved to the People tend to render the King honourable and great, and the Prerogatives of the Crown are in order to the Protection and Safety of the People. Every Subject of GREAT BRITAIN has a fix'd fundamental Right born with him, as to the Freedom of his Person, and Property in his Estate, which he can't be deprived of, but either by his own Consent, or for some Crime for which the Law has imposed such a Penalty or Forfeiture. Our Liberties and Privileges are so great, that the Subjects of other Nations would think themselves Princes, if they might enjoy them; and are such, as the greatest Princes in Foreign Parts, who are not absolute and independent Sovereigns, can scarcely pretend to be Possessors of. We enjoy Privileges unknown to the antient *Greeks* or *Romans*, and are the Noblest, I may say almost, the only Remains of the *Antient Northern Liberty.* [5]

And next to that of having a Share in the Legislature, it is one of the most valuable Parts of our Constitution, that no Man can be convicted, or attainted of any Crime, before two Juries pass on him, of at least 24 Persons; The one a Grand Jury, to present the Offence for Tryal; and the other a Petit Jury, to try the Truth of that Presentment. The Grand Jury coming from all Parts of the County, City or Liberty, for which they serve, and the other, viz. the Petit Jury, of the very Neighbourhood where the Offence was committed; who, according to the Evidence given them, determine thereupon and bring in their Verdict. And that the Evidence may be the clearer, and the better to be depended upon, written Depositions are not admitted, but upon mere Necessity: The Witnesses being to appear personally, and to be examined *Viva Voce*; a Method of coming at the Truth peculiar to this Nation, no [6] other having, or practising the like. For look abroad into Foreign Countries, almost where you will, you'll find the Subjects under such Laws, as render their Lives, Liberties, and Estates precarious, and liable to be dispos'd of at the Discretion of Strangers appointed to be their Judges, generally mercenary, and Creatures of the Prerogative; sometimes Malicious and Oppressive, and too often Partial and Corrupt; or suppose them ever so Just and Upright, yet still has the Subject no Security against Subornations, and the Attacks of false and malicious Witnesses: And often, when there is no sufficient Evidence, upon Suspicion only, they are obnoxious to the Tortures of the Rack, which may make an innocent Man consent himself guilty, merely to get out of present Pain; and then with seeming Justice he is executed. Or if he doth with invincible Courage endureth Question (as they call those Torments) yet he comes off with [7] disjointed Bones, and such Weakness, as renders his Life a Burthen to him ever after.

Deservedly therefore is this Tryal by Juries a part of the Great Charter, and ever rank'd amongst the choicest of our Fundamental Laws, which whosoever shall go about to suppress, or craftily undermine, by over-awing or corrupting Juries, and thereby rendering them only a Formality, breaks asunder the Fences of our Government, and is an Enemy to his King and Countrey; for which Reason, our Parliaments have always been most zealous for preserving this Great Jewel of Liberty; no one Privilege besides having been so often remembred there. One Instance thereof (amongst many others) was the Case of the Lord Chief Justice *Keyling*, who usurping an Arbitrary Power over a Grand-Jury of *Somerset-shire*, by commanding them to find a Bill of Indictment, Murder, for which they saw no Evidence; and upon their Refusal, he threatned and fined [8] them: But upon the Complaint of Sir *Hugh Windham*, their Foreman, to the Parliament, (tho' a Parliament of King CHARLES the Second, and much attached to the Court) yet even they could not bear such a bold Invasion of ENGLISH Liberty; the Commons brought that Chief Justice to their Bar, and there made him acknowledge his Fault.[1] When the one and the other Jury act as they ought, with Courage, Diligence, and Impartiality, we shall have just Reason, with the wise Lord Chancellor *Fortescue*,[2] to celebrate that Law that instituted them; to congratulate with our Countrymen the Happiness we enjoy, since the meanest amongst us is protected by the Laws of his Country in as secure a manner as the greatest.

And what compleats our Happiness is, that we may now take the most delightful View of our Excellent Con-[C-9] stitution and Laws; not as in former Reigns, struggling with Arbitrary Power and Tyranny, but as most safe and secure, under the best of Princes, his *Sacred Majesty*, our most Gracious Sovereign; whose Nature, Inclination, and Religion, all conspire to make him truly the Father of his People, delighting in their Happiness as in his own, and who makes the Laws of the Land the Rule of his Government. With such a King we are blest in a Queen, the Delight of the Nation, and the Glory of her Sex; whose known Piety is made still more exemplary by being joined with a fine Understanding, cultivated by the Study of the *Belles Lettres*, and improved with all useful Knowledge: We have also a numerous Royal Issue, to be form'd for the Support of our Religion and Liberties by these bright Examples; so that all the inestimable Blessings we enjoy under his Majesty's Reign, are likely to be entail'd down to future Ages, under a lasting Succession of

[1] *Journals of the House of Commons, 11 & 13. of* Decemb. 1667

[2] *Fort. de Laud. Leg. Ang. Cap. 26.*

[10] Protestant Princes. And may there never want one of this Royal Progeny to Rule over these Nations till Time shall be no more.

Gentlemen,

It is for the preservation and Support of this our excellent Government, by the due Execution of the Laws, that we are met together: And though the Court doth not doubt of your Ability to perform your Duty as *Grand Jury Men*; yet being sworn (amongst other Things) to enquire of such Matters, as shall be given you in Charge, it has always been the Custom, and therefore now proper to inform you, what Crimes and Offences you ought to enquire of, which otherwise perhaps might not occur to your Memory.

In the first Place, I shall recommend to your Enquiry all such Offences that concern Almighty GOD, and his [C 2-11] Holy Religion established amongst us.

It is for the Honour and Interest of every Government, that all Vice, Immorality, and Profaneness should be suppress'd, because they are prejudicial to it; and the contrary Virtues tend to the Good and welfare of Society. All manner of Wickedness, even in those Instances, where it doth not directly injure any private Person, nor disturb the Publick Peace, has an ill Influence upon Society, tends to make Men bad Subjects, and worse Neighbours, and indisposes them for the due Discharge of the Relative Duties of Life. And it has been observed, that a Contempt of GOD, and a Neglect of Religious Duties, is generally the Inlet to, and Forerunner of almost all manner of Wickedness.

I exhort you therefore to present all, that shall blaspheme, vilifie, and ridicule the Name, Nature, and Attributes of GOD, and all other Offences [12] against the Act of the Ninth Year of King WILLIAM the Third, *For the more effectual Suppressing of Blasphemy and Profaneness*. [9.W.III]

You are also to take notice of all other Offences mentioned in His Majesty's Royal Proclamation just now read to you: Particularly all profane Swearing and Cursing, Drunkenness and Breach of the Sabbath.

The horrid Oaths and Curses that abound in our Streets, are very shocking to Religious Foreigners, who come here; no such publick Profanation of GOD's holy Name being known Abroad, even in Popish Countries. Besides, the Offending GOD, the Injuring our Souls, and Affronting sincere Christians (in an Age which pretends to good Breeding) by Treating that GOD with Indignity, whom they worship and adore, are Things of such a Nature, which are worthy of our Notice. The common Practice of [13] profane Cursing and Swearing is exceedingly injurious to Civil Society; for whilst Oaths are reckoned the greatest Securities of Government, if they are once render'd slight and common, it will by Degrees lessen Men's Awe and Regard for them on more solemn and necessary Occasions; and when all Regard for the Obligation of Oaths are lost, there is an End of our Courts of Justice. We have no other Way to judge of Right or Wrong, Truth or Falshood, nor any Security left for our Lives and Properties, when the Reverence for this solemn Appeal to the All-seeing GOD is once extinguished in our Minds. So that upon Civil, as well as Religious Considerations, you ought to set your Faces against this Sin, and present all Constables, negligent or remiss in this Part of their Duty, in Taking up and Giving Information against Common Swearers.

Drunkenness is not only a Transgression of the Laws of GOD, and the [14] Law of the Land, but a Violation of the Law of our Nature: It deprives Men of their Reason, and levels them with the Beasts. Presentment and Indictment in Session is one Method appointed by the Statute of the Fourth of King JAMES I. for the Punishment of Drunkenness. [4. Jac. I. Cap. 5]

It has been the Honour of our Government, that the Observation of the LORD's Day has been more strictly enjoyn'd by our Laws, than any other Nation whatsoever; and it is Pity that such excellent Laws have not been better executed.

The Statute of the Twenty Ninth of King CHARLES II. for the better Observation of the Lord's Day, requires all Persons to exercise themselves thereon in the Duties of Piety and true Religion, publickly and privately, and prohibits all bodily Labour, and worldly Business [29. Car. II. c. 7]. And since this Law forbids Carriers and Waggoners to travel upon their honest [15] and necessary Business on that Day, it surely cannot be supposed to allow any in the Profanation of it by Races, which some Persons have presumed to appoint to be run on Sundays. But His Majesty hath thought fit to discourage such Practices, and commanded the Justices of the Peace of this City and Liberty strictly to put in Execution all the Laws against the Profanation of the Lord's Day, and to the utmost of their Power to discourage and punish any Breach of the Laws in this Behalf [1. Car. 1 c. 1 - 3. Car. I. c. 2.]. His Majesty's Pleasure herein having lately been signified by a Letter from the Right Honourable the Lord *Townshend*, one of His Principal Secretaries of State, his Lordship's Letter shall be presently read in Court.

Since therefore His Majesty's pious Care for the Good of his People is so great, 'tis hoped that so illustrious an Example will inspire you with a Zeal [16] to do your Duty, by Presenting all that shall make default in coming to Church, or some Religious Meeting tolerated and allowed by Law, every Sunday: And all that shall spend their Time on that Day in any Sports or Games whatsoever, especially Gaming Assemblies. [1. Eliz. c. 2.- 23 Eliz. c. 1 - 3 Jac. I. c. 4.-1 W. & M. Sess. 1. c. 18.]

The Devout Observation of the LORD's Day has hitherto, and ever will be, the most probable Means of preserving a Sense of, and keeping up a visible Face of Religion in the World; which (should these Races and other Diversions on this Day prevail) would soon be lost among us.

[5 Eliz. c. 9.] Enquire of all Perjury in Oaths judicially taken: All Subordination of Perjury and Forgery: And also of all Books and Pamphlets wrote against Religion, or the Sacred Scriptures; or that are *Contra bonos Mores*. [D -17

There are such Books published, daily sold in Shops, and advertised in the Publick News-Papers, that ought rather to pass the Fire than the Press; and are a Scandal to any Christian Country. If you can't find out these detestable Authors, present the Printers and Publishers. All these in their Nature seem to be the more immediate Offences against the Divine Majesty.

After the Duty we owe to Almighty GOD, with which nothing ought to come in Competition, the next Duty we owe is to our King and Country; and for the Preservation of these, I must recommend to you to enquire into all Treasons.

It is High-Treason, To Compass or imagine the Death of the King, or Queen, or the Death of their Eldest Son and Heir, and to declare the same by some Overt-Act. [25 Edw. III c. 2.] It is also High-Treason, To levy War against the King; adhere to his Enemies, or to give them Aid or [18] Comfort, in the Realm or elsewhere. To Counterfeit his Great or Privy Seal; To Counterfeit his Coin, or bring false into the Realm; To kill the Lord Chancellor, Lord Treasurer, Justices in Eyre, of Assize; and Justices of Oyer and Terminer, being in their Places doing their Offices.

There are some other Species of High Treason, which because you'll have no Occasion to enquire into, I need not trouble you with the Particulars. I shall only put you in mind of that Excellent Statute of the Sixth [6 Anne c. 7.] of the late Queen *ANNE*, whereby it is made High Treason to maintain by Writing, or Printing, That the Kings and Queens of this Realm, by the Authority of Parliament, are not able to make Laws of sufficient Force to bind and limit the Descent of the Crown; or that the Pretender hath Right to the Crown; or that any other Person hath Right to the same, otherwise than according to the Acts of Settlement. And if the Offender maintains the same by Words only, it is a Praemunire. [D 2-19]

And here, GENTLEMEN, I would observe to you, That by a former Act of Parliament, made in the Thirteenth Year of the Reign of Queen ELIZABETH, to assert and maintain, That the Queen and Parliament could not bind or limit the Descent of the Crown, was made High Treason during that Queen's Life. [13 *Eliz.* c. 1. Rast. 27. - 3 Inst. 6, 10, 12, 14.- *Coke*' s Instit. 4. *part* 36.] By this Law it appears, that the Patriarchal Scheme, and the Doctrines of indefeisible unalienable Hereditary Right are of mere modern Invention, and neither known nor believed by our Parliaments or Clergy in the Glorious Reign of QUEEN ELIZABETH.

So that you see, the Title of his present Majesty King GEORGE is unquestionable, and most agreeable to our Antient Constitution and Laws.

You are also to enquire of Misprision of Treason; which is barely a Concealing it, without Evidencing a Consent to it, for that is High Treason: By the Statute of the Fourteenth of Queen ELIZABETH [14 *Eliz.* c. 7], it is [20] Misprision of Treason to Counterfeit any Foreign Coin not current here. You are to present all Treasonable and Seditious Words and Speeches, reflecting on His Majesty's Sacred Person and Government, for they are indictable at Common Law.

The Third and last Sort of Offences, that I shall recommend to your Enquiry, are those that concern your Fellow-Subjects. Of these some are Capital, and some are not Capital.

Of the Capital You are to present Petty Treason, which is an inferior Degree of Treason, and is committed against a Subject between whom and the Offender the Law presumes, there is a special Obedience and Subjection due [*25 Edw. III c. 7.*]: It is a Petty Treason therefore, for a Servant to kill his Master, or Mistress, or Master's Wife, or a Wife her Husband, or an Ecclesiastical Man his Prelate.

You are to enquire of Burglary, which is a Breaking and Entering into a House by Night, with an Intent to com-[21] mit some Felony, whether the felonious Intent be executed or not. By the Statute of the Eighteenth of Queen ELIZABETH, Clergy is taken away in all Burglaries. [18 *Eliz.* c. 7.]

Your are to present all Sorts of Felonies; as Murders, Robbery on the Highway, Picking of Pockets; but these common Thefts are so well known to you, that I shall not suspect your Knowledge and Understanding so much, as to think you stand in need of any Detail of them, or that I should define them to you.

Of Offences not Capital there are very great Numbers: I shall only mention some, that are most recent amongst us, and therefore likely to fall under your Cognizance and Enquiry. You are to present Petty Larceny; All Buyers and Receivers of stolen Goods, knowing them to be so; all forcible Entries and Detainers of Land and Tenements by Force. All Riots, Routs, and unlawful Assemblies. [5 *R.* II c. 7 - 8 *H.* VI. c. 9.- 31 *Eliz.* c. 11- 21 *Jac.* I. c. 15- 34 *Edw.* III c. 1] Affrays, Assaults, [22] Batteries; and in general, All Breaches of the Peace; All that buy or sell by false Weights or Measures; All that deceitfully get into their Hands other Men's Goods by false Tokens, Pretences, or Counterfeit Letters; All Forestallers, Regrators, and Ingrossers of Corn and other Victuals; All that shall sell corrupt and unwholesome Victuals; All common Barretors, and Stirrers up of Suits and Quarrels, either in the Courts of Justice, or in the Country amongst the King's Subjects, who otherwise would be in Peace. [17 *Rich.* II. c. 8- 13 *Hen.* IV c. 7- 19 *Hen.* VII. c. 13-

11 *Henr.* VII.c. 4- 22 *Car.* II. c. 8- 33 *H.* VIII. c. 1- 5 & 6 *Edw.* VI. c.14 - 51 *Hen.*III. Stat.6. An. Dom. 1266.- 1 *Edw.* III c. 14 - 20 *Edw.* III. c.4 - 1 *Rich.* II. c.4] By Presenting some Barretors, you'll vindicate the Honour of our Laws, by Turning the Edge of them, and the Eyes of your Country upon such Men, who so much abuse the one, and are a Nusance to the other: That Great Man, the Lord Chief Justice HALE, us'd to say, that it was of more Service to the Publick [23] to convict one common Barretor, than ten Highwaymen: Present also all Keepers and Maintainers of Common Gaming Houses, which are indictable as Common Nusances at Common Law, as well as punishable by the Statute of the Thirty third of King HENRY the Eighth. [33 *H.* VIII. c. 7.]

Present likewise all Common Gamesters, who draw in and ruin young Gentlemen of Estates, and others. Enquire of all Bribery and Extortion in any Officers or Ministers of Justice, in taking Money where none is due, or more than due, or before it is due, and particularly of the Extortion of Gaolers. [*12 Rich. II. c. 2- 4 Hen. IV. c. 5.- 5 & 6 Edw. VI. c.16 - 3 Edw I. c. 26.*]

Present all Bawdy-Houses, and all disorderly Houses; under which Denomination you ought to reckon those many Houses and Shops, where such Numbers of the lower Sort of People get drunk with Geneva, and other spirituous Liquors; a growing Evil, of more mischievous Consequence to the Publick, than can well be exprest. [24] And because our Excellent Laws are often render'd useless, through the Remisness and Neglect of the inferiour Officers, who are to execute them,

Enquire, if any Constables omit to make Presentments of any publick and notorious Offences in their respective Parishes or Wards; if they refuse or neglect to execute Warrants delivered to them; if they neglect Watch and Ward; or the Suppressing Vagrants; or if they wilfully neglect or omit any other Part of their Duty.

[2 & 3 *Edw.* VI. c. 15.] Present all Tradesmen, Workmen, and Artificers, that conspire together not to sell their Goods at, or to work, but at certain Rates and Prizes; and all such exercise Mechanical Trades, to which they have not been Apprentices Seven Years, according to the Act of the Fifth of Queen ELIZABETH. [5 *Eliz.* c. 4.]

Present all that shall contract with Artificers to go out of the Kingdom, contrary to an Act of the late King GEORGE. [E -25] You are to enquire of all Highways, and Bridges out of Repair, and who ought to repair them; of all Cheats; and of all publick Nusances: And here I hope you will not forget the very bad Condition of the Streets, and Pavements in many Parts of this City and Liberty, which gives great Offence to every Body, and is detrimental to the Health of the People; and is occasion'd chiefly through the Neglects of the Scavengers and Rakers, and partly by the Remisness and Carelessness of the Servants and Agents of the several Companies of Water-Works, who, when they have broke up the

Ground, to put in or mend their Pipes, lay down the Pavements again in those Places in a very loose, irregular, and unworkmanlike Manner.

These, GENTLEMEN, are all Matters very Proper for your Enquiry, and the Court doth not doubt of your Care therein; but there is one Thing more, which I must at this Time particularly recommend to you, and that is, to [26] present the Authors, Printers, and Publishers of all Libels.

It is a Shame to our Nation, that there should be any Persons belonging to it so little sensible of the Happiness which we enjoy, as to libel and disturb such a King, and such an Administration; yet this Offence is now grown so common, that if a Man goes into a Coffee-House, it is uncertain whether he lays his Hands upon a News-Paper, or a Libel.

I would not have any imagine, that there must be express Words of Scandal, and Persons Names at length, to make a Libeller Criminal; if our Laws require this, they are very weak; and it would be strange, that all Mankind must understand a Libeller's Meaning, except the Court and the Jury, who are to try him.

Indirect or Oblique Scandal hath in all Times (especially since the Abolition of the Court of Star-Chamber) [16 Car. I. c. 10] been prosecuted, and the Offenders convicted and punished in the ordinary Courts of Jus-[27] tice; and if it were otherwise, the subtle or cunning Contrivance, which aggravates the Crime, would prevent the Punishment. And therefore it is, that Ironical Scandal, nay, even Dumb Scandal, (Scandal by Pictures or by Signs) as is mentioned in the Case *de Libellis Famosis*, in my Lord COKE's Fifth Report, is indictable in this Court. The only Caution necessary in these cases is, that the Interpretation be not forc'd or strain'd. [*Coke*'s 5th Report.]

I shall conclude with Putting you in Mind of that Part of your Oath, which obliges you to Present all such Matters and Things, as come to your Knowledge touching this present Service, as well as such Offences, that shall be given you in Charge. You are, or ought to be summoned from the several Quarters of this populous City and Liberty, to the Intent that no Offences in your respective Parishes, or Streets, or probably throughout the whole Liberty, may escape the Knowledge of one or other of you. In Finding only such Bills, that [28] are brought to you by private Prosecutors, you'll do but one Part of your Duty, which a Jury return'd out of one Parish or Street might do as well. But if you'll have a due Regard to your Oaths, you must present all notorious and publick Offences in your respective Neighbourhoods; which, if Grand Juries would every where do, would tend much to reform the vicious Part of Mankind.

Gentlemen,

Your Office is as Antient as our Laws, and (as you have heard) the great Bulwark of our Liberties. And it is with Pleasure, I see this great and important Trust now reposed in Persons of your Credit and Reputation, Knowledge and Experience; who, I doubt not, will perform every Part of your Duty, and acquit your selves like such, as have a strict Regard to Justice, and the Proceedings and Authority of this Court.

FINIS.

THE **CHARGE** TO THE *GRAND JURY* OF THE City of BRISTOL and County of the same City, At the General Quarter-Session of the Peace, held in the Guild-Hall there, *April* 30, 1728. By WILLIAM CANN, Esq; Steward of the Sheriff's-Court. *LONDON:* Printed in the Year MDCCXXVIII.

To the Gentlemen of the Grand Jury of the City of *Bristol* and County of the same City.

GENTLEMEN,

Could I with any Decency have excused my self from printing the following Speech after your Commands to publish it, the same, being no more intended for the Press than it is fit for it, had never thus appear'd abroad. The only Recommendation of this Charge to your least Notice, were those slight Touches in it relating to our happy Establishment: And your View in having it thus come into the World, I look upon as kindly giving me a proper Opportunity to clear my self from the Aspersion mention'd in your Presentment, which I hope the following Pages will effectually do. I am,

Gentlemen,
Your Most Obedient and
Most Humble Servant,
WILLIAM CANN.

[7]

Gentlemen of the Grand Enquest,

The Season of the Year convenes us together to put the Laws in Execution, in order to a Continuance of the Quiet and Repose of this antient City. And when I mention Laws, I would not be understood to mean those given to Mankind by Providence, as a perpetual and inviolable Rule of Action, (which is usually term'd the Moral Law), but that peculiar Scheme of Laws which hath been carved out and formed by Human Understandings, and which exact some special Duties, and prohibit some particular Crimes, under the Sanction of Temporal Rewards and Punishments. And in this Sense (I think) Divines also understand that Passage in the Sacred Writings, which takes Notice that *the Laws were not made for the righteous Man, but for the lawless and disobedient, for ungodly and for sinners, for unholy and profane.* [1]

This being then (as I humbly conceive) the Nature of those Laws which concern the Security of our Persons and Properties, it may not be amiss to consider (by way of Charge) the Excellency and Perfection of our National Laws in general, and thereby implicitly endeavour to persuade and induce you to a cheerful Attendance here in this ensuing Session of the Peace, to the end, that [8] such of them as particularly relate to the Administration of Justice in this Court, may have their due Effect.

And this, Gentlemen, may appear on our taking only a transient View of the Frames of other Neighbouring Governments, and considering the manner their Subjects pass their Days in Subjection under them; and then comparing the happy Lives we lead in this Kingdom with theirs; for by Comparisons is the true Value or Worth of any thing ever best and most surely try'd, as the Difference of Briliants is the more easily discover'd when the Artist examines them together in the same Light.

And here, Gentlemen, it must be so far admitted, that in those Nations I hint at, you find their Sovereign ever in a State of Grandeur and Show, in human Appearance full of Majesty and Dominion, and encompass'd with those great Honours and Attendants which do so properly accompany the Supream Head: But then when we look into the Spring and Fountain from whence these flow, we discover their Original to be in a great Measure and Degree owing to the forced Subjection of their unwilling Subjects, their Patience of bearing Ills, and their tame Submission to the uncontroul'd Will of their Prince, as well in respect to their Religious as Civil Rights and Liberties, from which, and the like Incidents, his Splendour and [9] Glory are found chiefly, if not entirely, to proceed.

You have the Property of those under him sunk and diminish'd in a Moment to half its Value, at his own Arbitrary Will and Pleasure, with the Dash of the Pen, perhaps with his Glove on, and their Consciences (tho' ever so tender) dragoon'd into one Form of Method of Divine Worship,[2] (and that too little else but Pageantry), unless they betake themselves to distant Kingdoms for the Relief and Quiet of their uneasy Minds in this particular. Certainly if such a King receiveth Homage from his Vassals, the same cannot be real and from the Heart, but proceeding from Terror only, as the Indians are reported to worship

[1] Tim. 1: 9.

[2] This is an evident allusion to the methods used by Louis XIV to convert French Protestants back to Roman Catholicism, when his Dragoons were quartered in Protestants' houses, after the Revocation of the Edict de Nantes, 1685. The comparison between the two kingdoms is a permanent feature of these texts, and of the century in general. But conversely, not a word is said of English subjects who were Roman Catholics.

meerly thro' Fear. Thus it really fares with some of our Neighbours: But Things appear with a quite different Face, when we survey our own well contrived Establishment, the peculiar Glory of the *English* Nation; our Sovereign is ever alike circled with the utmost Majesty and Honour, has all the Rule and Dominion over his willing Subjects that a good Prince can either hope or wish for, without breaking in, either upon their Religious or Civil Rights and Liberties, both which they enjoy in as full and ample Manner and Form, as they in their fondest Expectations can reasonably covet or desire. [10] From hence it is, that this Splendour, like that of the Sun, proceeds from himself only; there are no Chasms in his natural Brightness that need any supply like borrowed Moon-light; or at least, if any part of his Sun-shine be owing to any Foreign Cause, it is the cheerful Obedience of his willing Subjects under him.

If there should ever be a Prince amongst us here, who might but attempt to make a vitiated Will his Law, (but thank God there's not the least shadow of any such at present) we have a Parliament entrusted with our Liberties and Properties to moderate and correct it: not, Gentlemen, like that of *France*, which is merely Nominal, and without Action, but one that can and will stand by us, and by interposing on our Behalfs at such a Juncture, dare endeavour to protect us from the Injuries even of Majesty itself.

It is to this Happiness of the Constitution (no doubt) owing that so much Blood and Treasure were with Consent nay Chearfulness, spent in the late War, to support and guard it from the Insults of Foreign Powers, and from its being infected and corrupted with Popery, and arbitrary Government, which so much imbitter the Pleasures, and disturb the Calmness of Life in those unhappy Countries where they are established. These Considerations, without [11] Question, animated and invigorated our Veteran Troops and with additional Courage and Resolution, to defend us from these last mentioned Evils and Calamities, and so deservedly esteem'd by this Nation, and which now indeed we can by no means dread or fear, since the Prospect of that invaluable Blessing (Universal Peace) seems to be so near at Hand, under the Influence of which we may securely hope both our Religious and Civil Rights will for ever rest free from Interruption by the ineffectual Power of any Foreign Restless Prince whatsoever; so that every Man may sit down content under his own Vine in the full Fruition and Enjoyment of his Liberty, one Moment whereof (as a great Man once finely observ'd) is worth a whole Eternity in Bondage.

And having mentioned Religious Rights, it might look partial, should I not take Notice that it hath been sometimes objected, and by those of known Worth and Learning, that too great a Latitude in Matters of that kind hath obtained, and the Indulgence that was originally intended by our Governments to Persons really Scrupulous touching the establish'd

Form of Worship of the Nation, (the best I think in the Universe) hath of late been so much extended as to let in Numbers of illiterate Pretenders, to become Rectifiers of Mens Lives, who be-[12] fore more properly employed themselves perhaps in mending their Shoes,[1] to the apparent rendering our Holy Religion obnoxious to the Censure and Reflection of our Neighbours, who Smile within themselves to see so many silly aukward Wretches playing the Mountebank in those sacred Things, which ought to be touched by such only, whom a liberal Education hath fitted and prepared for so great an Undertaking: And perhaps, Gentlemen, there may be some seeming Weight in the Objection, and it must appear very odd and unaccountable to some, when they take Notice what a stir and adoe there hath been about varying and amending that which though it may be alter'd, is yet incapable of more Perfection than it hath already; and it may be still farther surprizing to observe what sorry Workmen are frequently employ'd in the Business; as if an ordinary Stone-Cutter should go about to rectify a supposed Defect in the Legg or an Arm of a fine Image carv'd by Phidias or Praxiteles: However this Objection, palpable as it is, yet I think is by no means sufficient to call in Question the Prudence of the Government in winking at their Indulgence being thus abused; for (besides it's obliging weak Minds thereby) these Empiricks in Divinity, and their few empty Followers enjoy their Short-lived Per-[13] suasions without Interrupting the State; and being to inconsiderable to be observ'd by it, they soon shrink, and dwindle into nothing: A late Instance of which we had in this City, where, (as I have been credibly inform'd) a Fellow just from the Plough, and countenanced by a Journey-man Weaver only, obtained under the before-mentioned Favour of the Law, a License to preach (as he impudently call'd it) but within a few Months the Place where he vended his wretched Wares became a Stable for Horses, Creatures he before was accustomed to govern, and lead, and to which Employment he is again properly returned.[2]

In fine, Gentlemen, so long as Sense and Reason have a Place amongst us to enable Mankind to distinguish between Right and Wrong, there can be no Foundation even to suppose that these new sprung Teachers (and such only I mean) will be capable of ever gaining many Proselytes by the frivolous Jargon they utter amongst their Scanty Flocks, who I think may be properly enough said to follow, not the true Shepherd, but the Sheep with the Bell; for indeed their Nonsense can have no other

[1] An allusion to the number of self-appointed itinerant preachers, who had left shoe-mending to become preachers or mountebanks. See J. Swift, *A Tale of a Tub*, 1710, 5th ed., Section 1; R. Graves, *The Spiritual Quixote*, where Jeremiah Tugwell, a cobbler, is going to accompany young Wildgoose in his preaching and this, as late as 1773. See I, vi.

[2] I have not been able to trace the origin of this fact.

Recommendation in the World, but that of being noisy, and delivered extempore.

On the other Hand we find our Clergy universally esteem'd to be (as they certainly are) the most learned Body of Men in the [14] Christian World, and they do therefore not only command, but deserve all manner of Respect from us: It's no Objection to their Merit as a Society of Men, to say that the Actions of some few crept in amongst them, may not perhaps be exactly squared by the strict Rules of Virtue and Morality; their Sacred Order is notwithstanding still the same, as the Soveraign's Image alike remains to be such, whether Stampt on Gold or Copper.

Amongst the many and singular Virtues and Perfections which adorn and set off her present Majesty, I think it to be none of the least, that she shewed so early a regard on her first Arrival here, her Continuance of it ever since verified as often as Opportunities present themselves, and which were always welcome to her, and her late bounteous Liberality to their indigent Widows and Orphans, joined with gracious Hints, which heightened the Value of the present, that under her Shade they might rest assured of Protection from the many Ills which ever attend Poverty and Want.

To these Learned Gentlemen it belongs to temper and humanize our Passions and Affections, as it does to the Magistrates and Grand Jurors to correct and punish us, when we suffer them to grow excessive, [15] and to break out in the Outraging one another.

And having mention'd Magistrates, I might here take Occasion (if time permitted) to consider of what publick Use and Blessing they are when Justice and Wisdom have their Seat amongst them.

The Value of such is finely imagined in the following Conceipt, which a very Venerable and Learned Man had of them, when he said, *They were Blessings as extensive as the Community to which they belong, whatsoever that relate to this Life; secure to us the Possession and enhance the Value of them all; which render the Condition of the happiest amongst Men still more happy, and the State of the meanest less miserable than it would otherwise be; and for the Enjoyment of which no Man can well envy another, because all Men in their several Ranks, and according to their several Proportions and Degrees so alike Share in it.* And then he alludes to an apposite Passage in Holy Writ, where the precious Ointment is represented as running down from the Head to *Aaron*'s Beard, and thence to the Skirts of his Garment. [1]

Gentlemen, We need no Perspectives to discover such Magistrates as these I hint at; nor (when I perceive Persons of your Figure here) Men capable of assisting them in a due Administration of Justice. [16] It would be mispending time to detain you with any Repetition of the several well known Parts of your Office, which all or most of you have heard so

[1] An allusion to Ps. 133: 2.

frequently, and fully dictated from this Place, by the learned Gentleman for whom I now Officiate. Let it suffice that I just remind you of the Oath you have even now ta'en, enjoining the Performance thereof, and that I only recommend your diligent and chearful Attendance here in this ensuing Session, in Order to a faithful Discharge of that Duty you all so well understand.

FINIS

THE **CHARGE** OF Sir *John Gonson* Knt. TO THE **GRAND JURY** of the Royalty *of the* Tower *of* London, *and Liberties and Precincts thereof.* At the General Quarter-Sessions of the Peace for the said *Royalty*, &c. held the sixteenth Day of *July* 1728. at the *Court-House* on *Great-Tower-Hill.*

Printed at the Desire of the Justices of the Peace *for the said* Royalty, *and of the* Grand Jury.

LONDON: Printed by Charles ACKERS, in *Great-Swan-Alley*, St. *John's -Street.* MDCCXXVIII.

Turr' & Libertat. Turr. London. } ss. *Ad Generalem Quarterialem Sessionem Pacis Domini Regis tent' apud le* Court-house *super* Towerhill *magna infra Libertat' Turr' dicti Domini Regis* London. *Praedict' in & pro Libertat' Praedict' & Praecinct' ejusdem, Die* Martis *(scilicet Decimo Sexto Die* Julii, *Anno Regni Domini* Georgii *Secundi, nunc Regis* Magnae Britanniae, *&c. Secundo.*

WHEREAS Sir *John Gonson* Knight, Chairman at this General Quarter-Sessions of the Peace, held for the *Tower* of *London* Liberties, and Precincts thereof, having this Day given to the Grand Jury, sworn at this present Sessions of the Peace, held for the said Liberty, a Loyal, Learned and Ingenious Charge, and tending much to the Promoting of Virtue and Religion; it is unanimously Agreed and Ordered by this Court, That the Thanks of this Court be, and the same are hereby given, to the said Sir *John Gonson* for such his Charge. And further, the Court desires, that he would be pleased to cause the same to be Printed.

Per Curiam
BRUNCKER.

[A 2]

To the WORSHIPFUL

Sir *John Gonson* Knt.

CHAIRMAN of the General Quarter-Sessions of the Peace, held for his Majesty's *Royalty* of the *Tower* of *London*, the sixteenth Day of *July*, 1728.

We the Grand Jury, sworn to enquire for the Body of the Royalty *of the* Tower *of* London, *having this Day received a most Loyal, Learned, and Ingenious Charge by your Worship, Do hereby return you our most hearty Thanks for the same; and [4] pray, that you will be pleased, to cause the same to be Printed.*

Henry Willoughby.
Henry Dean.
Ralph Arnold.
James Wood.
Peter Gayd.
Thos. Hutchinson.
Wm. Hookham.
Will. Higgins.
Sam. Knowles.
James Swaine.
John Smith.
Charles Woolmer.
Wm. Harper.
Wm. White.
John Harper.

[5]
THE
CHARGE
OF
Sir *John Gonson* Knt.

Gentlemen of the Grand Jury,

IT is the peculiar Happiness and Glory of us in *Great-Britain* to be in the strictest Sense a free People, and to live under a Constitution of Government so admirably fram'd, that it secures as great Powers and Prerogatives to the Crown, as any wise and good Prince can desire, who will own his People as Subjects and not as Slaves; and at the same Time reserves most va-[6] luable Rights and Liberties to the People. There is that due Balance in Property, Power and Dominion in our Constitution, that, like the ancient Government of *Sparta*, it may be call'd an Empire of Laws, and not of Men. Every Subject of Great-Britain has the same Right to what he can acquire by his Labour, and Industry, as the King hath to his Crown; no Man can be Imprisoned, unless he has trangressed a Law made by the representatives of his own Choosing, nor be tried but by a Jury of his Neighbours. A greater Inheritance (saith my Lord *Coke*) is derived to us by our Laws, than from our Parents. For without the former what would the latter signify?

AND as this most happy Constitution hath been maintained at the Expence of Millions of Treasure, and came down to us swimming in the Blood of our Ancestors, who always esteemed it the most valuable Legacy, which they could leave their Posterity: so GOD Almighty, by a kind and over-ruling Providence, hath [7] still preserved us a free People; our Government having stood the Shock of Ages from its Original; particularly of the last, when so many Attempts were made to turn our limited Monarchy into Tyranny. And this inestimable Blessing we ought the more to value, if we look Abroad in to the Kingdoms, that lie nearest and are best known to us; in some of which we shall not find the Shadow of Liberty left; and in many there is no more than the Name remaining.

Spain, Portugal, Sweden, Denmark and *France* were all, an Age or two ago, limited Monarchies, govern'd by Princes well advised by Parliaments or Cortes[1], and not by the absolute Will of one Man. But now all their valuable Rights and Liberties are swallowed up by the arbitrary Power of their Princes; whilst we, happy *Britons*, are in many Things the Envy as well as the Wonder of other Nations, and almost the last of the *Northern* Kingdoms of *Europe*, that have preserved this our ancient and well balanced Government. Remarkable is that Account [8] which we read concerning *Monsieur Mezeray*, the famous *French* Historian who towards the Close of the last Century,[2] discoursing with a Person of Quality of our own Nation [Mr. Hampden][3], about the Difference of Government in *France* and in *England*, broke out into these Expressions. " We had once in *France* (says he) the same Happiness and the same Privileges, which you have; our Laws were made by Representatives of our own Choosing; our Money was not taken from us, but by our Consent; our Kings were subject to the Rules of Law and Reason: But now alas! we are miserable, and all is lost. Think nothing, Sir, too dear to maintain these precious Advantages, and if ever there be Occasion, venture your Life and Estate, and all you have, rather than submit to the Condition, you see us reduced to. "

THUS sensibly did this great Man lament the lost Liberties of his Country. [B-9]

AS to the Excellency, Wisdom and Justice of our Laws, the daily Benefits and Avantages, which we all receive from them, give them a Character beyond all the Rhetorick imaginable.

WE of this Age enjoy such a Collection of Blessings, as ought to be viewed with the highest Sentiments of Joy and Thanksgivings to Almighty GOD. A King upon the Throne form'd for the Happiness of all, that live under his Government, who is ever Securing and inviolably Maintaining all the legal Rights and Liberties of his Subjects, and whose only Ambition is to make them all easy and happy. And with such a King we have a most Virtuous, Pious and Excellent Queen, and a numerous Royal Progeny, eminent for all princely Virtues and Endowments, promising Happiness to our latest Posterity at different Ages.

Gentlemen,

OUR most admirable Laws preserve their Honour, and best exert their Power [10] and Force, by a due impartial and vigorous Execution, and an equal Distribution of Justice. And our Lives, Liberties, and

[1] The Spanish equivalent of the Parliament.

[2] François Eudes de Mezeray (1610–83) wrote an *Histoire de France* (1643–51) then an *Abrégé chronologique* (1668).

[3] John Hampden, 1594–1643, the famous parliamentary opponent of Charles I's arbitrary policy.

Properties, in a great Measure, depend upon the due Execution of that great Power, which, by the Wisdom of our Constitution, is intrusted with Grand Jury and Petty Juries. You are therefore summoned here, and sworn to enquire, and present to us all such Crimes and Offences, as fall within the Cognizance of this Court.

ALL Manner of Crimes are presentable by you, from the highest to the lowest Offences, from High Treason to Trespass: But tho' High Treason, Petty Treason, Burglary, and Felonies of all Sorts are enquirable by you and every Grand Jury; yet because Bills of Indictment for these Crimes are seldom or never brought before you at this Quarter-Sessions, but prosecuted at another Place,[1] I shall omit to give you in Charge any Capital Offences, and confine myself to those Offences only, that are both Enquirable and Punishable here. [B 2-11]

IN the first Place the Honour and Service of Almighty GOD, ought to be our chiefest Care. And we should all endeavour, if possibe, to put a Stop to that Deluge of Profaneness, that has so overspread the Nation, and it were happy if our Holy Religion did not suffer as well from its Enemies Diligence to corrupt our Principles, as from the wicked Lives of its Professors.

THEREFORE you are to enquire of all Offences against the Act of the ninth Year of King WILLIAM the Third, [9 & 10 *W.* III. c.32] for the more effectual Suppressing Blasphemy and Profaneness, and particularly of all Books and Pamphlets wrote against the *Christian* Religion, or the divine Authority of the Holy Scriptures: There are several late Writers, who go under the Names of *Deists*, but are really *Atheists*, without GOD in the World, renouncing his Providence, and *even denying the* LORD *that bought them* [2 Peter II. i]; pretending [12] indeed an Enquiry after sensible Ideas of the spiritual and supernatural Truths of eternal Life: Whereas, with all their boasted Reason, they are not able to given an Idea of the Breath of natural Life, nor can tell the Composition of the least Pile of Grass; and yet, by rational Demonstration, would determine and judge of Things invisible, which can only be the Objects of Faith in the Word of GOD. Several of these Authors deny the Immortality of the Soul, and the future State of Rewards and Punishments, and would subject Mankind to a Baseness and Wretchedness inferior to the worst of Brutes, and thereby also dissolve the Bond of Security and Peace among all human Societies, and Relations, which can only consist in the Fear of GOD, and the Practice of Religion.

IF you cannot find out the Authors, present the Printers and Publishers of all these Wicked and Blasphemous Books. [13]

[1] Such offences were tried by judges under commissions of Oyer and Terminer, and Gaol Delivery. They dealt with capital crimes, whereas the Q-S. magistrates could not inflict the capital penalty.

YOU have heard his Majesty's Proclamation read to you, for the Encouragement of Piety and Virtue, and for the preventing and punishing of Vice, Profaneness, and Immorality, and the Causing it to be thus publickly read, is one Part of the Duty of the Court, but not the whole;[1] for his Majesty therein commands his Judges of Assize at their Assizes, and his Justices of the Peace at their General Quarter-Sessions, to give strict Charges for the effectual Prosecution and Punishment of the Offenders of all Sorts and Kinds mentioned therein: And also of all Persons, that, contrary to their Duty, shall be Remiss and Negligent in Putting these good Laws in Execution. The Offences, expresly mentioned in this most Excellent Proclamation, are, Excessive Drinking, Blasphemy, Profane Swering and Cursing, Lewdness, Profanation of the LORD's Day; all publick Gaming, and Gaming-Houses, and other lewd and disorderly Practices. [14]

DRUNKENNESS is a Vice, that calls aloud for your Redress upon a double Account; 1. Upon a Religious one, as it is an Offence against Almighty GOD; and, 2. Upon a Political one, because it reduces whole Families to Poverty and Ruin. One of our Statutes fixes this infamous Character upon the Vice of Drunkenness, [4 Jac. 1. c. 5.] That it is Odious and Loathsom, the Root and Foundation of Blood-shed, Stabbing, Murder, Swearing, Fornication, Adultery, and such like enormous Sins, to the great Dishonour of Almighty GOD, and of our Nation, the Overthrow of many good Arts and Manual Trades, the Disabling of divers Workmen, and the general Impoverishment of many good Subjects, abusively Wasting the good Creatures of GOD.

IF this was a lively Description of the sad and fatal Consequences of this brutish Immorality at the Passing of this Act, which is above a hundred and twenty Years ago, when the Nation in general was, comparatively speaking, much [15] more Virtuous than it is now; what abundant Reason have we to do our utmost to suppress this Vice, that is at present so recent amongst us, and which, daily Experience shews, often drowns the best Natural Parts, and renders Men wholly unserviceable to the Community?

A common Drunkard is Indictable in Sessions, as well as Punishable in a summary Way, and yet we seldom hear of any Offenders of this Kind presented by Grand Juries, notwithstanding this Offence is so common and notorious.

A common Swearer is a Nusance to the Place where he lives. I am sorry that it is still too true, what that great and good Man, Arch-bishop TILLOTSON, says in a Sermon against Swearing, That a Man cannot walk the Streets without having his Ears grated with this hellish Noise. We may justly wonder at the Patience and merciful Forbearance of our

[1] Most likely George II's proclamation dated 5 July 1727.

Great GOD, in not punishing these Impious Wretches, by an immediate [16] Stroke of his Almighty Vengeance, in not Sinking them quick into that irrecoverable State of Damnation, which they so often and earnestly imprecate upon themselves, for the Confirmation of some trifling Matter, and sometimes of a downright Falshood. And as this is a Sin very dishonourable to GOD; so it is in this Particular extreamly Dangerous to human Societies: For profane Cursing and Swearing contributes much to the Growth of Perjury. Oaths are little minded when commun Use has sullied them, and every Minute's Repetition has made them cheap and common; Who can believe, that a Man, who hourly provokes GOD by rash and vain Swearing, should stick at a false Oath, whenever his Ambition, his Covetousness, or his Revenge prompt him to it, and importunately Demand to be gratified tho' at so vast a Price? Besides, at so low a Rate do such Men value their Souls, who expose them to the Wrath of GOD, and Eternal Damnation, by a [C -17] Sin, from which they cannot reap the least Profit or Pleasure?

IF any Constables are Remiss or Negligent in their Duty, in Taking up and Giving Information against these Offenders, it is your Duty to Present such Constables, that they may be Punished and Fined.

THE Profanation of the LORD's Day is of late very Notorious, and yet pleaded for by some among us as Warrantable. Whatever Disputes there may be about the Morality of the Fourth Commandment, it is generally agreed amongst pious Christians, that this Day ought to be devoutly and religiously observ'd and kept holy [1 Car. I c. 1.; 3 Car. 1. C. 2; 29 Car. II. c. 7.]; this the *Homilies* of our Church and our Laws require. The Lord Chief Justice HALE, who was an excellent Christian as well as a great Lawyer, made it his Observation, that the more strictly he kept Sunday, the better Success he always had in his worldly Affairs the Week following. [His Life by Dr. *Burnet* late Bishop of *Sarum*][1]. [18]

YOU are to present to this Court, all such Persons who do not come to Church, or some Religious Meeting, allowed by Law, every Sunday. [1 Eliz. C. 2- 23 Eliz. c. 1.- 3 Jac. I c. 4 - 1 W. & M. Sess. 1.c. 18]

YOU are to enquire of Perjury, and Subornation of Perjury, which, as I observed before, does, in a great Measure, owes its dreadful Encrease to the impious Custom of profane Cursing and Swearing in common Conversation. These Offences of Perjury, and Subornation of Perjury, are more Heinous, and deserve a severer Punishment, because they are committed with Thought and great Deliberation, and carry along with them a high Affront to the Majesty of GOD, and great Injustice and Injury to Men, the Consequences of them are the Ruin of innocent Persons, who sometimes lose their Lives, and often their Estates, and good Names, by the false Oaths of perjured Wretches.

[1] G. Burnet, *The Life and Death of Sir Matthew Hale*, 1682 (3 eds.; transl. into French, 1689).

ALL these in their Nature are more immediate Offences against Almighty [C 2- 19] GOD, and his Holy Religion established amongst us.

YOU are likewise to enquire of such Offences, as are committed against your Neighbours, or Fellow Subjects, and which Injure them in their Persons, their Properties, or their Reputations.

YOU are to enquire of Petty Larceny, which is Stealing any Thing under the Value of twelve Pence.

YOU are also to present all Assaults, Batteries, Affrays; and in general, all Breaches of the Peace, all forcible Entries, and Detainers of Land and Tenements by Force.

A forcible Entry is, where one or more Persons, with Weapons not usually born, have violently entered into the House or Land of another; or where one or more have entered peaceably, the Door being open, and there have forcibly put another out of Possession [5 *R.*II c. 7 - 15 *R.*II c. 2- 8 *H.* VI c. 9- 31 *Eliz.* c. 11 - 21 *J.* I. c.15]. [20]

A forcible Detainer is, where one or more have entered peaceably into the House, or Land of another, and then have detained the Possession thereof with Forces and Arms.

YOU are to enquire of all Riots, Routs, and unlawful Assemblies.

A Riot is, where three Persons or more are met together to do an unlawful Act so as to beat a Man, lay open his Fence, and the like, and have done the same [34. *E.*III c.1- 17 *R.* II c.8- 13 *H.*IV c.7- 19 *H.* VII c.13].

A Rout is, where three Persons or more have met together to do an unlawful Act, and move from the Place where they first met, but afterwards parted without doing the Act.

AN unlawful Assembly is, where three Persons or more meet together to so an unlawful Act, and part without doing the same, or moving forward for that Purpose.

YOU are to present all Forestallers, Regrators, and Ingrossers [5 & 6 *Ed.* VI c. 14] [21] These our Laws esteem great Offenders, who without any real Cause, enhance the Price of Corn, and other Victuals, and thereby occasion Uneasiness, Discontent, and Murmuring, especially among the lower Sort of People.

FORESTALLING is, Buying up Commodities by the Way, before they come to Market.

REGRATING is, Buying Corn or other Victuals, in the Market, and Selling it again in the same Market, or in any other within four Miles.

ENGROSSING is, Buying up great Quantities of Corn, or other Victuals, and Selling the same again.

THESE Offenders, for the first Offence, forfeit the Value of the Goods, and are to suffer two Months Imprisonment: For the second Offence, double the Value of the Goods, and Six Months Imprisonment: And for the third Offence they shall forfeit all their Goods, stand in the Piillory, and be Imprisoned during the King's Pleasure. [22]

YOU are to enquire of Barretry, Maintenance, Champerty, And Embracery: These are also great Crimes, and it is Pity, that they are not oftener prosecuted.

33 *E.*I. Stat.2] BARRETRY is, Stirring up of Suits and Quarrels amongst the King's Subjects, which otherwise would be in Peace.

1 *E.* III c. 4- 20 *E* III. C.4- 1 *R.* II c.4] MAINTENANCE is, the Taking in Hand, Bearing up, or Upholding of Quarrels, or Sides, to the Disturbance or Hinderance of common Right.

33 *E.*III Stat.-3 *Ed.* Ic.25- 33 *E.* I Stat.3.] CHAMPERTY is, the Maintaining and Carrying on of Suits and Causes, at their own Costs and Charges, to have Part of the Land or Thing in Question, or Part of the Gains.

38 *E.*III c. 12- Noy's Reports, Fol. 102] EMBRACERY is, and an Embracerer is, one, that when Matter is at Trial, comes for a Reward to the Bar, being no Lawyer nor Witness, and speaks in Fa- [23] vour of one of the Parties, or labours the Jury, or uses any unlawful Practice, to make them give their Verdict as he would have them.

YOU are to present all Bawdy-houses, Gaming-houses, disorderly Houses, and unlicensed Houses. Those Houses and Shops, where People frequently get drunk with *Geneva*, or other sipirituous Liquors, are Indictable as disorderly Houses, whether they have or have not Licences.

NOTHING is more destructive either to the Health or Industry of the poorer Sort of People, on whose Labour and Strength the Support of the Community depends so much, than the immoderate Drinking of *Geneva*. It is common for a starving Sot, intoxicated with this or the like Liquors, to behold his Rags and Nakedness with a stupid Insolence, and either in senseless Laughter, or in low and insipid Jests, to banter all Prudence and Frugality, drowning his pinching Cares, and losing, with his Reason, [24] all anxious Reflections on a Wife, or Children, perhaps crying for Bread in a horrid empty Home. In hot Tempers, it lets loose the Tongue to all Indecencies and Rudeness of the most provoking Language, as well as the most hellish Oaths and Curses, and which is frequently followed by Quarrels and Curses, and somtimes [sic] has been the Cause of Murder. Besides all this, these Houses and Shops are the Receptacles of Thieves and Robbers, and often the Original of them too; for when a Wretch has spent and wasted that, which should support him, and his Family, it is here, that they Associate and turn House-Breakers, and Street-Robbers, and so, by quick Progressions at last make an Exit at the Gallows.

OUR Laws have not only taken a great Deal of Care to punish all Breaches of the Peace; but also in several Instances what only tends to a Breach of the Peace, as Challenging another to Fight; Also Libels against private [D - 25] Persons are Indictable. For it is as just, that Reputation should be guarded and defended by Law, as that Property should.

THEREFORE Writing a scandalous Letter concerning any one, directed either to the Party himself, or a third Person, is punishable in this Court; and putting such a Letter into the Post, hath been adjudged a Publication of the Libel.

YOU are to enquire if the Clerk of the Peace, Coroner, Gentleman Goaler, and all other Officers of this *Royalty,* perform their respective Duties.

WHETHER they, or any other judicial Officers, are guilty of Bribery, by Taking Gifts or Rewards to pervert Justice; or are guilty of Extortion, by taking Fees, where none are due, or before they are due; or greater Fees than by Law are due to them; and particularly enquire of the Extortion of Goalers and Bailiffs. [26]

YOU are to enquire, whether the Offenders sent to the House of Correction are set to work as they ought, and receive their due Punishments; and whether the Gouvernour or Keeper thereof doth his Duty therein. Of which a true Account is to be render'd every Quarter-Sessions.

IF any Constables omit or neglect to make Presentments to this Court of any Annoyances, common Nusances, or notorious Offences in their respective Neighbourhoods; you ought to present such Constables.

YOU are also to present all treasonable and seditious Libels against his Majesty and his Ministers of State, or other great Men, or Magistrates; these are Indictable at common Law.

YOU are to enquire of all publick Nusances, the Want of due Repairs in common Highways, Streets, and Pavements. But I refer you, for a most [D 2-27] distinct and particular Account of these Offences, to my Charge given to the Grand Jury of the City and Liberty of Westminster, at the last Easter Quarter-Sessions held there, which that Court was pleased to Order to be Printed and Published; a Copy of which I have directed to be given to each of you, GENTLEMEN, who are sworn upon this Grand Jury, for your Use of this present, or any future Service of this Kind.

Gentlemen,

The OATH, that you have taken, obliges you to present all such Matters and Things, as come to your Knowledge, touching this present Service, as well as such Offences that shall be given you in Charge; and by the Statute of the Third of King HENRY the Seventh, [3 *H.* VII c. 1] if a Grand Jury Conceal any Thing, which they ought to present, the Justices may, within a Year, impanel another Jury to enquire of such Concealment, and upon Conviction, Fine every one of the former Jury at [28] the Discretion of the Court. So earnestly the Law insists upon your doing your Duty. Therefore you must present all Nusances, Annoyances, Houses of Lewdness, and common Gaming; disorderly *Geneva*-shops, common Gamesters, common Drunkards, and Disturbers of the Peace, and all other Offenders within this *Royalty,* as far as shall come to the Knowledge of any of you; which if you neglect to do, and leave any unpresented for Love, Favour, Affection, Gain, Reward or Hopes thereof, you'll break your promissory Oath; I mean, that solemn Appeal you lately made to the GOD of Truth, who will not fail to avenge it upon your selves, and your Families; *for he will not hold him guiltless, who takes his Name in vain.*[1] But that you may the better keep your Oaths, and Discharge your Duty with the greater Sincerity and Diligence, let me advise you seriously to think of the general Appearance, which we must all [29] one Day make before the Awful Tribunal of the Great GOD, in Comparison of which, the most Solemn and August Judicature here upon Earth, (tho' it may faintly represent it to our Thoughts) is but a Piece of formal and vain Pageantry.

FINIS.

[1] Exod. 20: 7.

THE **Second CHARGE** OF Sir *John Gonson* Knt. TO THE GRAND JURY of the City and Liberty of Westminster, &c. at the General Quarter-Sessions of the Peace, held the eleventh Day of *July*, 1728, at the *Town Court-House* adjoining to *Westminster-Hall.* AND ALSO ***HIS CHARGE*** to the GRAND JURY of the *Royalty* of the *Tower of London*, and the Liberties and Precincts thererof, at the General Quarter-Sessions of the Peace for the said *Royalty*, & c. held the sixteenth Day of July, 1728, at the *Court-House* on *Great Tower-Hill.*

Printed at the Desire of the Justices of the Peace in both the said Commissions, and of the respective *GRAND JURIES.*

LONDON:
Printed by CHARLES ACKERS, in *Great-Swan-Alley*, St. *John's -Street.*
MDCCXXVIII

Civitas, Burgus, & Villa Westm. *in Com.* Middx. { *ss. Ad Generalem Quarterialem Sessionem Pacis Domini Regis tent' apud* Westm. *pro Liberta' Decani & Capituli Ecclesiae Collegiat. beati* Petri Westm. *Civit', Burgi, & Villae* Westm. *in Comitat.* Midx *& Sancti* Martini le Grand, London' *die* Jovis *scilicet undecimo die* Julii, *Anno Regni Domini* Georgii *Secundi, Dei Gratia nunc Regis* Magna Britanniae, *&c secundo.*

Forasmuch as the Charge this Day given by Sir *John Gonson* Knight, Chairman of this Court (in the Absence of the Right Honourable *John* Lord *Delawar* the present Chairman[1]) to the Grand Jury, and Jury of Constables, assembled and sworn at this present Sessions of the Peace held for this City and Liberty, is a Religious, Loyal, and Elegant Charge, tending to promote the Practice of Virtue and Religion, and also fully demonstrating the Happiness of our Constitution and Government, under the auspicious and glorious Reign of his present Majesty, and his wise Administration: It is unanimously Agreed, and Ordered by this Court, That the Thanks of this Court be, and the same are hereby given to the said Sir *John Gonson* for his said Charge; and this Court doth desire, that he will be pleased to cause the same to be printed and Published.

[1] John West, 1st Earl Delaware, 1693-1766. Cf *D.N.B.*

Per Curiam
MIDDLETON.

[A 2]
To the WORSHIPFUL
Sir ***John Gonson*** Knt.

CHAIRMAN of the Quarter-Sessions, *&c.* held for the City and Liberty of *Westminster*, the eleventh Day of *July*, 1728.

We the Grand Jury, sworn to enquire for the Body of the City and Liberty of *Westminster*, having received a most Excellent, Learned, and Loyal Charge from the Chair given by your Worship, Do hereby return you our most hearty Thanks for the same; and pray, thay you will be pleased, for the Publick Good, to cause the same [4] to be Printed, to remain to Posterity, &c.

James Webb.

Edm. Purse	Tho. Fayram
Tho. Mitchell	Wm. Holmes
John Richards	Sam. Mallings.
Jos. Pagett	Peter Wood
Charles Steward	Tho. Baker
Tho. Farraine	John Chadworth
John Parker	Sam. Vale
Tho. Stocken	Tho. Hamley
John Gouleton.	

[5]
THE
Second CHARGE
of
Sir *John Gonson* Knt.

Gentlemen of the Grand Jury,

As the principal End of Civil Government and Human Laws is to secure Property, to oblige Men, out of the Fear of Penalties, to live honestly and justly, and that each Individual may be defended against Injury and Wrong; so where the Fundamental Laws and Constitutions of any Government have been wisely adapted to these [6] Ends, such Countries and Kingdoms have encreas'd in Virtue, Power, Wealth, and Happiness.

Oratio pro Publio Sextio. TULLY, who takes it from ARISTOTLE, tells us, That the ultimate End of Government, and the Mark, that all Rulers ought to aim at, is to acquire Peace with Reputation.

TOWARDS attaining this End, he mentions the several Particulars, which it requires the greatest Application and Vigilance of good Governours to promote and maintain; and the chief Branches, as he enumerates them, are, Religion; the just and legal Powers and Rights of the Legislature; and of the Magistrates subordinate to that; a due Administration of Justice, the Publick Treasure and Credit; and concludes with *Laus Publica*: which indeed is the Result of a good Administration of the several Branches mentioned. For Praise, both at Home and Abroad, will always attend good Management. [7]

It is apparent to any one, that will but reflect upon all these Particulars, That in no Age hath there ever been in this Nation, or any other, a more universally Glorious Administration, than we now enjoy under his Sacred Majesty King G E O R G E the Second.

To begin with Religion. The Church of England by Law establish'd is in no Danger, but in a most safe and flourishing Condition; all her Immunities, Rights, and Privileges are secur'd to her by the strongest Laws; and at the same Time the Protestant Dissenters are easy and happy under the Act of Toleration. And, as his Majesty was pleased to take Notice in his Speech to the last Parliament, [His Majesty's Speech to both Houses of Parliament, July 17. 1727]" Such mutual Forbearance is diffused throughout the Kingdom, that the National Church repines not at the Indulgence given to scrupulous Consciences; and those that [8] receive the Benefit of the *Toleration*, envy not the *Establish'd Church* the Rights and Privileges, which they by Law enjoy."

It was quite otherwise in former Reigns, when Popery and Tyranny had almost prevailed to the Ruin of our Church and State. The Protestants of these Kingdoms, by the Artifice of Papists, and the Tools of Arbitrary Power, were miserably divided and set against each other, that by such Divisions, Popery and Tyranny might more easily be establish'd among us. But such have been the good Effects of the *Act of Toleration*, as to unite his Majesty's Protestant Subjects in Interest and Affection; many of the Dissenters are become sincere Converts to our Church, and their Prejudices wear off: The Members of our Church, and the Dissenters, notwithstanding their lesser Differences, now generally behave themselves towards each other, as becomes Fellow Subjects and Fellow Christians, [B -9] as Children of the same heavenly Father, and Heirs of the same Promises; agreeable to the Advice of our present most pious and excellent Metropolitan, in his admirable[1] Sermon and Exhortation for mutual Charity and Union among Protestants, preached before King WILLIAM and Queen MARY, at *Hampton-Court*, May 21, 1689.[2]

[1] *Sermons and Discourses on several Occasions, by the Most Reverend Father in GOD*, WILLIAM, *Lord Arch-Bishop of* Canterbury. *The Second Edition*. 1716. pp 192, 193.

[2] This sermon was that preached at Hampton-Court, 21 May 1689, "Sermon and Exhortation for Mutual Charity and Union among Protestants." The 2nd edition quoted

THE great Learning, Piety, truly Christian Moderation, extensive Zeal, and Christian Charity of those most Reverend Prelates, who now adorn the Mitre, will, in all human probability, raise the Lustre and Reputation of the Church of England to such a Degree, that as the Steddiness of his Majesty's Counsel, and the Wisdom of his Administration justly entitles our Nation at present to hold the first Rank; so shall our Church be look'd upon as the Mother of all the Reform'd Churches [10] in Europe, and will become a Praise in the whole Earth; our learned Divines, for their Excellent Writings and virtuous Lives, being famous Abroad, and highly esteem'd even at Geneva.

As to the just Rights and Powers of the Legislature, no Prince ever had a more tender Concern for them than his present Majesty. The true Interest of the Nation is steddily pursued, and the great Fences and Boundaries of our Religion and Liberties inviolably maintained, and all farther Securities, for the Preservation and Advancement of both, are chearfully granted.

PUBLICK Justice is duly and impartially Administer'd. In the chief Court of Equity presides a noble Lord, justly esteem'd by all for his great Learning, Probity, and admirable Temper;[1] and in the other Courts of Justice there are such excellent and learned Judges on the Bench, that have been the Ornaments of the Bar, not the Blemishes of it, as a great Man truly said of Judges in former Reigns, [B 2 -11] some of whom had wickedly given up the Constitution, by allowing the King a Power to dispense with the Laws; and tho' the Mildness of King WILLIAM and Queen MARY's Government was such, that King JAMES the Second's Dispensing Judges and Lawyers suffer'd no other Punishment, yet they are branded by Act of Parliament, and their Names left on Record to Posterity, as Betrayers of the Rights and Liberties of the People.[2 W. & M. Sess. 1. C. 10.]

As to the Treasure and publick Credit of the Nation, Was it ever rais'd to such a Height before, as it is now? Or the Purse ever in better Hands? Such a Confidence the People have in the publick Management, and are so well satisfied, that what we pay is punctually apply'd to the Service to which it is appropriated, and the whole manag'd with such exquisite Conduct and Frugality, by those honourable Persons who preside over the Treasury,[2] that never were Taxes more freely complied with, nor [12] such large Sums raised so speedily, and at so low an interest.

AND what crowns all our Happiness, is that we have a King upon the Throne, who is possessed of all the Royal and Human Virtues that

---

here is dated 1717, ed. R. Baker, London: Godwin, Tooke & Pemberton. B. L. 226 h 10 [16].

[1] It might be Lord King, Lord Chancellor from 1 June 1725 until 1733.

[2] The persons presiding over the Treasury would be: R. Walpole, Sir Chas. Turner Bt, Geo Dodington, Sir Geo. Oxenden Bt, Wm Clayton.

can endear a Prince to any People; and what adds to the Glory of his Majesty's Government, is, that he scorns to be the Head of a Party, and King only of one Part of his People; but extends the Blessings of his Reign to all his Subjects without Distinction: He has no other Views but to make them all easy and happy, to unite their Hearts and Interests, and render them as well affected to one another, as all ought to be to him. And with such a King, we have a Queen renown'd over all the World for her Virtue and Goodness, and for her sacred Regard to the true Protestant Religion, which will make her History the Delight of good Men in Ages to come.[1] We are also blest with a numerous and hopeful Progeny, sprung from these great Parents, educated by their royal Cares, and form'd [13] by their Examples, and who cannot fail of perpetuating to these Nations the Felicity, which we enjoy under their Most Excellent Majesties. In a Word, we have such a Scene of Good at present, as few Nations have ever enjoyed, and such a Prospect of Good to come, as calls the Blessings of future Times into our own, and adds to the Happiness of the Age, a Taste of the Happiness of their Posterity.

Gentlemen,

FOR preserving the publick Peace, and restraining the Lusts, unruly Passions, Frauds, and Violences of Men, our Laws have several Ways wisely provided Remedies, and constituted many Courts of Judicature: Amongst which I may reckon one of the Chiefest to be this Court of Quarter-Sessions, which is held four Times in a Year in every County; and also many Cities, Corporations, and Liberties, have their Quarter-Sessions, and their Grand and Petty Juries; and these being drawn by our excellent Constitution [14] from the several Parts of each County, City, and Liberty, there can be no notorious Breach of the Law, morally speaking, committed within this Kingdom, that can escape their Knowledge. This is a Court so honourable, that it receives its Authority by a special Commission from his Majesty; in which the greatest Subjects in Great-Britain think it an additional Dignity and Privilege to have their Names inserted; and several Noblemen of illustrious Extraction, magnificent Titles, and splendid Fortunes, have lately qualified themselves to act as Justices of the Peace for this City and Liberty; whose hereditary Candor and Generosity, inherent in noble Blood, inseparable from the Birth and Education of Peers, renders them eminently qualified for the Administration of publick Justice, and must needs give great Satisfaction to the People to think, that their Causes are to come before, and their Differences to be determined by such noble Judges, who are neither to be sway'd by Hopes, over-ruled by Fears, [15] nor misled by any false

[1] Caroline of Brandenburg-Anspach, 1683–1737, daughter of the Margrave of B-A. Johan Frederick, and his 2nd wife Eleanor of Sachs-Eisenach.

Prejudice or Passion, but will decide every Cause with the strictest Impartiality, Equity, and Honour.

AND as our Office is honourable, so it is likewise very Ancient; for, besides the Reason, which we have to believe that this, or something very like it, was contemporary with the Original of our own, and other of the *Gothic* Governments in *Europe*, our *Chronicles* inform us, that WILLIAM the First, [Hollingshead. Baker] commonly call'd the *Conqueror*, about the Fourth Year of his Reign, which is six hundred and sixty Years ago, appointed Justices of the Peace; tho' the first particular Statute, which we meet with concerning them, is in the first Year of the Reign of EDWARD the Third. [1 Ed. III Cap. 16] How generally useful and serviceable to the Country, this our Authority has been found to be, needs no other Proof, than the considerable Enlargement it hath since that Time received in almost every Reign. [16]

WHEREAS the High Commission Court, the Star-Chamber, and the Court of Wards and Liveries, and several other Courts having exceeded their Jurisdiction, and being found to deviate from their original Institutions, and instead of giving Ease Relief, and Security, to become Burthensome and Oppressive to the Subject, have been suppressed by Authority of Parliament. But the Wisdom of the Legislature, instead of vacating our Power, hath in many Particulars extended the Limits of it; for they could not but be sensible of the vast Advantages that every Man receives by so frequent, and so regular, so cheap, and so easy an Administration of Justice.

THE Oath, that you have taken to present all such Matters and Things that shall be given you in Charge, seems to imply an Obligation on me, to acquaint you with those Crimes and Offences, that the Commission of the Peace, and divers Statutes appoint to be either enquired of or punished in this Court, at [C -17] least, with such of them as are most likely to fall under your Cognizance and Enquiry. And these Articles of your Charge, for Method sake, are usually divided into three general Heads.

I. SUCH Offences as concern Almighty GOD, and his holy Religion established amongst us.

II. THE King. And,

III. OUR Neighbours, or Fellow Subjects.

As to the First of these. Tho' Religion hath a much higher and nobler End, yet it is so very necessary for the Support of human Societies, that it is impossible, they can subsist without acknowledging some invisible Power, that concerns himself with human Affairs, and will punish the Immoral and Vicious, and reward the Good and Virtuous in another Life. And the Awe and Reverence of this divine Being [18] makes Men more effectually observe those Duties, in which their mutual Happiness consists, than all the Punishments of the Magistrate. If it's reasonable for the Magistrate to punish one, who does any Injury to a single Person, he ought certainly to punish him who injures the whole Society, by openly denying the Being of a GOD, or that he governs the World, or presides over human Affairs; such a one may justly be esteemed an Enemy to the whole Race of Mankind, as subverting the Foundation on which their Preservation and Happiness is chiefly built.

To punish such bold and impious Offenders as these, an Act of Parliament was made in the ninth Year of the Reign of King WILLIAM the Third, whereby it is enacted, That if any Person, having been educated in, or at any Time having made Profession of the *Christian* Religion within this Realm, shall by Writing, Printing, Teaching, or [C 2 -19] advised Speaking, deny any one of the Persons in the Holy Trinity to be GOD, or shall assert and maintain, that there are more Gods than one, or shall deny the *Christian* Religion to be true, or the holy Scriptures of the *Old* and *New Testament* to be of divine Authority; being lawfully convicted by the Oath of two credible Witnesses, shall for the first Offence be adjudged incapable and disabled in Law to all Intents and Purposes, to have, hold, and enjoy any Office or Employment, Ecclesiastical, Civil, or Military whatsoever; and if at the Time of Conviction he is possess'd of any Office, &c. such Office, Place, or Employment, shall be void: For the second Offence, he shall be disabled to Sue, Prosecute, Plead, or use any Action, or Information, in any Court of Law or Equity; or to be a Guardian, Executor, or Administrator, or capable of any Legacy, or Deed of Gift; or of any Office Civil or Military, or Benefice Ecclesiastical; and shall suffer three Years Imprisonment without [20] Bail, from the Time of the Conviction.

THIS Act was not made to punish the Error, but the Impudence of the Offender. And if ever there was Occasion to put it in Execution, it is now, when several wicked Authors, in their pernicious Books, dare to blaspheme that holy Name, by which we are call'd, and even in a ludicrous Manner to write against the Deity, the Miracles, and meritorious Sufferings of our Blessed Lord and Saviour.

PRESENT all, that shall speak or do any Thing in contempt of the Holy Sacrament, contrary to the Act of the First of King EDWARD the Sixth; And all that shall disturb any Preacher allowed, in his open Sermon and Collation, or be procuring or abetting thereunto. [1 Ed. VI. Cap. 1.- 1 M. 1 Sess. 2 Cap. 3.- 1 W & M. Cap. 18].

YOU are to take Care, that the Laws against Immorality and Profaneness be strictly put in Execution, in pursuance of the excellent Proclamation just now [21] read to you. We neither want good Laws, nor due Encouragement from our Superiors, nor yet good Magistrates; but many of the Constables, and other inferior Officers, are so negligent and remiss in their Duty of Informing against, and prosecuting common Swearers, Drunkards, Sabbath-Breakers, &c. that often renders our Pains as it were ineffectual, for the Promoting a general Reformation of Manners. Therefore make a strict Enquiry into, and make a due Presentment of all the Neglects, or Connivances of all Officers of Justice concern'd in the Execution of the Laws, especially those against Immorality and Profaneness; for since we find by Experience, that they have so little Regard to the Glory of GOD, the Good of their Country, or their Oaths, it is highly conducive to their own Good, and to the better Demeanour of their Successors, that they should be made publick Examples of, and suffer Fine and Imprisonment, as the Court shall think fit.

THE Second general Head relates to the King.

The greatest Offfence against him is High Treason.

BEFORE the Statute of the Twenty fifth of King EDWARD the Third, what was High Treason at the Common Law being very uncertain, this Statute was made to reduce the several species of Treason to a Certainty.

25 *Ed.* III C. 2 By this Act, Compassing or Imagining the Death of the King, or Queen, or their eldest Son and Heir, and Declaring, by an open Act, a Design to depose, imprison, or murder the King, *&c.* is High Treason; so is levying War against him, or adhering to his Enemies, within the Realm or without; and also counterfeiting his Great Seal, Privy Seal, or his money current within the Realm. The several other Species of High Treason I omit to give you in Charge, because not likely at present to fall under your [23] Cognizance and Enquiry. But before I proceed to other Things, I must mention to you one Act of Parliament made for Securing to us, and our latest Posterity, that invaluable Legacy of the *Hannover* Succession, left us by the great King WILLIAM of Glorious and Immortal Memory. And this is a Statute made in the Sixth Year of the Reign of the late Queen ANNE, whereby it is made High Treason to maintain by Writing, or Printing, that her then Majesty was not lawful Queen; or that the Pretender hath any Right to the Crown; or that any other Person hath any Right to the same, but by the Acts of Settlement; or that the King and Parliament cannot limit or bind the Succession of the Crown: And if the Offender maintain the same only by Words, it is Premunire; but then, Information for the Words must be made before one or more Justices of the Peace, upon the Oaths of two credible Witnesses, within three Days after they are spoken, and the Prosecution must be within three Months after the [24] same. This is necessary to bring the Offender to suffer the Punishment for a Premunire; but the like Words, without these Circumstances or Qualifications, are Indictable as a High Misdemeanour at the Common Law, as being against the Duty and Allegiance of every Subject. And here I would remark to you, that Altering or Limiting the Succession of the Crown is not unprecedented; for in the Reign of King HENRY the Eighth, he,

with his Parliament limited, order'd and settled the Succession as they pleased; and in the thirteenth Year of Queen Elizabeth, an Act was passed, that made it High Treason for any one during her Life, and a Premunire afterwards, to deny that such Power was invested in the Queen and Parliament. [13 Eliz. C. 1. Rast. 27-3 Inst. 6. 10. 12.14.- Coke's Inst. 4. Part 36.]

You are also to enquire of Misprison of Treason, which is a bare Knowledge of Treason without Assent to it. [D -25]

AFTER Treasons, and Misprison of Treason, you are to Enquire of Felonies committed against the King, and which, for Distinction sake, may be call'd publick Felonies. Debasing the current Coin, and unlawfully Diminishing it are made Felony, by the Acts of Sixth and Seventh; and the Eighth, and Ninth of King WILLIAM the Third. [6 & 7 W. III. c.17 - 8 & 9 W. III Cap. 25] And so is Attempting to kill, assault, or wound any Privy Counsellor in the Execution of his Office, by an Act of the the Ninth of the late Queen ANNE. [9 Annæ Cap. 16]

ANY Person going beyond the Seas, to serve any foreign Prince, without taking the Oath of Allegiance before his Departure, is to suffer Death as a Felon, by the Statute of the Third of King JAMES the First.[3 Jac. I. Cap. 4].

EMBEZZELING his Majesty's Armour, Ordinance, Shot, Powder, and other Habiliments of War, or Victuals provided for Soldiers, by any Persons [26] having the Charge or Custody of the same, to the Value of twenty Shillings, tho' at several Times, is made Felony by an Act of the Thirty first of ELIZABETH. [31 Eliz. Cap. 4] And so is stealing or embezzeling his Majesty's Naval Stores, by an Act of the Twenty second of King CHARLES the Second.

COUNTERFEITING the King's Stamps, or Uttering, Vending or Selling any Vellum, Parchment, or Paper with counterfeit Marks, knowing them to be so, is Felony by the Statute of the Tenth of King WILLIAM the Third. And so is privately and fraudulently Using any Stamps, to defraud his Majesty of his Duties, by two Acts of Parliament, one of the Tenth, and the other of the Twelfth of Queen ANNE. [10 Annae Cap. 19.26. 12 Annae Cap. 9. 19.]

YOU are also to present the Authors, Printers and Publishers of all treasonable and seditious Books, Pamphlets and Ballads reflecting upon his [D 2- 27] Majesty's sacred Person, or his Administration.

The third general Head of Offences concerns your Neighbour, or Fellow Subject.

Of these, some are Capital.

1. SUCH as are committed against his Life, as Murder, which is a voluntary Killing of another with Malice prepensed, expressed, or implied; or Manslaughter without Malice when two quarrel and fight instantly before they grow cool again, and one of them is kill'd; or

sometimes Chance medly, as doing a lawful Act without an Intent to hurt, and Death ensues.

2. SUCH as concern his Goods, as Grand Larceny, or a Felonious and Fraudulent Taking or Carrying away, but not from his Person, or out of his House, above the Value of Twelve Pence; Petty Larceny, if under that Value. Robbery, [28] which always supposeth the Taking away of the Money, of Goods, from the Person, or out of his House, he or his Family living in it, to be with Force and Violence; otherwise being privately and secretly done, it is call'd Larceny from the Person.

PICKING a Pocket, or Cutting a Purse, is a capital Offence by the Statute of the Eighth of Queen ELIZABETH. SO is Horse-stealing, by the Second and Third of King EDWARD the Sixth and other Statutes. [8 Eliz. C. 4.-2 & 3 Ed. VI. C. 33- 37 Hen VIII. C.8.- 1 Ed. VI. C. 12.]

BY an Act of the Third and Fourth of King WILLIAM and Queen MARY, if any Person take away, with an Intent to Steal, any Goods to the Value of forty Shillings, which they are to use in their Lodgings, it is Felony without Clergy [3 & 4 W. & M. C. 9.]. As it is by the Statute of the Twenty first of King HENRY the Eighth, for a Servant of the Age of Eighteen, and not an Apprentice, [29] to withdraw himself with the Goods of his Master or his Mistress, with an Intent to steal the same; or without their Assent or Commandment, embezzel their Goods with the same Intent, to the Value of forty Shillings.

By the Statute of the Tenth and Eleventh of King WILLIAM the Third, Stealing out of any Shop, Ware-house, Coach-house, or Stable, by Night or Day, to the Value of five Shillings, tho' the Shop, *&c.* be not broke open, or any Person put in Fear, is Felony without Clergy: So is Assisting, Hiring, or Commanding any Person to commit such Offence [10 & 11 W. III. C. 23.].

STEALING to the Value of forty Shillings, or more, out of a Dwelling-house, is also Felony without Clergy, by an Act of the Twelfth of Queen ANNE. [12 Annae C. 7.]

COUNTERFEITING Bank Notes, Exchequer Bills, South Sea Bonds, or Lottery Orders, are capital Offences by several Statutes made in [30] the Reigns of King WILLIAM, Queen ANNE, and the late King GEORGE [8 & 9 W. III. C. 19- 7 & 8 W. III. C. 31- 8 & 9 W.III. C. 23- 3 Annae C. 13 -7 Annae C.7. 9 Annae C. 7 - 1 Geo I. C. 12-9 Annae C. 21.- 12 Annae C. 2.]

COUNTERFEITING or Forging, or Assisting in the Conterfeiting and Forging any Letter of Attorney, or other Authority, to transfer the Shares of any Proprietor in the Capital Stock of any Body, or Bodies Politick, or Corporate, established by an Act of Parliament; or falsely Personating the true Proprietor of any such Shares, *&c.* or Receiving, or Endeavouring to receive the Money of such Proprietor, as if he was the true Proprietor, by Counterfeiting his Name, &c. is Felony without

Clergy, by the Statute of the Eighth of the late King GEORGE [8 Geo I. C. 22.].

3. YOU are to Enquire of such Offences, as concern your Neighbour's Habitation, as Burglary, or Breaking and Entering the Mansion-House of another in the Night Time, with an Intent to commit some Felony; and House Burning, [31] which takes in the voluntary and malicious Burning of Outhouses, Stablings, or Barns with Hay, or Corn in them, as well as the Mansion-House strictly so call'd.

THERE are likewise many other Offences enquireable by you, which are made Felony by several Statutes. I shall mention some of them.

AS all Rapes and Ravishments of Women, by the Thirteenth of King EDWARD the First, and the Sixth of King RICHARD the Second [13 *Ed.* 1 Cap.34; 6 *R.* II. C. 6.]. And also forcibly Marrying Women of Substance in Goods or Lands, against their Wills, and receiving such Offenders, knowing thereof, or abetting the same, is made Felony, by the Third of King HENRY the Seventh, [3 *H.* VII Cap. 2. - 39 *Eliz.* C.9.] and the Thirty Ninth of Queen ELIZABETH. To lie with any Woman Child under Ten Years old, tho' with her Consent, is Felony, by the Eighteenth of Queen ELIZABETH. To cut out the Tongue, [32] or to put out the Eyes of any Person, is Felony, by the Fifth of King HENRY the Fourth. [5 *H.* IV Cap. 5 - 22 & 23 *Car.* II. Cap. 1] And by the Twenty second and Twenty third of King CHARLES the Second, commonly call'd the *Coventry Act*, all such on Purpose, and of Malice aforethought, and by Lying in Wait, unlawfully to cut out or disable the Tongue, put out an Eye, slit the Nose, cut off a Nose or Lip, or cut off or disable any Limb, it is Felony in him, his Aiders and Abettors.

IF any Owner, Captain, Master, or Mariner, or other Officer belonging to a Ship, shall wilfully cast away, burn, or destroy the Ship, or procure the same to be done, to the Prejudice of any Person, who shall underwrite any Policy of Insurance thereon, or of any Merchant that shall load Goods thereon, it is Felony, by an Act of the Fourth of the late King GEORGE. [4 *Geo* I. Cap. 12] [E -33]

A listed Soldier, departing from his Captain without Leave, is Guilty of Felony by the Eighteenth of King HENRY the Sixth, and the Second of EDWARD the Sixth. [18 *H.* VI. Cap 19.- 2 Ed VI. Cap. 2] And any Soldier raising a Mutiny in the Army, or refusing to obey his superior Officer, or resisting any Officer in the Execution of his Office, or striking, drawing, or offering to draw, or lift up any Weapon against his superior Officer, is also guilty of Felony, by an Act of the tenth Year of the Reign of Queen ANNE. [10 *A* . C. 10].

STEALING or Taking away any Record is Felony by the Statute of King HENRY the Sixth, and is so acknowledging any Bail, Recognizance, Statute, or Statutes, or Deed inrolled in the Name of another, not privy or consenting thereunto, by the Statute of the Twenty first of

King JAMES the First; [21 *Jac.* I. Cap. 26] and Forging a Deed, after a former Conviction [34] for the like Offence, is made Felony by the Fifth of Queen ELIZABETH [5 *Eliz.* c. 14.]

A Felon's escaping before Transportation, or Returning from Abroad before the Time expired, for which he was ordered to be Transported, is made a capital Offence, by the Sixth of the late King GEORGE. [6 *Geo* I. C. 23.]

IF eight Persons, or more, Assault or Wound any Officers of the Customs in the Execution of their Duty, it is Transportation for seven Years, and if the Offender return within that Time, then he is to suffer as a Felon, by an other Act of the Sixth of the late King GEORGE.[6 *Geo* I. C. 21].

MALICIOUSLY Setting on Fire, Burning or Causing to be Burnt any Wood, Underwood, or Coppice, or any Part thereof, is made Felony, by an Act of the First of the late King GEORGE. [*1 Geo I. C. 18*].

IF twelve Persons, or more, are riotously and tumultuously assembled [E 2 -35] together, and by Proclamation made by a Justice of the Peace, Mayor, Bayliff, or other head Officer, they are commanded to disperse themselves, and depart to their Habitation, &c. and if they continue for an Hour after, it is Felony without Clergy, by an Act of the First of the late King GEORGE. [1 *Geo* I C. 5.] As it is by the same Act to demolish and pull down any Church, Chappel, or any Meeting-House for Religious Worship, certified and registered according to the Statute of the First of King WILLIAM and Queen MARY, [1 *W. & M.* sess. 1. C.18] or any Barn, Stable, or other Outhouse, or knowingly to hinder or hurt any Person beginning to make Proclamation, whereby such Proclamations shall not be made, is also Felony; as it is in the Rioters, to whom it should have been made, if they do not disperse themselves, but continue together an Hour after such Let or Hindrance. [36]

BANKRUPTS, Removing, Concealing or Embezzeling any Money, Effects, &c. to the Value of twenty Pounds are Guilty of Felony, by an Act of the late King GEORGE. [5 *Geo* I. C. 9.]

TRANSPORTING live Sheep, or Lambs, out of the King's Dominions, is Felony for the second Offence, by an Act of the Eighth of Queen ELIZABETH. [8 *Eliz.* C. 3.] The Punishment for the first Offence is Forfeiture of Goods and Chattels, and Loss of the Offender's left Hand, which is to be cut off in some open Market, and Imprisonment for a Year. Maliciously and Willingly Killing any Horses, Sheep, or other Cattle in the Night time, is Felony, by the Twenty second and Twenty third of King CHARLES the Second. [22 & 23 *Car.* II c. 7.] Marrying a second Husband or Wife, the former being alive, is also Felony, by the Act of the First of King JAMES the First [1 *Jac.* I C. 11]. [37]

BY the Statutes of the Fourth and Sixth of the late King GEORGE, [4 *Geo* I. c. 11, 6 *Geo* I c. 23] to take Money or Reward, Directly or

Indirectly, under Pretence, or upon Account of Helping another to stolen Goods or Chattels, unless such Person apprehends the Felon, who stole the Goods, and brings him to Tryal, and gives Evidence against him, he shall suffer, as if he had stolen the Goods himself. The late Jonathan Wild was Convicted and Executed for this Crime.

PERSONS going arm'd, having their Faces blacked, or otherwise disguised, appearing in any Forest, Chase, Park, Paddock, *&c.* Hunting, Wounding, Killing, or Stealing any Red or Fallow Deer; or Robbing any Warren, or Place, where Conies or Hares are usually kept; or stealing any Fish out of any River or Pond; or maliciously Killing or Wounding any Cattle; or Cutting down, or otherwise Destroying any Trees planted in any Avenue, or growing in any Orchard, or Plantation for Or-[38] nament, Shelter or Profit; or Setting fire to any House, Barn or Outhouse or Stack of Corn, Straw, Hay or Wood; or wilfully and maliciously Shooting at any Person in any Dwelling-house; or knowingly sending a Letter without a Name subscribed thereto, or sign'd with a fictitious Name, demanding Money, Venison, or other valuable Thing; every Person, offending in any of these Particulars, is guilty of Felony without Clergy, by an Act of the late King GEORGE. [9 *Geo.* I. C. 22]

I shall mention but one Crime more, that is a Felony by Statute, and that is, The most Detestable and Unnatural Sin of Sodomy: A Crime, that GOD Almight punished with one of the most signal and remarkable Judgments, that he ever inflicted upon any Nation or People. [25 *H.* VIII C.6- 32 *H.* VIII C.3.- 2 & 3 *Ed.* VI. C. 29- Repealed by 1 *M.* C. 1. Revived and made Perpetual by 5 *Eliz.* C. 17.] And may we not expect some extraordinary Punishments [39] from Heaven, when the vilest Abomination of the Heathen World, and a Sin, not to be named amongst *Christians*, prevails in a Nation, that for so many Years has enjoy'd the Light of the *Gospel* in the Power and Purity of it? It is not only under our own Constitution, but in all civilized Nations, that the Laws have severely punish'd this execrable Crime. I hope therefore you will do your Duty, not only in Finding out and Punishing these abominable Offenders against GOD, the Law, and human Nature; but also by Presenting those Houses, that harbour and entertain them; several Persons for keeping Disorderly Houses of this Kind have lately been Pilloried, Fined and Imprisoned. And I hope, that the rest of these Miscreants will be brought to condign Punishment, that so this horrible Wickedness, that 'till of late rarely appear'd in our Histories and Records, may be intirely suppress'd, and rooted out from amongst us.[40]

2. OF Offences not Capital, you are to present all Riots, Routs, and unlawful Assemblies, Assaults, Batteries, and all other Breaches of the Peace. All common Nusances, Houses of common Lewdness and Gaming, and disorderly Houses. Those Houses and Shops where People frequently get Drunk with Geneva, and other Liquors of that kind, are

Indictable as Disorderly Houses, whether they have or have not Licences.

YOU are to enquire of all Want of due Repairs of Bridges, Common Highways, Streets, and Pavements; and of all Kinds of Trespasses and Misdemeanours whatsoever. But for a more particular Account of these Offences of a lower Kind, I refer you to my Charge the last Quarter-Sessions, which the Court was pleased to Order to be printed and publish'd. A Copy of which I have directed to be given to every one of you, for your [F -41] Use on this present, or any future Service of this Nature.

To Conclude, GENTLEMEN, As you are to enquire of, and present all Offences against the Laws of GOD, and the Laws of the Land, so I hope, that you will acquit your selves with all Honesty, Diligence, and Impartiality; and we shall find by your Presentments, that you have a well grounded Zeal for the Honour and Glory of Almighty GOD, a true Love to your Country, a most sincere and affectionate Loyalty to his sacred Majesty King GEORGE the Second, upon whom, and his Royal Progeny, next under GOD, our Safety and Happiness depends; and a tender and conscientious Regard to the solemn Oath, which you have taken in the Face of this Court, for the true Performance of your Duty; always Remembering the strict Account that you must give at the last Day, of all your publick and private Actions, before [42] the great Tribunal. And now, GENTLEMEN, without Detaining you any longer, I dismiss you to your Enquiries.

FINIS.

THE **Third CHARGE** of **Sir *John Gonson* Knt**. TO THE **GRAND JURY** OF THE *CITY and LIBERTY of* Westminster, *&c.* At the General Quarter-Sessions of the Peace, held the ninth Day of *October* 1728, in WESTMINSTER-HALL.

Printed at the Desire of the Justices of the Peace *for the said City and Liberty, and of the* Grand Jury.

***LONDON*:** Printed by Charles ACKERS, in *Great-Swan-Alley*, St. *John's-Street*. MDCCXXVIII.

Civitas, Burgus, & Villa Westm. *in Com.* Midd. } ss. *Ad Generalem Quarterialem Sessionem Pacis Domini Regis tent' apud* Westm. *Pro Libertat' Decani & Capituli Ecclesiae Collegiat.beati* Petri Westm. *Civit', Burgi, &c Villæ* Westm. *in Comitat.* Midd. &. *Sancti* Martini le Grand, London' *die* Mercurii *sicilicet nono die* Octob. *Anno Regni Domini* Georgii *Secundi, Dei Gratiâ nunc Regis* Magnae Britannia, *&c secundo, coram Justiciariis, & ibidem.*

HIS Majesty's Justices of the Peace for the City and Liberty of *Westminster*, assembled at this present General Quarter-Sessions of the Peace, being of the Opinion that the Charge, this Day given by Sir *John Gonson* Knight, as Chairman (in the absence of the Right Honourable *John* Lord *Delawar* the present Chairman) to the Grand Jury sworn to enquire for our Sovereign Lord the King, for the Body of this City and Liberty, and to the High and Petty Constables there, is a *Learned, Loyal, Judicious and Useful Charge, highly tending to the Service of his Majesty, and his Government*: Have unanimously agreed, that the Thanks of this Court be, and the same are hereby given to the said Sir *John Gonson* for his said Charge, and they desire that he will cause the same to be Printed and Published.

Per Curiam

MIDDLETON.

[A 2]

To the RIGHT WORSHIPFUL
Sir *John Gonson* Knt.

CHAIRMAN of the General Quarter-Sessions of the Peace, held for the City and Liberty of *Westminster*, &c. the ninth Day of *October* 1728.

We the Grand Jury, impanelled and Sworn to enquire for our Sovereign Lord the King for the Body of this said City and Liberty, having received from your Worship, as Chairman, a very Learned, Loyal,

Ingenious and Useful Charge, Do hereby return you our most humble Thanks for the same; [4] and desire, that you will be pleased to cause the same to be Printed and Published for the better Information of the Inhabitants and Officers within this City and Liberty, in the Discharge of their respective Duties, &c.

John Farmer
Charles Fullwood.
James Jarman.
Samuel Cotterell.
John James.
John Hind.
Robert Halliwell.
Christopher Hammond.
Daniel Turman.
John Walker.
Charles Capell.
John Rumbold.
H. Tabel.
Joseph Tull.
Richard Hunton.
John Hopkins.
Edmund Osborne.
Solomon Ranger.
Richard Pick.
John Wells.
John Shepherd.

[5]
THE
Third CHARGE
of
Sir *John Gonson* Knt.

Gentlemen of the Grand Jury,

HUMAN Societies, and human Laws are the Effect of Necessity and Experience. If Men, in their Behaviour, lived up to the Precepts of the Law of Nature, none would ever spill his Neighbour's Blood, hurt his Person, or invade his Property. But because Men are so [6] apt to violate those equitable Laws to gratify their Passions and corrupt Inclinations; and, when left to the boundless Liberty, which they claim from Nature, every Man would be Interfering and Quarrelling with another, every one would be Plundering the Acquisitions of another, the Labour of one Man would be the Property of another, Weakness would be the Prey of Force, and one Man's Industry the Cause of another Man's Idleness.

HENCE came the Original of Government, which was the mutual Contract of a Number of Men, agreeing upon certain Terms of Union and Society, and putting themselves under Penalties if they violated those Terms, which were called Laws, and put into the Hands of one or more Men to execute: Thus Men quitted their natural Liberty to acquire civil Security, and were willing to part with some Privileges and Rights, which they have by Nature, in Order to secure the Rest from Violence. [7]

THE Judicious[1] Mr. HOOKER thinks, that the first Government was Arbitrary, by a single Person; 'till it was found by Experience, That *to live by one Man's Will became the Cause of all Mens Misery.*

AND this he concludes was the Original of inventing Laws. "The lawful Power of making Laws (says he) to command whole politick Societies of Men, belong so properly to the same intire Societies, that for any Prince, or Potentate of what Kind soever upon Earth, to Exercise the same of himself, and not by express Commission immediately and personally received from GOD, or else by Authority derived, at the first, from their Consent upon whose Persons they impose Laws, is no better than Tyranny." This is the more Worthy of Consideration, being the Judgment in a Point of Religion, not of an Historian or a Lawyer, but of a [8] Reverend Divine, and such an one who hath been so great a Champion for Authority and Government, and for strict Conformity to our excellent Church.

ABSOLUTE Monarchy, indeed, may rather be esteemed a Species of Anarchy, than any form of civil Government: For surely, when Men entered into Society, they never agreed or intended, that all of them, except one, should be under the Restraint of Laws, and that he alone should still retain all the Liberty of the unrestrain'd State of Nature, corrupted with Flattery, arm'd with Power, and made Licentious by Impunity, and at the same Time that the People should be totally deprived of the Safety and Security in civil Society, for which it was at first Instituted, and for which only they enter'd into it.

IT is certain then, that the Limitation of Power, and the Superiority of Laws, in Matters of Government, had an Original in the early Ages of the World; [B -9] the *Lacedæmonian* Government was the same with that of *Crete*, and the Basis of each was settled upon this Maxim, That Liberty is the chiefest Good of civil Society, because it is that which makes every Thing we possess our own; without this Liberty all Property centers in those who govern, and not in them who are governed. By Liberty is not meant Licentiousness, or for Men to act without Controul, but under the restraint of good Laws; so far free and at Liberty as reasonable Creatures would wish to be, and so far only restrain'd, as is necessary for the Peace and Good of Society.

THE Constitution of different Countries are indeed various, but the Obligations between the Governing and the Governed are every where mutual; the Office of a King, a Senate, or of the executive Power in a popular State, is to protect the People in their Lives, Liberties, and Properties; and to this End they claim the Allegiance, Obedience, and Assistance of their Subjects. The [10] *Roman*, and most of the *Græcian* States, were built upon the Republican Plan; but when the *Goths*, and

[1] Eccles. Polity, *Lib.* 1. *Sect.*10.

other *Northern* Nations destroy'd the *Roman* Empire, and extended their Conquests into far distant Countries; they establishedd, wherever they came, a mixt form of Government, which, like the World, subsists by the Opposition of the Elements, of which it is composed: The Preservation of this Constitution depending upon the Balance between the King, Nobility, and People, the Legislative Power was lodged in these three Estates, call'd by different Names in different Countries; in the *North* Diets, in *Spain* Cortes, in *France* Estates, and in *England* Parliaments. For tho' the Word Parliament, as my Lord COKE in his first Institute observes, is not above seven or eight hundred Years old; yet Assemblies of the People, or their Chiefs and Representatives, in most Nations of *Europe,* upon emergent publick Occasions, to consult and determine of their own Af- [B 2 - 11] fairs, has been a Practice so universal, as to Time and Place, that the Histories of all Nations, now extant, afford plain Footsteps in this Matter. The Style and Title of such Assemblies may indeed change with Language, which is a Thing continually changing[1], and the Name and Designation of the Constituents may alter; but it has ever been the immutable and constant Practice of civilized and well governed Nations to meet in general Assemblies, to advise, debate, and finally determine concerning their publick and national Concerns.

THAT this was our Case in Britain before Our SAVIOUR's Time, is clear from JULIUS CESAR's *Commen-*[12] *taries* [2]. And TACITUS, in his *Germania* [3], gives the like Account of that Country. And one of our most ancient Law Books, call'd *The Mirror of Justice,*[4] cited by my Lord COKE in his first Institute, mentions an Assembly of the Counties, *&c.* in[5] King ALFRED's Reign; to descend lower would exceed [13] my Bounds. And the Subject had been unanswerably maintained by Mr.

[1] Sir HENRY SPELMAN in his *Glossary* says thus, under the Word Gemotum, "Wittenagemot idem apud Anglo-saxones, quod apud nos hodie Parliamentum, parumque à Folemoto defferebat, nisi quod hoc annuum esset, & è certis plerumque Causis, illud ex arduis Contengentibus, & Legum Condendarum gratiâ, ad Arbitrarium Principis indictum."

[2] CAESAR. Comment. Lib. 5. Summa Imperii bellique Administrandi communi Concilio permissa est Cassivelano.

[3] De Minoribus Rebus Principes consultant, de Majoribus omnes.

[4] See the ed. by J. Whittaker (London: B. Quaritch, 1895).

[5] The Mirror of Justice was written in the Saxon Times, as it appears from the Book it self, and it was revised, and some Things added to it, by the learned and wise Lawyer ANDREW HORNE, who lived in the Reigns of King Edward the First, and King Edward the Second.

MYRROR, page 10.

For the good Estate of the Realm, King ALFRED cause the Counties to assemble, and ordained it for a perpetual usage, that twice a Year, or oftener if need were, in Time of Peace, they should assemble at London, to sit in Parliament, for the Guidance of GOD's People, how the Nation should keep themselves from Sin, live in Quiet, and receive Right by certain Usages, and holy Judgments.

PETYT, in his *Antiquity and Power, &c of the House of Commons,*[1] and by Mr. TYRREL, in his *Bibliotheca Politica,*[2] and the learned Preface to his *History of England,* which no Writer of Note has hitherto undertaken to confute; and last of all by Mr. Rymer in his *Fœdera*[3]. The Excellency of this mixt Government consists in that due Poize, or Balance between Rule and Subjection, so justly observed in it, that by the necessary Concurrence of the Nobility and Commons, in the making and Repealing all Laws, it hath the main Advantages of an Aristocracy and a Democracy, and yet free from the Disadvantages and Evils of either of those Kinds of Government.

BUT Length of Time, and a Succession of Folly and Vice, in two Parts of the Legislature, and of Cunning and Success in the Third, has driven it almost out of *Europe*. In *Spain, France, Denmark, Bohemia, Hungary,* and Part of *Germany,* the Monarchy, or rather [14] Tyranny, has now swallowed up the ancient Constitution; in *Switzerland* and *Holland* the two other States have yielded to the Commons: Whilst we in *Great-Britain* have still happily preserved this noble and ancient *Gothic* Constitution, which all our Neighbours once enjoy'd, as well as we, who are the Wonder and Glory round about us. And we may truly apply to our selves the Words of a inspir'd Author, *What Nation is there so great, that hath statutes and judgments so righteous as those, which our GOD hath given us*!

THE several Charters, especially that stiled *The Great Charter*, in the ninth Year of King HENRY the Third, in and by which our Rights and Privileges stand secur'd, sworn, and entail'd down to us and our Posterity, were not voluntary Abatements of the King's original Power, nor the Grants and Concessions of our Princes (as FILMER, BRADY, LESTRANGE, HICKS, LESLEY,[4] and other advocated for Arbitrary Power [15] would make us believe) but Recognitions of what we had reserved unto our selves in the original Institution of our Government, and of what had always belonged to us by common Law, and most ancient

[1] W. Petyt: 1636–1707, *Antiquity and Power of the House of Commons*, 1739; *The Ancient Right of the Commons of England Asserted*, 1680.

[2] James Tyrrel, 1642–1718, *Bibliotheca Politica*, a series of 14 political Dialogues published between 1692 and 1702, in which he treated of the constitutional issues raised by the later Stuarts and the Revolution, and gave a Whig view of the question. They were collected into one vol. in 1727.

[3] Thos. Rymer 1641–1713, *Fœdera, Conventiones, ...ab 1066 ad nostra tempora,* 15 vols (1704–13)

[4] Sir Robert Filmer, 1588-1653, author of *Patriacha*, circa 1650; Robert Brady, died 1700, wrote several books on the history of England: *An Historical Treatise of Cities & Burghs, or Boroughs, showing their Original, &c*, 1690 in the preface of which, he showed that 'they have nothing of the greatness and authority they boast of, but from the bounty of our ancient kings and their ancestors."; Sir Roger Lestrange,1616-1704, journalist and writer of political pamphlets; Dr George Hicks, 1642-1715, Bishop of Thetford, and linguist; Charles Lesley, 1750-1722, non-juror, partisan of James II, attacked William III, then attached himself to the Pretender after 1715.

Custom: And tho' these Liberties and Privileges came to be more distinctly expressed in *Magna Charta*, than they had been before; yet they had not only been acknowledged, and transmitted down in the Laws of King EDWARD *the Confessor*, as the Birthright of every *Englishman*, which also WILLIAM the First, commonly called *the Conqueror*, ratified as such; but they had long before been collected into a Body by King EDWARD *the Saxon*, and were only revised, repeated, and confirmed by EDWARD *the Confessor*.

BRACTON, who was a Judge in the Time of King HENRY the Third, calls the Laws of *England*, *The Ancient Judgments of the Just*. And BRITON, Bishop of Hereford, who published his Book in the fifth Year of King ED- [16] WARD the First, by the Command of that King, as as written in the Name of that King; and Sir GILBERT DE THORNTON,[1] who was a Chief Justice in the same Reign, and reduced the Book of BRACTON into a *Compendium*; and likewise Sir JOHN FORTESCUE, who was Lord Chancellor in the Reign of HENRY the Sixth, in his Book *De Laudibus Legum Angliae*, all write to the same Effect, and speak of the Laws of England as the Birthright of the Subject. And with these now mentioned concur all the eminent Authors in the Profession of the common Law, who, being so learned and so ancient, are therefore the most competent Witnesses of the *English* Constitution. Generally speaking, the whole Body of our Statute Laws, together with the Petitions of Right, and the *Habeas Corpus* Acts, are but Declarations and Confirmations of the common Laws of the Kingdom. And soon after the happy Revolution, under the Great and Glorious King WILLIAM the Third, which [C -17] restored and improved our Constitution, was passed the famous Bill of Rights, wherein the ancient and fundamental Rights and Liberties of the Subject are distinctly stated, in thirteen Articles, and ratified and confirmed to is and our Posterity, and here acknowledged to be our most rightful Inheritance. [1 W. & M. An Act declaring the Rights and Liberties of the Subject &c.]

OF all the inestimable Advantages derived to us from this our wise Frame of Government, none more deserves to be highly prized and valued than that peculiar Birthright of ours, Tryal of Causes, whether Civil or Criminal, by Juries; an undoubted Part of the Gothic Constitution. This hath always been held so sacred, that King ALFRED [2] put one of his Judges to Death for Passing Sentence upon a Man, when three of the twelve disagreed in their [18] Verdict from the Rest. And the same King put another of his Judges to Death, for Passing Sentence of Death upon an *Ignoramus* returned by the Grand Jury. And a Third,

[1] Sir Gilbert de Thornton, composed a *Summa* at the end of the 13th century.

[2] Nath. BACON's *Historical Discourse of the Uniformity of the Governement of* England. [Nath. Bacon, half- brother of Francis, 1593-1660).]

for Condemning a Man upon an Inquest taken *ex Officio* (as before the Coroner, and the like) when the Criminal had not put him self upon his Country, that is, to be try'd by a Jury.

GENTLEMEN,

IT is for Putting in Execution of this great and invaluable Privilege that we now met together, and you are summoned here, and sworn to enquire of, and present to us, what Violations have been made of the Laws of GOD, and the Laws of the Land, by any Person, or Persons whatsoever, within the City and Liberty of *Westminster.*

IN the Course of your Enquiries, the Honour and Service of Almighty GOD, [C 2- 19] and his Holy Religion demands your first and principal Care.

A Sense of Religion, or the Fear of GOD, so manifestly tends to preserve the Peace of Society and the Welfare of Kingdoms, that it is not more the Duty than it is the Interest of all Governours, to support and Maintain it in its highest Esteem. Says TULLY,[1] Take away Religion, and you take away with it mutual Faith and human Society, and the most Excellent of Virtues, Justice itself. And MACHIAVEL, who had as little Respect for Religion as most People, ascribed the Prosperity of Rome to their Care of Religion, and the Strictness of their Morals; and tells us, That all Princes and Commonwealths, who would keep their Government intire and uncorrupt, are above all Things to take Care of Religion, and preserve it in its due Veneration: [20] *For in the whole World (says he) there is not a greater Sign of imminent Ruin, than when GOD and his Worship are despised.*[2]

A general Dissoluteness of Manners in any Community certainly tends to its Destruction: The *Wise Man*'s Observation being founded in the Nature of the Thing, as well in the Decree of Almighty GOD, *That righteousness exalteth a nation* ; *but sin is a reproach to any people.* [Prov. XIV.34.] As the Virtue of a Kingdom encreaseth or diminisheth, so doth its Strength at home, and Credit abroad; and the Experience of all Ages and Nations teacheth us this great Truth, that no Government can long flourish, which doth not discourage and punish Vice and Profaneness.

TO incite your Zeal in Doing your Duty, you have an illustrious Example before you. His Majesty, in his Excel- [21] lent Proclamation just now read to you, hath declared it to be his Royal Purpose and Resolution, to Discountenance and Punish all Manner of Vice, Profaneness, and Immorality in all Persons of what Degree or Quality soever. And gives these Reasons for it, That it is an indispensable Duty on him (and consequently on all of us who act by his Authority) to be careful,

[1] Lib. 1. De Nat. Deorum. *Fides etiam & Societas humani generis & unâ excellentissima Virtus Justitia tollitur.*

[2] MACH. Disc. Page 284.

above all Things, to Preserve and Advance the Honour and Service of Almighty GOD, and to Discourage and Suppress those Vices, which are so highly displeasing to GOD, and a Reproach to our Religion and Government; and as these Vices have a fatal Tendency to corrupt Persons, otherwise religiously and Virtuously disposed; so they may, if not timely remedied, draw down the divine Vengeance upon us.

HOW piously, and with what an unfeigned Concern, doth his Majesty express himself for the Good and Welfare of his Subjects, is evidently demonstrated, if you will but peruse the Proclamation [22] it self, which his Majesty also commands to be given in charge, at every Assizes, and at every Quarter-Sessions.[1]

AND therefore I hope, that you who (among other Things) are sworn diligently to enquire, and make true Presentment of all such matters and things, as shall be given you in Charge, from the due Regard, which you have for his Sacred Majesty, as well as for the Prosperity and Happiness of your Country, will, to the utmost of your Power, exert your selves in Putting these good Laws in Execution; and not suffer Blasphemy, profane Swearing and Cursing, Drunkenness, Profanation of the LORD's Day, and all other lewd and disorderly Practices, mentioned and described in this most Admirable Proclamation, to be practised and committed every Day with Insolence and Impunity, whilst every thing that is Good, Virtuous, and Laudable, is reviled, contemned and ridiculed. [23]

AFTER a due Concern for the Honour and Glory of Almighty GOD, the Honour and Safety of his Vice-gerent, our Most Gracious Sovereign, his Virtuous and Most Excellent Queen, and his Illustrious Royal Progeny, justly claim this next Place in your Thoughts.

THE greatest Offence, that can be committed under a Monarchical Government, is High Treason.

BEFORE the Making of the Statute *de Proditionibus*, in the Reign of King EDWARD the Third, in the Time of the *Barons* Wars, and during the Minority of that King, Treason was variously described, and according to the Temper of the Times, Facts were declared or not declared to be Treason, which kept the People in such continual Fear, and under such dreadful Apprehensions (the Punishment for this Offence being the most Severe which our Laws do inflict) that in the twenty fifth Year of that King's Reign, this Law was made [24] which reduces the Species of High Treason to a Certainty; and this was then thought of so great a Benefit to the Subject, that the Parliament who made it, as my Lord COKE tells us, was called *Parliamentum Benedictum*, or the *Blessed Parliament.*

BY this Act, Compassing or Imagining the Death of the King, the Queen, or their their eldest Son and Heir, is High Treason. So is Levying

[1] The same proclamation of 5 July 1727.

War against the King, Adhering to his Enemies, Giving them Aid or Comfort, in the Realm or elsewhere. Counterfeiting his Coin, or Bringing false into the Realm; Killing the Lord Chancellor, Lord Treasurer, Justices in Eyre, of Assize, and Justices of *Oyer* and *Terminer*, being in their Places doing their Offices. It is likewise High Treason by this Act, to Counterfeit the Great or Privy Seal; and Counterfeiting the Privy Signet, or Sign Manual, is made High Treason by another Act of the First and Second of PHILIP and MARY. [D - 25]

BY an Act of the Thirteenth and Fourteenth of King WILLIAM the Third, it is High Treason, to hold any Correspondence with the Pretender, who is himself, by this Act, attainted of High Treason.

ENDEAVOURING to Hinder, or Deprive the next Successor in the *Protestant* Line, from Succeeding to the Crown, is made High Treason, by an Act of the First of the late Queen ANNE.

BY a Statute of the Sixth of Queen ANNE, it is High Treason to Maintain and Affirm, by Writing, or Printing, that his Majesty is not Lawful and Rightful King of these Realms; or that the Pretender hath any Right to the Crown; or that any other Person hath any Right to the same, but by the Acts of Settlement; or that the King and Parliament cannot bind or Limit the Succession of the Crown. And if the Offender maintains the same by Words only, then it is a Premunire.[26]

IN the Reigns of King CHARLES the Second, and King JAMES the Second, there were several hard and irregular Prosecutions for High Treason; as that of the Lord RUSSEL, the Honourable Mr. SIDNEY, Mr. CORNISH, and others, whose Attainders, soon after the Revolution, were reversed by Parliament.[1] And it was one of the Blessed Fruits of this Glorious Revolution, that the Laws concerning High Treason were altered for the better, and greatly in Favour of the Subject. Formerly Men were committed for Treason, and their Friends were not admitted to come near them, nor were they allowed either Counsel to assist them, or Pen, Ink, or Paper, or Informed for what Treason they were committed, or by whom accused; and tho' they had a Liberty to except against any of the Jury, they were never allowed to have a Copy of the Pannel to make Advantage of it. But now, by the Statute[2] of the Se-[D 2-27] venth of King WILLIAM the Third, a Person committed for Treason, or Misprision of Treason, shall have a Copy of the whole Indictment five Days before his Tryal, to Advise with Counsel, &c. and a Copy of the Pannel two Days before his Tryal: And shall be allowed to make a full Defence by his Counsel learned in the Law, and his

[1] Lord William Russell, 1639-83, & Algernon Sidney, 1622-83, were leaders against the Court's policy, at the time of the Exclusion Bill crisis; they were executed after the Whigs were defeated. Henry Cornish, d. 1685, merchant and alderman of London, was convicted on trumped up charges, for his unconciliatory attitude to James II.

[2] *An Act for Regulating of Tryals in Cases of Treason, and Misprision of Treason.*

Witnesses shall be examined on Oath, and he shall not be Convicted, but by the Oaths of two Witnesses to the same Species of Treason.

YOU are to enquire of Misprision of Treason, which consists in the bare Knowledge and Concealment of High Treason.

YOU are to present the Authors, Printers, and Publishers of all seditious and treasonable Libels, against his Majesty's Sacred Person, his Illustrious Family, or his Administration; and of all the Libels that have been published of late, none exceeds the Malignity of that Villanous One of *Mist's Journal* of the twenty [28] fourth of August last,[1] which the Grand Juries of Middlesex and Bristol have worthily presented, as a most Wicked and Treasonable Libel, reflecting on his Sacred Majesty, and the Ever Blessed Memory of his Royal Father; which Presentments being printed in the *London Gazets*, I presume most of you have seen.[2]

GENTLEMEN,

IT is to his Majesty, as a common Father, that we owe all the quiet uninterrupted Enjoyment of our civil and religious Rights and Liberties, which we are at present blest with; and from the Succession in his Royal House we can only expect to have them continued to our Posterity. And as it cannot be doubted, but that you wish well to your selves, and your Families; so I hope you will do your Endeavour to Punish all those wicked Men, who would by their Libels, or other Devices, change so glorious a Prospect into Error, and Super-[29] stition in the Church, and Tyranny and Arbitrary Power in the State, under an inraged *Popish* Pretender, who has been harboured ever since he was five Months old among Arbitrary Princes, and been a constant Attendant at Courts, where no Law was ever talked of, besides the Will of the Prince.

AFTER your Duty to GOD and the King performed, your Neighbours, or Fellow Subjects claim your Justice.

YOU are to enquire of Petty Treason, which is where a Servant kills his Master or Mistress, a Wife her Husband, or an Ecclesiastical Man his Prelate.

YOU are to present Burglary, which is the Breaking and Entering into a House, in the Night Time, with an Intent to commit some Felony.

YOU are to present all Sorts of Felonies, whether against the Person, [30] Goods, or Habitation of Man; and all Accessories before and after the Facts; all Petty Larcenies; all Assaults, Batteries, Affrays; forcible Entries, and Detainers of Lands and Tenements by Force; Riots, Routs, and unlawful Assemblies; Neglect or Breach of Duty in publick Officers, especially of Constables who Neglect or Refuse to execute Warrants

[1] *Mist's Journal*, first appeared in Dec. 1716, continued as *Mist's Weekly Journal*, then as *Fog's Weekly Journal* until 1737.

[2] Here are probably meant London newspapers generally, for no newspaper was called the Gazette, or had the word Gazette in its title at this date, except the *Weekly Journal, or the British Gazeteer.*

delivered to them; Bribery; Extortions; all publick Nusances; all that Sell corrupt and unwholsom Victuals; all Houses of common Lewdness and Gaming; disorderly *Geneva* Shops; Night Houses; and those Houses which harbour Inmates, especially those that are kept open all Night, and which receive great Numbers of idle and disorderly Persons, lodging all Comers for a Penny or Two-pence per Night. A vigorous Prosecution of these Sort of Houses will be one Way of Preventing the numerous Robberies which we have lately heard so much of. You are also to enquire of all Highways and Bridges out of Repair, and of all broken Pavements; and in [31] general, of every thing that is an Offence against the publick Peace.

YOU are, GENTLEMEN, of so good Understanding and Capacities, and so well Experienced in the Nature of this Service, that it will not be necessary to give you a long Catalogue or Detail of the many and various Kinds of Offences enquirable by you; but least any thing which you ought to enquire of should not occur to your Memories, I refer you to my former Charges, printed by Order of the Court, and at the Desire of three several Grand Juries; and I have directed printed Copies of all those Charges, to be given to every one of you GENTLEMEN, who are sworn upon this Grand Jury, for your Use on this present, or any future Service of this Nature.

THESE Matters and Things, GENTLEMEN, that have been given you in Charge, with whatever else shall come to your Knowledge, touching this present Service, you are Impartially to lay [32] before this Court by your Presentments, in Order to have the Offenders punished, and the Grievances redressed, by the effectual Putting our excellent Laws in due execution. And upon any Doubts, or Difficulties, which in the Course of your Enquiries you may meet with, the Court, upon your Application, will give you all due Assistance.

FINIS.

A **CHARGE** TO THE **GRAND JURY** OF THE *CITY and LIBERTY of* Westminster, *&c.* At the General Quarter-Sessions of the Peace, held the third Day of *July*, 1729, in WESTMINSTER-HALL. **By Sir JOHN GONSON Knt**.

Printed at the Desire of the Justices of the Peace, *for the said City and Liberty, and of thew Grand Jury.*

LONDON: Printed by Charles Ackers, in *Great-Swan-Alley*, St. *John's - Street.* 1729.

Civitas, Burgus, & Villa Westm. *in Com.* Midd. } *Ad Generalem Quarterialem Sessionem Pacis Domino Regis Regis tent' apud* Westm. *pro Libertat' Decani & Capituli Ecclesiæ Collegiat. Beati* Petri Westm. *Civit', Burgi & Villæ* Westm. *in Comitat.* Midd. *& Sancti* Martini le Grand, London' *Die* Jovis *scilicet tertio die* Julii, *Anno Regis Domini* Georgii *Secundi, Dei Gratiâ, nunc Regis* Magnæ Birtanniæ, *&c Tertio.*

This Court taking into their Consideration the most Religious, Learned, Useful, and Excellent Charge, this Day delivered by Sir JOHN GONSON Knight, Chairman of this Court, to the Grand Jury, sworn to enquire for our Sovereign Lord the King, for the Body of this City and Liberty, at this present Session of the Peace; doth hereby Order, that the said JOHN GONSON have, and he hereby hath the Thanks of this Court for the same; and the said Sir JOHN GONSON is hereby desired to cause his said Charge to be forthwith Printed and Published.

Per Curiam

MIDDLETON

[A 2]

To the WORSHIPFUL
Sir *JOHN GONSON* Knt.

CHAIRMAN of the General Quarter-Sessions of the Peace, held for the City and Liberty of *Westminster*, &c. the third Day of *July*, 1729.

WE the Grand Jury impanelled and sworn to enquire for our Sovereign Lord the King, for the Body of the said City and Liberty, having (with due Respect and Attention) received from your Worship, a most Eloquent and Useful Charge, tending to the good Government and Information, not only of this City and Liberty, but to the universal Guidance and Direction of all Persons whatsoever, in the Execution of the several Offices and Trusts in them respectively reposed; Do therefore return our most humble Thanks for the same, and intreat that you will be pleased to cause the said Charge to be Printed, for the better Improving tbe Knowledge of his Majesty's Subjects in the Laws and Customs of this Realm.

Samuel Bever,
John Hodson,
William Boon,
Lawr. Neale,
John Hathaway,
Wm. Barber,
Jos. Mines,
John Buck,
Tho. Paulin,
Samuel Cockey,
Moses Holloway,
Edward Shepherd,
Rich. Williams,
Jos. Caldecott,
Richard Clayton,
Geo. Shute, Jun.
Cuthbert Cornforth,
John Bladwell,
John Dunkarton,
Peter Le'Cott
Tho. Gisbon.

[A 1]

CHARGE
TO THE
GRAND JURY, &c.

Gentlemen of the Grand Jury

GOVERNMENT in general is an orderly constituted Power, for publick Good. Orderly, to prevent Anarchy and Confusion; Constituted Power, to prevent Usurpation; For publick Good, to prevent Tyranny and Oppression.

THE Use and Necessity of Government is so obvious to all Men, that [2] there never was Age or Country without some Sort of civil Authority. But as Men are seldom unanimous in the Means to attain their End; so their Difference in Opinion, in Relation to Government, has produced Variety of Forms of it in the World. To enumerate them would be to recapitulate the History of the whole Earth. But they may, in general, be reduced to one of these Heads; either the civil Authority is delegated to one or more, or else it is still reserved to the whole Body of the People. Whence arises the known Distinction of Government, into Monarchy, Aristocracy, and Democracy.

MONARCHY it's probable was the first and most natural Government, because the most simple and easy for Men to light on. And in the first Ages of the World, before Ambition and Luxury had debauched the Minds of Princes, it was doubtless the best Sort of Government. But the Setting up so many Commonwealths on the Ruin [3] of Monarchies, shewed that Men found great Mischiefs and Inconveniencies in that Sort of Government, when it once grew tyrannical, or else they had never departed from it. And this made them, as BRUTUS said, at the Beginning of the *Roman* Commonwealth, to invent other Sorts of Government, which might partake of all the Benefits, without the Inconveniencies of absolute Monarchy.[1]

WE can never enough admire the Wisdom of the antient *German* and *Go*-[4] *thic* Nations, who preferred a limited Monarchy to all other Forms of Government, as an excellent Medium between the Mischiefs of Arbitrary Power, and those Inconveniencies that attend Republicks, where either the common People or the Nobility must govern. And of this ancient Constitution our Government is the Noblest, and almost the only Remains. Our Legislature is in the King, and the two Houses of Parliament. The executive Power is in the King, who is to govern his People by Laws of their own Choosing. The King is owned to be the Supreme of these Authorities, and in some Cases the Crown is the sole Power of the Kingdom. As for Instance, the Power of making War or Peace is intirely in the Crown. So is the executive Part of the Law. But then to Restrain this Power, even where it is Absolute, from Exerting to any Thing unreasonable or unjust, there is first, as to Making an unreasonable War, no Mo-[B -5] ney to be raised for Carrying on this War or for any Thing else without a House of Commons. In the next Place, to Redress erroneous Judgments, or Decrees upon which Executions would follow. These Judgments, or Decrees, made by the King's Courts, may be reversed by an Appeal to the House of Lords, which is the supreme Court of Judicature, and from whence no Appeal lies in the Crown. For where Kings are not the whole entire Power, the Case of *Meum* and *Tuum* is often disputed between the King and the Subject. And the Judges are under an Oath to give a Judgment according to Law; not only in all Causes between one Subject and another, but also between the King and the Subject. And this Way the Crown is controuled, even by those who act by the Crown's Commission. This original happy Frame of Government is truly and properly called an *English* Man's Birthright, a Privilege not to be exempt [6] from Law, but to be freed in Person and Estate, from arbitrary Violence, and Oppression.

And the Institution of Grand and Petit Juries is one of the most antient, and valuable Parts of our excellent Constitution, and the greatest Fence and Bulwark of our Lives, Liberties, and Properties.

[1] Hooker's *Eccl. Polity, lib.* 1. *sect.* 10. At the first, when some Kind of Regimen was once appointed, it may be that nothing was then farther thought upon for the Manner of Governing, but all permitted unto their Widsom and Discretion which were to rule. 'Till by Experience they found this for all Parts very inconvenient, so as the Thing, which they had devised for a Remedy, did indeed but increase the Sore, which it should have cured. They saw, that to live by one Man's Will became the Cause of all Men's Misery. This constrained them to come to Laws, wherein all Men might see their Duty beforehand, and know the Penalties of Transgressing them.

Gentlemen,

IT is for the Exercise of this great and invaluable Privilege, that you are now summoned here, and sworn. And you are to present to this Court all Offences against the Rules, either of *Moral* or of *Civil* Justice. Under the former is included all Vice, Immorality, and Profaneness. And under the latter, all Offences committed against your King, and your Country.

THE Honour and Service of Almighty GOD ought to be our first and principal Care. The most famous Writers of Politicks, from PLATO down to [B 2 - 7] MACHIAVEL, shew, that Vice is always attended by Corruption, and is the Pest and Bane of every free Community. Every one, who has read the Roman History, which is now in the Hands of almost all the World, must be satisfied, that the Reason, why the *Romans* expelled the *Tarquins*, and establish'd Liberty upon a lasting Foundation, was, because they were at that Time a most religious and virtuous People. And the Reason, why they could not recover them, upon the Extinction of the Race of the CESARS, was, because they were then a more profligate, vicious, and luxurious People, than ever the World has known in any other Nation. All the famed Legislators of the World, MOSES, LYCURGUS, SOLON and NUMA founded their Laws, their Governments, and political Institutions upon Religion and Virtue.

YOU are therefore, as you honour your King, and love your Country, to take Care, that the Laws against [8] Immorality and Profaneness be strictly put into Execution, as the most excellent Proclamation, just now read directs, and which I am Commanded to enforce to you, and particularly those against profane Cursing and Swearing, Drunkenness and Breach of the Sabbath.

AFTER those Offences, which more immediately concern Almighty GOD and his holy Religion, you are to enquire of Offences against *Civil* Justice, which are such Crimes, as are committed against your King and your Country.

The greatest of these is High-Treason.

IN the *Saxon* Times there was no other Treason known, than that of Treachery to their Country, and Deserting it in Time of Danger[1]. Even Plotting against their King was no more than Felony, as appears by the *Mirror of Justice*[2]. An Indictment [9] for an Offence of that Nature, against King EDMUND, concludes only *felonice*. Whereas Indictments in the other Case, concluded *felonice & proditorie*. The Punishment of the one was Loss of Life, and Forfeiture of the personal Estate only; of the other, Loss of Life with Forfeiture of the whole Estate, both Real and Personal.[3]

[1] Tacitus *Ger. cap.* 10. *Proditores & transfugas arboribus suspendunt.*

[2] Mirror, *cap. 2, sect. 11.*

[3] *Leg.* Edw. *cap.* 38.

Treason, which thus antiently related to the Kingdom only, we find, by the Chief Justice Glanville,[1] who wrote in K. HENRY the IId's Reign, to have been then extended to the Person of the King; for that Author puts them both on the same Foot, and makes one as well as the other to be *Crimen læsæ Majestatis*. And the Reason of this, no Doubt, was the great Interest, which the Kingdom had in the Safety and Preservation of that Prince.

OFFENCES against the Safety and Honour of the King's Person, being then become Treason, made it so extensive [10] and rendered it of so uncertain a Nature, that Persons were often involved in Treason before they thought of it: For as yet Treason was under no other Regulation, then what the present Sense of the Judges (not always above the Influence of angry or covetous Princes) should determine to be so; of which those Times afforded but too many sad Instances. To obviate there this Mischief, was the Statute of the *25* th of King EDWARD III. [cap. 2][2] made, as a Rule whereby the Judges were intirely to govern themselves, who otherwise might have retained to this Day, a Power to declare any Thing to be Treason, which they apprehended to be highly prejudicial to the Kingdom. And tho' the Parliament, for very good Reasons, thought it necessary to confine inferior Jurisdictions to one Rule; yet they still reserved to themselves a Power of Judgment what shall be Treason in particular Cases, that were not expressed in this [11] Statute, as appears by the Proviso at the latter End of it[3].

BY this Act of the *25* th of King EDWARD III. Compassing or Imagining the Death of the King or Queen, or their Eldest Son, or Heir, and declaring by an open Act a Design to Depose, Imprison, or Murder the King, &c is High Treason. So is Levying War against him; or Adhering to his Enemies, within the Realm or without; and also Counterfeiting his Great Seal, or his Privy Seal, or his Money current within the Realm. The several other Species of High Treason, by this and latter Acts, I omit to give you in Charge, because] [12] not likely at present to fall under your Enquiry. And I shall only mention to you the Statute of the *6th* of Queen ANNE, [Cap. 7] whereby it is made High Treason, to Maintain and Affirm, by Writing or Printing, that his Majesty is not

[1] GLANV. *de Leg. lib.*1, *cap.*2, *&* *lib.*14, *cap.*1. [Ranulph de G., became chief justiciar to Henry II in 1180.]

[2] See *A Discourse concerning High Treason* (London: R. Mead, 1683, in-fol.)

[3] Sect. 12 " And because many other like Cases of Treason may happen in Time to come, which a Man can't think or declare at this present Time, it is accorded, that in any other Case, suppos'd Treason, which is not above specified, doth happen before any Justices; the Justices shall tarry, without any going to Judgment of the Treason, till the Cause be shewed and declared before the King and his Parliament, whether it shall be judged Treason, or other Felony."

lawful King of this Realm; or that the Pretender hath any Right to the Crown; or that any other Person hath any Right to the same, but by the Acts of Settlement; or that the King and Parliament cannot Limit and Bind the Succession of the Crown. And if the Offender Maintains the same by Words only, then it is a Premunire.

AND here I must observe to you, that Altering and Limiting the Succession of the Crown, by Parliament, is no such new or unprecedented thing, as some of the Enemies of our present happy Establishment would make us believe; but it is most agreeable to our Antient Constitution and Laws, and exercised and practised Ages before the Revolution. Of [C-13] which many Instances might be given, from our Histories and Records. Allow me to mention a few. King HENRY VII. had several Titles, yet he thought fit to wave them all, and get the Crown settled upon him, and the Heirs of his Body, by Parliament[1]. Accordingly an Act passed in the first [14] Year of his Reign to this Purpose, in which it is remarkable, that there is no Recognition of any antient Right; but only an Establishment of the Possession, which he then had. And this, Act was passed before he married with the Princess ELIZABETH, eldest Daughter to King EDWARD IV. and Heiress of the House of *York*. Nothing therefore can be more evident, then that he depended on his Parliamentary Title. He would never own that of the House of *York*, or suffer his Queen to join with him in any Act of Government, and this perhaps might be the Reason, why he never repealed the Act of the First of K. RICHARD III. by which she was declared Illegitimate.[2] And whatever the Title the House of *Lancaster* had, it could not avail him, because his Claim was under one, who was also Illegitimate.[3] Besides, his Mother [C 2-15] the Countess of *Richmond*, was alive during

[1] Bacon's *Hist.* H.VII. *Engl. Ed. fol.* 7, 8, 11, 12, 16. BUCK's *Hist. of* RICH. III. Unprinted Statute still upon the Roll, the Title of which is *Titulus Regis.* And it runs in these Words: " To the Pleasure of Almighty GOD, the Wealth, Prosperity, and Surety of this Realm of *England*, and to the singular Comfort of all the Kings Subjects of the same, and in avoiding all Ambiguities and Questions. Be it Ordained, Established, and Enacted, by the Authority of this present Parliament, that the Inheritance of the Crowns of the Realms of *England* and of *France*, with all the Preeminence, and Dignity Royal to the same Pertaining, and all other Signories to the King belonging beyond the Sea, with the Appurtenances thereto, in any wise due or pertaining, be, rest, remain, and abide in the most Royal Person of our now Sovereign Lord King HENRY the VII*th* , and in the Heirs of his Body, lawfully coming, perpetually, with the Grace of GOD, so to endure, and in no other".

[2] Collect. of Records, *p.* 709, 714.

[3] John of *Gaunt*, duke of *Lancaster*, had by CATHERINE SWINFORD, before Marriage, four Illegitimate Children, HENRY, JOHN BEAUFORD (afterwards D. of Somerset) THOMAS and JOAN, and in the 20th Year of K. RICHARD II. he, by Act of Parliament, makes them Legitimate, COKE's 4 *Inst.* 36, 37. K. HENRY VII. Was Son to EDW. HADDAM, Earl of *Richmond*, and MARGARET his Wife, Daughter and Heiress of the above mentioned JOHN BEAUFORD, Duke of *Somerset.*

his whole Reign, and did not dye 'till after the Accession of King HENRY VIII.[1]

As K. HENRY the *8th* 's Grandmother was alive, when he came to the Crown, and as he succeeded by Virtue of a Parliamentary Entail;[2] so he trusted but little to any Hereditary Right. As appears plainly from the several Acts of Parliament he procured for Settling his Succession. By the Act of the 25 th of his Reign,[3] the Lady MARY was Bastardized, and the Crown, for Defaults of Heirs Male of his Body, lawfully begotten on Q. ANNE BULLEN, was Limited to the Lady ELIZA [16] BETH, and her Heirs. And after this there is another Statute of the 28 th of K.H. VIII.[4] repealing the former Act, and declaring the Lady MARY and the Lady ELIZABETH to be both Illegitimate, and settling the Crown upon himself and the Heirs of his Body by Q. JANE; and for Want of such Heirs, with Power to dispose of the Crown, by his Letters Patent, or his last Will, to what Person or Persons, and for such Estate in the same, and under such Conditions, as should please his Majesty. And lastly, another Act passed in the *35th* Year of his Reign,[5] altering the Succession again, and settling the Crown first on his Son, Prince EDWARD and his Heirs; then on the Lady MARY and her Heirs; afterwards on the Lady ELIZABETH and her Heirs; and the Remainder over to such Persons as the King should appoint, by his Letters Patent, or his last Will [17] as before. By Force of this Act K. EDWARD VI. succeeded, and after him Q. MARY, and Q. ELIZABETH; both of which, being under a Sentence of Bastardy, could pretend to no Right, but what was given by this Statute of the 35th of K. HENRY VIII.[6] From hence it is evident, that in the Reigns of K. HEN. VIII. and Q. ELIZABETH, these Parliamentary Settlements of the Crown were held, and esteemed Good and Effectual to those that Claimed under them, against all Pretenders to the Contrary. And this, according to the Opinions of the greatest Men, and the most learned Lawyers, who lived in those Days. We have it from the Lord HERBERT's History of K. HENRY VIII.[7] that Sir THO. MORE, who was Lord Chancellor in that Reign, and RICHARD RICH, then Sollicitor General, and afterwards Lord RICH,[8] in their Debate about the Supremacy, both agreed it to be the known Law of *England* and laid it down as a first Prin-

[1] Lord HERB. *Hist. of* H.VIII.- *Compl. Hist. of Engl. vol. 2 p.* 4.[Edward Baron of Cherbury, *The Life and Raign of King Henry VIII*, 1649.]

[2] 'a decision by Parliament to create an entailed interest or estate.'

[3] 25 H. VIII. *cap.* 22. An Act concerning the King's Succession.

[4] 28 H.VIII. c.7. An Act concerning the Succession of the Crown.

[5] 35 H.VIII. c. 1., An Act for the Establishment of the King's Succession.

[6] 35 H. VIII. cap. 1.

[7] 35 H. VIII. cap. 1.

[8] Richard Rich,(1496?-1567) 1st Baron Rich, Lord Chancellor.

[18] ciple, that the Parliament could Alter and Limit the Succession of the Crown. And some great Lawyers, in a Parliament of Q. ELIZABETH,[1] declared the same Thing. Mr. YELVERTON,[2] afterward Speaker and a Judge, said, that to Assert that the Parliament had no Power to Determine of the Crown was High Treason. And Mr. MOUNSON Affirmed, that it was horrible to say, that the Parliament had no Authority to Determine of the Crown. For then would ensue (says he) not only the Annihilating the Statute of the 35th of K. HENRY VIII. but the Statute made in the first Year of this Queen's Reign of Recognition should also be made Void. This, and much more to the same Effect, may be found in Sir SIMON D'EWE'S Journal.[3]

AND by a Statute of the First of K. EDW. VI[4] all Usurpations of the Crown, against the Act of the 35th of HEN. VIII. are made High Treason. And when [19] the duke of *Northumberland* (who had married his Son to the Lady JANE GRAY) had prevailed upon K. EDWARD VI. in his Sickness, to Nominate that Lady by Will for his Successor. The Judges, and others the King's Council, told him in express Terms, that such Designation would be of no Force against the Act of Settlement[5], by which the Crown, in Case of K. EDWARD's Death without Issue, was Limited to his two Sisters, the Ladies MARY and ELIZABETH.

INDEED, the Author of the Book of the *Hereditary Right of the Crown of* England *Asserted*, &c[6] published in the last Year of the Reign of Q. ANNE, is very positive, that Q. MARY and Q. ELIZABETH had no Occasion for this Act of Parliament, being both Legitimate Descendants of K. HENRY VIII. as he would make his Readers believe. Yet it's plain, that K. HENRY VIII. and his Lawyers and Divines, were of another Opi-[20] nion. And as to this Author's Argument to prove their Legitimacy, this one plain Answer may be given, That they are all of them founded upon the Rules of the Canon Law. Which, unless Confirmed by Act of Parliament, is of no Force here,[7] especially when it stands (as in this Case) in direct Contradiction to the Laws of England. And as to Q. MARY it is plain, at her coming to the Crown, she could not be looked upon as Heir by Right of Blood, because, by the afore-mentioned Statute of the 25 th of HENRY VIII. his Marriage with Q. CATHERINE her Mother was declared Unlawful, and the Crown settled on the King,

[1] 13 ELIZ. 1571

[2] probably Sir Henry Y., 1566-1629, judge under James I & Charles I.

[3] *Page* 164, 176.[Sir Simon, 1602-50, M.P., left a diary containing parliamentary records and proceedings.

[4] Cap. 12, sect. 9.

[5] Burnet's *Hist. of the Reform.* part 2, fol. 223.

[6] Page 213, 214, 215, 216. [1714].

[7] GLANV. *l.* 7, *c.* 15. COKE 2 *Inst.* 96,97. *Stat. of Merton, c.* 9. 23 H. VIII.*c.* 38. 12 C.II *c.*33.

and on the Heirs of his Body by Q. ANNE BULLEN, as I mentioned before. And besides all this, she was but Sister by the Half Blood to K. EDWARD VI. and so could not Inherit as Heir to him. And tho', in the first Year of her Reign, the Parliament ('tis true) took [D - 21] off her Illegitimacy, and repealed so much of the Acts of the 25th and 28th of K. HENRY VIII. as declared her Illegitimate;[1] yet in this the Parliament seems rather to provide for the Honour of her Descent, than to declare her Succession to be Inheritance by Right of Blood. Because this Statute of the 35th of K. HENRY VIII. whereby the Crown was settled upon Prince EDWARD, and the Heirs of his Body; and the Remainder upon the Ladies MARY and ELIZABETH, and whereby the King had also Power given him to Dispose of the Crown, by Letters Patent, or by Will, was not at all repealed, but still remains in our Statute Book. And after the Death of Q. MARY, it was agreed by both Houses of Parliament, that Q. ELIZABETH should be proclaimed ac [22] cording to the Act of Settlement, of the *35 th* of K. HENRY VIII.

AND in the Act of Recognition of her Right, Imo ELIZABETHAE,[2] the same Act of Settlement is referred to, and declared to be, and remain the Law of this Realm for ever. And it is evident, that this Glorious Queen thought her Right to the Crown to be so well established, by these Acts of Parliament, that, as it is very well observed by Dr. WELWOOD in his *Memoirs* [3], she scorned to repeal, even the Act which declared her Mother's Marriage to be Illegitimate, and incapable to succeed. But still the Title of Q. ELIZABETH being scrupled by the *Romish* Party, produced and occasioned the Statute of the 13th of her Reign[4]. Whereby it was made no less than High Treason, during the Queen's Life, and Loss of Goods and Chattels, afterwards to Affirm and Maintain, that the Queen [D 2 - 23] to, and with the Authority of Parliament, was not able to make Laws and Statutes of sufficient Force and Validity to Bind, Limit, Restraint, and Govern all Persons, their Rights, and their Titles, that in any wise may, or might Gain any Interest or Possibility in, or to the Crown of *England*, in Possession, Remainder, Inheritance, Succession, or otherwise howsoever.

THOSE that are truly Loyal to our present most Gracious Sovereign, have Reason to recognize, with high Satisfaction, that such a Power of Alteration and Limiting the Descent of the Crown, is duly lodged in the King and Parliament. For under the Authority of an Act of

[1] *Rast.* 4, 1 M I, *sess.* 2, *cap.* 1, An Act declaring the Queen's Highness to have been born in just and lawful Matrimony, and also Repealing all Acts of Parliament, and Sentence of Divorce, made or had to the contrary.

[2] I ELIZ. c. 3. sect. 1.

[3] WELWOOD's *Memoirs*, p. 5. [*Memoirs of the most material Transactions in England, for the last Hundred Years, preceding the Revolution in 1688…* 2nd ed. corr. (London: 1700)

[4] 13 ELIZ. c. 1.

Parliament, we derive to our-selves the Happiness of his Government.

IT is owned, that the Monarchy of *England* is Hereditary, and not Elective. But neither our Monarchy, nor any other Monarchy upon Earth, is Hereditary in such a Sense, that is must necessarily descend by Right of [24] Birth, without Distinction to those who are Incapable, as well as to those who are Capable of it. If in a Hereditary Monarchy the next Heir should happen to be an Ideot, does the Order of his Birth make it necessary, that he should be a King? No body will say that. And yet such a natural Incapacity does not unfit Prince for Government, more than an Incapacity arising from Principle. He that professes Principles destructive of the End and Design of any Government, is more Dangerous to that Government, and therefore more unfit and uncapable of it, than an Ideot. One could not Protect it, the other would destroy it. But no one is born to destroy the Happiness, and inflict Misery on any Part of Mankind. No Man is born under an Obligation to submit to any Power applied to such unnatural Purposes. But still the Monarchy of *England* is Hereditary; for our Laws and Customs have made it so. But then there is no Natural or Divine [25] Right of Succession to Crowns, different or abstracted from the Civil and Political Laws, and Constitutions of particular Kingdoms. The Hereditary Right is not unalterable, but subject to the Laws of each Country; and a Person may be Heir to a Crown in one Country, that cannot be so in another: As for Instance, in *France* Females cannot Inherit; whereas in *England* they may. And MARIANA in his History tells us, that antiently in the Kingdom of *Arragon*, the Brother of the King was to Inherit before the Daughter.[1] The People of *Great Britain* have not therefore a Right to Choose whom they please to be their King; but are obliged to accept of, and to submit to, as such, that Person whom the Legislative Power shall appoint, capable of Answering the End and Design of this Government. By this Rule they guided themselves at the Re-[26] volution,[2] and considered

[1] Juan de M., S.J. *Historiæ de rebus Hispaniæ libri XX*, Toleti 1592. transl. into English, *The General History of Spain*... trans. by Captain J. Stevens, London: 1699.

[2] 1 W. *and* M. *sess.* 2, *cap.* 2; *sect.* 7 And whereas it has been found by Experience, that it is inconsistent with the Safety and Welfare of this *Protestant* Kingdom, to be governed by a *Popish* Prince, or by any King or Queen marrying a *Papist*. The Lords, Spiritual and Temporal, and Commons, do further Pray, that it may be enacted, and it was thereby enacted, That all and every Person, or Persons, that is, are, or shall be Reconcilied to, or shall hold Communion with the See, or Church of *Rome*, or shall profess the *Popish* Religion, or shall marry a *Papist*, shall be excluded, and be for ever incapable to Inherit, Possess, or Enjoy the Crown and Government of this Realm, and *Ireland*, and the Dominions thereunto belonging, or any Part of the same; or to have, use, or exercise any Regal Power, Authority, or Jurisdiction within the same. And in all and every such Case, or Cases, the People of these Realms shall be, and are thereby absolved of their Allegiance. And the said Crown and Government shall, from Time to Time, descend to, and be enjoyed by such Person, or Persons, being *Protestants*, as should have inherited and enjoyed the same; in Case the

the Right of Primogeniture as far as it was consistent with the Safety of our Church and Nation. They Transferred their Allegiance from a *Popish* Prince, who was absolutely Incapable by Principle, of Continuing in the Exercise of this Govern-[27] ment, to the next Protestant in the Hereditary Line capable of it. By this Rule the Government is at present happily Established, upon our most Gracious Sovereign[1]. And by this Rule I hope it will descend to his Royal Progeny, and that Popery will never come nearer the British Throne, than the Acts of Settlement do allow of.

YOU are therefore to be very careful in Presenting all that shall by Writing, Printing, or Speaking, deny his present Majesty's Title to the Crown. Or Maintain, that the Pretender hath any Right to the same. Or that the [28] King and Parliament are not invested with sufficient Power to Bind or Alter the Succession of the Crown, that these Offenders may be brought to condign Punishment, and be Convicted, either of High Treason, or Premunires, as the Excellent Statute of the *6th* of Q. ANNE directs.

AFTER High Treason, you are to Enquire of Misprision of Treason, of Petty Treason, of Burglary, and of all Sorts of Felonies, either at Common Law, or by any particular Statutes. The Felonies by Statutes are very numerous, and I have given an Account of most of them in my Charge, at this Quarter-Sessions, in *July* last, in which, and in my three other Charges, printed by Order of Court, and at the Request of the several Grand Juries, you will also find an Account of the various Sorts of Crimes and Offences committed against the Lives, Habitations, Properties, and Welfare of Mankind, and of the highest and lowest Offences, and therefore, instead of [E-29] Troubling you with a Repetition of the same Things, I have ordered Printed Copies of all those Charges, to be given to every one of you for your Use, on this present or any future Service of this Nature. I shall therefore only take Notice of a very few Offences, some of which were made Felonies by Acts of the last Session of Parliament. By an Act of the 12th of the late K. GEORGE, for the Building a Bridge cross the River of *Thames* from *Fulham* to *Putney*, wilfully and maliciously Burning, Blowing up, Pulling

---

said Person, or Persons, so reconcilied, holding Communion, or Professing, or Marrying, as aforesaid, were naturally dead.

[1] By an Act of the 12*th* of W.III. *cap. 2* The Princess Sophia, Electress and Dutchess Dowager of *Hanover* is declared next in Succession, after his Majesty (K. WILLIAM) and the Princess ANNE, and their respective Issue. And that then the Crown, &c. shall remain to the said Princess SOPHIA, and the Heirs of her Body, being *Protestants*. And there is a Proviso, that all Person who may inherit the Crown, by Virtue of this Act, and are reconcilied to the Church of *Rome*, or shall marry a *Papist*, shall be subject to the Incapacities of the said Act of 1 W. *and* M.

down, or Destroying the said Bridge, or any Part thereof, or Attempting so to do, is made Felony without Benefit of Clergy.

AND by an Act of the last Session for Relief of Insolvent Debtors, any Person forswearing himself, in any Particular, in Order to have the Benefit of the said Act, is to suffer Death as a Felon. And by another Act of the last Session, Forgery is also made [30] Felony[1] without Benefit of Clergy; as it is by the same Act, to steal Bonds, Notes, and other Securities, for the Payment of Money. And likewise by the same Act, any Person convicted for Perjury, or Subornation of Perjury, besides the Punishment by Law before to be Inflicted for those Crimes, is to be Sent to the House of Correction to hard Labour, for a Time not exceeding seven Years; or else to be Transported for a Time not exceeding seven Years, as the Court shall think proper. And if any Person so committed to the House of Correction, or Transported, shall voluntarily Escape, or Break Prison, or Return from Transportation, such Offender shall suffer Death as a Felon, and may be tried for such [31] Felony, either in the County where he so escaped, or where he shall be apprehended.

AND for the more effectual Suppressing of Gaming Houses, and Enabling the Justices of the Peace to punish the Gamesters, our Legislature hath now thought fit, by a Clause in an Act passed last Session, to revive certain Laws, *&c.* to Impower the Justices of the Peace, upon the Oaths of two Witnesses, to bind, with sufficient Sureties, any Person found Playing in a common Gaming House, to play no more so long as he lives. Whereas it was held before,[2] that no Person could be bound with Sureties, according to the Statute of the *33d* of HENRY VIII.[3] unless he was so found playing upon the personal View of the Justices.

THERE is one Thing more, that I must particularly Recommend to your Care, before I dismiss you. And that [32] is to present the Authors, Printers and Publishers of all seditious Libels, either against his Majesty's Sacred Person, his Illustrious Family, or his Administration. It should incite your Zeal against these Offenders, if you consider how mild and gracious a Sovereign now reigns over us. And I dare answer for it, we shall have more and more Reason to bless Almighty GOD for Bringing him to the Throne, and to pray that he may long sit thereon, and be succeeded (in his good Time) by a Race of Virtuous and Religious Protestant Princes; that do all the invaluable Blessings of the present Reign, may be transmitted down to latest Posterity.

FINIS.

[1] An Act for the more effectual Preventing, and further Punishment of Forgery, Perjury, and Subornation of Perjury; and to make it Felony to steal Bonds, Notes, and other Securities for the Payment of Money.

[2] Rex versus la Serre & Parmentier Hill, 7 Geo I. 1720.

[3] Cap. 9.

THE **CHARGE** OF J.... *P*.... TO THE Grand Jury of *M* — — *x*, On *Saturday May 22. 1736. LONDON:* Printed in the Year MDCCXXXVIII. [*Price Fourpence*]

[A 2]

A CHARGE to the Grand Jury of M.......x by J...ge P....

Gentlemen of these Juries

It is with great Pleasure I meet you at this Time: *A Time! Gentlemen*, in which every honest Man, every True *Englishman*, ought to rejoice with great Pleasure, and Joy, and Satisfaction.

This Nation, *Gentlemen*, never flourish'd more than at this Time; and I dare venture to affirm, *Gentlemen*, on my own Knowledge, that *England* never was so happy, *both at Home and Abroad*, as it is now. [4]

It was but lately, *Gentlemen*, very lately! but a little while ago; 'tis within all your Memories, *Gentlemen*, that *Europe* was over-clouded; our neighbouring Princes engag'd in a bloody and dreadful War; and had it not been for our *Wise King Gentlemen*, we might have been in the same Condition.

War, *Gentlemen*, is a sad thing! a very sad thing! and worst of all, *Gentlemen*, when in one's own Country. Desolation of Houses, Destruction of Thousands of innocent People; Lands laid waste; Fine Men! Brave Men! Men of great Abilities and Quality; Men of great Possessions, either kill'd, dead, or ruin'd, and reduc'd to Necessity.

These, *Gentlemen*, are the Miseries of War; and had we, *Gentlemen*, enter'd into these Affairs, This might [5] have been our Case; but, thro' the Providence of God, and the *great Wisdom of the King*, we have been preserv'd from it. And does not this, *Gentlemen*, afford great Matter of Joy and Pleasure, and Satisfaction, to every true-hearted *Englishman*!

'Tis a pleasurable Thing, *Gentlemen*, to think what a *Wise King* this Nation is *bless'd* with! So *Wise* a King, *Gentlemen*, never *before* sat on the *English* Throne; and no King, *Gentlemen*, ever carry'd *the Glory of this Nation* to *such a Height* as he has done! The Report, *Gentlemen*, of his *Wisdom* and *Conduct*, has brought *POWERFUL* Princes to seek Protection under him; and what an Honour it is to us, *Gentlemen*! what *Joy*, and *Pleasure*, and *Satisfaction*, to have so *Wise* a King to rule over us!

Such, *Gentlemen*, is the *Wisdom*, such is the *Goodness* of our King, that he is [6] *ever watchful, ever studying, ever contriving* for our *Good*, when we, *Gentlemen*, least think on't. Nor does his Majesty, *Gentlemen*, confine his

Care for us to the *present* Time, but when he is remov'd from us; which, *Gentlemen*, every honest Man, every good *Englishman* will wish and pray may be *late! very late!*

Gentlemen, in order to make us happy, his Majesty, in his *great Wisdom*! marry'd his eldest Daughter to a *Prince* nearly related to that Prince to whom we owe all that we enjoy at this Day;[1] for had not King *William*, *Gentlemen*, rescued us, in the *very Nick of Time*, from Arbitrary Power, our *Liberty* and *Property*, and every thing else, had been taken from us, and *We*, Gentlemen, *had all been made Papists*!

The *Wise King*, *Gentlemen*, for a further Assurance of our Happiness, has marry'd his Son, the Prince of *Wales*, [7] *Gentlemen*, a *promising Prince*, *Inheritor* of all his Father's Virtue and Wisdom[2]. Him, *Gentlemen*, his Majesty has marry'd to an excellent Princess, acknowledg'd by all and every body, *both those that have seen her, and those that have not seen her*, to be an agreeable Lady. Besides, *Gentlemen*, she is a *Protestant Princess*, descended from a Family that is united by Blood, by Marriage, or *by one thing or other*, to all the *Protestant* Families in *Europe*. What a *Glorious Alliance*, *Gentlemen*, is *This*! This Alliance, *Gentlemen*, will bring such *Strength*, and such *Security* to *Us* and our *Religion*, that *nothing can hurt us!*

These *Great Things! Gentlemen*, his Majesty has done for us; and every honest Man, I am sure, every true *Englishman*, ought to be thankful to God Almighty, and to *the great Wisdom* of the King, for them. This, *Gentlemen*, I thought proper to observe [8] to you upon this *Happy Occasion*. And now,

Gentlemen , I must beg Leave to represent to you some Nuisances, which it is your Business to rectify. We have very good Laws, *Gentlemen*, and I doubt not but you, all of you, do your Duty: But those under you, *Gentlemen*, I am afraid, are negligent.

There are, *Gentlemen*, two sorts of Laws that are both erroneous: Those that are too weak, and those that are too severe. If the Laws are too low and weak, they let Offenders escape; if they are too rigid, they make Men desperate. Our Laws, *Gentlemen*, are happily temper'd between both, and these Laws *Englishmen* love, and delight to be govern'd by.

There is one great Evil, *Gentlemen*, lately grown up amongst us to an ex-[B-9] orbitant Height: and that is, *Gentlemen*, Drinking of Spirituous Liquors. Our *Wise* King, and the *Wisdom of Parliament*, have provided against it; but before that Law takes Place (not till Michaelmas, Gentlemen!) many Persons may be destroy'd, many Enormities commited, unless you take Care to restrain them. You have, *Gentlemen*, in every Corner of the Streets, Tippling-Houses, where these Spirits are

[1] Anne, Princess Royal, b. 1709, m. William IV of Orange, 1734.

[2] The Prince of Wales was Frederick, 1707–51; married Augusta, daughter of Frederick II of Saxe-Gotha.

sold. These Tippling-Houses, *Gentlemen*, are Harbours for Rogues and Thieves, and disorderly Persons; and in them they *Burrow like Rabbits*. Here, *Gentlemen*, they drink till their Blood and Spirits are inflam'd, and they are made fit for any desperate Attempts; then out they issue, and no sooner is a Fact committed, than *Whip-Stitch* they are gone, away they fly to one of these Houses, that receives both them and their Booty; and if you pursue them, no, they know nothing of the Matter; there are no [10] such Persons there; tho', at the same time they lye conceal'd and lurking in their Berry.

'Tis not these only, *Gentlemen*, but your very Servants and Trades-folks, Men and Women, that have taken to drink these pernicious Liquors. Ask them to drink a little Beer or Ale, no, no Beer nor Ale, but a *Sneaker*, a *Sneaker*, or a *Dram* ; nothing less; and even Children in Arms they will give it to unmix'd, *Arrack*, *Rum*, or *Punch*.[1]

Gentlemen, 'tis a melancholy thing to see brave, stout, jolly *Englishmen* dwindled away to Shrimps; but so it is, *Gentlemen*: And this Evil has even spread to all the Country over, insomuch, that in the Inns, when our Duty obliges us to travel, we have much ado to keep our Servants sober. The first thing in a Morning, out comes my Landlord, *Gentlemen*, with a Bottle in his Hand; a *Dram*, ay, a *Dram*, will [B 2 -11] comfort the Coachman, and every other Servant must have the same.

It is a very happy thing, *Gentlemen*, when the Farmer pays his Rent well: The Landlord is very please'd with it; but in the Country, *Gentlemen*, where I have the Honour to live, a Farmer that rents a Hundred a Year, lives better than the Owner of the Land. His Wife and Daughter must drink Tea and Coffee; and when the Good-man comes from his Work, he must do so too. Tea, *Gentlemen*, is but a thin Liquor, not apt to raise the Spirits, rather sinks them: Why then, *Gentlemen*, a *Dram!* A Dram to qualify it, feels warm and comfortable to the Stomach; and thus they learn to love it.

I very well know, *Gentlemen*, that 'tis said, putting down these wretched Spirits will hurt the Farmers, will sink the Price of Corn, and will spoil the [12] Market. This, *Gentlemen*, is alledged under a Pretence, that these Spirituous Liquors are made from Barley, and consequently are wholesome for the Bodies of Men.

Barley, *Gentlemen*, is a great Support to this Kingdom; but that great Consumption they pretend to make of it, is not true. And indeed how can it be? For I am well informed, that they can afford to sell these Spirits, and get good Profit by them, at so low a Price as 10 *d. per* Gallon : Whereas Raising the Corn, Malting it, and afterwards Working it, will cost at least double the Sum. But when, instead of these vile Spirits, the

[1] A sneaker = a small bowl, 18th century language; Arrack, any spirituous liquor of native manufacture, in Eastern countries.

People take to drinking good Ale and Beer, they will then be able to work, the Consumption and Price of Corn will increase, and both Farmer and Landlord will be the better for 't. But, instead of Barley, what do you think, *Gentlemen*, these pretended [13] wholesome Spirits are made of? You will scarce imagine; but I will tell you, *Gentlemen*, *What you have been drinking all this while!* These Spirits are made of such Stuff, such vile Stuff! *Gentlemen*, that the very Mention of it will surfeit you; even no other nor better, than your common Lay-stalls. [1]

Another Nusance, *Gentlemen*, which falls under your Care, is the High-ways. Every Parish, *Gentlemen*, is by Law obliged to mend their own Roads; the Turn-pikes come in only in Aid; and if the High-way is not mended, the Parish ought to be Indicted. The High Road's not being mended, *Gentlemen*, is an evil thing! a very evil thing! I am sure I have found it so, having often been oblig'd to *go through Ways that are unpassable.*

There are, *Gentlemen*, besides these, many Nusances, many Abuses, many Offences, which *You, Gentlemen who* [14] *Walk*, and come from distant Places, have a better Opportunity of seeing, and knowing, than I have; and yet I, and *all Gentlemen that Ride in Coaches*, meet with many Inconveniencies.

There are, *Gentlemen*, your *Coach-makers*, nothing more common with them, than turn the whole Street into a Shop, and spread it all over with Coaches and Carriages; and then, *Gentlemen*, as you drive along, *slap* you come against some of them, *down* comes your Coach; perhaps a Wheel, an Axle-tree, or your Pole broke, if not your Neck: And what care they? It makes Business for some of them, and that's all they care. But this, *Gentlemen*, is a great Abuse, and contrary to Law.

The Care of the Streets, *Gentlemen*, seems in a great Measure to be at an End. If a Man wants to pull down, or repair a House, immediately the Street [15] is cover'd with Rubbish; perhaps, *Gentlemen*, you think, in order to save the Charge of carrying it away; but, *Gentlemen*, it is for quite other Purposes. I will tell you for what. Wheels and Carriages, by going often over this Rubbish, grind it to Powder. This, *Gentlemen*, they sift, and of this they make Morter, and with this rotten Stuff, they build your Houses; by which Means, *Gentlemen*, you are never safe; and great Odds, *Every Night, but you find your Houses tumbled about your Ears in the Morning.* And this, *Gentlemen*, is a very great Evil!

I might tell you, *Gentlemen*, of many Mischiefs of this kind; but as Gentlemen of your Learning, Parts and Fortunes, know these things better than I do, I shall trouble you no further; only I beg Leave to observe, *Gentlemen*, and desire, That as we have a *Wise King*, and a *Gracious King*, that does all he can for us, that you, *Gen-*[16]*tlemen*, will do your

[1] *O.E.D.*: a burial-place; a place where refuse or dung is laid.

Part too. Then every thing will go well, PEACE and PLENTY will *Flourish*, and we shall be *Happy*!

FINIS

Guilford Muniment Room LM 1066 / 1-10.
Mid-summer Quarter Sessions at Guilford. 1736.

Gentlemen of the Jury,

We are met here on the solemn Occasion of putting those Laws into Execution wch relate to the Preservation of the Peace; & as the Necessity of Government flows from the Corruption of Human Nature so the thought the Glory and Honour of it consist in the regular Administration of Justice, & as without it the one Societys cannot be upheld, so without the other all communitys would be little better than well modell'd combinations to oppress, cheat & ruin the weaker & submitting part of mankind. Not but that the advantages of a political union are so inconsiderable, yt it may be doubted whether Tyranny it self tho never so unlimited, never so grievous, be not rather to be chosen than a wild & corrupt state of anarchy. This state exposes men to the frauds & violence of their neighbours & the extravagant Caprices of the People, the other Subjects whole Nations to the mad Frolicks, & brutal Passions of a Flatter'd & [2] an abus'd Tyrant. Both Extreams are very dreadful & as much to be deprecated as the raging pestilence or any Common calamity; while the mean between them from wch they Both so far deviate, is a Copy well drawn from ye great & not to be equalled Original of God's Government of the World. Whose only End is to promote the Happiness of His Creatures; as the Peace, Safety & publick Good of the People ought to be no less ye aim of all Rulers than it is the Reason Why Government was first instituted. How happy therefore & how much to be valu'd are the Laws of England, & whereby we are deliver'd from Both Extreams. We neither lye under ye Terror of an arbitrary Power, nor are we cast loose to ye Wildness of ungoverned Multitude. Our Laws are neither writ on Sand nor with Blood; for they are neither easy to be defac'd, nor cruel in their Execution; but are a known & establish'd Rule, whereby we are taught how to administer Justice, & whereby as Men's Rights are limited, so their Passions are restricted & the publick Peace is settled on a secure & steady foundation. The Quality of our Law is so dissuasive & extended, so well calculated & adapted to the Good of [3] the Whole, yt the Meanest Person shelters himself within the Protection of its Care & the greatest is not without the Reach of it's Power. Prerogative & Property, wch are so much abus'd as pretences for oppression on the One hand, & Sedition on the Other are there so well dispos'd & regulated, that being twisted together in a Mutual Defence they afford our Island a Safer Protection than the Ocean yt surrounds it. The subject I am upon is so copious & pleasant yt should I please my own Inclinations I should wast that time in Speaking wch may be better spent in Acting for the Good of our Country. For sure I am they serve the Government but tho' they may want Eloquence to give It's due praises, but have Courage enough to defend & preserve it when disturb'd by any of its Enemys, in wch Number are to be reckon'd All Prophane, Lewd, Traitorous Seditious Lawless & disorderly Persons; who blaspheme God & dishonour their King, Country & Themselves; who conspire the Ruin of the Government under [4] whose Protection they live & censure it's Proceedings who rob Murther & oppress the Innocent & in a Word disturb the publick Peace. Of all wch Sorts of People I may truly say, that as they are a Scandal & reproach to Human Nature, So they do naturally weaken ye Foundations of any Constitution & must in time, if not duly repressed & punished, occasion its overthrow. Therefore the Laws of England have Several Ways wisely provided Remedys for so great an Evil & Preservations against so dangerous a Distemper. Amongst which I may account one of the Choicest to be the Court of Quarter Sessions, wch is generally four times a year held in every County. A Court Ancient & Honourable, so Honourable it receives its Authority by a special Commission from His Majesty, in wch the Highest Subjects in England think it an additional dignity and Priviledge to act for the Publick Good, & in [5] relation whereunto the King himself is by our Laws Stiled the Principal Conservator of the Peace a Title Glorious without Pomp & clearly descriptive of the brightly Burthen annex'd to Royalty! And how generally useul & serviceable to the Country this One Authority hath been found to be, needs no other Proof than the considerable Enlargements it hath since this time (viz. D° the IIId) recorded. For the Government could not but be sensible of the vast advantages that Every Man receives by so frequent & so regular, & so cheap & so easy an Administration of Justice, whereby all violences are checkt & nipt in ye bud, & the disturbers of ye Publick Peace are hindered from triumphing in their unpunish'd Villenys. Therefore yt this Good End may be attained & ye Country receive ye full Benefitt of those Laws it is recommended to you (Gent^{n} of the Jury) to Search & enquire after, inform against & prosecute according to Law all Offenders against the Rules of Justice, wch as it relates to different Objects, [6] I shall distinguish under these two General Heads of Moral & Civil Justice. Under the former is comprehended all Prophaneness, Vice & Immorality; & under the Latter all Treasons, Felonys, & Breaches of the Publick Peace, and all other Crimes. Which you are sworn to enquire into, & present according to the best of Yr Skill & Knowledge; & I dont doubt but you will acquit yourselves of this yr Duty with all honesty diligence & Impartiality, remembering the solemn obligation you have laid upon your Souls by Yr Oath.

Gent: The Offenders against Moral Justice are those Who are guilty of

1st Profane cursing & Swearing
2 Breach of the Sabbath
3 Drunkenness
4 Bawdry
5 Offences against the Established Church

And first (Gent:) the daily increase of Cursing & Swearing is a thing sadly & seriously to be considered. This is an Immorality so unworthy of any who professes himself to be a Christian yt even an honest Heathen [7] would have blusht to be Surpris'd in it, for tho' their Religion was false & their Gods were factitious, yet they were rather guilty of an Immoderate Superstition than any thing bordering on Prophaneness. As this Sin is very dishonourable to God So it is in this particular extreamly dangerous to Human Societys, in that it makes Men less careful & inconsiderate in what they assert or Worship, tho they confirm it with the most solemn Oaths. For from a Custom of Swearing Men easily slide into Perjury, and how can it be consistent with Reason that a Man who hourly Invokes God by rash & vain Swearing, should boggle at a False Oath, whenever his Lust, his Covetousness, his revenge & his Ambition prompt him to it & importunately demand to be gratifi'd tho' at so vast a price?

Present then (I strictly charge you) common Swearers. The Second Immorality wch calls aloud to be redressed is Drunkenness, a Vice on which one of our Statutes (viz. 1 Jac: 1. c. 5.) fixes this infamous Character That it is odious & loathsome, that is the Root [8] and Foundation of Bloodshed, Stabbing, Murther, Swearing, Fornication Adultery, & such like Enormous Sins, to the Dishonour of God & of our Nation, the overthrow of many good arts & manual Trades the disabling of divers Workmen, abusively wasting the good Creatures of God. This Charge tho' it may seem severe, yet it is, as our Experience informs us, a very true & lively description of this Brutish Immorality. Therefore for the repressing this Vice, our Laws have provided a Punishment not only for the Drunkards, but also for the Inn Keepers, Victualling-Houses & Ale-houses that harbour entertain & encourage them. For as the Preamble to one the Statutes relating to the matter (viz. I Jac:1 c. 9) informs us, The ancient, true, & Principal Use of Inns, Alehouses & Victualling-Houses is for the receipt, Relief & lodging of Travellers & for the Supply of the Wants of People, who are not able to buy in their provisions of Meat & drink in [9] greater Quantitys; but was never meant for the Entertainment & harbouring of Lewd & Idle People to spend & consume their Money & their time in a lewd & drunken Manner. Gent: the Offences against these Statutes concerning drunkenness, disorders in Alehouses are to be diligently enquired into & duely presented at Every

Quarter Sessions: as likewise are all defaults of Under Officers in conniving at them & Neglecting to bring them to condign Punishments I doubt not but you will do your parts in it, & you may assure your selves we shall deal with them as severely as the Law directs. You are likewise to enquire & present all Persons who presume to keep Alehouses without a Licence from the Justices of Peace, yt they may undergo the Pains & penaltys appointed by Law.

Gent: You are in the next place to present all those Infamous Houses of Bawdry; All Masters & Mistresses of these Infamous Houses & all Frequentors of them fall under the Cognizance & Censure of the Law. For Bawdry is an Offence Temporall as well as Spiritual, & is against the Peace of the Land. Therefore you are [10] to take Care to enquire & present all such Persons who being duly Convicted before us, shall suffer ye utmost Severitys ye Law will allow of: And as for those Persons of Publick Houses, who contrary to their Licences maintain, harbour & abett those or any other disorders, (whereby the Youth of the Nation are corrupted & rendered unfit to Serve their Country) Upon Yr Presentment of them, we will take Care not only to punish them by Fine & Imprisonment, but also to Supress them & to have the forfeitures of their Recognizances estreated into the Exchequer. Gent: You are also to present all those that absent themselves from Church or any Protestant assembly of divine Worship (tolerated by Law) on Sundays & Holy days. Those who do not receive ye Sacrament once a year and those who deprave it by Word of Mouth or otherwise. Gent: You are to present Sabbath Breakers in any Respect either for Pleasure or Profitt, but Works of Charity, Piety & Necessity are excepted on that day. [11] For Sports & pastimes, Revellings & disorders [are] certainly inconsistent with ye duty of that day, as buying & selling, travelling of waggons, driving of Cattle to Markets or Fairs or exercising any Trade or Calling whatever; all wch Offences are to be presented & are punishable in this Court.

Civill Justice is of a very large extent but as High Treason, Misprisions of Treason, Petty Treasons, Præmunires & all Felonys above Petty Larceny are under the Cognizance of the Superior Courts I shall not trouble you with them, tho' they are enquirable & presentable here. Gent: Petty Larceny is the Felonious taking & Carrying away ye Personal Goods of another, but not from his person nor out of his House, & ot exceeding the Value of 12 d. [12] Present Forcible Entrys & detainers, Riots, Routs, & unlawful assemblys, & all other Breaches of the Publick Peace. Present all Publick Nusances, such as Publick Bridges & Highways out of Repair & ditches unscowered. Present Offences against Publick Justice such as Perjury, Subornation of Perjury, Bribery, Extortion of all Officers under ye Colour of their Office, and the negligence of Constables, Headboroughs & Tithingmen & all other Officers intrusted with a particular Administration of Justice; all those Offenders (& many more could I mention) may by the Law be bound to their good behaviours or Imprison'd Indicted or Fin'd, & of such I charge you carefully to enquire, & present them. Gent: Tho I may have omitted Several Particulars, that does not excuse you from Presenting all Offences yt come to Yr Knowledge, wch [13] but you will do without Favour, Affection or Malice, yt so your Oaths may be uprightly & honestly perform'd, God Honour'd, Your King Serv'd, & Right done to Yr selves & Country: And I must add further, that as we are so fortunate to have a Prince on the Throne, the End of whose Government is the Happiness of his People, Whose greatest Pleasure is the due Execution of his Laws; (witness the Proclamation wch has been read to you)[1] as his Royal Consort the Queen is so full & well-drawn a Pattern of all Private & Publick Virtue and is at Present the Guardian of these Realms,[2] and as we are in this Country so immediately under his Royal Eye, This Consideration, Gentlemen, should incite you (and I dare say it does) and all of us in our several stations to do our dutys in the livelyest & most effectual manner, that by a due observation of the Peace of the Country, we may, as far as in us lyes, render his Majesty's [14] Government both easy & Secure, otherwise we should be so unworthy of the Name of a Loyal & Grateful People, which, Gentlemen, should any one attempt to take from us, I dare say, would fire Every Breast here with a just & generous Resentment & disdain; And so, Gentlemen I dismiss you to your several Enquirys.

At Guilford, 1738.

Gentlemen of the Jury

Were nature perfect & always upright, as at its first Institution; were Men no ways drawn aside & byass'd, by ambition, avarice or any inordinate Passions of the Mind to the Prejudice & hurt of Others; there would be no Occasion for any Laws, & consequently of the meeting at these times for enforcing their Execution. But as the Nature of man has so greatly fell from its original Goodnesss & Purity, & plunged itself into a Generall State of depravity, wch breaks out into Crimes & offences of different kinds, it lays Every wise & well regulated Government under a Necessity of providing Remedys against these Evils that daily arise, & of contriving Laws rightly adapted to the Nature of every Offence in order to check their Progress and Growth. [2]

Those Forms of Government are the mildest & Best that so temper their Justice & Mercy, that the One is neither born away nor effac'd by the other; But where Both are left free & unrestrain'd, to operate properly

[1] It might be A Proclamation for putting into Execution the Laws made to prevent Tumults and Riotous Assemblies, 5 Feb. 1736?

[2] Refers to a time when George II was away in Hanover.

upon the Actions of Offenders, according to the several degrees & Qualitys of their Offences. Where Justice is not let loose to range at large in an Arbitrary cruell Manner, & carry its avenging Sword without controll; but there is always room left, for Mercy to Shed a Silver Tear, & soften the Severity of the Blow. Such, Gentlemen, is the Government of wch we justly boast. As No Man is compleatly wicked at Once, but becomes so insensibly by a gradation of wickedness, wch would continually gain Strength by Impunity, till the Offenders loosing all Sense of fear & remorse, grows steel'd & harden'd to the Commission of Crimes of the deepest dye: And Capital Crimes must be attended with [3] Capital Punishments. Therefore Gentlemen to prevent these Consequences, the Wisdom of the Government has provided This Court of Quarter Sessions & arm'd it by Several Statutes with Proper Powers to nip Offences in the bud, & lash Offenders by gentle Chastisements into a due Sense of what they owe, their King, their Country, & themselves, before their Offences grow too extream - For as all are the Object of Government, so Every well constituted State extends its power to the Protection of all, for which Reason this Court has Power & Jurisdiction to prevent, as well as punish all breaches of the peace; that by a wise & timely restraint, the hand of Oppression & force may not bear down a helpless Submission & an ability to defend; that artifice & fraud may not prevail over Innocence & Simplicity, that One Man's Person or Property mayn't be exposed to the violence of another [4] and the Common Bonds of Society by that means be broken & dissolv'd, but that All things may rest in a Peace inviolate under the Protection of the Laws & yt the weakest amongst the People may find a sure Sanctuary in ye Publick Authority.

But as all Laws, tho' made with the utmost foresight & wisdom of ye Contrivers, are no more than a dead letter, except they are enliven'd & actuated by a fair & due Execution; Tis you, Gentlemen of the Jury, that are the first Springs of their action, who by a diligent & impartial of yr Dutys, are to give them that life & motion they otherwise want, & without which they would lose their intended Course & influence, & be entirely defeated of their End. Therefore that the County may not loose the good Effects of those wholesome Laws, wch create at once the Glory as well as the Strength of this Constitution, but that [5] the full Benefit of them may be receiv'd, I recommend to you Gentlemen to enquire of & prosecute according to law, all Offenders against the Rules of Justice; which as it relates to different Objects, I shall distinguish under these two general Heads, of Morall & Civil Justice. Under the former is comprehended all Profaneness, Vice & Immorality, and under the latter all Treasons, Felonys, & Breaches of the Publick Peace, & all other Crimes, wch you are sworn to enquire of & present according to the best of Your Skill & knowledge. Gentlemen, the Offenders against Morall

Justice are those, who are guilty of Offences against the Establish'd Church, Breach of the Sabbath, Profane Cursing & swearing, Drunkenness & Bawdry.

And first, Gentlemen, I think I cannot recommend any thing better, than for you to enquire of and [6] present all Offences against the Establish'd Church & our Holy Religion, as being the great basis & foundation, the truest well spring & source of all Morall & Social Virtues. You are to present all those that absent themselves from Church or any Protestant assembly of Divine Worship, tolerated by Law, on Sundays & holidays. Those who dont receive the Sacrament at least once a year, Those who deprave it by Word of Mouth or otherwise. You are to present Sabbath Breakers in any respect either for pleasure or profit, but Works of Piety, Charity, & Necessity are excepted on that day. For Sports & Pastimes, Revellings & disorders are certainly as inconsistent with the Duty of that Day, as buying & Selling, travelling of Waggons, driving of Cattle to Market or Fairs, or exercising any trade or Calling whatsoever. [7]

You are to present all Disturbers of any Assembly for divine Worship, all Disturbers of Ministers when they are officiating, & all Fighters & Strikers in Churches or Church-yards; all which Offences are cognizable by, & punishable in this Court. The Antients had that high Veneration for their Gods, that they made it a Rule never to form or begin any Enterprize of consequence without first consulting ye divine Will & imploring its protection. Even they consider'd that the Prudence & foresight of Man is very short & their views very limited; that they cannot penetrate into future things, & yt many times what they imagine to be most for their advantage, proves as often their overthrow & ruin; whereas, the Gods, being Eternal, know all things future as well as past, & inspire those they love, to undertake such things as are expedient for them; which is a Favour & Protection, they owe to the Man, & grant only [8] to those yt invoke & consult them. These were ye Notions of the Greatest & wisest men among the Heathens; upon this Basis they rested their Assurance of Success in all their Undertakings. And shall we, that are Christians be suppos'd to have less Zeal for the Support & Honour of Our Religion, than the Heathens had for theirs? Surely no.

Although ye Objects of their Worship were false & fictitious, yet the End & Intention of it was both wise & good. For we all cannot but know & be convinc'd, what a noble Impulse & ardour of Mind, arises & flows, from a due Sense of the Deity & his Religious Worship, towards Actions, that are truly great & benevolent, what a check and Barr it is, against those privately concocted Crimes, that No Human Law can reach, no human wisdom prevent. And of this, Gentlemen, we may be assur'd, & see it [9] but too often verify'd, yt That Man who does not serve his God, will never serve his King & Country as He ought. For which reason the Execution of those Laws, that are ye fences & safeguards of our Holy Religion, can never be too strongly recommended to you & enforc'd.

In the next Place, Gentlemen, I think the daily increase of Cursing and Swearing is a thing Sadly & Seriously to be consider'd. It is a vice of that pernitious & extensive Tendency yt strikes at the very Root of All Credibility of Evidence & Testimony: for a Man that accustomes himself to a Habit of Swearing cannot be so thoroughly affected, as He ought to be, by the Impression of an oath, when He takes it in Solemn & Serious Cases; and as the Heart of Man is unsearchable by any other Means, How can the real & naked Truth that is implanted there, & There only, be drawn out of him, & discover'd, whenever He for ye sake [10] of Ambition, fear, revenge, or any indirect Notion of Self Interest thinks fit to disguise or conceal it? And then how insecure & Precarious must the Persons & Propertys of all men be, when all Contests relating to Both, are decided & determin'd for ye most part upon Evidence given upon Oath? Present them & prosecute all common Swearers.

The next crying Immorality is drunkenness, a Vice on wch One of the Statutes (viz: 4th Jac. 1st) Stamps this Infamous Character; yt it is loathsome & Odious, yt it is the Root & foundation of Bloodshed, Stabbing, Murder, Swearing, Fornication & suchlike enormous Sins; to ye Dishonour of God & our Nation, the overthrow of many good Acts & manual Trades, the disabling of divers Workmen abusively wasting the good Creatures of God. This Charge although it is a very heavy one & of large Extent also, Yet we find by daily Experience [11] that it is but true, & especially Since the drinking of Gin & other Spirituous Liquors has been so much the vogue amongst the Common People amongst whom Robberys, House=breakings & all sorts of Villanys, have become more frequent & are more daringly committed, than was known to our Ancestors. Insomuch yt the Legislature have been forc'd to make a new Law on Purpose to discourage & restrain ye drinking of those Liquors, & an Order has been issu'd out by the King and Councell to ye Justices of Peace to See it duly & Steadily put into Execution. When the Government apprehended such hurtful Consequences from it exert themselves in so particular a manner; it is right to awake & alarm Us all in our Severall Stations to cooperate vigilantly & Strenuously with it; that Nothing may be wanting in Us, whereby so good & necessary a Law (wch I am sorry to say) may be hindred from having a proper & desir'd Effect. [12]

Our Laws, Gentlemen, have provided a Punishment not only for ye Drunkards, but also for the Inn=keepers, Victualling=houses and Ale=houses that harbour & entertain in them. For as the Preamble of one of the Statutes relating to this Matter (viz: 4th Jc.1st) informs us, That the antient true & principall Use of Inns, Victualling Houses & Alehouses was for the receipt, relief & lodging of Travellers, & for the Supply of the Wants of those people who were no able to buy in their provisions of meat and drink in greater Quantitys; but was never meant for the entertainment & harbouring of lewd, Idle & disorderly people, to spend & consume their money & time in a lew & drunken manner; & by that means bring their Familys to be maintained by ye Parish, & to ye Cost & Impoverishment of Honest & industrious men. Gentlemen, the Offences against those Statutes concerning Drunkenness & all disorders in Ale=houses are to be diligently [13] enquir'd into & diligently presented at Every Quarter Sessions; as are likewise All defaults of Under Officers conniving at these & neglecting to bring them to condign Punishment. Were They to do their duty in that Respect as they ought; the many disorders yt take their rise & beginning in those Houses would be in a great Measure Suppress'd, & not be able to spread themselves over the Country in so generall a Manner as we daily hear they do. For which reason I particularly Charge you with this Branch of Yr duty, & we for our parts shall not fail of giving you ye Assistance & encouragements to it that we can. You are likewise, Gentlemen, to enquire of & present All persons who presume to keep Ale=houses without a License from the Justices of ye Peace, that they may undergo the Pains & Penalties of the Law; And as they are not bound in any Recognizance to keep good Order in their Houses, as the Others are; they are much more dangerous to ye People, & more destructive of the Quiet & [14] Good Order of the Country, than the licensed Houses, for which Reason we shall deal with them with all the Severity of the Law, as they will deserve. Gentlemen, You are in the next Place to present all Houses of Bawdry, all Masters & Mistresses of those Houses, & all Frequenters of them fall under the Cognizance & Censure of the Law. For Bawdry is an Offence Temporall as well as Spiritual, & is against the Peace of the Land. Those Houses are the great Nurserys & Seminarys of Debauchery; where the Youth of the Nation, are as it were initiated into all the Mysterys of Vice; from whence follows a general corruption of their Manners, & whereby they are rendered not only unserviceable to the Publick, but miserable in their private Familys & oftentimes as long as they live; yt you cannot be too strict in Yr Enquirys on that Head.

Civil Justice is of a very large extent, but as High Treasons, Misprisions of Treason, Petty Treasons [15] Præmunires & all Felonys above Petty Larceny, are under ye Cognizance of the Superior Courts, tho they are enquirable of & presentable Here I shall not take up Yr time in defining & explaining them to you. Gentlemen, Petty Larceny is the Felonious taking & carrying away ye Personal Goods of another, but not from his Person nor out of His House & not exceeding the Value of Twelve Pence.

You are to present all those who Speak ill words of the King, His Ministers or Magistrates; all the Authors, Printers & Publishers of

Seditious Libels against the Government, Officers of State, Privy Councellours, or any Noble Peer of the Realm. Present all forcible Entrys, forcible Detainers, Riots & Routs & unlawfull Assemblys, & all other Breaches of the Publick Peace. Present all Publick Nusances, Such as Publick Bridges out of Repair, & Highways not Mended, Ditches unscowred, Hedges not Shrip'd according to the Statute. Present Offences against Publick Justice, Such as [16] Bribery, Extortions of all Officers under ye Colour of their Offices; The Negligence of Constables, Headboroughs, Tithingmen, & all other Officers intrusted with a particular Administration of Justice, Present especially those who treat the Warrants of Justices of Peace with the least disrespect & contempt, & those Officers that presume to be negligent & careless in the Execution of them: for Obedience is the very Essence of the Law; & it is a great discouragement & disheartening to poor people to apply to justice for Redress, when it cannot be obtain'd without a tedious & unnecessary attendance & loss of time, wch to them is valuable, thro' the slackness & dilatoriness of the officers in the discharge of their Duty. Those, Gentlemen, we shall be Sure not to spare, but punish Severely as they deserve. All those Offenders (& Many More I could mention) may be by the Law bound to their good [17] behaviour or Imprison'd, Indicted & fin'd, of such I charge You carefully to enquire & present Them. I think, Gentlemen, that I have mentioned the Most Material things that are to be the Subject of Yr Enquiry, & that tho' I may have omitted Severall Particulars, Yet You are to Present all Offences that come to Yr knowledge, which I dont doubt but You will do, & without fear, affection, or Malice according to the Tenor of the Solemn Oath which You have just now taken.

Gentlemen, I cannot forbear observing to You, that of late years there hath Sprung up amongst us a general looseness of Manners & a greater Disregard of All things both Civill & Sacred than was ever known in these Kingdoms; a Want of Reverence to the Laws & Magistrate, & an Abuse of Liberty under our Mild & happy Constitution; a Want of Care in Parents & Masters of Familys in training up their Children [18] in Reverence & Awe, keeping their Servants in discipline & good Order, & instructing them in morall & religious Dutys; a great Increase of Idleness, Luxury & Gaming; & an excess in the Use of Spirituous & Intoxicating liquors. That these Observations are but too true I believe, Gentlemen, You are All but too Sensible of; that Surely there was Never More Reason to put the Laws strictly in Execution than Now; And as we have the Happiness to live in a Country where the Laws must freely & fully take place; as we are govern'd by a Prince who makes the Law his Will, & not His will the Law; Nothing, Gentlemen, can interrupt this happy Freedom of ours, if we act unanimously in our severall Stations for the publick Good, & are No Ways wanting to Our selves. I think, Gentlemen,

I cannot Conclude better than in the Words of a very famous & learned Author, who wrote of Laws in [19] Generall; & after he had well weighed & explain'd the Nature of all Laws, both Divine, Naturall & Human; & Shew'd their Severall Operations & Effects, ends in these admirable Words. Wherefore of Law there can be no less acknowledged, than that Her Seat is in the Bosom of God; Her Voice the Harmony of the World; All things in Heaven & Earth do Her Homage; the Least as feeling Her Care, & the Greatest not exempted from Her Power; Both Angels, & Men & Creatures of what Condition soever, tho' Each in different Sort & Manner, Yet all in Uniform Consent admiring Her, as the Author of their Peace & Joy.

Qr Sessions At Guilford 1740

Gentlemen of the Jury

As the Nature of Man has greatly fell from its Originall goodness & purity & plung'd itself into a general State of depravity, wch continually breaks out into Crimes & Offences of different kinds, it lays Every wise & well Constituted State under a Necessity of providing Remedys against those Evils that daily arise, & of contriving Laws rightly adapted to the Nature of every offence in order to check their Progress & Growth. Those Forms of Government are the mildest & best that So temper their Justice & Mercy, that the one is neither born away nor effac'd by [2] the Other. but where both are left free & unrestrain'd to operate properly on the actions of Offenders according to the severall degrees & Qualitys of their offences. Where Justice is not loose to range at large in an arbitrary cruell manner & carry its avenging Sword without control, but there is always room left for Mercy to interfere & Soften the Severity of the Blow. Such Gentlemen is the Government wch we have the great happyness to live under. As no man is compleatly wicked at once but become so insensibly by a gradation of wickedness, wch would continually gain Strength by Impunity, till the Offender loosing all Sense of fear & remorse, grows harden'd to the Commission of Crimes of the deepest Dye, & Capitall Crimes must be attempted with Capitall [3] Punishments. Therefore, Gentlemen, to prevent these Consequences, the Wisdom of Government has provided this Court of Quarter Sessions & arm'd it with Proper Powers to nip Offences in ye Bud. & deter Offencers by gentle Chastisements into a due Sense of what they owe their King, their Country, & themselves, before their Offences grow too Extream. For as the whole Body of a People is the Object of Government, so every wise & well Constituted State extends its Power to the Protection of all; for which reason this Court has Power & Jurisdiction to prevent as well as punish all breaches of the Peace; that by a wise & timely restraint, the high hand of Oppression & force may not like a Tempest bear down before it an helpless Submission & where there is no Ability to [4] defend; that Arbitrary & fraud may not Prevail over Innocence & simplicity, that One Mans Person & Property may not be exposed to the Violence of Another, & the common Bonds of Society by that means be broken & dissolv'd; but that all things may rest in a peace inviolate under the Protection of the Laws, & that the weakest among the People may find a Sure Refuge in the Publick Authority. But as All Laws tho' made with ye utmost foresight & the wisdom of the Contrivers, are no more than a dead letter, except they are enliven'd & actuated by a fair & due Execution; Tis by You, that are the first Springs of their Action, who by a diligent & impartiall discharge of Yr Dutys, are to give them that life & motion they want, [5] And without which they would loose their intended Course & influence & be entirely deafeted of their End. Therefore yt the Country may not be depriv'd of the good Effects of those wholesome Laws wch are at once ye Glory as well as the Strength of this Constitution, I recommend to You, Gentlemen, to enquire of & present & prosecute according to Law, all Offenders against the Rules of Justice, wch as it relates to different Objects I shall distinguish under these two general Heads of Morall & Civil Justice. Under the former is comprehended All the Profaneness, vice & immorality; And under the latter of all Treasons, Felonys & breaches of the Publick Peace, & All other Crimes wch you are sworn to enquire [6] & present according to the Best of Yr Skill & Knowledge. Gentlemen the Offenders against Morall Justice are Those who are guilty of Offences against the Established Church, - Breach of the Sabbath, Profane Cursing & Swearing, Drunkenness & Bawdry.

And first Gentlemen, I think I cannot recommend anything better than for You to enquire of & present all Offences against the Established Church & our Holy Religion, as being the great Basis & Foundation, the truest Well spring & source of all Morall & social virtues. You are to present all those that absent themselves from Church or any Protestant assembly of divine worship tolerated by Law on Sundays & Holydays. Those who dont receive the Sacrament at least once a year, & those who deprave it [7] by word of mouth or otherwise. You are to present Sabbath breakers of any kind either for Pleasure or Profit, but Works of Piety, Charity & Necessity are excepted on that day. For Sports & Pastimes, Revellings & disorders are as certainly inconsistant with the Dutys of that day as buying & selling, travelling of Waggons, driving of Cattle to Fairs & Markets, or exercising any trade or calling Whatsoever. You are to present all disturbers of any Assembly for divine Worship, all Fighters or Strikers in Churches or Church Yards; All which Offences are cognizable by & punishable in this Court. The Neglect of the Dutys of this Sacred Day is one great Source of that Torrent of Iniquity that overspreads the Land: Condemn'd Criminals often confess just before their Execution, that [8] this was the beginning of their Vicious life & the first occasion of bringing them into wicked Company; from wch they proceeded from One degree of Vice to another till they came to that unhappy End.[1] For which reason the Execution of those Laws that are the Fences & Safeguards of our Holy Religion can never be too strongly recommeded & enforc'd.

In the next Place Gentlemen I think the daily increase of Profane Cursing & Swearing is a thing Sadly & Seriously to be consider'd. It is now become ye Common language of ye Streets in both Sexes, & amongst Many degrees of Men; to which there being no possible Temptation, One would think People used it only to Shew how wicked they dare be, & to defy Ye Divine Displeasure. To these frequent Oaths in Common Conversation, it is likewise owing that they are so little regarded on Solemn Occasions [9] in our Courts of Judicature, of which We have lastly had Such Notorious Instances, & it were heartily to be wish'd, that Some Method might be found out to put an effectual Stop to them; & especially as this Common habit of Swearing Strikes at the very Root of all Credibility of Evidence & insensibly Slides into an Habit of Perjury. Appeals to Heaven, are the strongest Pledges Man can give of their Veracity & the Making these instrumentall to the perverting of Justice, is an Iniquity that Shakes the very foundations of Governement. It invades the Right of our Neighbours, undermines the Power of the Prince, & affronts the Attributes of God to whom Vengeance belongeth. Present them and prosecute All Common Swearers. The next crying Immorality is Drunkenness. A vice on which one of the Statutes (4th Jac. 1st) stamps a Most infamous Character, yt it is the foundation of Blood-shed, Stabbing, Murder [10] and such like Enormous Sins. This Charge although it is a very heavy One, Yet we find that it is but too true. The prodigious Increase of those infamous Shops, wch Sell Spirituous Liquors is too visible; where People may be cheaply drunk to the ruin of their own Constitutions & those of their Posterity. And we owe to those Inflaming Liquors that such daring Villainys, as Housebreakings, Robberys, Murders, are risen to such a height of insolence unknown to our Ancestors.[2] Our Laws, Gentlemen, have provided a punishment not only for the Drunkards, but also for the Innkeepers, Victualling Houses, & Ale=houses that harbour & entertain them. For as the preamble of One of our Statutes (4th Jac: 1 st) informs Us The ancient True & Principall

[1] This is an allusion to the usual *Dying Speech and Confession of A.B.…* often written and published by the Ordinary of Newgate; for which see P. Linebaugh, "The Ordinary of Newgate and His Account," in, *Crime in England 1550–1800*, ed. J.S. Cockburn (London: Methuen, 1977), 246–69.

[2] A frequent complaint that in former ages, criminality was of lesser extent and lesser range, and to be found under the pen of many writers of the 18th century.

Use of Inns, Victualling Houses & Ale-houses was for ye Receipt, relief & [11] lodging of Travellers & for ye supply of the Wants of those People who were not able to buy in their provision of Meat & drink in greater Quantitys; but was never meant for the entertainment & harbouring of lewd Idle & disorderly people to Spend & consume their Mony & time in a lewd & drunken Manner & by that Means bring their Familys to be maintained by the Parish, to the Cost & impoverishment of Honest & Industrious Men. Gentlemen, the Offences against the Statutes concerning Drunkenness & all disorders in Ale house are to be diligently enquired into & presented at Every Quarter Sessions are likewise all defaults of Under Officers in conniving at these & neglecting to bring them to Condign Punishments. Were they to do their Duty as they ought, in that respect; the Many disorders that take their rise & beginning in those Houses would be in a great Measure suppress'd, [12] & not to be able to Spread themselves in so general a Manner over the Country as we daily hear they do. For wch Reason I particularly charge You with this Branch of Yr Duty; & we for our Part shall not fail of giving You all the assistance & encouragement in it that we can.

Gentlemen You are in the Next Place to present all Houses of Bawdry; all Masters & Mistresses of those Houses & all Frequenters of them fall under the Cognizance of this Court. For Bawdry is an Offence Temporall as well as Spiriuall & is against the Peace of the Land. Those Houses are the Great Nurserys & Seminarys of debauchery; But who can without Horror think of those Emerit Harlots, who having Spent a great part of a Miserable Life in Lust & wantonness in their declinging years take upon them the Office of tempting & Soliciting Others? Who stand ready to Seize unsuspecting Innocents at their first arrival, & under pretence [13] of hiring them to honest business use all their Arts to betray them into Lewdness.[1] Who at once despoil them of their Virtue, health & all the comforts of this life & all the happiness of another. Description cannot reach their Guilt, nor is any Punishment too severe for their Persons.

Civill Justice is of a large Extent, but as High Treasons, Petty Treasons Premunires & all Felonys above Petty Larceny are under the Cognizance of the Superior Courts, tho' they are enquirable of & presentable here, I shall not take up Yr time in defining & explaining them to you. Gentlemen Petty Larceny is the Felonious taking & carrying away the Personall Goods of Another, but not from his Person nor out of his House, & not exceeding the Value of Twelve Pence. You are to present all those who speak ill Words of the King, His Ministers or Magistrates; All the Authors, Printers, [14] and Publishers of Seditious Libels against

[1] Cf Hogarth, *The Harlot's Progress*, Plate 1, (1732). Mother Needham and the infamous Colonel Charteris were still in everybody's memory.

the Government, Officers of State, Privy Councellors, or any noble Peer of the Realm. Present all Riots, Routs & unlawfull assemblys, & all other Breaches of the Publick Peace. Gentlemen, you are to present & prosecute all Forestallers, Regraters & Ingrossers. If any Person shall buy any Merchandize, Victualls or any other thing whatsoever before it shall be bought to Fair or Market to be sold; or shall make any Price or dearer Selling or any Such things; disswade or Move any Person not to come thither, shall be accounted a Forestallers. Any Person who doth buy or get into his Hands in any Fair or Market any Corn, fish, Butter or any other dead victualls whatsoever brought thither to be sold, & shall Sell the Same again in ye Same Fair or Market or any other within four Miles thereof, shall be taken for a Regrator. [15] Any Person that gets into his Possession by buying or Contract (unless by Grant of Lands or Tithes) Corn on the Ground, or any Corn or dead Victualls with intent to sell same again shall be deem'd an unlawful Ingresser. Present all publick Nusances, such as Publick Bridges out of repair and high ways not mended, Ditches unscowre'd & hedges not Shrip'd up according to ye Statutes. Present all Offences against Publick Justice, Such as Bribery, Extortions of Officers under the Colour of their Office: the Negligence of Constables, Tithingmen, & all other Officers intrusted with a particular Administration of Justice. Present especially all those that treat the Warrants of Justices of Peace with disrespect & Contempt & those Officers that presume to be negligent or Careless in the [16] Execution of them: for Obedience is the very Essence of the Law; & it is a great discouragement & disheartening to Poor People to apply for Justice for Redress when it cannot be obtained without a tedious & unnecessary attendance & loss of time, wch to Men is valuable, thro the Slackness & dilatoriness of the Officers in the discharge of their Duty. Those, Gentlemen, We shall be sure not to Spare, but punish Severely as they deserve. All these Offenders and many more I could mention, may be by this Court bound to their good Behaviour or imprison'd, indicted & fin'd; & of Such I charge you carefully to enquire of & present them. I think Gentlemen, that I have mention'd the Most Materiall things that are to be the subject of Yr Enquiry; & tho' I may have omitted Severall Particulars, [17] Yet you are to present all Offences that come to your knowledge wch I dont doubt but you will do & without fear, favour or Malice according to the solemn Oath wch you have just now taken.

Quarter Sessions 1741

Gentlemen of the Jury

We are met on the solemn occasion of putting those Laws in execution which relate to the preservation of the Peace; and as the necessity of Government flows from the Corruption of Human Nature, So the

Strength, the Glory & the Honour of it consist in a regular Administration of Justice, and as without the One Society cannot be upheld so without the Other All Communitys would be but little better than Well-modelled Combinations to oppress, cheat & ruin the weaker & defenceless Part of Mankind.

As the Peace, Safety & Publick Good of the People ought to be No less the Aim of All Rulers than it is the reason why Government was at first instituted; [2] How happy therefore & how much to be valu'd are the Laws of England, that We, by a Well=balanced, well hung Constitution, Set free & fearless of All Extreams of Power, that are alike destructive. We neither lye under the Terror of an Arbitrary Nod, nor are we cast loose to ye Wild & extravagant Caprice of an ungovern'd Multitude. Our Laws are neither easy to be effac'd, nor cruell in their execution, but are a known & establish'd Rule, whereby We are taught to administer Justice; & whereby, as Mens Rights are limited, so their Passions are restrain'd, & the Publick Peace is Settled on a Solid & lasting foundation. The Quality of our Law is so dissuasive & extended, yt We All, in our Several Stations, Partake of its Virtue & Effects; The Least as feeling its Care, & [3] the Greatest as not Exempted from its Power. Prerogative & Power, wch are so much abus'd as Pretences for the Opposition on the One hand, & Sedition on ye Other, are here so well dispos'd & regulated, that being twisted together in a Mutual defence, they afford Our Island a Safer Protection than the Ocean that surrounds it. But as the Best Law in ye World is of itself but a Dead Letter; & of his force or valifity without proper Persons to put it in Execution; as these Statutes of themselves have neither Ears to hear our Cause nor feet, nor hands to hasten to defend us; but all the assistance that Justice gives Us is convey'd by its Ministers. I Must urge You Gentlemen of Ye Jury Who are the Primum mobile, & Set all the Other Springs agoing, to an active, vigorous & diligent discharge of your Dutys, that the Excellency of our Laws [4] may not loose its Proper & intended Course & Influence.

And first, Gentlemen, what relates to God and Goodness must stand in the Front. wch is not only what ought to be of it self, but what our Good Great King has commanded Us by His Royal Proclamation (wch was just now read to Us) to do, as the Basis & ground of our Actions here: And, indeed, unless we are Good Christians it is impossible to be loyal & good Subjects, Religion being the best Support & Prop of a State. Now, what more immediately concern the Honour of God, are these two Vices viz: Customary Swearing & Drunkenness. I much question whether the first was done more frequent in this Nation than it is at present; That Great & tremendous Name being as familiarly used as the Meanest Thing. To swear even in a Passion, or under the Highest Provocation, is by no Means Justifiable; but to fill [5] our Mouths with

Oaths, when Cool, in temper & in our Common discourse, is shocking & dreadfull. Present then (I strictly charge You) Common Swearers. Drunkenness is the second Vice yt calls aloud for Yr Redress; it is So universal Now that it is become a National Reproach, People of all Ages & Sexes being infested wih it. There ought to a Reformation in this Particular upon a double account a Religous One, because the Honour of God suffers so extreamly by it; and upon a Political One because not only whole Familys are reduc'd to poverty & ruin by it, & become Chargeable to ye Parish they live in, but Men themselves are rendered wholly unserviceable to the Publick. One Great Step towards it would be to curtail the Number of Ale=houses (wch are grievously degenerated) from their Original Institution) & to be Sharp & Severe with the Keepers of them, who make nothing of breaking ye Conditions of their Recognizances [6] by wch they are bound at their Licensing to Keep good order & rule in their Houses, & not to suffer continual Tipling; wch notwithstanding they do, even on Sundays, & in time of Divine Service too, most Manifestly & scandalously.

To go to the Root therefore of this Evill I woud have you present not only those who resort to & frequent Ale=houses, & Sit tipling there till be drunk, but the Ale=houses keepers themselves, who Suffer such doings in their Houses & all Constables who are Careless in this particular Part of their Office: & to suppress this & the Former Vice more effectually, Informers ought to be encouraged, that these Offenders may more readily be apprehended & brought to Justice.

These two Articles I more especially recommend to Yr Inquiry, because they so immediately concern the Peace & Happiness of the Publick, & I make no doubt, Gentlemen, but you will regard them as Such. [7] Present Those who absent themselves from Church or any Protestant assembly of Divine Worship tolerated by Law on Sundays & Holy=days.

Those who receive not the Sacrament once a year, and Those who deprave it by Word of Mouth or otherwise. Disturbers of Preachers in their Sermons; Fighters or Strikers in Churches or Church yards. Gentlemen, as to Felonys of an High & Capitall nature as they are only Inquirable of but not Punishable in this Court, I shall not take up Yr time in Mentioning & Defining them to you, but Petit=Larceny is Punishable here: And Petit=Larceny is a Felonious taking & carrying away the Personal Goods from Another, not from his Person nor out of his house & not exceeding ye value of 12 d. Present all those who Speak ill Words of the King, His Ministers or Magistrates. All the Printers Publishers & Authors of Seditious Libels against the Government, Officers of State & Privy Councellours. [8] Present all Forcible Entrys, Forcible Detainers; Riots, Routs & unlawfull assemblys, & all other breaches of the Publick Peace. Present all Publick Nusances, as Publick

Bridges out of repair, & Highways not mended, Ditches not scowr'd, & Hedges not Shrip'd up according to the Statute. Present all offences against Publick Justice, Such as Bribery, Perjury, Extortions of Officers under ye Colour of their Office, The Negligence of Constables & Tithingmen, & all Other Officers intrusted with a Particular Administration of Justice: for Many Offences and Misdemeanours yt are so frequent amongst us are in a great measure owing to the remissness of Officers in ye discharge of their Dutys, and that naturally draws on a Contempt of Authority, which shoud be always look'd upon as Sacred when duly exercised; Obedience being the very Essence of ye Law. [9] Those Offenders Gentlemen, we shall be Sure not to Spare but punish severely as they deserve. All these Offenders (& many more I coud mention) may be by the Law bound to their good Behaviour or Imprison'd, Indicted or Fin'd; & of such I charge You carefully to enquire & present Them.

I think, Gentlemen, that I have mentioned the Most Materiall things that are to be the Subject of your Enquiry; & tho' I may have omitted Several Particulars, yet You are to Present all Offences that come properly to Yr Knowledge, which I dont doubt but you all Impartially do, according to the Tenor of that Solemn Oath, wch You have just now taken for that Purpose.

This Gentlemen is a very Criticall time; and a Time that calls for the Greatest Care and Circumspection in Preserving the Peace of [10] the Country at Home, when We are engag'd in a Foreign War abroad;[1] and we dont know how soon the Enemys may be Even at our Doors. For although We have the Best of Kings upon the Throne and as Wise & Vigilant an Administration as Ever was; Yet we have found by very late Experience, that the Most Wise & best concerted Measures, are not always carryed into Execution with Equal Success. This Consideration Shoud have such an Effect upon the Minds of All True Englishmen, (and I dare say, Gentlemen, it has so upon Yours) that We shoud lay aside all Little Party=heats & Divisions amongst our Selves, & be Ready as One Man to join against the Common Enemy; as Well as against Those, that under any Colour or Pretence whatsoever, [11] Woud Sow the Seeds of Division amongst Us, & alienate our Affections from the Government; Woud undermine the Strongest Pillars of the State; & hazard the Danger of a Generall Confusion, Rather than not Gratify their Own Ambition & Prejudices; That have the Good of their Country allways in their Mouths, but their Self=Interest alone allways at their Hearts.

Of These Men, Gentlemen, it behooves Us All to be exceedingly aware; least We shoud be made Sensible by Sad Experience (& when it

[1] War was declared on Spain, 19 October 1739.

is too late) that although They have the Voice of Jacob, Yet their Hands are the Hands of Esau; Hands full of Treachery, and Rapine, and Bloud.[1]

At Guilford **Midsummer Qr Sessions 1742.**
In Court Ld Onslow
Mr Edwards
Mr Woodford
Mr Hind
Mr Anston

Gentlemen of the Jury

Were Nature perfect & in its Original Simplicity: Had no inordinate Passion or Desire crept into the Mind of Man; but were That Law, wch is written in Every Mans heart, & wch tells him privately from within, when he does wrong; Were that Law fully to take place & allways to Regulate our Conduct; We should have little occasion for Courts of Justice, or to attend Here to enforce the Laws of our Country against any of our Fellow Subjects. But, Gentlemen, as the Case is quite otherwise, & a great Corruption of Manners but too plainly prevails amongst us; from which, as from a Fountain that is foul, flows almost an Infinite Variety of offences; [2] This will always oblige every Wise Government to branch out its Power in a proper Manner, & Suit its Several Punishments to the Nature & Quality of every Offence. For as all are the Object of Government, so Every well constituted State extends its Power to the Protection of All: for which reason this Court has power and Jurisdiction to prevent as well as punish All Breaches of the Publick Peace: yt by a timely & Wise restraint the Hand of Oppression & force may not bear down the Innocent & helpless Person: that one Man's Person & Property may not be expos'd to the Violence of another, & the Common bonds of Society be broken & dissolv'd but yt all things may rest in an undisturb'd peace under the protection of the Laws, & yt the weakest amongst the People may find a Sure Sanctuary in the Publick Authority. [3]

But as all Laws tho' made with the Utmost Wisdom & foresight of the Contrivers, are No more than a Dead Letter, except they are enliven'd by a Vigorous & due Execution; Tis You, Gentlemen of the Jury, that I must excite to a diligent & Impartial discharge of Yr Dutys, yt those Wolesome Laws, which are as well the Glory as the strength of this Constitution, may have their proper Effect & Virtues. First, Gentlemen, I must recommend to you to enquire & present all offenders against Morall Justice: Those who are guilty of Offences against the Established Church, Breach of the Sabbath, Profane Cursing & Swearing, Drunkenness & Bawdry. You are to present All those that absent themselves

[1] Gen: 27, 22.

from Church or any Protestant assembly of Divine Worship tolerated by Law on Sundays & holidays. Those who dont receive the Sacrament at least once a year, & those who deprave it by word of mouth or [4] otherwise. You are to present Sabbath Breakers of any kind, either with respect to Pleasure or Proffit; but Works of Piety, Charity or Necessity are excepted on that Day: for Sports & Pastimes, Revellings & disorders are as certainly inconsistent with the Duty of that day, as buying & selling of Cattle, travelling of Waggons or exercising any trade or Calling whatsoever. You are to present all Disturbers of any asssembly for Divine Worship; all Disturbers of Ministers when they are officiating, & all Fighters & Strikers in Churches or Churchyards; All wch Offences are Cognizable by & punishable in this Court. In the next place, Gentlemen, Profane Cursing & Swearing is an Offence Sadly & Seriously to be consider'd. It is a Vice of that pernitious & extensive tendency, yt it strikes at the Root of all belief of Testimony & Evidence. [5] And then how precarious & insecure Must the Persons & Propertys of All Men be, when all Causes relating to Both are for the Most part determined by Evidence given upon Oath? Present & prosecute all Common Swearers.

The next Crying Immorality is Drunkenness, on which One of the Statutes (4 Jac:1st) Stamps this Infamous Character; yt it is loathsome & odious; yt it is the Root & foundation of Bloudshed, Stabbing, Murder, Swearing, fornication & such like Enormous Crimes &c. This is a Heavy Charge, tis true, but yet we see it verifyed but too frequently. Our Laws, Gentlemen, have provided a punishment not only for the Drunkards, but also for ye Innkeepers, Victuallors & Ale=house keepers that harbour and entertain them. For as the Preamble to One the Statutes (1st Jac1st) relating to this Matter informs us; the Antient, true, & principall use of [6] Inns, Victualling=Houses & Ale=Houses was for the Receipt, relief, & lodging of Travellers, & for the Supply of the Wants of Those people who were not able to buy in their provisions of Meat & drink in greater Quantitys; but was never meant for the entertainment & harbouring of lewd, Idle & disorderly people to Spend & consume their Money & time in a lewd & drunken manner; and by that Means bring their family to be maintained by ye Parish, & to the cost & impoverishmt of Honest & industrious Men. Gentlemen, these offences against these Statutes concerning Drunkenness & all disorders in Ale=houses are to be diligently enquired into; & duly prosecuted at Every Quarter Sessions; as are also all defaults of under officers in conniving at them, & neglecting to bring them to Condign Punishment. For which reason I particularly charge you with this branch of Yr Duty; & We for our [7] Parts shall not fail of giving you all the Assurance & encouragement in it that we can. You are likewise, Gentlemen, to enquire of & present all persons who presume to keep Ale-houses without a licence from the Justices of Peace, yt they may undergo ye Pains & Penaltys of the Law: for as they are not bound by any Recognizance to keep good Order in their houses, as the others are, they are much more dangerous to the People, & more destructive of the Quiet & good Order of the Country than ye licenc'd houses; for wch reason We shall deal with them with all ye Severity of the Law, as they will deserve. Gentlemen, You are in ye next place to present all houses of Bawdry; all Masters & Mistresses of those Houses, & all Frequenters of them fall under ye Cognizance & Censure of the Law. For Bawdry is an Offence Temporal as well as Spirituall, & is against the Peace of the Land. The Consequences of frequenting those Houses is so grievous, & ye Evills flowing [8] from them so Many & so miserable, that You cannot be too strict in Yr Enquirys on that Head.

Civill Justice is of a very large Extent but as High Treasons, Misprisions of Treason, Petty Treason, Premunires & all Felonys above Petty Larceny are under ye Cognizance of the Superior Courts, tho they are enquirable of & presentable here, I shall not take up Yr time in defining them & explaining them to you. Petty Larceny, Gentlemen, is the Felonious taking & carrying away ye Personall Goods of Another but not from his Person nor out of his House, & not exceeding the value of Twelvepence. You are to present all those who Speak ill words of the King, His Ministers or Magistrates; All the Authors Printers & Publishers of Seditious Libels against the Government, Officers of State, Privy Councellors, or any Noble Peer of the Realm.[9] Present all Forcible Entrys, forcible detainers, Riots, Routs, & unlawfull assemblys, & all other Breaches of the publick Peace. Present all Publick Nusances, such as Bridges out of Repair & High Ways not Mended, Ditches unscowr'd & Hedges not Stript up according to ye Statute. Present all offenders against Publick Justice, such as Bribery, Extortions of all officers under Colour of their Office: The Negligence of All Constables & Tithingmen & all other Officers that are intrusted with a particular Admininstration of Justice; all these Offenders (& many More coud I mention) may be by ye Law bound to their good behaviour or imprison'd, Indicted or fin'd; & of such I charge You carefully to enquire of & present them.

I think Gentlemen, yt I have mention'd the Most material things that are to be ye Subject Matter of yr Enquiry, [10] and tho' I may have omitted several Particulars, yet You are to Present all Offences that come to Your Knowledge, which I dont doubt, Gentlemen, but You will Impartially do, without fear, favour or malice, according to the Tenor of the Solemn Oath which you have all just now taken.

Quarter Sessions at Guilford – July ye 12 th 1743.

In Court
Ld Ayleresford
Ld Onslow
Mr. Denzill Onslow

Mr Woodford
Mr Hind
Mr Anston
Mr Fullman
Mr Woodroff
Mr Dolriff
Mr Henry Weston

Gentlemen of the Jury

As Liberty & Property are the most valuable Blessings of Life, so it has been the Chief Aim of the Greatest & Wisest Legislators to defend & Secure them by all the best means they coud possibly invent. The Great & Chief End originally of Mens uniting into Civill Societys & putting themselves under Government, was the Preservation of their Propertys. By the Generall Name of Property, I here mean their Lives, Libertys & Estates. For Men being Originally in a State of Nature, (and wch is a State of Perfect Freedom to Order their Actions, & dispose of their Possessions & Persons as they think fit, within the Bounds of the Law of Nature, without asking leave or depending on the Will of any other Man) Men, I say, in this State, woud never divest themselves of that Naturall Liberty, [2] and put on the Bonds of Civill Society, by agreeing with other Men to join & unite into a Community; but for their Comfortable, safe and peacable Living One amongst another, in a secure enjoynment of their Propertys, & for a greater Security against any Persons, that are not of it, & woud any ways invade it. To this End, in the state of Nature, there are many Things wanting.

First, there wants an Established, Settled, Known Law, receiv'd & allow'd by Common Consent to be the standard of Right & Wrong, & the Common Measure to decide all Controversys between Men by; for tho' the Law of Nature be plain & intelli[gi]ble to all Rational Creatures; yet Men being biass'd by their Interest, as well as ignorant for want of study of it are not apt or willing to allow of it, as binding to themselves, in ye application of it to their particular Cases. In the next Place, In the State of Nature, there [3] the Power Every Man has of punishing the Transgressions of others, make them take Sanctuary under the Established Laws of Government, & therein seek the Preservation of their Property. Tis this Makes them so willingly give up, Every One his Single power of Punishing, to be exercis'd by Such alone as shall be appointed to it: & by Such Rules as the Community, or Those authorized by them to that Purpose, shall agree on. And in this We have the Originall Right & Rise of both Legislation & Executive Power in all States, as well as of the Governments & Societys themselves.

At first, when some certain kind of Government was once approv'd, it may be, Nothing was thought upon for the Manner of Governing, but all permitted to their Wisdom & Discretion, which were to Govern; till by Experience they found this for all parts of the Community very inconvenient: So that the means which they had de [4] vised for a Remedy, did indeed but increase the Sore, which it shoud have Cured. They Saw, yt to live by One Mans Will, became ye Cause of All Men's Misery. This constrain'd them to come to Laws wherein All Men Might see their Duty beforehand, & know the Penaltys of transgressing it.

And Gentlemen, These Forms of Government are always the Best where the Good of the Publick is the Great & Sole Object of the Legislators; Where the Constitution is so wisely fram'd, yt there is a due Balance preserv'd between the Legislative & Executive Power of it: Where Justice & Mercy are so rightly temper'd together that they go, as it were, Hand in Hand, & Materially assist Each Other in their Severall Operations. Hence arises that Resistless Harmony in Government whose Perfection is so pleasing to all; Where No Offender undergoes the Punishment wch is due to his Crimes, but under a full, tho' possibly unwilling Conviction in his Mind, of the Impar [5] tiality of the Sentence, wch is past upon Him; where No Offender escapes by the Clemency of a Pardon; but at the Same Time yt He is ready to adore its Mercy, He trembles at its Justice. Such Gentlemen, is the Happiness of this Constitution of which We are members. A Constitution, which, as it is the Strength & Glory of this Country; So it is the Envy of the Nations around us.

But as all Laws are No More in themselves than a Dead Letter, unless they are enliven'd by a due Execution; Tis you, Gentlemen of the Jury, that are, in this Court, the first Springs of their Motion; Who by a diligent & Impartial discharge of Your Dutys, are to give them that life and vigour they otherwise want, & without which they woud loose their intended influence & End. Wherefore I must direct you to enquire of & present All offenders against ye Rules of Justices, wch as it relates to Different Objects, I shall distinguish under these two Generall Heads of Morall & Civill Justice. Under the Former, is comprehended All Profaneness, Vice and [6] Immorality: And under the latter, All Treasons, Felonys & Breaches of the Publick Peace; and all other Crimes wch You are Sworn to enquire of & present according to ye best of Yr Skill & Knowledge. Gentn, The Offenders against Morall Justice, are those who are Guilty of Offences against the Establish'd Church, Breach of the Sabbath, Profane cursing & Swearing, Drunkenness & Bawdry. And first, Gentn, I recommend to you to enquire of & present all Offenders against our Holy Religion; as being the great Basis & Foundation, the truest Well Spring & Source of All Morall & Sociall Virtues. You are to present All those that absent themselves from Church or any Protestant assembly of Divine Worship tolerated by Law, on Sundays & Holidays:

Those who dont receive the Sacrament once a Year, & those who deprave it by word of Mouth or otherwise. You are to present Sabbath breakers in any Respect, either for Pleasure or Proffit; but Works of Piety, Charity & Necessity are excepted on that day. You are to present all Disturbers of any Assembly for Divine Worship; and all Fighters or Strikers in Churches or Churchyards; all which offences are Cognizable & punishable in this Court. [7] In the next Place, Gent[n], I think ye daily Practice of Profane Cursing & Swearing is a Matter Sadly & Seriously to be consider'd; not only with regard to its Impiety in point of Religion, but with regard to its Evill tendency in ye Civill Government. For a Man that uses himself to an Habit of Common Swearing, is very apt to make light of an Oath, even When He takes it on ye Most Serious & Solemn Occasion. Be Sure to present all Common Swearers.

The next crying Immorality is Drunkenness; a Vice upon which One of our Statutes Stamps this most Infamous Character; yt it is loathsome & odious; that it is the Root & foundation of Bloudshed, Stabbing, Murder, Swearing &c. This We find to be too true allmost every day. Our Laws, Gentn, have provided a Punishment not only for the Drunkds. but also for all Publick Houses, yt Harbour and entertain them. For as we are inform'd by ye Statutes relating to this Matter. The Ancient true & Principall use of such Publick Houses was for the Receipt, relief & lodging of Travellers; & for the [8] Supply of the wants of Such People, who were not able to buy in their Provisions of Mean & drink in greater Quantitys; but was never meant for ye harbouring & entertaining of Lewd, Idle & Disorderly People, to riot & wast both their time & Substance in, & by yt Means oftentimes bring large Familys to ye Parish. Gent:[n] The offences against these Statutes concerning Drunkenness, & all Disorders in Alehouses are to be diligently enquired of, & presented at Every Quarter Sessions. In the next Place, You are to present all Houses of Bawdry; all Keepers of Such Houses & all Frequenters of them fall under the Cognizance & Censure of the Law. For Bawdry is an offence Temporall as well as Spiritual; & is against ye Peace of the Land. Those Houses are the Great Nurserys & Seminarys of Debauchery; where the Youth of the Nation are, as it were, Initiated into all the Miserys of Vice: yt You cannot be too Strict in Yr Enquirys on that Head.

Gentlemen, Civill Justice is of a large Extent, but High Treasons, Misprisions of Treason, Petty Treasons [9] Premunires & all Felonys above Petty Larceny, are under the Cognizance of the Superior Courts, I shall not take up yr time in defining them to you.

Gent[n], Petty Larceny is the Felonious taking & carrying away ye Personall Goods of Another, but not of his Person, nor out of his House, & not Exceeding the value of Twelve pence. You are to present all those who Speak ill Words of the King, His Ministers or Magistrates; all the

Authors, Printers & Publishers of Seditious Libels against the Government, Officers of State, Privy Councellors, or any Noble Peer of the Realm. Present all forcible Entrys, forcible Detainers, Riots, Routs & Unlawful Assemblys, & all other Breaches of the Publick Peace. Present all Publick Nusances, as Bridges out of Repair, Highways not mended, Ditches unscowred & Hedges not Striped up according to the Statute. Present all offences against Publick Justice, as Bribery, Extortions of all officers under Colour of [10] their Office; The Negligence of Constables, Tithingmen, Headboroughs & all other officers intrusted with a Particular Administration of Justice; those we shall be sure not to spare, but punish severely as they deserve.

All these Offenders (and many more I coud Mention) may be by the Law bound to their Good Behaviour, Indicted, fin'd or Imprisoned.

I think Gentlemen, that I have mentioned ye Most Material things that are to be the Subject Matter of Your Enquiry; & tho' I may have Omitted Several Particulars, yet You are to present all offences that come to Yr knowledge; wch I dont doubt, but You will do, & without fear, affection or Malice according to the Tenor of the Solemn Oath wch You have just now taken.

At Guilford Quarter Sessions 1744.

In Court

Ld Ayleresford & Ld Onslow

Mr Woodford Mr Edwards Mr Austen Mr Woodrett Mr Denzill Onslow

Note: From a simple comparison with the other texts of the same series, it clearly appears that this one seems an abridged version of all others; there are more abbreviations, the usual formulas are not fully developed, and the text is shorter.

This Charge was given also again at Guilford Quarter Sessions 1746 when the last Paragraph was added to this Charge: & given instead of the paragraph wch is immediately foregoing to it.

In Court

Ld Aylesford & Ld Middleton

Mr Woodford Mr Edwards Mr Asten & Parson Hillman.

Gentlemen of the Jury

As No Government can subsist without it is strongly compacted & bound together by good & wholesome Laws; & as the Best Laws are of No force & efficacy without a due & vigorous Execution of them; it is the Duty as wall as the Interest of Us all in our Severall Stations, to use our Utmost Endeavours to promote & forward so Necessary & useful a Work. Coud that Great Law wch is written in Every Mans Heart, of Doing as He woud be done unto, take place & prevail amongst us: Coud that Law lift up its voice within, So as to [be] heard with a due Attention, Our Case woud be Happy indeed: but Gent[n], the Heart of [2] Man has so Strong an Alloy of Passion, Prejudice & Interest interwoven & blouded with it, that, I am afraid, We shall never listen to the Voice of That Charmer, Charm He never so wisely. This makes it necessary for all Governments to invent & contrive Such Laws, as may both Suit the Genius of the People, & at the same time answer all the Ends of the Constitution That the Weak may be Secur'd from the Violence of the Strong; & that Every Man may find, both as to His Person & his Property, a Secure Refuge under the Shelter of the Publick Authority. We Gentle[n], are so fortunate as to have a Constitution so well adapted to these Ends, that is is not only the Strength & Glory of this Country but the Envy of all the Neighbouring Nations. Then how [3] Blameable shoud we all be? How unworthy of receiving ye good Effects of these Wise Laws, shoud we omit any Opportunity of Carrying them into a due Execution, especially when call'd upon by the Duty of our Stations for yt End? This, Gentle[n], I need not tell you, is the Business of this Day, as far as these Laws relate to the Jurisdiction of this Court.

Therefore, Gentle[n], I must direct You to enquire of & present all offenders against Morall Justice; under wch Head is comprehended all Profaneness, Vice & Immorality. You are to present all those who are guilty of Offences against the Establish'd Church, Breaches of ye Sabbath, Profane Cursing & Swearing, Drunkenness & Bawdry. And first, Gentle[n], You are to enquire of & present all those that absent themselves from Church or any Protestant [4] Assembly of Divine Worship tolerated by Law, on Sundays & Holidays. Those who deprave the Sacrament by word of Mouth or otherwise. You are to present Sabbath breakers in any Respect, either for pleasure or proffit; but Works of Piety, Charity or Necessity are excepted on that Day. You are to present all Disturbers of any Assembly for Divine Worship; & all Fighters & Strikers in Churches or Churchyards: all which offences are Cognizable by & punishable in this Court. In the next Place Gentle[n], I think, the daily practice of Profane Cursing & Swearing, is a Matter Sadly & Seriously to be consider'd; not only with Regard to its Impiety in point of Religion; but with regard to its Evill Consequences in the Civill Government. For a Man that uses Himself to an Habit of Common Swearing, is very [5] apt to make light of an Oath, even when He takes it on the most Serious & Solemn occasion. Be sure to present then all Common Swearers. The next Crying Immorality is Drunkenness & that crys loud enough to be heard by Us all; Drunkenness is a Vice upon which One of our Statutes Stamps this Most Infamous Character; that is is loathsome & odious; yt is the Root & foundation of Bloudshed, Stabbing, Murder, Swearing, & Many other Enormous Crimes. Our Laws, Gentle.[n], have provided a Punishment not only for the Drunkards, but also for all Publick-Houses, that Harbour & entertain them. For as we are inform'd by the Statutes relating to this Matter, The antient, true & Principall use of Such Publick Houses was for the Receipt, Relief & lodging of Travellers; [6] and for the Supply of the Wants of Such People as coud not buy in their provisions of Meat & drink in greater Quantitys; but was never meant for harbouring & entertaining of Lewd, Idle & Disorderly People to riot & wast their time & Substance in, & by that means oftentimes bring large Familys to the Parish. Gentle.^{n}, the Offences against these Statutes concerning Drunkenness & all Disorders in Ale= Houses are to be diligently enquired into, & presented at every Quarter Sessions. In the next Place, You are to present all Houses of Bawdry; all Keepers & Frequenters of Such Houses, fall under the Cognizance & Censure of this Court. For Bawdry is an Offence Temporall as well as Spirituall, & is against the Peace of the Land. Those Houses are the Great [7] Nurserys & Seminarys of Debauchery; where the Youth of the Nation are Initiated, but too early, in all the Misterys of Vice; yt You cannot be too Strict in Yr Enquirys on that Head. Gentle^{n}, You are to present all offenders against Civill Justice; but as High Treasons, Misprisions of Treason, Petty Treasons, Premunires & all Felonys above Petty Larceny are under ye Cognizance of the Superior Courts, I shall not take up Yr time in Defining them. Gentle^{n}, Petty Larceny is the Felonious taking & carrying away the Personall Goods of Another, but not of His Person nor out of His House, & not exceeding the value of Twelve pence. You are to present all those that speak ill words of the King, His Ministers or Magistrates; All the Authors, Printers and Publishers of Seditious Libels against the [8] Government, Officers of State or Privy Counsellours. Present all Forcible Entrys, forcible Detainers, Riots, Routs & unlawful Assemblys, & all other Breaches of the Publick Peace. Present all Publick Nusances, such as Bridges out of repair, High Ways not Mended, Ditches unscowr'd, & Hedges not Strip'd up according to the Statute. Present all offences against Publick Justice, as Bribery, Extortions of All Officers under Colour of their Office; The negligence of Constables, Tithingmen, Headboroughs & all other Officers intrusted with a particular Administration of Justice. These We shall be sure not to Spare, but punish severely as they deserve.

All these Offenders (and many more I coud mention) may be by the Law bound to their Good Behaviour, or Imprison'd, Indicted & Fin'd, & of [9] Such I charge You carefully to enquire and present them.

Gentlemen, as this is a time of particular & Eminent Danger, we cannot be too Carefull & vigilant in preserving ye Peace of the Country. When we are engag'd with the most Perfidious of Enemys abroad, & have very narrowly escaped an Invasion at Home: An Invasion, which must in the Nature of it have overwhelm'd Us with Bloud & Confusion. I hope We shall not fail on all occasions, but especially at this time, to have a Watchfull Eye over their Conduct, who by their Religion or Principles are anyways disaffected to the Government. As We are but too fully convinced that No Tenderness towards Them will reclaim their Hearts, We Must take Care to Dissarm their Hands; and Since there are many Good Laws in force [10] against them, there is great reason that they Suffer the Penaltys that are provided for them: Especially those of Them (if any such there are) Who having taken the Oaths to the Government, and notwithstanding that sacred Tye omit no Opportunity of Shewing by their Words & Actions, their Malevolence to the Present Royal Family & Government. We may then Judge of the Tree by its Fruit.

Against such Men, as Those, we cannot be too much upon Our Guard; least We shoud be made Sensible by Sad Experience (and when it is too late) That allthough their Voice, is the Voice of Jacob; Yet, Gentlemen, their Hands are the Hands of Esau; Hands full of Treachery, Cruelty & Bloud. [11] And now, Gentlemen, as we have had in Those Parts a Great & Providential Escape from a most unprovok'd & unnatural Rebellion at Home, wch was added & assisted by our Most Inveterate & Perfidious Enemys abroad, (the Bloudy & wasting Effects of which, the Northern Parts of these Kingdoms have Severely felt, and the Wounds of it are amongst Us all in some Shape or another, as it were, still Bleeding) it Behooves us to to have a Most Watchfull Eye over all These, who by their Religion or Principles, who have Reason to Suspect to be any ways Disaffected to His Present Majesty or his Government: And Those are chiefly, Popish Recusants, Nonjurors & Protestants, who, altho' they have taken the Oaths to His Present Majesty, & enjoy the Benefit of his Protection, do yet make it their Business to [12] Libell & Censure the Government & in their Words & daily Behaviour Shew themselves Disaffected; and to give them their Due Character, They are but one Degree from Traitors. Therefore since Nothing will make Such Men Friends to this Government, Prudence directs us to use the best Caution against their designs; & since there are many good Laws in force against them, there is great Reason that they suffer those Penaltys, that are Provided for Them. For a Government legally Established & Regularly Administered (as ours is) must not Suffer the Insults, or the Depreciating of any Sort of Men Whatsoever; and those whom neither Prudence nor Modesty will Restrain within the Limits of their Duty, Must be taught it, by the Severe Discipline of the Law. Therefore, Gentlemen, it is your Business diligently to enquire, and duly to present [13] all Such Disaffected & Seditious Persons, & we will take care to See them Punish'd according to the full Measure of their Deserts.

Memdum. The Statute of Concealments of Jurys is ye 3d of Henry ye 7th C. 1 st.

At Guilford, Midsummer Quarter Sessions 1745

In Court

Ld Onslow Mr Edwards Mr Woodford Mr Fullham Mr Denzill Onslow Mr John Ellwell Mr Merchiss Mr Moreton.

Given also at ye same sessions in 1750. In Court Ld Onslow Mr Woodford Mr Edwards Mr Fullham.

Extracted chiefly from Mr John G [illegible]

Five charges printed for W. Meadows at the Angel in Cornhill, & C. Ackers on St John Street.

Gentlemen of the Jury

Liberty is One of the Chiefest Goods of Civill Society; because it is That which makes Every thing we possess Our Own: without this Liberty all Property centers in those who govern, & not in them who are governed. By Liberty is not meant Licentiousness, or for Men to act without Controul, but under the Restraint of Good Laws; So far free & at Liberty as Reasonable Creatures woud wish to be; & so far restrain'd, as is necessary for the Peace & Good of Society.

The Constitutions of Different Countrys are indeed various, but the Obligations between the Governing & the Governed are every where Mutual. The Office of a King, a Senate or of the Executive Power in a Popular State, is to protect the People in their Lives, Libertys & Propertys; and to this End they claim the Allegiance, Obedience & assistance of their Subjects [2] The Old Roman & most of the Græcian States were built upon Republican Principles; but when the Goths & other Northern Nations destroy'd the Roman Empire, & extended their Conquests into far distant Countrys; They establish'd, wherever they came, a Mixt form of Government; the preservation of which Constitution depending upon the Balance between the King, the Nobility and the People, the Legislative Power was lodg'd in these three Estates, call'd by different Names in different Countrys: & in this Country at this day by the Word Parliament. The Excellency of this Mixt Government consists in that due Poize or Balance between Rule & Subjection, wch is so justly observ'd in it, & which is the Strength & Measure of its Duration.

But length of Time, & a succession of Folly & Corruption in Two parts of the Legislature, & of Cunning & Success in the Third, have driven it almost out of Europe: Whilst We in Great Britain have still happily preserv'd this Noble & Ancient Gothick Constitution, which all our Neighbours once enjoy'd, as well [3] as We, who are the Wonder & Glory of all the Kingdoms round about Us.

But of all the Inestimable Advantages deriv'd to Us from this Our wise Frame of Government, None more deserves to be highly priz'd & valu'd, than That particular Birthright of Ours, Tryals of Causes Whether Civill or Criminal, by Jurys; an undoubted part of the Gothick Constitution. Our Most Excellent Laws preserve their Honour & best exert their Power & force by a due, impartial & vigorous Execution, & an Equal distribution of Justice. And our Lives, Libertys & Propertys in a great Measure depend upon the due Execution of that great Power, wch by the Wisdom of Our Constitution, is intrusted with Grand & Petty Jurys.

You, Gentlemen, are therefore Summon'd here, & Sworn to enquire of & present to Us all Such Crimes & offences as fall within the Cognizance of this Court. All manner of Crimes are presentable by You, from the Highest to the Lowest offences, from High Treason to Trespass: But tho' High Treason [4] Petty Treason, Burglary & Felonys of all Sorts are enquirable of by You & Every Grand Jury: yet because Bills of Indictment for these Crimes are Seldom or never brought to You at the Quarter Sessions, but prosecuted at another Place; I shall omit to give You in Charge any Capital Offences, & confine My Self to those Offences only that are both Enquirable of, Presentable and Punishable Here.

In the first Place, the Honour & Service of Almighty God ought to be Our Chiefest cares and We shoud all endeavour to put a stop to that deluge of Profaneness that has overspread the Nation: and it were happy if our Holy Religion did not suffer, as well from its Enemys diligence to corrupt our Principles, as from the wicked lives of Its Professors. You have heard His Majesty's Proclamation read to You, for the encouragement of Piety & Virtue, and the preventing & punishing of Vice, Profaneness & Immorality. [5] The offences expressly mention'd in this Most Excellent Proclamation are, Excessive Drinking, Blasphemy, Profane Cursing & Swearing, Lewdness, Profanation of the Lords Day, all Publick Gaming & Gaming houses & other Lewd & disorderly Practices. Drunkenness is a Vice, that calls aloud for Yr Redress upon a double account; First upon a Religious One, as it is an offence against Almighty God; & Secondly upon a Politicall One, because it reduces whole Familys to Poverty, Ruin & the Parish. A Common Drunkard is Indictable in Sessions, as well as punishable in a Summary Way. A Common Swearer is a Nusance to the Place where he lives: and as this is a Sin very dishonourable to God, so it is in this Particular to Human Society: for profane Cursing & Swearing contributes much to the Growth of Perjury. Oaths are little minded, when Constant & habitual Use has sully'd them, & Every Minute's Repetition of them has made them cheap & Common. Who can believe that a Man who Hourly provokes God by Rash & vain Swearing, shoud stick at a false [6] Oath, whenever his Ambition, his Covetousness or his Revenge prompt him to it, & importunately demand to be gratify'd, tho at so vast a price! You are to present to this Court all such Persons who do not come to Church, or some Religious Meeting allow'd by Law on Sundays; and the profanation of the Lord's day is of late become very notorious. All these offences are in their Nature more immediate offences against Almighty God & his Holy Religion establish'd amongst us.

You are likewise to enquire of such offences as are committed against Yr Neighbours or Fellow Subjects & wch injure them in their persons, their Propertys or their Reputations. You are to enquire of Petty Larceny; Petty Larceny is the Felonious taking & carrying away ye Personall Goods of Another, but not of his Person, nor out of his House, & not exceeding the value of Twelve pence. You are to present all assaults, Batterys & affrays, & in generall all Breaches of the Peace. You are to enquire of & present all Riots, Routs & unlawfull assemblys. You are to present all Forestallers, Regrators & Ingrossers. [7] Forestalling is buying up Commoditys by the way before they come to Market. Regrating is buying Corn or other Victualls & Selling the same again in the same Market, or in any Other within four Miles. Engrossing is buying up Great Quantitys of Corn on the Ground or other Victualls, & Selling the same again. Those our Laws esteem great Offenders, who without any real Cause, enhance ye Price of Corn & other Victualls & thereby occasion uneasiness, Discontent & Murmuring, especially amongst the Lower Sort of People. You are to present all Bawdy Houses, Gaming Houses, unlicens'd Ale Houses & all Disorderly Houses of what Sort soever. Those Houses, & Shops where People get frequently drunk with tipling Geneva & other Spirituous Liquors, are Indictable as Disorderly Houses, whether they have, or have not Licences. Nothing is more destructive, either to the Health or Industry of the Poorer Sort of People, on whose Labour & Strength the Support of the Community so much depends, than immoderate drinking of those Liquors. You are also to present all Treasonable & Seditious Libels against His Majesty or his Ministers of State, [8] or other Great Men or Magistrates. These at [= are] Indictable at Common Law. You are to enquire of & present all Neglects or Connivances of all Officers of Justice concern'd in the Execution of the Laws: Whether they are guilty of Bribery, by taking of Gifts or rewards in Order to prevent or delay Justice; or are Guilty of Extortion by taking fees, where none are due, or before they are due; or greater than by Law are due to them. You are to enquire of all Publick Nusances, the want of Repairs in Bridges & Common Highways, Whether Ditches are scowr'd & Hedges Strip'd up according to the Statute.

Gentlemen, The Oath that You have taken obliges You both to present all such Matters & things as come to Yr Knowledge touching this present Service, as well as such Offences as shall be given you in Charge; and by the Statute of the Third of Henry the Seventh; If a Grand Jury Conceal any thing, wch they ought to present, the Justices may within a Year, Impannell another Jury to enquire of such Concealment, [9] and upon Conviction, fine Every One of the Former Jury at the Discretion of the Court: so earnestly the Law insists upon your doing Your Dutys.

You are, Gentlemen, of so good Understanding & Capacity, & so well experienc'd in the nature of this Service; that it will not be necessary to give You a longer detail of the many & various kinds of Offences enquirable of by you: and I have no Doubt but You'll Impartially lay before this Court by Yr Presentments, as well what things I have given you in Charge, as Those that you know to be Cognizable here, in order to have the offenders punish'd, the grievances redress'd, by the Effctual putting the Laws in due Execution. And upon any doubts or difficulty, wch in the Course of Yr Enquirys You may meet with, The Court upon Yr Application to it, will give You all Due Assistance.

At the Guilford Qr. Sessions 1748.
In Court
Mr Woodford Mr Lee Major Clark.
and at the Guilford Quarter Sessions 1749
In Court
Mr Edwards Mr. Austen Mr Willoughby Mr Woodroft Mr Walters.

Gentlemen of the Jury
Government is necessary to the welfare of Mankind, because it is ye great band of Human Society, the guard of its Peace, & the Security of Every Man's Person & Property. Without it Mankind woud be unavoidably Miserable, & Society woud presently disband & all things woud run into Confusion. Without Government there coud be no such thing as Property in any thing; for Nothing but Laws can make property: and Laws are the effect of Government and authority: Nay we have no Security of our Persons & lives, much less of any thing yt belongs to us & is at present in our Possession. Were we not protected by Laws, we coud have no Safety, no quiet enjoynment of any thing; but Every Man must be upon his guard against all the world, & expos'd to Continual violence & Injurys from Those, who are too many & too Strong for Him; So that all our Quiet and Security from Fear & Danger, [2] from the fraud & oppression of those who are more crafty & powerful than ourselves; from endless Confusions & distractions, & from a state of perpetual feud & War with all mankind, is entirely due & owing to Civil Government. And This alone is so unspeakable a Benefitt; as all the wit & sagacity, all the Cunning & Contrivance, which Mankind has above the Brute Creation, woud otherwise but enable them to do so much the greater Mischief, & to devise & find out more powerful & Effectual means & Instruments, to harm & destroy one another. It is a Branch of the Civil Government of this Country, that Empowers Us, Gent., to meet here to day, & put in Execution those Laws, wch relate to the Jurisdiction of this Court. For all Laws (be they never so god, never so wisely contriv'd to answer their Prospective Ends) are, but as a Dead letter if they are not carry'd into a Proper Execution; by which alone they receive Life, & vigour & operation; & without which, We can

never Sensibly receive the Benefitts that are intended to flow from Them. This habitually leads me to the Point in hand; which is to lay before You, the Proper Objects of Your severall Enquirys & Presentments in this Court.

Gentlemen, You are to enquire of & Present all [3] Offenders against Morall Justice; under which Head is comprehended, all Profaneness, vice & Immorality. You are to present all those that are Guilty of Offences against the Established Church, Breach of the Sabbath, Profane Cursing & Swearing, Drunkenness & Bawdry. And first, Gent: You are to enquire of & present all those who absent themselves from Church, or any Protestant assembly of Divine Worship tolerated by Law on Sundays & Holidays; Those who are Sabbath Breakers in any Respect, either for Profit or Pleasure; but Works of Piety, Charity or Necessity are excepted on that day. All which offences are Cognizable by & punishable in this Court. In the next place You are to present all Those who are guilty of Profane Cursing & Swearing Which Immorality, by reason of its Great & Evill tendency, & its daily encrease amongst us, the Legislature has thought fit lately to enact a new Law, in Order to punish all offenders of that kind more severely, than they were by any Former Statutes. The next Crying Immorality is Drunkenness; upon which vice, One of our Statutes Stamps this most Infamous [4] Character; that it is Loathsome & odious; that it is the Root foundation of Bloudshed, Stabbing, Murder, Swearing & many other enormous Crimes. Our Laws, Gent: have provided a punishment not only for the Drunkards, but also for all Publick Houses, that harbour & entertain them. For, as we are inform'd by the Statutes relating to this Matter, the Antient, true & principall use of Such Publick Houses, was for the Receipt, relief & lodging of Travellers; & for the Supply of the Wants of such People, as coud not buy in their Provisions of Meat & drink in greater Quantitys; but was never meant for the harbouring & entertaining of Lewd, Idle & disorderly people, to riot & wast their time & Substance in; By which Scandalous Impoverishment of themselves, they many times bring Large Familys to the Parish, in order to be fed & maintain'd by the Hard Labour, & at the great Expence of Honest & Industrious Men. You are to present all Houses of Bawdry; all keepers & Frequenters of such Houses: For Bawdry is an Offence Temporall, as [5] well as Spirituall, & is against the Peace of the Land, all keepers & Frequenters of such Houses fall under the Cognizance & Censure of this Court. Gentlemen, You are to present also, all Offences against Civill Justice, but as High Treasons, Misprisions of Treason, Petty Treasons, & all Felonys above Pett Larcenys, are under the Cognizance of the Superior Courts, I shall not take up the time of the Court in defining them to you.

Gent: Petty Larceny is the Felonious taking & Carrying away the Personall Goods of Another, but not of his Person nor out of his House, &

not exceeding the value of Twelve Pence. You are to present all these that speak ill Words of the King, His Ministers or Magistrates; all Authors, Printers & Publishers of Seditious Libels against the Government, Officers of State & Privy Councellours. Present all Riots, Routs & unlawful assemblys, & all other Breaches of the Publick Peace. Present all publick Nusances, as Bridges out of Repair, Hedges not properly Shript up, Highways not amended, or which are any ways annoy'd by the laying of Carrion, or dung or any other Filthy thing in or near them to the Offence of Passengers; or by ye laying of Timber, [6] Stones, or any thing or near them, that may any ways endanger Travellers as they pass along. Present all offences against Publick Justice, as Bribery, Extortions of Offices under Colour of their office; The negligence of Constables & Tithingmen, & all other Ministeriall Officers of Justice; and also all Such Men as Refuse to aid & assist Constables & Tithingmen & Such like Officers, in the Execution of their office; When they are call'd upon, & warn'd by them so to do, & which of late is become a very Frequent Practice, to the great delay & Hindrance of Justice.

Loseley MSS / 10 (Guilford) [probably post 1757]

Gentlemen of the Jury,

That Flow of Liberty, wch both distinguishes & renders this Country so remarkably free & Happy beyond all others, that we either know or read of in History, is owing to the Wise & admirable Constitution of its Laws. These Laws, whilst they are preserved & executed with their due Force & Vigour, Must stand like so many Rocks of Defence, no ways to be impress'd upon by the High Hand of Tyranny or Arbitrary Power, nor in the least to be shaken & over born by any Torrent of Popular Commotion or Confusion.

The Common Law of this Realm receiving their Grounds, Principally from the Laws of God & Nature (wch Law of [2] Nature, as it related to Man, is call'd also the Law of Reason) And these Laws being, for their Antiquity, Those whereby this Realm was govern'd many hundred years before the Conquest; the Equity & Excellency of Them is such; as that there is no Human Law so apt & profitable for the Peacable & prosperous Government of this Kingdom; and so necessary for all Estates & for all Causes concerning Life, Lands or Goods, as those Laws are. And for that purpose at the Common Law (long before Justices of the Peace were made) there were several Persons to whose Charge the maintenance of this Peace was recommanded, & who with their other Offices, had (& still have to this day) the Conservation of the Peace annex'd to their Charges, as a thing incident & inseparable from them. And [3] Yet they were & are called by the Names of their Offices only; the Conservation of the Peace being included therein. Given in charge from this Place at ye Session in 1757. Peace, Gent:, in effect & in its largest Extent (as a great & able Writer on this subject) is the Amity, Confidence, & Quiet that is between Men; And he that breaks this Amity or Quiet, breaketh the Peace. Yet Peace (in our Law) is taken for An Abstinence from Actuall & Injurious force & so is rather a Restraining of Hands, than an uniting of Minds. And for the maintenance of this Peace, chiefly, were ye justices of Peace first made. The Breach of this Peace (as you are to Consider it) is any Injurious force or violence against the Person of another, his Goods, Lands, or other Possessions, whether it be by threatening words, or by furious Gesture, or force of Body, or Arms, or any other force used in Terrorem. And the Business of this Court, Principally, is to suppress & Bring to punishment Persons using such Injurious force or [4] Violence. But Gent:, Since the first Granting of ye Commission of the Peace, & the Institution of this Court, The Power of it is greatly enlarg'd by severall Subsequent Acts of Parliament; & Several other Offences, then what were Orignally ye Subject Matter of its Cognizances, have been brought under its Jurisdiction; But all of them as having more or less Tendency directly or indirectly, towards the main Design in view, wch was the Preservation of the Peace in General. This makes it necessary for me, Gent: to enumerate and lay before you the proper Objects of your Severall Enquirys & Presentments in this Court. Gentlemen, you are to enquire of and present all (&c)

the Preamble of my Charge at Guilford Qr Sessions 1748

And at D° Sessions 1751 In Court then Ld Onslow Mr Edwards Mr Woodcroft Mr Austen

D° at D° Sessions 1752 In Court Ld Aylesford Mr Edwards Revd Mr Phillips Mr Garrell

D° Sessions in 1753 In Court Mr Weston & Mr Austen

A **CHARGE** TO THE GRAND-JURY AT THE *QUARTER - SESSIONS* HELD AT BARNSLEY in Yorkshire, The Fifteenth Day of October, 1741. By *RICHARD WITTON*, of *Lupset*, Esq; *Y O R K*: Printed by WARD and CHANDLER. 1741.

Mr *WITTON*'s Charge, &c.

Gentlemen,

I find by *Bracton*, and Other the oldest Books in the Law, That the Justices, upon holding their several Courts of Sessions, did deliver in Writing to the several Grand Inquests certain Articles of Heads of Inquiry, which were commonly stilled *Capitula Placitorum Coronæ*; which were as Rules or Directions how they were to proceed in their Inquiries, for the better Performance of their Duty and Office.

When this Method came to be laid aside and disused, it became usual for some One of the Justices to Charge the Grand Inquest by Word of Mouth with those Articles or Heads of Inquiry, and by later Practice to observe to them the great Happiness of our Constitution, and the Justness and Equity of our Laws, which, when ever set forth in their true Light, will appear to be most excellent;[1] happily suited to the Genius and Temper of the People, and wisely tending to secure to the King his just Prerogative, as well as to the People their Lives, Liber-[4] ties and Properties; and tho' this be not observed by every Body, nevertheless it is most certainly true, that the King's Prerogative, justly exercised, is the greatest Security to the People's Liberties.

When ever the mad and unruly Passions of the People of this Nation have been, or at any Time hereafter shall be so overheated by factious and wicked Leaders, (pretending always the publick Good but in Reality intending only their own private View and Interests) as to endeavour to deprive the King of that Prerogative which the Laws have wisely given him for the Honour and Support of his Imperial Crown; Farewel then the People's Liberties, and Adieu to Every Thing but Anarchy and Confusion.

Witness the Times of good King *Charles* I. a Prince more wise and virtuous than any Throne in Europe was at that Time blessed with; but traduced and maligned nevertheless, by the Tongues and Pens of factious

[1] This is an interesting note, for it proves Witton's knowledge of the customs of the time.

Miscreants, Sons of *Belial*, and Enemies to all Government, unless they themselves were Rulers.

And it is very proper and necessary for us at this Time to observe their Infernal Policy.

They did not directly attack his then Majesty's Person or Character, which were both sacred and unspotted.

They only pretended, that in some Instances he had been misled by evil Ministers and Counsellors; And therefore, if in Compliance with their good and wholesome Advice, he wou'd but remove Those whom They think fit to call so, and, (as their true Intent and Meaning is) put them in their Places, then the Nation would be perfectly easy and happy, and the Throne established in Righteousness; and as Christ rules in Heaven, so the Saints wou'd then govern upon Earth. [5]

But let the Consequence be ever remember'd.

For when God, for the just Punishment of our Sins, and to compleat the Character of that good and great Prince, by shewing his great Patience in Suffering, and thereby to exhibit him to all the World as the greatest Christian Hero. I say, when the Wisdom of the Almighty, to crown his Virtues, and compleat our Miseries, was pleased to make him a Martyr, and to deliver Him up into the Hands of an enraged Multitude, what Tongue can express the Miseries of this poor Nation and People.

The Constitution was broken in every Part; our Nobles walked on Foot; and the vilest Dregs and Scum of the People rode in Chariots; our *Jerusalem* weeped, and was laid in Ashes but had none to pity her; she mourned daily in the Street but found no Compassion, nor any to help her; God hid His Face from us, and therefore we were in trouble; such Trouble and Adversity indeed, as no *British* Eye had ever seen, cou'd it enter into the Heart of any *Free Briton* so much as conceive, had we not daily felt the intolerable Burthen of it.

I wish every Man who now hears me, making a true though very imperfect Representation of those miserable Times, wou'd seriously consider how near a Resemblance they bear to the present.

God has blessed us with a King now reigning, who, as he has in his Veins the same Blood Royal with the Blessed Martyr before-mentioned, so he inherits his Royal Virtues; who, though he be great in War, and shewn his Martial Courage in so many eminent Occasions, yet, for the Good of his People is rather desirous of Peace, for the Sake whereof, how long did he endure the Insults and Depredations of a Nation, whom, for its Weakness and the Folly of its Councils, he could not despise? [6]

How long was the *British* Lyon passive? But the Nation being at last wearied out with so many repeated Injuries, did by their proper Representatives, beseech our most merciful Prince to draw his Sword. He, ever ready to take their Advice, and redress their just Grievances, at last declared War, providing such military Forces both by Sea and

Land as no former Times have equall'd.[1] And if all the Success which might be expected from so great a Military Force, under the Conduct of the wisest Concils, has not attended our Enterprizes, yet all unprejudiced Persons will, I am sure, agree with me, That our proud Enemies have at least suffer'd so much, that they will in all Probability be very cautious for the future how they provoke the Vengeance of the *British* Nation.

Has not the wise Schemes of our most gracious King and his Ministry been, from the Beginning of the War to this very Day, greatly crossed and obstructed by the wicked Designs of Enemies at Home, who will never be quiet when out of Place, our Efforts might in all Probability have been attended with much better Success.

But what great Matters can be expected from a divided People, and how heavily must the Wheel of Government go when so many clog and obstruct it? Could we ever be so happy as all to unite for the publick Good, *Great Britain* from hence, and the Happiness of its Situation, might justly defy all the Powers of Europe; and all Nations would both dread her, and (as her Councils are just and wise) make her a Mediator in all their Differences, applying to her as to the *Romans* of old, for Protection against all their Enemies.

But such is the Corruption of the present Age, that to talk in this Manner, is like framing some *Utopian* or other such fan-[C-7] tastical State, a mere Child of some extravagant Brain or fruitful Imagination.

Let us take the World as it is; doubtless the best Way of procuring a General Reformation would be for every Man to reform Himself.

But 'tis hard and very unjust upon our good King and his Ministers, to be blamed for ill Success by those who have in a great Measure occasion'd it; who, for private Ends, and from personal Quarrels, have opposed the best concerted Councils, and wou'd rather see all Things in Disorder and Confusion, than the Nation safe and happy under any Administration wherein they do not preside.

But to draw nearer to the present Occasion, and speak what better becomes my private Station in Life: As I have observed to You before the Excellency of our Laws, so I must beg your Patience while I reflect a little upon the great Justice and Equity which is used in their Administration.

Times were, when the Benches were filled with such Men as were a just Reproach to the Bar; and indeed when the Design of the Court was to overturn the Laws, they, who least understood their Beauty and Excellence, were the fittest Instruments for that Purpose.

But as I have lived in happier Times in the Day-Spring of the Revolution, when *Westminster-Hall* was honoured with those great Men,

[1] The war declared in Spain in October 1739, and which, begun as a colonial war, widened into a European conflict.

Sommers, Holt, and Treby,[1] those great Oracles of Law and Equity, and who had for many Years before been the great Honour and Ornaments of the Bar, to whose Memories all who knew them do now pay the greatest Reverence, I cannot forbear congratulating both You and Myself upon the near Resemblance which the present Times bear to these happy Days: Tho' I have for many Years discontinued any practice at the Bar, yet some Business having the last Winter called me to [8] Town, I could not forbear often visiting with Pleasure that venerable Hall of Justice; and' tis with as great Pleasure I tell you, that the Seats there are now filled with as learned Sages as ever adorned them. Therefore under so righteous a King, we may securely trust and confide, that our Lives, Liberties, and Properties are better secured than they have been at any Time within Memory: And, that our King and his Ministers have no other Design but to support and establish them.

It has long been observed, that Judges and Times are usually suited to one another; And a Prince, who is truly *Pater Patriæ*, shewing towards his People the like Love as a natural Parent does to his own Children, will always be careful to fill the Benches with such Persons as are both learned and upright.

And this being at present our happy State, may I not well say of us *Britons*, *Oh! Fortunati nimium sua bona norint.*

But tho' we are so blessed, yet by the Art and wicked Cunning of some prevailing over the Weakness of others, we hear many still complaining in our Streets. Neither the Lenity of our King, nor even the Mercy of Almighty GOD, by granting and restoring to us at this Time such Plenty of Corn, can make us easy and contented: So truly are we described by an old *British* Bard, who in a celebrated Poem most justly calls us:

God's pamper'd People, who, debauch'd with Ease,
No King can govern and no God can please.

And now, *Gentlemen*, begging your Pardon for so long a *Preface*, I will come close to the Business in Hand, and briefly mention to You such Crimes and Misdemeanours as I think most properly belong to your Inquiry and Presentment; [9] And give You some Directions as to the Manner of your proceeding therein.

Gentlemen,

By the King's Commission [which has been now read to You] You will observe this Inquiry is very large and extensive, so as to comprehend Offences of the highest Nature, as well as those of lowest Degree.

But as the former more properly belong to the Cognizance of his

[1] John, 1st Lord Somers, 1651–1716; Sir John Holt, L.C.J. 1642–1710; Sir George Treby, ?1644–1700. All famous lawyers.

Majesty's Judges of *Oyer* and *Terminer*, there seems but little Occasion to trouble You with any particular Enumeration of them.

I shall therefore only mention to You some such Articles as are usually inquired of, and presented, at every Quarter-Session of the Peace. And they are these,

1. Such Larcenies as simple Felonies as are within the Benefit of Clergy, and for which either a corporal Punishment is to be inflicted, or else Transportation.

Next to these,

All Breaches of the publick Peace, either by Affrays, Assaults and Batteries, forcible Entries, and Wilful Trespasses, or by Riots, Routs, or unlawful Assemblies.

You are to Inquire also concerning all Nusances and common Annoyances, which are Things done or suffered to the general Grievance of the King's Subjects.

And these relate principally to the King's Highways; with respect to which, You are to inquire,

1. Whether they be duly repaired?

2. Whether any Encroachments have been made thereon? [10

3. Whether the Hedges and Ditches next the same be duly cut and scower'd; so that Travellers may not be endanger'd, hinder'd or obstruct'd, by any Default or Neglect herein.

You are to inquire of and present all Frauds and Deceits, and more especially such as are committed by false Weights and Measures.

And here it may be proper to mention to You the Offences concerning your Markets, by Forestalling, Ingrossing, and Regrating, which tend to inhance the Price of Victuals, to the common Prejudice of all Buyers.

It is very fit and necessary, that You Inquire, How all Officers, subordinate to this Court; such as Constables, Bailiffs, Overseers of the Poor, and Surveyors of the Highways, have acted and demeaned themselves in their several and respective Offices.

And if you find any of them to have been either corrupt, or remiss and negligent therein, You must not fail to present them.

Our Laws, Gentlemen, tho' excellent, and most wisely calculated to make us the happiest People upon Earth, yet of themselves are but a Dead Letter, unless we give Life and Spirit to them, by a vigorous and impartial Execution.

For this End, the Law has appointed Officers of several Orders, Ranks and Degrees;

Some properly accountable to his Majesty and the High Court of Parliament, some to the King's Superior Courts in *Westminster* Hall, and others (such as I have particularly before named) to this Court, and subject to your Cognizance as the Grand Inquest of the same. [D- 11]

Whose Misdemeanours and Neglects, if you do not duly present, you are not only injurious to the Publick, and to yourselves, as Members thereof, but you highly offend against your own Consciences, by wilfully breaking that solemn and sacred Oath, which you here have all now taken.

As to the several good Laws for punishing Vice, Immorality, and Prophaneness, those have been so particularly mentioned in his Majesty's Proclamation just now read to you, and you are there so strictly enjoined by his Majesty to put the same in due Execution; that is it is needless for me to make a Repetition of them, so if the pious and zealous Charge there given you by his Majesty Himself, for your vigorous Execution of the same, will not move and excite you to use your utmost Endeavours for this good End, it would be great Presumption in me to think, that any Thing coming from my Mouth should be of any Avail with you.

If you may be supposed to have need of any Direction, as to the Manner of Proceeding upon such Bills, or Presentments as shall be brought before you, this, I think, will be best done by putting you in Mind of the wise End and Design of the Law, in the Institution of Grand Juries,

Which was this;

That no Man's Life, Liberty, or even good Name, should be brought into publick Question, till there had been first a private and previous Inquiry, by a Jury of Gentlemen of good Estates and Fortunes in the Neighbourhood (and this under an Oath of Secrecy, not to disclose the Evidence that should be given them) whether there was a problable and reasonable Cause and Ground for bringing the Party suspected or accused, to an open Trial. [12]

Gentlemen.

Where there is such a probable Cause, it is your Duties to find the Bill; but where there is not, you ought to reject the same.

Gentlemen,

Your Oath itself, expressly requires you both to be Diligent and Impartial, in these your Inquiries and Presentments.

It strictly enjoins you, not to conceal or hide any Thing, for Favour, Fear, Promise, or Hope of Rewards, nor to present any one out of Hatred or Malice.

All Parts of Which Oath, I Doubt not but you will duly consider, and honestly perform, both to the Satisfaction of your Consciences, and the Good of your Country.

FINIS.

A **CHARGE** DELIVERED TO THE **GRAND JURY**, AT THE SESSIONS of the PEACE HELD FOR THE City and Liberty of *Westminster*, &c. On THURSDAY The 29th of JUNE, 1749. by ***HENRY FIELDING***, Esq; CHAIRMAN of the said SESSIONS. Published By Order of the COURT, and at the unanimous Request of the Gentlemen of the GRAND JURY. *LONDON:* Printed for A. MILLAR, opposite Catherine-Street, in the Strand, 1749.

City, Borough, and Town of Westminster, *in the County of* Middlesex } *At the General Quarter Session of the Peace* *of our Lord the King, holden at the Town Court-House near* Westminster-Hall, *in and for the Liberty of the Dean and Chapter of the Collegiate Church of St.* Peter, Westminster, *the City, Borough, and Town of* Westminster, *in the County of* Middlesex, *and* St. Martin le Grand, London, *on* Thursday *the Twenty-ninth Day of* June, *in the Twenty-third Year of the Reign of our Sovereign Lord* George *the Second, King of* Great-Britain, *&c. before* Henry Fielding, *Esq; the Right Hon.* George *Lord* Carpenter, *Sir* John Crosse, *Baronet,* George Huddleston, James Crofts, Gabriel Fowace, John Upton, Thomas Ellys, Thomas Smith, George Payne, William Walmsley, William Young, Peter Elers, Martin Clare, Thomas Lediard, Henry Trent, Daniel Gach, James Fraser, *Esquires, and others their fellows, Justices of our said Lord the King, assigned to keep the Peace of the said Liberty, and also to hear and determine divers Felonies, Trespasses, and other Misdeeds done and committed within the said Liberty* .

HIS Majesty's Justices of the Peace for this City and Liberty of *Westminster*, now assembled at this General Quarter Session of the Peace, held for the said City and Liberty, being of Opinion that the Charge this Day given by *Henry Fielding*, Esq; the Chairman of this Session, to the Grand Jury sworn to inquire for our Sovereign Lord the King for the Body of this City and Liberty, and to the High and Petty Constables of the same, is a very loyal, learned, ingenious, excellent and useful Charge, highly tending to the Service of his Majesty and Administration and Government, have unanimously agreed and resolved, That the Thanks of this Court be, and the same are hereby given to the said *Henry Fielding*, Esq; for his said Charge. And we do desire that he will be pleased to cause the same to be printed and published, for the better Information of the Inhabitants and public Officers of this City and Liberty in the Performance of their respective Duties.

By the Court.

FORBES.

[B]

A **CHARGE** Delivered to the **GRAND JURY**, *&c.*

Gentlemen of the Grand Jury,

THERE is no Part in all the excellent frame of our Constitution which an *Englishman* can, I think, contemplate with such Delight and Admiration; nothing which must fill him with such Gratitude to our earliest Ancestors as that Branch of the *British* Liberty from which, Gentlemen, you [8] derive your Authority of assembling here on this Day.

THE Institution of Juries, Gentlemen, is a Privilege which distinguishes the Liberty of *Englishmen* from those of all other Nations: For as we find no Traces of this in the Antiquities of the *Jews*, or *Greeks*, or *Romans*; so it is an Advantage, which is at present solely confined to this Country; not so much, I apprehend, from the Reasons assigned by FORTESCUE, in his Book *de Laudibus, cap.* 29. namely, *because there are more Husbandmen, and fewer Freeholders, in other Countries*; as because, other Countries have less of Freedom than this; and being for the most Part subjected to the absolute Wills of their Governors, and not under the Protection of certain Laws. In such Countries it would be absurd to look for any Share of Power in the Hands of the People. [B 2-9]

AND if Juries in general be so very signal a Blessing to this Nation, as FORTESCUE, in the Book I have just cited, thinks this: *A Method,* says he, *much more available and effectual for the Trial of Truth, than is the Form of any other Laws of the World, as it is farther from the Danger of Corruption and Subornation*; what, Gentlemen, shall we say of the Institution of Grand Juries, by which an *Englishman*, so far from being convicted, cannot be even tried, not even put on his Trial in any Capital Case, at the Suit of the Crown; unless, perhaps, in one or two very special Instances, till Twelve Men at the least have said on their Oaths, that there is a probable Cause for his Accusation! Surely, we may in a kind of Rapture cry with FORTESCUE, speaking of the second Jury, *Who then can unjustly die in* England *for any criminal Offence, seeing he may have so many Helps for the Favour of* [10] his *life, and that none can condemn him, but his Neighbours, good and lawful Men, against whom he hath no Manner of Exception.*

TO trace the Original of this great and singular Privilege, or to say when and how it began, is not an easy Task; so obscure indeed are the Foot-steps of it through the first Ages of our History that my Lord *Hale*, and even my Lord *Coke*, seem to have declined it. Nay, this latter in his Account of the Second or Petty Jury, is very succinct; and contents himself with saying, that it is very antient and before the Conquest. [*Co. Lit. 155 b.*][1]

Spelman in his Life of *Alfred, lib.* 2 Pag. 71 will have that Prince to have been the first Founder of Juries; but in Truth they are much older, and very probably had some Existence even among the *Britons*. The *Normans* likewise had antiently the Bene-[11]fit of Juries, as appears in the *Custumier de Normandy*[2]; and something like Grand Juries too we find in that Book under the Title *Suit de Murdyr*.

Bracton, who wrote in the Reign of HENRY the Third, in his Book *de Corona chap.* 1. gives a plain Account of this Matter: And by him it appears that the Grand Juries before the Justices in *Eyre*, differed very little at that time from what they now are, before Justices assigned to keep the Peace, Oyer, and Terminer, and Goal-Delivery, unless in the Manner of chusing them, and unless in one other Respect; there being then a Grand Jury, sworn for every Hundred; whereas at present one serves for the whole County, Liberty, *&c.*

BUT before this Time, our Ancestors were sensible of the great Importance of this Privilege, and extremely jealous of it, as appears in the 29th Chapter of the Great Char-[12] ter, granted by King JOHN, and confirmed by HENRY the Third. For thus my Lord *Coke*, 2 *Instit.* 46 expounds that Chapter. *Nullus liber homo capiatur*, &c. 'No Man shall be taken, that is (says he) restrained of Liberty, by Petition or Suggestion to the King and his Council; unless it be by Indictment or Presentment of good and lawful Men, where such Deeds be done.'

And so just a Value have our Ancestors always set on this great Branch of our Liberties, and so jealous have they been of any Attempt to diminish it, that when a Commission to punish Rioters in a summary Way, was awarded in the Second Year of RICHARD the Second, 'it was,' says Mr. *Lambard* in his *Eirenarcha*, fol. 305. 'even in the self-same Year of the same King, resumed, as a Thing over-hard (says that Writer) to be borne, that a Freeman should be imprisoned without an Indictment, or other Trial, by [13] his Peers, as *Magna Carta* speaketh; until that the Experience of greater Evils had prepared and made the Stomach of the Commonwealth able and fit to digest it.'

[1] It is not easy to assign a precise origin to the institution of the jury. Chambers, *Lectures*..., I, 103,: "we may still trace the Saxon institutions in the use of juries, though the forms of indictment... seem better to correspond with the...Norman practice"; Stubbs, *Constit. Hist.*, makes it a Saxon adaptation of a Norman custom, I, 313, passim; *The Oxford Companion to Law*, 686, mentions an ordinance of King Ethelred II, circa A.D. 1000, but also thinks of a Norman origin, "of a system of inquisitions in local courts by sworn witnesses."

[2] Also called *Grand C(o)ustumier de Normandy* = the book of the customs of Normandy, quoted by Sir Wm Chambers, vol. I & II.

AND a hard Morsel surely it must have been, when the Commonwealth could not digest it in that turbulent Reign, which of all others in our History, seems to have afforded the most proper Ingredients to make it palatable; in a Reign moreover when the Commonwealth seemed to have been capable of swallowing and digesting almost any thing; when Judges were so prostitute as to acknowledge the King to be above the Law; and when a Parliament, which even *Echard* censures, and for which Mr. *Rapin*, with a juster Indignation tells us, he knows no Name odious enough, made no scruple to sacrifice to the Passions of the King, and his Ministers, the Lives of the most distinguished Lords of the Kingdom, as well as the [14] Liberties and Privileges of the People. Even in that Reign, Gentlemen, our Ancestors could not, as Mr. *Lambard* remarks, be brought by any Necessity of the Times, to give up, in any single Instance, this their invaluable Privilege.

ANOTHER considerable Attempt to deprive the Subject of the Benefit of Grand Juries was made in the eleventh Year of HENRY the Seventh. The Pretence of this Act of Parliament, was the wilful Concealments of Grand Jurors, in their Inquests; and by it 'Power was given to the Justices of Assize in their Sessions, and to Justices of the Peace in every County, upon Information for the King, to hear and determine all Offences and Contempts (saving Treason, Murder and Felony) by any Person against the Effect of any Statute.'

MY Lord *Coke* in his 4th Institute fol. 40. sets forth this Act at large, not as a Law which in his Time had [C-15] any Force, but *in Terrorem*; and, as he himself says, that the like should never be attempted in any future Parliament.

'THIS Act, says Lord COKE, had fair flattering Preamble; but in the Execution, tended diametrically contrary; *viz.* to the high Displeasure of Almighty GOD; and to the great Let, nay, the utter Subversion of the Common Law; namely, by depriving the Subject of that great Privilege of being indicted and tryed by a Jury of their Countrymen.'

BY Pretext of this Law, says the great Writer I have just cited, EMPSON and DUDLEY did commit upon the Subject insufferable Pressures and Oppressions. And we read in History that soon after the Act took place, Sir WILLIAM CAPEL, Alderman of *London*, who was made the first Object of its Tyranny, was fined Two thousand seven hundred Pounds, Sixteen hund-[16] dred of which he actually paid to the King, by way of Composition. A vast Sum in these Days, to be imposed for a crime so minute, that scare any Notice is taken of it in History.

OUR Ancestors, however, bore not long this Invasion on their Liberties; for in the very first Year of K. HENRY VIII. this flagitious Act was repealed, and the Advisers of all the Extortions committed by it were deservedly sacrificed to the public Resentment.

GENTLEMEN, I shall mention but two more Attacks on this most valuable of all our Liberties; the first of which was indeed the greatest of all, I mean that cursed Court of Star-Chamber, which was erected under the same King.

I SHALL not before you, Gentlemen, enter into a Contest with my Lord COKE, whether this Court had [17] a much older Existence, or whether it first begun under the Statute of 3 HENRY VII. For my Part I clearly think the latter.

1. BECAUSE the Statute which erected it mentions no such Court as then existing, and most manifestly speaks the Language of Creation, not of Confirmation.

2. Because it was expressly so understood by the Judges, within Five Years after the Statute was made, as appears by the Year-Book of 8 HENRY VII. *Pasch. Fol.* 13. *Plac.* 7.

LASTLY, Because all our Historians and Law-writers before that Time are silent concerning any such Court; for as to the Records and Acts of Parliament cited by my Lord COKE, they are most evidently to be applied only to the King and Council, to whom, in old Time, Complaints were, in very extraordinary Cases, preferred. [18]

THIS old Court, my Lord COKE himself confesses, sat very rarely; so rarely indeed, that there are no traces left of its Proceedings, at least of any such as were afterwards had under the Authority of the Statute. Had this Court had an original Existence in the Constitution, I do not see why the great Lawyer is so severe against the before-mentioned Act of the 11th of HENRY VII. or how he can, with any Propriety, call the Liberty of being accused and tried only by Juries, the Birth-right of an *English* Subject.

THE other Instance was that of the High Commission Court, instituted by Parliament in the first Year of Queen ELIZABETH.

THIS Act likewise pretends to refer to an Authority in being. The Title of it is, An Act restoring to the Crown the antient Jurisdiction, *&c.* By which, saith Lord COKE, 4 *Inst.* 325, the [19] Nature of the Act doth appear; *viz.* that it is an Act of Restitution.

AND hence the Court of Common-Pleas, in the Reign of JAMES I. well argued, that the Act being meant to restore to the Crown the antient ecclesiastical Jurisdiction, the Commissioners could derive no other Power from it than before belonged to that ecclesiastical Jurisdiction.

BUT however necessary, as my Lord COKE says, this Act might have been at its first Creation, [4 Inst. 326] or however the Intention of the Legislature might have been to restrain it, either as to Time or Persons, certain it is, that the Commissioners extended its Jurisdiction in many Cases, to the great Grievance of the Subject, and to the depriving them of that Privilege which I have just mentioned to be the Birth-right of an *Englishman.* [20]

THE Uses made of these Courts, and particularly under that unhappy Prince CHARLES I. need not be mentioned. They are but too well known. Let it suffice, that the Spirit of our Ancestors at last prevailed over these Invasions of their Liberties, and these Courts were for ever abolished.

AND, Gentlemen, if we have just Reason to admire the great Bravery and Steadiness of those our Ancestors, in defeating all the Attempts of Tyranny against this excellent Branch of our Constitution, we shall have no less Reason, I apprehend, to extol that great Wisdom, which they have from time to time demonstrated, in well ordering and regulating their Juries; so as to preserve them as clear as possible from all Danger of Corruption. In this Light, Gentlemen, we ought to consider the several Laws by which the Morals, the Character, the Sub-[21] stance, and good Demeanor of Jurors are regulated. These Jurors, Gentlemen, must be good and lawful Men, of Reputation and Substance in their County, chosen at the Nomination of neither Party, absolutely disinterested and indifferent in the Cause which they are to try. Upon the whole, the Excellence of our Constitution, and the great Wisdom of our Laws, which FORTESCUE, my Lord COKE, and many other great Writers, have so highly extolled, is in no one Instance so truly admirable as in this Institution of our Juries. [1]

I HOPE, Gentlemen, I shall not be thought impertinent, in having taken up so much of your Time to shew you the great Dignity and Importance of that Office which you are now assembled here to execute; the Duties of which it is incumbent on me concisely to open to you; and this I shall endeavour in the best Manner I am able. [22]

THE Duty, Gentlemen, of a Grand Juror, is to enquire of all Crimes and Misdemeanors whatsoever, which have been committed in the County or Liberty for which he serves as a Grand Juror, and which are anywise cognizable by the Court in which he is sworn to enquire.

AND this Enquiry is in a twofold Manner, by way of Indictment, and by way of Presentment.

WHICH two Words, Mr. LAMBARD, *fol.* 461. thus explains:

A PRESENTMENT, says he, I take to be a meer Determination of the Jurors themselves; and an Indictment is the Verdict of the Jurors, grounded upon the Accusation of a third Person: So that a Presentment is but a Declaration of the Jurors, without any Bill offered before; and an Indictment is [D -23] their finding of a Bill of Accusation to be true.

THE usual Method of Charge hath been to run over the several Articles; or Heads of Crimes, which might possible become subject to the Enquiry of the Grand Jury.

[1] This was evidently a purely theoretical view: English history will amply demonstrate otherwise, from the trial of Archbishop Sancroft in 1687 to the political trials of 1794.

THIS we find in BRACTON, who writ so long ago as the Reign of HENRY III. was the Practice of the Justices in Eyre, *l.* 3 *c.* 1. And my Lord COKE says, 4 *Inst.* 183. That the Charge to be given at the Sessions of the Peace consisteth of two Parts; Laws Ecclesiastical for the Peace of the Church, and Laws Civil and Temporal for the Peace of the Land. And Mr. LAMBARD, in his *Eirenarcha*, gives the whole Form of the Charge at Length, in which he recapitulates every Article which was at that Time enquirable in the Sessions. [24]

BUT, Gentlemen, I think I may be excused at present from taking up so much of your Time; for tho' we are assembled to exercise the Jurisdiction of a very antient and honourable Liberty, yet, as there is another Sessions of Justices within that County of which this Liberty is a Part, before whom Indictments for all Crimes of a deeper Dye are usually preferred, it seems rather to savour of Ostentation than Utility, to run over those Articles which in great Probability will not come before you.

AND indeed a perfect Knowledge of the Law in these Matters is not necessary to a Grand Juror; for in all Cases of Indictments, whether for a greater or lesser, a public or private Crime, the Business of a Grand Jury is only to attend to the Evidence for the King; and if on that Evidence there shall appear a probable Cause for the Accusation, they are to find [D 2-25] the Bill true, without listening to any Circumstances of Defence, or to any Matter of Law.

AND therefore my Lord HALE, *vol.* 2. *fol.* 158. puts this Case. "If *A.* be killed by *B.* so that the Person of the Slayer and Slain be certain; and a Bill of Murder be presented to the Grand Jury, regularly they ought to find the Bill for Murder, and not for Manslaughter, or *Se defendendo*; because otherwise Offences may be smothered without due Trial; and when the Party comes on his Trial the whole Fact will be examined before the Court and the Petty Jury; for if a Man kills *B.* in his own Defence, or *Per Infortunium*, or possible in executing the Process of Law upon an Assault made upon him, or in his own Defence on the Highway, or in Defence of his House against those that come to rob him (in which three last Cases it is neither Felony nor Forfeiture, but upon Not Guilty pleaded he ought to [26] be acquitted) yet if the Grand Inquest find an *Ignoramus* upon the Bill, or find the Special Matter, whereby the Prisoner is dismissed and discharged, he may nevertheless be indicted for Murder seven Years after; "whereas, if upon a proper Finding he had been acquitted, he could never afterwards be again arraigned without the Plea of *Autrefois acquit.*

THIS Doctrine of the learned Chief Justice you will apply to whatever Case may come before you: for wherever you shall find probable Cause, upon the Oaths of the King's Witnesses, you will not discharge your Office without finding the Bill to be true, shewing no Regard to the Nature of the Crime, or the Degree of the Guilt; which are Matter proper for the Cognizance and Determination of the Court only.

H.P.C. ii. 157. I MUST not, however, omit, on the Authority of the last-[27] mentioned Judge, "that if, upon the hearing the King's Evidence, or upon your own Knowledge of the Incredibility of the Witnesses you shall be satisfied, you may then return the Bill *Ignoramus*."

IT is true my Lord HALE confines this to Indictments for Capital Offences; but I see no Reason why it may not be extended to any Indictment whatever.

ONE Caution more occurs on this Head of Indictment; and it is the Duty of Secrecy. To have revealed the King's Counsel disclosed to the Grand Jurors was formerly taken to be Felony; nay, Justice SHARD, in the 27th Year of the Book of Assises, *Placit.* 63. doubted whether it was not Treason; and tho' at this Day the Law be not so severe, yet is this still a very great Misdemeanor, and fineable as such, and is moreover a manifest Breach of your Oath. [28]

I COME now, Gentlemen, to the Second Branch of your Duty, namely, that of presenting all Offences which shall come to your Knowledge.

AND this is much more painful, and of greater Difficulty than the former; for here you are obliged, without any direct Accusation, to inform yourselves as well as is possible of the Truth of the Fact, and in some measure likewise to be conusant of those Laws which subject Offences to your Presentment.

UPON this Head therefore I shall beg Leave to remind you of those Articles which seem to be most worthy of your Enquiry, at this Time; for indeed it would be useless and tedious to enumerate the whole Catalogue of Misdemeanours that are to be found in our Statutes; many of which, though still in Force, are, by the Changes of Times and Fashions, become an-[29]tiquated, and of little Use. *Cessante ratione Legis, cessat & ipsa Lex*;[1] and there are some accidental and temporary Evils which at particular Seasons have, like an epidemic Distemper, affected Society, but have afterwards disappeared, or at least made very faint Efforts to corrupt the public Morals. The Laws made to suppress such, tho' very wholesome and necessary at the Time of their Creation, become obsolete with the Evil which occasioned them, and which they were intended to cure. But, Gentlemen, there are Evils of a more durable Kind, which rather resembles chronical than epidemic Diseases; and which have so inveterated themselves in the Blood of the Body Politic, that they are perhaps never to be totally eradicated. These it will be always the Duty of the Magistrate to palliate and keep down as much

[1] = the reason for passing a law disappearing, the law itself disappears.

as possible. And these, Gentlemen, are the Misdemeanors of which you are to pre-[30] sent as many as come to your Knowledge.

AND first, Gentlemen, I will remind you of presenting all Offences committed immediately against the Divine Being; for tho' all Crimes do include in them some Degree of Sin, and may therefore be considered as Offences against the Almighty; yet there are some more directly levelled at his Honour, and which the Temporal Laws do punish as such.

AND, 1. all blasphemous Expressions against any one of the Sacred Persons in the Trinity, are severely punishable by the Common Law; for, as my Lord HALE says, in *Taylor*'s Case, I VENT.293. [3 Keb. 607. 621. S. C.] "Such Kind of wicked blasphemous Words are not only an Offence against GOD and Religion, but a Crime against the Laws, State, and Government;" and in that Case the Defendant for Blasphemy, too [31] horrible indeed to be repeated, was sentenced to stand three Times in the Pillory, to pay a great Fine, and to find Security for his good Behaviour during Life.

IN like Manner, all scandalous and contemptuous Words spoken against our holy Religion, are by the Wisdom of the Common Law made liable to an Indictment; for "Christianity" (says that excellent Chief-Justice, in the Case I have just cited) "is Parcel of the Laws of *England*: therefore to reproach the Christian Religion is to speak in Subversion of the Law. "And to the same Purpose is *Attwood*'s Case, in CRO. JAC. 421. where one was indicted before the Justices of the Peace for saying, that the Religion now professed was a new Religion within fifty Years, *&c*. For as to the Doubt concerning the High Commissioners, started in that Case, and then, as it appears, over-ruled, that is now vanished. [32]

NOR are our Statutes silent concerning this dreadful Offence; particularly by 1 ELIZ. *c.* 2. *sect.* 9. a severe Punishment is enacted for any Person who shall in any Interludes, Plays, Songs, Rhimes, or by other open Words declare or speak any thing in derogation, depraving or despising the Book of Common Prayer, *&c.*

MR. LAMBARD, I find, mentions this Act in his Charge, though the Execution of it be in the Counties confined to the Justices of *Oyer* and *Terminer* and of Assize; but the 22nd *Sect.* of the Statute seems to give a clear Jurisdiction to this Court, at two of our Quarter-Sessions.

THE last Offence of this Kind which the wicked Tongue of Man can commit, is by profane Cursing and Swearing. This is a Sin expressly against the Law delivered by God him-[33] self to the *Jews*, and which is as expressly prohibited by our blessed Saviour on his Sermon on the Mount.

MANY Statutes have been made against this Offence; and by the last of these, which was enacted in the Nineteenth Year of the present King, every Day-labourer, common Soldier, common Sailor and common Seaman, forfeits One Shilling; Every other Person, under the Degree of a Gentleman, Two Shillings; and every Person of or above that Degree, five Shillings.

AND in case any Person shall after such Conviction offend again, he forfeits double; and for every Offence after a second Conviction, treble.

THOUGH the Execution of this Act be entrusted to one single Magistrate, and no Jurisdiction, unless by Appeal, given to the Sessions; yet I could not forbear mentioning it here, when I am speaking in the presence of many [34] Peace-Officers, who are to forfeit 40 Shillings for neglecting to put the Act under Execution. And I mention it the rather to inform them, that whenever the Offender is unknown to any Constable, Petty Constable, Tithingman, or other Peace-Officer, such Constable *&c.* is empowered by the Act, without any Warrant, to seize and detain any such Person, and forthwith to carry him before the next Magistrate.

AND if these Officers would faithfully discharge the Duty thus enjoined them, and which Religion as well as the Law requires of them, our Streets would soon cease to resound with this detestable Crime, so injurious to the Honour of God, so directly repugnant to his positive Command, so highly offensive to the Ears of all good Men, and so very scandalous to the Nation in the Ears of Foreigners.

HAVING dispatched those Misdemeanors (the principal ones at least) [35] which are immediately committed against God, I come now to speak of those which are committed against the Person of the King, which Person the Law wisely holds to be sacred.

BESIDES those heinous Offences against this sacred Person which are punished *ultimo supplicio*, there are many Articles, some of which involve the Criminal in the Guilt of Præmunire, and others are considered in Law as Misprisions or Contempts. The former of these is by Mr. Serjeant HAWKINS, in his Pleas of the Crown, divided into two general Heads: *Viz.*

Into Offences against the Crown.

AND Offences against the Authority of the King and Parliament.

UNDER the former Head he enumerates nine several Articles; but as these chiefly relate to such Invasions of the [36] Royal Prerogative as were either made in popish Ages in favour of the Bishops of *Rome*, or in those Times which bordered on the Reformation in favour of the Church of *Rome*, and are not practised, at least not openly practised in these Days, I shall have no Need to repeat them here.

UNDER the latter Head he mentions only one, which was enacted in the Reign of Queen ANNE, 6 *Ann.* c.7. If any Person shall maliciously and directly, by Preaching, Teaching, or advised Speaking, declare, maintain and affirm, that the pretended Prince of *Wales* hath any Right or Title to the Crown of these Realms, or that any other Person or Persons hath or have any Right or Title to the same, otherwise than according to the Acts of Settlement; or that the Kings or Queens of this Realm, with the Authority of Parliament, are no able to make Laws to Limit the Crown and [37] the Descent, *&c.* thereof, shall incur a Præmunire.[1]

A MOST wholesome and necessary Law. And yet so mild hath been our Government, that I remember no one Instance of putting it in Execution.

MISPRISIONS or Contempts are against the King's Prerogative, against his Title, or against his sacred Person or Government.

UNDER these Heads will fall any Act of public and avowed Disobedience; any denying his most just and lawful Title to the Crown; any overt Act which directly tends to encourage or promote Rebellion or Sedition; all false Rumours against his Majesty, or his Councils; all contemptuous Language concerning his sacred Person, by cursing, reviling him, *&c.* or by uttering any thing which manifests an Intention of lessening that Esteem, Awe and Re-[38] verence which Subjects ought to bear to the best of Princes.

THESE are Offences, Gentlemen, which I must earnestly recommend to your Enquiry. This, Gentlemen, is your Duty as Grand Jurors; and it must be a most pleasing Task to you, as you are *Englishmen*; for in Proportion as you love and esteem your Liberties, you will be fired with Love and Reverence towards a Prince, under whose Administration you enjoy them in the fullest and amplest Manner.

BELIEVE me, Gentlemen, notwithstanding all which the Malice of the Disappointed, the Madness of Republicans, or the Folly of the Jacobites may insinuate, there is but one Method to maintain the Liberties of this Country, and that is, to maintain the Crown on the Heads of that Family which now happily enjoys it. [F - 39]

IF ever Subjects had Reason to admire the Justice of the Sentiment of the Poet *Claudian, That Liberty never flourishes so happily as under a good King*, we have Reason at present for that Admiration.

I AM afraid, Gentlemen, this Word *Liberty*, though so much talked of, is but little understood. What other Idea can we have of Liberty, than that it is the Enjoyment of our Lives, our Persons, and our Properties in Security; to be free Masters of ourselves and our Possessions, as far as the known Laws of our Country will admit; to be liable to no Punishment, no Confinement, no Loss but what those Laws subject us to! Is there any Man ignorant enough to deny that this is the Description of a free People; or base enough to accuse me of Panegyric, when I say this is our present happy Condition? [40] BUT if the Blessing of Liberty, like that of Health, be not to be perceived by those who enjoy it, or at least must be illustrated

[1] The Jacobite attempt of 1745 was still very recent, together with the threat for the dynasty. Neither was his political journalism very old....

by its Opposite, let us compare our own Condition with that of other Countries; of those whose Polity some among us pretend so much to admire, and whose Government they seem so ardently to affect. *Lettres de Cachet,* Bastiles, and Inquisitions, may, perhaps, give us a livelier Sense of a just and mild Administration, than any of the Blessings we enjoy under it.[1]

AGAIN, Gentlemen, let us compare the present Times with the past. And here I need not resort back to those distant Ages, when our unhappy Forefathers petitioned their Conqueror *that he would not make them so miserable, nor be so severe to them, as to judge them by a Law they understood not.* These are the very Words, as we find them preserved in *Daniel*; in Return to [F 2-41] which, the Historian informs is, nothing was obtain'd but fair Promises. I shall not dwell here on the Tyranny of his immediate Successor, of whom the same Historian records, that " seeking to establish absolute Power by Force, he made both himself and his People miserable."

I NEED not, Gentlemen, here remind you of the Oppressions under which our Ancestors have groaned in many other Reigns, to shake off which the Sword of Civil War was first drawn in the Reign of King *John,* which was not entirely sheathed during many successive Generations.

I MIGHT, perhaps, have a fairer Title to your Patience, in laying open the tyrannical Proceedings of later Times, while the Crown was possessed by four successive Princes of the House of *Stuart.* But this, Gentlemen, would be to trespass on your Patience indeed: For to mention all their Acts [42] of absolute Power, all their Attempts to subvert the Liberties of this Nation would be to relate to you the History of their Reigns.

IN a Word, Gentlemen, all the Struggles which our Ancestors have so bravely maintained with ambitious Princes, and particularly with the last mentioned Family, was to maintain and preserve to themselves and their Posterity, that very Liberty which we now enjoy, under a Prince to whom I may truly apply what the Philosopher long ago said of Virtue, THAT ALL WHO TRULY KNOW HIM MUST LOVE HIM.

THE third general Head of Misdemeanours, Gentlemen, is of those which are committed against the Subject, and these may be divided into two Branches.

INTO such as are committed against Individuals only: [43]

AND into such as affect the Public in general.

THE former of these will probably come before you by Way of Indictment; for Men are apt enough to revenge their own Quarrels; but

[1] It is to be noted that the same argument will be used 40 years later by the supporters of the established order against the French revolutionary doctrine of liberty: see Burke and his followers.

Offences *in commune nocumentum* [1] do not so certainly find an Avenger; and thus those Crimes, which it is the Duty of every Man to punish, do often escape with Impunity.

OF these, Gentlemen, it may be therefore proper to awaken your Enquiry, and particularly of such as do in a more especial Manner infest the Public at this Time.

THE first of this Kind is the Offence of profligate Lewdness; a Crime of a very pernicious Nature to Society, as it tends to corrupt the Morals of our Youth, and is expressly prohibited by the Law of God, under [44] Denunciation of the severest Judgment, in the New Testament. Nay, we read in the 25th Chapter of *Numbers* the exceeding Wrath of God against the Children of *Israel* for their Fornication with the Daughters of *Moab*. Nor did the Plague which on that Occasion was sent among them, and which destroyed Four and twenty thousand, cease, till *Phineas*, the Son of *Eleazar* and Grandson of *Aaron*, had slain the Israelite together with his Harlot.

AND this, Gentlemen, though a spiritual Offence, and of a very high Nature too, as appears from what I have mentioned, is likewise a temporal Crime, and, as Mr. LAMBARD (122) says, against the Peace.

My Lord COKE, in his third *Institute*, 206, tells us, that in antient Times Adultery and Fornication were punished by Fine and Imprisonment, and were enquirable in Turns and Leets. [45] And in the Year-Book of HENRY VII. [1 *H*. 7. fol. 6. plac. 3] we find the Custom of *London* pleaded for a Constable to seize a Woman taken in the Act of Adultery, and to carry her to Prison.

AND though later Times have given up this Matter in general to ecclesiastical Jurisdiction, yet there are two Species which remain at this Day cognizable by the Common Law.

The first is, any open Act of Lewdness and Indecency in public, to the Scandal of Good-manners.

AND therefore in *Michaelmas* Term, 15 *Car*. 2. B. R. Sir CHARLES SIDNEY was indicted for having exposed himself naked in a Balcony in *Covent-Garden*, to a great Multitude of People, with many indecent Words and Actions, and this was laid to be contrary to the King's Peace, and to the great Scandal of Christianity. He confessed the Indictment and SIDERFIN, [1*Sid*. 168], who reports the Case, tells [46] us, that the Court, in Consideration of his embarrassed Fortune, fined him only 2000 Marks, with a short Imprisonment, and to be bound three Years for his good Behaviour. An infamous Punishment for a Gentleman, but far less

[1] A nuisance to the public. F. points out a state of facts: probably less than one in ten crimes, offences, etc. were actually punished, either because people did not care to report such misdeeds, because they could not attend to the lengthy process; or because they did not care to have some one hang for a trifle, or because there was no organised police force that could pursue and arrest malefactors.

infamous than the Offence. If any Facts of this Nature shall come to your Knowledge, you will, I make no Doubt, present them, without any Respect to Persons. Sex or Quality may render the Crime more atrocious, and the Example more pernicious; but can give no Sanction to such infamous Offences, nor will, I hope, ever give Impunity.

THE second Species which falls under this Head, is the Crime of keeping a Brothel or Bawdy-House. This is a kind of common Nuisance, and is punishable by the Common Law.

IT is true, that certain Houses of this Kind, under the Name of pub- [G-47] lic Stews, have been sometimes tolerated in Christian Countries, to the great Scandal of Religion, and in direct Contradiction to its positive Precepts: But in the thirty-seventh Year of HENRY the Eight, they were all suppressed by Proclamation. And those infamous Women who inhabited them were not, says Lord COKE, either buried in Christian Burial when they were dead, nor permitted to receive the Rites of the Church when they lived.

AND Gentlemen, notwithstanding the Favour which the Law in many Cases extends to married Women, yet in this Case the Wife is equally indictable, and may be found guilty with her Husband.

NOR is it necessary that the Person be Master or Mistress of the whole House; for if he or she have only a single Room, and will therewith accommodate lewd People to perpetrate [48] Acts of Uncleanness, they may be indicted for a Bawdy-House. And this was the Resolution of the whole Court, in *the Queen* and PEIRSON. SALK. 332.

NOR is the Guilt confined to those who keep such Houses; those who frequent them are no less liable to the Censure of the Law. Accordingly we find, in the select Cases printed at the End of Lord Ch. J. POPHAM's *Reports*, that a Man was indicted in the Beginning of CHARLES the First, at the Sessions for the Town of *Northampton*, for frequenting a suspected Bawdy-House. And the Indictment being removed into the *King's-Bench*, several Objections were taken to it, which were all overruled, Judgment was given upon it, and the Defendant fined.

If you shall know, therefore, Gentlemen, of any such Crimes, it will [G 2 -49] be your Duty to present them to the Court.

FOR however lightly this Offence may be thought or spoken of by idle and dissolute Persons, it is a Matter of serious and weighty Consideration. It is the Cause, says my Lord COKE, of many Mischiefs, the fairest End whereof is Beggary; and tends directly to the Overthrow of Men's Bodies, to the wasting of their Livelihoods, and to the indangering of their Souls.

TO eradicate this Vice out of Society, however it may be the Wish of sober and good Men, is, perhaps, an impossible Attempt; but to check its Progress, and to suppress the open and more profligate Practice of it, is within the Power of the Magistrate, and it is his Duty. And this is more immediately incumbent upon us, in an Age when Brothels are become in an Manner the Seminaries of Education, and that especially of those Youths, [50] whose Birth makes their right Institution of the utmost Consequence to the future Well-being of the Public: For whatever may be the Education of these Youths, however vitiated and enervated their Minds and Bodies may be with Vices and Diseases, they are born to be the Governors of our Posterity. If, therefore, through the egregious Folly of their Parents, this Town is to be the School of such Youths, it behoves us, Gentlemen, to take as much Care as possible to correct the Morals of that School.

AND, Gentlemen, there are other Houses, rather less scandalous, perhaps, but equally dangerous to the Society: in which Houses the Manners of Youth are greatly tainted and corrupted. These are those Places of public Rendezvous where idle Persons of both Sexes meet in a very disorderly Manner, often at improper Hours, and sometimes in disguised Habits. These Houses, which pretend to be the [51] Scenes of innocent Diversion and Amusement, are in reality the Temples of Iniquity. Such Meetings are *contra bonos mores*; they are considered in Law in the Nature of a Nuisance, and as such, the Keepers and Maintainers of them may be presented and punished.

THERE is a great Difference, Gentlemen, between a morose and over-sanctified Spirit, which excludes all Kind of Diversion, and a profligate Disposition which hurries us into the most vicious Excesses of this Kind. "The Common Law," says Mr. PULTON in his Excellent Treatise *de Pace, fol.* 25. *b.* "allows many Recreations, which be not with Intent to break or disturb the Peace, or to offer Violence, Force, or Hurt, to the Person of any; but either to try Activity, or to increase Society, Amity, and neighbourly Friendship." He there enumerated many Sorts of innocent Diversions of the rural Kind, and [52] which for the most Part belong to the lower Sort of People. For the upper Part of Mankind, and in this Town, there are many lawful Amusements, abundantly sufficient for the Recreation of any temperate and sober Mind. But, Gentlemen, so immoderate are the Desires of many, so hungry is their Appetite for Pleasure, that they may be said to have a Fury after it; and Diversion is no longer the Recreation or Amusement, but the whole Business of their Lives. They are not content with three Theatres, they must have a fourth; where the Exhibitions are not contrary to Law, but contrary to Good-Manners, and where the Stage is reduced back again to that Degree of Licentiousness which was too enormous for the corrupt State of *Athens* to tolerate; and which, as the *Roman* poet, rather, I think, in the Spirit of a Censor than a Satyrist, tells us, those *Athenians*, who were not themselves abused, took Care [53] to abolish, from their Concern for the Public.

GENTLEMEN, our News-Papers, from the Top of the Page to the

Bottom, the Corners of our Streets up to the very Eves of our Houses, present us with nothing but a View of Masquerades, Balls, and Assemblies of various Kinds, Fairs, Wells, Gardens, *&c.* tending to promote Idleness, Extravagance, and Immorality, among all Sorts of People.

THIS Fury after licentious and luxurious Pleasures is grown to so enormous a Height, that it may be called the Characteristic of the present Age. And it is an Evil, Gentlemen, of which it is neither easy nor pleasant to foresee all the Consequences. Many of them, however, are obvious; and these are so dreadful, that they will, I doubt not, induce you to use your best Endeavours to check the further Encrease of this growing Mis-[54] chief; for the Rod of the Law, Gentlemen, must restrain these within the Bounds of Decency and Sobriety, who are deaf to the Voice of Reason, and superior to the Fear of Shame.[1]

GENTLEMEN, there are another Sort of these Temples of Iniquity, and these are Gaming-Houses. This, Vice, Gentlemen, is inseparable from a luxurious and idle Age; for while Luxury produces Want, Idleness forbids honest Labour to supply it. All such Houses are Nuisances in the Eye of the Common Law; and severe Punishments, as well on those who keep them, as on those who frequent and play at them, are inflicted by many Statutes. Of these Houses, Gentlemen, you will, I doubt not, enquire with great Diligence; for though possibly there may be some Offenders out of your Reach, yet if those within it be well and strictly prosecuted, it may, perhaps, in Time have some Effect on the others. Example in this Case may, [H-55] contrary to its general Course, move upwards; and Men may become ashamed of offending against those Laws with Impunity, by which they see their Inferiors brought to Punishment. But if this Effect should not be produced, yet, Gentlemen, there is no Reason why you should not exert your Duty as far as you are able, because you cannot extend it as far as you desire. And to say the Truth, to prevent Gaming among the lower Sort of People is principally the Business of Society; and for this plain Reason, because they are the most useful Members of the Society; which by such Means will lose the Benefit of their Labour. As for the Rich and Great, the Consequence is generally no other than the Exchange of Property from the Hands of a Fool into those of a Sharper, who is, perhaps, the more worthy of the two to enjoy it.

I WILL mention only one Article more, and that of a very high Na-[56]ture indeed. It is, Gentlemen, the Offence of Libelling, which is punished by the Common Law, as it tends immediately to Quarrels and Breaches of the Peace, and very often to Bloodshed and Murder itself.

[1] This argument, of a fury after pleasures, Fielding developed again in his *Enquiry into the Cause of the recent Increase of Robbers*...,1751. See my edition. of this text (Toulouse: P. U. M., 1989).

THE Punishment of this Offence, saith my Lord COKE, is Fine or Imprisonment; and if the Case be exorbitant, by Pillory and Loss of Ears.

AND, Gentlemen, even the last of these Judgments will appear extremely mild, if we consider in the first Place the atrocious Temper of Mind from which it proceeds.

Mr. PULTON, in the Beginning of his Treatise *de Pace*, says of a Libeller, "that he is a secret Canker, which concealeth his Name, hideth himself in a Corner, and privily stingeth his Neighbour in his Fame, Reputation, and Credit; who neither knows from whom, nor for what Cause he receiv- [H 2-57] eth his Blows, nor hath any Means to defend himself:" And my Lord COKE, in his 5th Report (125) compares him to a Poisoner, who is the meanest, the vilest, and most dangerous of all Murderers. Nor can I help repeating to you a most beautiful Passage in the great Orator DEMOSTHENES, who compares this Wretch to a Viper, which Men ought to crush where-ever they find him, without staying 'till he bite them.

IN the second Place, if we consider the Injury done by these Libellers, it must raise the Indignation of every honest and good Man: For what is this, but, as Mr. PULTON says, "a Note of Infamy, intended to defame the Person at whom it is levelled, to tread his Honour and Estimation in the Dust, to extirpate and root out his Reputation from the Face of the Earth, to make him a Scorn to his Enemies, and to be derided and despised by his Neighbours." [58]

IF Praise, and Honour, and Reputation, be so highly esteemed by the greatest and best of Men, that they are often the only Rewards which they propose to themselves, from the noblest Actions : If there be nothing too difficult, too dangerous, or too disagreeable for Men to encounter, in order to acquire and preserve these Rewards; what a Degree of Wickedness and Barbarity must it be unjustly and wantonly to strip Men of that on which they place so high a Value.

NOR is Reputation to be considered as a chimerical God, or as merely the Food of Vanity and Ambition. Our worldly Interests are closely connected with our Fame: By losing this, we are deprived of the chief Comforts of Society, particularly of that which is most dear to us, the Friendship and Love of all good and virtuous Men. Nay, the Common Law indulged so great a Privilege to Men of good Reputation in their Neighbourhood, that in many [59] Actions the Defendant's Words was taken in his own Cause, if he could bring a certain Number of his Neighbours to vouch that they believed him.

ON the contrary, whoever robs us of our good Name, doth not only expose us to public Contempt and Avoidance, but even to Punishment: For by the Statute 34 EDW. III. *c.* 1. the Justices of the Peace are empowered and directed to bind all such as be not of good Fame to their good Behaviour, and if they cannot sufficient Sureties, they may be committted to Prison.

SEEING, therefore, the execrable Mischiefs perpetrated by this secret Canker, this Viper, this Poisoner, in Society, we shall not wonder to hear him so severely condemned in Scripture; nor that ARISTOTLE in his Politics should mention Slander as one of those great Evils which it is difficult for a Legislator to guard against; that the *Athenians* punished it with a very severe [60] and heavy Fine, and the *Romans* with Death.

BUT tho' the Libeller of private Persons be so detestable a Vermin, yet is the Offence still capable of Aggravation, when the Poison is scattered upon public Persons and Magistrates. All such Reflections are, as my Lord COKE observes, a Scandal on the Government itself; And such Scandal tends not only to the Breach of the Peace, but to raise Seditions and Insurrections among the whole Body of the People.

AND, Gentlemen, the higher and greater the Magistrates be against whom such Slanders are propagated, the greater is the Danger to the Society; and such we find to have been the Sense of the Legislature in the 2nd Year of *R.* 2. For in the Statute of that Year, *chap.* 5. it is said, "that by such Means Discords may arise between the Lords and Commons whereof great Peril [61] and Mischief might come to all the Realm, and quick Subversion and Destruction of the said Realm." And of such Consequence was this apprehended to be, that we find no less than four Statutes to prohibit and punish it; *viz. Westm.* I *c.* 33. 2 *R.* 2 *c.* 5. 12 *R.* 2. *c.* 11 and 2 and 3 *P. & c M. c.* 12. By this last Statute a Jurisdiction was given to the Justices of Peace to enquire of all such Offences; and if it was by Book, Ballad, Letter or Writing, the Offender's Right-Hand was to be stricken off for the first Offence, and for the second he was to incur a Præmunire.

THIS last Statute was afterwards prolonged in the last Year of Q. MARY, and in the first of ELIZABETH, during the Life of that Princess, and of the Heirs of her Body.

I HAVE mentioned these Laws to you, Gentlemen, to shew you the Sense of our Ancestors of a Crime [62] which, I believe, they never saw carried to so flagitious a Height as it if [read: is] at present; when, to the Shame of the Age be it spoken, there are Men who make a Livelihood of Scandal. Most of these are Persons of the lowest Rank and Education, Men who lazily declining the Labour to which they were born and bred, save the Sweat of their Brows at the Expence of their Consciences; and in order to get a little better Livelihood, are content to get it, perhaps, in a less painful, but in a baser Way, than the meanest Mechanic.

OF these, Gentlemen, it is your Business to enquire; of the Devisers, of the Writers, of the Printers, and of the Publishers of all such Libels; and I do heartily recommend this Enquiry to your Care.

TO conclude, Gentlemen, you will consider yourselves as now summoned to the Execution of an Office, of the [I-63] utmost Importance to the well-being of this Community: Nor will you, I am confident, suffer that Establishment, so wisely and carefully regulated, and so stoutly and zealously maintained by your wise and brave Ancestors, to degenerate into mere Form and Shadow. Grand Juries, Gentlemen, are in Reality the only Censors of this Nation. As such, the Manners of the People are in your Hands, and in yours only. You, therefore, are the only Correctors of them. If you neglect your Duty, the certain Consequences to the Public are too apparent: For, as in a Garden, however well cultivated at first, if the Weeder's Care be omitted, the Hole must in Time be over-run with Weeds, and will resemble the Wilderness and Rudeness of a Desert; so if the Immoralities of the People, which will sprout up in the best Constitution, be not from Time to Time corrected by the Hand of Justice, they will at length grow up to the most enormous Vices, will overspread the whole Nation, and [64] in the end, must produce a downright State of wild and savage Barbarism.[1]

TO this Censorial Office, Gentlemen, you are called by our excellent Constitution. To execute this Duty with Vigilance, you are obliged by the Duty you owe both to God and to your Country. You are invested with full Power for the Purpose. This you have promised to do, under the sacred Sanction of an Oath; and you are all met, I doubt not, with a Disposition and Resolution to perform it, with that Zeal which I have endeavoured to recommend, and which the peculiar Licentiousness of the Age so strongly requires.

FINIS.

[1] Cf the same image in Shakespeare, *Richard II*, Act III, sc. 4, the garden scene.

THE **CHARGE** OF THE Right HONOURABLE ***Thomas Marlay***, Esq; LORD CHIEF JUSTICE of his MAJESTY's Court of *King's Bench* in the Kingdom of *Ireland*, TO The GRAND JURIES of the County of the City of *Dublin*, and County of *Dublin*; on the sixth of November 1749, and printed at the Request of the said GRAND JURIES. — (By Leave of the said Chief Justice). *DUBLIN*: Printed by OLI. NELSON, in *Skinner-Row*, 1749.

I Direct OLI. NELSON to print this Charge, and that no other print the same.

THO. MARLAY.

[A]

THE **CHARGE** OF THE Right HONOURABLE ***Thomas Marlay***, Esq; LORD CHIEF JUSTICE of his MAJESTY's Court of *King's-Bench* in the Kingdom of *Ireland, &c.*

Gentlemen of these several GRAND JURIES,

YOU are called here together, on an Occasion which, tho' it frequently, and regularly happens, is (especially at this Time,) of the greatest Importance to the Interest of your several Counties.

THE Prosperity of all Countries depends upon a wise Frame of Government, equal and [3] prudent Laws to regulate Property, and to restrain and punish Offenders, and a due and exact Execution of those Laws.

WITHOUT these Blessings, the Advantages of Climate, Situation, nay even of Trade, and Riches, contribute but little to the Happiness of a People, and very often serve only to promote Luxury, Sloth, Oppression, and Rapine among the Subjects at Home, and to encourage Insults, and Invasions from their Neighbours abroad. So that a *Land flowing with Milk and Honey*,[1] where the Government is ill formed, or ill administered, becomes a Curse to the Inhabitants.

OUR Constitution is so wisely fram'd, the Powers given to the several Parts of the Legislature so properly balanced, such Provisions made to preserve the Authority, and Person, of the Sovereign, to protect the

[1] Exod. 3: 8, 17, etc.

Lives, Liberties, and Properties, the Peace, Credit, and Reputation of the Subject, that all great Legislators, all wise Nations, have, in all Ages, rather propos'd, and wish'd for, than enjoy'd a Form of Government, modell'd like that at present established in *Great-Britain* and *Ireland*.

Of Consequence, our Laws, where the Representatives of the People, and the principal Men of the Kingdom, for so very many Centuries, have had such frequent Opportunities of Meeting, to consult, and deliberate upon, to alter, and amend the old Laws, and make new ones, with the Consent of their Kings, many of whom have been the best, as well as the [5] greatest, Princes in Europe, and, like our present Sovereign, have never refus'd, or omitted, to do every Thing for the Good of their People, are the most prudent, and equal, the least severe, and at the same Time the most just, and reasonable, of any in the World.

NO Tortures allow'd, (a Practice used in every other Country in *Europe*), no Man capitally punished, unless the *Grand Jury*, the principal Persons of the County, think the Accusation probable, nor unless the *Petty Jury*, his Equals, find him guilty.

THE Liberty, and Property of every Man, and his Reputation, as valuable as any Property, are secured with equal Care. Such is the Excellency of our Constitution, and of our Laws; as to the regular Execution of those Laws, in your several Counties, it depends upon you, Gentlemen.

YOU are under the highest Obligation, from the Oath you have now taken, from your Interest, from your Duty to your King, and from the Regard you each of you have to his Character, to omit Nothing, to do every Thing, that may preserve the Peace of your Country, *without Fear, Favour, or Affection*.

FOR this Purpose, you are to enquire into all Offences committed within your several Counties, whether Capital, or against the Peace. [1] [6]

THE Capital Offences in Ireland, such as are punished with Death, are either High-Treason, or Felony.

High-Treason is an Offence more immediately against the Person of the King, and most severely punished, because the Safety, Peace, and Tranquillity of the Kingdom is highly concerned, in the Preservation of his Person, Dignity, and Government; and because, as the Subject hath his Protection from the King, and his Laws, he is bound by his Allegiance to be true, and faithful, to his Sovereign.

YOU, Gentlemen, have so often served your Country, in this important Trust, have so often been put in Mind of the several Species, and Kinds, of Treason, ascertained by the Satute of *Ed.* 3. and enacted by

[1] This is another oversimplified way of classifying offences.

the several Statutes made in this Kingdom since this Time, that I shall not now enumerate them, nor the several particular Species of Felony.

BUT shall put you in Mind, that counterfeiting the Coin, is by that Statute of *Ed.* 3. Treason, and the Clipping, Diminishing of it, is by subsequent Statutes, of Force here, made the same Offence.

MONEY is the Common Measure, and Standard of all Commerce; and in all Countries, is, and ought to be, under the immediate Care, and Inspection of the Sovereign. The publick attest the Weight, and Fineness of it. The [7] Practice of filing, and washing Guineas, and Half-Guineas, tho' High-Treason by Law, has been of late too commonly practis'd in this Kingdom; the late Proclamation, offering a Reward and pardon, has not yet had Effect. To detect these Robbers of the Publick, and bring them to Punishment, is a Thing worthy of your Enquiry.

THE Persons of Kings are in all Monarchies held inviolable, and the Design to destroy them, if manifested by any Overt-Act, is by our Law justly punished with the utmost Severity; the infinite Confusions, which follow upon the Murder of a King, hinder often those Offenders from being punished at all, who can never be sufficiently punished.

AND levying War against the King, is not only High-Treason of itself, but an Overt-Act of compassing his Death.

WHEN Posterity read that in this Age, a Rebellion was carried on in *Great-Britain*, without the least Colour or Pretence, of Oppression; nay, by many who had not even that false Pretence of Religion to palliate their Treason, against a Prince, one of the best, the most merciful, just, and generous, of our Royal Line, who had given the Fortunes of all Criminals, whether forfeited for Crimes against the State, or for other Offences, to their Children, or Relations, (a Grace never practis'd before;) who has expos'd his Person at the Head of his Armies, in Defence of the Liberties of his Kingdoms, and of *Europe*; and that *Ireland*, where much the greatest Part of the Inhabi-[8] tants profess a Religion, which sometimes has authoris'd, or at least justified, Rebellion, not only preserv'd Peace at Home, but contributed to restore it among his Subjects of *Great-Britain*. [1]

WILL they not believe that the People of *Ireland* were actuated by something more than their Duty and Allegiance? Will they not be convinc'd, that they were animated by a generous Sense of Gratitude, and Zeal for their great Benefactor, and fully sensible of the Happiness of being bless'd by living under the protection of a Monarch, who like the glorious King *William*, the *Henries*, and *Edwards*, his Royal Predecessors, has himself led his Armies to Victory, and despis'd Danger in the Cause of his People; and one from whom we not only expect, but

[1] This panegyric of George II alludes to his behaviour during the crisis of 1745.

are assured of, a Race of Princes, equally eminent for their Generosity, Prudence, and Courage.

BUT will not they be, are we not ourselves, astonish'd to find, that in the Capital City of this Kingdom, a City the most distinguished for their Duty, Zeal, and Affection to their Sovereign, within less than three Years, publick Encouragement should be given, to a most infamous, inconsiderable, and impudent Scribbler[1], who has dar'd in print to menace his Majesty; has dared most falsely, and scandalously, to calumniate and traduce both Houses of Parliament, the King's Ministers, Lord Lieutenants, and all Magistrates from the highest to the lowest; nay who has dar'd to attempt the utter Subversion of our Constitution, and to bring us into absolute *Anarchy* [B-9] and *Confusion*; who has dared to prescribe a *solemn League*, and *Covenant*[2] to be taken by such as set up for Representatives in Parliament, or for the considerable and lucrative Offices in the City; tho' the Writ, which impowers the Choice of Members to serve in Parliament, directs that they shall have *full* Powers.

NAY this impudent Scribbler, tho' the Proctors of the Clergy are excluded the House of Commons by an Act of Parliament in this Kingdom, has dar'd to introduce not only them, but all who have a Right to vote, above one hundred and fifty Thousand, into the House of Commons as Assessors; and says *They have a Right to sit there, and to bear, and to observe the Conduct of their Representatives*: Where will he find a Place capable to receive them?

THIS is indeed preaching up Anarchy.

THIS Scribbler, this Impostor, has fled from Justice; his Works (but I hope not his Influence) remain.

I HOPE we shall be no longer seduced by the Name, the Shadow of Liberty, and by catching at it, lose the Substance.

LET no more *Lambert Symnels, Perkin Warbecks*, or Princes of *Passow*, be countenanced or encouraged among us.[3] *Let us at last awake and vindicate the Constitution.* [10]

WE are and shall always continue free, have the same Right to acquire Honours, and Estates, in *Great-Britain*, as well as *Ireland*, and to tax ourselves, as any of his Majesty's Subjects, unless this Impostor can procure *an Army, to lead on any Emergency he shall think fit*, it may be, to put

[1] Here a ms note, adding: C. Lucas [Charles Lucas, one of the companions of Henry Flood.]

[2] An allusion to the Solemn League and Covenant signed in 1643 by the Scots and the English Parliamentary leaders to establish the Presbyterian church in England.

[3] Under the reign of Henry VII Lambert Symnel (in 1487) and Perkin Warbeck (1491–99) respectively claimed they were the true heir to the throne, Symnel for being Edward, Earl of Warwick, nephew of Edward IV, and Warbeck, for being Richard, Duke of York, second son to Edward IV. Symnel confessed that he was a counterfeit, and was pardoned; Warbeck was executed. He had tried his luck in Ireland as well as in England.

to Death the Collectors of the Duties of Customs, Excise, and Hearth-Money, whom he declares Pirates, and Robbers; and the Acts of Parliaments they are impower'd by, made in this Kingdom in the Reign of Charles the Second, to be Anticonstitutional, and void; or prevail upon us to renounce our Connexion with *Great-Britain.*

BUT you may ask, Gentlemen, what can we do in this Case? This Impostor, this Seducer, this false Preacher, is already declar'd an Enemy to his Country, by the GRAND INQUEST of the Nation.

DON'T deceive yourselves, Gentlemen; his Papers remain, and there are some deluded People, who are not yet cur'd of their Infatuation. *Those who are not against him, are for him*[1]; and those who abet, or encourage him, are equally guilty, and deserve his Fate.

'Tis in your Power, it is your Duty, to present all seditious Libels, the Authors, Printers, and malicious Publishers of them, in your several Counties; and this brings me to mention the Nature of Libels. [11]

A LIBEL is a malicious Defamation of any Person dead or living, express'd either by Writing, Printing, or Picture, and is most severely punish'd by the Law, because of the direct Tendency to the Breach of the Peace.

THIS was always a dangerous Offence: but is much more so, since the Invention of Printing, and since Printing-Presses have been so common. And let me observe to you, Gentlemen, *That nothing can preserve the Liberty of the Press, but an effectual Restraint of the Licentiousness of Printing.*

HOW miserable must be the Condition of all Men, in a Country where every Garret-Scribbler, every one who employs those Hours he ought to spend in his Shop, in defaming and reviling his Neighbours, and all in Authority over him, instead of following his lawful Trade and Occupation!

PRINTERS and Hawkers for their Penny, and Half-penny, take infinite Care to propagate the Scandal, and the injur'd Person has but seldom the Opportunity of a Vindication.

IF Reputation be what every good and honest Man ought to value; if Fame, tho' not the best, be one of the most common Motives to Great and Laudable, nay even to Charitable Actions, how pernicious a Wretch, [12] how much an Enemy to Mankind, must he be, who endeavours to take away the very Incitements to do Good, and persuade the World to set no Value on Reputation; which, by these Means, is in the Power of every infamous Scribbler to destroy!

DOES not this tend to the Subversion of all Morality, the very Tie and Bond of Human Society? To perpetuate Animosities, and create eternal Breaches of the Peace among private Persons? And where Libels

[1] Cf. Mat. 12: 30.

are against the Government, they tend to the Subversion of it, in my Lord Chief Justice's *Holt* 's Opinion.

TAKE away the Credit of Magistrates, and you, in a great Measure, take away their Authority.

WHILE the Validity of Laws, and the Power of the Legislature, are thus publickly declaim'd against, and revil'd, nothing but Force and Violence must prevail, and Mankind must live in the Condition of Beasts of Prey.

SHALL our Governours, our Parliaments, our Magistrates, lose all the Reverence due to them, because some infamous Writers dare defame them?

ARE Printers to make and repeal Laws? Must one of the lowest and meanest of Tradesmen, without Learning, without any Oppor-[13] tunity of conversing with Men of Knowledge, and Experience, dictate from behind his Counter to the Government, to the Magistrates of his Country, and not only pretend to instruct, but reproach and vilify them?

I wish some of these Political Preachers, these Mountebank Politicians, had at least read *Æsop*'s Fables, and there remember'd the Story of the War between the Members and the Belly.

THIS might have cur'd them of their Affectation of *Independancy.*

INDEPENDANTS were the People, who in the last Age destroy'd the Constitution; the King, first, the establish'd, then the Presbyterian Church, and at last themselves, and who brought these Kingdoms under Tyranny, and arbitrary Power.[1]

GOD Almighty has so form'd the World, that all Things are dependant on him, and on one another. In each System of Beings all are moved and act in their proper Sphere, and each contributes to the Advantage and Preservation of the other.[2]

Subordination is as necessary in Government, as in Nature.

BUT, Gentlemen, I neither say, nor think, that Men of the meanest Parentage, or lowest Occupation, may not deserve the highest Em-[14] ployments, Honours: it is one of the happy Circumstances of our Constitution, that they are capable of both, where they have deserv'd them; *that all Men, by Virtue, may attain to Honour.*

But surely *Want of Birth*, and *Want of Education are not alone Merit* !

GENTLEMEN, I am fully convinc'd that not one in forty of the Followers of that infamous Scribbler, *who has now fled from Justice,* knew his Principles, or considered the Tendency of them.

BUT I fear there may yet be some few among us who hope to make

[1] This is an allusion to the various circumstances of the civil war and its consequences, in the 17th century.

[2] This is yet another illustration of the famous theory of the chain of being, for which see the study of A. O. Lovejoy, *The Great Chain of Being* (Harvard U.P., 1936 and 1964). Similar reflexions are to be found in Grose's text, 1796. See infra.

their Advantage by our Confusion, and these may have Followers; for as Liberty is the most justifiable Cause, 'tis the most specious Pretence.

EXERT yourselves, Gentlemen, free us from these insolent Libellers, these abandoned Printers, and Publishers, these *Jack Straws, Wat-Tylers*, and *Jack Cades* of the Age.[1]

EVERY Thing, that tends to the Breach of the peace, is under your Inspection; let these Miscreants see that you have a just Indignation against them and their Works, and that you are resolv'd to execute the great Trust committed to you, without *Fear, Favour, or Affection.*

FINIS.

[1] Leaders of revolts against the king's authority: Tyler in 1381, Cade, the mid-1450s.

Norfolk County Archives Reel 191/4 -Grand Jury Charges 1749-1767. MC 36/171, 484 x 1.

[f. 1.] Charge Sept 1749.

Gentlemen of ye Grand Jury

I am desird by the Court & in the Absence of the Recorder it is my Duty to give you in Charge those Matters referr'd to in ye Oath you have just now taken & to remind you of the Duty & nature of ye Service you are now ingag'd in, & of such Parts of our Constitution as relate thereto & this ~~present~~ [p.1 v] Assembly in Conformity to an Ancient Custom which does great Honour to his Majesty & his Government by permitting thus publickly & in his own Courts the Equity Justice & Extent of it to be inquir'd into, & a Sort of Appeal to be made to ~~you~~ & all ~~here~~ present for the Reasonableness of our Subjection & Correspondance betwixt the Government & ~~Governed~~ People [f. 2.] not to be found in any other Country or indeed practicable in any, but where the Extent of ye Royal Prerogative & the Obedience of the Subject is Limitted & Ascertain'd by ~~the~~ Law ~~of the Land~~ & where the King holds his Authority by the ~~glorious~~ noblest Tenure that of Protecting the Rights & Liberty's of his People, that this was always intended by our [f. 2 v] Constitution is Evident from the Nature of it, but never three together hardly two & seldom any one of our former Kings or rather their profligate Minions have been contented with this Sacred & Most Honorable Post ~~appears from~~ all our Historys agree in so that it is owing to the ~~Glorious~~ Brave Struggles of our Ancestors in former Ages particularly in the last & more especially in the latter part of it [f.3] that we have had this happiness during four successive Reigns & ever Since the Revolution ~~continu'd in this happy Situation for they~~ When on this Condition and for this very purpose they gave the Crown to our Glorious Deliverer and such of the then Royal Family as ~~were~~ coud answer this End & in default of the Issue by them to his Majesty & his descendants being the next Protestants in the Royal Line By that Act of Settlement referr'd to in our Oath of Allegiance and by which [f. 3 v] this Succession became & is the first Principle of our Constitution in Church & State, which can be preserv'd under none, if not under a Race of Kings made so for this express purpose, By our Constitution in Church I mean as well those Laws made for Restoring & preserving to our Dissenting Brethren the common

Rights of Mankind to [f. 4] Worship Almighty God in such manner as appears to them most worthy of him, so as their principles and & practice be not dangerous to Society, & which are now happily a part of our Constitution, as well, as those made for the Honour & Protection of ~~the Established~~ ye most Excellent & pious Form of Worship Establish'd in our National Churches, By our Constitution in State no Body [f. 4. v] can mistake me that I mean the Body of Laws by which this Nation under his Majesty is Govern'd in its Civil consider'd distinct from its Religious concerns & particularly that part of them call'd the Crown Law which we are here assembled to inforce in this Jurisdiction as a Court of Oyer & Terminer & General Gaol Delivery. The Excellency of [f.5] this part of the Law consists not so much in punishing and restraining the Violent & open or the secret Invasion of the profligate & Wicked on our persons & properties, Which all Societies even those of Banditti themselves provide against & which an Absolute Government can prevent perhaps better than a Limitted one, but in ~~preventing~~ this that it is effectiually secured from being Subservient [f. 5.v] to the designs of the Ambitious & the Malice and Caprice of the great, and that whilst they are pretending to punish the Guilty they may be prevented from oppressing the Innocent, 'tis in this that the Security of our Lives and property & consequently our Liberty & Happiness as a People consist, And that we do not without Reason Value ourselves on the [f.6.] possession of this Happiness will appear from Considering where the Power of Judgment is plac'd with us & What helps there are in our manners & forms of Administration of Justice to the impartial Discharge of it & protection of the Innocent beyond what now is or ever was in any other Nation - Now with us Courts are open & never held but after [f.6.v] publick Notice or at stated Times where the Friends and Witnesses of the Accused & Accuser have equally access and Admittance, And are heard with equal indifference and impartiallity, but with them Justice, as they call it, is dispatchd not only in private Courts but in matters which relate to the publick & which require therefore the freest Examination [f.7] and Tryal in private Rooms and where the Friends of the Accus'd are so far from having access that without any Notice of the Place or Time of their Tryal they are frequently for the first time inform'd of their Fate by seeing them led to Execution nay sometimes they are actually executed before they know that they are Condemn'd —— With us the [f.7 v] Witnesses are publickly produc'd and confronted by the prisoner, Their Examination is free & not the Effect of that Infernal practice, Torture & the Wrack, & the Accus'd have not only the Encouragement but the Authority of the Court to compel such to appear ~~for them but~~ & be in like manner examin'd on their behalf as he desires; whilst, with them the Witnesses' Names or [f.8] their Depositions are seldom known or publish'd in State Affairs, except as an Extraordinary favour, & their Evidence is forc'd from them by Torture & Terror & a Witness appearing for them would only involve himself in the same misfortune with him. Our Judges are taken from amongst those who have made the Study of the Law the Business of their Lives, are constituted for Life & with such Honours & Allowances as (exclusive from further Favours from the Crown) [f.8 v] may well enable & encourage them to discharge their Trust faithfully, they are instructed and all the World can witness to their Honour, that they do consider themselves as the Councel of the Accus'd & that as such they are to exert all their knowledge & urge every thing that can fairly make for them in their Favour & whatever Opinion they give it is in open Court & with a Declar^t of the reason found^t of their Judgt [f.9] But Their Judges are chosen for the very purpose of murdering by Law the best of Mankind, when they presume to oppose the Worst, who have the power of appointing them as best serves their purpose from amongst the weak wretched or Cruel & perhaps known Enemys of ye Accused subject not only to be displac'd but in their Turn oppress'd if they prove refractory or unwilling to go through with their [f.9 v] Masters Drudgery and no Reason is ever by them given for their Judgment wt is also deliverd privately; With us the Charge is plain and founded on the Oaths of at least Twelve impartial Neighbors & on some known Law, with them it is Dark & Ambiguous subject to any construction these Worthy Judges will put upon it & made by an unknown Accuser. Had we therefore no other Security for an impartial Tryal [f.10] than these Circumstances an Englishman might justly be the envy of the rest of the world, But all this is inconsiderable to the most able and Valuable Right of Tryal by Jury as it is secur'd to us by that most excellent Law of the Habeas Corpus Act; This Blessing by which we are distinguish'd from all other Nations we owe to the Wisdom and [f.10 v] Foresight of our Saxon Ancestors who finding that all the Governments that had ever existed had degenerated into ~~Tyranny~~ Arbitrary power & its certain consequence Slavery, devis'd & form'd a new sort of Government by extracting what was Good from all others with such Additions as were thought Sufficient to make it morally perfect. They temper'd the Violence of the People [f.11] with the Dignity and Gravity of the Nobility, and check~~ding~~ their insolent pride with the Freedom & Liberty of the Community and regulated the whole with the Authority of the ~~King whom~~ Crown which they ~~would have~~ made Hereditary to deprive the Wickedly Ambitious from disturbing the peace of the Kingdom [f.11 v] & accordingly distributed the several parts of Government and particularly with regard to Judicial Matters which consists either in enacting Laws in Judging viz In pronouncing those Guilty or Innocent who stand accus'd of the Breach of them or in punishing those adjudg'd Guilty as was most suitable to the preservation and the security of the [f.12] Liberty of the Subject therefore they allowed the Nobility & Com[mon]s to enact

Laws with the consent of the King to whom they gave all the Honour of Governmt & appointed that the Courts & Laws should be in his Name & under his protection & Direction & as the Father of his People that he might endear himself to them permitted him only to moderate the Severity of the Law by the [f.12 v] heavenly Attribute of Mercy which they left wholly in him, but the great & most important part that of Judgment they tho't would never be so impartially executed as by the people themselves & that if they parted with it as other Nations had done, all the other Fences of the Liberty of the Subject wou'd be easily broke down they therefore [f.13] by their Original Contract reserv'd their power wholly in the Countrey or People in England & this appears from the form & Substance of our Tryals, The Accus'd here are not to depend on the Judgment of the King or his Ministers but of their Countrey & Fellow-Subjects for their acquital or Condemnation, The Jury are told that they are this Country & that they [f. 13 v] are to determine not for but betwixt the King & the prisoner & to pronounce him Guilty or Innocent & without whose Leave & Consent our King can punish no Man, from hence it appears that the Station of a Juryman is the most Honourable Useful & Important that a Subject can be in & that in the Institution of a Jury more properly than elsewhere may be found what [f.14] was lately call'd in the house of Commons the Majesty of the People of England & that of a petty Juryman is not less than that of the ~~Grand~~ other Jurymen from whose Judgment ye Appeal is made to them, and of this being the Case no Gentleman of this Town can sure think it any Disparagement to him to perform this Duty when he is wanted in capital Cases & as it is most unreasonable [f.14 v] to excuse himself from an Attendance on this Court by which they are exempted from a much more burdensome one on others ~~& for my own part~~ I shall think myself obliged to require & enforce it because I am persuaded I can never discharge the great trust committed to me so much to the honour & reputation of this Jurisdiction as with such Assistance [f.15] I should now proceed to show you how very greatly the H[abeas] C[orpus] Act is instrumental in securing to us these invaluable Rights but that wou'd be trespassing too much on your patience. I can now only refer you to the preamble of ye Act pass'd ye 32nd Car. 2 for the many Evasions by which the Benefit of this Tryal was eluded & to the Act itself for the provisions by which it is [f.15] secur'd & was thereby a very great means of bringing about the Revolution & ~~to~~ I proceed to that wch I mention'd as one of the privileges of an Englishman who is as such not only to be try'd but accus'd by his Fellow-Subjects this Gentlemen is your province & you are to try that inestimable Jewel Reputation & to enquire whether the Accusation is grounded on real Facts & proof of guilt or owing to Malice [f.16] revenge or private Resentment ~~if the former appears to you to be the case you are to consent to & authorise~~

~~this Court to proceed to the Tryal but if the latter you are to~~ & accordingly allow of or dismiss the Charge & save the Accus'd from the Burden of a Publick Tryal ~~and~~ consequently your Deliberations must be private But this great Charge is intrusted with you [f.16 v] under such Obligations to an impartial Discharge of your Duty yt it is manifest a publick acquittal from such unfortunate Circumstances or impious Perjury's as can induce you to think him guilty is become absolutely necessary for the sake of ye Innocent Accus'd or to satisfy ye Justice due to ye Publick by the Condemnation of ye real Guilty. For you are to [f.17] enquire viz Examine not carelessly or Indolently but diligently ~~into the Foundation & proofs but or which of your own knowledge may be in support of any Bill of Accus. & consider of the Circumstances & facts attested by and thereby or from their known characters to~~ and then Judge of the Credibility of the Witnesses & Facts asserted by them ~~whereby this means you are fully~~ and [f.17 v] being satisfy'd of the Truth of ye Charg you are to present it to this Court as such ~~I say Gentlemen fully satisfy'd for tho' it is sometimes said that a probable Ground is sufficient yet it is to be consider'd yt you~~ upon your Oaths assert the fact to have been committed ~~it is absurd to say you only~~ not that it has been probably or as you only suspect or slightly believe it & therefore you are [f.18] not to present a Bill as true till you have such a Satisfaction by the Evidence as wou'd in your Opinion be Sufficient to Convict the Party upon his Trial if he had nothing to alledge in his defence that this conviction is the Truth, wh you are sworn to present is manifestly prov'd by Sr John Hawles in the case of the Ld Shaftsbury & that to [f.18 v] allow of any less is to destroy the very end of a Grand Jury; & besides Gentlemen it may be of great disservice to the Publick Justice to present Bills on imperfect Evidence for the Guilty may thereby & do too often Escape. But whatever your Reasons be for finding a Bill or not whether from the Evidence or your own or your fellow Jurors Knowledge & Opinions[f.19] notwithstanding the strange practice to the Contrary in defiance of the clearest part of your Oaths You are to keep ye same Secret if not always wh I think ~~you are bound to do~~ best at least 'till the matter in Question is finally determin'd, to disclose the Evidence given to a Grand Jury was formerly esteem'd Felonious & is now punishable as a great Misdemeanour & most [f.19 v] ~~justly~~ deservedly for if it be dishonoble to discover what passes or is said in a private Room or Clubb it ought to be esteem'd infamous to do so out of ~~a~~ Company call'd together by Publick Authority & where every one is oblig'd to disclose & speak his true & real Sentiments -- And that you may ~~be under the most solemn obligation to~~ discharge this Office as good Men you swear to lay [f. 20] aside all Malice & Hatred, & to be free from the biass of Favour or Affection & especially of Reward, yt is any advantage to arise to you from the determination of the matter in question & to use your utmost Skill in discharging faithfully your trust, The matters you are to enquire of are in general all Sort of Crimes and Offences committed either against the Antient & Common or [f.20 v] the Statute Laws of this Kingdom they ~~are~~ may be more particularly ~~distinguished~~ divided into Offences against Religion against the King's Person & Government or against the Lives Persons Habitations & Property's of the Subjects --Those against Religion I mention in the first place from the Dignity of ye Subject not that with regard to temporal Punishment they are [f.21] now of so great consequence for tho' under the two Capital Offences of Heresy & Whitchcraft but particularly from the 2 Hen 4th wn they first ~~Law that~~ were enabl'd ~~them~~ to burn Hereticks was the common pretence by wh the Popish Clergy made dreadful havock wth all the Good & Pious that differ'd from them ~~by pronouncing them full of Church Treason which they call'd~~ of Heresy ~~tho' what it was no more than Treason is in other Countreys was never defin'd & then by delivering them~~[f. 21 v] ~~over to the Flames by means of their executing the Laity not the Venom of this proceeding was~~ Yet the Danger was in great Measure eradicated in the first of Q. Eliz. when Heresy & the proceedings on it were Limitted & ascertained & the Sting finally taken away by ye 29th Car. 2. which abolish'd all Capital Punishment in pursuance of Eccl.[l] Censures & left the Clergy to make what they [f.22] wou'd of it in their own Courts & we pleasantly enough are now quitt of the other ~~Capital Offence of Witchcraft~~ ~~tho' that constituted till his present Majesty's Reign~~ for by the 9 Geo. I. it is now no Offence to be but to pretend to be a Witch & to tell fortunes & ye like is by that Statute most severely punisht all inferior Offences relating meerly to Religion are only such as are affronts & disturbances of the practice of piety & Religion such as Ludicrous and Profane Songs & Plays reflecting upon [f.22] the Establish'd Church not Resorting to any Church or protestant Place of wors[h] which are punishable by 1 Eliz or Offences against the 9 & 10 Wm as Blasphemy or profaneness & especially Books wrote against the being and Attributes of Almighty God ye Doctrines of the holy Trinity the Christian Religion & the divine Authority of the holy Scripture yet that must [f.23] be intended of such ~~Books~~ as are wrote in a Ludicrous & profane way by no means suitably to the sacredness and importance of the subject & not to a candid serious & decent argumentation of even those sacred Truths, you a~~re al~~ways also to present ye Offences mention'd in his Majesty's proclamation All reviling the Sacrament of the Lord's Supper profane cursing & Swearing & Sabbath [f.23 v] breaking & Drunkenness & all open & scandalous Acts of profaneness & Lewdness & particularly the nurseries of them all lewd & Disorderly Houses whether publick or private - Offences against the King & his Government are either high Treason which in other Nations is almost any thing the Government please to call so but with us is described & ascertain'd by [f.24] 25th

Edw. 3 ~~or subsequent~~ & Statutes Subsequent to ye 1 Mary wch chiefly relate to Dangers from the Popish Religion or the Popish Pretender & his Adherents either in or out of the Kingdom or Contempts against the King's Authority in his Palace or Courts of Justice but which I need not particularly enumerate because I can't suspect any such Offences can be committed in [f. 24 v] this Loyal & Protestant Town or if there were it wou'd not be proper to try them before any but the Rever'd ye Judges of the Kingdom. Offences against the Subject are either ~~against his Life~~ Homicide wn comitt'd with express or imply'd [intent] is term'd as Murder ~~which~~ when committed by a Servant on his Master or Mistress a Wife on her Husband or a Clergyman on his Prelate is petty Treason. [f.25] & Manslaughter or in defence of himself his Person or Habitation or by Misadventure ~~or~~ Offences against his Habitation are Burglary which is the breaking or entring a dwelling House in the Night Time with intent to commit tho' no felony be actually Committed or by wilfully setting fire to it all which are most [f. 25 v] justly Capital Offences as al~~ways~~ so the detestable Crime of Sodomy & the cruel one of Rape which is the knowing a Woman against her Will if above the Age of 10 Years or ~~of her~~ either With or Without her Will if a Child under that Age when she ~~can't be presumed to~~ is not allowed to give her Consent as also many a Woman another Sort of Rape against her Will Other Offences [f.26] are Thefts or as we call them Larcenary meerly so, or mix'd and attended with such Circumstances as render them Capital or at least more heinous the first & ~~most heinous~~ greatest of which is Robbery this is a Violent taking from the person or in his presence any part of his property after putting him in fear & it differs from other Felony's in that however small the thing taken be it is robbery & Capital with these Circumstances whereas in others ~~Felonys~~ there must [f.26 v] be some certain value taken 12 at the least & so up to 40 s or more & by a late Act even the Assault & putting in fear with intent to rob is also Felony. When this Robbery is committed in or near a Highway it is made Capital by the 23rd Hen. 8. When a Robbery is committed by privately stealing from the Person tho' without Violence & Terror it is ~~always~~ also Capital by the [f.27] 8 Eliz ~~if it is to the value of 12 or more~~; And in like Manner all Robbery in Dwelling Houses by Night or Day or in a Booth or Tent in a Fair or Market ~~Whilst the owner his Wife Children or Servant are therein & ye~~ accessorys before or after is also by several Statutes made Capital. Before I quit these Capital Offences I can't [f.27 v] omit mentioning some that the Misfortunes of our Times have produc'd, but wch do not fall under any of these Heads ~~I have mention'd~~ as the too common Offence of 3 or more Assembling together to Aid or Assist in running Goods which is a Species of Treason as it is carry'd on in defiance of Governmt & is therefore justly & of Necessity made Capital & I mention this not so much for the [f.28] Sake of the

Guilty who before they can become so in this manner must be desperate & incorrigible but to warn their unwary Friends & Acquaintance from giving them Assistance to escape from Justice either by harboring on them secreting them till a proper time or by furnishing them with Money or other helps to get off especially when process is out ~~against them~~ & the Officer thereby prevented from taking them [f.28 v] for by so doing they will involve themselves in the same punishment tho' innocent of their Crime. Riotously Assembling together & but beginning to pull down any Religious Place of Worship or dwelling or Work-house is also made Capital or even Countinuing so Assembled for the Space of one hour after Notice given from the Magistrate to depart [note: 22 & 23 Car. 2. 1 Annæ Stat. 2 c. 9.] [f.29] Offences not Capital are either Misprisions by concealing Felonys & encourage'g and assist'g the perpetrators of them either before or after the Commitment thereof where they are not by so doing made accessary as in most Cases they are Or they are such as amount to a Breach of the Peace ~~cannot~~ committed by one or more as Assaults Batterys Affrays forcible entrys & [f.29 v] Detaining & Riots Routs Unlawful Assembly's or meer Misdemeanours without Violence where there is no Breach of the Peace such as Bribery & Extortion in the Officers & publick Ministers of Justice by taking Fees where none are due or more than their due Or by other Persons either such as are grossly infamous & Scandalous as Perjury Forgery notorious Cheats & Conspiracy's [f.30 not numbered] & Contrivances for that purpose & Libells & defaming Others whether by printing writ'g, or other abusive descriptions as dr'g them hang'g on the Gallows or in ye Pillory or the like which must not be permitted for the sake of Society even where the Object ever so well deserves it for that the Law is to determine ~~if~~ such Offences as are not in their [f. 30 v] nature infamous but are detrimental to the general Order & good of Society such as Nusances in High Ways or Bridges publick Keys & Commons, disorderly publick Houses & Tavern & Gaming Houses Trades or Employments carryd on in such manner as to be dangerous to the Health or Habitations of the Neighbourhood Monopolies Forestalling regretting & engrossing [f.31] [another handwriting] using false weights & Usury wh bear hard upon & are in their Consequences the certain ruine of the Poor Barratry & the like whereby the Law wh shoud be the protector is turnd to the ruine of many. To enter more minutely into these several crimes woud be ~~a means of~~ the preventing and of promoting the end of this Assembly by delaing you too long from business & it is unnecessary as the Court will readily explain & clear up any Doubts you may be under as soon as informd of them. You may therefore now proceed to consider of these matters & when you have compleated your Exa'n you may depend on being dismissd from any further Attendance.

[f. 1] **1750** [no other mention; in another writing]

Gentlemen of the Grand Jury

You are now under the most sacred obligation to assist this Court of O. & T. by presenting to it those matters which I am directed to give you in Charge after a Carefull and attentive Examin^{n} that is diligent Enquiry & after a free debate which is evident can never be fully so unless secret, so that to discover what passes on this occasion woud be dishonourable if the clearest part of your Oath did not make it wicked, perhaps at any Time which if it can be avoided I think most adviseable, but at least [f.1. v] till the matter is finally determind to disclose what passes amongst you was formerly esteemed felonious and is at this Time very Penal. As Honest Men you are required and I doubt not will steadily pursue that excellent Directory your Oath and lay aside not only all resentmt & Malice but even that Favour & Affection which ye English good Nature ~~of an Englishman~~ can't refuse even to ye Guilty For you will consider that such Compassion at this Time is Injustice to the rest of Mankind [f.2.] And therefore should any of you be in such a situation that may induce a Suspicion of your being interested in the Affair in Question or that you are affected by any particular Circumstances to favour or prejudice to the party accused it will be decent to retire from your Fellows whilst his Case is under their Consideration. The truth requird by your Oath and on which you positively assert the Charge is such a Belief of it as may induce the other Jury to affirm your Verdict when travers'd by the Prisoner. [f.2 v] If nothing further is alledg'd by him in his Defence than what you are appriz'd of To find a Bill on probable Evidence not sufficient in your Opinion (tho uncontradicted) to convict besides the wicked Absurdity of affirming on Oath what you are not fully satisfyed is true, may be very Detrimental to the Prisoner if innocent, who ought to be protected in that Case by you the Guardians of his Reputation and to be dismiss'd in the first instance without the [f.3] Fatigue and Ignominy of a publick Trial, and if Guilty the Publick may be deprived of the Justice due to them by a premature prosecution For you cannot presume that fuller Evidence will be offer'd ~~to the~~ in Court than is given to you. Having ment'd these general Rules for your Conduct & before I proceed to the particulars of your Charge give me leave in conformity to an Ancient and laudable Custom on these publick occasions and which does Honour to his Majesty's Governmt to observe as farr as the Time will permitt me on the Nature & excellency [f.3 v] of the Executive Part of our Constitution in Criminal Matters

[Marginal note: The Crown Law] to inforce which pursuant to the very extensive Powers granted to this Corporation is the Business of this

Assembly. Now this Excellency consists not so much in punishing and restraining any attacks upon his Majestys Person and Governmt. & the open and violent or the secret Invasion of the Profligate on our Persons & Properties which all Governmts and Societys provide agt & which an absolute Governmt can [f.4] Perhaps better prevent than a limitted one as no express Law can so fully take in every Case as a Judgmt upon ye Particular Circumstances of it but in this - that it is effectually secured from being Subservient to the designs of the Ambitious the Malice or Caprice of the Great or the wicked Conspiracy of the little and that whilst they pretend to punish the Guilty they may be prevented from oppressing the Innocent. For by this Security of our Lives and Propertys & dependance of Protection whilst we [f.4 v] Do not offend against any known Law and consequently our Liberty & happiness as Freemen is seen & felt. Whether this be our Case must be known by considering the form & manner of Administration of Justice and in whom the right of judging is placed with us and how far in these particulars it excells or is inferior to the Laws of other Countrys This Enquiry will afford us a most pleasing Satisfaction and cannot but be the best because the most [f.5] Rational Reason & Encouragement for us to do ~~for~~ & even risque~~ing~~ Every Thing in support of it as Every Thing worth possessing is secured by it For here we shall find the Courts of Justice are ~~open~~ held after a Sufficient Publick Notice or at stated Times openly & to which the Friends and Witnesses of the accused and the accused have the same access & Admittance and are heard with equal indifference and impartiality that here ye Witnesses on either Side are publickly produced confronted and sifted free from all Terror and Violence not only of that [f. 5 v] Infernal and in other Countries universal Practice of Torture & Rack but as farr as human Prudence can guard against the least Byass or influence where the accused have not only the encouragement but the authority of the Court to compell Witnesses to appear for them. The Judges are those who have made the Study of the Law the Business of their Lives they are not removable at the pleasure of the Prince & have such Honours and Allowances as without further expectations may [f.6] Well enable & encourage them to discharge their Trust faithfully They are required & nothing is better known than that they do consider themselves as Counsell for ye Prisoner and that not to exert all their knowledge and urge every thing that can fairly make for his Defence is a high imputation upon their Ability & integrity, their Conduct & their Opinions, & the Reason for their Judgmts are given & submitted to the Publick a greater Security than which can not be against a bad Heart or weak head or more likely to procure [f.6 v] the Removal of such a Monster or misfortune ~~that may~~ if it ever intrude and gain a place on our Benches. No person can be accused unless by the Oath of Twelve at least of the most considerable & impartial of his Countrymen & on a

Charge grounded on some known Law. I will not at this time enlarge on these Circumstances As the bare mention of them are sufficient to prove the impartiality of our Tryals and for which an Englishman might justly be ye Envy of all other Nations where the [f.7] Contrary practices in almost Every one of these particulars prevail And as they are altogether inconsiderable to the great Priviledge our Speedy & effectual Tryal or discharge by the provisions of the habeas Corp: Act and by our Glory & peculiar Right of Tryal by our own selves commonly called the Jury who are the actual Representative of the Country. This Blessing by which we are distinguished from all other Nations we owe to the Wisdom & foresight of our Saxon Ancestors who finding that all the Governmts which had ever [f.7 v] Existed had degenerated into Arbitrary power and its certain Consequence Slavery having devis'd a new form of Governmt extracted what was good from all others ~~with such~~ & added such as were tho^{t} sufficient to make it morally perfect Thus they temper'd the violence of the people with the Dignity of the Nobility and check'd their insolence and Pride with the freedom and liberty of the Commons and restrained the whole with the Authority of the Crown which they made hereditary [f.8] to Deprive the wickedly ambitious from disturbing the Peace of ye Kingdom ye Consequence of all Elective Monarch^{es}. In Judicial Matters as ~~a Bill~~ well as in the other parts of the Constitution they placed all the Honour of Governmt in the King and appointd the Laws ~~should~~ to be enacted & Courts held in his Name and under his protection & direction ~~and that~~ but as the Father of his People & that he might endear himself to them permitted him only to moderate ye severity of the Law by the Heavenly Atribute of Mercy Yet the Power & Majesty of [f.8 v] Judgemt they by their original Contract reserved to and wholly placed in the Country or People of England this appears from the form and substance of our Tryals where the accused do not depend on the King or his Ministers but on the Judgmt of his Fellow Subjects under ye direction of Gods good Providence or as we express it on God and his Country for his deliverance The Jury are told (as the fact is) that they are the Country on which he hath put himself for [f.9] Good or ill and that they are to determine not for but betwixt him and the King and pronounce him guilty or innocent of ye Charge This is such a Publick Acknowledgmt of the Majesty of the People of England and that without their Authority the King himself can punish no Man as is not to be found at this Time in any other Constitution and even what appearance there was of it in the ancient Roman or Græcian States was so partial and imperfect that it can bear no Comparison with ours. How great then is the indolence of [f.9 v] Leaving ye important and most Honourable Station of a Juryman in Capital Cases to the most inferior illiterate and perhaps stupid of the Comunity that this has not been generally the Case in this Borough has been very much to their

Creditt and when their [sic] is such a Weight of Business as now appears on the Kalendar it cannot but be very greatly to the Honour & Reputa^{n} of the Publick Justice of this Town that the Pannell is composed of its principal inhabitants and as [f.10] their Attendance on ye Publick behalf will in a particular manner deserve the thanks of the Court in General ~~on the publick behalf~~ I cant help this early expressing for my own part the very great obligation and satisfaction I shall have in finding the Absence of the Revd & learned the Judges and my own incapacity in the Tryal of such Capital Offences so well supplyed if not improv'd but lett it always be remembere'd that all this noble Structure and Barrier of our Libertys might as it has been [f.10 v] become Insufficient witht the Hab. Corp. Act for by this only can we be assur'd of the Benefit and Comand ye use of it By this most excellent Law it is enacted under ye heaviest Penaltys that the Chancellor & Judges on Application to any of them shall grant ye Writt of H.C. in favour of any person not in Prison for a Treason or Felony plainly exprest in their Warrt or order of Comittmt. and that every [f.11] Gaoler shall within Three Days or more according to ye distance obey such Writt by bringing his Prisoner to ye Judge who order'd it who is thereupon to Bail him if his Case allows it and who is not to be again Comitted for the same offence or Charge tho Colourably varyd in form And that no Person shall be imprison'd in Scotland Ireland or any other of His Majesties Dominions or Garisons beyond Sea or removed from one Prison to another but in ye reasonable & necessary Cases excepted in the Act and no [f.11 v] Pretence after the Assize is proclaim'd but to be brought to that Court & there openly dealt with according to Law. Gaolers are also to deliver within Six hours after demand to ye Prisoner or any Person requesting it on his behalf a Copy of ye Warrt or order by which he detains him and that those who are comitted for offences not Bailable may have speedy deliverance it is provided that upon their Prayer or Petition in open Court the first day of the Sessions of O. T. & G.D. or the first Week ~~of~~ in any Term to be tryed they shall be Indicted & tryed [yt] Session [f.12] or discharged on the last Day thereof unless it be proved on Oath that the Witnesses coud not be ready and even then if not tryed and convicted the 2d Term or Session shall be discharged. these Gentn are the great Priviledges of this Law which may be justly termed the 2d Great Charter and cannot be too much valued by us the Protection of which has been claimed by the greatest of our Nobles even in the Reign of King William

The Priviledges procured to us by it are such that tho' [f. 12 v] it is Evident they ought to be enjoyed by every free People yet they never were so by any either antient or modern till we had obtained this Law by the glorious Struggle of ye Patriots of those Days & ye Providential Pleasantry or if K.R. Author of our History tells us of one of them so near were we loosing this great national Blessing ye want of wch had been felt so severely felt by the best of our Ancestors in the last Age and amongst the rest [f.13] By the Great Selden who under the pressure of a 16 Years Imprisonment on ye false Charge of moving Sedition & in which but for the interposition of the Long Parliament he had probably spent all his Life had yt greatness of mind to exert all his vast Abilities & knowledge for the Honour of his King & Country in many but particularly that Treatise of his in which he asserts the Dominion of the British Fishery. I proceed now to be the subject matter of your Enquiry which is in [f. 13 v] General by whom any sort Crimes have been comitted agt either ye antient Common or Statute Law & which relate to his Majestys Person & Governmt. the Lives Persons Habitations & Properties of the Subject or against Religion in Reverence to which they are first to be consider'd tho' as to Temporal Punishmts they are now inconsiderable. Under ye Papal Tyranny Heresy and [f.14] Witchcraft were terrible Instrumts to destroy every good and pious Man that differd from them but all Capital Punishmts of Ecclesiasticall Censures were abolished by ye 29 Car 2d. It is at this Time no offence to be a Witch but to pretend to be so which is very penall by ye 9 Geo: 2d ~~and~~ so that it is now established as the indefeasible Right of every man that ~~every mortal~~ he may worship Almighty God in the Way he Judges most Worthy of him provided he does not disturb [f.14 v] or Endanger ye Peace of the Society And all offences relating merely to Religion are reduced to such as are Affronts and Disturbances to ye general Practice of Piety such as Ludicrous & Prophane Plays & Songs reflecting on ye Established Church Blasphemy or prophaneness & especially Books wrote agt ye being & Attributes of Almighty God ye Doctrines of ye Holy Trinity ye Christian Religion & ye Divine [f.15] Authority of the Holy Scripture by which is intended such as are not wrote with a Candour Seriousness & Decency suitable to those Sacred & important Subjects which in this way may be enquir'd into for their more evident manifestation as we find by Dayly experience. You are also to present ye Offences mentd in his Majesties [f.15 v] Proclamation now read all reviling of ye Sacramt of ye Lords Supper prophane cursing and swearing Sabbath breaking & Drunkenness and all open and scandalous Arts of prophaneness & Lewdness & particularly ye Nurserys thereof all Lewd and disorderly Houses whether publick or private Offences agt the King Vide ye former Charge [Feb.?/ Fol.?] 23e

11th Sep 1751

[f.1] *Gentlemen of ye Grand Jury*

You are now by that excellent Sumy of your duty the Oath wch has been administd to you under the most sacrd Obligations to assist this Court by diligently & carefully & attentively to enquire after & present whether any of the offences & Misdeamrs I am directed by this Court to give you in charge have been & by wh[om] committed & done in this Jurisdiction who You probably or even vehemently suspect to be guilty, but such as woud from what you know, or shall have given you in Evidence be by you [f.1 v] pronounced Guilty on their Traverse if Nothing further was offer'd in their defence, To say otherwise is to affirm that for truth on your Oaths wn you only suspect to be so & thereby contrary to the very end of your Inst (wch is to be ye Guardians of the reputation of Mankind & to protect) you may put an Innocent Person in hazard of his Life or at least subject him to ye Ignominy & disgrace of appearing as a Criminal, or by a premature Trial suffer a very guilty one to escape, That you may be fully inform'd & assisted in this Enquiry & free from any restraint you are required to conceal the Kings council i.e. the Evidence & ye opinions of your selves & your Brethren, To discover [f.2] This after such an Engagement is wicked, & without it woud be dishrble [dishonourable] & mischevious It was formerly deemd felonious, & is now highly pœnal notwithstanding the strange practice to yr contrary on this and other occasions where Oaths of Office tho explicit & clear are impiously disreguarded; I'm perswaded I need not remind you to lay aside malice & Revenge & shall rather press you not to let the good nature of Englishmen too far biass & prevent you, from bringing to Justice those who are proper Objects of it & particularly the Offenders agst ye Peace decency & good order of Society. The natural & most certain Seminarys of all other Crimes & indeed tis by this Enquiry that you must at this time discharge your Duty to God & [f.2 v] & your Country as I have the pleasure to observe very few of ye greater crimes in ye Calendar but before I mention ye particulars of your Charge let me remind you & let us all rejoyce in the exercise of that great Nationl Blessing the Judicial part of our Constitution wch we are now Assembled to execute & wch therefore more immediately deserves our present Consid. The Excellency of the pride & glory of an Englishman appears from ye nature of it by wch contrary to that of all other Nations, The Right of Judgement is reserved & remains in the people where reason & experience assure us it is best placed For give it to the King, tho we might be at ease during his Majestys reign, we must tremble for our selves [f.3] or our Posterity under such of his Successors as will not remember his Example. Give it to ye Nobility tho those in this Country have contributed more to its Libertys than those of other Nations have done for theirs, yet the Consequence is most obvious from ye Experience of all Ages & People by whom they have been found excellent Legislators but very different Judges. Keep it where it now is by the method of Jury who are a fair unexceptionable representative of the people & Country & its blessing & influence may be derived from us to our latest Posterity for it is one of the few Institutions that cant [f.3 v] degenerate to ye Injury of those it shoud protect, unless they will themselves desert this most Hble Post & thro' Indolence or worse motives leave it to be executed by the weak or wicked, but this I may reasonably hope will never happen in this Jurisdiction, from ye chearful & most laudible example & (with a single exception) unanimous compliance of its principal Inhabts by their attendance on ye last Genl Sess when the Capital Criminals then before the Court required ye Assistance of those, who by their Inward Integrity & Ability might insure the Equity & candour of & in spite of the mis-representations of the peevish morose or rash ~~Judges~~ preserve [f.4] that Reputation to its Judgemts so necessary to be supported by all who expect from it that Protection & Security to themselves & familys & will deserve that releif & ease by it from personal tedious & expensive attendance on ye County Court wn this therefore useful & valuable priviledge & Liberty intended to give to ye Justices of this Borough but wn without such assistance on all proper occasions might become useless if not distructive. I have on former Occasions in this place endeavord to explain how this right of Judgemt in ye people (in wh their Majesty may be said to consist) - remains with them as a part of our Original Contract & Constitution of Goverment wn indeed it is morally [f. 4 v] certain had they once parted with, no Goverment woud ever have return'd us that. I will not now enlarge upon it & shall only say that the whole cannot but be so, when every circumstance and form in our method of Tryal remind us of & proves it & which therefore when assisted by its faithful Ally the Habeas Corpus Act can never be lost but by our own fault & by this we may be assur'd that the glory of our Constitution will ever be continued to us especially under his Majestys protection for the continuance of wch there can sure be none now so stupid as not most heartily to pray & that thereby the distractions of a Minor or the hazard of a very young King may be [f. 5] averted from these Kingdoms a prospect of wch it has pleased the divine providence to open to us by the unexpected & inexpressible Loss of his late Royal Highness & if in these our Times The Trial of Several Offences have been taken out of this Constitutional Method of Trial by Jurys, it becomes our Duty to suppose our Representa^{ve} in Parlt (with whom our Lives & Libertys are instrusted) woud not have consented to such Innovations, but from the Malignity evil Tendency & danger of Letting them go unpunishd & ye absolute necessity for the preservation of ye whole community to bring those guilty of them at all events to Justice, & by these new enacted methods since ye ordinary course of Justice was found ineffective [f. 5 v] and this shoud engage us all to assist in giving them their just force & Effect as well by example as otherwise that even still grea[r] may not be enacted & this may be the case of the Act in ye last Sesns against excessive drinking Gynn & strong Waters wch however severe it may be must & will be inforced if the mischeif thereby intended to be is not effectually Stoppd or distroyd.

You are Gentln to present all offences as well as such comd agst & in contempt of Divine authority [f.6] & holy Revelation & Institution or such human laws as have been made for ye presevation & support of Religion such as Blasphemy & profaness & espec[ially] Books wrote against the being & attributes of Almighty God ye Doctrines of ye holy Trinity the Christian Religion & ye divine authority of the Holy Scriptures the several offences mentioned in his Majesties proclamation now read to you profane cursing & Swearing & Sabbath breaking Lewd & Ludicrous & profane Songs, plays pictures & devices tending to promote Lewdness debauchery or reflecting on Religion & religious Acts & particularly the Established Church wh as well for its innate excel [f.6 v] lency as for that it is the law of the Land deserves first to be remember'd yet so as not to forget the protection due to our fellow Subjects & Christians the other congregations of protestant Dissenters whilst they are exercising the Common right of Mankind & ye Liberty of Englishmen & therefore any insults on such religious Assemblys & places of meeting are most deservedly highly pœnal by Law (& to be presented by you) & so are all such who do not resort to their parish church or some of these yt have & so are all open Acts of Lewdness & Debauchery both indecent & offensive to ye community & [f.7] distructive of the good order of it. Or such Laws as concerns us meerly as a society of men whether Capit'l or not or Offences at Common Law or by some Subsequent Statutes The Greatest of all these is High Treason wh being levelled either directly at the Kings person or Goverment the basis of our happy Constitution such as manifestly tend to the distruction & confusion of ye whole Comnty is therefore to be in the first place prevented upon wh plain principle infamously wrestl'd & misapplyd under colour of Just the Cruelest Murders of the best & wisest men have been & daily are committed in other Country. [f. 7 v] Whilst here Treason is defind & so discribd & requird to be provd that as all all laws shoud it can only protect not destroy. Next to Treason are Felonys i.e. Acts perpetrated with a wicked disposition agst the Life Body goods or Habitn of ye Subject as Murder wh is in general depriving another of Life directly or indirect with deliberation & designedly either actually provd or manifestly implyd in the nature & from ye circumstances of ye Action & every Manslaughter is so presumed to be in the first instance & to be so presented by you tho in favour [f.8] of passion & human Nature ye punisht of Death may be afterwards mitigated yet even ye most accidental killing another is attended with heavy forfeitures & even further punisht at ye discretion of ye Court. In ye next place are publick Felonies respecting the Coin and money of ye Nation. Treasble attempts agst ye King or his Councellors in his pallace or Judges doing their Duty Subjects without Licence entring into foreign Service Distroy & embezlg the Shipps of War Mercht Shipps in danger or Military Stores by those intrusted with them & their recieving Popish priests or holding correspon[dence] [f.8 v]] with ye Popish See, the being notoriously Assembled & not dispersing at ye proclamation or but beging to demolish any place set apart for Religious Worship or by going out to ye Numbr of 3 or more to assist in running unaccustomed goods or by brea[king] of prison & escape for Felony these with other publick Felonys such as forging of Fund Deeds & publick Securitys or the Notes Orders & Seals of ye publick Companys distroy'g Ships by the Master or Mariners intrusted with ye Navigation of them with many other local Felonys as also other Felonys comitted [f.9] agst the person goods & Habitation of ye Subject &ye rights of Marrg & evil examples of others as all sorts of Larcenarys or Thefts & Robbery & Pyracy Burglary Firing Houses & Outhouses & House breakg all wh I pass over & barely mention to you to avoid unecessary delay as it appears to me it woud be at this time to enlarge more particularly on these heads few of wh will probably come under your consideration at this Ssns but that the same pleas[ant] prospect may be continued in the Succeeding ones give me leave [f.9 v] to remind you of the lesser Offences & Misdeamrs wh tho not Capital will very soon & almost of necessity consequently produce Capital Offences & whether they be such more immediately relate to Religion & the practice of Piety just now mentiond or such relating in ye first Instance to Man only as such these are commonly calld Nusances the Principal of wh are publick houses of Entertainmt or provided for ye practise of Lewdness & immorality. The detecting & punishing of any one offence will be a most useful & proper discharge of your [f.10] Duty to God your Country & your selves & as there are the nurserys of great Crimes so are others of great mischief & Inconveniences to Society you are therefore to prevent all Bribery corruption & Misdemeanors in ye Off[ic]ers of Justice all Barreters Maintainers & Incouragers of Vexatious Suits & illegal proceedings under colour of Law all conspiracys & attempt to injure others in their person reputation & property in defiance of Law as Batterys Riots & Affrays forcible Entrys & detainers Libells & defamats pict[ures]& description all offences in cary on trades in a manner or in their nature dangerous to ye habitations or the Health or in general unreasonable [f.10 v] Hurtfull to ye Neighbourhood & Community Offences ags Publick Trade as Usury forestallg ingrosg regratg Monopol[y] deceits & Cozinage in Weights & meas[ures] by wh in a more particular manner the poor &

needy are oppressd & ruind for the emolument of some few of the most Worthless of Mankind & lastly such as tend to ye neatness & convenience of ye wholes [i.e. holes] in ye Publick Highways Streets passages drains & easments wh if not kept in due order by this natural & antient method of Correction must in the end come to be supported [f.11] here as elsewhere by the grievous method of Taxation wh every individual will then find infinitely more burdensome than any private Service now required from them All these Misdemeanors are to be punished by Fine & imprisonment at least & sometimes corporally accordg to ye degree & nature of the Offence I will not doubt Gentln of your Steady Strict & Just performance & discharge of your present Great Trust & from wh I will detain you no longer that you may be dismissd the first minute the publick Service will permitt it & will not dismiss before you will not desire it

Lent 1752

[f.1] The Great and extensive Jurisdiction of this Town and the Power of holding Courts of Oyer & Terminer of equall Authority in this Populous District with those held before the Revd the Judges in the Countys at large from whence it has been taken cannot be duly executed unless kept as frequently as in them since it is an Injury either to the Publick or to the accused if by any Delay here they are prevented from coming at that Judgmt which ought always to be given with the utmost Convenient Expedition to Answer the just Ends of it, and therefore [f.1 v] an implyed Trust and Confidence that it woud be executed at least as speedily as in the Circuit, this Renewal of the Antient and Custom[y] Time of holding these Courts agreeable to the Trust implyed in their grant of it wch certainly was that it should be held as previously does Honour to the Corporation and the Magistrate who presided when this Resolution was taken and confers a fresh obligation on the Inhabitants of this Town for whose Protection and great Ease and Benefitt this Priviledge was granted & is continued and who may therefore be reasonably expected chearfully to assist and attend upon and defend its Acts wh is cleerly their Interest and Duty agt any rash malevolent or invidious misrepres- entations. And Gentn I have [f.2] The Pleasure to find by the Calendar that this faithful discharge of the great Trust is in fact the principal duty of our present meeting & that there will not probably fall under your Consideration any of the great and Capital Crimes and felonys And therefore I shall in General only give you in Charge to enquire after the Perpetrators of any felonys if any such there be which may appear to you to have been here committed and shoud you be in any Doubt abt the Nature of them or in what manner they are to be prevented You may depend on our imediate advice and assistance but at present it seems unnecessary to give you any Directions or to spend any further Time about them which may be more usefully & agreable too as it is ye source of the greatest earthly happiness employed in Considering the Nature of that part of our Constitution which is ye occasion of the present Assembly [f.2 v] And this may be the rather expected on these publick Occasions because whilst the excellency of our Legislature or Parliamt has been the Subject of the ablest Pens of this Nation the Great & important executive part of Governmt with regard to Criminal prosequtn has been if at all only Cursorily ment[d] by them and left to be treated of by the Lawyers only and from a strange indolence we content ourselves with saying (most truly indeed) that Jurys are the Honour Blessing & Birthright of these People But why they are so or the Nature of them have been little attended to so that they have been of late Years given up in many instances almost without a Sigh and certainly without a struggle. Nor those of superior Station do not reflect that the Jury are in Fact discharging [a?] [f.3] Most Honourable & important part even of Sovereignty itself and that for which the whole so far as respects our Domestick Concerns was instituted; For when ye World grew too populous for the natural and Primitive Patriarchal Governmt it became necessary to establish certain Laws or Rules for the Governmt of Society and to subject every Member thereof accused of any Breach of them to the Judgemt of others, which in all Ages & Countrys has been found to be the Sovereign Power to which all other Parts of Governmt are only Ministerial & subordinate & whether placed in the King & ye Nobility [f.3 v] or a Select Number of ye People became in Time absolute Master of the whole in spite of any Councells Restrictions or Limitations and which has always ended in such an abuse of Power as was either overturned by the justly Provok'd People as in time reduced them to such a State of Slavery and Indolence that they became an easy Prey to the Invader & this was so natural and usual that they [?] the Vices of these their Conquer'd Slaves became in their Turn subject to the same miserable Condition - But the antient Invader of these Kingdoms finding a brave Resistance from our Ancestors not so much by corrupted by the Wealth or enervated by Luxury as [f.4] The Inhabitants of better Climes bravely resisted their Invader & coud hardly be said to be conquered as they preservd the essentials of their own const[ution]in ye new established Governmt & amongst others that form & Method of Tryal which in Magna Charta is by way of emphasis stiled the Law of the Land & at this time commonly called a jury that is they reserved the Power of Judgemt as the Basis of Government to the whole People by whom they saw it only woud not be abused for thus placed it is the Interest of those who are to exer to it to preserve & use it for its Original Intents & Purpose And as this Authority ended with ye Verdict no Opportunity is given to wrest it to [f.4 v] other Purposes than what it was designed for and which can never be the Case unless executed by such Ordinary and weak People as will suffer themselves to be intimidated by and corruptly accept the Wages of Iniquitys from the great Ministers and Engines of Power which may be always prevented if the Gentry and more Substantial part of the Comunity be but true to themselves and not reject this Honourable Station by throwing it on their Poorer or Weaker Neighbours contrary to the very Design & End of the Institution That this is in reality ye State of this Noble Priviliedge is evident from ye [f.5] Common form of arraigning the Prisoner & Charge to ye Jury when they & ye Publick are told that ye Prisoner has put himself for Tryal not on the King ye Court or his Ministers but on the Jury by him admitted & allowed the impartial Representation of his Country to determine not for or agt but betwixt ye Prisoner & ye King who as the Guardian of ye Peace & quiet of his Subjects is the Accuser By your Allegeance or Presentmt from whence ye Importance of your Station & of how much Consequence it is for ye Publick Security to have it well executed is manifest Since you are on the one hand to take Care that ye Kings Name is not made Subservient to Private Ends [f.5 v] Malice & Resentmt to the Destruction or Oppression of ye Innocent not even in their Character & Good name So you are on ye other Hand to determine when it is properly used for the Great End & design of governmt and of the Royal Authority in bringing to Justice Malefactors & Disturbers of ye Peace & quiet of Society And this you cant fail of doing by attending to that excellent Summary of your Duty and Directory in the proper Execution of it The Oath of Office you have now taken in the Discharge of which I shall only at this Time particularly recommend to your Consideration [f.6] Such Misdemeanors & Offences as if not restrained & nip'd in ye Bud will in Time be productive of ye greatest Crimes And in the first Place such as Relate to ye Honour of Almighty God & his Worship All Blasphemous & Impious Opinions vented by Writing Printing teaching or advised speaking open Acts of immorality Profaneness & Lewdness agt. which sevl good Laws have been made & his Majestys Proclamation now read reminds us of putting them in execution But indeed every Mans own Interest will do so as these Offences unavoidably weaken the Obligations to the Performance of the Duties of Social Life & lead directly [f.6 v] To all Wickedness and Injustice by searing Mens Consciences & taking away the motives that a due Sense of Gods Good Providence & Omnipresence & his Divine Revelation lays on Men to perform their Duty to him and their Neighbour There are also many Laws made for due Conformity to our national Church the effect of ye Diabolical Attempts of ye Popish Adherents in the Reign of Queen Elizabeth & her Successor & ye Violent & terrible Havock of ye Hypocritical Zealot In the Reigns of King Charles ye 1st and 2nd the last of which was in the 22d Year of Ch. 2d by wh and notwithstanding ye Superlative Charity and forbearance of ye Church [f.7] of England above all others it was no wonder that whilst smarting under their Wounds these Laws were enacted But upon the Happy Revolution all Conscientious Dissenters were freed from ye Penaltys of them and they were restor'd to ye Comon rights of Mankind under ye reasonable & easy Conditions of professing themselves good Subjects Protestants & Christians but all these Acts were left and are still in force and confirmed by the Act of Settlemt as a part of our Constitution & ought to be put in Execution agt such mad Wicked or weak Enthusiasts of the last Century who only by their Abuse of it can authorize any Attempt [f.7 v] To repeal that excellent Act of Toleration from which we have recd & enjoyed so much Peace & good Neighbourhood I coud have wish'd there had been no occasion to say so much on this Head but ye unhappy present State of ye Neighbouring City arising wholly from the abuse of this Law and the strong Neglect of those in Authority there will not entirely let me pass it by Not that I have any Apprehension of ye Contagion spreading to this Place where these Vagabond Cheats will I doubt not find a Wiser People and Impartial Magistrates who will not impiously pretend Conscience in opposition to [f.8] their Duty under those Laws they have sworn to Execute For here are none of those Inconsistent People called occasionale Conformists After these open Acts of Irreligion You'll Consider of and present the first Effects or rather Introduction to them Disorderly Houses whether Publick or Private Publick Houses are extreamly proper & Usefull for ye Refreshmt of the Working Hand who are as well entitled as their Betters & do probably enjoy more than them such Relaxations from their Labours Provided they [f.8 v] Are not carried to excess which then become their Destruction both here & hereafter In my Opinion Exercises & Open Recreations in ye Day Time & even now & then an hour or two in the Evening are rather advantageous to the Community than otherwise But when once the Night is far advanced and Cards or other House Games are begun there is no Mischief which may not be dreaded That none of these are prevented by ye Constables is very Astonishing Did they pay any Regard to their Duty or Oaths they woud not appear so Ignorant of what the Ears & Eyes of all others are Witnesses to [f. 9] There are Other Nusances which affect the Good Order of Society Such as Usury Forestalling Monopolize Deceits in Weight Measures by which in a Particular Manner ye Poor & Needy are oppressed for the Emolument of some of the most Worthless of Mankind - Trades carryed on in a manner or in their Nature dangerous to ye Health or Habitation or in General unreasonable or Hurtfull to ye Neighbourhood for People ought not for their own private Advantage or from Indolence or worse Motives Disturb others in ye Enjoymt of their own Habitations And for mutual Advantage allways shoud Contribute their Share & Proportions to ye Neatness and [f. 9 v] Convenience of ye Whole In the Publick Highways Streets Passages & Easemts. And as it is your Duty to prevent any Defects there it is the Part of ye Court to carry such presentmts into Execution And you may depend upon it they will not be intimidated from Doing their Duty by the Threats of the Litigious & Perverse & when those who now refuse Paymt to Rates which I am informed is the Case of ye last Surveyors are themselves obliged to have a Rate as they will when sumon'd on the presen[men]t at the last Sessions and which will be turned into a Bill of Indict^{mt} by you by wh they may feel the Unreasonableness & Hardships of such Opposition [f.10] You are also to present all Abusives in the Administration of Justice by its Officers from Bribery Corruption or otherwise, all Barretters Maintainers and Encouragers of Vexatious Proceedings under Colour of Law all Conspiracys and attempts to injure others in their Persons Reputation & property all Batterys Riots forcible & Violent Breaches of the Peace Libells Deformatory Pictures and Descriptions But as the freedom from great Crimes afford the best grounded hopes of their being very few smaller offences and is Proof of ye Good Order & Behaviour of the Inhabitants of this Jurisdiction & of the Vigilance of its residing Magistrates I hope you will have very little Trouble [f.10 v] In the Discharging of your present Trust and that this Day may be sufficient for your Enquiry when you may be assured of being dismissed from any further Attendance ~~on your Duty~~ from which I will therefore detain you no longer at this Time.

September 1752

Gent.

[f.1] As you now attend this Court in the same Honble Station & Duty in which you have so frequently served his Majesty & your fellow Subjects of this Borough and discharged it with that due Regard to the Solemn Obligation with which it then was and now is comitted to you and as you then were so fully instructed in the Nature of the Business which did or might come before you I am persuaded it is very unnecessary for me at this time to say any Thing to you merely on your own Account as I can have no doubt but that you will strictly adhere to that excellent Directory of your Duty the Oath now administered to you And [f 1.v] That you will with your utmost Care & Industry and that Honble secresy you have sworn to preserve consider of such matters as you do know or shall be informed are to be presented by you to this Court without any Regard either of favour or Affection or which is much less to be feared ill Will hatred or Malice and that upon the Whole you will do all that now is expected from you on this occasion But these & the like Addresses tho' imediately directed to you are also intended for the rest of the People assembled on these occasions to impress in them a just Sense & Reverence of the Authority as well as the Power of Government The Equity & reasonableness of it being thus [f.2] Openly explained and a Sort of Appeal made to them for the Justice of it. The Power of Government may be supported as in Turkey or France and their Subjects fully instructed in the Effect of it by Legions of Mercenary Bands But the Authority of it can only subsist in a free State and the willing Obedience of its Subjects ~~wholly apprized~~ satisfyed of the reasonableness of their Subjection and convinc'd that it is their Interest to preserve it as the means of procuring security and Happiness to every individual who will deserve it by their Behaviour & due Submission to Law and the Ministers of it But this is more especially so to those of the meanest and most inferior Stations who in Arbitrary [f.2 v] Governmts are the most oppressed because the last & upon whom the weight of Power descends with accelerated force and coud our inferior People be fully apprized of the Happiness they derive from our Constitution by which ye lowest is defended from the insult of ye Greatest Subject and the Enjoyment & Reward of their own Industry preserved and secured to them by it It coud not surely fail of creating in them and every one a Reverence for and thereby give Authority to their Protectors and best friends the Law & ye Magistrates and who woud be the better enabled to maintain and promote ye Publick Happiness and Ease of ye [f.3] Community intrusted to their Care by the Union of Authority & Power by which one if not both only can be preserved to answer any good End and woud prevent that licentious abuse of Liberty by which the only Arguments are furnished to its insiduous Enemies & Betrayers We seem indeed to have a Notion of this our publick Happiness and the Foundation of it by our manner of expecting of that Soul of our Constitution from which it almost wholly arises. The Right of Tryal by Jury or rather by ourselves of whom the Jury are only the Representative and by which we are distinguish'd as a free People from all other Nations of the World and happily for us [f.3 v] Our Forefathers were so fully convinc'd of the excellency of this Institution that the first End of every successfull struggle for Liberty hath been to confirm & fortify this Right by new Regulations and particularly by that most excellent Law the Habeas Corpus Act And these struggles seem to have succeeded better in this than in other Kingdoms as they have been directed here to honest & virtuous Purposes of publick security, which will always procure friends whilst there remains any publick Virtue in the Nation. This End & intention is the only Rule by which we may judge of the Justice and Laudableness of [f.4] Any Opposition that this publick Happiness & Security is in a manner entirely owing to the Institution of Juries tho' greatly assisted by ye Integrity & Ability of our Judges and that it more effectually Answers the Design of its Institution than any other Method of Tryals that doth or ever did exist in this or in any other Country. I have endeavoured to explain so lately to all or most of you in this Place that it woud be too much trespassing on your Patience to repeat at this Time what I then said and shall therefore only Remind you that Jurys are ye Representatives of the People of England in whom their Majesty appears and by whom they [f. 4 v] Virtually give Judgmt. tho the form & Effect of it is pronounced by the Court, that the most important part of Governmt The Power of Life & Death appears by this to be actually retained in ye Community and that it is the Ministerial Parts of Governmt only which [by ye original Contract] is granted to the King and his proper Officers. that it is this Right which hath in all Ages and must always preserve us as a free & independent People unless by Supineness & unpardonable Negligence we weaken its Authority by suffering it to be executed by the meanest & most ignorant [f.5] or totally perverted - by the Wicked & Profligate who will thereby be the Tools not the opposers of Power - In short when we cease to consider it as a sort of LightHouse which must Conduct the Bottom on which all our nationall Happiness is embark'd safely into Port from any Political Storm from which it may be threatened and which therefore it is our true Interest to preserve in perfect order and full Reputation in this Calm of fair Weather that it may be usefull in Tempestuous Times Let every Poor Man consider that by this Institution under the Divine Providence and the Protection of his Majesty his Liberty freedom and Ease is maintain'd Let every rich Man remember that it [f. 5 v] Is by this his Property is inviolably preserved And let them if they can find any other Security which has not been in other Countries & therefore may be in this diverted to the Destruction rather than the Preservation of the Subject and then lett them if they can refuse ye highest Reverence to its Authority or ever see any invasion or abuse of it with Indifference But this Admonition might perhaps be more necessary in any other Place than in this Jurisdiction where the Service of it has been usually better attended than I coud almost elsewhere ever observe And I therefore mention it rather as an encouragement [f.6] To persist in this Attendance which does publick Justice so much Honour This Institution consists of Two parts by one the accused are freed or finally condemn'd Yet with such Mitigation as their Crimes will admitt of consistent with the Justice due to the Publick This vast & important Charge is the part of the Petty Jury, by the other we are assured of not being disturbed or oppressed whilst innocent with the Ignominy of a Publick Tryal untill an imprudent Conduct or infortunate Accidents have render'd our behaviour so suspicious that it becomes the most desirable means of regaining or cleaning our sullied Reputation To Judge of [f.6 v] This Expediency is your Province. You are to hold ye Ballance determined betwixt and put an End to Rash or malicious Scandal or allow of a reasonable just and necessary Accusation. This is your Delicate & Honble Station & therefore intrusted with the most reputable of the Community This is in Generall your Charge but more particularly you are to enquire by whom & what offences have been comitted in this Jurisdiction In the first place such as may seem to be more directly comitted against the Divine Majesty None of which are Capital since the [f.7] Reformation & the Statute of the 29 Car 2d against executing Hereticks so called tho they have been frequently the most Learned and best of Men & the 9th of his present Majesty by which it is justly consider'd that the Offence is not in using Witchcraft and Sorcery but pretending to do so and what remains are such as are Affronts & Disturbances to the Practice of Piety & Religion in Generall such as Lewd and Ludicrous & prophane Books Plays Songs Sabbath Breaking Drunkenness Prophane Cursing & swearing & all other open Acts of Lewdness & Profaneness especially Books wrote against [f.7 v] the being & Attributes of Almighty God of the Doctrines of ye Christian Religion & Divine Authority of ye Holy Scriptures. And the other Offences mentioned in his Majestys Proclamation now read to you. Also Reflections & Insults on ye Establish'd Worship or Interruption to the Religious Acts of Conscientious Protestant Dissenters from it who as Men Christians & fellow Subjects have a Right to be protected in their exercise of their Religion under the very reasonable Terms and Conditions required from them The next in Order are Offences comitted imediately against his Majestys Person Crown & Dignity [f.8] which are called High Treason These are defined in our excellent Laws and the Method of our Conviction so restrained that no good subject can be in any Danger from them nor can I suspect any such will be comitted in this Loyal Borough Offences against the Subject are felonies or Misdemeanours against the Person, Habitation, Property, Reputation, and the Ease quiet & security of the Society — The Highest Degree of felonies are Murder Rapes Sodomys firing of Houses and Entring them in the Night Time with intent to comitt any felony tho no felony be actually comitted These have been Time immemorially Capital And the Protection of the House has been by [f.8 v] Severall Statutes extended to any sort of Robbery in Dwelling Houses Shops or Basement or any Outhouses belonging thereto or even in any Booth or Tent in a fair or mart which have been made Capital when such Robbery amounted to the Value of forty Shillings or in some Cases even to 5 s. Whether the Owner his Wife or Servants were therein or not or whether they were put in fear or not for ye Generall Division of Offences for felony by our Law was into great Larcenary or Theft amounting to the Value of 12 d. a considerable Sum in those Days wh was Capital or Thefts under that Value stil'd petty Larceny But the necessity of Things have made most felonies Capital when attended with particular Circumstances

[f.9] Such as that I have mentioned on the Dwelling or other Houses or from ye Person or in the Highway in which Case ye smallest Robbery is Capital or privately from his Person is also made Capital. But in these Cases the most tender Regard has always been had on the Tryal of them so as to preserve the Life of the Criminal where other Circumstances do not render him an Object unfitt for Mercy There are also many other Capital felonies which cannot be properly reduced under the Head of those I have mentioned such as Offences which relate to the Embezillmt or destroying or forging Records or the Notes and Books of the publick funds & monied Corporations [f.9 v] The Destruction of Cattle Ships & their Merchandize by the master or mariners, [?] the Effects of Bankrupts & forging of Deeds or securitys all which are render'd Capital and which of these shoud be any Occasion for your farther Consideration of them & so as to occasion any Doubt amongst you will be fully explained by the Court as soon as they are made acquainted with it as well as with any other Offences that may possibly come before you and which therefore I will not enlarge upon at this present but in these & all other Offences where the Enormity of them arise from [f.10] The particular Circumstances with which they were comittted the fact of those circumstances so charged in the Indictmt is as much to be attended to and proved to your Satisfaction as the Principal Act which indeed is so plain that I shoud not have mentd it but for the contrary practice which has of late prevailed in this and a Neighbouring Country. The last sett of Misdemeanors & Offences proper for your Consideration are so in Respect of ye publick Justice Ease Trade & Health & Conveniency of ye Community And in the first place are such as tend to ye Comission of those immoralitys & Offences against Religion which I have formerly mentd such as the great foundation of them all disorderly & Lewd publick or private Houses All Assaults & Affrays [f.10 v] All Extortion in the Ministers of Justice all Barretors & encouragers of Vexation & like actions or Usury forestalling Deceit or Cozenage among particular People especially if comitted in Weight or Measure In the Sale of their Resp[ect-]ive Comodity all conspiracys & unlawful attempts to invade the property of them. All Nusances and incroachmts on Highways Rivers or Comon Streets or Annoyances & Hindrances to the free use of of them by all his Majestys Subjects all Trades carried on in a manner dangerous or Destructive to the Habitations persons or Health of the Neighbourhood But I will not enter into a fuller Description of these matters of which you are I doubt not fully apprized and that they are a part of your Duty to prevent that I may detain you no longer from ye public service to wh you were sworn.

Sept 9 1767

[f.1] *Gentn of–.*

Before I give you in charge the Matters refer'd to in that excellent Directory for the due discharge of it the Oath now administ[d] to you I find my self oblig'd by an[ot]her usage by prefacing it by some Considn suitable to ye publick meeting as far as time will permitt what Introduc'd this Laudible Custom viz the publishing & explaning any new Laws and ye Satisfying the people in the Reasonable[ness] of any Alteration in Government is now quite unecessary from the Care taken by the Government to publish by the Prints the Account & Abst[tracts] of such General Laws as are of the most publick Concern; & from that Conviction w^{h} after above 50 years experience every one must feel of the happiness secur'd to us by the Act of Settle[ment] of the Crown on his Majesty & his Royal Family whom may God long preserve Yet it may still be retained to many useful purposes particularly at this time to remind those who do, & inform those who do not know upon what principle it is that we only have so long preserved, whilst it is lost to all other Nations, our liberty & Property [f.1 v] Which is not what is often used for a pretence to Licentiousness & to do what we please, but that perfect assurance every subject with us has of the quiet Enjoyment of all Religious & Civil Rights whilst he continues Obedient to ye Laws & yt when he is accused of any Crime he shall have a speedy Tryal be judged by those by himself admitted Impartial Whilst in other Countrys the greatest & best Subject if he happens to displease ye Ministry, knows not whether he may be dragged to a Gaol unknown or inaccessible to his Friends, to a perpetual Imprisonment or to a cruel Execution after a farce of a Trial before the most Exceptionable Judges

This our Liberty we owe to ye prudent Circumspection of our Ancestors who that they might transmitt to their posterity those Libertys & possessions which they had bravely kept or got wisely devised the only Method hitherto found Sufficient to Restrain absolute Government w^{h} considers the Wisest Laws as [?] when contradictory to themselves [f.2] They Judged the Regal & Hereditary Form of Gover^{t} most suitable to these Kingdoms & therefore placed All the Visible Splendor & Authority in ye King & his Ministers insomuch that any Disobedience to ye Law is aptly said to be an Offence against the Honour of his Crown & Dignity, & of that Peace & Order among his subjects w^{h} it is his peculiar Duty to maintain by his Ministers who are therefore to be respected as exercising his Royal Authority. But then they obligd him w^{h} distinguished our Government from all Others, to have the Concurrance of his People without w^{h} his most positive Commands, w^{h} other Kings term their Will & pleasure were to have no force, & therefore it is said the King can do no wrong, Nothing being absolutely & without Controul left to him but the Heavenly attribute of Mercy hereby to Endear him to his people as their Father & Protector, Speaking Emblematically they placed the Sword in his hand but w^{h} he is not permitted to unsheath without this Consent of the whole people given by their [f. 2 v] Representatives the Jury for they justly Suppose the unanimous Opinion of 12 Impartial men assisted by the Court woud be the General Sence of the Country

All this is most Evident from ye judicial Form of Arraigning the Prisoner w^{h} tho too frequently Gabled over by the Clerk deserves the Attention of every Englishman for he informs the Jury they are Elected to Judge betwixt the King & the Prisoner (Can there be a more Exalted Station?) who being accused of Such or Such a Crime has denyd his Guilt & for a proof of his Innocency Submitted it under the direction of Gods Good Providence to ye Judgment of the Jury the Representatives of his Country for so the Words (wh command you are) plainly Impart & the Court has thus Joynd Issue or agreed on ye Trial with him after the humane prayer for his Acquittal Thus you see how hrble is the Station of a Juryman by whom the Original Majesty of the People of England is preservd & continued by this Exercise of the high Act of Sovereignty, & it is for this reason that the Judgmt must be unanimous as being that of the Country whilst [f.3] other Judges giving only their own Opinion determine by plurality of Votes, this is real Liberty & Property (not the too frequent Licentious Abuse of it in our days both by the Great as well as the Little the consequence of w^{h} is terrible to think of.

The Contemptible (in modern Language) addition of Petty is not given to ye other Jury as descriptive of its Authority because being appealed to from yours it is in nature superior & so more Hn^{ble} but as being limitted to the Offences comitted by the Prisoners at ye Bar Whilst you are to enquire of all Offences committed in the Jurisdiction.

But great as this our Priviledge is, it might be as it was, in great measure defeated for want of a Speedy Trial ~~before~~ untill that was also Secur'd to us (by some others) but more espetialy the Habeas Corpus Act a ~~more valuable~~ greater & at ye same time more just Acquisition from Goverments, than was ever obtaind by any People But our Constitution is tender of the Reputation as well as of ye other property of ye Subject w^{h} is not permitted to be drawn in question without a serious Enquiry into the Reasonableness of the Acccusation [f. 3 v] This Enquiry must in its nature be private Apart from, & without ye Immediate Assistance of ye Court, & therefore this delicate Trust is comitted to those of Superior Rank & Reputation at least for prudence & Integrity such as it is to be presumed, the publick Councellors of a Corporate Town are, at least shoud be, not thereby to exclude them from the more Important Service on the other Jury, & You have here Solemny Engaged to make this Enquiry Dilligently, & carefully, secretly, cooly, candidly, & without favor or Afection your Charge is truly to present to, or inform the Court of such Offences as you shall find to have been comitted & by whom & which have not already been presented in this Jurisdiction, for all from the Highest to the Lowest Offence may be presented by you tho perhaps (coud it be possible to be at this time com^{d} here) High Treason must be tryd in another place I need not be very particular in them at this time as the Vigilance of your Local Magistrates woud doubtless name timely disorder & brot the persons of the supposd offenders before the Court of whom I have the pleasure which [?] by the Kal[ende]r these are [f. 4] I shall therefore only just name them. Offences are in general divided into Capital & those not so & into those comitted against Humane Laws & against those which relate to the Honour & Reverence of Almighty God & his Worship w[h] are therefore first to be mentiond for there is not happily with us now any such Capital The two terrible & most distructive Capital supposed Crimes under the Papal Tyranny & folly of Heresy & Witchcraft are no more so. All Executions in pursuance of Ecclesiastical Judgments for Heresy being taken away by [blank space] & the other is pleasantly got rid of by ye 9 Geor 2 by w[h] it is now no Offence to be but to pretend to be a Witch & by this it is that our Religion wh always accompanys Civil Liberty & Freedom of thought is Establishd. But there still remains due punishmt for what will probably be the most useful part of your Enquiry. All such publick & immoral Behaviour as inevitably in ye Consequences lead to ye Greatest Disturbance of Society & are therefore proper Objects of Temporal Laws & the extirpation of yt practice of true Piety & the Corruption of all Good Manner the best support of any Nation. [f. 4 v] Such are Lewd & Blasphemous Speeches & behaviour - profane Cursing & swearing & breach of ye divine & most holy ordynance of the Sabbath Drinking & all other Acts of open Wickedness & Bad Manners & particularly the great Nursery of such Behaviour disorderly & lewd houses whether Publick or private against w[h] his Majesty has warnd you by his Royal Proclamation now read & to w[h] he has the greater Reason to expect our Obedience from his own Rare Royal Example of Religion & Virtue.

Civil Capital Offences are first that which dissolves all Society & the only one by our new Law attended with any cruelty in ye punishmt calld High Treason w[h] by another happy part of our Constition is defined by the Act 25 Ed 3 & some other w[h] cheifly relate to the Popish Religion & the Popish Pretender & his whilst in other Countrys High Treason is every thing the government as Heresy is every thing the Preists call so but this Enquiry will take up very little here of your time if it possible can be elsewhere [f.5] Other Offences are either agst ye Subjects person as first Murder or Homicide calld Petty Treason when committed by a Servant on his Master or Mistress or Wife on her hus[d] or Religious agst his Prelate designedly as it is legally Termd of Malice Aforethought either actually so, or implyd by such a Brutal & cruel or passionate Behaviour as occasions Death & is most justly punishable according to ye Divine Law by the Blood of the Offender tho comited in otherwise a lawful Act & Correction as where a Master beats his Servant, or pupil, immoderately or with a Mortal Instrument as a Handspike or the Like or against his Property Calld Robbery (which is a Violent taking from the Person or in his presence putting him in fear the Smallest Value & by a late Act the Assault & putting in fear with intent tho' no felony committed is made felony, these with the cruel & Brutal Offence of Rape & Sodomy & that agst the Habitation calld Burglary w[h] is the breaking & Entring a House Church or Walld Town in the Night with Intent to Committ tho no Felony actually be done were almost the [10] only Antient Capital Offences but the Increasing Iniquity of the Times have obliged the Legislature to ad all Kinds of Robbery to a certain Value by breaking & entring or in a Dwelling House Stable Shop Warehouse Tent or Booth in a Fair or Market in or near the Highway or privately from the person - Counterfeiting the Stamp Dutys publick or private Security Notes Bills or Orders for ye Receit of Money or Goods agst Commanders or Masters abusing their Trust & voluntary losing their Ships together with ye Accessory before or after the fact - Riotously Assembling & begining to pull down places of Religious Worship dwelling or other Houses & continuing such [f.6] Acts after his Majestys Proclamation of wh we have so lately had the most melancholy Example which I hope may be prevented by the few (thro his Majestys & his Ministers great Lenity) Examples of Justice to w[h] I ad Running goods by 3 or More Arm'd or Harboring & concealing knowingly any such Offenders. Offences Not Capital are Misprision by Concealing Offences or encouraging Offences before or after the Fact where they are not made as in most cases they are by Stat. Accessorys espetially that most dangerous one of knowingly Receiving Stol[n] Goods of w[h] a small parcel of comparatively to ye real Value a very small value is naturally & properly great Evidence & is punishd with 14 Years Transportation without Mitigation.

[f. 6 v] Other Offences are Breaches of the Peace properly so calld by one or more as Assaults Batterys Afrays forcible Entry Riots Routs & tumultuous Assemblys for the doing of any Act whether otherwise lawful or not - Misdemeaners without Violence as Bribery & Corruption in ye Ministers of Justice Infamous & dangerous to Society as Per[jur]y forgery Conspiracys Libells by writing printing or provoking Pictures & descriptions nusances to the Habitation as Offensive or dangerous Trades or neglect & Stopage of the Highway Streets Keys or publick & Common Conveniency & in general whatever is Detrimental to ye good Order peace Health & ease of Society & their reasonable & necessary Enjoyment Such as that cruel hardship on ye poor Usury Forestalling Monopoly & the like & that shameful Abuse [f.7] of the Law the protector otherwise of all Barratry & litigious & malitious prosequtns, all wh if necessary will be more fully explaind in the several Bills presented to you & the Court will as soon as infmd with pleasure satisfy any of your doubts yt may arise upon them.

FINIS

A CHARGE DELIVERED TO **THE GRAND JURY**, AT A GENERAL QUARTER SESSIONS OF THE PEACE, HELD FOR THE TOWN AND LIBERTY OF BERWICK, THE 15TH. OF JULY, 1754. — Published at the Request of the GRAND JURY. — LONDON: Printed for G. FREER, at the *Bible* in *Bell-Yard*, near *Lincoln's-Inn*, and Sold by the Booksellers of *London* and *Westminster*.

M. DCC. LIV.

[A]

A CHARGE DELIVERED TO **THE GRAND JURY**.

Gentlemen,

The Preservation of Civil Order in the Society was the original Design and End of the Institution of Justices of the Peace: And the primary Jurisdiction of this Court was to superintend it, by making an Enquiry into every Violation, and punishing every Breach of it. [2]

TO aid in this Enquiry, it has the Assistance of a Double Jury, of Twelve Men at least; whom the Law requires to be *disinterested* and upright, and who are to present every Offender against the Laws upon their Oaths, without Bias, from Favour, or Affection to, or Malice and Resentment against, any Person whatsoever. This Institution of Juries, in the Trial of all Criminal Facts from the highest Offence to the lowest, does the greatest Honour to, and is the peculiar Privilege of the *British* Constitution: And whilst the sacred Regard and Veneration are paid to Oaths, which so solemn and awful an Appeal to the Supreme Being demands, and the Laws of Society presume, in the Administration of them, it must continue to be the [3] highest Security, which any Man could wish to have, for enjoying every Right which is most dear to him: But whenever the Members of Society in general, become so profligate and abandoned, as to prostitute their Oaths and their Consciences, to the lowest and vilest Purposes, whether from Considerations of falsly estimated Gain, (for what pecuniary Gain can compensate the Loss of so many valuable Privileges) or to gratify brutal Resentment; this noblest of Institutions must be totally subverted, and rendered useless; and the Decision of private Property, as well as the punishing every publick Offence, must become precarious; and the *Lives*, *Liberties*, *Reputation*, and every *Valuable Possession* of the Honest and Well-Meaning, must be in [4] the Power of the most abandoned Profligates in the Society.

THE shocking Crime of PERJURY must be attended with many other fatal Consequences to Society; as it must necessarily destroy all mutual Confidence and Faith in Peoples Intercourse of Commerce, and all other Dealings with each other: For who can be supposed, to be so absurdly credulous, as to believe Persons will contract with Faithfulness, in their ordinary Dealings, who shew such a Contempt and Disregard to Truth, even where there is the sacred Sanction of an Oath to confirm it, and where they make a Sport and Mockery of the highest Ob-[5] ligation they can possible be under, to declare the Truth?

THE Consequences to the Persons themselves must be no less *fatal.* How must these Traitors against HEAVEN and the Society appear, even in the Eyes of those very Persons, whose Purposes are effected by their *Perjury*, or by such who are engaged in the same Schemes? Surely no one, who has the least *Moral Sense* remaining, however they may find themselves benefited by the Treason, but must think with the greatest Horror and Detestation of the Traitor!

A noted Instance of the Truth of these Observations is given us by an ancient famous Historian, who tells [6] us, the *Greeks* were reduced so law in their Credit and Reputation, by the Disregard they shewed to their Oaths, that the most solemn ones they took, to confirm the Truth of what they said, could not give to the Relation the smallest Credit, nor did any one think themselves safe in lending any of them Money, though they had given the highest Securities and Engagement for the Repayment.

AT the same Time, from a contrary Conduct of the *Romans*, an Oath was looked upon as the most binding Obligation upon their Consciences, and the greatest Security, to Persons who had any Dealings with them. The Reason assigned by the Historian, for this Difference of Con-[7] duct is, that at that Time, the Doctrine of *Epicurus* was introduced amongst the Grecians, and consequently the Belief of *Infernal Torments*, as well as that of a *Providence*, was discountenanced.

I am sorry, a *late Occasion* has laid me under an indispensible Obligation to say something to you, as to the Nature of an Oath; since the Notoriety of the Manner of many Persons swearing at *that* Time, as well as the Method made use of by those, who *prompted* them to it, shewed too plainly, that the Design of both was, rather to obscure the Meaning of it, and Stifle any Convictions of Conscience, which might arise in the Mind of the Taker, than explain the Meaning of the [8] one, or the Foundation of the other. Nay, an honest Endeavour to do this, from *this Place*, raised such Indignation, that it was attempted to be ridiculed in the most wretched *Grubstreet Rhime* and sung in their *Bacchanal Cabals*, by as *mean* and *contemptible* Performers.

TO endavour to extinguish all Sense and Obligation of an *Oath*, is undoubtedly *Atheism* in Practice: For where, amongst the Vilest, can be found one, who really believed a *Supreme Being*, and *Superintending Providence*, that would be so audacious, as to offer such an Affront to such a Being, by calling upon Him to be a Witness to the Sincerity of his Heart, and the Truth of his Words, and to renounce all Hope of his [B-9] Mercy and Protection, if he endeavoured to deceive, in what he affirms to be the Truth, (which is the allowed Construction put upon such an Appeal) when at the very Time he is vainly attempting to deceive Him, by such absurd Evasions, and foolish Salvo's, by which he cannot even impose upon his Fellow-Creatures.

BUT however consistent it may, with the Principles of some refined *Epicurean* Gentlemen, (whose Schemes in Life ill comport with the Restraints, which the Belief of a Providence, and the Obligations which Oaths lay them under) to endeavour, by their Songs, to delude the unthinking Vulgar: Yet every one, whose Education has given him an [9] Opportunity of knowing our Constitution of Government, and the Benefit, which the Use and Regard to Oaths is of, in the Administration of Justice, (as they are the highest Security for the Sincerity of the Relation of Facts), should have been restrained, by this Consideration alone, from making the Attempt to explain the true Meaning and Intention of Oaths, the Subject of low Wit and Ridicule; had no former Instances of Behaviour shewed the *Person* too plainly to be divested of all Sense of Character, as well s Decency of Conduct.

AS this Court has a Jurisdiction of all Matters, which may affect the Peace of the Society, either immedi-[10]ately, or consequentially; I would recommend at present more particularly to your Consideration and Enquiry, all *Assaults*; an *Assault* is only an Attempt to do a corporal Hurt to another; as by holding up a Person's Fist, presenting a Gun, or using any other Instrument in a threatning Manner, where the Person threatned is within the Reach, or Effect of it: All *Batteries*; which are any the smallest Injuries, done to a Man in an insolent or angry Manner: All *Affrays* ; which are, where an Intention appears, by evident Circumstances, or threatning Words, to commit such Act of Violence, which must necessarily occasion Fright and Terror.[12]

YOU must enquire of all Riots; which are, where three, or more, meet, and agree mutually to assist each other, in the Execution of a Matter of a private Nature, and afterwards execute it in a violent Manner, to the Terror and Disturbance of the Neighbours; whether the Act was lawful, or unlawful in itself: And where Persons form themselves into Parties, in order mutually to assist each other, in order to execute any Act of Violence, either to the Person of any one, or his Possessions; This is a Riot, not only in the Persons first assembled to execute it, but in every one, who joins with, and assists such Persons, after they are actually engaged; though he did not [13] assemble with them, from the Beginning.

YOU must enquire of all *Perjuries*, and *Subornations of Perjuries*. By the V. of *Eliz.* Perjury is defined to be a *wilful, false Oath*, in any Proceedings, in any of the Courts therein mentioned, where it is of Consequence to the Point in question, where Lands or Tenements, Goods or Chattels, Debts or Damages are concerned.

SUBORNATION of *Perjury* is, where any Person *corruptly* procures *another*, by Rewards or Promises, or any other sinister and unlawful Means, to commit wilful and *corrupt Perjury.* [14]

THE *perjured* Person forfeits twenty Pounds; the Suborner justly forfeits double the Sum: And in case either hath not Goods or Chattels to the Value, they are to be set upon the *Pillory* for an Hour, and imprisoned for Six Months.

SUBORNERS are the most dangerous Wretches who have ever infested and *disgraced* Human Society; who throwing off all Regard to the Deity themselves, and consequently, all Regard for Oaths, lay themselves out to pervert and Draw in the Ignorant, Unwary and Profligate, to effect their wicked and detested Purposes, by gilding over Oaths by such ensnaring Means, and absurd Glosses, which are so eagerly laid hold of by such as on-[15] ly want a colourable Pretence for swearing, and would chuse to have any Construction put upon them, which may admit of their making a diabolical and gainful Traffic of them: Or by cooking up Oaths in such a Manner, as best to answer their Purposes, and afterwards gaining upon the most weak or wicked Persons, to swear to the Truth of the Facts; though they neither understand the Nature of an Oath, nor the equivocal Meaning, and Language, in which they are conceived and expressed.

THESE are Practices which *shock* every honest Man within this Jurisdiction, and give too just an Occasion to all their Neighbours, to look upon the whole of the Inhabitants, as the most [16] abandoned Set of Men, unfit to have any Correspondence, any Intercourse of Traffic with. But this, I am confident, can only be affirmed of the lowest and vilest Dregs of People; for I Can, with great Pleasure, from Knowledge and Experience declare, that the Men of Property and Traffic here, are Men of strict Honour in their Dealings, and who have the greatest *Detestation* of these *infamous Proceedings*; and Men, who who would not barter their Honour, or Consciences, for the most tempting Gain in Life.

I know of no other Means you have, to retrieve and rescue your Character from this infamous Charge, than by the Impartiality of your Enquiry, this Day, by presenting [C-17] every Offender of every Denomination, without Regard to party, or any other Distinction; and by that means make appear, the solemn and sacred Regard, you pay to this Institution of a Jury, which you are returned to serve upon; which is the great Support of the British Constitution, and the greatest Security of every Individual of the Community, whilst the most solemn Oath, you have taken, is duly reverenced, and which becomes the more important, as it is made use of in the Administration of Justice) which the Regard to the Supreme Being should oblige to the Observance of, and a proper Obedience to the Laws of the Society, which lays so great a Stress upon it, in the Administration of Justice requires. [18]

Besides this, you and all honest Men within this Liberty, should take every Opportunity, to shew your Resentment and Indignation against such *Profligates*, by setting a Mark of Distinction upon them. This will be a Declaration to the World, that they are abandoned by their Townsmen, who disclaim such *Practices*, as well as by their Neighbours.

These are Matters of the first Importance to this Community; and which, if not speedily reformed, must have the most fatal Consequences upon it, as to its *Character*, *Reputation*, Traffic and every other Thing, which can conduce to its Happiness and Welfare, and upon that Account demand your most serious Attention.

FINIS.

A **CHARGE** DELIVERED TO THE **GRAND JURY**, at the **General Quarter Session of the Peace**; Held at GUILDHALL, WESTMINSTER; On Wednesday, April 6th, 1763. By **Sir JOHN FIELDING**, Knt. CHAIRMAN of the said SESSION. Published at the unanimous Request of the Magistrates then present, and the GRAND JURY.

LONDON: Printed for CHARLES MARSH, at CICERO'S HEAD, Charing-Cross. MDCCLXIII.

[(i)]

A DEDICATION

To the Earl of NORTHUMBERLAND, Lord Lieutenant of Ireland, Knight of the Most Noble Order of the Garter, one of the Lords of His Majesty's most Honourable Privy Council, and Lord Lieutenant and Custos Rotulorum of the County of Middlesex, and City and Liberty of Westminster.

MY LORD,

As the following Charge is published at the unanimous request of the magistrates of the city and liberty of Westminster, present at the last quarter sessions held for the said city and liberty at Guild-hall, as well as that of the Grand Jury, to whom it was delivered, from their polite opinion, that it might be useful to mankind, methinks I feel their consent co-operating with my own inclinations, to dedicate the first fruits, even of a [ii] supposed advantage, arising from Guild-hall in Westminster, to your Lordship; as the origin and present existence of that court-house, so convenient and beneficial to this city and liberty, has been owing to your Lorship's public spirit and generosity. And I flatter myself, that its farther establishment will be much indebted to your care and attention. When public trusts are reposed in honest and disinterested hands, it gives universal satisfaction, and challenges unlimited confidence: sure I am, that I may most sincerely congratulate my brethren, the worthy magistrates of the city and liberty of Westminster, that the trust relative to our commission, is placed in the hands of a nobleman, who has already given the most satisfactory testimonies of his anxiety, to discharge it with fidelity to the crown, with honour to the commission itself, and with real advantage to this city and liberty. He who diligently examines into the judicial proceedings in this kingdom, provided he has a mind sufficiently enlarged to take in objects of such immense consequence, will find abundant reason to admire the wisdom of our laws, and to rejoice at the abilities, candour, and integrity, with which they are executed in our several courts of judicature; and he who looks down from hence to the lowest part of the civil power, must be filled with respectful ideas at the ample provision thereby made for the support and liberty, the peace, good order, and happiness of civil society.[iii- a]

If magistrates are well chosen, they cannot be too numerous, for wherever they are situated, they remain as pure fountains, constantly affording life, refreshment and protection to the neighbouring inhabitants. If magistrates of spirit, abilities, and integrity, are any way useful, where can they be more so, than in populous cities? for robberies and frauds will be the most frequent where property of value most abounds; and acts of violence, as well as other heinous crimes, arising from intemperance, will be most numerous, where expence and luxury furnish out the greatest variety of temptations to vice. If this be true, of what importance must be the commission of the peace for the city and liberty of Westminster appear to your Lordship? and though it has been treated with contempt, from the misconduct of a VERY few of its individuals, yet, as your Lordship has lately had an opportunity of seeing how respectable it is in its collective body, I doubt not, but in behalf of the liberty of the subject, in obedience to your Lordship's sentiments of justice and humanity, and agreeable to your obliging promise, that you will use your utmost endeavours to support its dignity, and thereby render it more beneficial to the inhabitants of this great city. And that your Lordship may enjoy all the confidence that is due to your disinterested conduct, and all the happiness that can arise from [iv] the exertion of true benevolence, public spirit, and generosity, is the ardent wish of

MY LORD,
Your Lordship's respectful friend,
and obedient humble servant.
JOHN FIELDING.

[(I)]

City, Borough and Town of Westminster in the County of Middlesex.

THE general quarter session of the peace of our Lord the King, holden at Guildhall in King-street, Westminster, in and for the liberty of the dean and chapter of the collegiate church of St. Peter, Westminster, the city, borough, and town of Westminster, in the county of Middlesex, and St. Martin le Grand, London, on Wednesday the sixth day of April, in the third year of the reign of our sovereign Lord George the Third, King of Great Britain, &c. before Sir John Fielding, Knt. Sir Henry Cheere,

Knt. William Kelynge, Henry Strachey, Francis Bedwell, John Spinnage, Samuel Pevison, Roger Jackson, Saunders Welch,[1] John Cox, Nicholas Spencer, Thomas Kynaston, Thomas Black, Thomas Miller, Gerard Howard, John Goodchild, Aaron Lamb, Samuel Wadding, Robert Quarme, Peter Plank, Jasper Aris, ----- Brocodale, Esqrs. and others their fellow-justices of our said Lord the King, assigned to keep the peace within the said liberty; and also to hear and determine divers felonies, trespasses, and other misdeeds done and committed in the said liberty.

[(2)]

City, Borough and Town of Westminster in the County of Middlesex.

The Names of the Jurors to enquire for our sovereign Lord the King, and the body of the said liberty.

Thomas Stephens, Gent. sworn Foreman   James Crofts

James Bellis	Kemp Bridges
John Cropley	John Tinckler
John Tatham	Thomas Woolhead
Thomas Pervill	Richard Francklin
John Gregory,	Thomas Heafford
Robert Haswittle	Thomas Billiffe
Edward Jones	James Wilchin
Thomas Mist	Edward Hutchinson
John Goodacre	John Knight
Thomas Whitmay	Edward Gray.

[B-1]

A Charge to the Grand Jury.

Gentlemen

THIS honourable, this important, and most necessary office, which your country now calls upon you to execute, has been so often and so ably explained, from the different benches in this kingdom, that the duties of it are almost as universally known as the office itself. To suppose then that I could add any thing new to this subject, would be an extraordinary instance of my vanity. However, as something is expected to be said on these occasions, the few observations I have to make, may serve rather to remind than to inform you in your duty; it being merely my intention to recall to the memory of those who have served this office before, and to raise in the minds of others who have never attended on these occasions, an adequate idea, if possible, of the immense conse-

[1] The well-known High Constable for Holborn, quoted in Henry Fielding's own *Charge*.

quence of that trust now reposed on you, for grand-juries, gentlemen, are the great bulwark of English liberty, the guardians of our property; and the security of our lives. [2]

In order to do this, I shall first consider the matter; that is to say, the objects of your enquiry; and then the manner in which it is expected, and were much to be wished, this enquiry should be made. Indeed, as to the former of these, if you have paid a due attention to the proclamation just read, it must give you a general idea of the business you are now assembled to execute; it being intitled, " A Proclamation for the Encouragement of Piety and Virtue; and for the Punishing of Vice, Prophaneness, and Immorality." And tho' indeed there is scare an offence, either towards God or man, that is not there pointed out for our prevention or punishment; yet, as you are the grand spring and fountain of all the proceedings on this court, it is evident, that, unless you diligently enquire, and faithfully present, the wicked must go on and prosper; and piety and virtue, if not totally extinguished, will be inevitably overshadowed by the rank and luxuriant branches of vice and immorality. [3]

OFFENCES

THE offences, gentlemen, that will be offered to your consideration, must either be by presentment or indictment; and of these there are an infinite variety: but, as I should be sorry to take up too much of the time of this court, or uselessly engross your attention, I shall confine myself to those only which may, probably, be submitted to your enquiry, and which are within the jurisdiction of this court to punish; and to these I shall speak in the following order: namely, Offences towards God, the King, to one another, and to the Public in general.

AND, first, as to the offences towards God. You are to present all who atheistically deny his being, or blasphemously ridicule his attributes; and, if we consider but one moment, how much the true happiness of each individual consists in an acknowledged dependence on the Supreme Being, and in such a faith in his Son, our blessed Redeemer, as may beget an unerring obedience to his laws, we shall find, that every man's happiness will be proportioned to that faith and obedience; and so will that of every [4] family, consequently of every nation, for national happiness depend on national piety and virtue. From hence you may gather, how essential a part of your duty it is to support the established religion of your country; and, though we are encouraged to the practice of piety and goodness by the promises of inestimable blessings as our reward; and are dissuaded, nay deterred, from vice and immorality, by the fear of eternal punishment; yet we find there has always been a necessity for the execution of human laws to enforce and punish the violation of those of the Almighty; and it is of these laws you are now called upon to give your assistance in the execution; for a little observation is sufficient to shew, that those punishments, which follow the commission of crimes in common people, are more likely to prove efficacious, than those that are at a greater distance.

AND, now I am speaking in an open court, I cannot sufficiently lament, that shameful, inexcuseable, and almost universal practice of prophane swearing in our streets: — A crime so easy to be punished, and so seldom done, that mankind almost forget it is an offence; and, to our dishonour be it spoken, it is almost peculiar to the English nation! I beg, Gentlemen, you would use your utmost endeavours to suppress this dreadful evil wherever you can; but this you will best do by your own example, as the offence is punishable in a judicial way before a magistrate. Nor should I [5-C] mention it here, was I not sensible that I am speaking in the presence of a great number of peace-officers, whose immediate duty is to apprehend such miscreants, and carry them before a magistrate; and who are not only blameable, but punishable, for the neglect of this duty.

THE last offence I shall mention on this subject is, the breach of the Sabbath, a practice as shameful as it is common: but as these are unworthy members of the church, and not only disgraceful, but noxious members of society, they will therefore, I doubt not, meet with the detestation of all pious and honest men, and consequently with every punishment due to such an insolent crime, which it may be in your power to inflict; for this sort of impious neglect partakes of the deepest ingratitude, from the creature to the Creator.

THE next offences I am to speak of, are those towards our Sovereign Lord the King; and these relate either to his Sacred Person, his Crown or Dignity. And here I have a fair opportunity to expatiate on the various kinds of Treason; but as offences of this high nature will scarc come before this court, nor, I hope, before any court in this kingdom: and as it is a more pleasing task to speak of advantages than crimes, permit me, for a moment to turn your thoughts towards our excellent Constitution; [6] observe well its dignity, examine how nobly it is calculated for the support of liberty; mark how, by its exquisite frame, our privileges are preserved, our properties secured, and our happiness established; and who will not rejoice that he is an Englishman. Then behold our most gracious Sovereign as an almost perfect man, presiding over this perfect human system of government; and happy indeed must it be for this nation, when he, who is the head of the Church, is one of the brightest examples of Piety in it; and where he, who is the supreme Governor of a free People, is the greatest friend to Liberty. Behold him in private life, and you will see the most amiable pattern of conjugal and parental affection, of filial duty and brotherly love. What motives are here for veneration and respect; what claims on our gratitude; what a solid foundation for lasting love and loyalty. Treason in a reign like this, would be the most unnatural of crimes, for we have nothing left, even in our wishes for a monarch, but for his health and long life; which, I am persuaded, must be the constant objects of the united prayers of his faithful people. Pleasing as this subject is, I shall conclude it by the mentioning of one circumstance, which does honour to the present reign, and will appear in history as the most glorious act of the best of Kings; I mean his Majesty's making his Judges independant, by increasing their salaries, and establishing them in their office for life; an additional security this, to the liberty of the subject, that words can give [7] but an imperfect idea of; and should his Majesty, as from that countenance with which he has lately honoured this bench, doubtless he will, extend his care and attention to the civil power throughout his kingdom. Government must be established on the most respectable footing, and the great advantages from it, viz. impartial justice; peace and good order be transmitted to our posterity; and that we may deserve the continuation of these blessings, as Christians and Englishmen, let us fear God, and honour the King.

THE next offences, Gentlemen, I am to recommend to your consideration, are those arising from the injuries we do to each other. These either concern our lives, our properties, or our reputations: as to the first of these, viz. murder, I thank God, considering how populous this kingdom is, and in what an abandoned luxurious age we live, instances of this horrid crime are rare; and I verily believe, that the severe blows, that intoxicating liquor, gin, has, within these years, received from the legislation, has made them more rare; nay, perhaps, that house-breakers, highwaymen, and other violators of the public peace, are not so cruel as formerly, may be owing to the same cause; for Gin is a special of liquid fire, that inflames the constitution, enrages the mind, does not cheer the heart, but makes men ripe for mischief. As felons of all kinds, as well as cheats, are the objects [8] of universal fear, being the declared enemies of their fellow-creatures; I am sure you need no other motive than a regard to the public welfare, to afford your utmost assistance in bringing them to condign punishment. And give me leave to point out the receivers of stolen goods, as a particular object of attention; for, if there were no receivers, there would be no thieves. In a trading populous city like this, in a country distinguished for bravery, distinguished for liberty, trials of manhood, must frequently happen, and assaults among the people, and some of a very cruel nature, will sometimes arise: these indeed deserve punishment; but as among these prosecutions, there are some of a litigious nature, where no real injury has been done, you will be watchful, by a nice enquiry, to defeat the designs of malice, who too often tempts her votaries to supply facts by perjury. Prosecutions like these, serve only to strip the rags from the backs of the poor, to place them on the shelves of the pawn-broker, and to bring their late unhappy possessors, and their families to the parish. Such Disputes should end at the reconciling bar of the candid magistrate.

THE next offence which comes in order to be spoke of is, the defaming and aspersing the reputation of our neighbour, commonly called a libel. Wood, in his institutes, says, "That a Libel is a malicious defamation of any person, expressed either in [D-9] printing or writing, signs or pictures, to asperse the reputation of any one who is alive, or the memory of one that is dead." This, Gentlemen, is an offence of the deepest dye, fatal in its consequences, and, from its nature, difficult to be guarded against. For my own part, I have ever endeavoured to persuade myself, that folly and ignorance have a greater share in these aspersions than malice: and where this is the case, caution should supply the place of punishment; but where there is evidence of malice, what punishment can be adequate to the crime of robbing a man of his good name; for he who maliciously invents, or propagates a falshood, to the injury of an innocent person, to serve the purpose, either of ambition or avarice, is a monster in human shape, that beggars all description. — A wretch like this deserves not friends nor confidence: for a good man values his reputation more than his life; nay, to enjoy it, is one of the great ends of his living. And as you, Gentlemen, are summoned to this place, because you are men of reputation, I am persuaded you are too sensible of the value of character yourselves, to suffer that of your neighbour to be wounded with impunity, if you can afford him redress.

THE next offences deserving your notice, are those that are committed against the public in general; of these there are a great variety, but I shall confine myself to the three following, [10] viz. public lewdness, bawdy-houses, gaming-houses. And first as to public lewdness.

IT is the observation of a moral writer of eminence, "That there is some degree of virtue in a man's keeping his vices to himself:" for, as example is allowed to be more efficacious than precept, in recommendation of virtue, where men act as it were in opposition to the depravation of human nature; how must the open and public example of lewdness draw men into the tide of wickedness, where their own passions and inclinations serve as winds to carry them down the stream! Men like these, deserve punishment as public as their crimes. But as this offence belongs to none but the most abandoned mind, I thank God it is not common; and perhaps it would be much less seen, were those persons punished, who exposed to sale the most abandoned prints of lewdness, and the most infamous books of bawdry, which are considerably bought by curious youths, to the danger of their modesty, the hazard of their morals, and too often to the total destruction of their virtue.

As to bawdy-houses, they are the receptacles of those who still have some sense of shame left, but not enough to preserve their innocence. [11]

THESE houses are all sufficiently injurious, and do great mischief. But those I would particularly point out to your attention, are the open, avowed, low, and common bawdy-houses, where vice is rendered cheap, and consequently within the reach of the common people, who are the very stamina of the constitution.

THESE are the channels thro' which rottenness is conveyed into the bones of the artificer, labourer, soldier, and mariner; by this means weakness and distemper are entailed on their offspring, whose utility to the public depends on their health and strength. These are the houses that harbour and protect undutiful children, idle servants, and disobedient apprentices. Let me then entreat you, as fathers, masters, and as tradesmen, to put an end to these sinks of vice in your respective neighbourhoods.

LET not that common vulgar error, of being afraid of these people, because they are litigious, desperate, and full of threats; for these fears are groundless, and should not, nay, I hope will not, deter you from this particular duty. — You present, and we will punish.

AS to gaming-houses; such numbers of persons of all ranks, have brought themselves, some to the greatest distresses, and others to most shameful and ignominious ends, by frequenting [12] these houses, where Gentlemen, sharpers, highwaymen, tradesmen, their servants, nay, often their apprentices, are mixed together; that when I mention the very name of a gaming-house, I am persuaded that it conveys to your minds such ideas of mischief to society, that you will not suffer any of them to escape that come to your knowledge. And by a particular attention to the last mentioned offences, you may be the happy means of preventing frauds, thefts, and robberies; most of which take their rise from these impure fountains of extravagance.

HAVING now gone through these objects of enquiry, that occurred to my mind, and endeavoured to explain the consequences of the offences themselves, in order to excite your attention to the offenders, I shall beg leave to say a few words concerning the manner in which it is expected this enquiry should be made. I am persuaded that I need not remind you, Gentlemen, that you have taken a most solemn oath to execute this office, with impartial justice, without resentment, without malice, without favour, without affection. And this I sincerely trust you will do. But when I mention the word oath; where shall I find language to express the hearty concern I feel, when I consider with what shameful insensibility, this great defence of our lives, this barrier of our liberties, this security of our properties, an oath, is treated by the lower rank of the community! I too much fear, [E-13] that one of the principal causes of this contempt, is the slovenly manner in which this solemn obligation is administered, which does not only take off the awe, but even the very idea of the presence of Almighty God.

INDEED, from unavoidable necessity, witnesses that come before you, are sworn in open court; where, I am sorry to say, neither that decency or silence can be easily preserved, which is so necessary on such solemn occasions: and it often happens, that there is a great distance of time between their being sworn, and their being examined. And though, Gentlemen, you are not authorized by law to re-administer the oath, yet it will be highly becoming, nay, it is absolutely necessary for you, to remind the parties that come before you, in the strictest terms, of the very solemn obligation they are under to speak the truth; and this should be done previous to your examination of their complaint: for, as you only hear one side, and as I have before observed, many prosecutions are founded on malice, prosecutors are often tempted at that time to go great lengths, it being out of power of those they accuse, either to contradict them, or to make a defence. Should they not then be also cautioned against advancing falshoods, which must be detected when they come to a trial; though trials, I fear, are studiously avoided by these prosecutors, who indict merely to intimidate or make a property of those they [14] accuse. Were I to unravel the various artifices which experience has informed me malice and oppression constantly use to impose on juries, there would be no time left either for you, or this court, to execute the business we are met upon.

BUT I cannot conclude this subject, without making one observation on a part of your oath, which, I fear, is not always preserved with that fidelity one would wish, and yet, I believe, is generally broke though with innocence. I mean that secrecy to which you are enjoined; for, I believe, it often happens, that those matters, which have been the objects of your enquiry in the morning, when in a collective body, are made the subject of an evening's conversation when separated; and, as this may be the means of defeating public justice, it would be but decent to defer such conversation till you are discharged this court.

HOWEVER, submitting what I have said to your own good sense, and your own integrity, and myself to your candour, I doubt not but you will execute your office in all respects suitable to its dignity, to the satisfaction of your consciences, and to the advantage of your country.

FINIS.

A **CHARGE** GIVEN TO THE GRAND JURIES OF THE COUNTY OF THE CITY OF DUBLIN, AND COUNTY OF DUBLIN, AT A SITTING OF His Majesty's Commissions of *Oyer and Terminer*, AND *General Gaol Delivery* For the said Counties, On SATURDAY the 3d Day of DECEMBER, 1763, BY THE RIGHT HONOURABLE **RICHARD ASTON**, Esq; Chief Justice of his Majesty's Court of Common Pleas. Published at the Request of THE CITY GRAND JURY. *DUBLIN*: Printed for SARAH COTTER, in Skinner-Row, 1763.

[A 2]

Gentlemen of these Grand Juries,

I HAVE the Honour to meet You on this solemn Occasion, which the Wisdom of Government, for the Sake of preserving Peace and Good Order, has made frequent and regular.

As the Well-being of every Country in a great Measure depends upon the wise Frame of their Laws, to regulate Property, and to restrain and punish Offenders, and on a due Execution of those Laws; it became absolutely necessary for the Sup-[4] port of Government, and the Safety of the Subject, that some Persons should be intrusted with the Inquiry into all Crimes and Offences whatsoever: And it was no less needful for the Security and Quiet of every Man, that such a Trust should be delegated to Men of Integrity and Indifference, who might not suffer the Guilty to escape Prosecution for their Crimes, or the Innocent to be oppressed by false, weak, or vindictive Accusations.

For this wise and necessary Purpose, GRAND JURIES were instituted, which are therefore generally composed of Persons of the first Rank, and best Credit in their Country, who, from their Number, Circumstances, and Characters, are the least liable to be awed by Power, byassed by Favour, or influenced by any undue Means whatsoever.

MANY of you, Gentlemen, have so often served your Country in that important Trust, and have consequently been so often put in mind of the several Branches of your Duty, that it may seem needless at present to enumerate them; and yet, the general expectation of the Duty required from this Bench, makes it necessary for me to offer some Matters for your Attention and Consideration, which I shall endeavour to adapt to the present State and Condition of Affairs within your respective Jurisdictions. [A 3-5]

IT is an undoubted Truth, that to maintain and recover the Peace when it is broken, shews more Power; but that to prevent the Breach of it shews more Wisdom; and therefore it is highly to be wished, that the vigilant Attention of the Magistracy, and the Influence and Example of the Gentry, might ever be so effectually exerted as to prevent those Means by which Disorders come : For in populous Cities, and in Government in general, as in private domestic Society, if the Power is not preserved and exerted in its proper Place, and a due Subordination formed in Consequence of it; if there is not Example, Regularity, and good Discipline; Disobedience, Disorders, and Confusion, will be the natural Fruits of such a neglected Police: And then, the Work of Reformation can only be brought about, by enforcing an Obedience to the Laws by Punishments suited to the Nature and Degree of the several Offences.

TO enquire into those Offences, to present the Offenders, is your Province; and your Power for that Purpose is co-extensive with the Criminal Law. As the Catalogue of Offences, as well as Capital as Criminal, within your Cognizance, are very numerous I will endeavour to class them, as far as I shall enumerate them, in such a Manner, that the Nature of the Offences may be distinctly understood, and the Wisdom and Utility of the Laws in the Suppression and Punishment of them clearly comprehended; whether the Of-[6] fence be more immediately against the Duty We owe to GOD, the King and his Government, Individuals, or the public Police: Under which four general Heads all public Crimes and Misdemeanors may be properly ranked and comprehended.

UNDER the first of these, all Offences against Religion are included; such as Publishing Books against its Truth, reviling the Sacrament, Blasphemy, Neglect of religious Worship, prophane Swearing, Drunkenness, and all Kind of Immorality.

To diminish the Credit, is to diminish the Influence of Religion; and We are well assured, that whatever tends to weaken that Influence upon the Minds of Men, is highly detrimental to the public Welfare. It is taking away an Encouragement to Virtue, and a Restraint upon Vice, a greater and more co-ercive Restraint than all the Wisdom of Human Laws, or the Terror of Human Judicatures can impose. It has been the peculiar Honour of our Government, that the Observation of the Sabbath has been more strictly enjoined by our Laws, than by any other Christian Community; and it would be a great Pity, that such excellent Laws should lose their Use for want of due Execution, or to be permitted to be defeated by any Houses or Places of Resort on that Day, for any

Wicked or unlawful Purposes, such as Gaming, Drunkenness or Debauchery: For there Youth are first seduced from [A 4-7] their native Innocence; there they imbibe those dissolute Principles upon which they afterwards act to the Destruction of themselves and others; there they first get involved into Difficulties, and become connected with a Set of Acquaintance, who are ever prompting them to Villainies to support their Extravagance, and ready to assist in carrying them into Execution. It is there they learn that detestable Habit of prophane Swearing, which, by Degrees, lessens the Awe and Regard for Oaths on just and necessary Occasions: And when the Reverence for that solemn Appeal to the Almighty is once lessened in the Minds of Men, they are led insensibly to Perjury itself, which is destructive of all the Fruits of Truth and Justice.

AMONGST other Immoralities prompting Men to a Neglect of their religious Duties, is Drunkenness, too frequently practised with Impunity, scandalous to the Profession of Christianity, and the Abhorrence of all good and wise Men: When once this Vice prevails, it infects the Manners of a People, it enervates and debases the natural Courage and Bravery of the lower Sort, and turns it into a barbarous Ferocity and Madness, the evil Effects of which We too frequently hear of in horrid Cruelties. In the Gentry, it extinguishes that Spirit of Emulation which excites them to noble Actions, and promotes public Virtue; for Men abandoned to this Vice, have nothing in View but its Gratification; they lose [8] the Ambition of doing well, and the Shame of doing ill: In short, it creates a Neglect of the Laws, destroys Order, produces Faction and ill Discipline, and is highly Injurious to Society, whether considered in a religious or civil Light.

I DOUBT not but Gentlemen of your Education, Understanding, Fortune, and Influence, do, by your Example, discourage the Growth and Increase of all these Immoralities; and will, upon your due Inquiry, present all Persons and Places which contribute to these Disorders. It is with a View to that laudable End, that his Majesty's Proclamation for the Encouragement of Virtue and the Suppression of Vice, Prophaneness, and Immorality, is directed to be read at the Commissions: His Majesty, by being himself the Pattern of Piety and Goodness, recommends the Practice of it to all his People, and promotes it by his own great Example.

THE next Duty We owe, is to our King, and his Government, for whose Preservation, it is ever Part of your Duty, to enquire of and present all Treasons and Misprisions thereof: But You, Gentlemen, have been so frequently reminded of the several Species of Treason, I shall not now think it necessary to enumerate them, as I am sure every one who hears me, is sensible that any Attempt to disturb the Happiness of his Majesty's Reign, by Conspiracy against his Sacred Person, or Rebellion against his Government, [9] would be an Attempt to subvert the happiest

Constitution that any Nation was ever blessed with. It is sufficient therefore to inform You, that the Laws have provided wisely against all Offences that even tend, though they do not amount, to High Treason; and that all opprobrious and seditious Libels or Discourses against the King or his Government, are indictable Offences, within your Cognizance, and deserve your most serious Attention and Regard, whenever they are laid before You.

NEXT to Offences against the King and the State, the Injuries done to Individuals fall under your Consideration; which respect their Persons, their Reputation, Habitations, and Property.

OF those respecting the Person, Murder is certainly the greatest, and is declared in this Kingdom to be High Treason; and every Design to commit Murder, though not carried into Execution, is a very great Misdemeanor. There are many Statutes made for the Security of the Individuals against the Violence of others, and which inflict Capital Punishments on the Offenders, which I shall not now take particular Notice of; but think it sufficient to observe, that all ineffectual Attempts with an Intent to commit those Crimes, are punishable as Misdemeanors.

ALL other Injuries to the Person, are reducible under the general Head of Assaults, which [10] differ sometimes so much in their Degree as to be distinguished even in the Indictment: But in most Cases the Indictment is found generally, and the Circumstances in Aggravation, or Mitigation, are left to the Judgment of the Court which inflicts the Punishment.

THE LAW extends its Protection likewise to the Reputations of the Subject, which are too frequently and violently attacked by the Publication of Libels: These are open, public Attempts to blast and ruin the Characters of Men, which to every one of a generous Mind, is dearer to him than his Property. It is therefore deemed an Indictable Offence; for the Liberty of the Press, is, like all other Liberties, to be used and enjoyed according to Law, which being a Law of Reason, and guarding against Force, Violence and Licentiousness in every Branch of it, will no more admit an injurious Insult on a Man's Reputation than a forcible one on his Person or Property. These Sorts of Offences demand our most earnest Attention; because a Libel in every Instance, is a gross Abuse of the Liberty of the Press, as it perverts that valuable Privilege in Favour of Public Liberties, into a mischievous Attack on the Happiness of private Persons.

AS to Injuries which respect the Habitations and Property of Men; the former are most affected by the Crimes of House-burning, and [11] Burglary; the latter by Theft, malicious Mischief, and Forgery. Such Offences against the Mansion and Habitation of Men, which is a Place that the Owner ought to enjoy in the utmost Security, do, in Point of reason, as well as the Eye of the Law, appear highly aggravated, whether

You consider the Manner or the Time of committing them; when Men are most liable to surprize, and least able to defend themselves, and when there is the least Probability of discovering the Offenders.

THE principal Aggravations of Larceny are, where the felonious taking is from the Person, or from the House; and where it is accompanied with the Circumstance of Violence and putting in Fear, the Offence is distinguished by the Name of Robbery. Many are the Statutes which relate to these Matters; various and numerous are the Articles which it is made Felony to steal, spoil, or destroy: For a large Share of the Property amongst Men being of such a Nature, as necessarily to be abroad and ever exposed to Theft or Mischief, which no human Precaution could be watchful enough to defend; it was therefore thought expedient by the Legislature, to enact penal and sanguinary Laws to guard the Property of Persons in that State of Danger, which a Civil Action was found insufficient to protect, or to prevent the Spoliation of. And here I cannot but observe, that where the Injuries to the Goods, Cattle, and Improvements of Men, [12] are done without any View of Profit to the Offenders, but proceeding from a mere Spirit of Malice and Mischief, nothing can be urged in the Mitigation of such Crimes, and they deservedly receive the utmost Severity in Punishment.

EXPERIENCE too well proves that the Crime of Forgery, which may affect either a Man's real or personal Property, is a Crime of the most dangerous and extensive Nature, and is become so easy to execute and so difficult to detect, that it has made its destructive Progress, with the Increase of Trade and Wealth, in such a Manner amongst a Commercial People, that the Precautions of the most Prudent have frequently been found an insufficient Security against it; for which Reason the Legislature have, with great Wisdom, made it a Capital Offence.

I shall now, Gentlemen, proceed to take Notice of some Offences against the Common Wealth, or Public Police, and which concern the Public Justice, and Peace, as well as the Trade, Health, and Domestic Order of this City.[1]

As there is not any Nation, happier in their Laws, every Endeavour should be used to preserve their Force and Influence; and every Opposition to their Execution, ought to be discountenanced as *criminal*: Obstructing therefore the Execution of the Process of Law, or pre-[13] venting its Effects by procuring Escapes, breaking Prison, or Rescue, are indictable Offences against the Public Peace, in some Cases as Felonies, in others as Misdemeanors. And when Offenders are led forth to Justice, to undergo the Punishment due to their Crimes (which Punishment is intended for Example to deter others from the like Misdoings, and to secure the Innocent in Peace) all Interruptions to the Executions of the

[1] This is an interesting new view of the magistrate's responsibilities in his Charge.

Sentence of the Law, which ought ever to be attended with an Order and Decorum suited to its Solemnity, are presentable and punishable as great Misdemeanors.

ALL Offences whatsoever, subject to Prosecution by Indictment, are considered by the Law, as Breaches of the public Peace: But the most flagrant Breach of the public Peace, is a Riot, supported by Numbers, and accompanied with the Circumstances of Terror. This Offence, unless timely suppressed, becomes dangerous to the Public, as well as to private Persons, and may finally overturn all good Order and Rule amongst us.

NO Man here can be a Stranger to the late tumultuous Insurrections in the remoter Part of this Kingdom; and I am very sorry to observe, that there have been of late very outrageous Proceedings of the like Kind in this City. Let the Pretences for such riotous assemblings and risings be what they may, all such daring and [14] licentious Mobs ought to meet the immediate Resistance, not only of the Magistracy and those in Authority, but of every Man who wishes to preserve the Government, the Laws, and this excellent Constitution.

EVERY Man who thinks seriously, must be sensible of the ill Consequences that are likely to flow from such repeated Disturbances; they are not barely to be considered as Breaches of the Peace, but as having a direct Tendency to dissolve all Bonds of Society, to destroy Property, and to endanger Government itself. Insurrections, therefore, for the Reformation of real or imaginary Evils of a public and general Nature, are, by Construction of Law, considered as High Treason, within the Clause of levying War in the Statute of Treasons: For tho' such risings are not immediately levelled against the Sacred Person of his Majesty, yet they are against his Royal Authority and the Dignity of his Crown.

THERE are Laws to redress all Grievances: If any Man thinks himself aggrieved, let him have Recourse to those Laws: If Men will attempt to do themselves that Justice they imagine they are intitled to, or to punish others for Offences committed towards themselves, they take the Sceptre out of the King's Hands, and the Power from the Laws: And it would be [15] impossible, Gentlemen, for any Government to subsist, under proper and reasonable Regulations, if the Subjects of that Government were permitted to be wiser than the Laws, to judge of their own Injuries, to carve out their own Remedies, and to punish the supposed Aggressors of their Rights. The Measure of Redress, as well as the Mode of obtaining it, would be so vague, so various, and so disproportioned, according to the different Opinions and Feelings of Men, that both the one and the other would be no less uncertain, and fanciful, than oppressive.

No Man, or interested Body of Men are to be trusted with such an Authority; possibly *no* Man is equal to it in his Nature, where *Self* is concerned: And therefore, Laws are adapted to the Universal Case of all Mankind united in one Society and Government, and *no* Man is to be his *own* Judge, or Avenger. And, Gentlemen, if those very Laws should err, or be defective in any Particulars (which, as being the Works of Human Wisdom only, they may) yet that is infinitely more supportable and more wise to submit to, than to leave the Law, and the Remedy, to that Incertainty and Oppression, which the Mode and Measure before described (when usurped by Individuals) will ever be subject to.

THERE are Laws therefore, Gentlemen, to punish Men for such Presumption; and I trust [16] they will ever be faithfully put in Execution. I have dwelt the longer on this Subject, as a Caution and Warning to the People in general, and that it may be known, how justly severe the Laws are against such Offences; and what Anarchy and Confusion might be introduced into the State by a Continuation of such daring Proceedings: I hope that my humble Endeavours on this Occasion may have their desired Effect, that future Mischiefs may be thereby prevented, and that We may not be laid under the disagreeable Necessity of punishing the Offenders. I thought it my Duty to say thus much, and I think I could not say less upon such an Occasion.

As to Offences which concern Trade; they are such as more immediately affect the Revenue of the Crown, by Smuggling to its Prejudice; or the Subject, by a Variety of Frauds and Oppressions in carrying it on: Amongst the rest, none better deserves your Notice, than that Offence, which in the several Shapes of Forestalling, Regrating and Engrossing, raises the Price of Provisions; and to satisfy the Avarice of a few, oppresses and adds to the Calamities of the Poor. An Offence so wicked in its Principle, and so pernicious in its effects, that the Number it distresses will induce You to present all Offences of that Sort within your Jurisdiction. [B-17]

ALL COMBINATIONS by those of a Trade to raise the Price of the Commodities, tho' done in the Shape of Contracts, or Covenants not to sell under a set Rate, are condemned by the Law, and held illegal by Lord *Holt*, in a Case, called the *Plate Button-makers Case*. By the particular Statutes of this Kingdom, as well as by the Common Law, such Practices are forbid; and all Workmen and Artificers combining to advance the Wages and Rate of their Labour, or to lessen their usual Hours of Work, though under the Form of By-Laws, Rules and Orders, are equally liable to the Punishments ordained by the Law: Their Clubs or Societies for that Purpose are also held unlawful, and the Persons who knowingly harbour them in their Houses for such Purposes, are deemed Keepers of disorderly Houses. I believe, no Principle is truer in Trade, than, that every Commodity, and the Labour attending it, will find its own true Value: That there should be one set Rate both for one and the other, seems to me unreasonable, as well as unpracticable; as it gives no

Encouragement to, nor makes any Allowance for superior Skill, Strength, Diligence and Honesty; but those, who least deserved it, would be the greatest Gainers by such a Measure.

I AM concerned to see so many Offences of this Sort in my Calendar, and, amongst the rest, *one*, which is the greatest Discouragement to virtuous Industry, as well as the most unrea-[18] sonable Restraint on the natural Rights of Mankind; I Mean that Sort of Combination amongst Journeymen, that no Man should work in his Trade without a Ticket, or Certificate from those Confederates, denoting that it was free and lawful for him to do so. How injurious this is to the Public, as well as oppressive to Individuals, at the Close of so long a War, is too evident to bear any Doubt.[1] The great Number of Forces necessarily discharged from the Sea and Land Service, adds a Multitude of Hands to the Community that may be usefully employed in Civil Capacities: And it would be unreasonable not to allow every such Person in this Kingdom, as in *England*, to pursue those honest Means to obtain a Livelihood, which his natural Bent and Genius prompted him to make Choice of. A different Conduct shuts the Door against Industry, and leaves those very Men, who have spent their Time, and risqued their Lives, in the Service of their Country, in a State of inactive Poverty, exposed to every Temptation to break the Laws, and to embrace a dissolute Course of Life, by being denied the Liberty of following a better; and, for aught I know, this may have tended to increase those very Disturbances, which, We have already heard too much of. But to whatever Set of Persons, the Rules and Orders made under these extraordinary Combinations are intended to extend, they are all equally illegal and void, and require the most immediate Interposition of the Law to punish and suppress. [B 2-19]

GENTLEMEN, what relates to Public Health, and the Domestic Order of the City, is next to be considered. Upon this Occasion, I cannot but take Notice of the Diligence and Activity of the Chief Magistrate, in constantly visiting the Markets, and frequently seizing the unwholesome Provisions there exposed to Sale: A Conduct, which being preventive of the ill Effects that, otherwise, might have attended the Health of the City, merits the Thanks and Commendation of the Public. The exposing of unwholesome Victuals to Sale, is an Offence of a very dangerous Tendency; as the Necessities of the numerous Poor, naturally lead them to buy, where they can purchase cheapest; and when once Diseases are contracted from such noxious Food, no Man can answer how far they may extend.

BESIDES these, many and various are the Nusances in this City, and which cannot escape the common Observation of every Man: Such as,

[1] The Seven Years War, the end of which was the Treaty of Paris, signed on 10 February.

great Heaps of Rubbish (the Consequence of Building and Repairs) left in the Streets for an unreasonable Length of Time. No Man, on Account of his own necessary Occasions is to prejudice the Public, and therefore, all Obstructions that may be attended with such a Consequence, ought to be removed in convenient Time.

THE abominable Condition of the Streets is much owing likewise to that intolerable Prac-[20] tice of throwing out of all Kinds of Dirt from the several dwelling Houses; which is not only unwholesome but illegal, and tends, I presume, to invite that Number of Swine, we see so frequently and familiarly feeding and passing in the Streets; Animals so noxious in their Nature, as ever to be held a Nusance, and not permitted therefore to be kept, in a large City. These are indictable Misdemeanors, and ought to be redressed for the Sake of Health and Neatness; Epidemic Disorders frequently arising from the continued Uncleanliness of Inhabitants, whose Indolence, or Fear of Expence, cannot be offered as an Excuse for laying the Public under so great and general an Inconvenience.

THE Great Number of Beggars in the Streets at all Times, is another Nusance that deserves your Notice; it being hardly possible to pass, without being saucily importuned by them in the Day, and audaciously attacked by Night; The many shocking Objects, which too frequently present themselves, ought to be removed, and all who are Impostors, should be exemplarily punished: I confess, Gentlemen, I think it is a Pity that there are not some Laws made for the better Regulation and Support of the Poor of this Kingdom.

BUT the worst of all Nuisances, and most destructive of the Domestic Order of this City, are Disorderly Houses; the most dangerous of which are Night-Houses, for the Reception of [21] the vilest of the People, and where the most abandoned of both Sexes are harboured; who are enured to a Habit of Laziness by Day, and Debauchery by Night. From these Places they issue forth at an irregular Season of the Night, primed with the most pernicious Liquors, and hardened to attempt the most daring Villainies, such as a civilized and well-regulated City should blush to own: And yet I must, with the greatest Concern, observe to You, Gentlemen, that these Enormities grow much too familiar, and that the Acts of Violence, We hear of so frequently committed in the Streets of *Dublin*, approach too near *American* Cruelty.

To suppress such Houses, and prevent the Growth of these Evils, is a Matter of public Concern; and it were fit that in the Appointment of the Nightly Watch in this City, the Age, Condition, Calling, and Character, of the several Persons in that Station, should be consulted, as far as may be, by those to whom their Nomination belongs; for though, *if the Lord keepeth not the City, the Watchman waketh but in vain*, yet we are not in these Cases to place a supine Reliance upon Providence, but it is our Duty to use the best of human Endeavours, and implore the Divine Protection in their Support.

HAVING thus stated to you Gentlemen the Nature of your Institution, and as many branches of your Duty, as upon the present Occasion seem [22] material, I shall briefly consider the Manner in which your Jurisdiction ought to be executed.

THOUGH Grand Juries were to consist of Persons of the best Distinction, yet the Law, ever Jealous of inferior Jurisdictions, would not entrust the Execution of so extensive a Power with any Body of Men, however unexceptionable they might appear, but under the Sanction and Solemnity of an Oath; than the Words of which, nothing can be more plain and expressive; The Language and Signification of it, seems impossible to be mistaken. "Diligent Inquiry into Crimes, True presentment, Secrecy, and Impartiality" are the Terms it enjoins, and you, Gentlemen, who have taken it, are bound to observe it in every Part.

WHEN Accusations are brought before you, You are confined to the Evidence produced on the part of the Crown; and are not to enter into the Circumstances that may be urged by way of Defence: Because the Party accused will have his full Advantage of those upon his Trial. Not that the Tale is to be told partially to you, but the whole Circumstances are to be candidly related to you, or extracted from the Evidence by your Examination and Inquiry; And if you are satisfied upon the whole Matter, that there is a reasonable Ground to warrant the Accusation, you ought to find the Bill. [23]

A METHOD has prevailed in this Kingdom of restraining this Inquiry to the reading of certain written Papers, annexed to the respective Bills of Indictment, which are commonly called Examinations, but are in general no more than Affidavits made before a Magistrate, the Contents of which the Examinant swears to be true: And these *Only*, exclusive of all other Lights, You have been taught to believe are the proper Evidence to inform and conclude your Minds of the Truth of every Accusation. Allowing these Examinations to be admissible Evidence for that purpose, yet there seems to me no legal Foundation to make them the *Only* One.

THE Rights of the Crown and the Liberties of the Subject, stand principally upon the Footing of the Common Law which Law, is *Wholly*, not *Partially* introduced and established in this Kingdom; and all Customs, and Usages contrary to the Spirit and Policy of that Law, are absolutely void. The Benefits therefore arising from that most excellent Institution, a Grand Jury, are alike extended to his Majesty's Subjects in one Kingdom, as in the other, and they are equally intitled to receive and inherit the full Advantages of that General Introduction without reserve. No Restraint therefore, Gentlemen, ought to be put upon Your Enquiry into the Truth of any Accusation brought before You, by a personal Examination of the Witnesses produced on the part of the Crown; as it in an inherent, Con-[24] stitutional Right in You, for the Safety of the Subject, grounded upon the Common Law, agreeable to the Terms of your Oath, recognized by Statutes made to prevent weak and false Accusations, and ratified by immemorial and uniform Usage in that Kingdom, whence this Law is derived.

THE usual Method, Gentlemen, of doing this, is by swearing the Witnesses produced in support of the Prosecution, in open Court, (no other Jurisdiction then having an Authority to administer that Oath[1]) The Names of the Persons so sworn, are indorsed upon the Bill of Indictment, which being delivered to the Grand Jury, is the proper Information to them on whom to call to give Evidence; And at the same time excludes all suspected possibility of the Defendant's Witnesses being clandestinely introduced to controvert the Accusation; As the Grand Jury have no Right to examine any other Witnesses, than such as are produced before them on the part of the Prosecutor, in the manner I have before mentioned: And this Method of swearing Witnesses and indorsing their Names upon the Bill of Indictment, I have, upon my own Search, found to have been practised [C-25] both in this City and the County of *Dublin*, in many Instances, soon after the Revolution.

IT must be obvious therefore, Gentlemen, to every Man of Understanding, how much more satisfactory this *Viva Voce* Evidence must be to the minds, and conscientious Feelings of a Grand Jury, than any Knowledge or Information that can be drawn by them from the written Examinations *Only*.

WHAT Diligence can be said to be exercised in placing an implicit Faith on the Examinations returned, without making actual Inquiry into the Circumstances themselves? The Injunctions of Diligence, Secrecy, and Impartiality, prove it was intended that the Jury should have all advantages which the several Cases would afford, to make the most effectual Inquiries. The Knowledge of the Accuser, or the Witness; their Fame and Reputation, and the manner of giving their Testimony, frequently afford such strong Lights to Men of Understanding, as cannot possibly appear in the same Form of Words reduced into Writing. Truth is frequently manifested by the Plainness, Ease, and Simplicity of the Person that is giving his Testimony; and Falseness and ill Design, may be alike apparent from a sort of Studiousness and Difficulty in answering: It would therefore be beyond Measure unreasonable to deprive You, Gentlemen, of these Opportunities of informing your Judgments, when you are expressly bound [26] by your Oaths, as well as the eternal Law of Justice, and loving your Neighbour as yourselves, to take heed of

[1] The Form of the Oath: "The Evidence you shall give to the Grand Inquest upon this Bill of Indictment *Against* A. B. shall be the truth, the whole Truth, and nothing but the Truth. So help you GOD."

Truth in your Presentment; and when the Difference is so material to the Party accused in point of Reputation as well as Expence, whether he shall be put upon his Trial as a Delinquent, or be judged by you innocent of the Charge.

BOTH these Methods of your Enquiry, as well by written Papers, as by Evidence *Viva Voce*; being admitted in this Kingdom to be equally legal; who can hesitate to prefer that Method which is best calculated for the Security of the Subject, suits best with the Obligations of your Oath, "a Diligent Enquiry," and is almost likely to produce the Satisfactory Effects of that Diligence, " a true Presentment "?

THAT Method therefore, Gentlemen, of examining the Witnesses themselves, I most seriously recommend to your Consideration and Practice; and under these Directions will no longer detain you from the Dispatch of your necessary Business, not doubting, but that you will discharge this important Trust, constitutionally reposed in you by the Common Law, to the Honour of yourselves, and the Advantage of your Country.

FINIS.

THE RIGHTS AND PRIVILEGES OF BOTH THE **UNIVERSITIES** AND OF THE UNIVERSITY OF CAMBRIDGE IN PARTICULAR DEFENDED IN A CHARGE TO THE GRAND JURY AT THE QUARTER SESSION FOR THE PEACE HELD IN AND FOR THE TOWN OF **CAMBRIDGE** THE TENTH DAY OF OCTOBER 1768. ALSO AN ARGUMENT IN THE CASE OF THE COLLEGES OF CHRIST and EMMANUEL. by JAMES MARRIOT, LLD. *CAMBRIDGE*, Printed by J. ARCHDEACON, Printer to the UNIVERSITY: Sold by T. & J. MERRIEL, and J. WOODYER in CAMBRIDGE J. FLETCHER and D. PRINCE at OXFORD; J. RIVINGTON, B. WHITE, JOHNSON & Co. J. BEECROFT, and J. WORRALL in LONDON. 1769 For the Benefit of the HOSPITAL at CAMBRIDGE.

(*Price* 1 *s.*)

IT is owing to certain misrepresentations that the following charge is printed: although the Person who delivered it as a Magistrate could have wished to have avoided the submitting to strict perusal words spoke without preparation, on a sudden occasion, when he was requested by the rest of the Bench to attend on account of a prosecution of much consequence. It will however be a very great satisfaction if the publication may serve a general purpose, and keep up for the future in the minds of the inhabitants of this place, the ideas which were meant to be impressed concerning the submission due to the good government of the Laws in general, and the preservation of the most valuable Rights and Privileges to this University in particular.

[A 2-3]

CHARGE

Gentlemen of the Grand Jury,

YOU have heard his Majesty's proclamation read against prophaneness and immorality: I dare say no motive for a discharge of the duty required by it can be wanting to you: and I am extremely happy to see, in point of character and property, a Grand Jury so very respectable: It will be the less necessary therefore for me to press upon your attention the importance of that trust which the constitution of your country reposes in you.

With you, Gentlemen, as a Grand Jury, the laws begin and end: I mean with regard to their effect: for unless bills are found by grand juries, no crimes against the public peace and the safety of persons or properties can be brought to punishment, and so future attempts discouraged and repressed; because without bills are found no persons can be tried. An ill-judged lenity therefore of Grand Juries, if occasioned by personal favour, or the fears or hopes of private connection, is a crime against the constitution of our country, and destroys the laws in the first entrance of justice.

The bench, however enlightened or supplied in any place, can do little more than explain and announce the laws; but you, Gentlemen, are in fact the Judges for your Country: for you are, as judges of the fact in the first instance, the Guardians of the peace, and properties, and lives of your fellow subjects; because you are to judge whether the bills preferred are such as are fit to be proceeded upon by a more exact trial of the parties charged. [4]

I know it has been attributed to an excess of lenity of former Grand Juries in this place, whether with or without a cause I know not, that crimes against the peace have escaped without farther trial. It this charge were true, the consequence would have been plainly the greatest public disorder, from a presumption of impunity. I inquire not into the cause, but what passed last winter is as obvious to your reflection as it is recent in your memories. Your houses were not safe: scarce a week passed without shops being robbed, or attempted to be robbed: the streets swarming at unreasonable hours with vagrants, and disorderly persons of both sexes. The magistrates and officers of justices intimidated in the discharge of their duties: a murder committed, without the actor of that barbary being yet discovered.

When I recollect a magistrate in this place, of the most respectable rank, being insulted by the populace in the streets upon the success of a certain cause, I cannot help observing to you the general disposition among the lower orders of the people to hold in contempt the authority of the magistrates; it has shown itself almost in every corner of the kingdom, and broke out into violent disorders: For my own part I tremble, lest the continuance of them should occasion remedies as terrible as the disease. While the licentiousness stalks abroad you cannot be too watchful, Gentlemen, to support your own property and safety. More particularly must you be attentive to stop the first sources of public evils: I know none more certain causes of them here, than the numerous small public houses, the pests of this town; and those which come under the general description of the law as disorderly houses, or houses of bawdry. From hence proceeds all that dissoluteness, and fa-[A 3-5] tal extravagance attending it, which induce young persons, by inflaming their passions, to destroy their constitutions, and to betray too often their trusts and their duties to their masters, their parents and families. Pilferings, robberies, and murders, flow from these places of vicious entertainment. You have a long list of prisoners: Among others, I see the son of a respectable inhabitant of this place charged with assaulting his own father, and afterwards of drawing a knife upon the magistrate. If this is so: it is madness; such as every greatly wicked person is possessed with: and to what can we attribute such sort of outrages if it is possible, but to such causes as these which I have mentioned?

You have in the calendar of prisoners several persons who are charged with keeping houses of debauchery: Among them is one who once was so successful as to obtain a verdict against a respectable magistrate who was unfortunately mistaken in the mode and forms of office. I think it necessary to observe here, for the sake of the audience, that this verdict, as was the declared opinion of the King's Judges in *Westminster* Hall, did not, and does not affect in any degree the jurisdiction of the magistrate, nor the right of the officers under him, nor the privileges of that body in which the magistrate presided, who acted upon that occasion.

By the laws of the land in favour of liberty, mistakes in form are always useful to the criminal; a defect in the nicety of pleadings, the negligence or want of judgement in any counsel who settles them; the prejudices, or a little too much firmness of opinion, in persons not versed in the laws which are out of their profession, are circumstances, any one of which may occasion at any time the loss of a suit: but such a case may happen [6] without destroying the general authority of the magistrates, or the legal privileges in the mode of exerting it, necessary to good order and government. There are great privileges existing within the district of this place. Those privileges remain the same: they were granted for great public purposes: they have always been supported by those whose duty it is to support them, on the best and surest foundation.

Should this woman, who has once triumphed, be now found guilty, I mean, if the evidence should be full, in your opinion, and in that of the rest of the jurors, it will only show that public justice, however evaded or insulted, however slow or obstructed, at last overtakes a criminal. But I would not prejudice you against the person: I only mean to awaken your attention to the nature of the crime; that if you see reason you may find bills in this and the like cases, in order to try the fact.

There are two other persons charged with the same offence of keeping a common house of bawdry, *Morris Bearfoot* and *Sarah* his wife. I must observe to you, Gentlemen, that there is a stile of vice, so much the more dangerous to the morals of this place as it is superior in elegance, and therefore it will deserve your serious attention.

In order to obviate any niceties or distinctions which may be taken by counsel as to the indictments of these two persons, it is proper for me to inform you that, by law, a wife may be indicted together with her husband, and condemned to the pillory with him for keeping a bawdy house: for this is an offence as to the government of the house, in which the wife has a a principal share [1];[A 4-7] and it is also an offence as may generally be presumed to be managed by the intrigues of her sex. And so it is laid down 1 *Haw. 2. ibid.* 74.

I must farther observe to you, that although two persons are prosecuted according to the 25 *Geo.* 2. which is made perpetual by the 28 *Geo.* 2. *c.* 19. yet that act only directs the mode of prosecution, and neither alters the nature of the offence, nor the punishment of it at common law.

This act is declarative of the common law, when this act says, *sect.* I. That the master or mistress are equally punishable, and that any person who shall at any time appear, act, or behave him or herself as master or mistress, or as the person having the care, government, or management of a bawdy house, gaming house, or other disorderly house, shall be deemed or taken to be the keeper thereof, and shall be liable to be prosecuted: For, according to Lord *Coke*, Inst. 205. and 1 *Hawkins* 196. it is held, that the keeping a bawdy house is an offence at common law, as well as ecclesiastical; being a common nusance, not only in respect of its endangering the public peace by drawing together dissolute and debauched persons, but also in respect of its apparent tendency to corrupt the manners of both sexes.

For punishment of such offences, antiently, the lords of leets had pillories: so 2 *Hawkins, p.* 73. and the sheriffs held the leet or view of frankpledge, where all persons appeared, and took oaths of allegiance, and swore to maintain the King's peace; and so great an effect, says Lord *Coke*, had this universally in keeping the peace, that before the conquest a man might have rode with a white wand, and much money about him, without weapon, throughout *England.* And although the view [8] of frankpledge, and the formal swearing of all persons to keep the King's peace is disused, yet it is a matter worthy the attention of all persons who hear me, that every man is at this day still bound by his natural allegiance, and by tacit obligation under which he is born: and in return for the benefit and protection of the laws, he is still held in duty to keep and maintain the peace of the King and the land.

[1] This is noteworthy because a married woman was usually considered as a *femme covert* = under the legal authority of her husband; even when they both committed an offence, she was considered as having obeyed the orders of her husband, therefore her responsibility was not so great as her husband's.

And it was upon the ground of this allegiance, in view of frankpledge, that the statute of Hue and Cry was made: all persons being charged in the King's name to aid and assist.

When I observe that this act of 25 *George* 2. is declarative of the common law, in respect to the punishment of the offence, it may be observed in general, that the penal statue law has grown to so immense a size[1] as to make us think less than we sometimes ought to do of the officers and penalties at common law. This act particularly regards the mode of process. The subterfuges of old offenders, more accurately versed in the means of escaping justice than even their own sollicitors or counsels, have occasioned acts of parliament to be made to reach offences with greater certainty in the process.

I know of no acts which the policy of the legislature has dictated in this view that deserves to be applauded more than the act by which these parties are prosecuted: and it does infinite honour to the Judge who drew it; not more distinguished by his birth than his talents, the Honourable Justice Mr. *Bathurst.*[2]

As this act, the 25th of *George* 2. *c.* 36. is but little known, and I believe this is the first instance [9] in which it has been made use of, and carried into execution in this place, it will be for the benefit of the people, who make the audience here, to be acquainted with its contents. By the 5th section of this act, the constable, upon notice of any two inhabitants of a parish paying scot and lot, that any persons keep a disorderly house, is obliged to go before a justice; they then, upon oath that they can prove, are to enter into recognizances of £ 20. each to give evidence; and £ 10. on conviction is to be paid by the overseers to each of the parishioners so informing, upon conviction of the offenders; and the overseers to be reimbursed by the parish.

So that the policy of this act is to oblige the overseers themselves to inform, in order to save the money of the parish. It also obviates the false notion of dishonour in laying informations of this kind, by rendering such informations necessary.

A common informer, that is to say, a person who make a general trade of it, is certainly an odious character, but in such cases as these, where the morals, peace, and even safety of families, in a whole neighbourhood is concerned, informations must be considered in a very different light. Ill Fame, Notoriety, Vicinity, and a general disorderly manner of living, will justify every such sort of prosecution, which is an act of merit towards the public.

[1] See for instance William Addington, *Abridgement of Penal Statutes*, the 2nd ed. London: J. Whieldon, 1782. 756 pp.

[2] Henry Bathurst, 1st Lord Apsley and 2nd Earl Bathurst, 1714–1794. By 1768 he was a Judge of the Common Pleas. He was made Lord Chancellor in 1771.

Having mentioned the words ill fame, and bad repute, it leads me to observe, that the common law has not defined or strictly drawn the line to show what sort of houses are houses of bawdry. An indictment may even be generally laid of infamy and bad repute, at common law: and so Lord *Mansfield*, and the court of King's Bench, held in [10] the case of *the King, v. Higginson*. No acts of parliament have defined the offence: in short, it was impossible to define that which the law has better left to the idea of a jury: who being of the vicinity themselves cannot fail of being perfect judges of what houses may rightly be held to be Houses of Bawdry, Ill Fame, or Disorderly, and the Keepers of them of course to be liable to the punishment inflicted by the laws.

With respect to evidence in such cases I must observe to you, that less evidence is necessary to induce a Grand Jury to find a bill, than may be sufficient to convict; because the evidence for the finding the bill is of the nature of the evidence upon examination of criminals in order to commitment; both being only in order to something farther, and as a foundation for a trial.

In speaking of evidence I must observe, that in cases like those now before you, the turpitude of any witness is no objection either to their competency or credibility; unless there appears revenge against the criminal: for without the evidence of persons of ill fame, and disorderly lives, those persons who are the principal abettors, persuaders, and maintainers of such evil and miserable courses, cannot be brought to justice.

Gentlemen, I have endeavoured to clear the way for you; and I enter the more willingly into this detail upon account of the audience[1]; and that the proceedings in the criminal law may be well understood, in order that they may be well executed.

So full and large a dissertation is the more proper for me, and in my place, in order that many of the young persons of this University who are near me, and who are destined, some of them, one day or other [11] to profess and practice the law, may understand the admirable constitution of their country in these particulars, and may admire with you, that which we are all equally bound to support, the elegant simplicity of the laws in criminal trials, which our ancestors, having built up with so much solidity, consecrated to liberty.

I cannot conclude this charge, Gentlemen of the Jury, without publicly commending the zeal and diligence of a very good officer, the present high constable, and saying a word of the nature of his office. It is an office of great trust and powers, and of a much antienter date as conservator of the peace by common law than that of the justices of the peace, who

[1] This is one of the cases where the magistrate insists on the importance of his Charge to the public in the court-room.

were created by statute; and whose powers in some respects are thought to break in upon the line of the Great Charter. This officer may do many things upon view: and the petty constables, who, I desire will take notice what I say, are to obey him as their commanding officer, or to suffer upon complaint duly made and proved for their disobedience; subordination being the life of civil as well as military discipline. I fling this out this because there has been lately an assault upon this officer in the discharge of his duty. And now I mention him as a conservator of the peace, I cannot omit speaking of other conservators of the peace of a higher rank and character; lest any person should imagine, that their power is ceased, or to be resisted with impunity. I mean the Proctors of this University. By common law and usage, and by the charters and privileges of both the Universities of this land confirmed by act of parliament, the Proctors in both universities are the nightwatch and ward established by immemorial custom, and may *apprehend* and *detain* disorderly and *suspected* persons, and those who break the peace, *upon their own view without special warrant to apprehend and* [12] *detain*, in the same manner as any other peace officers and persons keeping watch and ward in cities and great towns by law may do. For which see the Statutes 13 *Ed.* 1 c. 4. 5 *Hen.* 4. c. 3.

Many people have entertained absurd notions, and others have industriously cultivated them, that the verdict at the assizes in the case of *Mart* and his wife was decisive against the power of the Vice-Chancellor and the Proctors of the University.

In the case of *Mart* and his wife against Dr. *Elliston*, Vice-Chancellor, and others, upon a motion for a new trial in the King's Bench, Lord *Mansfield* is said, upon good authority, to have expressed his surprize that any set of men should have looked upon this cause as a popular one; or wish to loosen the discipline of the University: that the cause was tried under particular circumstances; and that the general rights and privileges of the University remained unimpeached by the verdict at the assizes. Sir *Eardly Wilmot* observed, that from what appeared on the trial the rights of the University were rather established than impeached; because it appeared, that no suit has been commenced in consequence of the exercise of those rights for 200 years: so that they never had the sanction before which they have now had.[1]

This case of *Mart* against Dr. *Elliston* had been much talked of, and little understood in this place. I will state it fully; because it will have its uses in the future government of this place: and it will remove, I am confident, many prejudices and errors.

This cause in the first instance, I mean on the trial at the assizes there,

[1] Sir John Eardley Wilmot 1709–92. In 1755 a judge of the King's Bench, C.J. of the Common Pleas, 1766–71.

turned upon a special plea. The declaration of the plaintiff was for imprisonment of the plaintiff by the Vice-Chancellor and Proctors *for* 12 *hours* without reasonable or probable cause. The plea of the defendants was first generally of the charters and privileges of the University and its officers exercised by antient usage in taking up disorderly and suspected women; and it justified the detention of the plaintiff *one hour* only: So that the plaintiff proving a detention of more hours than one, a verdict was found by the jury for the plaintiff; of necessity, because the defendant justifying but one hour, and the plaintiff proving 12 *hours*, 11 hours according to the logic of the law remained *not justified*. Besides it might be, that the plaintiff was not in her *then* circumstances a proper object. Any justice of the peace or other peace officer might have erred in the same manner, both as to the object of detention, or as to the mode of supporting his act by his proper pleadings. So that this case does not affect in the least the jurisdiction of the Vice-Chancellor, or the powers of the peace officers of the University.

I dare say, Gentlemen, you wish with me, that the public insults on the chief acting magistrate of the University, and on the body which he represents, may be buried in oblivion. I cannot however press too strongly upon your attention in these times the necessity of a perfect union between the magistrates of the Town and University; as I will do my best endeavours, while I have the honour of being in office, to maintain the inseparability of that authority which is so naturally and closely linked together in the chain of all constitutional government. - There are privileges for great public purposes which must be supported. There is an alliance in the exercise of legal discipline, which none but the enemies of both the Town and the University, and of every useful national establishment, ever attempted or wished to separate. [14]

I will now conclude. I have taken up, Gentlemen, much of your time; but with this view, that less of it may be taken up for the future; and I have hazarded the fatiguing your patience in hearing me, for the sake of all these good people here, who deserve to be instructed: for altho' they are apt to be misled and inflamed by persons who make it their business to cultivate popular prejudices, yet I have ever observed, that natural good sense and good humour are qualities common among our countrymen even of the lowest degree; and that they are generally satisfied with just reasoning, if it is but clearly and diligently laid open and adapted to their capacities. They must be sensible that without public order men cannot either eat, drink, or sleep; walk forth, or breathe fresh air in safety. In few words we all know that one must govern, or that all must be miserable: And certainly, as there are but two ways of governing mankind, either by military force, (an instrument too apt to get the better of its master) or by the respect due to the laws and the magistrate, it is much better for every community to be armed with laws, than to be awed by arms; and reduced into a slavish subjection, fit only for irrational creatures.

Let me then, Gentlemen, once more exhort you to satisfy the duties expected of you: do justice to these people, and to yourselves; to your own peace, you own properties, and your own characters, and to the person who has the honour to speak to you. If you shall see sufficient reason, you will find the bills; if you shall not see sufficient reason, you will reject them: but in every case you will remember your Oaths, and SUPPORT THE LAWS.

A **CHARGE** to the GRAND JURY of the COUNTY OF MIDDLESEX. DELIVERED At the General Quarter Session of the Peace, holden at Hick's Hall in the said County, on Monday the Eighth Day of January 1770. By JOHN HAWKINS, Esq. One of His Majesty's Justices of the Peace for the said County, and CHAIRMAN of the Court of Quarter Session for the same. — LONDON: Printed for J. WORRALL and B. TOVEY, at the Dove in Bell-Yard, near Lincoln's Inn. — M.DCC. LXX.

[5]

MIDDLESEX

At the General Quarter Session of the Peace holden at HICK's HALL, in Saint-John-Street, in and for the County aforesaid, on Monday the Eighth Day of January 1770, before Bartholomew Hammond, Saunders Welch, John Spencer Colepeper, Elisha Biscoe, Edward Jennings, Henry Lamb, William Timbrell, Joseph Keeling, Esqrs. Sir Robert Darling, Knt. Nathan Carrington, Stephen Cole, John Barnfather, Charles Dod, Jeremiah Bentham, Peter Lewis Perrin, Rupert Clarke, Joseph Newsom, George Mercer, John Cox, Benjamin Cowley, David Wilmot, Burford Camper, and Thomas Edmonds, Esqrs.

Unanimously resolved and ordered, That the thanks of this Court be, and the same are hereby returned to John HAWKINS, Esq; for his learned and excellent Charge, delivered to the Grand Jury, at the opening of this session. And the Court doth desire, that he will be pleased to cause the said Charge to be printed and published as soon as conveniently may be. And it is further ordered, That the Chairman have a copy of this order, and that the Clerk of the Peace do wait on him with the same immediately. [7]

To the Worshipful

JOHN HAWKINS, Esq;

Chairman of the General Quarter Session of the Peace, holden at HICK's HALL, and in and for the County of Middlesex, on Monday the 8th Day of January, 1770.

WE the Grand Jury sworn to inquire for the county of Middlesex, having this day received from your Worship, being in the chair, a most learned and excellent Charge, do hereby return our most sincere and humble thanks for the same, and pray, you will be pleased, for the public good, to cause the same to be printed and published.

Sampson Jessop
John Tuach,
John Marneau,
William Collier,
Samuel Dean
Robert Miller,
John Chant,
John Clothworthey,
John Inman,
William Bradley,
Richard Jenkinson,
William Worland,
John Goodbern,
John Dean,
Peter Abraham De Brissac,
William Benn,
John Cater,
Samuel Ament,
James Lard,
Robert Leblond,
Samuel Flaxmore.

[B-9]
A
CHARGE
to the
GRAND JURY
of the
COUNTY OF MIDDLESEX.

Gentlemen of the Grand Jury,

YOU are chosen out of the body of this county, and called upon to the discharge of a duty, which, as it is of great importance to the lives, the liberties, and properties of your fellow-subjects, is highly worthy of your most serious attention. [10]

The law of this country, founded as it is in wisdom and justice, improved by the accumulated experience of many ages, and favourable to the liberties of the subject in a degree that admits of no comparison with the laws of other countries, has given you a primary and original jurisdiction in criminal matters; and, except in some particular cases, where the complaint is made to a superior court of criminal judicature, has postponed all enquiry touching the delinquency of such as offend against it, to the presentment of a Grand Jury.

And in this institution we may discern the equity and moderation with which the law of this country distinguishes between civil and criminal causes. In the former, which draws into question the title to a man's estate, or subject him to a demand of reparation in damages for meer personal injuries, the delinquent is immediately called upon to answer the charge of his adversary; and this, though the subject matter of it be ever so groundless, frivolous, or vexatious. But in criminal matters the case is otherwise; for over and above the advantages which the law reserves to the person accused upon a trial by his peers, his neighbours, and [B 2-11] possibly his friends, it has exempted him from the necessity of vindicating his own innocence, until you, by your presentment, shall have pronounced, not only that the offence wherewith he is charged is cognizable by law, (that is to say, either against the public peace, or prohibited by some statute,) but that the same is substantially true. In this presentment of your a majority will concur, and the law has farther provided, that that majority shall at least be twelve; so that before the person accused can be convicted, two juries must pass upon him, making together twenty-four persons; one to ascertain the relevancy, and the other to determine the merits of the charge.

Such, in a general view of it, is the authority with which you are invested; to the faithful execution whereof, it is hoped, you will need no other incentives than your regard for the public, and that respect which all reasonable men are disposed to pay to the laws of their country, and the government that protects them.

In the discharge of this your duty, reason and justice require you to lay aside all party [12] distinctions, local attachments and prejudices; and, in short, whetever else might tend to fix a bias on your judgments; and this not so much because you are by your oath restrained from presenting any thing *for malice or evil will*; and obliged *not to leave any thing not presented for love, favour, affection, reward, or any hopes thereof*; but because it would be wrong, repugnant to the first principles of natural justice, nay, offensive to the Divine Being itself, to do otherwise. And here it may be necessary to mention, as well for the information of yourselves as others, that there is an antecendent obligation on all men, independent of oaths and promises, to act agreeable to the dictates of truth and justice; and that tho' your oath may *superadd to*, it does not *create*, the obligation you are under to acquit or condemn according to the evidence, which from time, shall be produced to you.

The offences properly cognizable by you, are either capital, which are punishable by loss of life and forfeiture of goods; or finable, which subject the offender to imprisonment, and a discretionary fine, proportionable to the nature and degree of his offence. [13]

Under the first head of this division are comprehended the crime of treason; which is of two kinds, that is to say, high-treason and petit-treason; and felonies, which are divers, some at the common law, and others by statute. And so extensive is your authority, that every species of offence, from high-treason down to trespass, which is the smallest infraction of the public peace punishable by our laws in a criminal way, are equally within your jurisdiction.

The security in which his majesty holds his crown, the mildness of his government, and his own regal and private virtues, have removed to a great distance the probability that that species of treason, which consists in the compassing or imagining the death of the king, the queen, or the prince, their eldest son and heir, or the levying war against the king, will ever come in judgment before you. However, an offence less atrocious, it is true, but very mischievous in its consequences, namely, that of libelling his ministers, and arraigning his councils, may possibly be subjected to your enquiry; in the course whereof you will do well to consider, that for all misbehaviour of persons in office, [14] as well the king's ministers, as others, the constitution has provided a sufficient remedy, by making them responsible at a proper tribunal; and that the publication of written and printed slander has no better a tendency, than to lessen that confidence in the widsom and integrity of those, who have the direction of the public councils, which it is as much their interest to merit as to possess.

This, in the eyes of those persons, may seem a small evil; and to justify the practice of libelling, it may possibly urged, that every subject in the kingdom has a right to censure the conduct of those employed in the administration of government. But admitting such a right, does it include in it the idea of power and ability sufficient for the exercise of it? Before a man presumes to form a judgment on the act of another, in all reason let him thoroughly understand the motives to, and the ends of it: that is what is required in the common occurrences of life; and how less than a competent knowledge of the subject can be sufficient to qualify a man to judge of the operations of government, or the characters or abilities of those employed in the business of it, it is hard to [15] conceive. If this be the case, and a certain degree of skill in the constitution of this country, its laws, its history, its connexions, and its interests, be necessary, as most assuredly it is, to enable a man to form an adequate judgment of the conduct of those, who, from time to time, have the direction of its councils, the exercise of this liberty, which is so loudly contended for, must necessarily be confined to a very few.

But supposing a person possesed of all the knowledge requisite for the above purpose; supposing him to be what almost every man now affects to be thought, a consummate politician, is such a one under no restraint in this respect; shall he excite jealousies in the minds of his fellow-subjects; shall he traduce and villify, not only blameless, but respectable characters; shall he blow the trumpet of faction, and sound an alarm to rebellion with impunity? Let the law answer this question, and declare, as it does by the mouths of its oracles, that libelling is a great offence, as it tends to the breach of the peace[1]; that every libel made against a private person merits a severe punishment, because it provokes all the family of [16] that person to revenge; that if it be against a magistrate, it concerns not

[1] 23 Co. 35 Edwards v. Wootton.

only the peace, but it scandalizes the government; that a libeller is punishable by indictment at common law, and that according to the greatness of the offence, either by fine or imprisonment, or by the pillory[1]; that not ony the writer, but the publisher of a libel, is liable to this punishment[2]; and that in a prosecution for a libel, the law considers, not whether the person libelled be of good fame or not, nor whether the subject matter of the libel be true or false, but will punish the libeller even though it be true[3].

These arguments are adduced to shew, as well the iniquity as the unreasonableness and danger of the practice of libelling. Attend to others of a more serious nature.

We have lived to see the time when all the uneasinesses arising from a disputed title to the crown of this realm, and all apprehensions of a change in the national religion, are happily subsided. Our enemies abroad are reduced in their numbers, and in their power to hurt us. [C-17] Nothing can affords them so strong a temptation to disturb the tranquillity we at this time enjoy, as the prevalence of faction among us; and nothing has so great a tendency to promote faction, as the uncontrouled licence of the press, and the liberty of uttering sedition and defamation with impunity.

The crime of Treason, the first general head in the above division of offences, is branched out into many particulars, other than those already mentioned; as namely, to adhere to the enemies of the King, to counterfeit his great, or privy seal, or the current coin of the realm: these, and some other offences, are high treason. There is yet another species of treason, which the law calls petit-treason; and this is defined to be homicide committed on a subject, between whom and the offender the law supposes a special obedience and subjection; as from the wife to her husband, from a servant to his master, or from a clerk to his bishop or diocesan. These, in a general view of them, make up the whole of the offences included in the general appellation of Treason. [18]

Felonies, which are the second species of capital offences, are murder, robbery, burglary, larceny, and other crimes, sufficiently understood, either as being so declared by the common law, or enacted by statute.

The second class of offences comprehends those that subject the offender to fine and imprisonment; and these are either against public justice, or the King's peace, or the profit or health of his subjects; among which are perjury, bribery, extortion, maintenance, riots, routs, and unlawful assemblies and combinations; assaults, and other injuries to the persons of the individuals; forestalling, regrating, and ingrossing; frauds

[1] 3 Co. 125. The case de libellis famosis.
[2] 9 Co. 59. b. Lamb's case. Moor 813. S.C.
[3] 5 Co. 125.

and deceits of tradesmen, artificers, and such as prepare or sell unwholesome food. Under this general head are also included nusances, which consist in acts either injurious to the ease, the health, or the morals of the people: such are annoyances and obstructions in the public streets and highways, the exercise of noxious trades and businesses in particular places, and the keeping of houses for the purposes of lewdness. [C 2-19]

In this cursory enumeration of offences cognizable by you, you cannot but discern some, which, at this time, demand your particular attention. You whose habitations are mostly in the eastern part of this county, need not be told, that it is the seat of a manufacture, which has long afforded the means of a comfortable subsistance to thousands. In consequence of the encouragement it has met with, those habits of industry and parsimony, which attended its introduction into this kingdom, have given way to a spirit of licentiousness, which has manifested itself in outrages of the most daring kind; combinations have been formed, contributions exacted, houses have been entered and plundered; manufactures, and the engines employed in carrying them on, destroyed; fire and destruction have been threatened to individuals; and this under pretence of promoting the interests of the inferior manufacturers, whose success in these their illegal attempts would be their ruin.

The general flourishing state of the manufacture now spoken of, the rate of wages paid to the workmen employed therein, dis-[20] proportionably greater than most of other artificers require; and, above all, the indulgence which the legislature has, from time to time, shewn to this exotic manufacture, by restraining, not to say prohibiting, the wear of foreign commodities, have left these men without any reasonable cause of complaint. And in this state of things you will see the necessity of punishing the promoters of illegal combinations, and such as take part in riots and unlawful assemblies; the *ultimum supplicium*, the utmost punishment, has been inflicted, the judgment of the law has been executed on such of the capital offenders in this way, as the hand of justice could reach; this court has exerted its authority in the punishment of some who have been found guilty in a less degree; and it now remains to see, whether the sacrifices which have been made to public justice, will restore to such of this body of manufacturers, as are disposed to be peaceable, the liberty of maintaining themselves and their families by their own honest labour and industry.

Injuries to the persons of the King's subjects, by assaults or battery, are the lowest offences subject to your enquiry. These partake in a [21] great measure of the nature of civil action, inasmuch as the fine upon conviction, though nominally given to the King, is in most instances imposed with a view to a pecuniary satisfaction to the injured party; and though in many cases the injured complained of, may be so small as hardly to entitle the sufferer to a recompense, yet where the fact is proved to your satisfaction, it will be safer for you in respect of your oath, and more for the public benefit, by finding the bill, to subject the matter to a farther enquiry, than to discharge the injured party without his remedy. The reason of this is, that in the case of assaults the hope of redress from the law suspends the emotions of revenge. In other countries, a blow is frequently returned with a stab; and in this, were it not for the wise provision of the law, and that generous spirit discernable even among the lowest of our people, indictments for assaults would be less frequent than for mayhem or murder.

Of nusances none will appear to be more worthy of your notice, than those that have a tendency to corrupt the manners of youth. Such are gaming houses, and places of lewd resort. In these the habits of idleness and debauchery are first contracted, connections of the worst kind are [22] formed, and all the ends of a virtuous education frustrated.

Over and above the power to punish the offences already enumerated, the law and the constitution of this country have in a great measure intrusted to you the care of Religion; the importance of which you will easily conceive, when you are told, that civil sanctions have been found too weak to restrain men from violence, and that without the belief of a God, of Providence, and a future state, society could in no way subsist.

It is for these reasons that public seminaries are instituted, and a peculiar order of men exempted from the necessity of secular pursuits, the better to qualify them for the employment of public instructors; all which care would be to little purpose, were religion left exposed to that insult and contumely, with which some have taken the liberty to treat it; and it is for this reason that the legislature, after declaring christianity to be part of the law of the land, has invested you with a power to controul and check that licentious and daring spirit,which leads men to deny its authority, or controvert its [23] precepts, and by consequence to weaken, if not dissolve, the bonds of society.

In all the provisions which the law has made for the establishment of a national religion, and the guarding it from insult, such a latitude is left for private judgment, and such is the indulgence given to scrupulous minds, that no man is left to complain that the rights of conscience are in any degree violated, excepting those, who profess a religion subversive of the constitution of this country, and which, for that reason, has not the least claim to a toleration.

Taking then the religion of this country to be such as the law has made it, it is the duty of the civil magistrate to promote its interests, and it is yours also, under the authority of particular statutes, to put into a course of punishment all such, as by writing, printing, teaching, or advised speaking, deny the existence of God, or assert that there are more than one, or that deny the truth of the christian religion, or the authority of the scriptures, or that shall revile the sacraments, or speak in derogation of the book of common-prayer[1], farther, and for reasons of a political nature, and [24] which enter not into the truth of its doctrines. The law has made it highly penal to exercise the Romish religion in this country, and has subjected those to severe punishments who shall endeavour to spread the infection of popery, and thereby alienate the minds and affections of the people from their rightful sovereign.

The frequency of sessions in this county, and the means of information which, as being resident therein, you severally have in your power, touching the nature and extent of your authority, make it unnecessary to be more particular in the enumeration of the several matters cognizable by you as a Grand Jury. But as the nature of your office, and indeed the terms of your oath, require that your presentments be agreeable to truth, which can only be discerned by means of the evidence produced before you, it may not be amiss to give you some information touching the nature and kind of evidence which the law requires as the ground and foundation of your judgments. And this is the more necessary, as an opinion has of late been propagated with a degree of confidence that would disgrace even truth itself, namely, that the *same degree of evidence is necessary to warrant a Grand Jury to find a* [D-25] *bill of indictment, as would justify a petit Jury to find a verdict against the prisoner.*

And first, that you may understand the nature of an indictment, you are to know, that it is an enquiry, finding some offence against the king; that it is the king's action, whereupon the party shall be arraigned and put to answer, and tried, by another jury, and that every strong suspicion of such an offence, though it be felony, appearing on record hath the force of an indictment.[2]

And next it is to be observed, that an indictment[3] is no part of the trial of any offence, neither is the presentment thereof by the Grand Jury, in [26] the language of the law, ever termed a *verdict*; the consequence whereof is, that an enquiry by a Grand jury is not of necessity to be directed by those rules of evidence which the law has prescribed in the case of a trial by a petit Jury; and it is no derogation from your authority to say, that a petit Jury may *extenuate* an offence, and make it less than you, by your presentment, shall have found it.[4] In short, it is

[1] 9. & 10. W. III. cap. 32. 1 Edw. VI. cap. 4. 1 Eliz. cap. 2. § 9.

[2] *Babington*'s Advice to Grand Jurors in Cases of Blood, 82.- *Finch* of Law, 25.

[3] An indictment is no part of the trial, but an information, or declaration, for the king; and the evidence of witnesses to a Grand Jury is no part of the trial, for by law the trial in that is not by witnesses, but by the verdict of twelve men, and a manifest diversity between the evidence to the Jury, and a trial by Jury. If the indictment were part of the trial, then ought he that is a nobleman, and lord of parliament, to be indicted by his peers; but the indictment against a peer of the realm is always found by freeholders, and not by peers. 3 Inst. 26.- Vide also I. Inst. § 194.- *Fortesc.* de laud. cap. 26.- *Staundf.* Plees del Coron. Lib. 2. fo. 90.

[4] Sir *James Astry*'s general Charge to Grand Juries, 15. 21.

your office to *inquire of*, and that of the petit Jury, to *try* the fact; and for the former of these purposes, *probable* evidence is not only sufficient, but it is all that the law requires, as a the foundation of a presentment by a Grand Jury.[1]

The arguments that have been adduced in favour of the contrary notion, either prove nothing, or they prove too much. Of the first sort [D 2-27] are those, for which no other authority is produced than the opinion of certain most approved, but anyonymous *lawyers* ; of the latter, are those that represent it as *shocking to humanity to see an innocent person brought to his trial for an offence* with almost *any evidence to support the charge.*

It is doing too much honour to arguments of this kind to enter into a formal refutation of them. It might be easily shewn, that the admitting a Grand Jury to find an indictment upon probable evidence, is in favour of the subject. Lord Chief Justice Hale puts a case[2], which proves it beyond the possibility of a question. And, waving the arguments dedu- [28] cible from the constant and uniform practice of Grand Juries under the direction of the wisest and ablest Judges that have ever presided in our courts of justice, let it suffice to say, that in favour of the contrary opinion, we have no judicial determination, nor in short any thing deserving the name of authority whatsoever.

To this caution, respecting the nature of the evidence, which the law requires as the ground of your presentments, it may be necessary to add another touching your conduct in the course of your proceedings during your attendance on this court.

You will recollect, that by the oath you have just taken, you have

[1] Advice to Jurors in cases of blood, 16, 63, 125, et passim. Sir *James Astry*'s general charge to Grand Juries, 14. - Billa vera is the endorsment of the Grand Jury, upon any presentment or indictment which they find to be probably true, *Terms de la ley*. - Delationem aut in judicium postulationem nihil aliud esse quam duodecem virorum prejudicium quo finem tamen pricnpali negotio nullum affert, sed conjecturam aut opinionem verius, quo circa de asbsentibus etiam inquiritur et de noncitatis. *Thos. Smith*, de Repub. Anglor. Lib. ii. cap. 26. - [=an accusation is nothing but a preliminary inquest, which however does not put an end to the matter, but rather brings about an hypothesis or an opinion, it is why an inquest is led about persons absent or not brought to the bar.] - State Trials, Vol. iii. 416. Vol. v. 3.

[2] If A. be killed by B. so that it doth *constare de persona occisi et occidentis*, and a bill of murder be presented to them, regularly they ought to find the bill for murder, and not for manslaughter, or *se defenso*, because otherwise offences may be smothered without due trial; and when the party comes upon his trial, the whole fact will be examined before the court, and the petit Jury; and in many cases it is a great disadvantage to the party accused; for if a man kill B. in his own defence, or *per infortunium*, or possibly in executing the process in law upon an assault made upon him, or in his own defence upon the highway, or in defence of his house against those who come to rob him, in which three last cases it is neither felony nor forfeiture, but, upon not guilty pleaded, he ought to be acquitted; yet if the grand Inquest find Ignoramus uppon the bill, or find the special matter whereby the prisoner is dismissed and discharged, he may, nevertheless, be indicted for murder seven years after. 2. *Hale*'s Hist. Plac. Coron. 158.

severally engaged *the king's counsel, that of your fellows, and of your own, well and truly to keep secret.* The meaning of which words is, that you [29] are not to reveal the evidence of any of the witnesses that shall be produced to you, nor discover what you amongst yourselves shall have counselled, advised, or debated, in the business before you; such discoveries have been productive of great mischief, and may subject you to a severe punishment.

It was once a doubt with a very reverend and learned judge, whether the revealing the king's council, disclosed to the Grand Jurors, was not *treason*;[1] others have thought it be *felony*[2]; and to seti it at the lowest, Lord Chief Justice *Coke* says, that certain it is, that such discovery is accompanied with perjury, a great *misprision*, to be punished by fine and imprisonment.[3]

These are the heads of your duty, in the discharge whereof you will do well to consider the obligations you are under, arising from the terms of your oath, the nature and ends of public justice, and the relation in which you at present stand to that community of which you are a part. [30]

The latter of these considerations will make you sensible of the error of those, who imagine, that freedom may exist in opposition to the laws. It will further teach you to reverence the constitution of your country; and, lastly, convince you, that it is the indispensable duty of every one that participates in the blessings of it, to contribute his utmost towards its support, and to animate and invigorate those laws, which have for their ends the protection of property, the preservation of the the public tranquility, and the diffusing among the people the blessings of peace and liberty.

FINIS.

[1] Lib. Ass. anno 27. Placit. 63. *George*'s case.

[2] Staundf. 35.

[3] 3 Inst. 107.

A CHARGE to the GRAND JURY of the COUNTY OF MIDDLESEX. DELIVERED AT THE GENERAL QUARTER SESSION OF THE PEACE, holden at HICK'S HALL in the said County, on *Monday* the Eleventh Day of *September*, 1780. — By Sir JOHN HAWKINS, Knt. Chairman of the Quarter and General Sessions of the Peace and Oyer and Terminer for the same County. — LONDON: PRINTED FOR EDWARD BROOKE, AT THE DOVE, IN BELL-YARD, NEAR LINCOLN'S INN. — M.DCC. LXXX.

[A 2]

MIDDLESEX

At the General Quarter Session of the Peace holden at HICK'S HALL, *in* Saint-John-Street, *in and for the County aforesaid, on* Monday *the Eleventh Day of* September 1780, *before the Reverend Sir* George Booth, Baronet, Thomas Cogan, William Gregson, George Alcock, *Esquires, and others their Fellows, Justices of our Lord the King assigned to keep the Peace in and for the said County.*

IT is unanimously resolved and ordered, That the Thanks of this Court be, and the same are hereby returned to Sir JOHN HAWKINS, Knt. Chairman of the Sessions of the Peace for this County, for his Charge delivered to the GRAND JURY, at the Opening of this Session. And the Court doth desire, that he will be pleased to cause the same to be printed and published as soon as conveniently may be. And it is further ordered, That Sir JOHN HAWKINS have a copy of this order, and that the Clerk of the Peace do attend him therewith immediately.

[4]

To the Worshipful
Sir JOHN HAWKINS, Knt.

WE the GRAND JURY sworn to inquire for the county of *Middlesex*, having this Eleventh Day of *September*, 1780, received from your Worship a learned and eloquent CHARGE, do hereby return our most sincere Thanks for the same, and pray that, for the public Good, you will cause the same to be printed and published.

George Friend,
Robert Walford,
Roger Griffin,

Edward Gateward,
Robert Chapman
Samuel Adshead,

Thomas Nowell,
Joseph Mainwaring,
Hugh Morgan,
John Rivington,
John Robinson,
John Bacon,
Richard Palmer,
Lawrence Green,
Thomas Fazakerly,
Joseph Faikney,
John Woolly,
John Barton,
Joseph Odell,
Henry Wright,
George Hickman,
Richard Rees,
Jasper Weaver.

THE TRAVERSE JURY, consisting of the under-named Persons, make the same Request.

James Whiskin,
John Banbury,
James Dashper,
John Byfield,
Matthew Graham,
William Newcomb,
Edward Millington,
Mark Stanley,
Edward Cooper,
William Luff,
Elijah Jeffries,
William Smith.

[A 3-5]

A **CHARGE** TO THE **GRAND JURY** Of the County of MIDDLESEX.

Gentlemen of the Grand Inquest,

AT the Opening of the last Session I was led, by a Retrospect on the Transactions of the preceding Month, to give to the Grand Inquest, then attending on this Court, in a Charge, which, as having neither Leisure nor Opportunity to prepare myself for any other, was unpremeditated, some general Directions for their Conduct in the Execution of their Office, together with some information touching the Nature and Extent of their Authority, adapted particularly to that Crisis.[1]

Whether the like Kind of Necessity yet subsists, I have neither inquired nor am informed; I trust it does not; and that there remain but few of those who were found active in the late daring Outrages, that have not either satisfied the Justice of the Law, or experienced that Clemency, which, in all favourable Cases, his Majesty is disposed to extend.

Nevertheless, while there exists a Possibility that, in Consequence of recent Information, or some other warrantable Ground for Prosecution, you may be called to the Exercise of that Power and Authority which the Law has entrusted with you, in the bringing to a legal Trial the Disturbers of the public Peace. I hold it my Duty to give you, that now attend for that Purpose, such Instruction and Advice as I am able, for

[1] Most probably the Gordon Riots, of early June 1780.

the faithful and conscientious Discharge of your Office: And to this I think myself the more obliged, by the Consideration that there may be some among you to whom, as never having attended in this Capacity before, such Instruction and Advice may be necessary.

To all which I add, that this Court being possessed of no Power of controuling your Deliberations, or of rectifying, other than in Matters of Form, any of the Mistakes, Errors, or Imperfections you might innocently fall into, or which might appear on the Face of any of your Presentments, it cannot but be of Importance to the Properties, the Liberties, and even the Lives of your fellow Subjects, as also for the Ease and Quiet of your own Minds, and greatly for the Benefit of the Public, that your Judgments should be well informed as to the Nature and Extent, and the Reason that oblige you to the conscientious Exercise, of your Authority. [A 4-7]

Upon this Ground, and before I proceed to enumerate the several Heads into which the criminal Law of this Country is branched out, I must inform you, that your Jurisdiction extends to all such Offences as the Law, no less emphatically than truly, declares to be against the King's, or, which is the same, the public Peace.

The Motives to peaceable Conduct, or, in other Words, of Submission to that legal Power, the chief End whereof is the Preservation of the Peace and its consequent Blesssing Liberty, are of various Kinds; but with the generality of People there is one that human Laws have ever had in View, namely, the Penalty that follows the Violation of public or private Rights; but Penalties have very little Effect on the Mind, they operate only on the Will; and it is a higher Principle than the Dread of Punishment that must dispose Men to be either good Subjects or good Neighbours. By this higher Principle I mean nothing less than that Reverence for legal Government, which, in the Opinion of the Wise and Judicious in all Ages, is but its Due.

I shall not need to trouble you with any of those Notions touching the Origin of civil Government, which have employed the Thoughts and Pens of speculative Politicians: As little do I mean to decide upon that [8] controverted Question, whether the Power of the supreme Magistrate be the Grant of God, or the Gift of the People; and the rather, because there is, in my Apprehension, a middle Hypothesis which removes all the Difficulties that have hitherto embarrassed this subtle Question[1]. It

[1] Touching the Origin of civil Government, there are two Opinions severally maintained by the Writers on that Subject; the one termed *patriarchal*, which supposes the Right of Dominion to be founded on the express Donation of God, the other called the *popular* Scheme, which supposes the same Right to be the Gift, or to arise from the Consent, of the People. Of the former, Sir *Robert Filmer*, *Hobbes of Malmesbury*, and a few others; of the latter, Mr. *Locke*, and if I remember right, Bishop *Hoadley*, are the Abettors.

The middle Hypothesis above hinted at, that the Rights, the Powers, and Privileges of

Dominion are from God, but the Choice of the Person who shall exercise them is the Right of the People.

A late very ingenious Writer, the Rev. Mr. *Henry Grove*, of *Taunton*, was the first, in his own Opinion, that discovered this Middle Scheme, concerning which he speaks as follows: "There may possibly be Advantages peculiar to each of these [the popular and the patriarchal] Schemes, and whether the Patrons of them will own it or not, there are Difficulties and Objections too that embarrass both. – Now if there be any third Hypothesis, which, having the main Advantages of these two, provides against the ill Consequences of each, it ought certainly to have the Preference. I am mistaken if the following does not bid fair for it: This Hypothesis in short is this, That all Power is directly from God, not by his positive Appointment, but as he pleased to signify his sovereign Will by the Nature of Things, leaving it to the Choice and Discretion of People among whom Governments are not yet established, in what Form, by what Persons, and on what Conditions this Power shall be exercised. The Power itself flows from the Will of the Creator, declared with that Plainness and Evidence that no Part of Mankind can be ignorant of it." See an Essay on the Origin and Extent of civil Power among the Miscellanies of the Rev. Mr. *Henry Grove*, Octavo, 1739.

But this Author seems to have been little aware that the very same Doctrine is the Subject of an Essay upon Government, written by Dr. *Thomas Burnett*, Rector of *West Kington*, in the County of *Wilts.*, and printed first in Duodecimo in [1716] and again in Octavo in 1726, wherein he declares his Sentiments: "As the Welfare of Society is the End and Reason of all Government, so the different Interests of different Societies is the Reason of the different Forms of it: And as it cannot be doubted, but these different Forms were devised by Men, so though the Authority of Government be from God, yet the Appointment of the Persons to execute that Authority is purely and intirely of the Ordinance of Man. And this gives an Account of the Expression, 1 *Peter* ii. 13. of being subject to every Ordinance of Man for the Lord's Sake; by which is meant, that those who are intrusted with the Government of Societies in any Kind of Form, are only the Ordinance of Men; but yet, though they are so, they are nevertheless to be submitted to, for the Lord's Sake, because they execute that Power in Behalf of the Society, which every Society has from God." Lib. cit. Page 33, Edit. 1726.

The Coincidence of Opinions between these Two Writers is very remarkable, seeing that, without being conscious of so doing, they illustrate the Arguments of each other; and it cannot but be Matter of Surprise to find, as the Reader may, the very same Doctrine maintained by that very able and judicious Writer on Government, Hooker, in the following Passage, in the eighth Book of his Ecclesiastical Polity, Page 444, Edit. 1682. " On whom Power is bestow'd at Men's Discretion, they do hold it by Divine Right: If God, in his revealed Word, hath appointed such Power to be, although himself extraordinarily bestow it not, but leave the Appointment of Persons to Men; yea albeit God do neither appoint nor assign the Person; Nevertheless, when Men have assigned and established both, Who doth doubt but that sundry Duties and Affairs depending thereupon are prescribed by the Word of God, and consequently by that very Right to be exacted? For Example Sake, the Power which *Roman* Emperors had over foreign Princes, was not a Thing which the Law of God did ever institute: Neither was *Tiberius Cæsar* by especial Commission from Heaven therewith invested, and yet Payment of Tribute unto *Cæsar*, being now made Emperor, is the plain Law of *Jesus Christ*: Unto Kings by human Right, Honour, by very *divine* Right, is due. The Doctrine above advanced is finely illustrated by the same Author in the following apt Comparison: " The Law appointeth no Man to be a Husband; but if a Man hath betaken himself unto that Condition, it giveth him Power and Authority over his own Wife."

These Citations seem abundantly to prove against the Notion of a Grant in the one Scheme, or a Donation in the other, yet comprehending both; that the Authority of the Magistrate does, by divine Appointment, result from, or arise out of, the Relation between is sufficient here to say, that Government was originally instituted of Necessity; and being calculat-[9] ed, not merely to avert the Evils to which a State of Nature must have exposed Mankind, but to promote and ensure all the various [10] Blessings of Society, and by directing, controuling, and regulating the social Offices in this Life to fit and prepare us for a better, it is, and must be ever deemed, an Object of high Veneration.

Omitting then an Inquiry into the Origin; let us look to the Ends of Government, which we shall find to be no other than the Good of the People, or, in other Words, the promoting, by Laws and political Institutions founded in Wisdom and Justice and corresponding with the revealed Will of God, the Happiness of those who are the Subjects of it, or over whom it is exercised: Whatever are the Distinctions, the Honours, the Emoluments with which they are in- [11] vested, who hold or which accrue from the Exercise of great Offices in the State, these are merely accidental: In a Word, not for the sake of the Governours, but of the governed, was civil government first instituted.

But as the Ends of Government cannot be answered without Subordination and legal Submission on the Part of those who derive Benefit from it, there necessarily results an Obligation on the People, of Obedience to the legislative and executive Powers, in what Hands soever lodged: And not to Obedience only, but to Respect and Veneration, without which Government is in Fact, what all Laws do but presume it to be, Coercion; and those Restraints will be looked on as little better than Slavery, which are in Truth the greatest possible Security of Liberty. For if we admit, as we must, that there is a Principle in Men that disposes them to resist Authority, what is Government but Force? and that there is such a Principle no one can deny, who is at all acquainted with human Nature.[1] [12]

That such Respect and Veneration as is here mentioned is due from thh People to their Governours, is not only deducible from the Principles of natural Reason, and the uniform Tenor of the Sacred Writings, exhorting us to a dutiful Subjection, and Obedience to lawful Authority,[2]

---

him and his People, in like Manner as that of a Husband does from the Relation between him and his Wife. – Editor's Note: Dr Burnett's book=*An Essay upon Government: or, the Natural Notions of Government demonstrated.* London: Baker & Warner, 1716, in-8°, not in-12°-2nd ed., 1726, in-8°.

[1] Laws politic, ordained for public Order and Regimen amongst Men, are never framed as they should be, unless presuming the Will of Man to be inwardly obstinate, rebellious, and averse from all Obedience unto the sacred Laws of his Nature: in a Word, unless presuming Man, in regard of his depraved Mind, little better than a wild Beast, they do accordingly provide, notwithstanding, so to frame his outward Actions, that they be no Hindrance unto the common Good, for which Societies were instituted: Unless they do this, they are not perfect. *Hooker*'s Ecclesiastical Polity, Page 85.

[2] Vide *Rom.* xiii. 1. *Titus* iii.1. 1 *Peter* ii. 13.

but the Exercise of these Dispositions, so necessary to the Existence of Order and the Promotion of national Happiness, is clearly discernible in the Conduct of Mankind and the Œconomy of the World from the earliest Ages to the present; and that not only in Countries and Nations where the Arts of civil Life, the Refinements of human Policy, and the Precepts of Religion have been equally unknown; but in those enlightened Regions where the Power of Reason and Reflection have been cultivated to the Height of Philosophy.

These Arguments, drawn from the Nature and End of Government, the Sanction of Holy Scripture, and the general Assent and Practice of Mankind, might be thought sufficient to establish so simple a Position as that the Obligations of Government, or, to adapt the Term to our own Constitution, of the Prince and his People, are reciprocal; so that if the Duty of one be to afford Protection, that of the other is to [13] yield Obedience; yet may they be further enforced, by a Reflection on the Utility of Government, as manifested in the Blessings it dispenses, as well in the Executio n as the framing of Laws for the Benefit and Security of the Subject. Blessings which can only be estimated by a Comparison that places the Enjoyment of Wealth, the Fruits of Industry, and the Sweets of domestic Felicity on the one Hand, and Terror, Rapine, and Desolation on the other.

To the Arguments arising from the Benefits to Society which Government ensures, I might add the many others deducible from the Miseries that attend the Want of it; but these are evident. Nevertheless, I cannot omit to mention a political Artifice, a cruel one I confess, which we are told was formerly practised in one of the four great Monarchies pointed out by the Prophet *Daniel*; I mean that of the ancient *Persians*; among whom it was a Custom, immediately on the Death of their Kings, to proclaim a Suspension of the Laws, and Impunity to Offenders for five Days; during which Interval the Ravages and Depradations of Robbers, and other lawless Men, were usually so great, as to drive the People to an Impatience for the Restoration of Government, and a willing Submission to that [14] Authority which uninterrupted national Felicity frequently induced Men to undervalue, if not to contemn.

From these Considerations on the Nature and End of Government, the Transition is obvious to those Laws that tend to the Support of it; and here let me observe, that, although in common Speech we are frequently led to say, that the Laws are the King's Laws, and in the Bill preferred to you Offences are said to be against the King's Peace, yet are the Laws no less the Laws of the People than of the King; these, and all the Benefits arising from them, the Freedom of his Person, the Security of his Property, the Protection of his Dwelling, and of his Wife and Children, these, I say, an *Englishman* regards as the Price of his Allegiance, and claims and challenges as his Birthright.

I shall now proceed to an Explanation of the Nature of your Office, and an Enumeration of the several Offences of which it gives you Cognizance. As to the first, you are to understand, that in all Cases which draw into Question the Life, the Liberty, or the Property of the Subject, the Judgment of the Law is founded on the Determination of twelve Men; which Determination, as it is supposed to result from a careful Investigation and Inquiry into the Truth of a Cause, is called a Verdict. This is the ordinary [15] Process in civil Cases, which go no farther then to draw into Question a Man's Title to his Estate, or subject him to a Demand in Reparation of Damages for mere personal Injuries: In these Instances the Delinquent is immediately called upon to answer the Charge of his Adversary, even though the subject Matter of it be groundless, frivolous, or vexatious: But in criminal Matters, that is to say, in Treason, Felony, and Breaches of the Peace, which subject the Offender to the Loss of Life, the Restraint of Liberty, or the Payment of a discretionary Fine, the Law is abundantly careful, that it interposes between the Complaint and the Trial of the Offence, an Inquiry into the Nature and Motives of the Prosecution; to the End, that if less than probable Evidence shall be produced in Support of it, the Person accused shall be dismissed by your Return of Ignoramus. In these Presentments of a Grand Jury, consisting generally of twenty-three Persons, a Majority must concur, from whence it follows, that before a Person can be convicted on a criminal Charge, two Juries must pass upon him, making together twenty-four Persons; the one to repel frivolous, vexatious, and malicious Complaints, the other to review such as have received your Sanction, admitting in Evidence and Argument every possible Circumstance of Exculpation. [16]

I have further to inform you, that an Indictment or Presentment by a Grand Inquest is no part of the Trial of the Offence, but merely an Information or Declaration for the King: ' For were the Indictment Part of the Trial, then ought he that is noble and a Lord of Parliament be indicted by his Peers; whereas the Indictment of Peers of the Realm is always by Freeholders, and not by their Peers.' I cite this as the Opinion and express Declaration of one of the ablest Lawyers that ever filled the Seat of Justice in this Country,[1] and draw this Inference from thence, as also from the uniform Practice of every Court of criminal Jurisdiction in the Kingdom, that an Inquiry by a Grand Jury is not directed by those Rules of Evidence that are prescribed in the Case of a Trial by a Petit Jury, but that probable Evidence is in all Cases a legal and justifiable Ground for your finding an Indictment a true Bill[2] [B-17]

[1] III Institut. 26. Vide also *Co. Litt.* Sect. 194. *Fortesc.* de laudib. cap. 26. *Staundf.* Plees del. Coron. Lib. 2. Fo. 9O. [Co. Litt.=Coke upon Littleton]

[2] [same note as Hawkins 1770, p. 26.]

The Offences cognizable by you are such as either immediately or remotely tend to the Disturbance of the Public Peace; and these are either capital, and punishable by Loss of Life and Forfeiture of Goods, or fineable, subjecting the Offender to a discretionary Fine; and, in atrocious Cases, to the Imprisonment of his Person.

Under the first Head of this Division are comprehended the Crime of Treason, of which there are two Species, that is to say, High-Treason and Petit-Treason, and Felonies of which there are divers, some at the Common Law, and others by Statute; of the former it may be observed, that High-Treason is an Offence against the State, and of the others that they are each Offences of a less public Nature, Petit Treason being the Term appropriated by Law to homicide committed on a Subject, between whom and the Offender a special Obedience and Subjection is supposed; as from the Wife to her Husband, from a Servant to his Master, or from a Clerk to his Bishop or Diocesan: The other, that is to say, Felony, is of various Kinds, the most obvious of which are Murder, Robbery, Burglary; and in general, every Kind of Larceny, or Stealing.

And it is my Duty to inform you, that in the higher and lower Offences, that is to say, High-Treason and Larceny, the [18] Law makes no Distinction between the Principal and the Accessary. So that, in these Offences, not only the Actor, but he who shall stand by, and by Words or Gesticulations abet, instigate, or excite him to, or encourage him in the Commission of the Offence, such a one I say is, in the Judgment of the Law, equally culpable with the Actor: And for this Reason you may discern a most cogent Reason; for in some Instances you will in Fact find the Accomplice to tbe the Principal in the Offence; as where a Boy is employed in the burglarious Entry of a House, while another stands by and encourages him to venture in; or where a Mob are excited to Outrage by the Counsel, Persuasions, Directions, or Acclamations of one or more particular Persons: In both these Cases, and they are such as very frequently happen, the Abettors and Encouragers are equally responsible in Law with the immediate Perpetrators of the Mischief.[1]

From a Retrospect to the late Instances of Tumult and Outrage, and those Insurrections which gave rise to them, it is to be feared that some are involved in the Guilt of High-Treason: I shall be extremely cautious in my Directions to you on this Head, and shall choose rather to deliver the Sense [B 2-19] of the Laws in the Words of the Law itself, and of its ablest Expositors the Judges of the Land, than risque the misleading you by any mistaken Conceptions of my own.

In the earlier Times, the Judges and Laywers held a Diversity of Opinions respecting the Crime of High-Treason; many Offences being then included under that Denomination, which the Law has since

[1] I *Hawk.* P.C. 37.

thought proper to reject. At this Day the several Kinds of Offences that constitute this Crime stand enumerated in a Statute of the 25th of *Edw.* III which, as it is the only legal Test of Treason, has ever been looked upon as the Subject's great Security: Among other Acts of Violence it is thereby expressly declared to be 'High-Treason to levy War against our Lord the King in his Realm, or to be adherent to his Enemies in his Realm:' Upon the form of which Clauses the uniform Determination of the Judges has been, 'that those who make an Insurrection, in order to redress a Public Grievance, whether it be a real or pretended one, and of their own Authority attempt with Force to redress it, are said to levy War against the King, although they have no direct Design against his Person; inasmuch as they insolently invade his Prerogative, by attempting to do that [20] by private Authority, which he by public Justice ought to do, which manifestly tends to a downright Rebellion; as where great Numbers by Force attempt to remove certain Persons from the King; or to lay violent Hands on a Privy Counsellor; or to revenge themselves against a Magistrate for executing his Office; or to bring down the Price of Victuals; or to reform the Law or Religion[1]. The same is asserted upon equal Authority, of ' those who assemble in great Numbers for the Purpose of breaking Prisons, and delivering or setting at Liberty Persons therein confined[2].'

And although the Idea of levying War seems to include the bearing or carrying offensive Arms, such as Guns, Swords, *&c.* yet the Want of these Circumstances has been held of no Weight; the Number of the Insurgents supplying the Want of Military Weapons.[3]

The true Test and Criterion of an Insurrection is, The Intent and Purpose for which the Parties assemble. If it be on Account of some private Quarrel, or to take Revenge on some particular Persons, it amounts to no more than a Riot; but if it be with a more ge-[B 3-21] neral View, and for any of the Purposes above-mentioned, especially with a display of Flags and Colours; the beating of Drums, or other Incentives to Tumult and Outrage; and where the Insurgents are provided with Axes, Crows, and other Tools of the like Nature, proper for the Mischief they intend to effect; such an Insurrection, such an Assembling as this, though not immediately against the Person of the King, is doubtless levying War against him, and by necessary Consequence High-Treason within the Statute[4].

The capital Offences next in Degree to Treason are Felonies, and these are divers; some being at the Common Law, and others by Statute.

[1] I *Hawk.* 37.
[2] *Hale*'s Hist. Plac. Coron. Vol. I. 133.
[3] *Foster*'s Crown Law, 208.
[4] *Foster* , 208, 209.

In the former class are included Murder, Larceny, Robbery, Burglary, and an Offence termed in our Law *Arson*, or the maliciously and voluntarily burning the House of another by Night or Day[1]; Felonies by Statute ar much more numerous; and the present Occasion calls upon me to direct your Attention to a Statute made in the first Year of King *Geo.* I. by which it is enacted, 'That if any Persons, to the Number of Twelve, or more, being unlawfully, riotously, and tumultuously assembled together, to the Disturbance of the Public [22] Peace; and being required or commanded by any Justice of the Peace, Sheriff of the County, or Under Sheriff; or by the Mayor, Bailiff, or Bailiffs, or other Head-Officer or Justice of the Peace of any City, or Town Corporate, where such Assembly shall be, by Proclamation to be made in the King's Name, immediately to disperse themselves, and peaceably to depart to their Habitations, or to their lawful Business, under the Pains of the said Statute, shall afterwards unlawfully, riotously, and tumultuously continue together by the Space of one Hour after such Proclamation made, or after a wilful Let or Hindrance of a Justice of the Peace, *&c.* from making the said Proclamation, they shall be adjudged Felons without Benefit of the Clergy.

And it is further enacted by the said Statute, 'That if any Person or Persons shall, with Force and Arms, wilfully and knowingly oppose, obstruct, or in any Manner hurt any Person, *&c.* who shall begin to proclaim, or go to proclaim, according to the Proclamation appointed by the said Statute, whereby such Proclamation shall not be made, they shall be adjudged Felons without Benefit of Clergy.'

And by the same Statute it is further enacted, 'That if any Persons unlawfully, [B 4-23]riotously, and tumultuously assembled together, to the Disturbance of the Public Peace, shall unlawfully, and with Force, demolish or pull down, or begin to demolish or pull down, any Church or Chapel, or any Building for religious Worship, certified and registered according to I. *Will.* & *Mar.* 18. which is commonly the Toleration Act; or any Dwelling-House, Barn, Stable or other Out-House, they shall be adjuged Felons without Benefit of the Clergy.[2]

It would take up more of your Time than can well be spared, were I to enumerate all the several Offences that the Law has subjected to the Inquiry of a Grand Inquest. Of those that remain unspoken of the chief are Larcenies, or Felonies of the lesser Kind, Perjury and Subornation thereof, Nusances and Affrays.

Under the first Head are comprehended the stealing Things of small Value, without any Circumstances of Terror to the Owner; and it affords a very melancholy Proof of the increasing Depravity of the Times, and

[1] I. *Hawk.* P.C. 105.

[2] Vide I. Hawk. 167.

of the little Regard paid by the common People to the Laws of God, and the Precepts of Religion, that the gradual Improvements of Theft and Depradation seem to have out-gone those of the Law, and to have eluded and set at nought [24] all possible Contrivances for the Security of Property. Not to mention the various Methods of privately Stealing from Persons in the Streets or in Public Assemblies, our Humanity is affected by the Consideration that, in the Villages adjacent to the Metropolis, scarce any one resident therein, be his Condition ever so low, can call any Thing his own: and that this is truly the Case, who needs to be told who sees posted up in every Contry Retirement, a Caution importing no less than the Loss of a Limb to him who shall attempt the stealing from thence a favourite Plant, Fruit, perhaps unripe, or it may be a Handful of Flowers? This it is well known in a recent Expedient for the Security of rural Property, and argues a Change of Manners, among the lower Order of People, which is but one Way to be accounted for.

From Crimes that affect the Persons and Properties of Men, I pass to such as tend to the Obstruction or Hindrance of public Justice; the most atrocious of which are Perjury, and Subornation theerof. The Credit of human Testimony is of such Importance to Society, that, where it fails, the Laws are either rendered of no avail, or are perverted to Purposes the most injurious, and resemble wholesome Nutriment con-[25] verted into Poison. By Means of Perjury the innocent are condemned, and the guilty suffered to go free; and upon this Offence I Cannot omit to point out to you an Observation that has frequently occurred to me in the Exercise of my Office of a Magistrate, that in giving Evidence, Men frequently practice a Sort of Casuistry, which they think absolves them from the Guilt of Perjury, distinguishing in their own Minds between swearing to the Hurt, or for the Benefit of another; and I have known a Witness, for Fear of incurring the Guilt of Perjury, scruple swearing to the Person of an Offender, in order to his Conviction; who I have been persuaded, to exculpate him, would not have hesitated falsely to depose, that at the Time of committing the Offence the Person charged was sleeping in his Bed[1]. [26]

[1] Very little short of the Case here supposed, was the following one of an Offender, a few Years ago tried before me at the *Middlesex* Session. Some Custom-House Officers being in Search of smuggled Goods, the Mob rose and resisted them with a Discharge of Fire Arms; and a Riot ensued. The Prisoner was apprehended as one of the Rioters, and being carried before a Magistrate, alledged in Proof of his Innocence, that at the Time of the Riot he was ten Miles from the Place where it arose, viz. at Croydon, in Surry. Forgetting this his Defence before the committing Magistrate, he at his trial produced a friendly Witness, who swore, that for a certain Period, commencing and ending with the Riot, the Offender was in his own Room, having locked himself in; and that he, the Witness, through the Chinks of an adjoining Apartment, saw him remain there till the Tumult was over. It happened, however, that the committing Magistrate being in Court, produced the Examination taken before him; and, the same being properly attested, and the Evidence

Of Nusances there are many and various Kinds. These stand opposed to private Injuries; and in judicial Proceedings, are ever laid as against the King's Peace, and to the Annoyance of his Subjects. Under this Head are comprehended Obstructions of the public Highways, Buildings and Erections for the carrying on of noxious Trades and Businesses, Gaming-Houses, Places of lewd Resort, and Places of public Diversion not licensed according to an Act of Parliament, made in the Reign of the late King. The Mischiefs severally arising from these are obvious; and it is Part of your Duty, as they shall come to your Knowledge, or fall within your Observation, from Time to Time, to present such Offences and Places, in order to the Punishment of those Persons who by Law are made responsible for their Act in the one Instance, and their Conduct in the other.

Affrays and Assaults on the Persons of Individuals, though nominally Offences against the King, and therefore fineable at the Discretion of his Justices, are, nevertheless, near- [27] ly similar in their Nature to the civil Action of Trespass; inasmuch as the Fine upon Conviction is in most Instances imposed with a View to the pecuniary satisfaction of the Prosecutor. In Complaints of this Sort, where the Injury is but small, the Magistrate, to whom the Complaint is first made, cannot better exercise his Humanity, and I may add, his Wisdom, than by persuading the Parties to Peace and reconciliation; an Expedient which I have seldom known to fail; yet if he thinks proper to bind the Offender over, your Duty is, upon probable Evidence, to find the Bill.

I will not at this Time trouble you with the particular Mention of the many Statutes that have from Time to Time been made for the Support and Encouragement of Religion; nor farther enlarge upon that Topic, than to inform you, that of political Institutions the Wisest suppose the Being of a God, the Belief of a Providence that over-rules and directs the Actions of Men, and a future State of Rewards of Punishments: and as the fullest Evidence of these important Truths is contained in the sacred Writings, the Founders of our excellent Constitution have recognized the Christian Religion, and by an Ecclesiastical Establishment declared it to be Part of the Law of the Land. [28]

I am sufficiently aware that a Religion protected, as that of this Country is, by Laws and Statutes that make it penal to controvert its fundamental Precepts, notwithstanding that it gives to scrupulous Consciences every reasonably Indulgence[1], is by its Enemies termed the

---

of his being active in the Riot appearing full and clear, the Jury found the Offender guilty; and, if I do not mistake, the Court committed the witness for Perjury.

[1] This Indulgence has been farther extended by a very late Act of Parliament; and it is but Justice thus publicly to declare, and it will afford Satisfaction to many to be informed that the same has been gratefully accepted; many of the most eminent Dissenting Teachers

Religion of the Magistrate: in one View it may, perhaps, appear so; yet, were the Countenance and Support of the civil Power wanting in this Instance, it is much to be questioned whether among us we shoul have any Religion at all.

But be the established Religion what it may, it is at least your Duty to protect it: from Infidels and Sceptics it has nothing fear; for such has been the Effect of the Researches of learned and inquisitive Men, of a Profession to which we are under the greatest Obligation, who with unremitted Care and the msot sedulous Application have set themselves to search the Scriptures that the Evidence of its divine Authority, its Truth, and Excellency is every Day accumulating; so that our own Experience seems to coincide with the Assurance of the Gospel[1], [29] "That the Gates of Hell shall not prevail against it." I say, from such Enemies as these Christianity has little to fear; nevertheless from Insult and Contumely it looks to you for Defence; and to this End, Laws have been enacted, and continue still in Force, that subject to your Notice, and subsequent Punishment, all such as by Writing, Printing, Teaching, or advised Speaking, deny the Existence of God, or assert that there are more than One, or that deny the Turth of the Christian Religion, or the Authority of the Scriptures, or that shall revile the Sacraments, or speak in Derogation of the Book of Common-Prayer[2].

To this extensive Jurisdiction, which I have attempted to delineate, the Law has added the Correction of the public Manners, and has given you Authority to inquire of and present Offences *contra bonos Mores*, or, in other Words, against the Rules of Decency: under this Head are comprehended Bathing in public Places adjacent to Highways and Foot-paths, and the Violation of the Rights of Sepulture.

Having taken Occasion to mention the Subject of Religion, it cannot be amiss if I apply it to the Circumstances of your present [30] Attendance, by reminding you, as I do now, of its Obligations; and of them the least that can be asserted is, that they bind you by the Hope of the greatest Rewards, and the Dread of the severest Punishments, to the Observance of an Oath, perhaps the most solemn and awful that the Wit or Ingenuity of Man can devise; for you ought to remember, as I trust you do, that it is meant to restrain you from presenting any Thing from Malice or ill Will, and obliges you not to leave any Thing unpresented for Love, Favour, Affection, Reward, or any Hopes thereof.

In these two emphatical Sentences are comprised the Study of a Grand

---

in this Country having legally qualified themselves for the Exercise of their Function, by complyig with the Terms thereof.

[1] *Matt.* xvi, 18.

[2] 9 & 10 Will. iii. Cap. 32. - 1 Edw. VI. Cap. 4. - 1 Eliz. Cap. 2 § 9.

Inquest: I refer you to your Consciences for the Discharge of it, and dismiss you to the Dispatch of that Business, which by this Time calls for your Presence.

FINIS.

Lord Loughborough's Charge to the Grand Jury of WILTS, at the late Assizes at Salisbury,

August 6, 1791.

This is not a complete Charge, but a newspaper summary of the speech delivered by Lord Loughborough. There are two printed sources: one is *Wool Encouraged without Exportation, or Practical Observations on Wool and Woollen Manufacture. In two Parts*....By a Wiltshire Clothier, F. A. S. [Henry Wansey] London: T. Cadell, 1791. The other is from the *Salisbury and Winchester Journal*, 15 August 1791. The two summaries are different; but they report the same substance. Prisoners were indicted for destroying of Scribbling Machine at Bradford. If they had grievances about the use of such machines, they could have tried a legal remedy; but the use of violence was inexcusable. The original text could not be found.

The Charge of Sir William Ashhurst.

The text given here is that to be found in the following book:
The Advantage of a National Observance of Divine and Human Laws. A Discourse in Defence of our Admirable Constitution. By a Country Post-Master. To which is added, Mr. Justice's Ashhurst most excellent Charge to the Grand Jury, for the County of Middlesex. Ipswich: J. Bush, 1792. [ms superscription: July 26. From the Author. P. Deck, Post-master at Bury with several other Copies.] 22 pp. [B.L. 8135 b. 19.]

There exist several other editions of the text of Ashhurst's Charge, among which, one translated into Welsh. The *Charge* begins p. 23, and is thus introduced:

"The Charge of Sir William Ashhurst delivered to the County of Middlesex, November 19, 1792... breathes so much the true Spirit of the English Law, and is so well suited to the curb the Presumptious Spirit of the Times, that it must be read with Pleasure by every true Englishman."

Gentlemen of the Grand Jury,

I have the honour upon the stated return of this solemnity of putting into execution the Criminal Law, and of bringing such Offenders to justice as have been guilty of a breach of the Law. Gentlemen, there is no Nation in the world that can boast a better System of Government than that under which we have the happiness to live. Here no man is so high as to above the reach of the Law, and no man so low as not to be within the protection of it. — The Power of the Crown on the one hand, and the Liberty of the Subject on the other, are both effectually secured, and at the same time kept within their proper limits. Gentlemen, the Law of this Country only lays such restraints on the actions of individuals, as are necessary for the safety and good order of the Community at large; and such restraints are so far from being infringements on Civil Liberty, that Civil Liberty could not subsist without them: for if every [24] man were left to the free and uncontrouled impulse of his own mind, as in a state of Nature, no man could be secure of his person or property, and the weak would become a prey to the strong. But in a state of Civil Government, each individual grows strong in the strength of the community.

Gentlemen, it is Civil Liberty that is the parent of industry, and consequently of wealth. For in a state of Nature, there was no security to property, and no man thought of property further than for the momentary supply of his own immediate necessities. But when men have entered into society, the consciousness that their property is secure, induces to habits of industry. Man in that state does not bend his pursuits to the mere supply of his present wants, but looks forward to future ages. The mutual wants of men produce a mutual supply: this leads to Trade and Commerce, and extend a man's connections beyond the narrow limits of his own family: and thus mutual wants bring mutual happiness. But, Gentlemen, as a preliminary step to the procuring of these enjoyments, it was necessary that mankind, on entering into Society, should give up into the hands of Government that species of Liberty which resulted from the perfect equality of man, and where no man had a right to impose on another a rule of conduct, but every man, as far as his strength carried him through, followed his own will. But, Gentlemen, a state of society cannot subsist without Subordination; there must be general rules laid down by the coercive power of the State wherever it resides, as a standard by which the actions of men are to be measured and punished, so as to prevent them from being injurious to the rights and happiness of their fellow-citizens. And there must be a coercive power in such hands as the Constitution has thought fit to place it, to enforce such law and rules of actions as the wisdom of the State has prescribed. Happily for us, Gentlemen, we are not bound by any laws but such as are ordained by the virtual consent of the whole kingdom, and which [25] every man has the means of knowing; and if men judged aright, they would be persuaded their happiness entirely depended on a due observance and support of these Laws. There have, however, under the best systems of Government, been found men of corrupt principles, who, having, forsaken honest industry, wish to throw every thing into confusion, and to live by rapine and plunder; when that is the case, it is become necessary for the coercive power of the State to lend its restraining hand, and to punish offences of such a flagrant nature. There is no prospect of Reformation till such corrupt members be cut off, to prevent others being contaminated by their example. But, though crimes must not go unpunished, I may venture to affirm, that there is no Nation whatever that is so careful of the natural Liberty of the Subject, or has made such humane provisions for offenders, as the Nation in which we live.

Gentlemen, the ordaining of this preliminary step – the Inquest, such as that on which you now appear, composed of Gentlemen of rank and figure in the Country – is a guard and caution unknown in every other Country. And after you have given your opinion that the matter is fit for another enquiry, the accused has a right to have his Indictment tried by a Jury, which is a most invaluable privilege.

The Law, Gentlemen, is no less careful in protecting men's civil rights. There is no Country where the Law is more uprightly or more impartially administered. For this blessing we are indebted to the wise and prudent form of our Constitution, and to that security which naturally results from it. Hence it is that our Commerce has been extended beyond the example of all former ages. And we all know that this is the case of every Manufacturing Town in this Country. Such is the flourishing state of this Kingdom, and such the happy Fruits of Liberty and Peace, one would suppose there was not a man in the Kingdom [26] who did not feel it, and feel it with a grateful heart; and yet, I am sorry to say, there are men of dark and gloomy hearts, who would wish to overturn the general fabric of our Constitution, which has been the work of Ages, and would give us in return a system of universal Anarchy and Confusion. There have been Publications in which the the Authors disclaim any idea of Subordination, as inconsistent with the natural rights and equality of man, and recommend the example of a neighbouring Nation as a model for our imitation. Alas! Humanity is called upon to pity the deplorable situation of that Country: but it is a very ill chosen example of imitation to hold forth to a Nation in a most flourishing state of happiness; and it is pretty extraordinary, that, with our eyes open, we should wish to plunge ourselves into the same abyss of misery with that neighbouring Nation. One might have naturally expected that doctrines so absurd, so nonsensical, and so pernicious, would have been treated with that contempt they deserve, and would have sunk into oblivion. But when one not only finds such tenets held, but Societies of men formed, who meet with the express purpose of disseminating such doctrines, and who hold a regular correspondence with other societies in a neighbouring Nation, it is time for every sober man who is at all interested in the safety and welfare of his Country, as much as in him lies, to endeavour to crush such unconstitutional and pernicious doctrines. Gentlemen his Majesty, who is always anxious and watchful over the safety and prosperity of his People, did sometime ago issue his Royal Proclamation[1], which received the approbation of every good Citizen in this Kingdom. And, Gentlemen, I am afraid the circumstances which gave rise to that Proclamation are not yet so totally at an end, as to make it unreasonable for me to recall them to you recollection. Gentlemen, His Majesty states, that Divers Wicked and seditious Writings &c.[27] (*Here his Lordship recites the substance of the Proclamation*) Gentlemen I cannot help expressing the happiness I feel, that his Majesty's Proclamation has been received with every mark of respect through the Kingdom; and there are scarcely any Parts of the Kingdom that have not presented an Address to His Majesty in consequence of it, and who have not expressed their hatred and abhorrence of such pernicious doctrines, and shewn that they are not to be duped out their happiness by the shallow artifices of such men as have nothing to lose, and who would enrich themselves by the destruction of all Government. His Majesty's Servants and Min-

[1] Probably that dated 22 May 1792.

isters have paid due attention to this Proclamation, so far as to have instituted proceedings against several Libellous and Seditious Publications. But, Gentlemen, though the Proclamation has tended to produce the desired effect, it has done it so effectually as to prevent the disseminating of such kind of Writings; and all sober men out to be diligent in supporting the cause of Order and Government.

Gentlemen, I trust your minds will be impressed with these ideas, and that you will be assiduous in supporting our present form of Government. Such of you as are in a private station, will endeavour, by your examples, to discountenance such kind of doctrines; and those of you who are cloathed with the Robes of Magistracy, will be diligent in exerting yourselves to bring to Justice all who have been guilty of a breach of the Law, by publishing tenets of that pernicious nature.

I will take up no more of your time, but recommend it to you to proceed with all due dispatch to the Public Service; and I have no doubt that you will discharge your duty in a manner honourable to yourselves, and so as to deserve the Thanks of your Country.

A **CHARGE** DELIVERED TO THE *GRAND JURY* OF THE COUNTY OF MIDDLESEX AT THE GENERAL SESSION OF THE PEACE, HELD AT THE SESSIONS HOUSE ON CLERKENWELL-GREEN, ON MONDAY THE 10TH OF DECEMBER 1792, By WILLIAM MAINWARING, Esq. CHAIRMAN. PRINTED at the REQUEST of the GRAND JURY.

A CHARGE, &c. &c.&c.

Gentlemen,

BEFORE you retire from the Court to proceed to your Business, I must request you will permit me to call your Attention to some Measures of great Importance to us all, in which the Tranquillity and Hap-[6]piness of the Country are most materially concerned, and which it is your particular Province at this Time, as the Grand Jury for this great and populous County, to enquire in to and present.

His Majesty has found it necessary to issue a second Proclamation, in which it is set forth, *that the utmost Industry is still employed by evil-disposed Persons within this Kingdom, acting in concert with Persons in Foreign Parts, with a View to subvert the Laws and established Constitution of this Realm, and de-*[B 2-7] *stroy all Order and Government therein; and that a Spirit of Tumult and Disorder, thereby excited, has lately shewn itself in Acts of Riots and Insurrection.*

The Methods which have lately been pursued by evil-disposed Persons, to disturb the Peace and good Order of the Kingdom, to introduce Anarchy and Confusion among us, to alienate the Minds of the People from a due Regard to the Laws and our happy Constitution, are of so alarming a Nature, as to call upon all good Men, upon all who have Property [8] to defend, or who wish to transmit to their Posterity the Blessing they enjoy under a mild and free Government, to aid and assist in bringing such Offenders to Justice.

Gentlemen, the Constitution of this Country hath long been the Envy and Admiration of other Nations. – The Liberty, the Security, the Protection which every one enjoys in his Person and Property, by the Wisdom of our Laws and the Purity of their Execution, have made this Country the desired Asylum of the [B 3-9] wretched and oppressed. – Here all Ranks are alike protected, all are alike amenable to the Laws, all subject to the same Punishments, and equally compellable to make

Retributions for Injuries committed. – In this Country the Law is no Respecter of Persons. – In our Courts of Justice all are equal: high and low, rich and poor, all are alike the Care of our Laws. This is the happy Equality which every one is entitled to, and enjoys, in this Country – and it is the only Equality consistent with any Form of Govern-[10] ment, without any System of Society. Equality, in the Sense in which it is now attempted to be inculcated into the Minds of the People, by crafty and designing Men, is, in the Nature of Things, impossible.

The wildest Savages, in the rudest State of Nature, look up to some one as their Chief or Head, to lead and to protect them. The Author of our Being has not made us equal – we cannot make ourselves so. We were meant for Society, and endowed with different Power and Faculties to assist each other; the strong [B 4-11] must protect the weak, the weak will contribute to the Convenience and Accommodation of the strong. – It is the superior Blessing, which God has bestowed on the human Race, to unite us together by mutual Dependence on each other; from this arise all the Comforts and Endearments of human Life.- Of all Creatures upon Earth Man would be the most wretched out of a State of Society; no Society can exist without Laws and Regulations for the Support of it; and those established here are confessed by all Na-[12] tions to be the best adapted to give Security, Comfort, and Happiness.

You, however, Gentlemen, are no Strangers to the Fact, (for it is too notorious) that Doctrines have of late been maintained and propagated, and Writings most industriously dispersed, with a View to create in Men's Minds Discontent with our Constitution and present Form of Government.- Attempts are daily making to persuade Men they have not those Rights to which they are entitled – to delude and impose upon weak Minds, and excite them to [13] Proceedings, which, if not put a Stop to, may be of very serious Consequence to us all.

The Liberty of the Press is one of the glorious Privileges of Englishmen – it is essential to the Liberty of the Subject, to the Existence of a free State, while exercised for lawful and just Purposes; but when it is made use of as the Instrument of Slander and Detraction, to destroy the Comfort and Happiness of Individuals, or to disturb the Harmony and good Order of the State, to mislead and impose upon the weak and [14] ignorant, it becomes the most mischievous and destructive Engine that can be put into the Hands of wicked and ill-designing Men. A Man may injure his Country and violate the Law by the Publication of seditious and inflammatory Writings more than by any other Method; inasmuch as the Poison which such Writings contain is more extensively disseminated, more effectually and secretly infused into Men's Minds than it could be by any other Mode of Proceeding.

GENTLEMEN, many well-dispos-[15] ed Persons who would shudder at the Thought of committing an Act of Treason, will innocently take a

Book to their Closet, and read it; some from mere Curiosity, some from a Desire of Information; and if they have not Judgment to detect, and strength of Mind to resist, the fallacious Arguments and false Reasonings made use of by artful and evil-minded Men to impose upon and mislead, they insensibly fall into the Snare prepared for them; and though they may not perhaps, at first, be worked up to Acts of Out-[16]rage and Violence, are gradually lulled into a State of Indifference for the Preservation of that Constitution which they are taught to believe is oppressive, and withholds from Men their just Rights.- These, and a long Train of Evils, are the Consequences of seditious Publications. That we may examine our Constitution-the Principles on which it is founded -may point out Inconveniences- may suggest Improvements- may examine the Conduct of the Ministers of the Government- all these, GENTLEMEN, are Privileges which [17] every British Subject enjoys.- But the Publication of libellous and seditious Pamphlets and Papers having a direct tendency to subvert and destroy the Constitution, to irritate Men's Minds, to fill with them with groundless Jealousies and Discontents, and to bring together a deluded Populace, for the Purpose of altering the Constitution, or coming to Resolutions contrary to the established Laws of the Country. – All this is at once sounding the Trumpet of Rebellion, and inviting evil-disposed or misguided Men, whose Minds have been poisoned by [18] the Promoters of Sedition, to commit Acts of Violence and Outrage, by which the Life and Property of every good Subject will be in danger, and at the Mercy of a lawless Mob, pushed on to desperate Measures by the Hope of Plunder, and establishing an imaginary Equality. When Writings of this Sort appear, it is the Duty of every one to use his Endeavours to suppress them, and bring the Offenders to Justice. – But *you*, Gentlemen, in the Situation in which *you* stand, are more immediately called upon to bring forward Offences of this Sort. – If [19] it is within your own Knowledge who the Writers or Publishers are, you are to present them.– If Charges against such Persons are brought before you by Indictment, you will consider them seriously; and if upon the Evidence you hear, you find them proper for further Enquiry, you will declare them TRUE BILLS, that the Party accused may be made amenable to the Law, and, if Guilty, may be brought to Punishment. – You are not to try - not to hear and determine the Offence, but only to say whether the Party accused ought [20] to be put upon his Trial.- Such is the Caution and Humanity of our Constitution in favour of the Liberty of the Subject, that without your Assent Prosecutions for the highest Crimes which can be committed must stop.- This is a great and important Trust committed to you; in the wise and just Exercise of which, the Safety of the State, the Rights of the People, and the Preservation of the Constitution, are deeply concerned.

However great and heinous Offences may be, the even-handed

Jus-[C-21]tice of this Country proceeds by known, regular, and stated Rules. You must first declare that the accused ought to be tried; another Jury must hear the Accusation and Defence, and pronounce whether he be guilty or not: so that two Juries must give Sanction to the Proceeding, before Punishment can be inflicted.- Such is the Security which every one has in an English Court of criminal Judicature.

One would have thought the melancholy Fate of those unfortunate and deluded Persons, who suffered the [22] dreadful Sentence of the Law in Consequence of the active Part they took in the Riots[1] which disgraced this Metropolis in 1780, would have been a Warning, at least, as long as that Scene of Confusion and Mischief was recent in every one's Mind - but, alas! those Examples do not seem to have had the desired Effect.- Efforts are making by the Enemies to our Prosperity and Happiness to check our Career of Glory, and to destroy this beautiful Fabrick, THE ENGLISH CONSTITUTION, reared and perfect- [C 2-23] by the Wisdom and Experience of many Ages.

That Meetings convened, and Associations formed, for the Purpose of forcing an Alteration in our Laws, and changing the Constitution, are highly criminal, cannot but be obvious to every one of common Understanding, who will give himself a Moment's Time for Reflection. Where three or more Persons assemble together, to do an Act not justifiable by the Form of our Constitution, such a Meeting is an unlawful Assembly- and it is [24] the Duty of all Magistrates and others, to suppress and prevent such Meetings. The Purpose of the Meeting makes the Assembly unlawful, though the Purpose is not carried into Execution.

If a Number of Persons riotously and tumultuously assemble together, to redress (what they term) Public Grievances, or to alter the established the Law of the Land; or attempting, by Intimidation and Violence, to force the Repeal of Laws, or compel the enacting of new ones it is an Act of Treason.[25]

Gentlemen, I need not, when I am addressing myself to Men of your Experience and Situation in Life, detail the several public Offences on this Subject. It is enough to say, that every Act tending to produce a Breach of the Peace -to disturb the Tranquility and good Order of the Kingdom, to create Discontent in Men's Minds with our Constitution and Form of Government, either by Actions, seditious Writings, libellous and indecent Prints, or in any other Way, are all high Offences and Misdemeanours, pro-[26] per for your Inquiry and Presentment.

I cannot dismiss you without adding one Word more, on a Matter which it is fit that *all* should know, if there are any that are ignorant of it.

[1] The famous Gordon Riots, led by Lord George Gordon, mainly against Roman Catholics. Lord Gordon was declared insane and locked up.

That every One residing here, and enjoying the Protection of the Law, is bound to Allegiance and Obedience to it.- Obedience to the Law necessarily follows Protection under it.

Therefore it is, that Foreigners dwelling among us, and enjoying our [27] Protection, from whatever Country they come, are equally amenable to the Laws, and equally liable to be punished as Traitors, for Acts of Treason committed by them, or for any other Crime they may be guilty of, as if they were natural-born Subjects.

I will detain you, Gentlemen, no longer. I have thought it proper shortly to mention these several Matters to you, with a View to bringing them to your Recollection at this particular Time – not doubting, however, but that you are well [28] acquainted with this, and every other Particular of your Duty, and that you are come hither well disposed to exercise the Power with which the Constitution has invested you, with prudent Firmness, with Justice, and with Mercy.

FINIS.

A **CHARGE** GIVEN TO **THE GRAND JURY** OF THE HUNDREDS OF KIRTON AND SKIRBECK, IN THE PARTS OF HOLLAND, IN THE COUNTY OF LINCOLN AT EPIPHANY-SESSIONS, HELD AT BOSTON, 14TH JANUARY 1793. CONCERNING THE STANDARD MEASURE OF CORN; AND CONCERNING SEDITIOUS PUBLICATIONS. **BY SAMUEL PARTRIDGE, CL. M.A.** CHAIRMAN AT THE SAID SESSIONS. WITH AN ADMONITION TO THE KEEPERS OF INNS AND ALEHOUSES. LONDON: PRINTED FOR THE BENEFIT OF THE FRENCH REFUGEE CLERGY; AND SOLD BY C. NICOL, BOOKSELLER TO HIS MAJESTY, PALL-MALL. 1793.

To
THE RIGHT HONOURABLE
EDMUND BURKE,
THIS CHARGE,
AS A HUMBLE TRIBUTE OF THANKFULNESS,
FOR THE TIMELY ALARM BY HIM SOUNDED
AGAINST THE
FOREIGN AND DOMESTIC INCENDIARIES
OF GREAT BRITAIN,
IS OFFERED AND INSCRIBED BY
THE AUTHOR.
Boston, Lincolnshire, 11th Feb. 1793.

[7]
A CHARGE, &c.

Gentlemen of the Grand Jury:

IT was my design, a short time since, to address you this day on a subject of a nature altogether peaceful and agreeable: I mean, the reformation so much and so long wanted, and now likely to prevail universally, in the practice of MEASURING CORN. But I must speak to you concisely on this subject, that I may hasten to one of incomparably greater importance.

I will state to you the purport of the most material acts of parliament forestablishing ONE measure of corn throughout the kingdom: that you may be apprized of your duty respecting presentments or indictments for offences against those acts: first premising, that by a [8] late decision of the Court of the King's Bench, these acts remain unchanged.

There have been no less than twelve statutes relating to weights and measures, made in different reigns prior to that of Car. I. The earliest of which is in the 9 of Hen. III.; that is, in the year 1225. But it will be sufficient to our *present purpose*, as it will comprehend all that is now material on the subject, if I begin with stating to you the purpose of 16 Car. I. c. 19.

It is enacted, that there shall be but ONE measure, according to the standard of the Exchequer. Mayors, or other head officers, or their deputies or agents, are to execute the office of clerk of the market. If any mayor, or other officer, having power to inquire of any abuses in measures, shall seal or give allowance to any other measure than according to the standard of the Exchequer; or shall, [9] upon reasonable request and warning, refuse to seal such measures as are according to the said standard, on paying the legal fee; he shall forfeit *5 £*.-

22 Car. II. c. 8. If any person shall sell any corn, in open market, or any other place, by any other bushel or measure, than what is agreeable to the standard of the Exchequer, commonly called the Winchester Measure, containing eight gallons to the bushel, and no more or less, and strucken even by the brim, and sealed and directed, he shall forfeit for every offence 40 *s*.

And if any mayor, or other head officer, shall knowingly and wilfully suffer any person to buy or sell corn by any other bushel or measure than that prescribed, and sealed as directed; he shall for every offence, upon conviction by presentment or indictment before the justices for the *county*, at their quarter sessions, forfeit *5 £*. [10]

If any mayor, or *other person* authorized by law to seal measures, shall neglect or refuse (being required) to seal any bushel, half bushel, or peck, duly gauged, he shall forfeit, for the first offence, *5 £*. and for every other offence, *10 £*. And if any person shall exact more than one penny for sealing a bushel, or more than one half-penny for half a bushel or peck, he shall forfeit for the first offence, *5 £*.; for the second, *10 £*.; and for every other offence, *20 £*.

That there may be a just and certain measure to determine all controversies, one measure of brass shall be chained in the publick market-place, at the charge of the persons having the tolls thereof, on pain of forfeiting *5 £*.

And constables are impowered and required to search and examine if any persons use measures contrary to this act: and in case they shall find any unsealed measures, to seize and break the same, [11] and present the offenders at the ensuing sessions.-

22 and 23 Car. II.c. 12. Every person who shall buy or sell any corn *without measuring*, being thereunto required; or in any other manner than is directed by 22 Car. c. 8., shall forfeit and lose (besides the penalty of that act) all corn so bought or sold, or the value thereof to the persons complaining.

On complaint of any offence against this act, the proof shall lie upon the defendant, that he did buy or sell corn in every respect according to this and the said former acts.

GENTLEMEN; for the more certain and perpetual inforcement of the measure of corn agreeably to these acts of parliament, in which the public interest is so nearly concerned, and for the prevention, or the more ready determination of any differences, I strongly recommend, that in your respective parishes the constables be forthwith provided with a bushel sealed as these acts direct. [12]

GENTLEMEN; I ought not to quit this subject without making an observation, in which you have probably anticipated, and in which I am sure you will concur with me. And that is, we cannot forbear to admire those wise and excellent provisions which the laws of our country have made in this, as in other instances. The practice which lately prevailed in most parts of the kingdom, of buying and selling corn by a measure uncertain, but always larger than the true one, was in no respect the fault of the laws, nor yet of those persons by whom they are enforced; but it was owing solely to the inadvertence and negligence of husbandmen themselves, for whom every just provision had been long since made: who will, I trust, in future, be duly attentive to their own fair interests; and ready also to assist, by all lawful means, the endeavours of magistrates to distribute to every man his due.

But, GENTLEMEN; the concern and in-[13] terest which you, and the country in general, have in this business of measuring corn, is of very small importance, when compared with another matter, on which his Majesty has commanded his Justices of the Peace to address the several Grand Juries throughout the kingdom at this present general quarter sessions.

In the month of May last, his Majesty, who is constantly solicitous for the welfare and happiness of his people, found, "*That divers wicked and seditious writings had been printed, published, and industriously dispersed; tending to excite tumult and disorder, by endeavouring to raise groundless jealousies and discontents in the minds of his subjects: and also had reason to believe, that correspondences had been entered into with sundry persons in foreign parts, with a view to forward those criminal and wicked purposes.*"

His Majesty thereupon, being resolved to repress such seditious practices, issued [14] most seasonably his royal proclamation; – "*Solemnly warning his subjects to guard against all attempts of the nature above-mentioned, which aimed at the subversion of all regular government within the kingdom, and are inconsistent with the peace and order of society.*"

Gentlemen; I am persuaded you rejoice with me in knowing, that this proof of his Majesty's watchfulness for the good of his subjects, has been received by them throughout the kingdom with a most grateful attention. And I am especially happy in believing (from the observation and experience of several years), that in no part of the kingdom are the people more thankful for the happiness they enjoy under his Majesty's government, nor more inclined to deserve that happiness by conducting themselves as faithful subjects, than the people in those hundreds out of which you are returned to serve your country upon this [15] Grand Jury. From all general affirmations some exceptions must be made; but your neighbours are generally industrious, orderly, and peaceable: I do hope to see them still more so, when the great superfluity which there is of ALEHOUSES, in many of our villages, can be properly reduced. ALEHOUSES! THAT DEPLORABLE SOURCE OF MOST OF THE DISORDERS AND TUMULTS, VICES AND CRIMES, POVERTY AND POOR-RATES IN THE KINGDOM.

But, Gentlemen; little as our part of the country is at present infested with discontent and sedition, it still becomes us all to be very vigilant that they be not introduced amongst us. For, his Majesty finding, "*that the dispersion of seditious writings had lately been renewed with much activity in different parts of the kingdom,*" has directed, that it should be given in charge to you, Gentlemen of the Grand Jury, and I do accordingly [16] charge you, – "*diligently to inquire, and true presentment make, of all such wicked and seditious writings, published and spread within your hundreds, as shall be given in you in charge, or shall otherwise come to your knowledge; in order that the authors, printers, and publishers of all such writings as aforesaid, may be severally dealt with for their offences according to law.*"

Gentlemen; it is scarcely credible, with what diligence and activity the sowers of sedition have lately been at work in all corners of the land. Books and papers without number have been circulated, either gratis, or at the lowest possible price, by societies of various denominations: boldly proposing, not the IMPROVEMENT, but the UTTER SUBVERSION of our Constitution and Government. Insomuch that within these few weeks it has been (though I trust it has now ceased to be) a question, Not, – whether the produce of your farms should be [B-17] delivered by a lawful measure; but, – whether that produce should be your own property, or go into the hands of lawless plunderers;- whether you should have any servants and labourers to till your farms, or any farms to till? For, various bodies of men had associated (in undoubted connection and concert with persons in AND FROM foreign parts) for the purpose of recommending to, and forcing upon, THIS happy nation, an imitation of the proceedings of that most wretched of all the nations upon the earth - FRANCE.

The miseries under which that devoted country now groans, are probably known to us but imperfectly. However, we know, that public credit is destroyed; - a flourishing commerce ruined;- property of every kind, and the products of THE EARTH in particular, at the mercy of a lawless multitude;- of liberty and of justice not the shadow remaining;- [18] innocent persons without number massacred or banished;- personal safety so precarious (at least in the metropolis and the greater towns) that no man whose fortune is an object of plunder, or who is not attached to the ruling faction of the day, can lay himself down to rest, with any assurance that a band of murderers have not devoted him to die before the morning; – "*God and the King*," who WE are justly taught to "*fear and honour*," alike dishonoured, reviled, renounced and rejected -:

In short, the contest seems now reduced to this single point, - Whether those who HAVE PROPERTY shall not divide it EQUALLY with those who have NONE. And all these enormities;- this rapine, these murders, and massacres,- not only remain unpunished; but have been countenanced, and even applauded in the seat of legislation itself.

Thus have the French done all that [B 2-19] men can do, to injure the fair cause of LIBERTY, and to check the progress of it in the world. For, what monarchs will not be afraid to yield, nay, what wise subjects will not be afraid to demand, even a just extension of liberty; while consequences so fatal to both parties, as those which France exhibits, are fresh in the recollection of mankind?

But let us hope, for the quiet and safety of human kind, that these sanguinary monsters have nearly run their execrable race.[1] [20]

From this horrid spectacle, let us turn out thoughts to the actual situation of this country of OURS.

Our public credit is still high, notwithstanding warlike preparations: -

[1] At the time of speaking these words (14th January, 1793) there remained one great step in this race of crimes. And that step, alas, was taken SEVEN DAYS AFTER.

I do not hear that any amongst the ENGLISH APOLOGISTS FOR THE FRENCH, IN ANY PLACE, has failed to express his abhorrence of this barbarous, iniquitous, and cowardly act.

Of all the maxims which licentiousness has lately taught, this (which seems to be adopted in France) is the most horribly licentious: - THAT MURDER FOR LIBERTY IS NO CRIME. I once hoped, that if perfect liberty could be procured to the whole world by the MURDER OF ONE INNOCENT MAN, few Englishmen would be found who would not decline THE GLORIOUS AND IMMORTAL WORK. But I have shuddered to hear some of them coolly say,-That the first of the late French Revolutions was accomplished with as little unnecessary bloodshed as possible. A LITTLE MURDER! AND LIBERTY CHEAP AT SUCH A PRICE! These principles have produced in France their proper fruits. God forbid they should thrive in a British soil! Alas! when man has learned to dip his hands in THE BLOOD OF MAN, no beast of prey seems to be so dreadfully ferocious as he is.

foreign commerce flourishing beyond all past example; and by the vast capitals, the honourable name, and the enterprizing spirit of our merchants, increasing in all quarters of the globe:-inland trade rapidly making its way, by new channels, into every corner of the kingdom, [21] and connecting the distant parts of it:- manufactures in so much request for their goodness and cheapness, that the markets for them cannot be sufficiently supplied: - the general face of the country so improved and improving (especially, as you know, by vast undertakings in DRAINAGE) that it seems as if in a few years there would hardly be an acre of land, which stagnant water will continue to cover and retain in an unprofitable and disgraceful state: - personal safety, liberty, and property, secured to every honest and industrious man by just and equal laws: - and those laws ADMINISTERED with an impartiality that is above reproach.

Gentlemen; if such be the condition to which we have attained, and in which we are daily advancing, under our present happy Constitution; can there be any wisdom or patriotism, in recom-[22] mending the example of the FRENCH to our imitation?

For, do we live (as they did a few years since) under an ARBITRARY and DESPOTIC government? which in that country justly called for GREAT ALTERATIONS; suppose even a revolution; yet no such an INSANE revolution, as they have lately by a second, and that a most desperate experiment resorted to.

Some blemishes and defects may be discerned in our laws and institutions; as in what that is human may there not? But shall we, to remove them, voluntarily incur a great hazard of having NO laws to protect us; by letting loose (as in FRANCE) the MULTITUDE to reform us? As well might you pray for a SUCCESSION OF HURRICANES, for the benefit and improvement of your fields and villages.

Let us rather entrust all improvements to the circumspect wisdom of our consti-[23] tutional legislators, the King, Lords, and Commons; than whom; perhaps, the world cannot shew a body of men more watchful over, and more devoted to the welfare of any people.

Gentlemen; it is THUS the nation appears now to judge.

For, his Majesty's faithful subjects, sensible of the blessings they enjoy under his paternal government, are now declaring with one voice, raised in all parts of the kingdom, that they are cordially attached to that Government, and to the existing Constitution of their country. Never, I believe, on any occasion, was the sense of the nation expressed in so full and unequivocal manner. In consequence of which, and of the wise and vigorous public measures that have been pursued, DISLOYALTY AND SEDITION, which lately ventured abroad with an insulting and menacing air, have shrunk and hid themselves from the view of an [24] an indignant people. But disloyalty, baffled and disconcerted, will not be hastily converted into loyal attachment. Probably, pent up in the narrow cell of the guilty bosom, it rages with a malignity made tenfold by the disappointment. We must not, therefore, fall into an indolent security. The first storm, which threatened us, is happily blown over: we must anxiously watch the face of the sky, and make provision against a second.

It cannot be necessary, Gentlemen, to remind persons of your experience and years; but it may be useful to some who stand around us, to observe: - That while we contend most zealously for the support of our happy Constitution, we must be careful to do so in a legal and constitutional MANNER. Should there be found amongst us any men weak or wicked enough to aim at the destruction of our happiness by treasonable or sedi-[25] tious practices; let the justice of their country fall upon them by the course of A LAWFUL TRIAL. But if ever their persons or property should be threatened in ANY OTHER WAY; prevent (I pray you), by all your influence and exertions, that most dangerous mode of injustice, the rash and summary justice of A RIOTOUS MULTITUDE.

Do this for your own sake, as well as for the sake of what is right and fit: for ANARCHY and VIOLENCE do not long continue to be RESPECTERS OF PERSONS.

Gentlemen: The obvious conclusion from all that has been given you in charge, is this: - That you are bound, as you regard whatever can be dear to yourselves and your posterity, to cherish in your minds, and to infuse into the minds of others, as far as your influence extends, a spirit of thankfulness to Divine Providence, and of profound respect towards the memory of your fore-[26] fathers, for the invaluable blessings which you possess, in the security of your lives, liberties, and properties, under our most happy system of laws, and under the just and mild execution of them by a most benevolent and truly patriotic KING.

An interesting document is to be found on the last page of this volume: it is the copy, in a neat hand, of a letter sent to the Rev. S. Partridge. It reveals the importance attributed to the influence of these Charges, and is therefore reproduced here:

White Hall, 7th March 1793

Sir,

I have received and laid before the King your Letter of the 21st ulto. inclosing the Charge given by you to the Grand Jury at the last General Quarter Sessions, of the Hundreds of Kirton and Skirbeck in the County of Lincoln, and I am commanded to acquaint you that His Majesty views your Conduct upon that occasion in a very favourable Light.

I am,

Sir,

Your most obedient &
humble Servant
Henry Dundas

Rev: Samuel Partridge,
Boston, Lincolnshire.

A **CHARGE**, DELIVERED TO THE **GRAND JURY** OF THE COUNTY OF DUBLIN, At the General Quarter Sessions of the Peace, held for the said County, at KILMAINHAM, on the 15th of January, 1793. **By ROBERT DAY, Esq**. One of His Majesty's Counsel learned in the Law, and Chairman, of the Quarter Sessions for the said County. Published at the Request of the HIGH SHERIFF and MAGISTRATES of the COUNTY of DUBLIN. DUBLIN: Printed by HENRY WATTS, *Law Bookseller*, N° 3, Christ-Church Lane.

1793.

The HIGH SHERIFF and MAGISTRATES of the Country of DUBLIN, beg leave to return ROBERT DAY Esq., the Chairman, their sincere Thanks for his most Seasonable and Constitutional Charge, and desire his Permission to publish the same.

Signed by order of the Meeting,
JOSEPH ATKINSON, Sheriff.

[A 2 -5]

CHARGE, &c

Gentlemen of the Grand Jury,

"YOU are brought together at this periodical return of our General Sessions of the Peace, to discharge a duty of great and vital importance to the county of Dublin, and the community at large: to call forth into life and action the criminal law; to deliberate upon, and weigh in the scale of equal and dispassionate justice, such charges as shall be submitted to you against divers of your fellow-subjects; to put such of them in a course of trial as shall be made out to your satisfaction, either upon the evidence of your own senses, or upon the *viva voce*, or written evidence of accusers; and thus to vindicate and promote the general police and good order of your county. I am sensible that the duration of each Session, and the frequent return of this duty in the county of Dublin, are attended with no inconsiderable inconvenience to country gentlemen; but you will reflect how small a price you pay in this occasional trouble, for the essential advantages derived upon yourselves and the [6] public, from a conscientious and diligent discharge of your duty. In order to impress you with a just sense of the importance of this trust, it may not be amiss, particularly at this critical juncture, to trace briefly, the criminal law of your country from its elementary principles.

"When civil society was instituted, it was found necessary, that the constituent members should resign a certain portion of their natural liberty, (or to use the cant expression of the day, a certain portion of the 'Rights of Man,') in order the secure the remainder. The unlimited enjoyments of every individual in a state of nature, were found incompatible with human happiness, or the existence of civil society for which man was obviously formed; for the weak it is evident, must in that state be victims to the strong – the simple and honest must be the unprotected dupes of every designing or daring knave. To obviate these evils it was that civil government was established, wherein rules of conduct and the moral obligations of justice from man to man were prescribed, the impulses of appetites controuled by commensurate penalties, strength and power ceased to be the arbiters of property, and universal and equal protection was substituted for the wild excesses and dominion of passions. How far that professed object of all civil government has been at-[7] tained in other states, it is not our business now to enquire; it is enough for us to know, that every peaceful subject who reposes under the shade of the British Constitution – '*the proudest Monument of human Wisdom and Integrity*,' (the expression of a great man most egregiously misapplied) enjoys the most perfect security for his life, liberty, property and reputation. The means whereby that important end is obtained, are the civil code, and the criminal code; the latter of which is your peculiar and appropriated province; a code instituted for, and competent to the punishment and controul of public offences, and which, with the impartiality of death, knows no distinction between the Prince's palace, and the poor Man's cottage.

"But while the British Constitution provides adequate punishment for guilt, it has encompassed innocence with impenetrable lines of defence and security. The life and liberty of an Irishman are sacred; the law doth tender them so dearly, that no man can be convicted but on the oaths of 24 at least of his equals; 12 at least of the Grand Jury (whose condition is likely to raise them above undue influence,) must concur to find the bill of indictment, and 12 Petit Jurors, (secured by the privilege of challenge against all prejudice to the prisoner) must concur to convict upon that bill. – I ask you, Gentlemen, is there a man among you who is not conscious, and feels not that under the British Constitution, to be innocent is to be secure? To be innocent [8] is to be independent of, and beyond the reach of power? We know of but one Law for the proudest Peer of the realm, and the poorest Peasant who crawls upon the earth; a mild and equal code, which, like the Deity, is no respector of persons, but pervades, controuls, and cherishes alike the whole system! The poor man's friend – his shield and security against the strong arm of power! The popular order of the state, in fact, is the most essentially interested in maintaining inviolate the law, under whose happy influence and protection, industry, ingenuity, and personal exertion, (the only patrimony of that class of mankind) are stimulated, fostered, and invigorated.

"The British Constitution is so familiarized to us by uninterrupted enjoyment, that no wonder if weak or thoughtless minds surveyed its beauties without much emotion or sensibility. The charming scene always lying in our view, one is too apt at last to behold with apathy and indifference. But, gentlemen, who that has a heart to feel, or an understanding to reflect upon the calamities of France, but must be rouzed to an animated sense of the unrivalled excellencies of *our* Constitution, and of the rational liberty, which is our indefeasible birth-right? Mark the effect of these distractions upon your fellow-subjects of Great-Britain, that nation of philoso-[9] phers; that sober, dignified, and manly people: they know the value of their Constitution, and they venerate it with the enthusiasm of idolaters – a happy combination of the highest degree of practical liberty, with the energy and vigour of the monarchical form – a well-pois'd system of Government, perfected and mellowed by the wisdom of ages, admired and celebrated by the most enlightened sages of ancient as well as modern times – 1700 years ago, by the Roman historian in its cradle, and in the present century by the French philosopher in its maturity.[1] If sedition assail the venerable fabric, they embrace its columns, resolved to stand by it or perish in the ruins- they rally round the Throne of their good, their beloved King, and drown the storm with acclamations of loyalty, from end to end of the island. They laugh at the malignant folly of those human devils, who offer them wild theory for substantial enjoyment; and under pretence of amending their condition, would substitute for genuine liberty the vilest and most savage of all dominations, the tyranny of an unbridled multitude. If our system, say they, has in the lapse of years past contracted specks, there is a recuperative quality in the constitution, which enables it to purge and slough off without innovation of violence its own impurities. Judge, Gentlemen, of the tree by its fruit – prosperity unexampled in the world, a gigantic growth in commerce and manufactures, wealth, arts and learning, and [10] corresponding and still more rapid growth in the wealth and prosperity of this kingdom since the year 1782, when we were restored to the enjoyment and usufruct of that Constitution.

"Gentlemen, the same restless and evil spirit has been busy here too. In fact, the richest [s]oils will often throw up the most noxious weeds.

[1] The Roman historian: Tacitus ; the French philosopher: it could be Voltaire, with his *Lettres sur les Anglois*, later *Lettres philosophiques*, 1733–34; it could also be Montesquieu who, in *De l'esprit des lois*, 1748, greatly admired the parliamentary régime of Great-Britain.

So in the best constructed systems of Government, there will be found men of misguided and vicious propensities, who discover too late, that honest industry is the straitest road to wealth, and a just application of talents the road to honest fame. Bankrupt in fame and character, they sicken amidst the universal prosperity of their country, they survey with envy and disgust, that general happiness which they do not share, and they confederate without remorse against the most revered establishments, as a compendious mode of advancing themselves upon the ruins. Such men, as long as they escape the public executioner have an interest in agitating the country; they have nothing to lose – and in a scramble they may gain something. Who can behold without affliction, the desperate labours of parricides to disturb this peace and interrupt the growth of this flourishing kingdom? Fictitious grievances, and chimerical expectations of I know not what new-fangled equality, are held forth to delude the credulous and uninformed classes of the people; tho' it is certain that [11] one of the peculiar advantages of these countries, is in the diversified *Inequality* and gradual subordination which obtains among us, as various as the various talents and capacities of man, and the support which our several ranks and classes administer to each other. The most pernicious doctrines are circulated in news-papers, cheap pamphlets, and hand-bills. Bodies of the people have actually been invited, with the most unparalleled audacity, to arms. Indefatigable pains are taken to disaffect the public against the Legislature; to bring the Executive Authority of the Land into contempt; to hold forth as a model for our imitation a bankrupt and distracted nation, stained with the blood of her best citizens, and exulting, perhaps at this moment, in the murder of a mild and innocent Sovereign; a nation lately the seat of arts, elegance, refinement and science – now undone in the pursuit of a fantastical, implacable liberty, whose religion is atheism, and whose politics are universal conquest, and the dissolution of all legitimate government.

"Gentlemen, the alarm became so serious and general as to call loudly for the interposition of Government, and it must be owned that the Government has stepped forth with the most laudable vigour and the happiest effect. A seasonable Proclamation has been issued by the Lord-Lieutenant and Council, warning those disturbers of [12] the peace, of the dangerous precipice on which they stood. – Fortunately the hint was taken; for let me tell you gentlemen, that the raising and keeping together, numbers of armed men, against the express command of the executive authority, particularly if for the reform of imaginary or even public real grievances, has been adjudged to be a constructive levying of war against the king, and of course High Treason. The constitution avows no course of proceeding for a redress of grievances but by petition to any one or all the three branches of the legislature, conducted in a peaceable, orderly and respectful manner; a right disputed by the arbitrary and infatuated House of Stuart, but unequivocally asserted at the glorious Revolution in the famous Bill of Rights. But Gentlemen, an attempt by intimidation and violence to coerce a redress of grievances, to force the enacting of a new, or the repeal of a subsisting Act of Parliament, is a proceeding of a very different complexion indeed; it is in construction of law nothing less than to wage war against the King – it is High Treason. The government has also taken vigorous measures to crush every symptom of insurrection and tumult in the country; and to apprehend and to bring to justice all sowers of sedition. And let me remind my brethren the Magistrates in the solemnest manner in the presence of the County, that a more than ordinary vigilance and exertion is expected from them at this crisis, when the friends of anar-[13] chy and confusion are unusually active and industrious. They are called upon to disperse all meetings of a seditious tendency, to seize and commit all persons distributing seditious writings, or holding seditious and treasonable conversations. For, Gentlemen, though mere words cannot amount to an overt act of treason, unless uttered in contemplation of some traitorous purpose, yet when spoken in contempt of the King or his Government whereby his Majesty may be lessened in the esteem of his subjects, I say such words are highly criminal and punishable by fine and imprisonment, and even pillory. Much more criminal must seditious writing be, as writing imports a deliberate act, and if published may under certain circumstances amount to an overt act of High Treason. – The Magistrates are also particularly called upon, to caution all publicans and victuallers within their jurisdiction, against suffering their houses to be converted into dens of sedition and confederacy, under pain, not only of being stript of their licences, but of being held responsible for the crimes of those who they harbour.

"But vain will be the exertions of Magistracy, vain the interposition even of Government, if the gentlemen of influence and authority among us do not step out and second those exertions. We must not content ourselves with merely wishing well to our country; the time is come when men must act, when every friend to social order will [14] form round our unrivalled Constitution, and by a spirited conduct in his neighbourhood, sustain the Magistrate in preserving the public peace. Whatever speculative differences may exist in the country, depend upon it every man loves order in proportion as he loves liberty – in short, the very existence of that sacred liberty, without which we should be but tenants at will of all we hold dear in this life, depends upon a vigorous execution of the law and a prompt co-operation with the magistrate.

"One word more before I dismiss you. At a former Session, I had occasion to deplore the fatal spirit of combination which raged in our part of the capital to which our jurisdiction extends. That baneful spirit happily hath been suppressed through the vigour of some of our Magistrates, and some seasonable examples made by this Court, and the artizans have once more returned to their looms, and to the peaceful exercise of their several occupations. Nay more, it is well known that much pains have been taken to inflame and to excite some of the neediest and most desperate among the journeymen, and to *affiliate* them into subordinate Jacobin Clubs, for the blackest and most atrocious purposes; but that they have in general had the virtue and good sense to resist the infamous proposals. Thus deporting themselves, they have an irresistible claim upon our best offices and exer-[15] tions, while they are employed in honest industry, and in advancing the manufactures of their country, it behoves us to see that forestallers and ingrossers do not enhance the necessities of life and add further burdens to our tradesmen already struggling under too many difficulties. Gentlemen, this abominable practice demands your most serious enquiry; you ought not to wait for the return of informations upon the subject, but are bound by your oath (if any of you know of the practice) to discover the offender that he may be indicted or presented. And let me address one word to you out of your capacity of Grand Jurors, as Gentlemen of feeling and sensibility: Let me recommend to you an Association - nay, start not at the word-an association for the relief of distressed Artizans. If we must have associations among us, for God's sake let us set the example of one for a virtuous purpose - not for preserving game, not for preserving covers and propagating vermin, not for circulating libels and sedition - in short, not to administer to the luxuries, the folly or malignity of mankind: Let us all associate for the relief of the poor manufacturers of the Liberty, whose sufferings at this dear and pinching season, challenge our sympathy, and [16] whose patience and good conduct under these sufferings demand our warmest approbation and applause.

"Gentlemen, I have detained you too long from the discharge of your duty, and of the important public business which awaits your consideration."

FINIS.

A CHARGE, delivered to the GRAND JURY of the COUNTY of CHESTER, at the QUARTER-SESSIONS held at Chester, on Tuesday the 15th of January, 1793; By the Reverend ROGER JACSON, Chairman.

Published at the particular request of the Magistrates, Grand Jury, and the Committee of the Association of the City of Chester.

Gentlemen of the Grand Jury,

I AM directed to make it part of my charge to you, on this occasion, that you diligently inquire and true presentment make of all wicked and seditious writings that have come to your knowledge. --- This, Gentlemen, is one of the means that Government has adopted to suppress such publications, as you all know have remarkably abounded of late in this kingdom, justly alarmed, as it should seem, at the danger threatened thereby to our happy constitution. And it is a means, which at the same time that it bespeaks a proper vigilance in those that have the present direction of our affairs, exhibits to us an ample proof of the excellence of the government under which we live: It is a luminous display of the perfect civil liberty which Englishmen actually enjoy; that however wantonly provoked, the executive power dares not lift the hand of punishment against the meanest of its citizens, before a dispassionate enquiry is made into the probability of his guilt, by a jury of his fellow-citizens and equals, previous even to his being brought under the hazard of a trial for his offence. If we recollect the methods that other countries have taken to silence such writings, and stifle such opinions, as they rulers might happen to dislike; if we remember the large pecuniary fine attached to the publication of such writings by the house of Austria, by the summary and decisive operation only of a manifesto or a proclamation, and that too distributing that fine in such a manner as to invite information and persecution; if, I say, we compare for a moment these proceedings with those of England, we are directly in possession of a capital distinction between this and all other countries; of that ground, upon which we can maintain the opinion, that however they may have reason to desire a Revolution, we have none; that we are already in possession of more than all political *illumination*, all civil *regeneration*, can bestow, if it disdains to take the Constitution of England for its basis, or its guide. To the exercise of this part of your duty, I am particularly to call you; that by making a presentment, as a Grand Jury, of any offences against the Government, which may have come to your knowledge, if any such have come, you furnish the court with a proper cognizance of them, which, by turning your presentment into the more artificial mode of an indictment, may bring the offender to condign punishment. And it is indeed with some degree of exultation that I reflect, that I can now press this duty upon you with great confidence; when the regular and constitutional progress of liberty has freed me from the fear of involving the unwary in the punishment due only to malignant guilt; since the act of the last sessions of Parliament for regulating the judicial proceedings in the case of libels,[1] has given to the *Jury* a full and final power of deciding, not only upon the fact of publication, but upon the malicious intention, and every other circumstance that can at all make a publication criminal. – I conceive it, Gentlemen, not to consist entirely with the duty of my office to omit altogether to explain to you the law upon this subject; and tho' I shall not undertake to give you an extensive and critical rule, that you may apply to all cases, a difficult task perhaps for those who are possessed of the best information in this matter; yet, in general, you may take a libel to be any thing that is a contumely or reproach, published to the defamation of the government, of a magistrate, or a private person; and it may be in writing, or not, and so it may be published by *speaking, singing,* or *delivery* to another. – If, then, Gentlemen, you know of any matters that fall under these descriptions, that you think, either from the malicious and disaffected temper of the publisher, or the diligence and assiduity with which they are published, are likely to affect the peace of this country; it is your duty to that country, to place the offender in such a situation, as that he may satisfy the justice of the laws, if that has any demands upon him: which is precisely the regular effect of your presentment. And it is not, I am sorry to say, an ordinary call that you have to the exercise of this duty; but instructed and supported as I am in the opinion, by great men of all parties in this kingdom, I hesitate not to produce it to you as an argument for your attention in this matter, that we stand at this moment in a great and important crisis - that everything valuable, our properties, our lives, our liberties, are set upon the hazard: For I, for my part, see, and I lament that every one whose sincerity of attachment to our constitution is only impeached by this wilful blindness, does not equally see with me, that there actually exists a design, that there have been attempts, to subvert every thing in this country, which is either the glory or happiness of Englishmen; and that these attempts are supported by the natural enemies of these kingdoms - for in the insolent hour of success, those persons have avowed an intention of interfering in the domestic concerns of every nation under heaven; an intention which they took care to reprobate in all others; and which, if their sense of national honor had not forbad those other states to adopt,

[1] 32 Geo III c. 60.

these men had not now existed in their present form, to degrade the public character of one of the first countries of the world, and to violate the rights of nations and of humanity. When we combine with this extraordinary declaration, the recommendation and the praises of their proceedings, as fit models for our imitation, the constant appeal to their principles as the standard of all that is perfect in legislation, the open wished for their success, the establishment of societies for the express purpose of correspondence with them, and that correspondence actually opened by formal deputations, all which are facts notorious to every body; without mentioning their direct employment of the emissaries of sedition, which is however a fact, I fear, put now beyond the possibilities of a doubt; we have at once the clearest evidence indeed of the object of the proceedings amongst us, and of the necessity there is for us all, in our several stations, and with our utmost vigilance and care, to stand upon our guard, and exert the powers we have, while, Gentlemen, we have yet them, to deliver down our posterity, unsullied and[1] unimpaired by passing thro' our hands, the inheritance and the birth-right of Englishmen.

But I am happy that I can with propriety inforce my argument, by animating your hope, as well as by alarming your fears; – and, Gentlemen, the spirit of constitutional loyalty, of late so remarkably displayed throughout this kingdom, cannot fail to encourage you in the discharge of this part of your duty; for at the same time that its almost entire unanimity proves to you how inconsiderable, in points of numbers, your opponents are, it assures to you the good wishes, the approbation, the assistance, and the protection, of the greater and the better part of your fellow-citizens and subjects. United with such respectable associates, called in such a deliberate manner, by the unanimous voice of your country, there is nothing can deter you from your duty; and, among other things, let me intreat you to pay no regard to the objections and the calumnies that have been thrown out against those meetings, that have been held of late for the purpose of offering to you, and all good citizens who come forward in the discharge of their public duty, a proper countenance and support. Are you told, that they are spreading an unnecessary alarm? Recollect the grounds they have for their proceedings, in the observations I have just now made. – Is it said, that they may endanger the liberty of our country? that they may let in such a full tide of approbation of the measures of the government, as may sweep before it all the barriers of our freedom? Confront the assertion with their several declarations, that they will maintain the constitution and government of these realms, as by *Law* established. – Are they represented as enemies to the liberty of the press? as hostile to liberal inquiry and a

[1] Here begins the second column.

free discussion of opinions? Repel the foul slander with the remark, that the object of their censure is not the opinions, but the alarming abuse that is made of them; that as we cannot argue from the abuse of any thing, against the use of it; so neither can we with justice conclude, that he would restrain the abuse, is therefore hostile to the use, of that glorious privilege. – Is it apprehended that such associations will stop all wholesome reforms, and secure the continuance of any abuses of government, which some persons might wish to see removed? It surely is a groundless apprehension from these associations, for the declarations of all of them that I have seen are conceived, very properly, in such general terms, as to admit person of all descriptions, of all parties, of all sentiments, in politics, except Republicans and levellers, of all who wish the present prosperity of England any duration, of all who prefer the security of perfect liberty, before anarchy and national misery. – But, Gentlemen, tho' not one of these defences could with justice beset up, yet would I, I declare it without reserve, yet would I have been an associator; for dear and valuable as many of the principles alluded to are dear to me, things yet more dear, yet more valuable, are at stake - for the question before us, is not, whether an inveterate system of oppression and misrule shall be overturned, the subversion of which might be cheaply purchased with many sacrifices and even with many evils; but, whether a constitution, the consumate "contrivance of human wisdom"; the accumulated wisdom of ages, should be razed at once to the ground, and draw with it a wide and hideous ruin, for no better reason, than to make the experiment, whether something better might not possibly be contrived? – Is it with singular modesty proposed to the people of these realms, to contest for forms of government like fools, when we are actually in possession of that, which, from its nature, secures to it the privilege of being best administered, and is therefore best.– For it is indeed with a respect approaching to reverence, with a gratitude from the bottom of the heart, that I consider the English constitution, in all the latitude of its benefits and its excellence: Bred in independence, inclined by an inquisitive mind, and assisted by a liberal education, to seek the truth and venerating, with all the other blessings of civil and religious liberty, the power of discovering her, amidst the confusion of opposite opinions, by free and uncontrolled inquiry; at the same time attached by all the bonds of society, and the dearest domestic ties, to all those several relations that form the tenderest interests, and fill with the most anxious cares the human heart; not insensible to the refined and innocent pleasures of polished society and advanced civilization, I offer the warmest thanks to the Great Disposer of events, that I was born an Englishman: – For where can I boast my independence, or my inquiries after truth be gratified, so amply and so securely, as amidst the toleration, amidst the extensive sources of science, which this land of liberty has opened for her use? Where can the social affections be so fully indulged as amidst her perfect freedom of private intercourse? Where can the parental anxieties repose in such perfect confidence, as upon the security to all property which her laws afford, and the lucrative emoluments which her extensive commerce and her establishments hold out? Where can truth be gratified, if not in the perfection of the arts which her liberal patronage and her extensive protection of the lives and properties of all her subjects, justly boasts of as its happiest consequence and effect? In a word, wherever I turn, I find the wants of every situation, and every character, in life, amply provided for by her prudent laws and wise institutions - and shall we rashly forego these numerous advantages, shall we be slow in taking the alarm, when things so precious are threatened even with *distant* danger? The people of this country have happily shewn, that they deserve not this reproach: Let us all catch the animating flame; let us join with one heart and one voice in the support of our constitution, under King, Lords, and Commons as the government best able to resist the corruptions which wealth and prosperity never fail to introduce; as the government which not only give us present happiness, but has proved, by the experience of more than a century, that it is able to secure it to us upon lasting foundations.

Printed by ORDER of the COMMITTEE.

J. EDWARDS, Secretary.

A **CHARGE** DELIVERED TO THE **GRAND JURY** OF *NORFOLK*, AT THE GENERAL QUARTER SESSIONS HELD ON WEDNESDAY, JAN. 16, 1793, AT THE SHIRE-HOUSE ON THE CASTLE-HILL, *NORWICH*, by **HENRY JODRELL, ESQ.** CHAIRMAN. PUBLISHED AT THE REQUEST OF THE MAGISTRATES. PRINTED BY RAINGTON AND BACON. Norwich

[A 2-3]
A CHARGE, &c.

Gentlemen,

AS the Grand Jury of this County you are now assembled for the purpose of discharging a weighty and considerable trust; it has therefore been usual for the Court to point out to you the general outlines of your duty.

GENTLEMEN, the inquest now established in your persons is one of those institutions which we owe to the wisdom of our ancestors, particularly calculated to the free spirit of the English Law, and the peculiar policy of this country. You are invested with an absolute, and also a discretionary superintending, power; the former in respect to the finding or reject-[4] ing of such bills of indictment as may be brought before you, the latter in presenting to the Court such crimes, misdemeanors, and other offences, as may have been committed, and should be the subject of public notice and observation.

THE offences which will be brought before you by indictment, though numerous, are confined to one species of crimes, namely larceny.

YOUR duty as an inquisitorial power between the crown and the subject is to enquire into the nature of the offence, and the evidence to support the charge; you only hear the evidence on the part of the prosecution, and you should have no difficulty to find a bill a true bill, if the charge is so satisfactorily substantiated that you are persuaded of the truth of the evidence, and that there is reasonable ground to call upon the person accused for a denial and defence: twelve of you must agree to find the bill, for so tender and vigilant is the law of this country over the life, the liberty, and the property of the subject, no man can be convicted at the suit [5] of the King, unless by the unanimous voice of twenty four of his equals, and his neighbouring twelve of the Grand Jury in the first place assenting to the accusation, and the whole Petty Jury of twelve more afterwards finding him guilty on his trial.

THE other branch of your authority, that of presentment, is a great Constitutional trust, for you are chosen out of the body of this county to represent every particular member of it, and for such service you are summoned to appear to-day.

PRESENTMENT is the notice taken by the Grand Jury of any offence, either of commission or omission, arising within the extent of their jurisdiction, and which, by communicating to each other from their own knowledge or observation, they are enabled to bring forward without any indictment laid before them at the suit of the King; upon such presentment the officer of the Court frames an indictment, and the party is bound to answer it. Gentlemen, it has often occurred to me, that the exercise of this power has not been sufficiently attended to by Grand [6] Juries, and yet it is a most salutary institution, and is founded upon that great principle of the English Law – that to prevent is better than to punish. The power is in you to look around the several districts to which you belong; for which purpose you are directed to be summoned from various parishes and different hundreds, that by bringing, in your persons, the whole county into one spot, you may be able, collectively, to redress what, in your private capacities, you have had occasion, individually, to complain of: under this authority, therefore, of presentment, you are invested with complete cognizance over the peace, the comfort, and the safety of mankind; and having that authority, offences of every description, subordinate officers, all regulations respecting the public police, are immediately included; in you therefore is placed a superintending controul over the constables, persons licensed to keep public houses, the surveying of the highways, the overseers of the poor, and all such persons in whom the law has reposed its confidence, or has invested with power, that you, by your wisdom, may correct their abuses, and, by presenting to the Court any breach or neglect of duty, [7] may make them more vigilant and active for the future. And here, Gentlemen, I must observe, that the disorders which prevail in many parishes evince the truth of the very negligent manner in which the presentments of the constables are frequently delivered: the constable is an officer of considerable trust, he is, by law, immediately the protector of the police and regular deportment of the particular township or parish over which he is appointed to preside; and the internal state of such district, in respect of the peace and security of it, is under his care, and should be the subject of his vigilance and observation: the presentments therefore which the Constables are directed to make are, by law, intended to be the result of those parochial observations which have naturally occurred to them in the exercise of their duty, and which, if properly made, would be a timely check to those evils which should be a subject of complaint; instead of which, the presentments are signed certainly without much notice or attention, for there is generally one common answer – *nothing to present* –; and the fourteen articles contained in them, many of which are wisely calculated for the good order of [8] the parish to which they apply; are reduced to mere form; this, in my judgment, is a neglect of duty, and the Magistrates would do well never to receive such presentments but upon oath:– However, Gentlemen, such constables, as well as other persons, who are by law invested with authority, or in whom any parochial trust is imposed, are answerable to you, and may become, by your presentments, fit subjects of criminal correction: if therefore, to your knowledge any such peace officers have been negligent of their duty, and have suffered disorders and licentiousness to prevail; if public houses, which are licensed not for the wickedness but the comfort of society, are permitted to be the receptacles of disaffected, wicked and disorderly persons, *under whatever specious pretensions they may think proper to assemble*; if the paupers of any parish are suffered to be idle and abandoned in the towns or places where they belong; these are abuses which it is your duty to present, and the law will apply the remedy. Gentlemen, thank God, we live in a country where the law has provided for every individual: no man is so great as to be above its power, no man is so [B-9] humble as to be below its protection ; in every parish the old, indigent and infirm, are the objects of relief; the idle of employment; the disorderly and viciously inclined of correction; the criminals of punishment; and each description should be properly attended to: if the old and infirm are neglected, the bounty of society is betrayed; if the idle are not employed, they are naturally driven into vice; if vice is not corrected, crimes are committed, and punishment must necessarily ensue; and I am afraid it is the case of many an unfortunate victim to the injured laws of his country, to have suffered more from original neglect than bad disposition.

AND here, Gentlemen, let me observe, in doing which, I address myself more to you as respectable Farmers and Gentlemen, under whom laborers and the lower classes of society are employed, it should ever be your duty, as presiding over the parishes to which you belong, to attend from time to time to the price of corn, and those articles of life which are proper for the comfort and support of the inferior sort of people, – to compare their possible earnings with their neces-[10] sary expenditures; – there is power in the Magistrates at the sessions under an old law to regulate the price of wages of people in husbandry; however, to attempt an universal rule in this respect would be attended with more difficulties and inconveniences than the law was meant to remedy, on which account that statute has got into disuse; but the honest, laborious, and industrious man is entitled to the necessaries and enjoyments of life proportioned to the relative situation in which he is placed; if his labor is not equal to the support of his family with comfort and propriety, Charity is more kindly received, either by lessening the number of his family and placing out the children to honest callings, or by supplying him with the necessaries of life, by the procurement of the parish officers, at a lower price than he can otherwise obtain them, proportioned to the quantity of money he can possibly earn; by so doing you will encourage the efforts of honest labor, diffuse a spirit of chearful industry throughout the parish, and by communicating the blessing of a competent sufficiency procure health and strength to all the family; the weights and measures should be also from [B 2 -11] time to time attended to in every township and place, to see that the same correspond with what the law has prescribed; for the lower kind of people, who purchase every thing in small quantities, and by retail, are much affected by abuses of this kind. I am happy to find that the Magistrates of this county, with great wisdom and propriety, have taken the same into their consideration.

GENTLEMEN, these are the observations which have occurred to me to make to you in the ordinary discharge of your duty; it behoves you, as I have said before, to consult with each other, particularly at this season of the year, when ill-disposed persons are more easily secreted, and of course the property and safety of individuals exposed to the greater danger, to look around the different parishes which immediately fall under your knowledge and observation, and by your presentments to endeavor, if possible, to prevent those crimes which may otherwise be unavoidably committed; in so doing you will feel this great satisfaction, that by an early application of the remedy to the evil, you will not only prevent the innocent from being injured, [12] but the wickedly-disposed from being protected & strengthened in the principles of vice.

GENTLEMEN, having said so much to you on any other occasion, I should only, on the part of the Court, have desired of you dispatch in the exercise of your duty with an apology for my having detained you so long; but as the present hour is of great importance to this country, I feel it necessary to lay before you, and the county at large, what his Majesty, by his royal Proclamations, has deemed proper to divulge, and draw your attention to what is the duty of every honest citizen at this time particularly to regard.

GENTLEMEN, his Majesty, who has at all times shown himself the father as well as the protector of his people, ever anxious for their safety and happiness in the month of May last thought proper to issue his royal proclamation, which stated, "That wicked and seditious writings had been published and dispersed with a view to excite tumult and disorder, and to raise groundless jealousies in the minds of his subjects, respecting the laws and constitutions of the country, and [13] with a design to vilify and bring into contempt the provisions made at the time of the glorious

Revolution. That there was great reason to believe correspondences had been entered into with sundry persons in foreign parts, with a view to forward the criminal and wicked purposes beforementioned; his Majesty therefore, expressing his most earnest desire to secure the public peace and prosperity, and to preserve to his subjects the enjoyment of their rights and liberties, civil and religious, in his royal favor," strictly warned "his subjects against such seditious practices, and commanded the Magistrates of every description, in their several and respective stations, to be watchful for the public happiness and for the public peace, and particularly to be diligent in the discovery of the authors, printers and dispersers of such seditious publications."

GENTLEMEN, this gracious Proclamation of the King was received by his subjects with all that respect and affection due from duty and allegiance, and addresses from many parts of the kingdom were presented, expressive of [14] the people's hatred and abhorrence of those pernicious doctrines which had been endeavored to be inculcated into the minds of the unwary. But the machinations of the dark and designing minds are not so easily brought to light, and it afterwards appeared that the activity of those persons whose particular duty it is to suppress libellous publications and treasonable confederates was not in proportion to the dangers that ensued.

GENTLEMEN, perhaps to one of the characteristic virtues of this country, benevolence or charity, we owe in a great measure the impending storm that was ready to burst upon our heads. The hand and heart of an Englishman is ever open to relieve the distressed; this country, blessed with prosperity and peace, became the happy asylum of the wretched and oppressed; amongst the number of miserable objects who took refuge from a neighbouring country, deprived of every thing but what the generosity of Englishmen could bestow, it is much to be feared were some with minds full of the most dangerous contrivances, and with opinions destructive of all Government, and fraught with those black [15] designs which have prevailed elsewhere. What his Majesty in his royal Proclamation had before declared he had occasion to believe too clearly appeared to the executive Magistracy of the country, and it became necessary, in a moment of great impending danger, no further back than December last, for his Majesty to issue a second Proclamation, in which he is graciously pleased to declare "That the utmost industry is still employed by evil-disposed persons within this kingdom, acting in concert with persons in foreign parts, with a view to subvert the laws and established constitution of this realm, and to destroy all order and government therein, and that a spirit of tumult and disorder thereby excited has lately shown itself in acts of riots and insurrection"; and so alarming was the crisis, the Parliament was summoned to meet before its appointed time, in consequence of the Militia of many counties being drawn out and embodied, to act in case of necessity to support the civil Magistrate.

GENTLEMEN, in such a moment as the present, it is particularly the duty of Grand [16] Juries to watch the constitution and the law, and by their presentments to bring forward all such offences as may have been committed against the peace, the safety, and the security of the public.

GENTLEMEN, one could hardly have supposed, had it been less notorious than it is, that there could exist persons so blind to the interests of this country, or so wicked or ignorant as to believe that clubs or associations of persons met together to conspire against the established government, with a view to effect what they please to call a reform, can be colored with any artifice or tolerated with impunity. The constitution of this country, thank God, is not open to the attacks of such daring innovators, and the wisdom of the law has provided a remedy not only against the actual endeavors, but against the workings and secret contrivances of wicked and ill-disposed minds.

GENTLEMEN, every insurrection, which in judgment of law is intended against the person of the King, be it to dethrone or imprison him, or to oblige him to alter his [C-17] measures of government: these risings all amount to levying war within the statute of treasons, whether attended with the circumstances of open war or not, and every conspiracy for these purposes, tho' not treasons within the clause of levying war, yet is an overt act within the clause of compassing the King's death. All insurrections to effect innovations of a public nature are, by construction of law, treason, within the clause of levying war, for they are levelled at the King's crown and royal dignity, and have a tendency to dissolve the bonds of society, and to destroy the established government of the country. But, Gentlemen, the law does not begin here, there is a crime anterior, which is the knowledge and concealment of treason, without taking any active part to effect it; as if one, having notice before hand that persons designed to meet in order to conspire against the government, go into company and hear their treasonable consultations, and conceal them; or if one who has been in such company incautiously, and heard such discourse, meet the same company a second time, and hear such like discourse and conceal it; in as much it is the duty of every good subject, and in-[18] cluded in his allegiance, to discover all such illicit practices; the concealment is what the law calls a negative misprision, and is punishable as a high misdemeanor: the being apprized therefore of treasonable practices and of not revealing them, or if any person speaks or writes against the King's person or government, or does any thing that may tend to lessen him in the esteem of his subjects, and thereby weaken the state and raise jealousies in the people, is a great contempt, and to be punished as such: persons therefore who assemble, avowing their discontent to the established government of the country, and who, by deliberations, speeches and declarations, labor to overturn the constitution, and those who frequent such Meetings and conceal their purposes, are either guilty of actual treasonable conspiracy or the crime of misprision of treason, as I have before stated.

GENTLEMEN, that the most wicked and dangerous libels, tending to inflame the minds of the people, not only against he government and constitution of this country, but with a view to subvert all subordination, and thereby to destroy the principles of soci-[19]ety, under the specious pretence of the equal rights of mankind, were not only published and sold in open day, but at a price even below the necessary expence of preparing them, and industriously distributed among the lower orders of people, to hinder them in the pursuit of their honest callings, and to infuse into their minds discontent and treason, is a melancholy truth, and was too long suffered with impunity; however, Gentlemen, I hope by this time every body knows that a vast daring, wicked and shamefully-boasted publication has already received the verdict of an English Jury, and notwithstanding the assistance of one of the greatest advocates that ever adorned this or any other country for the defendant, yet the power of truth prevailed, and the bold and daring assertions of this wicked and desperate libeller were so strongly marked, that a most respectable Jury could not hesitate for a moment, and without any statement from the Judge, pronounced him guilty; a triumph of the law over the efforts of sedition.[1]

GENTLEMEN, it is your duty, in the faithful discharge of the trust that is reposed in [20] you, particularly to take into your charge the authors, publishers and dispersers of libels and treasonable publications, and the frequenters and abettors of such clubs and meetings where sedition is proclaimed, and the minds of his Majesty's subjects excited against the laws and government of the country, – wicked and deluded men who, in the end, must be the fatal instruments of their own destruction.

THE SPIRIT OF THE BRITISH NATION IS RAISED; associations dutiful and loyal, from every quarter, are met to counteract these dangerous conspiracies, and to assert the authority of a Constitution as established at the glorious Revolution.

[1] Thomas Paine's *The Rights of Man* was published in two parts, the second part being available on 16 Feb. 1792. It was mainly on account of this text that the proclamation of May '92 was issued. Paine was not present at the trial of his pamphlet since he was in France, having been elected the representative for Calais at the National Assembly. The trial took place before Lord Kenyon in the King's Bench on 18 Dec. 1792, the jury being a 'special jury', the counsel for the defence was Thomas Erskine. See *The Whole Proceedings on the Trial of an Information exhibited ex officio by the King's Attorney-General against Th. Paine*, London, 1793.

UPON these Principles his Majesty holds his Crown; upon these principles, I trust, we shall ever defend, and faithfully transmit to our posterity, that Constitution we received from our ancestors unaltered, unimpaired.

ENGLISHMEN, I hope, are not to be duped out of the blessings they enjoy.[21]

I will not distress you by drawing your attention to the miseries of a neighbouring country. I trust that every man is too sensible of the blessings he enjoys here to need such a contrast; but if any thing were necessary to excite in the minds of men a love for the regular government of the country and respect for the law, you have only to compare the misery of one with the prosperity of the other.

GENTLEMEN, to the active exertions of Juries, to the active exertions of Magistrates, – and here let me observe that the thanks of the county are due to the Most Noble the Marquis of Townshend, the Custos Rotulorum, and the other Justices who assembled for the purpose of declaring their resolution to support the Executive Government of the country, and to counteract the efforts of sedition, – a larger Meeting of Justices upon any occasion never assembled in this county, and I am sure some who were absent were prevented by unavoidable duty elsewhere.

GENTLEMEN, as I have said it is to the exertion of Juries, to the activity of Magis-[22] trates, and to the due execution of the law, we must rest our support, – WE HAVE ONLY TO ENLIST UNDER THE BANNERS OF THE BRITISH CONSTITUTION, TO SUPPORT THE CAUSE OF LIBERTY AND TRUTH.[1]

[1] There exists a second ed. of this text, also dated 1793, with the following differences: pp. 16/17: levying / war; 17-18: illicit / practices; 18-19: equal / rights. Furthermore, pp. 20–22 are also different: the last two paragraphs of p. 20, beginning with: THE SPIRIT OF THE NATION... are in small capitals, which modifies the page numbers. The rest, without any further modification.

A **CHARGE** DELIVERED TO THE GRAND JURY AT THE GENERAL QUARTER SESSIONS OF THE PEACE FOR THE COUNTY OF SUFFOLK, HOLDEN, BY ADJOURNMENT, AT IPSWICH ON FRIDAY, JANUARY 18, 1793. **By JOHN LORD CHEDWORTH.** PUBLISHED AT THE INSTANCE OF THE COURT AND THE GRAND JURY. *IPSWICH:* PRINTED AND SOLD BY J. BUSH, BOOKSELLER; SOLD ALSO BY DECK, GEDGE, AND RACKHAM, BURY; CROUSE AND STEVENSON, AND PEARSON, NORWICH; DOWNES AND MARCH YARMOUTH; HORTH, ECCLES; LODER, AND RIDLEY, WOODBRIDGE; AND KEYMER, COLCHESTER.

[A]

Gentlemen of the Grand jury,

YOU are now called upon to exercise one of the highest Privileges that can be enjoyed by the Citizens of a free State, that of assisting in the Administration of the criminal Justice of your Country. It is your Duty, in Virtue of the Office which You have now taken upon You, not only to decide on the Truth of all such Bills of Indictment as shall be laid before You, but likewise to present all Offences against the Public Peace, Convenience, and good Order which You know of from your own Knowledge.

Gentlemen, His Majesty having being informed that divers wicked and seditious Writings have lately been published and industriously dispersed in different Parts of the Kingdom, with a View to excite Discontents, Tumults and Disorders in this Realm, has thought to signify his Pleasure that it should be given in Charge to You, diligently to enquire, and true Presentment to make, of all such wicked and seditious Writings that have been published and industriously circulated within this District; in Order that the Authors, Printers, Publishers and Distributers of all such wicked and seditious Writings may be dealt with according to Law. In Obedience therefore to His Majesty's Commands, I do direct and charge You, diligently to enquire of all Writings of a seditious Nature which have been published and circulated in this District, and to present the Authors, Printers, Publishers and Distributers of them.

Gentlemen, Every Lover of Peace and good Order, every Friend of his Country must lament that it should have been found necessary to issue such a Direction: but it is notorious that Writings of a very pernicious Nature, calculated to captivate the Minds and inflame the Passions of the lower Classes of the People, and tending to subvert, not only the excellent Constitution of this Country, but [2] all Government and Subordination whatever, have of late issued from the Press. This is a Mischief which certainly deserves serious Attention, for it must be observed to every one capable of the least Reflection that no State of Society could possibly exist, no Security or Comfort be enjoyed, without a Government and Laws.- The Occasion and End of this Institution of Government have been extremely well set forth by a late Writer, whose Words I shall borrow:[1] " If we could suppose such a State of human Nature, as that all Mankind should by regulated only by the Principles of Justice, that no selfish Motives should bias, no Folly mislead, and no Passions disturb them; in other Words, if Man were a perfect Being, there would be no Occasion for Government among Men; for Government being designed to restrain such Actions as are injurious, if Actions were always wise, and just, and beneficial, the very Idea of Government would not exist at all. But as such a State of Things, however it may have been imagined in the golden Age, by the Fancy of Poetry, exists not; and as the human Bosom is equally the Repository of the malignant Passions that deform, and of the tender Sympathies that embellish, Life, it has been found necessary to use some Means that might restrain the vicious Inclinations of Men from breaking into Action, and disturbing the general Happiness. – No means so effectual for this purpose could be devised, as the social Union, by which the Force of the many, under a certain Organization, which is called Government, is always ready to be employed in the Restraint or Punishment of such Individuals, as affect by their Actions the public Tranquillity: for though it happens that all Men are not perfectly just and impartial in Matters that concern themselves, yet, as a Nation or Community consists of a Multitude of Individuals, the private Actions of Men can relate in their greatest possible Extent, only to a very few others, when proportionally considered to the whole. But all the other Members of the Community are greatly concerned in preserving inviolate, or in punishing the Violation of, certain Principles, without which there could be no Stability to the Acquisitions of Industry, no Security to the natural Possession of Life and Liberty; the united Force, therefore, somehow concentrated, of all the other Members of the Community, will always be directed, from a Sense of

[1] White on Governement.

common Utility, towards supporting these Rights in all, or in punishing the Infringements of them, for the Sake of Example. "Thus we see, (as Sir *William Blackstone* observes[1]) that "every Man, when he enters into Society, gives up a Part of his natural Liber-[A 2-3] ty, as the Price of so valuable a Purchase; and in Consider- ation of receiving the Advantages of mutual Commerce, obliges himself to conform to those Laws, which the Community has thought proper to establish. And this species of legal Obedience and Conformity is infinitely more desirable than that wild and savage Liberty which is sacrificed to obtain it. For no Man, that considers a Moment, would wish to obtain the absolute and uncontrolled Power of doing whatever he pleases; the Consequence of which is, that every other Man would also have the same Power; and then there would be no Security to Individuals in any of the Enjoyments of Life. Political therefore, or civil Liberty, which is that of a Member of Society, is no other than natural Liberty so far restrained by human Laws (and no further) for the general Advantage of the Public. Hence we may collect, that the Law, which refrains a Man from doing Mischief to his Fellow-Citizens, though it diminishes the natural, increases the civil Liberty of Mankind: "for "no Person is free[2] where any Person is suffered to do wrong with Impunity." For this end (says the Roman[3] Orator) do we become the Servants of the Law, that we may be free."

Enough, I trust, has been said, to shew the Necessity of Submission to Government. Religion likewise inculcates it as a Duty. For it is the Will of the Supreme Being (whose Goodness is equal to his Power) that the Happiness of human Life should be promoted. Now nothing conduces more to the Promotion of human Happiness than Civil Society, which we see cannot be maintained without Obedience to Government. The holy Scriptures therefore enjoin us to be subject to the higher Powers, to honour the King, to obey Magistrates, and this not only for Wrath, (for fear of the Punishment which human Laws may inflict,) but also for Conscience's Sake.

With regard to the particular Form of Government under which it is our Happiness to live, it is not easy to speak in Terms of too high Commendation. It fully merits the Eulogium which has been pronounced on it by a celebrated French Writer (the President *Montesquieu*,) who declares,[4] that it has civil Liberty for the direct End of its Constitution. It is extremely remarkable, that the great Roman Philosopher and Statesman, *Cicero*,[5] supposes the most excellent Form [4] of Government to be made up of a Combination of the three different Kinds, the regal, the

[1] I. B. c. 125.
[2] Ferguson on Civil Society, p. 261.
[3] Cic. pro A. Cluentio, 53.
[4] Sp. of Laws, B. 11. c. 5.
[5] Fragm. Cic. Edit. Amst. 1724. p. 3943.

aristocratic, and the popular; a Species of which no Example (as far as is known) existed at that time: and the profound and sagacious *Tacitus*[1] admits the theoretical Excellence of such a Constitution, though he doubts the possibility of its ever being reduced to Practice.

It is impossible for me at present to enter into an Examination of this admirable System. I am persuaded, the more it is scrutinized, and the better it is understood, the greater Degree of Approbation will it receive from every unprejudiced Mind capable of forming a Judgment on such a Subject. The Time will only suffer me to call your Attention to one or two Particulars, which are suggested by the Duties which we are at this Moment employed in discharging.- The French Writer I just now quoted observes[2] that the political Liberty of the Subjects consists in a Tranquility of Mind arising from the Opinion each Person has of his Safety. In Order to have this Liberty it is requisite, says he, that the Government be so constituted that one Man need not be afraid of another. Now mark with what anxious Care and Vigilance this is provided for by our excellent Laws. It is declared by Magna Charta that no Man can be taken or imprisoned but by the lawful Judgment of his Equals, or by the Law of the Land. – This Immunity is farther secured by the Habeas Corpus Act,[3] which has been justly styled a second Magna Charta; "a Statute (which as has been observed[4]) we must admire as the Key-Stone of Civil Liberty: a Statute which forces the Secrets of every Prison to be revealed, the Cause of every Commitment to be declared, and the Person of the accused to be produced, that he may claim his Enlargment, or his Trial within a limited Time. No wiser Form was ever opposed to the Abuses of Power." A further Security is raised by[5] that two-fold Barrier, which (as Sir *William Blackstone* says) the Founders of the English Law have with excellent Forecast placed between the Liberties of the People and the Prerogative of the Crown, a Presentment and a Trial by Jury; by which Institution it is provided, with a Tenderness and a Delicacy peculiar to the Law of England, that no one, not even the lowest of the People, shall be publickly arraigned for any Crime amounting to Felony, till twelve, at least, of his Countrymen have, after a previous Enquiry, declared on their Oaths, that there is Evidence suffici-[5]ent to induce them to believe that the Party accused is guilty of the Offence imputed to him: and that the Truth of every Accusation, whether preferred in the shape of Indictment, Information, or Appeal, should be afterwards confirmed by the unanimous Suffrage of twelve of the accused Party's Equals and Neighbours, indifferently chosen, and superior to all Suspicion. It must,

[1] Ann. IV. 33.
[2] Sp. of Laws, B. 11. c. 6.
[3] 31 Car.2. c. 2.
[4] Ferguson, 279.
[5] 4 B.C.c. 27.p. 349.

I think, strike every one, that the Institution of your Office, Gentlemen, is a mighty Bulwark for the Protection of the Subject: a signal Instance in proof of which occurs in the memorable Case of the *Earl of Shaftesbury* in the Reign of Charles the II. a Nobleman whose Influence and Abilities had rendered him extremely obnoxious to the Court, whose Measures he opposed: it was therefore determined to crush him by a Prosecution for High Treason; but this Design was defeated by the Bill of Indictment's being rejected by the Grand Jury of the City of London, notwithstanding some very unusual Steps had been taken in Order to get it found.

Gentlemen, I cannot attempt to enter on an Examination of the various Fallacies which have been made use of in the seditious Writings before spoken of in Order to render the People of this Country dissatisfied with the Established Form of Government.- Indeed, I am very little acquainted with these Writings, perhaps less so than I ought to but I cannot forbear noticing one or two of their Doctrines. One principal Topic employed by these Writers is the natural Equality of Men; whence it is inferred that there ought to be no Distinction of Rank in Society, and that the Idea of Property should be abolished, and that all Things should be in Common, since every Man has an equal Right to every Thing. These are certainly Positions extremely well calculated to excite Disturbances, by working out the Passions of the inferior Orders of Men. History will inform us that they are a Sort of Common-place usually resorted to by the Instigators of Sedition.[1] But surely these despicable Sophistries cannot impose on any but the most unthinking of Mankind.- Equality thus understood is perfect Nonsense: it can never subsist in any State whatever.- A very little Attention will enable any one to see that it is manifestly the Intention of the Supreme Ruler of the Universe that there should be Inequality in this World, the Comforts of which, are not distributed according to Merit; if they were, this World would not be what it is evidently intended for, a State of Probation and Trial. This unequal Distribution of Things affords the strongest Argument of [6] which Natural Religion is in Possession for a future State, to which we must look for the Rectification of these Irregularities.- In Conformity to these Ideas the Scriptures tell us that the poor shall never perish out of the Land; and the respective Duties of the rich and the poor towards each other are interspersed through the whole of the sacred Volume.- Even if we could suppose ourselves reduced to a State of Nature, (which, if it could happen, would be the greatest Calamity that could befal a People; for a State of Nature, is a State of Warfare and Violence,) we should find that even there, Equality did not exist: bodily Strength and

[1] See particularly Walshingham, 275. Rapin, Vol. I, 457. Hume's Hist. of England, Vol. 3, p. 7. 8vo Edit. 1789.

Ability of Mind are not bestowed on all Men in equal Proportion; and in a State of Nature, the weaker must submit to the stronger, which last would take from his Inferior, his Hoard of Nuts and Acorns, and would Drive him from the Shade in which he was reposing, if he (the stronger) wished to occupy it.

Another Position which has been advanced by the Enemies of our Constitution is[1], that there can be no true Liberty in any Constitution in which Royalty exists. This is a bold and unfounded Assertion, which, as those who have made it have not thought proper to support it with any Arguments, it is sufficient to deny. A limited Monarchy like ours, the Prerogative of which, (as Sir Henry Finch observes[2]) stretcheth not to the doing of any Wrong, a Monarchy which is subject to the Control of the Laws, and the Ministers and Advisers of which are responsible to the Nation for their Conduct, is consistent with the most perfect civil Liberty, as a very little Consideration of the Nature of Government will convince us.

Gentlemen, It is not only our civil Government that has been assailed; Attacks have likewise been lately made on our ecclesiastical Institutions: The Necessity of any religious Establishment has been denied, and Endeavours have been used (with no small Degree of Industry) to render odious the Mode which the Law has provided for the Payment of the Clergy.- Now it is to an ecclesiastical Establishment (by which I understand a legal Appointment of Ministers for the purpose of performing Divine Service and instructing the People in the Doctrines of the Religion supported by the State, with a suitable Provision for the Maintenance of its Ministers,) and to the Setting apart of stated Seasons for divine [7] Worship and religious Instruction, that we are indebted for the Preservation of any Degree of Religion among us. The Extinction of Religion, considered merely in a temporal View, would be a most deplorable Calamity. As little Religion as there seems to be in the World, it has nevertheless a very great Influence in promoting the general Tranquility, and restraining Men from the Commission of Crimes.[3] "It supplies the Defects of human Policy, by implanting a real Principle of Virtue in the Heart, and by influencing the moral Conduct from the Corrections of Conscience, and a sense of the Divine Authority." The Chances of escaping human Punishments are so many, that Numbers of Men would run that Risk if they were not deterred by the Fear of being called to an Account for their bad Actions in a future State. As to the Sabbatical Institution,[4] "Whoever considers how much that conduces to

[1] Address to the United States of America, read in the National Assembly of France, Dec. 22. 1792.

[2] Finch's Law, B. 2. c. 1. p. 85.

[3] Dr. Thorpe's Sermon at Cambridge.

[4] Paley's Moral and Polit. Philosophy, B. 5. c. 6.

the Happiness and Civilization of the labouring Classes of Mankind, and reflects how great a Majority of the human Species these Classes compose, will acknowledge the Utility, whatever he may believe of the Origin, of this Distinction; and will perceive it to be every Man's Duty to uphold the Observation of Sunday, let the Establishment have proceeded from whom or from what Authority it will." – The Expedience of an Appointment of Persons to perform the Offices and teach the Doctrines of Religion being once admitted, the Necessity of making a suitable Provision for their Maintenance, will follow of course.[1] "For besides the positive Precepts of the New Testament, where we are told, that it is the Divine Will[2] "That they who preach the Gospel, should live of the Gospel," natural Reason will tell us, that an Order of Men, who are separated from the rest of Mankind, have a Right to be furnished with the Necessaries, Conveniences, and moderate Enjoyments of Life at their Expence, for whose Benefit they forego the usual Means of providing them." – With Regard to the particular Mode provided in this Country for the maintenance of the Clergy, I must observe that their right to Tithes stands precisely on the same Ground as the Title of any Man to his Estate, viz. the antient Law of the Land;[3] so ancient, that the Time when Tithes were first introduced into this Country, cannot be ascertained. It certainly was very early, for they are mentioned in a Constitutional Decree made in a Synod holden in the Year 786; wherein the Payment of Tithes is strongly enjoined: and this Canon, or [8] Decree, (which at first bound not the Laity) was effectually confirmed by two Kingdoms of the Heptarchy in their Parliamentary Conventions of Estates.

Gentlemen, Notwithstanding the Propagation of the seditious Doctrines I have taken Notice of, I confess I am not myself under any Apprehensions for the Safety of our excellent Constitution: for though there may be among us a few discontented and malignant Spirits who repine at the Tranquility and Happiness of the County, a few

"moody Beggars starving for a Time
Of pell-mell Havock and Confusion,[4]"

Yet I hope and believe that the Number of these is very small, and that among them there are few indeed who are of any Consideration on Account of their Rank or Circumstances. There is in the People of this Country a Fund of good Sense, which enables them to see the Benefits of the Form of Government under which they live, and which will prevent their being seduced by designing and visionary Writers, to risk

[1] 2 Blackst. Com. 25.
[2] 1 Cor. ix. 14.
[3] 2 B. C. 25.
[4] Shakesp. 1st Pt. of H. 4th. Act 5.

the Peace and Happiness of the State from the Hope of gaining some imaginary and perhaps unattainable Advantages. The general Attachment of the Nation to the Constitution cannot be doubted: it has strongly manifested itself by the Associations that have been formed, and the Declarations that have been made, in every Part of the Kingdom.- This, however, is no Reason for suffering seditious Writings to pass unnoticed.- They are (as has been justly observed[1]) the more dangerous form because some of the Principles which they contain are true, though Consequences of the most pernicious Tendency, which the Premises will not warrant, have been unfairly drawn from them: and as every Reader may not be able to detect the Fallacy of such illogical Conclusions, mischievous Doctrines may by such Artifices be propagated, and therefore the Punishment of the Authors and Publishers of these Writings is the more necessary. Gentlemen, I am sure there is no Occasion for me to press on You an Attention to His Majesty's Commands: but being on the Subject of Libels, (which is the Term used by the Law to denote all Sorts of Criminal Publications,) I cannot omit taking notice of the Act passed in the last Sessions of Parliament for removing Doubts respecting the Function of Juries in Cases of Libel. – Before the Passing of this Act it was a Matter of perpetual Controversy, (and there were high Authorities on both Sides,) whether it were competent [B- 9] to the Jury to give a Verdict upon the Whole of the Matter in Issue, or whether the Question of the Criminality of the Paper charged to be a Libel were now wholly out of the Province of the Jury, and belonging exclusively to the Court. – Without enquiring into the Foundation of the opposite Opinions entertained on this Point, it is sufficient at present to remark that this Act now removes all Doubt respecting it, by enacting that on every Trial of an Indictment or Information for a Libel, the Jury may give a general Verdict of Guilty or Not Guilty upon the whole Matter put in Issue, and shall not be required or directed by the Court or Judge before whom such Indictment or Information shall be tried to find the Defendant Guilty merely on the Proof of the Publication by the Defendant of the Paper charged to be a Libel, and of the Sense ascribed to the same in such Indictment or Information. - Gentlemen, it is very justly observed by *Mr. Justice Blackstone*,[2] "that by the Punishment of Libels, the Liberty of the Press, properly understood, is by no means infringed or violated.- The Liberty of the Press is indeed essential to the Nature of a free State; but this consists in laying no *previous* Restraints on Publications, and not in the Freedom from Censure for Criminal Matter when published. Every Freeman has an undoubted Right to lay what Sentiments he pleases before the Public: to forbid this is to destroy the Freedom of the

[1] Plowden's Jura Anglorum.
[2] 4 B. C. 151.

Press. But if he published what is improper, mischievous, or illegal, he must take the Consequences of his own Temerity. To subject the Press to the restrictive Power of a Licenser, as was formerly done, is to subject all Freedom of Sentiment to the Prejudices of one Man, and make him the arbitrary and infallible Judge of all controverted Points in Learning, Religion, and Government.-But to punish (as the Law does at present) any dangerous or offensive Writings, which, when published, shall on a fair and impartial Trial be adjudged of a pernicious Tendency, is necessary for the Preservation of Peace and good Order, of Government and Religion, the only solid Foundation of civil Liberty. Thus the Will of Individuals is still left free; the Abuse only of that free Will is the Object of legal Punishment. Neither is there any Restraint hereby laid on Freedom of Thought or Inquiry; Liberty of private Sentiment is still left; the dissemination, or making public, of bad Sentiments, destructive of the Ends of Society, is the Crime which Society corrects. A Man (says a fine Writer on this Subject) may be allowed to keep Poison in his Closet, but not publickly to vend them as [10] Cordials. And to this we may add, that the only plausible Argument heretofore used for the Restraining of the just Freedom of the Press, that it was necessary to prevent the daily Abuse of it, will entirely lose its Force, when it is shewn (by a seasonable Execution of the Laws) that the Press cannot be abused by any bad Purpose, without incurring a suitable Punishment: whereas it can never be used to any good one, when under the Control of an Inspector. So true will it be found, that to censure the Licentiousness, is to maintain the Liberty of the Press." Gentlemen, if You present the Authors, Printers, Publishers, or Distributers of any Libels, You must select and set out in your Presentments the Passages which You present as criminal; for whatever is necessary to constitute the Crime must appear on the Record. If You agree on any Presentment of this Sort, the Court will, on your Application, direct their Officer to attend You, in order to assist You in drawing up your Presentment: he will explain to You the Meaning, the Use, and the Application of Averments and Innuendos, which are the necessary Explanations of the Libel; [as by stating the Subject of it, (as when in the Case of the King and Horne[1] the Libel was charged to be "of and concerning His Majesty's Government" which is an Averment;) or by assigning the Meaning of the Words used, (as when in the Case of the King and Matthews,[2] these Words "I will conclude with three Remarks: first, that every Assertor of hereditary Right must be a Jacobite," are thus explained: "I (meaning himself the said John Matthews) will conclude with three Remarks: first, that every Assertor of hereditary Right (meaning the hereditary Right to the Crown

[1] II St. Trials, 264.
[2] 9 St. Trials, 682.

of this Kingdom) must be a Jacobite (meaning a Favourer of the Person in the Life-time of King James II late King of England, &c pretending to be the Prince of Wales, and after the Decease of the said late King, pretending to be, and taking upon himself the Title of King of England by the Name of James III.") which Explanations are Innuendos: and whether the real Meaning of the Libel is that which is ascribed to it in the Indictment or Information is a Point of which the Jury who try the Cause are to judge:] but the Passages which You present as libellous must be selected by Yourselves, without the Assistance of the Officer, for those Passages constitute the Substance of the Offence, which must be found by You. It does not appear to me to be necessary to go farther into the Law of Libel at present; should any Doubt occur to You on the Subject, if You will [B 2- 11] come and state it, the Court will be ready to give You the best Assistance in their Power.

Gentlemen, As a Friend to rational Liberty, I mean a Liberty founded on Law, (for, as Mr. *Locke* observes, where there is no Law there is no Liberty,) I heartily lament the extreme Licentiousness of the Writings before alluded to. – Liberty is by Nothing so much endangered as by Licentiousness. – Because extravagant and mischievous Tenets have been inculcated in a Book called the *Rights of Man*, some People have concluded that Man has no Rights at all! – In like Manner the Cause of Peace, good Order, and Obedience to Government must suffer by the Revival of the exploded Doctrines of unlimited passive Obedience and Non-resistance; Doctrines that revolt the general Sense and Feelings of Men, and directly impeach the Principles of the Glorious Revolution of 1688.- For preaching these Doctrines Dr.*Sacheverell* was impeached by the Commons, and condemned by the Lords in the Reign of *Queen Anne.*[1] Attempts have been made to support these Doctrines by wresting and misinterpreting Passages of Scripture. But though Christianity, being intended to promote Men's temporal as well as their eternal Happiness, enjoins Obedience to Government in general, yet[2] "with Regard to the Extent of our civil Rights and Obligations, she hath left us precisely where she found us. She hath neither altered nor ascertained it. The New Testament contains not one Passage, which, fairly interpreted, affords either Argument or Objection applicable to Conclusions upon the Subject, that are deduced from the Law and Religion of Nature." This has been demonstrated by some of the ablest Divines of our Church; a full Refutation of the contrary Opinions may be found in the Arguments which were used on the Trial of Dr. *Sacheverell.*

Gentlemen, I must earnestly recommend to You to discourage as far as lies in your Power every Thing which can have the remotest Tendency

[1] A.D. 1709.
[2] Paley's Mor. and Polit. Philosophy, B.6. c. 4.

to produced Riots, Tumults, and Disorders, which (as we are told in His Majesty's Royal Proclamation issued in May last) on whatever Pretext they may be grounded, are not only contrary to Law, but dangerous to the most important Interests of the Kingdom. Gentlemen, If it were in my Power I certainly would prevent [12] the Burning of the Effigy of a Person of whom we have heard much, and who has lately been convicted of being the Author of a very seditious and inflammatory Libel; I mean THOMAS PAINE; because all such tumultuary Proceedings do very much endanger the public Peace and Safety, and tend to the Terror of the Neighbourhood. If that Person has really any considerable Number of Admirers, (which I am not willing to believe,) it is not a very unlikely Thing that a Body of them might sally out to rescue the Representative of their Hero from the intended Disgrace; an Affray might then take Place between the two incensed Mobs, in which it is possible that Life might be lost. I should therefore think it my indispensable Duty as a Friend to Quietness and good Order, but more especially as a Magistrate and Conservator of the Peace, to discourage by all the Means in my Power such disorderly Proceedings.

Gentlemen, I must do the lower People of this District the Justice to say that as far as my Observation has extended I have found them quiet and well-disposed. I have not discovered among them the smallest Symptom of any Disposition to Outrage. Since I have sat in this Court I have not tried a single Indictment for a Riot. – I hope they will persevere in that inoffensive Behaviour: – I have no reason to think they will not. If at any Time they think they have a Complaint, I hope they will represent their Case in an orderly and peaceable Manner, by which they are much more likely to obtain Redress than by having Recourse to Violence, and seeking to enforce their Demands by riotous and illegal Methods; in which Case they will certainly find that the Magistrates are firm, and determined to do their Duty.

Gentlemen, As we know from Experience that Nothing is more likely to produce Tumults and Disturbances than those violent Animosities which Men are apt to entertain toward each other on Account of Differences in their political and religious Opinions, I think it my Duty to call on You to use your best Endeavours to discountenance such intolerant Notions, to allay the Fervours which Diversity of Sentiment may occasion, and to promote a general amicable and benevolent Disposition towards Men of every Persuasion. While the Judgment of Man continues frail and fallible, as long as human Nature exists in this World, it is vain to hope for a perfect Uniformity of Sentiment on any [13] Point. The Tyrant who resolved that all his Subjects should be exactly of his own Height, and in Order to bring them to that Standard, lopped those who were taller, and stretched those who were shorter than himself, was certainly not more absurd than he who expects that all Men should think alike. Men's Persons do not differ more than their Minds. – It is related of a great Prince,[1] who was a violent Persecutor of the first Protestants, that having quitted the Toils of Empire, and retired to end his Days in a Convent, he amused himself in the Intervals of his Devotions with Works of Mechanism, and was particularly curious with regard to the Construction of Clocks and Watches; and having found after repeated Trials that he could not bring any two of them to go exactly alike, he reflected with a Mixture of Surprise and Regret on his own Folly, in having bestowed so much Time and Labour in the more vain Attempt of bringing Mankind to a precise Uniformity of Sentiment concerning the intricate and mysterious Doctrines of Religion. - I am sorry to say that at this Time a Spirit of Illiberality and Rancour between Persons differing in Opinion on the Subjects of Religion and Politics seems to be remarkably prevalent. This it is the Duty of every good Citizen to discourage, as having a direct Tendency to endanger the Peace of the Community, and to embitter Life, by destroying one of its chief Blessings, the Freedom of social Intercourse. It is the Practice of some Men to represent all who entertain Opinions different from their own as Latitudinarians in Religion and Republican in Politics. The extreme Disingenuity and Baseness of such an Artifice needs no farther Reprobation than the bare Statement of it. As a masterly Writer has justly observed,[2] "If one Class of Men are disposed to uphold the Power of the Crown, and another to enlarge the Freedom of the People, we have no Right to conclude that the former wish to be fettered with the Chains of Slavery, or that the latter are preparing to let loose the Ravages of Anarchy. The Advocate for Monarchy is not necessary the Foe of Liberty, nor is the Love of Liberty incompatible with Reverence for Monarchy. Experience puts to Flight those chimerical Accusations which issue from the narrow Spirit of System, or the frantic Vehemence of Party." – The Intemperance of Zeal on such Occasions is so far from being accorded to Knowledge, that, in general, it is in a directly inverse Proportion to it. Political Animosities are generally strongest in those who have scarcely a Glimmering of Political Knowledge; [14] and many of these violent Partizans, if they were to be asked the Meaning of certain Words which they have perpetually in their Mouths, would find themselves in the Situation of the Spanish Poet,[3] who, being asked the Meaning of one of his Odes, honestly confessed that that was a Circumstance he had never thought of. I am afraid few of these vehement Politicians have Candour enough to make a Confession similar to that of the Poet. With regard to religious Differences it is remarked by an excellent Writer of our own

[1] Robertson's History of Charles 5th. B.12.
[2] Letter from Irenopolis.
[3] Lopez de Vega.

Church,[1] that " Circumstances out of their own Power must determine the Religion of the Bulk of Mankind. To be born in such a Country, to be educated under such Parents, to be placed in the midst of Persons professing such a Sect of Religion, are Circumstances entirely out of our Power, and to be referred to only to the wise Disposition of Almighty God. It can be no Man's Fault that these are not different from what they are: yet these are the Things which must determine the Religion of the Bulk of Mankind. Were we ourselves born in such a Country, or of such Parents, can we be confident that we should not rank ourselves under a Religion which now perhaps we look on with Aversion and Contempt? – Could we divest ourselves of all the Prejudices of Education? Could we have Courage enough to oppose our own Opinions to all the Weight of Example and Authority? Could we have Integrity enough by avowing such Opinions to sacrifice our worldly Interests, and to incur Infamy and Reproach?" – I could wish indeed that those who dissent from established Opinions were less strenuous for the Propagation of their own Notions, less infected with the Zeal of Proselytism. But even for this Conduct, however we may lament it, Candour will make Allowance. The Opinions for the Propagation of which they are so earnest, they hold to be Truths of the highest Importance, and they conceive it to be their Duty to be active in the Dissemination of them. Though we may differ from them on this Point, yet, as we know that Integrity is perfectly consistent with Error, we may suppose them to be wrong, and at the same time give them Credit for Rectitude of Intention. To judge of Motives is in most Cases extremely difficult: they can be known with Certainty by him alone to whom all Hearts are open, and from whom no Secrets are hid. We certainly ought not to put the worst possible Construction on Men's Actions. [15] Whatever tends to exasperate the Minds of Men towards each other, or to perpetuate the Dislike which Men are apt to entertain for those of different Sentiments from themselves ought at this Time to be particularly avoided; and therefore I cannot but disapprove of all Clubs and Institutions, under whatever specious Names or plausible Pretences disguised, which have a Tendency to cherish Animosity and Rancour. – When I say this, I trust, I shall not, in the utmost Perversity of Construction, be understood to mean the slightest Allusion to those Associations which have been formed for the very laudable Purposes of declaring People's Attachment to the Constitution, and for the Prosecution of seditious Publications; which Purpose, whatever Opinions may have been entertained to the contrary, I conceive to be perfectly legal. These Associations have certainly had this good Effect, that they have shewn the Enemies of our Constitution that the general Sense of the Nation is united in Favour of the existing

[1] Sturge's 16th Discourse.

Form of Government. I must however remark that it would be an extremely unwarrantable and injurious Conclusion, that every Man who has not enrolled himself in the List of an Association is an Enemy to the Constitution. He who does not associate may be as firmly attached to the Constitution as he who does; but he may forbear to become a Member of an Association because, as the same Object will appear differently to different Minds, he is not convinced of the Necessity of it; or generally approving of Associations, because he has Objections to some of their Proceedings; or for a Variety of Reasons which it is not necessary to state. Every Man ought to be left at full Liberty to associate or not as he thinks fit; no Man ought to be censured for not associating.

Gentlemen, I am persuaded You will all of You use your Endeavours to cultivate a Spirit of Loyalty to the King, and a Reverence for the Laws. And I must repeat that You can by no Means render a more effectual Service to your Country than by promoting Benevolence and Candour towards Men of all Persuasions. Even supposing the Principles of those who differ from us to be as bad as some People choose to represent them, they are not likely to be reclaimed from their Errors by perpetual Abuse and Invective. If they are indeed Enemies, by constant Irritation and Opposition they will become ten-fold more Enemies; by Gentleness and Moderation the fiercest Tempers are sometimes softened. To the Dissemination of those violent and intolerant Opinions [16] which have been reprobating, may in a great Measure be ascribed the shocking Outrages at Birmingham which will remain an indelible Disgrace to the Annals of this County. On the Contrary, Nothing is more conformable to the Dictates of our Holy Religion (the very Essence of which is Peace and Good Will towards Men) than that benevolent and candid Disposition I have recommended, which all who sincerely wish to secure the public Tranquility, and a general Obedience to the Laws will earnestly Endeavour to promote, and that for the Reason assigned by the Apostle: "Love worketh no Ill to his Neighbour, therefore Love is the fulfilling of the Law."

I cannot conclude without again calling to your remembrance His Majesty's Commands respecting seditious Writings, and reminding You that in whatever You do it is necessary that Twelve of You should agree, for without the Concurrence of Twelve no Act of a Grand Jury is valid. - I am extremely sorry to have trespassed so long on your Patience; but in the present Conjecture of Affairs I thought it my Duty to lay these Sentiments before You. I shall add no more : I know too well the Value of Time to waste it farther by a fruitless Apology.

THE END.

CHARGE, DELIVERED TO THE GRAND JURY, OF THE CITY & COUNTY of NORWICH, ON FRIDAY, Jan. 18, 1793 BY *CHARLES HARVEY, Esq. Steward*. PUBLISHED AT THE REQUEST OF THE GRAND JURY AND THE MAGISTRATES. *NORWICH:* PRINTED BY J. CROUSE AND W. STEVENSON. 1793.

[A 2-3]

A

CHARGE, &c.

GENTLEMEN,

IT is always with peculiar pleasure that I embrace any opportunity of addressing you in the character and office in which you are this day assembled, namely, as a Grand Jury, to enquire for the body of this city and county.- Those who reflect on the many and important benefits which the community derive from the services resulting from the impartial and diligent execution of the trust reposed in you, cannot but contemplate with satisfaction so wise and excellent an institution, and cannot but feel happy in enumerating and particularising the various duties which, by that institution, are confided to you.- Your oath, which is so properly adapted equally to convey instruction in your duty, as to enforce the obligation to the performance of it, renders it unnecessary for me to enlarge on the general outline of the great trust, which you are this day called on to discharge; I shall only say that it consists in making diligent enquiry in whatever offen- [4] ces may exist, and to present the offenders to the Court, unawed by fear, unbiassed by prejudice, uninfluenced by reward.

As under every form of Government there must be some laws by which the peace of society is preserved, its rights and liberties ascertained and defended, and persons and properties protected, it is equally necessary that there should be some tribunal to take cognizance and to punish a breach of those laws, to which an appeal may at all time be made, and to which every man and every subject of the realm indiscriminately may resort for redress of wrongs and for distribution of justice. - The process by which all offences of this country are tried, is too well known to need any description here; the beginning of it however in all cases, (except in very few instances indeed) is by a presentment or indictment found by a Grand Jury, twelve of whom at least must concur in the finding, before any subsequent criminal proceeding can take place; and surely, Gentlemen, whilst such an institution as this exists in this country, there will exist at the same time a barrier equally efficacious in resisting, in suppressing, in punishing the guilty, as in affording protection and encouragement to the innocent, the virtuous and the deserving.

It will be unnecessary for me to enumerate the various matters which may this day become the subject of your enquiry, acquainted as you all must be with the nature of the crimes which at our Sessions are usually the objects of it, and having, I am confident, all of you, both from [5] your judgment and repeated experience, a clear and accurate knowledge of your duty.

Indeed, Gentlemen, I should at any other time have thought it needless to have entered into any discussion of any single branch of that duty, but at the present juncture, I deem myself called on by the commands of my Sovereign, which have been signified to every Magistrate who officiates in a similar situation to that which I have long had the honour to hold in this City. – Those commands it is my duty to obey, and I feel a sensible pleasure arising from that obedience, as the purport of them is congenial with the sentiments and inclinations in which I was early educated and instructed, which I have long cherished and maintained, and in which I trust I shall constantly persevere, from a confirmed conviction that they are founded on the most loyal principles, and on the soundest policy and wisdom.

The Magistrate to whose province it is assigned to deliver a Charge to the Grand Jury, has been enjoined to call their attention to some offences, which have lately become so prevalent and alarming, and have threatened so much danger to the general interests of the state, as to demand the interposition of the Executive Government to check, to controul, and if possible to suppress them. These offences are the publishing and circulating seditious and inflammatory libels, with a view to overturn and destroy our present excellent Constitution, and the holding seditious Meetings with the avowed purpose of effecting a similar object. And here, Gentlemen, it will [6] be proper to observe to you what our law defines to be a Libel and punishable as such. – A Libel then, in a strict sense, is "the malicious aspersion of any one, expressed either by printing or writing, tending to blacken the memory of one who is dead, or the reputation of one living, and personally expose him to hatred, ridicule and contempt; in a larger signification it may be extended to any defamation whatever: these Libels are against private Men, or Magistrates and public persons; those against Magistrates deserve the greatest punishment; a libel against a private man may excite the person libelled, or his friends, to revenge and to a breach of the peace; a libel against a Magistrate is not only a breach of the peace, but a scandal to Government and stirs up sedition." – This, Gentlemen, is the definition of libel as laid down by that great authority my Lord Coke, and has been so constantly adhered to as an invariable rule, and confirmed by so many determinations in the Courts of Justice, as to constitute it now the law of the land – it is that law which we are bound to administer; for we are not assembled to make laws or even to judge of their propriety, but to be governed and regulated in our conduct by those which are made; you, the Grand Jury, bound on your oaths to inquire whether this law has been violated, we as Magistrates to try by the verdict of another Jury, whether the person presented is guilty of the offence charged on him.

Having thus stated the law and our mutual obligations in consequence of that law, the next subject of enquiry [7] will be, whether, any offence of that description has been committed within that jurisdiction, in which we have cognizance – and, Gentlemen, I am afraid that that fact is but too notorious; that writings and libels of the most seditious and inflammatory tendency have been industriously circulated, not only over this city, but over every part of the kingdom, that societies have been formed and subscriptions raised to encourage the authors, to recommend their publications, to print such cheap editions of their works as to cause them to be universally read, to distribute them gratuitously amongst those whose circumstances would not afford the purchase, and in short all means employed, which art or ingenuity could devise, to insure them a general perusal amongst the lower classes of the community, are facts of such notoriety, and must have fallen so immediately within the sphere of your observation, as to require no additional evidence from the Bench to authenticate – the purport and tendency of these libels is to make men dissatisfied with the present Constitution, to arraign it *in toto*, to persuade the common people that it is defective in every part of it, that our limited Monarchy ought to be abolished, that the Aristocratic Branch of our Government, the House of Peers, is insufferable, that all gradations of rank and title are absurd distinctions, that the Three Estates by which we are at present governed is a ridiculous farce and not a Constitution; to this are subjoined other schemes and forms of Government, in which a visionary and impracticable Equality, founded on some pretended rights, is speciously introduced, and recommended to [8] us as models of perfection, and patterns for our imitation-God forbid, Gentlemen, that any such recommendatory precepts should be listened or attended to by any man who has the welfare of his country at heart; God forbid, that such doctrines should be for one moment inculcated with impunity in this land of freedom; already indeed has the almost general voice of this nation exclaimed against such pernicious, such fatal tenets; already has it condemned to public execration those insidious wretches, who, under the pretence of bringing peace and blessings to this isle, have really been endeavouring to sow in it the seeds of discord, sedition and dissention; already has the most unexampled union of formerly contending party, now concurring in opinion, demonstrated to our public as well as private enemies, that this country is not to be duped by their cunning, is not to be misled by their faction, no more than it is to be intimidated by their menace, or overawed by their power; already has the same union, in declaring its veneration for their ancient constitution, firmly resolved to maintain and defend it at the hazard of their lives and fortunes; already like their ancestors, who, on a precedent occasion not much dissimilar to the present, proudly said, "*Nolumus Leges Angliæ mutare*," have they, animated with the same patriotic spirit, expressed their mark of disapprobation at having this glorious fabric touched or impaired, by men who are as ignorant perhaps or wilfully blind to its blessings, as they are strangers to its principles. – But should any man wish to substitute any other form of Government instead of that which we now possess, and un-[B-9] der which, in spite of the powers of Europe, but a few years since, hostilely leagued and combined against us, and not withstanding the great pecuniary difficulties in which that formidable combination involved us, we have arrived to the most envied superiority; our agriculture, our commerce, and the arts flourishing beyond any former period, our population increased, the ingenuity, skill, and invention of our artificers and manufacturers carried to the most unrivalled excellence, to what other system are we to resort to insure a greater portion of a national happiness and prosperity? Is there in the whole world a Constitution where the rights of the people are so well understood, and so effectually secured? Is there any other where the liberty and property of the meanest individual is so peculiarly ascertained and so securely guarded? Examine Magna Charta, examine the Bill of Rights as framed and passed at the Revolution, in which the inalienable Rights of Englishmen are declared and solemnly recognised as their Birthright and Inheritance, and ask whether these glorious monuments of our ancestors patriotism and virtue, are not more substantial securities for our liberty, than the novel and chimerical doctrines of self-created politicians, or the mere dicta of speculative Philosophers? Such an examination must convince the most incredulous, when he sees these valuable privileges incorporated into the body of our laws and statutes, that we are and I trust shall continue a free and prosperous country. [10

Let us now see, Gentlemen, what a neighbouring kingdom has acquired, after effecting a revolution, at the commencement of which every Englishman and every friend to freedom rejoiced, as it overturned the ancient despotism under which that country had long groaned, and afforded a rational expectation of its enjoying a well settled liberty - when that revolution was accomplished, a mild, benevolent, but also unfortunate Sovereign wished his subjects to adopt a constitution on a plan somewhat similar to our own; elevated and blinded by their newly acquired power, they rejected his offer, and in its room have substituted a tyranny far more dreadful and despotic than their former despotic Monarchy; a Government without law, where every species of violence, rapine, plunder, barbarity and murder, is practised without controul, and with impunity, with no fixed law as a standard and rule for mens actions; the Council, the supreme Council of the nation, awed and directed in its proceedings by mobs, and clubs, and societies, composed of the vilest refuse of the most licentious metropolis, their decrees sanctioned and revoked as the Assembly is influenced by the clamours of this [sic] lawless banditti, or intimidated by the pikes and daggers of assassins! Is this liberty, is this government, is this a constitution? Yet it is such a system of anarchy and confusion that has found in this country its votaries and partizans, and these men who have reduced a populous and comparatively once happy country, to a slavery far more oppressive than the most arbitrary tyrant could have devised, and to a state of civilization not to be en-[B 2-11] vied even by savages, have been extolled as patriots and legislators; wretches, who having discarded and disclaimed all the ties of moral obligations and religious duty, have yet arrogated to themselves the title of Philanthropists; the impious ruffians who have banished all religion from the land, who have defiled and plundered its holy altars, who have exiled and massacred its venerable priests, because they could not conscientiously submit to the imposition of Atheists, have been applauded as the promoters of peace and the patrons of humanity. – Yet, Gentlemen, in this country (sorry am I to observe it) a Society has been formed, hardy and wicked enough to commend to public perusal the works of an Author, inculcating those very principles which have been the immediate cause of all this devastation and bloodshed; and this Society has had the unblushing audacity to usher this production into the world, under the pretence of more extensively circulating useful constitutional information[1]- Good God, Gentlemen, when acts, from which all mankind shrink with terror, are not only palliated and executed, but when the perpetrators of them are openly espoused and countenanced, it is natural for men to inquire into the views and motives of their advocates; it becomes every man who has any stake in the present happiness and prosperity of this country, seriously to ask himself, for what prospect of greater advantage either to his personal interest, or to the public benefit, he is desired to hazard this rash experiment of change, reform, and innovation: it ought not to be a slight proof of a meliorated condition in our laws, our man-[12]ners, or our customs, which we should require in such a case; we should have actual demonstration

[1] The allusion is to the Society for Constitutional Information. But there were a handful of other societies with identical purposes. See H.T. Dickinson, *Liberty & Property. Political Ideology in 18th-century Great-Britain*, (London: Methuen, 1979).

before we could consent to barter and exchange our present real and certain enjoyments, for ideal, remote, and therefore uncertain advantages.- I would not, Gentlemen, have made this digression, had I not, in some measure, been compelled to it by those reflections which naturally suggest themselves to any one, who attentively considers the great mischief and confusion which a sudden deviation from ancient and fixed establishments unavoidably produces; it serves, likewise, to explain the grounds and reasons, as well as the propriety of enforcing those laws to which I formerly adverted. For if such mischief is produced, (and that it is, we have but too shocking and melancholy an example), it is wise in Government early to enforce those wholesome and salutary laws calculated to prevent it; it is for the benefit of the community, for whom that Government acts, to apply, as early as possible, a remedy to evils, which, without such an interposition, might become too formidable to check by its authority. Yet, in this instance, and at a crisis so alarming, our Government has not acted in any manner but that which is constitutionally directed; it demands no blind submission to its will, no inconsiderate obedience to its wishes, but it relies solely on the discretion and intervention of a Grand Jury to assist its endeavours for the preservation of internal peace and quiet; it calls on that Grand Jury to make diligent enquiry into these offences which threaten so much calamity to the state, and to present the offenders to the Court, [13] that they may be amenable to the violated laws of their country.- In this procedure no tyrannical power is employed, no overbearing influence is made use of to compel your judgment, but every man is left to perform his duty, as his conscience, bound by the solemn oath he has taken, shall prompt and direct him.

But it may be asked, and indeed (whether from any design of throwing impediments in the way of justice, or from what other motive I cannot possibly determine) it has been observed; what! may we not deliver and publish our opinions upon men and measures, upon modes of Government, and reason upon their respective excellence and merits, without incurring the penalties of the law, and risking the disgrace of punishment? Would not the liberty of the press (which we have been taught to consider as sacred) be violated by restraining the free circulation of mens thoughts on matters of public concern, in which every body are interested, and in which they have a right to be instructed? The answer to such arguments is as easy as putting the question which requires it. - Yes; any man may write his thoughts, any man may publish his opinions on Government, on the excellence of various forms of it, he may compare, and decide on their different merits, and give the preference to that which he thinks best adapted to promote the interests of those for whom it is framed; he may do this without fear, or without censure; these are mere speculative opinions, which every Author, who has leisure and talents for such investigations, has an undoubted right to discuss, and to support with such arguments as his [14] ability and ingenuity can furnish; but he shall not, under pretence of doing this, abuse and slander the existing Government of this country, or the characters of those who form its constituted authority; under pretence of reasoning on the advantages or disadvantages of Monarchy, he shall not vilify and reproach the present reigning Sovereign, and personally expose him to hatred, contempt or ridicule; nor in treating of that high office, limited and restricted as it is by law in this kingdom, shall he declare such a regal Government to be tyrannical and oppressive; he shall not assert that the illustrious House of Hanover is unfit to sway the sceptre of this nation, and thus slander the august family, in whom rests the hereditary succession of our future Monarchs; in examining into the propriety of admitting any aristocratic interference in our legislature, he shall not assert that the House of Lords have not their views directed, or that they are inimical to the good of their country, and thus calumniate that hereditary legislative body; in treating of our national representation, and explaining its meaning, under colour of promoting a Reform, he shall not declare, that that which now exists has not the power of making laws, and that those statutes which it has had its share in framing and enacting, are nugatory, and that they require therefore no obedience from the people; neither shall he, in speaking of the nature and policy of these two estates considered as a Parliament, assert, and cause it to be believed, that it is an unnecessary, wicked and corrupt establishment; this he shall not do; Why? Because the permitting such invec-[15] tives to be thrown out against an existing Government, would at once break asunder all the bounds by which society is united; it would tend not only to excite universal dissatisfaction, but would cause the people to rise and rebel against those, in whose hands the Constitution has placed the Government of the country; because this ceases to be discussion; it is no longer reasoning on a fair and well-grounded hypothesis in order to draw certain conclusions, but it is asserting and assuming facts for the purpose of lessening the authority of the laws, and thereby depriving us of that necessary restraint and controul, by which the passions of mankind are kept under due and proper subjection, and by which national tranquility and prosperity is preserved, instead of being a prey to all the horrors of ungovernable and licentious violence. Observe too, for one moment, the consequence of these libels, which invite men not to argue but to act; what would be the effect; after our Constitution was annihilated, and when our lives, our liberty and our property, were deprived of that known safeguard which has hitherto legally protected them, what hopes, what prospect should we have of being much longer secured against that ruin and destruction, the certain attendants on civil commotions and discords? - If this, therefore, was tolerated, no Government could exist, for men would always be found who would endeavour to destroy that system with which they were discontented. – Even the French Legislators have had the policy to provide against this evil; but they have adopted measures for its prevention which would not be endured [16] in any country, where the least semblance of liberty was preserved; they have by a sanguinary decree, which none but tyrants could have framed, and which none but slaves could have sanctioned, pronounced the sentence of death on any one who shall venture to publish an opinion that Monarchy ought to form part of their Government. – Nor is it any answer to contend that these Authors, if evidently wrong in their principles, may be refuted, and therefore that their writings cannot produce mischief; this is false argument, for if such productions are disseminated amongst the lower classes of the community, whose education cannot so readily supply the means of answer and refutation, if they are distributed among men of that rank of life who are likely enough to be captivated by the first impressions, which such flattering doctrines as the establishing Equality will probably create; who are but too prone to listen to those, who speak to them about the deprivation of rights, and who are willing enough to believe any one who boldly assures them that they have the power, and ought therefore to assert them; I say, if such illusions are thrown out, it is sometime before the arts and falsity of the deceiver can be exposed, and such favourite themes extirpated from their ideas. The poison may take too deep root before its antidote can be procured, and the same effect might be produced in the political as in the animal body, the Constitution would be destroyed before those medicines could be applied which were to avert the fatal consequences of the venom's deleterious quality. I would not, Gentlemen, have trespassed so [17] long on your time with these observations on this peculiar offence, had not the enormity of it been of late so glaring, to require the aid of Magistracy, and the active exertion of the well-meaning citizen to check and suppress it.

Having stated to you the nature and effect of these libels, it will be proper to observe who the law considers as amenable for the publication of them. – On this head I shall be as concise as the subject will admit, by stating very briefly how the law is appliable to it. In the first place, the Author of the Libel, if by any act of his own he consents to, or countenances the printing and dispersing it; but if he merely writes it and keeps it to himself, this is no offence, as it can produce no mischief - but if, after a Libel is written by one man, another take it either with, or without the consent of the Author and cause it to be published, the person so taking it puts himself in the place of the Author, and shall be amenable for the consequences – so too shall any one who sells and distributes it, whether principal or agent, for it is the duty of each to know that the works which they circulate are free from libellous matter –

nor is ignorance of the contents of such books a sufficient excuse for those who sell and distribute them; such a defence, if proved, might, after conviction, mitigate the punishment, in some cases perhaps it might induce a Jury to acquit, but this being mere matter of defence, and therefore a fact which a Petty Jury only can inquire, would be no bar to a presentment- and the reason for this distinction is obvious, for was ignorance alone [18] to be a valid excuse, how easy would it be for the artful and designing to impose on the illiterate and unsuspecting, who, whilst they were thus incautiously vending treason and sedition, might be the occasion of the real culprit escaping both detection and punishment.

Gentlemen, let it not be supposed that any thing which I have advanced has any the remotest tendency to violate the liberty of the press; I know too well how much we are indebted to that valuable privilege, to have the least desire to see it in the slightest degree infringed; I would personally hazard as much as any man for its preservation; but I know too that the best method of perpetually securing to us the enjoyment of this privilege, is to check any intolerable licentiousness of it; if we wish to have it the fountain of truth, honour, of virtue, of liberality and freedom, we must cleanse its spring from all pollution, and not permit it to flow in torrents of treasonable and seditious doctrines – this liberty, like the liberty of the subject, must have its legal definition and security, and as well might it be contended, that the liberty of the subject was infringed by the commitment of a robbery, as that the liberty of the press was violated by the punishment of a publisher of immorality, treason and sedition. To avoid the imputation of singularity in these observations, give me leave to explain them more fully, by reading to you the precise words of that eloquent commentator on the laws of his country, Mr.[19] Justice Blackstone, to whose sentiments on this subject I should do manifest injustice, were I to express them in any language less emphatic than his own: that elegant Author, in treating of this offence says: "In this and the other instances which we have lately considered, where blasphemous, immoral, treasonable, schismatical, seditious, or scandalous libels are punished by the English law, some with a greater, others with a less degree of severity; the Liberty of the Press, properly understood, is by no means infringed or violated. The liberty of the press is indeed essential to the nature of a free state: but this consists in laying no previous restraint upon publications, and not in freedom from censure for criminal matter when published. Every freeman has an undoubted right to lay what sentiments he pleases before the public: to forbid this, is to destroy the freedom of the press: but if he publishes what is improper, mischievous, or illegal, he must take the consequence of his own temerity. To subject the press to the restrictive power of a licenser, as was formerly done, both before and since the revolution, is to subject all freedom of sentiment to the prejudices of one man, and make him the arbitrary and infallible judge of all controverted points in learning, religion, and government. But to punish (as the law does at present) any dangerous or offensive writings, which, when published, shall on a fair and impartial trial be adjudged of a pernicious tendency, is necessary for the preservation of peace and good order, of government and religion, the only solid [20] foundation of civil liberty. Thus the will of individuals is still left free; the abuse only of that free will is the object of legal punishment. Neither is there any restraint hereby laid upon freedom of thought or enquiry: liberty of private sentiment is still left; the disseminating, or making public, of bad sentiments, destructive of the ends of society, is the crime which society corrects. A man (says a writer on this subject) may be allowed to keep poison in his closet, but not publicly to vend them as cordials. And to this we may add, that the only plausible argument heretofore used for restraining the just freedom of the press, 'that it was necessary, to prevent the daily abuse of it', will entirely lose its force, when it is shewn by a seasonable exertion of the laws) that the press cannot be abused to any bad purpose, without incurring a suitable punishment: whereas it never can be used to any good one, when under the controul of an inspector. So true will it be found, that to censure the licentiousness, is to maintain the liberty of the press."

But surely it needed not the argument and assistance of this learned judge to convince us of truths so self-evident: What? If we protect the religion of our country by inflicting punishment on the publisher of blasphemy and impiety; if we protect the morals of mankind, and of the rising generation, by passing an ignominious sentence on the vender of obscene and lascivious prints and publications; if we protect the private characters of individuals, by subjecting the slanderer to make ample compensation in damages to the injured, by [21] means of civil process, or to fine and imprisonment by a criminal prosecution; shall we not equally protect the established character of the Constitution from the attacks of its malevolent and designing enemies? shall we not extend the protection to defend the honour of a virtuous, religious and beloved Sovereign, and the reputation of the other two branches of our Government; or are we prepared to say, that whilst the meanest individuals can have redress for such wrongs, that the highest official characters in the country shall sue for it in vain? Gentlemen, such a proposition is too monstrous to be endured, and needs only to be stated to expose its absurdity.

In the present times too, there can be no just cause of apprehension that the culprit will be weighed down by the hand of power, or convicted by partial or prejudiced judges; the late bill respecting libels having now left to the jury of his Peers, the consideration both of the evil tendency of the publication and the malignity of its Author.

I ought, Gentlemen, to make some apology for having so long detained you from your duty, by dwelling so minutely on this offence; in regard to the other, viz. the holding seditious and illegal meetings I shall be more concise.

Such meetings, in some instances, may be a misdemeanour only, in others may amount to the crime of high treason.

Any meeting convened and assembled for the purpose of forcing the enacting, the repealing, or altering any law [22] or statute, or the change of any part of the Constitution; to intimidate Magistrates in their duty, or assuming to itself the power of its own authority to remove and redress grievances, or in short to do any act which is not warranted by the law and constitution of the realm, is an unlawful assembly; and is considered so, whether the purpose for which it was assembled is carried into execution or not.

But if such persons proceed further than mere deliberation, if by means of riot and tumult they endeavour to compel the execution of such measures, such acts would amount to the crime of high treason, for which the lives of the offenders would be responsible.

You, Gentlemen, who know how much the peace and welfare of society depends on well-regulated Government, and on maintaining a due and proper subordination, must clearly see the necessity of such laws and the propriety of sometimes enforcing them; I will not, therefore comment on their utility. Little reason indeed should we have to boast of our liberty, if either our Legislature or our Magistracy were to be influenced or controulled by the terrors of factious and clamorous misrepresentation. We live in a free country, under mild and equitable laws, equally binding on the rich as on the poor, both equally amenable to punishment for the violation of them – thank God, in this kingdom, the cottage of the peasant is as much his castle, and as much under the safeguard and protection of these laws, as the Palace of the Prince; oppression and tyranny can-[23] not enter to destroy the happiness or to injure the tenants of either: it is the equal security, extended to all ranks alike, which is the true criterion of Freedom combined with good Government. Our laws are not injurious to the honest, the peaceable, the industrious, they are levelled only against the idle, the dissolute and the abandoned: it is men of the latter description who are always to be found among the discontented, and who, in concert with the ambitious and the disappointed, endeavour to promote change and create confusion; the one to gratify a little selfish pride and acquire a temporarily ill-got fame, the other to participate in general plunder: I trust this nation has sense to distinguish the views of such men, has prudence to thwart them, and has courage and spirit to overcome them.

In what I have now said to you, Gentlemen, I have considered myself as addressing men, who are firmly attached to that Constitution which they have received from their ancestors, who esteem and value it as their dearest birthright and inheritance; to men, who will always be ready and willing to defend that Constitution, which has protected them in every thing which makes society endearing, and life valuable; to men, who wish to bequeath that inheritance to their children and to posterity, with all its rights, privileges, and immunities, unimpaired in its vigour, and undiminished in its lustre.

Gentlemen, I cannot now dismiss you from this Court, without expressing my thanks for your patient attention, or without assuring you of my perfect confi-[24] dence in your honour, your integrity and your loyalty, and that you will this day perform your duty with that firmness, impartiality and justice, as to merit the thanks and approbation of your county, in whose service you are now essentially employed.

FINIS

A **CHARGE** DELIVERED TO THE *GRAND-JURY*, AT A SESSIONS OF **Oyer and Terminer and General Gaol Delivery**, For the City, and County of the City of BRISTOL, Held at the GUIDHALL there, On *SATURDAY* the 6th of *April*, 1793. BY RICHARD BURKE, Esq; RECORDER OF THE SAID CITY. *To which is added*, THE ADDRESS OF THE GRAND-JURY, PRESENTED TO THE RECORDER, At the CLOSE of the SESSIONS. **BRISTOL**: Printed by J. RUDHALL; - and sold by J. NORTON, and all the BOOKSELLERS of *Bristol* and *Bath*; – and by G. G. J. AND J. ROBINSON, London. M C DDXCIII.

(flyleaf)

THE GRAND JURORS direct that this Charge be printed and published at their Expence. --- They likewise direct that the whole Produce of the Sale be applied at the Discretion of the Rev. Mr. Rimbron, to the relief of the Prisoners in Newgate.

From the well know Benevolence of the Recorder, they presume he will not disapprove of such a Distribution.

[A]

A CHARGE, &c.

Gentlemen of the Grand Jury,

AFTER the painful duties attached to this seat were fulfilled, I have had, at the close of every Session, the pleasing task of delivering to the several Grand-Juries, the thanks of the Court. The Task was indeed pleasing, because the thanks have always been well deserved. The punctual attendance, the diligent enquiry, the intelligence with which the Grand-Juries of this City have gone thro' the business prepared for them, have been meritorious and exemplary. [2] You have observed, Gentlemen, that I have now relaxed the strictness of the usual course. The Names of the Defaulters have not been called over. I understand that there are, unfortunately, circumstances in the present time which demand from many persons, I might perhaps not improperly say from all, an encreased attention to their private concerns. A proper attention to these concerns is at all times a duty; just now, perhaps, that Duty is imperious. The Court then, relieved by your chearful attendance, passes over the absent without censure, and confines itself to the more happy Office of observing and applauding the generous punctuality by which you have given to this City, even in this time, the benefit of a full and most respectable Grand Inquest.

I have had also, for several Sessions, the solid satisfaction of remarking, and drawing the public attention to the gradual decrease of Offences in this City; of such, at least, as demand the severe cognizance of this Court. I am happy to be now able to repeat the same observation. The Crimes [A 2- 3] upon the face of the present Calendar are few in Number, not exceeding twelve, and that in one entire year. The magnitude, the vast population, and all other circumstances of this City through the extent of its Jurisdiction considered, this becomes a just subject of congratulation, and furnishes an happy proof of the regulated manners of the lower classes of the Citizens, as well as an honourable testimony to the vigilance and discretion of your resident Magistrates.

I wish I could express the same satisfaction in every other particular, or that I could as truly say, that the number of Prisoners was small in proportion to the number of criminal facts. Unfortunately it is not. You will find, almost throughout the Calendar, that more than one, in some instances four persons, are involved in the imputation of the same offence. This circumstance discovers a beginning of combination of Offenders, an appearance of System in the conduct of Offences, that will particularly deserve your Notice. Solitary Offenders are easily subdued; embodied, they [4] often grow so strong and subtle, as to elude Justice.

The Quality of the Offences charged does not furnish any matter of felicitation. More than half are of a very grave nature; and when they shall be brought before you in bills prepared for your Examination, you will give them all that attention, which is demanded by the public Interest and Safety, on the one hand; and the other, by a due regard to the fatal consequences of conviction, to the accused.

Whilst I thus recommend the more weighty accusations to your deliberate examination, you will not imagine, that I mean to exempt the lighter from very careful Scrutiny. That care in enquiry is sometimes called for by the very lightness of the Offence, and it ought to be well ascertained, before the person charged is subjected to a trial. I have heard a trial called a blessing; but surely this thought must proceed from some confusion on the understanding, by which the Trial itself, is substituted for the [5] mode. Our whole judicial Constitution, and particularly the Trial by Jury, is indeed a blessing; but your own observation has informed you, your own hearts will tell you, that a trial is a serious misfortune, and that no man, after the clearest acquittal, is (to give it no harsher description) at all the better in Character, Respectability, or

Situation. On this account then, you will give a sober attention to the bills laid before you, for even the slightest Offences.

I have heard it as an opinion, and that from persons of no vulgar understanding, that a Grand-Jury ought, on very slight grounds indeed, to put the subject matter before them out of their own hands, and deliver it over, together with the accused, for further and more minute investigation, by trial of the ordinary Jury. This, as I think, would be to abandon their post, to renounce their functions, and reduce the great trust reposed in them to a mere matter of form, in the execution. But a Grand-Jury is not intended as a ceremonial form. It was instituted for nobler and more [6] important Purposes. Whilst it was intended, on one hand, as an inquisition after crimes, and as the public Accuser; on the other, it has the still more sacred Office of Guardian and Protector of Innocence; by standing as a Barrier against the Prosecutions of inconsiderate levity, of insidious malice, or of oppressive power. A Grand-Jury was instituted to arrest unjust prosecution in the very beginning of its march against the Life, the Liberty, or the Character of the Subject, and qualified to say to the proudest Prosecutor, and that effectually, *thus far thou shalt go, and not further.*

But on what kind of Evidence; under what degree of approach to certainty, a Grand-Jury should deliver the Prisoner over to further, and other Trial, is another consideration, and is, as I think, incapable of definition, and not subject to any known Rule, or admitting of any direction for your Government, from the Court. Were I to risque any thing by way of recommendation on this subject, I should first draw your at-[7] tention to the circumstance, of the accused not being permitted to make any defence before you, and then I should say, you ought to see that the Commission of the Crime itself, was fully established by Evidence, and then that such a presumption is raised by the Evidence of the Crime so established, being committed by the party accused, as to satisfy your judicial Understanding, that he is reasonable called on for a defence, and the the whole matter is worthy of further, and more detailed examination. In the application of these principles (which seem to me to be just) your own informed Understandings and enlightened Consciences must be your Guides.

Hitherto, Gentlemen, in what I have offered to you, I have confined myself to one branch of your Duty, under one head of your Competence. But you have another power, from which other duties arise, and those more important; because, when duly and discreetly fulfilled they are much more beneficial in their effects, as powerfully tending to the prevention of crimes, the [8] best, if not the sole purpose of vindictive justice in all its gradations of punishment, even in that by which life is taken away. The beneficent power of which I speak, is that by which you are authorized and called on to make voluntary presentments, from your own immediate knowledge, or as the result of such enquiries, as your reasonable apprehension of existing evils, may induce you to institute. Crimes actually committed, are not the sole object of this your inquisition. Whatever has a tendency to incite to crimes, comes within its scope. Whatever corrupts the morals; every thing which disturbs, or directly leads to the disturbance of the public peace; or which promotes and encourages disobedience to the law; whatever is defamatory of the Character, or injurious to the personal safety or the property of the subject, are all matters for its cognizance and animadversion.

Amongst these, as directly leading to criminal practices, by incitement to illicit pleasures, and the consequent extravagance of expence, which again excites to unlawful [B-9] and violent means of supply, it is hardly necessary to mention those houses, where youth generally experiences its first corruption of mind. Totally to suppress such places of resort, may surpass your power, or that of the Magistrate; but their numbers may be diminished; many of the evils arising from them, may be prevented; and vice may be rendered, at least, less contagious, by the continued vigilance and animadversion of those, to whom such animadversion belongs.

There is another and shameful nuisance, to which, if it exists in this city, as it does in London, I wish to direct your attention: I mean, the abominable practice of publicly exhibiting in shops, prints and pictures of the most indecent and lascivious nature. It would be superfluous to point out to you, the certain and most pernicious effects of such exhibitions, and respect for one part of the auditory, forbids me to dwell upon the subject. The same reasons induce me to merely mention books and writings equally indecent, and more mischievously seductive, as being more easily concealed, and by affording more [10] frequent and more deliberate means to the unfortunate reader, to imbibe their poison.

To these which go to the immediate corruption of the mind, especially the youthful mind, I must add another kind of publications, which by rendering an honest fame and clear character (at best an uncertain possession) totally insecure, takes away one very powerful incentive to a virtuous life, and lessens the horror with which the first deviation from rectitude is attended. You perceive, that I mean defamatory libels, which, sparing neither age nor sex, nor rank nor condition of life, have grown to an enormity of evil, beyond the example, I believe, of any former time.

Another and more mischievous species of libellous writing, and perfectly new in its kind, has grown up in our time, and within a few years, and has arrived, almost at once, to a most malignant maturity. You already perceive, that I allude to those pernicious [B 2-11] Doctrines, those destructive moral and political principles, leading, and, without disguise, exciting to the most ruining practices, which have lately issued from the press. These, for a few years past, have not been left simply to work their own way, but have been disseminated amongst, and with the most criminal diligence and industry, even obtruded upon, the subjects of this country, especially on the lowest and least informed orders of the people, to whom such books in general are not accessible on account of their price, as most likely from their simplicity to be the dupes of the doctrines, as well as, from their numbers, the most powerful instruments of the practices which they recommend. These doctrines have been, in several parts of the kingdom, propagated with a zeal and industry altogether without a parallel, and in publications of every shape and size, from a volume on the shop, through the columns of a news-paper, to the hand-bill in the street, and the sedition chalked upon the wall.

These doctrines, and these publications, and the activity of clubs and societies, in their [12] promulgation and dispersion, had their commencement about the same time, that similar principles and doctrines were avowed and inculcated in France. There they were immediately acted upon, and the practice instantly followed the theory. That practice has been much applauded by the writers and preachers I speak of, and recommended to your imitation here. To men who can look beyond their own domestic circle, and can follow those principles in their effect, the calamitous success of these doctrines in that country, which they have ruined and desolated, is the best answer, and the surest antidote against the operation of the poison. To be safe from the infection we needed only to turn our eyes to France.

Look at that Country! 'Till very lately, without doubt, under all its circumstances, notwithstanding several vices, and several defects in its Government, France was the greatest, most opulent, and most powerful on the continent of Europe, and second to none, except our happy Country, in any of those arts which make a nation flourish, [13] and a people happy. What is it now? Its freedom has been vaunted, its new form of Government has been held up to disgrace the Constitution of his Country. What in reality, has this boasted Government been for four years past, but a succession of daring factions, all producing anarchy upon system, and exercising the most ferocious Tyranny, through that wild confusion of uproar and misrule?[1]

Personal liberty and safety were promised, to a degree of perfection, and with securities for their enjoyment hitherto unknown. Observe the performance: The Bastile was destroyed; seven victims, under what degree of real criminality is unknown, of arbitrary imprisonment, were released. Instantly all the prisons of France were filled, even to overflowing, with thousands of men and women of all ages and conditions,

[1] This is an allusion to the several forms of government which were short-lived and succeeded one another between 1789 and 1793.

many of them even without the colourable suspicion of offence. In the prisons of Paris alone were shut up, without crime specified or alledged, in the course of a few weeks, and there massacred, a far greater number of per-[14] sons,[1] than had been imprisoned since the foundation of the Monarchy of France, by the mere will and command of all their Kings, and all their Ministers, from him who first sat upon their throne, to their last most mild and benevolent Sovereign, and most innocent of men, whom they cruelly and publicly murdered on a scaffold, with every circumstance of insolent indignity, which could aggravate the most savage inhumanity. This has been the liberty and safety of the subject in France; and that the same liberty and safety may be perpetuated and legalized, a law has been enacted, by which each citizen is empowered and commanded to arrest and commit to prison, every person whom he may think fit to *suspect* of disaffection to the new order of things; that is, to the ruling faction, to the changeable tyranny of the day.

Property was declared to be sacred;[2] and the law under which it was to be acquired, and by which the acquisition was to be secured, were to be just, forcible, and perspicuous. As leading to this happy system of Legislature and Jurisprudence, they abro-[15]gated all their laws concerning property; abolished all titles and tenures by which it was held, or through which it was transmitted; overturned all Tribunals by which it was adjudged and ascertained, and having seized and confiscated by whole orders and descriptions of men, and through thousands upon thousands of individuals; have left France, at this day, without law, either by letter or spirit; and without any Tribunal for decision, from which can be shewn, by what title or tenure any man can claim, enjoy or transmit, to purchaser or posterity, one acre of land through the whole of that vast territory.

The temporal interests of the subject thus happily provided for, their eternal interests were not forgotten. Religion, freed from all intolerance, and purged of all superstition, was to be established pure and undefiled, through a perfect toleration in its exercise, as dictated by each man's conscientious judgment. To give life to this long desired, and most tender regard to the empire of conscience, they began by a persecution of the re-[16] ligion of their forefathers, and to that day their own, by profession and establishment, such as has never wasted the Christian church, even under its fiercest Heathen persecutors. The ministers of that religion, through all orders and degrees, were first stripped most contumeliously and outrageously of all their property, without even the suggestion of offence on their parts. Tests, declarations, and oaths were then multiplied, varied and imposed upon them by the practical spirit of this unbounded

[1] This an allusion to the Massacres of September.

[2] By the Déclaration des droits de l'homme et du citoyen.

toleration, and these being refused, thousands of them were murdered, and the remainder, first hunted like wild beasts through all parts of France, were, by one sweeping decree, banished for ever from their country. You know, Gentlemen, that multitudes of them are here, a living, and splendid monument of their own piety, constancy and virtue, and of English benevolence, charity and liberality. A beginning so full of zealous exertion, has had its natural ending, and after Atheism is little short of being established by law, there is not at this day (I speak from undoubted information) one place open for religious worship, [C-17] of any kind or description, in the vast metropolis of that infatuated country.

But why detain you with these disgusting and frightful details! France, in a word, exhibits to the view, a country groaning under a Tyranny more ferocious than ever disgraced and oppressed human nature; a state, whose finance is grounded upon confiscation; whose ways and means are fraud, plunder, and robbery; whose internal police owns murder as its surest instrument; which avows assassination as a weapon in its war, and executes its treaties of alliance, fulfils its promises of fraternity, by pillage, sacrilege and slaughter.

This copy but slightly sketched, and faintly coloured from the original would have made all notice of the writings and doctrines useless, if two considerations did not render it not inexpedient to bring them before you. The first is, that these doctrines are taught to men, who readily imbibe the seductive principle, but are wholly unable to trace the practical consequences, which are not [18] under their eye. The next and most important consideration is this; that even to those who may have some idea of those consequences, as applied to other countries, from a self partiality natural to us all, may flatter themselves that, under like circumstances, the same consequences may not happen here. But human nature is, much the same in all countries.

As long, indeed, as we are convinced of the value of our own Constitution, no recommendation however warm, no applauses however rapturous, of the new inventions in France, could induce us to plant here, what in that country has produced such bitter fruit. But what could not be effected by an admiration of France, might be produced, by odium raised against our own system of Laws and Government.

For this purpose men have stood forth, who, with infinite diligence have endeavoured to render every part of that Constitution, under which we have so long, and so happily flourished, and through very branch of its [C 2-19] Administration, disgustful and detestable to the People. Their diligence has the additional danger of being attended with a cautious observance of times, and seasons. They can withdraw and repose themselves, when circumstances are unfavourable to their designs: when the alarm which they had raised is abated; when vigilance is, as they suppose, lulled into security; when the Heavens shew more auspicious signs, then, like flies after a storm, they again come forth, with unabated zeal, and renovated vigour. Many of these, especially in our common news-papers, assume a kind of Magistracy, whose office it is to enlighten the People. Judging of most of these by their productions, you will think, that whilst they charitably ray out light on others, they dwell themselves in the thickest darkness. Yet, by these dispensers of light and knowledge, are the People taught to consider all the authorities of this country, as fraudulent and abusive. By them, the laws are represented as unjust, unequal, and absurd in themselves; and the administration of those laws corrupt, partial and oppressive. Magistrates [20] are vilified and calumniated, from the most high and most sacred, down to those of the most ordinary functions. All our Establishment, Civil, Religious, and Military, are continually represented as the work of ignorance and superstition, and the instruments of tyranny and oppression; and to crown all, to lay axe to the root, the Legislature, from which all have emanated, and by which they are supported, is denyed to have a legitimate existence, and is held out, sometimes by direct falshood of assertion, sometimes under specious pretexts, and by sophisticated arguments, as wanting itself in all founded authority, and no better, through all it components parts, than an unwise contrivance; and even, in many particulars, a mere usurpation.

These doctrines, principles and practices, which prevail, I trust, more in other places than in this city, but which ought every where to be watched and discountenanced, become intimately connected with the duties which we are this day to fulfil. We are here to enforce obedience to those laws and [21] to those authorities, by the terror of punishments which we are bound to inflict upon our fellow creatures, and fellow subjects, who have, even in the slightest degree, offended against them. In doing this, we should take special care to have our consciences free.

Gentlemen, The best security for obedience to the laws, is certainly founded in morality drawn from a pure and religious sense of the existence, and a firm belief in the superintending Providence of the Supreme and Eternal Being, and a conviction that he is the Author of, and has ordained civilized and social order amongst men. He who endeavours to dissuade from, to annihilate, or even to weaken this belief, destroys, to the best of his power, the surest ground on which obedience to the laws can be expected. Have no attempts of this kind been made? I leave the answer to your own knowledge and reflection.

But, even if this source of morality should become less abundant, another might remain conducive to an orderly and regulated submission to the Laws and Institutions of our [22] Country. *Habitual Esteem*, inculcated in us from our first dawn of reason; experience of the benefits resulting from, and a cultivated respect and reverence for the Laws and Institutions of our Country; from these we may draw a species of morality, productive of the best effects to the society in which we live. Long, very long, has the Constitution of this Country, from which the laws, and the dispensers of these laws, have their existence, been the object of our fondest affection, the theme of our constant panegyric; and whilst this affection and exultation remained, the laws, and the property guarded or avenged by the law, had by them no mean support. The Doctrines of the day annihilate this support, and we now come here to execute in its rigour that law, which the People have been taught to despise; whose authority they have been instructed to deny. We come here to read its terrible judgments, even to death, against very small trespasses upon property, knowing that the most earnest endeavours have been used to render the law itself odious, and that the Doctrines have been zealously propagated, which tend to the destruction of every principle, upon which [23] property is claimed or possessed; and an exclusive claim to which, or its separate possession has been asserted, if not expressly, yet by obvious inference, to be no better than an usurpation on the natural, and inalienable rights of man. Can we execute these laws, can we thus guard and avenge property with a safe conscience, unless we have, individually, at least, abstained from all kind of even the smallest encouragement to such doctrines, and such principles; or if we do not, in our public capacities, exert every Authority with which we are invested, to discourage, to suppress, and to punish those by whom such principles are instilled, such doctrines promulgated to the people?

Such persons, then if they are known to you within your Jurisdiction, together with their means of disseminating, by books or otherwise, I recommend to your serious attention, and reprehension, by presentment to the Court. The Institution, Gentlemen, whose functions you are called on to exercise, is a Watchman and Out-guard of the Constitution, whose blessings and benefits you experience, in the safety of your per-[24] sons; in the security of your property; in every species of orderly and social liberty. If there are men who warmed and invigorated by the beams of the Sun, in the midst of a land fertilized and bursting with abundance by his blessed influence, in a Scene glittering with his splendid Rays; if there are men who will make no other use of his cheering light, than to discover and count the Spots upon his glorious Face; leave them to the cheerless enjoyment, whilst we partake his blessings, and look up with grateful hearts to Him, from whom have proceeded those Blessings, and that Sun.

I shall detain you no longer from the Duties from which you are called by the Laws and Constitution of your Country, than whilst I express the earnest wish of my heart, in which I am sure of your concurrence, that the Constitution which we have received from the Wisdom of our Ancestors, may, by our plain sense, and untainted Integrity, be transmitted inviolate, as a sacred Inheritance, to our latest Posterity.

To RICHARD BURKE, Esq;

SIR,

WE the GRAND-JURORS for the City and County of Bristol wish to convey to you, in the most respectful manner, our Acknowledgments for the very excellent Charge delivered to us at the opening of the present Gaol Delivery.

Impressed with Sentiments of Loyalty and Attachment to our King and Constitution, and sensible of the Benefits we enjoy under a mild and happy Government; we hold it our Duty, by every possible means, to promote and encourage such Dispositions as may best ensure a Continu- [26] ation of the Blessings of good Order and civil Liberty.

We have seen with Regret the Attempts which have been made in different Parts of the Kingdom to disturb the public Mind, and to disseminate wild and theoretical Opinions totally subversive of Peace and good Government. We are happy to assure you, Sir, if any such Attempts have been made in this City, they have been few and ineffectual; and we rejoice in the general Disposition of the Inhabitants which has left us nothing out of the usual Course, to present.

As we wish to preserve and diffuse the good Effects of the Admonitions conveyed in your Charge, We conceive it to be within the Line of our Duty to request you to [27] favor us with a Copy of the same, in order to lay it before the Public.

With great Respect,

We are,

SIR,

GRAND JURY ROOM,

10th April, 1793

Your most obedient humble servants,

James M'Taggart, Foreman,
Daniel Taylor Haythorne
John Cockburne,
Henry Bright
Thomas Partridge
George Roche,
John Winwood
Richard Vaughan, Junr,
Samuel Whitchurch
Thomas Hughes,
William Peter Lunell,
John Page,
Richard Llewellyn,
T. Tyndall, Junr.
Samuel Townsend,
Thomas Eagles
Richard George,
John Lean,
Samuel Shute
Thomas Hill.
Charles Payne
John Cave, Junr.

THE END.

THE CHARGE DELIVERED BY The Right Honourable Sir James EYRE, Lord Chief Justice of His Majesty's Court of Common Pleas, And One of the COMMISSIONERS Named in a Special Commission of Oyer and Terminer, issued under the Great Seal of *Great Britain*, TO ENQUIRE OF CERTAIN High Treasons, AND Misprisions of Treason, Within the County of MIDDLESEX, To the GRAND JURY, At the SESSION HOUSE on *Clerkenwell Green*, on *Thursday* the 2d Day of *October* 1794. Published at the Request of THE GRAND JURY; And sold by Thomas Payne, King's Mews Gate, Castle Street, Saint Martins. 1794.

[A 2]

GENTLEMEN of the Grand Inquest,

YOU are assembled under the Authority of the King's Commission, which has been issued for the hearing and determining of the Offences of High Treason and Misprisions of High Treason, against the Person and Authority of the King.

That which hath given Occasion for this Commission is that which is declared by a late Statute, namely, "*That a traiterous and detestable Conspiracy has been formed for subverting the existing Laws and Constitution, and for introducing the System of Anarchy and Confusion which has so lately prevailed in France* ;" A CRIME OF THAT DEEP MALIGNITY which loudly calls upon the Justice of the Nation to interpose, "*for the better Preservation of His Majesty's Sacred Person, and for securing the Peace, and the Laws and Liberties of this Kingdom.*"

The first and effective Step in this, as in the ordinary criminal Proceedings, is, that a Grand Jury of the Country should make public Inquisition for the King, [4] should diligently enquire, discover, and bring forward to the View of the criminal Magistrate, those Offences which it is the Object of this special Commission to hear and determine.

You are Jurors for our Sovereign Lord the King; you are so stiled in every Indictment which is presented; but let the true Nature of this Service be understood. The King commands you to enter upon this

Enquiry; but the Royal Authority in this, as in all its other Functions is exerted, and operates ultimately for the Benefit of His People. It is the King's Object, His Duty, to vindicate His Peace, His Crown and Dignity, because HIS PEACE, HIS CROWN AND DIGNITY, are the SUBJECTS' PROTECTION, THEIR SECURITY AND THEIR HAPPINESS.

It is ultimately for them that the Laws have thrown extraordinary Fences around the Person and Authority of the King, and that all Attempts against the one or the other are considered as the highest Crimes which can be committed, and are justly punished with a Severity which nothing but the *Salus populi* can justify.

The Business of the Day calls upon me (in order that you may the better understand the Subject which is to come before you) to open to you the Nature of that Offence, which I have spoken of in general.

An ancient Statute, 25 Edward III, has declared and defined it. I shall state to you so much of that Declaration and Defi-[5] nition as appears to me to have any probable Relation to the Business of this Day.

By that Statute it is declared to be HIGH TREASON *to compass or imagine the Death of the King*, provided such Compassing and Imagining be manifested by some Act or Acts proved (by Two Witnesses) to have been done by the Party accused in Prosecution of that Compassing and Imagination; that is, from the Moment that this wicked Imagination of the Heart is acted upon, that any Steps are taken in any Manner conducting to the bringing about and effecting the Design, the Intention becomes the Crime, and the Measure of it is full.

These Acts or Steps are technically denominated Overt Acts; and the Forms of Proceedings in Cases of this Nature require that these Overt Acts should be particularly set forth in every Indictment of Treason; and, from the Nature of them, they must constitute the principal Head of Enquiry for the Grand Jury.

The Overt Acts involve in them Two distinct Considerations; 1st. The Matter of Fact of which they consist; in the next Place, the Relation of that Fact to the Design.

With respect to the mere Matter of Fact, it will be for the Grand Jury to enquire into the true State of it; and I can have very little to offer to your Consideration respecting it: And with respect to the Question, whether the Fact [6] has Relation to the Design so as to constitute an Overt Act of this Species of Treason, which involves Considerations both of Facts and of Law, it is impossible that any certain Rule should be laid down for your Government; Overt Acts being in their Nature all the possible Means which may be used in the Prosecution of the End proposed; they can be no otherwise defined, and must remain for ever infinitely various.

Thus far can I inform you: that Occasions have unhappily, but too frequently, brought Overt Acts of this Species of Treason under Consideration; in consequence of which we are furnished with judicial Opinions upon many of them; and we are also furnished with Opinions (drawn from these Sources) of Text Writers - some of the wisest and most enlightened Men of their Time, whose Integrity has always been considered as the most prominent Feature of their Character, and whose Doctrines do now form great Landmarks, by which Posterity will be enabled to trace, with a great Degree of Certainty, the boundary Lines between High Treason, and Offences of a lower Order and Degree.

It is a fortunate Circumstance that we are thus assisted; for it is not to be dissembled that, though the Crime of High Treason is "*the greatest Crime against Faith, Duty, and Human Society,*" and though "*the Public is deeply interested in every Prosecution of this Kind well founded,*" there hath been, in the best Times a considerable Degree [7] of Jealousy on the Subject of Prosecutions for High Treason; they are State Prosecutions, and the Consequences to the Party accused are Penal in the Extreme.

Jurors and Judges ought to feel an extraordinary Anxiety that Prosecutions of this Nature should proceed upon solid Grounds. I can easily conceive, therefore, that it must be a great Relief to Jurors placed in the responsible Situation in which you now stand, bound to do Justice to their Country and to the Persons accused, and anxious to discharge that trust faithfully; sure I am that it is Consolation and Comfort to us, who have upon us the Responsibility of declaring what the Law is in Cases in which the Public and the Individual are so deeply interested; to have such Men as the great Sir Matthew Hale, and an eminent Judge of our own Times who, with the Experience of a Century, concurs with him in Opinion, Sir Michael Foster, for our Guides.

To proceed by Steps: From these Writers upon the Law of treason (who speak, as I have observed, upon the Authority of adjudged Cases) we learn, that not only Acts of *immediate* and *direct* Attempt against the King's Life are Overt Acts of compassing his Death, but that all the remoter Steps taken with a view to assist to bring about the actual Attempt, are equally Overt Acts of this Species of Treason; even the Meeting and the consulting what Steps should be taken in order to bring about the End proposed, has always been deemed to be an Act done in Prosecution [8] of the Design, and as such an Over Act of this Treason - This is our first Step in the present Enquiry. I proceed to observe that the Overt Acts I have been speaking of have Reference, nearer or more remote, to a *direct* and *immediate* Attempt upon the Life of the King; but that the same Authority informs us, that they who aim directly at the Life of the King (such, for instance, as the Persons who were concerned in the Assassination Plot in the Reign of King William) are not the only Persons who can be said to compass or imagine the Death of the King. *The entering into Measures which, in the Nature of Things, or in the common*

Experience of Mankind, do obviously tend to bring the Life of the King into Danger, is also compassing and imagining the Death of the King; and the Measures which are taken will be at once Evidence of the compassing, and Overt Acts of it.

The Instances which are put by Sir Matthew Hale and Sir Michael Foster (and upon which there have been adjudged Cases) are Conspiracies to *depose* the King; to *imprison* Him; to *get His Person into the Power of the Conspirators*; to *procure an Invasion of the Kingdom*. The First of these, apparently the strongest Case, and coming nearest to the direct Attempt against the Life of the King; the last, the farthest removed from that direct Attempt, but being a Measure tending to destroy the public Peace of the Country, to introduce Hostilities, and the Necessity of resisting Force by Force, and where it is obvious that the Conflict has an ultimate Tendency to bring the Person and [B - 9] Life of the King into Jeopardy; it is taken to be a sound Construction of the Statute of 25 Edward III, and the clear Law of the Land, that this is also compassing and imagining the Death of the King.

If a Conspiracy to depose or to imprison the King, to get His Person into the Power of the Conspirators, or to procure an Invasion of the Kingdom, involves in it the compassing or imagining of His Death, and if Steps taken in Prosecution of such a Conspiracy are rightly deemed Overt Acts of the Treason of imagining and compassing the King's Death; need I add, that if it should appear that IT HAS ENTERED INTO THE HEART OF ANY MAN, WHO IS A SUBJECT OF THIS COUNTRY, TO DESIGN TO OVERTHROW THE WHOLE GOVERNMENT OF THE COUNTRY, TO PULL DOWN AND TO SUBVERT FROM ITS VERY FOUNDATIONS THE BRITISH MONARCHY, THAT GLORIOUS FABRIC WHICH IT HAS BEEN THE WORK OF AGES TO ERECT, MAINTAIN, AND SUPPORT, WHICH HAS BEEN CEMENTED WITH THE BEST BLOOD OF OUR ANCESTORS; TO DESIGN SUCH A HORRIBLE RUIN AND DEVASTATION, WHICH NO KING COULD SURVIVE, A CRIME OF SUCH A MAGNITUDE THAT NO LAWGIVER IN THIS COUNTRY HATH EVER VENTURED TO CONTEMPLATE IT IN ITS WHOLE EXTENT; need I add, I say, that the Complication and the enormous Extent of such a Design will not prevent its being distinctly seen, that *the compassing and imagining the Death of the King is involved in it, is in Truth of its very Essence*. [10]

This is too plain a Case to require further Illustration from me. If any Man of plain Sense, but not conversant with Subjects of this Nature, should feel himself disposed to ask whether a Conspiracy of this Nature is to be reached by this Medium only; whether it is a *specific* Treason to compass and imagine the Death of the King, and *not a specific* Treason to conspire to subvert the Monarchy itself; I answer, that the Statute of

Edward III, by which we are governed, hath not declared this (which in all just Theory of Treason is the greatest of all Treasons) to be High Treason.

I said no Lawgiver had ever ventured to contemplate it in its whole Extent; the *Seditio Regni*, spoken of by some of our ancient Writers, comes the nearest to it, but falls far short if it: Perhaps if it were now a Question whether such a Conspiracy should be made a specific Treason, it might be argued to be unnecessary: That in securing the Person and Authority of the King from all Danger, the Monarchy, the Religion and Laws of our Country are incidentally secured; that the Constitution of our Government is so framed, that the Imperial Crown of the Realm is the common Centre of the Whole; that all traiterous Attempts against any Part of it are instantly communicated to that Centre, and felt there; and that, as upon every Principle of public Policy and Justice they are punishable as traiterous Attempts against the King's Person or Authority, and will, according to the particular Nature of the traiterous Attempt, fall within One or other of the specific [B 2- 11] Treasons against the King, declared by the Statute of 25 Edward III; this greatest of all Treasons is sufficiently provided against by Law.

Gentlemen, I presume I hardly need give you this Caution, that though it has been expressly declared, by the highest Authority, that there do exist in this Country Men capable of meditating the Destruction of the Constitution under which we live; that Declaration, being extra-judicial, is not a Ground upon which you ought to proceed.

In consequence of that Declaration it became a public and indispensable Duty in His Majesty to institute this solemn Proceeding, and to impose upon you the painful Task of examining the Accusations, which shall be brought before you; but it will be your Duty to examine them in a regular judicial Course, that is, by hearing the Evidence, and forming your own Judgement upon it.

And here, as I do not think it necessary to trouble you with Observations upon the other Branches of the Statute 25 Edward III, the Charge to the Grand Inquest might conclude; had not the particular Nature of the Conspiracy, alledged to have been formed against the State, been disclosed, and made Matter of public Notoriety by the Reports of the Two Houses of Parliament, now in every ones Hands: But that being the Case, I am apprehensive that I shall not be thought to have fulfilled the Duty, which the Judge owes to the Grand Jury, when Questions in the [12] criminal Law arise on new and extraordinary Cases of Fact; if I did not plainly and distinctly state what I conceive the Law to be, or what Doubts I conceive may arise in Law, upon the Facts which are likely to be laid before you, according to the different Points of View in which those Facts may appear to you.

It is Matter of public Notoriety that there have been Associations formed in this County, and in other Parts of the Kingdom, the professed purpose of which has been a Change in the Constitution of the Commons House of Parliament, and the obtaining of Annual Parliaments; and that to some of these Associations other Purposes, hidden under this Veil, Purposes the most traiterous, have been imputed; and that some of the Associations have been supposed to have actually adopted Measures of such a Nature, and to have gone into such Excesses as will amount to the Crime of High Treason.

If there be Ground to consider the professed Purpose of any of these Associations, *a Reform in Parliament,* as mere Colour, and as a Pretext held out in order to cover deeper Designs - Designs against the whole Constitution, and Government of this Country; the Case of those embarked in such Designs is that, which I have already considered. Whether this be so, or not, is mere Matter of Fact; as to which I shall only remind you, that an Enquiry into a Charge of this Nature, which undertakes to make out that the ostensible Purpose is a mere Veil, under which is concealed a traiterous [13] Conspiracy, requires cool and deliberate Examination, and the most attentive Consideration; and that the Result should be perfectly clear and satisfactory. In the Affairs of common Life, no Man is justified in imputing to another a Meaning contrary to what he himself expresses, but upon the fullest Evidence. On the other Hand, where the Charge can be made out, it is adding to the Crime meditated the deepest Dissimulation and Treachery, with respect to those Individuals, who may be drawn in to embark in the ostensible Purpose, as well as to the Public, against which this dark Mystery of Wickedness is fabricated.

But if we suppose these Associations to adhere to the professed Purpose, and to have no other primary Object; it may be asked, is it possible, and (if it be possible) by what Process is it, THAT AN ASSOCIATION FOR THE REFORM OF PARLIAMENT CAN WORK ITSELF UP TO THE CRIME OF HIGH TREASON? All Men may, nay, all Men must, if they possess the Faculty of thinking, reason upon every Thing which sufficiently interests them to become Objects of their Attention; and among the Objects of the Attention of free Men, the Principles of Government, the Constitution of particular Governments, and, above all, the Constitution of the Government under which they live, will naturally engage Attention, and provoke Speculation. The Power of Communication of Thoughts and Opinions is the Gift of God, and the Freedom of it is the Source of all Science, the First Fruits and the ultimate Happiness of Society; and therefore it seems to follow, that [14] human Laws ought not to interpose, nay, cannot interpose, to prevent the Communication of Sentiments and Opinions in voluntary Assemblies of Men; all which is true, with this single Reservation, that THOSE ASSEMBLIES ARE TO BE SO COMPOSED,

AND SO CONDUCTED, AS NOT TO ENDANGER THE PUBLIC PEACE AND GOOD ORDER OF THE GOVERNMENT UNDER WHICH THEY LIVE; and I shall not state to you that Associations and Assemblies of Men, for the Purpose of obtaining a Reform in the interior Constitution of the British Parliament, are simply unlawful; but, on the other Hand, I must state to you, that they may but too easily degenerate, and become unlawful, in the highest Degree, even to the enormous Extent of the Crime of High Treason.

The Process is very simple: Let us imagine to ourselves this Case: A few well meaning Men conceive that they and their Fellow Subjects labour under some Grievance; they assemble peaceably to deliberate on the Means of obtaining Redress; the Numbers increase; the Discussion grows animated, eager, and violent; a rash Measure is proposed, adopted, and acted upon; who can say where this shall stop, and that these Men, who originally assembled peaceably, shall not finally, and suddenly too, involve themselves in the Crime of High Treason. It is apparent how easily an impetuous Man may precipitate such Assemblies into Crimes of unforeseen Magnitude, and Danger to the State: But, let it be considered, that bad Men may also find their Way into such Assemblies, and use the innocent Purposes of their [15] Association as the Stalking Horse to their Purposes of a very different Complexion. How easy for such Men to practise upon the Credulity and Enthusiasm of honest Men, Lovers of their Country, Loyal to their Prince, but eagerly bent on some speculative Improvements on the Frame, and internal Mechanism of the Government? If we suppose bad Men to have once gained an Ascendancy in an Assembly of this Description, popular in its Constitution, and having popular Objects; how easy is it for such Men to plunge such an Assembly into the most criminal Excesses? Thus far I am speaking in general, merely to illustrate the Proposition, that Men who assemble in order to procure a Reform of Parliament may involve themselves in the Guilt of High Treason.

The Notoriety to which I have alluded leads me to suppose, that a *Project of a Convention* of the People, to be assembled under the Advice and Direction of some of these Societies, or of Delegations from them, will be the leading Fact, which will be laid before you in Evidence, respecting the Conduct, and Measures of these Associations; a Project, which perhaps, in better Times, would have been hardly though worthy of grave Consideration; but, in these our Days, having been attempted to put into Execution in a distant Part of the United Kingdoms, and, with the Example of a neighbouring Country, before our Eyes; is deservedly an Object of the Jealousy of our Laws: It will be your Duty to examine the Evidence on this Head very carefully, and sift it to the Bottom; to consider every [16] Part of it in itself, and as it stands connected with other Parts of it, and to draw the Conclusion of Fact, as to the Existence, the Nature, and the Object of this Project of a Convention, from the Whole.

In the Course of the Evidence you will probably hear of *Bodies of Men having been collected together, of violent Resolutions voted at these and at other Meetings, of some Preparation of offensive Weapons, and of the Adoption of the Language, and Manner of proceeding at those Conventions in France, which have possessed themselves of the Government of that Country*: I dwell not on these Particulars, because I consider them, not as substantive Treasons but, as Circumstances of Evidence, tending to ascertain the true Nature of the Object, which these Persons had in View, and also the true Nature of this Project of a Convention, and to be considered by you in the Mass of that Evidence; which Evidence it does not fall within the Province of the Charge to consider in Detail; my present Duty is, to inform you what the Law is upon the Matter of Fact, which in your Judgement shall be the Result of the Evidence.

I presume that I have sufficiently explained to you that A PROJECT TO BRING THE PEOPLE TOGETHER IN CONVENTION IN IMITATION OF THOSE NATIONAL CONVENTIONS WHICH WE HAVE HEARD OF IN FRANCE IN ORDER TO USURP THE GOVERNMENT OF THE COUNTRY, and ANY ONE STEP TAKEN TOWARDS BRINGING IT ABOUT, such as for Instance, *Consultations, forming of Committees to consider of the Means, acting in those Committees*, would be a [C - 17] Case of no Difficulty that it would be the CLEAREST HIGH TREASON; it would be compassing and imagining the King's Death, and not only His Death, but the Death and Destruction of all Order, Religion, Laws, all Property, all Security for the Lives and Liberties of the King's Subjects.

That which remains to be considered is, *the Project of a Convention having for its sole Object the effecting a Change in the Mode of Representation of the People in Parliament, and the obtaining that Parliaments should be held annually*; and here there is Room to distinguish. Such a Project of a Convention, taking it to be criminal, may be criminal in different Degrees, according to the Case in Evidence, from whence you are to collect the true Nature and Extent of the Plan, and the Manner in which it is intended to operate; and it will become a Question of great Importance, under what Class of Crimes it ought to be ranged.

In determining upon the Complexion and Quality of this Project of Convention; you will lay down to yourselves One Principle which is never to be departed from; THAT ALTERATIONS IN THE REPRESENTATION OF THE PEOPLE IN PARLIAMENT, OR IN THE LAW FOR HOLDING PARLIAMENTS, CAN ONLY BE EFFECTED BY THE AUTHORITY OF THE KING, LORDS, AND COMMONS, IN PARLIAMENT ASSEMBLED. This being taken as a Foundation; it seems to follow as a necessary Consequence, that *a*

Project of a Convention, which would have for its Object the obtaining a [18] *Parliamentary Reform without the Authority of Parliament, and Steps taken upon it, would be* HIGH TREASON *in all the Actors in it*; for this is a Conspiracy to overturn the Government. The Government cannot be said to exist, if the Functions of Legislation are usurped for a Moment; and it then becomes of little Consequence indeed, that the original Conspirators, perhaps, had only meditated a Plan of moderate Reform: It is, in the Nature of Things, that the Power should go out of their Hands, and be beyond the Reach of their Controul. A Conspiracy of this Nature is therefore, at best, a Conspiracy to overturn the Government, in order to new model it, which is, in Effect, to introduce Anarchy, and that which Anarchy may chance to settle down into; after the King may have been brought to the Scaffold, and after the Country may have suffered all the Miseries, which Discord, and Civil War, shall have produced.

Whether *the Project of a Convention, having for its Object the collecting together a Power, which should overawe the Legislative Body, and extort a Parliamentary Reform from it,* if acted upon, will also amount to HIGH TREASON, and to the specific Treason of compassing and imagining the King's Death, is a more doubtful Question. Thus far is clear; a Force upon the Parliament must be immediately directed against the King, who is an integral Part of it; it must reach the King, or it can have no Effect at all. Laws are enacted in Parliament by the King's Majesty, by and with the Advice and Consent of the Lords and Commons, in [C 2-19] Parliament assembled. A Force meditated against the Parliament, is therefore a Force meditated against the King, and seems to fall within the Case of a Force meditated against the King, to compel Him to alter the Measures of His Government: But, in that Case, it does not appear to me that I am warranted by the Authorities to state to you, as clear Law, that the mere Conspiracy to raise such a Force, and the entering into Consultations respecting it, will alone, and without actually raising the Force, constitute the Crime of High Treason. What the Law is in that Case, and what will be the Effect of the Circumstance of the Force being meditated against the King in PARLIAMENT, against the King in the Exercise of the Royal Function in a Point, which is of the very Essence of his Monarchy, will be fit to be solemnly considered, and determined when the Case shall arise.

It may be stated to you as clear, That *the Project of a Convention, having for its sole Object a dutiful and peaceable Application to the Wisdom of Parliament on the Subject of a wished-for Reform, which Application should be entitled to Weight and Credit from the Universality of it, but should still leave to the Parliament the freest Exercise of its Discretion to grant or to refuse the Prayer of the Petition*, (great as the Responsibility will be on the Persons concerned in it, in respect of the many probable, and all the possible, bad Consequences of collecting a great Number of People together; with no specific legal Powers to be exercised, and under no Government but that of their own Discretion), *cannot in* [20] *itself merit to be ranked among that Class of Offences* which we are now assembled to hear and determine.

Upon this last Statement of Fact of the Case, I am not called upon, and therefore it would not be proper for me to say more.

Gentlemen, You will now proceed upon the several Articles of Enquiry, which have been given you in Charge: If you find that the Parties, who shall be accused before you, have been pursuing lawful Ends by lawful Means, or have only been indiscreet, or at the worst, if criminal, that they have not been criminal to the Extent of these Treasons, to which our Enquiries are confined, then say, that the Bills which shall be presented to you ARE NOT TRUE BILLS: But, if any of the accused Persons shall appear to you to have been engaged in that traiterous and detestable Conspiracy described in the Preamble of the late Statute; or, if without any formed Design to go the whole Length of that Conspiracy, they have yet acted upon the desperate Imagination of bringing about Alterations in the Constitution of the Commons House of Parliament, or in the Manner of holding Parliaments, without the Authority of Parliament, and in Defiance of it, by an usurped Power, which should, in that Instance, suspend the lawful Authority of the King, Lords, and Commons, in Parliament assembled, and take upon itself the Function of Legislation; (which Imagination amounts to a Conspiracy to subvert the existing Laws and Constitution, differing from the former only in the [21] Extent of its Object), YOU WILL THEN DO THAT WHICH BELONGS TO YOUR OFFICE TO DO.

In the Third View of the Case of the accused Persons; that is, if you find them involved in, and proceeding upon, a Design to collect the People together against the Legislative Authority of the Country for the Purpose, not of usurping the Functions of the Legislature but, of over-awing the Parliament, and so compelling the King, Lords, and Commons, in Parliament assembled, to enact a Law for new modelling the Commons House of Parliament, or for holding Annual Parliaments; and that Charges of High Treason are offered to be maintained against them upon this Ground only; perhaps it may be fitting that, IN RESPECT OF THE EXTRAORDINARY NATURE AND DANGEROUS EXTENT AND VERY CRIMINAL COMPLEXION OF SUCH A CONSPIRACY, that Case, which I state to you as a new and a doubtful Case, should be put into a judicial Course of Enquiry, that it may receive a solemn Adjudication, whether it will, or will not, amount to HIGH TREASON, in order to which the Bills must be found true Bills.

Gentlemen, I have not opened to you the Law of *Misprision of Treason*, because I am not aware that there are Commitments for that Offence; and therefore I have no Reason to suppose that there will be any

Prosecution for that Offence. It consists *of the Concealment of Treason committed by others*, (which undoubtedly it is every Man's Duty to disclose), and the Punishment is extremely severe; but the Humanity of modern Times hath usually interposed, and [22] I trust that the Necessities of the present Hour will not demand, that the Law of Misprision of Treason should now be carried into Execution.

Gentlemen, I dismiss you with confident Expectation that your Judgement will be directed to those Conclusions, which MAY CLEAR INNOCENT MEN FROM ALL SUSPICION OF GUILT, BRING THE GUILTY TO CONDIGN PUNISHMENT, PRESERVE THE LIFE OF OUR GRACIOUS SOVEREIGN, SECURE THE STABILITY OF OUR GOVERNMENT, AND MAINTAIN THE PUBLIC PEACE, IN WHICH COMPREHENSIVE TERMS IS INCLUDED THE WELFARE AND HAPPINESS OF THE PEOPLE UNDER THE PROTECTION OF THE LAWS AND LIBERTIES OF THE KINGDOM.

A **CHARGE** DELIVERED TO THE **GRAND JURY** OF THE COUNTY OF DUBLIN, AT THE QUARTER SESSIONS OF THE PEACE, HELD AT KILMAINHAM, *on Tuesday the 12th of January* 1796. By ROBERT DAY, Esq. M.P. ONE OF HIS MAJESTY'S COUNSEL LEARNED IN THE LAW, AND CHAIRMAN OF THE SAID COUNTY. published at the request of the High Sheriff, Magistrates and Grand Jury. DUBLIN: PRINTED BY RICHARD EDWARD MERCIER AND CO.BOOKSELLERS TO THE HON. SOCIETY OF KING'S INNS. 1794.

KILMAINHAM, January 12th, 1796.

THE High Sheriff, Magistrates and Grand Jury of the County of Dublin, return their warmest Thanks to ROBERT DAY, *Esq; Chairman of the Quarter-Sessions, for his very able and Constitutional Charge this Day delivered to the Grand Jury; and conceiving that the Promulgation of it at this Juncture could be highly useful, they request his Permission to publish it.*

Signed by Order of the Meeting,
George VESEY, Sheriff.
George GRIERSON, Foreman.

[7]

A CHARGE, &c.

Gentlemen of the Grand Jury,

IT is impossible for any Irishman, not dead to all public virtue, to contemplate without exultation and just national pride, the Stability of these Kingdoms, amidst the Convulsions and disastrous Events which in the lapse of a few years have desolated the greater part of Europe. While we prostrate ourselves in great adoration before the throne of God for this his stupendous goodness, it may not be unprofitable to inquire into the more immediate Causes of our Exemption from those [8] awful Calamities, which it has pleased Providence to visit upon so large a portion of our Fellow-creatures. Such disquisitions, while they teach us to form a just sense of our Establishments, and of their importance and value, must lead every man of prudence and reflexion to sustain and cherish them, as the surest means of our preservation amidst this wreck of Nations.

The structure and frame of our Government is the greatest and primary Cause, to which under God we are indebted for our Security, Strength and Prosperity: – that mixed Government, in which Monarchy, Aristocracy and Democracy combine their several Energies and best Properties, and controul the vices and excesses of each other,- that Government, in which these three Rival Powers are tempered into an apt consistence; and so many advantages [B-9] seemingly irreconcileable, like the jarring Elements of Nature, conspire to produce this harmonious well-poised order of things. From this Form of Government, in which the interests of All are alike considered, result our System of just and Equal Laws, and the principles which regulate the administration of Justice amongst us. From the same source is derived the happy State of Civil Society in these Kingdoms; where Protection is extended equally to All, where there is one Law for All, and where abilities and integrity secure free access to the emoluments and honours of the State for All. When I look through these Countries, I perceive that it is not distinguished Rank or high Birth, but superior Talents and acknowledged Merit which indiscriminately conduct the possessors to the proudest Eminences of the State. When I look through our flourishing Capital, when I look [10] into the Jury-Box which you, Gentlemen, now fill, I cannot but recollect that Industry, Probity, good Sense and Skill, are the unerring guides to wealth, honour and distinction amongst us. – In a word, it is by the energy and the protecting influence of our free and temperate Constitution, lying midway between Tyranny and Licentiousness, that the British Empire has risen to its unrivalled greatness, and the People to the highest gradation in the Scale of Political and Civil happiness.

Among the various means employed to secure the Civil Rights and happiness of our People, which in truth are the basis of public Security and Strength, none is more distinguished than that which the present Solemnity draws into action. You perceive that I allude to the administration of Criminal Justice amongst us. Our whole Judicial [B 2-11] Constitution is indeed a blessing; but particularly the Trial by Jury. In the construction of our Criminal Tribunals, which are separated into distinct parts, the more effectually to guard against, corruption, caprice and error, the leading principle which has been steadily kept in view is Equality. The Grand Jury and the Petit Jury are composed of Men, who in their turn are liable to be tried by others of their Fellow Subjects discharging the same awful and important Trusts. That measure of Justice, which the Juror metes out to his Fellow-subject to-day, may be dealt to himself to-morrow; it behoves him therefore that it be a just measure. So also they are indiscriminately called to those Services, from time to time as each occasion requires, from the great body of Freeholders of the County; no distinction observed, save that of Character and a very moderate qualifi-[12] cation of Property. It must strike you therefore that being transitory and Occasional Bodies, they are not exposed, as a Permanent Jury would be, to the operation of any corrupt or undue Influence, which the Rich and Powerful can always best command.

Nothing can more clearly illustrate this Equality (and as long as the modifications of corporal and intellectual Strength continue innumerable, so long will any other Equality of Condition be impracticable) than the dire effects of a Permanent Jury in France. That wretched Country had got a glimpse of our Establishments, and she adopted from us the institution of Juries. But they were Juries in name only, and not in principle or construction. Instead of impannelling them for each distinct Occasion as it occurred, her sanguinary Legislators established Standing Juries; [13] not to exercise their judgment upon the Cases presented to them, but to sanction with their venerable name the most unparalleled Enormities. The consequences were what might be expected. These Permanent Juries soon became the convenient Organ of each succeeding Monster in power, and at his nod, even without the formalities of law, consigned daily Hecatombs of innocent Victims to Judicial Sacrifice. Gentlemen, your indignation rises at this horrid prophanation of the sacred institution of Juries! an Institution which you habitually contemplate as the sure refuge and Sanctuary of Innocence, the Poor Man's best Friend, his Tutelar God; the strong Curb of insolent Power and licentious Authority; the Terror of Guilt alone!

But as Equality of Justice requires [14] Juries shall be Occasional, so to an uniform, skilful and enlightened interpretation of the Law it is necessary that the Judge be Permanent. Independent of the Crown, stimulated by the Conditions of his Tenure to a pure and upright conduct, controuled even by the Publicity of all Criminal proceedings from yielding to prejudice, passion or any other corrupt affection of the mind, the Judge may safely be Permanent. And indeed of necessity he must be so, as long as we prefer a System of known and fixed Laws to novel and chimerical Opinions: as long as Jurisprudence is considered a Science founded on solid and fixed principles: – in a word, as long as industry experience, education and learning are essential Ingredients in the Judicial Character. – And in fact, if in such an assemblage of Excellence as the British Government it be conspicuous [15] in any one of its Component Establishments beyond the rest, it is in the administration of the Laws and the dispensation of Justice, Civil and Criminal, by the Superior Judges. However insufficiently filled, or negligently administered other Departments of the State may sometimes happen to be, it must be admitted that, on our several Judicial Benches, men are to be found of the most elevated characters; who unite industry with talents and science; and who, impressed with a deep and conscientious Sense of the sacred duties of their functions, devote the whole of their lives to the Service of the Public.

In a word, we may with truth assert, that there is no Nation under the Sun in which Justice is so Equally and impartially administered, as in these Realms. And of the Law, it may with no less truth be said, that as it [16] provides a remedy for every injury, so it affords that remedy Equally to the proudest and the Poorest.

One should suppose, that under so favoured and providential a dispensation of things, no man in his senses could wish to change his Political condition. No man it might be hoped, who was was not actually distempered in mind, or bankrupt in fortune or fame, could be seduced from a rooted sense of the singular advantages derived from a system of Laws, "as broad and general as the casing air."- But, alas! it can no longer be concealed, that the industry of Sedition and Treason has been too successful in both Kingdoms. The wicked Conspiracy happily has been traced through many of its ramifications in Great Britain and Ireland. What the pro-[C-17] ceedings of the[1] British Parliament and Courts of Justice have been these two last years, to probe the evil and check its progress, it would be going out of our way to detail. But we know that Treason, of late, has thrown off the mask in our Sister Kingdom, and disdains all concealment. The late direct and immediate attempt upon the person of the Sovereign no longer leaves the object of the Conspirators questionable, or the Treason matter of construction and inference.[2] It was [18] reserved for the peculiar and daring atrocity of modern principles to assail the FATHER OF HIS PEOPLE; surrounded by his devoted and exulting Subjects; in the exercise of that August Function, which dispenses happiness to Millions, which gives life and motion to the most sublime System of Legislation that History has recorded. Phrenzy alone it was thought could have armed itself against the life of a Monarch, as distinguished for his inviolable fidelity to the Constitution, as for his exemplary piety and domestic virtues;- whose Life, in addition to our Allegiance, challenges the tribute of our Love; and whose Death would be the bitterest calamity which could be inflicted upon his Subjects, and I might add at this juncture upon Europe. [C 2 - 19]

[1] Early in 1794 it appeared from the Reports of both Houses of the British Parliament, grounded upon uncontrovertable evidence, and in the course of the State Trials which were had at the Old Bayly in the October following, that a Traiterous Conspiracy had been formed and acted upon, by certain Societies and Individuals in different parts of England and Scotland corresponding and intimately connected, for subverting the established Laws and Constitution, pulling down the Monarchy, and for introducing in its stead that Anarchy and those extravagant Notions of false Liberty, which have transformed the fairest and once the most civilized region of Europe into a wilderness of Tygers.

[2] A stone was thrown at the King's coach in October 1795 on his way to Westminster.

In this country the Plot has been conducted with more colouring and disguise, but perhaps with a still deeper degree of malignity. The object of the Conspirators of Great Britain was to subvert the Monarchy, that glorious fabrick which it has been the works of ages to erect, preserve, and meliorate, and upon its ruins to raise a Republic; that is, to let in all the confusion and wild misrule of France. This daring project was to be accomplished by means of a National Convention, to be openly and avowedly held; to which those evil-minded Enthusiasts had the folly to hope, that the sober, solid, and virtuous people of that Island might be persuaded to transfer their allegiance and confidence, from their good King and legitimate Parliament. But the object here was no less than tho procure an Invasion from France; from a [20] People, in whose presence all Nature withers; whose progress has been invariably marked by devastation, famine and blood. *Gallorum gentem infestis-sumam nomini Romano intra mœnua arcessunt*. –This was to be seconded by a general Rising of the great Mass of our People, who were represented as semi-barbarous[1], ready for any change, and harbouring a settled and confirmed aversion to the British name and connexion - that Connexion, to which we owe every thing enlightened, prosperous, great and good amongst us - that magnanimous people, from who we derive our proudest and most inestimable possessions; our Religion, our Constitution, our Common Law, our Liberties; this Institution which we now commemorate, and which, like a Presiding Angel, watches over and guards the whole -[21] the Trial by Jury. Gentlemen, you know that to promote this diabolical purpose, Jackson visited this City, an accredited Minister from the Dæmons of France to certain Traitors and Parricides of Ireland. You know that, through the vigilance and address of Lord Westmorland's firm and vigorous government, that infortunate Man was apprehended with all the evidences of his guilt upon him; was afterwards brought to justice; and that his cabinet of Conspirators, taking the alarm, prudently fled, and escaped the punishment due to their crimes. But the seeds of Treason unhappily had been scattered through the Island, and it must be owned that they have produced an abundant crop. It now comes out on the clearest evidence that those deluded men stile *Defenders*, apparently but a lawless Rabble, confining their views as it at first seemed [22] to mere acts of Plunder and Felony, have in truth been regularly embodied and organized under Leaders and Committee-men. It appears, that the Plot had rooted itself so extensively, that the Insurgents, through no less than nine Counties, have been leagued together by the most sacred (or rather, the most accursed) obligations to Rise upon a concerted Signal; that All were bound by the same Oath to the National Convention, used the same mysterious Signs, acted in unison, and were moved as it

[1] See Jackson's Trial, p. 81 & passim.

were by one Spring. With the same traiterous purpose they have been disarming every man in those Counties, upon whose co-operation they could not count, and who wanted courage and public Spirit to resist them. With the same criminal view they learned the use of Arms, levied Contributions, purchased Ammunition, recruited avowedly for the [23] National Convention, employed Emissaries in the experiment, as vain as wicked, of debauching our brave and steady Soldiers; and in short took every step to strengthen themselves, and give effect to the long-expected Descent.- Meantime the Conspirators were not idle in the Capital. In a[1] City, so populous and so profligate, the most desperate Enterprize will not long want an army of Advocates. All men, goaded by bankruptcy, evil society, or conscious guilt, have an interest in confusion, and were pleased to find a Rallying-point. Neglected Apprentices, needy Journeymen, seditious Masters hoping to "ride on the whirlwind," here formed themselves into Societies, Committees and Clubs, and familiarly discoursed of Rebellion as the sacred birth-right of the People. [24] The *Philanthropic Society* enlarged with great sensibility on the virtue of Assassination and the use of the Poniard. The dregs of the dissolved *United Irishmen* thought a Civil War the best expedient for promoting a general Uniformity and Harmony of Sentiment. And there is reason to believe, that a Massacre upon a comprehensive Scale was in agitation, as the surest means of promoting Political Morality and the Christian Religion!

Such, Gentlemen, is the dark and formidable Conspiracy, which, through the signal Mercy of Providence, has been brought to light when at the very point of explosion. Much praise is surely due to Government, for the perseverance and energy with which this infernal Plot has been followed up and defeated. We have awakened on the brink of a Precipice. We have been walking in dull Security over a [D- 25]Mine, which by good fortune has not sprung under our feet. But though the Electric Cloud be passed, the sky still lowers. "We have scotch'd the snake, not kill'd it." The Diligence of Bad Men never sleeps, and has the additional danger of being mingled with a cautious observance of times and seasons. They can withdraw, when the aspect of things is unfavourable; but if the alarm, which they have raised, shall subside, if your vigilance shall be lulled into security, then, like Summer flies after a Storm, they will again come forth with keener acrimony and renewed activity. Can it be doubted, that Republican Agents and disaffected Men of no mean condition foment this traiterous spirit, and administer to the support of those deluded Wretches, who can have no resources of their own to rest upon through [26] this barbarous warfare, so long and obstinately waged upon all Order and Civil Government in the Country? – But it is to be

[1] "In tantâ tamque corruptâ Civitate, Catalina, &c. See Sallust in bello Catal:

hoped, that the danger which happily we have escaped, and this malignant and contagious phrenzy of our peasantry which "frights the Isle from her propriety", will awaken us from the stupid lethargy in which we have hitherto been plunged; will animate, to a more than ordinary vigilance and exertion, not only the Magistracy and Executive Power of the Country through all its gradations, but every Individual who has an interest in Social Order – who means not tamely to resign his property to depredation, and his breast to the midnight Murder. The Evil has invariably been frowned down in those Countries, where a steady and determined countenance had been presented against it; on the contrary, [D 2-27] it has raged most where the families of natural influence and power, with the timid and fatal policy of the French Emigrants, had deserted their habitations, leaving the defenceless Country to the mercy of a desolating Mob. Gentlemen, depend upon this Eternal Truth, that there is more danger in Cowardice than in Courage. The man who fights with the Law on his side is, alone, a Tower of Strength. Guilt is ever as Cowardly as Cruel.

Gentlemen, it is needless to trouble you with any Legal Observations of my own upon this important Subject. The Law has been[1] lately laid down distinctly by higher authority, the con-[28] curring authority of three learned Judges; and I cannot express it more clearly than in the words of the learned Baron, your late worthy Municipal Judge. "It is now evident (said he) that the *Defenders* are not merely Felons but *Traitors*. The Oaths and Tests, under which they are enlisted, declare expressly that they are concerned with the National Convention of France for the purpose of subverting our Government. And it is now fit it should be made known, that it is *High Treason* to incite and encourage a man to become a Defender; that it Treason to harbour, comfort or abet the Defenders, – all persons in any wise concerned are Traitors. And further, all men who know, and do not disclose to Government or the Magistrates their knowledge of the Defenders, and [29] of their Criminal actions or purposes, are guilty of *Misprision of Treason* " – the judgment for which, Gentlemen, is not less than that the Convict be imprisoned for Life, forfeit the profits of his lands for Life, and forfeit absolutely all his personal property.

These Observations, Gentlemen, I address not only to you, but to this assembled Multitude; in the anxious and fond hope, that every man who hears me will with his utmost industry circulate them, and impress the Law upon the minds of the deluded Peasantry in his neighbourhood. Say to them, that at the moment when Parliament had been most busy

[1] By Chamberlaine, J. Finucane, J. and George B. in the King against Weldon for High Treason at the Commission held 14th December 1795.

in ameliorating their Condition:- when the only[1] price which they paid to the [30] State for protection had been remitted, and the burden transferred to their Landlords- when they had been relieved, in a great degree, of Tythe, at the expence of the Protestant Clergy - when a liberal Provision had been appropriated to the Education of the Roman Catholic Clergy – and above all, when a Protestant Legislature, by a bold and enlightened policy, struck off these Religious and Political Fetters, which for a Century had galled the great body of our Fellow-Subjects: – tell them, that, false to the acknowledged Loyalty of their own Communion, the first use they [31] have made of long-lost freedom, the first record of their gratitude for this accumulation of Bounty, was a foul Conspiracy, with the Eternal Enemy of the British Empire, to dethrone that virtuous and beneficent Monarch who had himself become a Mediator for the Catholic Body with his Parliament of Ireland! to bend the neck of free-born Irishmen to the vile yoke of French Usurpers drenched in blood; of the fiercest Domination that ever blotted the pages of history, or scourged any portion of the human race! Tell them, that their Guilt is the highest in the Scale of Crimes – that the Punishment which awaits them is the severest known to the law – that the public indignation is at its height, and calls aloud for vengeance on them - and that no resource remains but that they return forthwith to their Allegiance, and to those long deserted paths [32] of Industry in which alone they can find competence, and comfort for their unhappy families, balm for their wounded consciences, and favour from their offended GOD. Tell them, finally, that the best evidence they can give of contrition, and the surest title they can have to Mercy, will be a voluntary disclosure (before any information shall be given against themselves) of their whole Plot, and of the nefarious Incendiaries who have thus led them to destruction.

The Detail in which I have so long detained you will not, I trust, be deemed altogether foreign to the Duties of this day. We are assembled here to let loose the terrible Judgments of the Law, even Death itself, upon comparatively small offences against property; knowing at the [E - 33] same time that Principles are instilled, and Plots conceived, which would confound all Property and its Owners in one undistinguishable ruin. Can we with a safe conscience execute those avenging Laws upon paltry Plunderers, unless we also, in our several capacities, exert our authority to stifle these levelling and pestilential principles, which have

[1] The Hearthmoney Act, which transferred that Tax from all Houses having but one Hearth to such as have more; the Barren Land Act, which exempted all Heath and waste unimproved ground from Tythe for seven years after improvement; the great Catholic Act, which gave to the Catholic, in common with the Protestant Peasantry, every political privilege of which that Order of the Community is susceptible - these liberal measures, calculated generally for the relief of the poor at the expence of the Rich, were among the many excellent Laws of the Westmorland Government.

generated so many and such enormous crimes? Unless we use our best endeavours to trace to their Sources, and cut off, those waters of bitterness which overspread and pollute our Land? If there be any Fiends amongst us capable of "this deep damnation," any who, skulking behind in dastardly concealment, have urged their unhappy Victims down the Precipice, such are the proper [34] objects to select for punishment, and who of course demand your most persevering and determined inquiry. And therefore all Persons and Societies of that description, if any be known to you within our jurisdiction, I recommend to your most serious attention and severest animadversion.- So also all Houses, in which those seditious and treasonable Associations and Committees assemble, of which you have any knowledge, or shall receive information, should be Presented as Common Nuisances. The Publicans, who knowingly suffer their Houses to be converted to such Criminal purposes, (and it is incredible that they can be Strangers thereto) are deeply implicated in the guilt of the Conspirators; and the only question upon their Trial would be, whether they were Principals in the Treason [E 2-35] for receiving and comforting Traitors, or guilty only of an atrocious and most penal Misdemeanor in concealing the Treason.- And the Magistrates will, I trust, forgive me, if I solemnly conjure them, in the presence of the assembled County, to be particularly chaste and cautious at this juncture in granting Licences – to have a vigilant eye upon all Public Houses in their several Vicinities – to proceed summarily and severely against all unlicensed Publicans- and to withdraw their Licenses from all Publicans, whose conduct and character justify Suspicion; but Those, above all, who keep their Houses open at unseasonable hours. It would indeed be a Regulation of great public advantage, to shut up all places of mean and obscure resort at an earlier hour, than might perhaps be necessary in times less [36] critical. There can be no hardship in requiring men to retire early to rest, who should rise early to earn their daily bread. It is in the Dead of Night, when all Nature seeks repose – all but Animals of Prey – that conspirators assemble, and hatch dark and bloody Crimes. And it is in those Hotbeds of corruption and debauchery, that the first seeds of Vice and Criminality are sown, which afterwards ripen into full-blown Guilt, and find such incessant exercise for this and every other Criminal Tribunal.

Upon the face of the Calendar two men appear committed for plundering a Dwelling-house of Arms, and two more for administering unlawful Oaths. Charges of so serious a nature at all times demand your gravest attention, but more especially when such are [37] known to be among the crimes of Defenders. Gentlemen, let me recommend to you in these Cases (as indeed I most seriously do on every occasion of importance and doubt) to call the Prosecutors before you, and to sift and search them with all your diligence. Such Personal Examination will not only enable you to form a competent and sound judgment upon these particular Charges; but may also lead you to further discoveries touching the general Plot, which I make no doubt it is your wish, as it is your duty and interest, to pursue through all its mazes and concealments.

Gentlemen, I shall not trespass farther upon your time than just to remind you, that you are the Constitutional Guardian of the Lives and dearest Interests of your Fellow-subjects; that you are the sacred Shield of [38] Innocence against the strong arm of Power, Wealth, and Malice; and that whenever a Grand Jury find a Bill of Indictment upon insufficient Evidence, they betray the important Post committed to them by the Law; they do an irreparable Injury to the Party accused, and degrade into a mere formality one of the noblest bulwarks provided for Civil Liberty by our unrivalled Constitution.

THE SUBSTANCE OF A **CHARGE** DELIVERED TO THE **GRAND JURY** OF THE ***COUNTY OF HERTFORD***, On *Monday* the 7th Day of *March*, 1796. BY THE **HON. MR. JUSTICE GROSE.** LONDON: PRINTED FOR JOHN STOCKDALE, PICCADILLY. 1796.

Price, Sixpence, Or One Guinea per Hundred.

[A 2]

MARCH 8, 1796.

At a MEETING of the GRAND JURY at the Assizes for the County of Hertford,

resolved unanimously,

THAT the Foreman be desired to convey to the Hon. SIR NASH GROSE, Knight, one of the Justices of his Majesty's Court of King's Bench, the respectful and cordial acknowledgements of the Grand Jury of this County, for the able, judicious, and well-timed CHARGE delivered by him from the Bench on the opening of the Commission of Oyer and Terminer, and General Gaol Delivery, at Hertford, on Monday the 7th of March instant, containing matter of the most important nature, and expressed in terms, which, whether [4] We consider the authority from which they are derived, or the excellence of the sentiments themselves, are most happily calculated to inspire and to confirm, in all ranks of men, a sincere veneration for our Holy Religion, a dutiful submission to the Laws, and a steady attachment to the true principles of our invaluable Constitution; and earnestly to request, in the name of the Grand Jury of this County, that he will consent to the printing and publication of the same.

(Signed)

William Baker, Foreman
John Houblon
Ralph Winter
Thomas Hope Byde
John Baron Dickenson
Michael Hankin
John Rooke
George Stanforth
Francis Carter Serancke
Phillip Hollingworth
Thomas Blackmore
James Packard Ince
James Lucas
John Ralph
Joseph Walker
Stephen Wilson
William Newdick
Justinian Casamajor

John Cheshyre
Adolphus Meetkerke
Robert Dimsdale.
Simeon Howard
William Smith

[A 3]
THE
SUBSTANCE OF A CHARGE,
&c. &c.

Gentlemen of the Grand Jury,

WORDS cannot better describe the general outline of your duty, than those of the oath which you have taken. – "You are diligently to enquire and true presentment make. – You are not to present any one for envy, hatred, or malice; nor leave any one unpresented for love, fear, favour, or affection. – But to present things, truly, as they shall come to your knowledge." Thus are you, Gentlemen, become the Grand Inquest for this County, called together by the King, for the purpose of administering justice to his people, and impanelled, under the sanction of an oath, to execute those laws, by which society in this kingdom is holden together. [6]

So long as the world is inhabited by finite, imperfect beings, it will happen that offences come – For the protection of those against whom they are committed, and the punishment of those who may commit them, restraints are formed, and laws are made.

The primary object of the law, is to preserve entire the Government of the country, as it has been constituted by our ancestors. – For this purpose are enacted the statutes respecting High Treason, and for this purpose have been instituted prosecutions against persons suspected of that crime; and against others, whose conversation, or writings, have tended to excite Sedition.[1]

That such prosecutions should have been necessary, to every good man must be matter of surprise and concern – of surprize, that men should attempt to subvert a Constitution, the laws of which are made, administered, and corrected, as occasion may require, by ourselves-a Constitution which it has been the work of ages to perfect, has been the pride of English-[A 4-7] men, the envy of surrounding nations, and which our ancestors have delivered down to us, with a jealous care; - of concern, because these attempts lead to the substitution of idleness, spoil, and plunder, for industry; of atheism, for religion; and of anarchy, for government.

I am happy that I am not called upon to address you more particularly

[1] Here, and in the following paragraph, Grose made an allusion to the political trials of 1794 and the aftermath of the first years of the French revolution.

on this subject, by any commitments in your calendar, from which I may presume, that the inhabitants of this county know, and feel, the blessings of the Constitution under which they live; the most prominent features of which are, that every class[1] of men is equally intitled to participate in the benefit of its laws – that the highest are not above the law - that the lowest are within its protection.

The next object of the law, is to protect our lives, our persons, and our propperty.

Happily for your feelings, and my own, there appears no charge in the calendar of any offence against the first of these, I mean murder, [8] or manslaughter -offences, at the bare recital of which, humanity must shudder.

The other charges are, in general, such as your experience has rendered you perfectly conversant with.[2] – I shall not, therefore, trouble you with any comment upon the nature of them, except one– I mean that of Robbery.

This offence consists in taking from the person, or in the presence of another, by force, or by putting him in fear substituted for force, any property, of however small value, belonging to or in the possession of, the person robbed.

Within this definition are included the acts of those who by force seize provisions, which have been brought, or are in their way to market, from the persons under whose care they are. – This offence is a very bad one, because it leads to a total disregard of property and of the law, and to the taking, what is called by such offenders, the law into their own hands. In any well-regulated state this ought [9] not to be done-in this country there is not a pretence for resorting to such a conduct; since, by the laws of the country, recourse may be had to the courts of justice, by any one who has a complaint to make, whether that complaint be of a publick or a private nature.

But the offence is as impolitic, as it is criminal; as these acts of violence tend to raise the price of provisions, by the terror excited in the minds of those who would otherwise supply the market, but who, fearing the loss of their goods, withhold them: – Still worse is the wanton destruction of the necessaries of life – it savors of folly, as much as of wickedness. – By both these offences, the end aimed at is defeated, by the means used to attain it: – the price of the commodity destroyed is raised to the consumer, by the increased scarcity; – the laws of property, which should be held sacred, are violated, and the public peace is endangered. The

[1] Note here the use of the word 'class', repeated throughout this text.

[2] The allusion made by this, as well as by many a, magistrate to the experience of the jurors is a proof that they were often called upon to sit, and were empanelled with a certain regularity. See J.S. Cockburn & Th. A. Green eds., *Twelve Good Men and True…* (Princeton U.P., 1988): P. J. R. King, "Illiterate Plebeians, Easily Misled…" 254–304.

offence is capital, and I mention it thus publickly, that the ignorant and deluded may be apprized of the extent of the offence, and that he, who, [10] knowingly, and obstinately, persists in the violation of the law, may know the the conviction of him will be indubitably followed by punishment.

The offence, constituted as our laws are, is without excuse - because, by those laws, the rich are compelled to relieve the poor.- So long as a rich man has a loaf of bread, the poor man, for his subsistence, is entitled to a share of it – not by force, but, by that peaceable allotment which the statutes made for the relief of the poor point out.

Without, however, resorting to compulsion, we know that it is not in the nature of an Englishman to suffer a fellow creature to perish for want, which it is in his power to relieve:– In proof of this assertion, I need only refer to the charitable donations existing in every county: and would further refer to the daily attention which has been, and still is, paid to this subject by the legislature, and generous individuals, who are straining every nerve to [11] remove, or lessen, as far as may be, the discomforts of the existing scarcity.

It is my duty now to address you upon his Majesty's proclamation, against profaneness, immorality, and vice.

It has been admitted universally, that when this proclamation issued, the vice and immorality of the times called aloud for this parental admonition. The success of it, I fear, has not been such, that we dare flatter ourselves, that our attention may not still, with propriety, be called to the same subject. I am not vain enough to suppose that I can urge any thing new– it is, however, my duty to submit to you what has occurred to me upon it.

The purpose of it is to inforce obedience, not only that law which concerns our present temporal happiness, but to that, which, promulgated by the revelation of a supreme Being, is to interest us here and hereafter; as such, it is addressed to a kingdom, inhabited by men who [12] yet believe in a God; by men, who, grateful for slavation imparted to them by a beneficent Redeemer, believe in a future state.

Into the minds of persons like yourselves, to whose examples, and whose precepts, the lower classes of men will look up; it cannot be too strongly inculcated, how fit it is by every method to promote the desirable purposes of this proclamation; to teach men to be virtuous, and to keep them so, by encouraging habits of industry, and the practice of every moral and religious virtue. The prevention of crimes is a God-like act, far better than the correction of them.

We are all links of one great chain- the stronger every link, the firmer the whole will be. – In the honest labour of the inferior classes of men the rich are interested, who from their abundance are bound to relieve the poor in sickness and want, in return for that which the useful exertions of the one contribute, not merely to the luxury of the other, but also to [13] the improvement of those means by which the happiness of the whole community is extended and secured. Thus, in the industry, the morality, the temperance, and virtue, of every individual, the body politick, in all its parts, is deeply interested. Virtue and happiness go hand in hand, even in this world:– and the greater the stock of moral and religious virtue is among men, the happier the general state of society will be.

By the laws and government of a country, the minds and morals of its inhabitants are formed; by inculcating obedience to those laws, virtue is propagated. Of that obedience the people of this country have known, and still feel, the good effects. They have for their reward, honour, freedom, happiness. They are arrived at a degree in splendor in arms, arts, in commerce, and in literature,-equalled by few nations,-exceeded by none. If I were asked how we may best deserve these blessings, and retain that proud pre-eminence which we have attainted among the nations of the earth, my [14] answer would be, " Let us fear our God, honour our King, obey the laws ourselves, promote and enforce obedience to them in others." To enforce this obedience is the purpose for which we are met; that purpose, I have no doubt, will be effected by your attention to the duty imposed upon you, to the honour of yourselves, and the satisfaction of the public.

Lord Kenyon's Charge to the Jury, from: **The Speeches** (at length) of THE HONOURABLE *T. Erskine, & S. Kyd, Esq.* at the COURT OF KING'S BENCH, WESTMINSTER, on Saturday, June 24, 1797, of the TRIAL OF T. WILLIAMS, for publishing *Paine's Age of Reason* ; SECOND EDITION CORRECTED. LONDON: J.S. Jordan, C. Chapple, and C. Wood. 1797.

p. 28 Lord Kenyon then made the following CHARGE TO THE JURY.

Gentlemen of the Jury,

Being now in possession of all the facts of this case, and convinced, in my own mind, what conclusion ought to be drawn from them, I am not sure, that it is necessary to say any thing at all to you upon the subject. Gentlemen, before you proceed to decide on the merits of this or any other cause, it is proper to see whether the parties litigating stand in a fair light before you. I was extremely hurt when the learned Counsel for the Defendant thought fit to state to you, with very considerable emphasis, and a very determined tone of voice, that this was a scandalous prosecution. I cannot help wishing that sentence had not been uttered. Who commenced this prosecution, I certainly know not. But from what fell from the very learned Counsel who has just sat down, I am inclined to suppose it proceeded from a society of Gentlemen instituted for the most important of all purposes, for preserving the morals of the people; a society composed of Clergymen and Laymen of the most respectable character in this kingdom, who, seeing how the country is overrun with profligacy and wickedness, which boldly raise their heads in defiance [29] of the law of the land, were determined to see whether, in the first place, by admonition and advice, they could not stop the torrent of vice and immorality; and secondly, if that should fail, to try what could be done by punishment. If people, with the very best intentions, carry on prosecutions that are oppressive, the end may not always perhaps sanctify the means. But the manner in which this prosecution has been conducted, is certainly not oppressive; for instead of proceeding in the more expansive mode, the Prosecutors went before a Grand Jury of the Country: and it was necessary to obtain the opinion of that Grand Jury before the party could be put in process.

Gentlemen, we sit here in a Christian Assembly to administer the laws of the land, and I am to take my knowledge of what the law is from that which has been sanctioned by a great variety of legal decisions. I am bound to state to you what my predecessors in Mr. Woolston's case (2 Strange, 834) stated half a century ago in this Court, of which I am an humble Member, namely, that the Christian Religion is part of the law of the land. Christianity from its earliest institution met with its opposers. Its professors were very soon called upon to publish their apologies for the doctrines they had embraced. In what manner they did that, and whether they had their advantages of their adversaries, or sunk under the superiority of their arguments, mankind for near two thousand years have had an opportunity of judging. They have seen what Julian, Justin Martyr, and other Apologists have written, and have been of opinion the argument was in favour of those very publications. The world has been lately favoured with another apology from a most learned and respectable prelate, who calls his work *An Apology for the Christian Religion.* I shall not decide between the merits of the one and the other. The publications themselves are in the hands of the world; and I sincerely wish in the concluding language of the work to which I have just referred (I do not affect to use the very words) I sincerely wish that the author of the work in question may become a partaker of that faith in revealed religion, which he has so grossly defamed, and may be enabled to make his peace with God [30] for that disorder which he has endeavoured to the utmost of his power to introduce into society. We have heard to day, that the light of Nature, and the contemplation of the works of creation are sufficient, without any other revelation of the Divine Will. Socrates, Plato, Xenophon, Tully – each of them in their turns professed they wanted other lights; and knowing and confessing that God was good, they took it for granted the time would come when he would impart a farther Revelation of his Will to mankind. Though they walked as it were in a cloud, darkly, they hoped their posterity would almost see God face to face. This condition of mankind has met with reprehension to day. But I shall not pursue this argument. Fully impressed with the great truths of religion, which, thank God, I was taught in my early years to believe, and of which the hour of reflection and inquiry, instead of producing any doubt, has fully confirmed me in.

I expected the learned Counsel for the Defendant would have differed the case of the Publisher from that of the Author of this work; that he would have endeavoured to convince you that whatever guilt might belong to the Author, nothing was imputable to the Publisher. He has, however, to my utter surprise, exactly reversed the case. He tells you, it was orignally published at Paris in 1794; that the feelings of the Author's friends were wounded by this work, which I call a nefarious publication, and that it was in a great measure forgotten; and you are now called upon to judge of the merits or demerits of the publisher, who has brought forth a still-born work, forgotten by every body, till he ventured in defiance of the verdicts of mankind on the Author's political works, to send it forth among the inhabitants of this country. Unless it was for the most malignant purposes, I cannot conceive how it was published. It is however for you to judge of it, and to do justice between the Public and the Defendant.

The Jury instantly found the Defendant – GUILTY.

A **CHARGE** TO THE GRAND JURY OF THE COUNTY OF GLOCESTER, DELIVERED AT EPIPHANY SESSIONS, JANUARY 10, 1797. BY THE REV. JOHN FOLEY, CHAIRMAN. PUBLISHED AT THE SPECIAL REQUEST OF THE COURT OF QUARTER SESSIONS And sold by HOUGH, WASHBOURN, and EVANS, Booksellers, in Glocester, and by all other Booksellers within the County, at six pence each.

[B]

GENTLEMEN OF THE GRAND JURY,

It gives me pleasure to acquaint you, that, on inspecting the Calendar of the Prisoners who are to take their trials at the present Sessions, I see nothing in the nature of their crimes, that requires any particular observation. The same remark may be applied to their numbers, which, [2] considering the extent and population of the county, are comparatively small. From the wise regulations and admirable system of police adopted in your places of confinement,[1] there is reason to hope, that these unhappy persons will return home, improved in their morals; that they will, by their future behaviour, make amends for their past misconduct; that they will gradually recover the stand of virtue, and become useful members of society. These pleasing hopes are in some measure justified by experience. Few examples are to be met with in your Gaol Register of second commitments: and it is with the utmost satisfaction I announce to you, that one instance has occured of a Prisoner who, though completely abandoned on his first admission, was yet so thoroughlky reformed by your Prison discipline, as to be hired on the expiration of his confinement into a respectable family, where his behaviour during the ensuing twelvemonth was so truly meritorious, as to entitle him to that reward, which the Penitenciary Act, with no less

[1] This is an allusion to the untiring efforts of Sir George Onesiphorus Paul to improve the jail of Gloucester, and life within it; see also J. Howard, *The State of the Prisons*...1776; the efforts, and the act sponsored by Alexander Popham to improve health conditions, etc. See J.M. Beattie, *Crime and the Courts in England 1600–1800* (Princeton U.P., 1986); G. Lamoine, *Littérature et justice pénale en Angleterre au 18e siècle,* (Paris: Didier-Erudition, 1987).

wisdom than [B2-3] humanity, holds forth as an encouragement to returning virtue.[1]

GENTLEMEN, Persuaded as I am, that you are fully competent to the office you are now called upon to execute, I shall not take up your time with giving you instructions, that must be needless and superflous. On one point alone, you will permit me to drop a few hints, which I wish you to consider on your return to your respective homes, and to give them that attention, which you shall think they may deserve.

That poverty, the sure offspring of idleness and ignorance, supplies your Gaols with the [4] greatest number of their inhabitants, is a truth that cannot be denied. Yet your Poor Rates have increased most rapidly, amounting now to the enormous and almost incredible sum of upwards of two millions and a half per annum, exclusive of the endowments of Hospitals and Infirmaries, not to mention the vast number of Parish Benefactions and Charitable Legacies and Donations distributed at stated seasons of the year.[2] Making every allowance for an increased population; for the weight of accumulated taxes; for the high price of provisions and necessaries of life; and the disproportion perhaps in some instances of the wages of labour; still it is evident that the aggre-[5] gate sum[3] ought to be, and in fact would be, if properly applied, more than adequate to the purposes for which it was raised. Yet the reverse we find to be the fact, and it is difficult to determine which of the parties express greater dissatisfaction, – the Payer of the Rates at the perpetual demands made upon his industry, or the Pauper at the scantiness of the allowance made to his misery. The evil is become so enormous as to call for Parliamentary interposition, and the Legislature are now busily employed in providing such remedies as shall be judges most likely to prove effectual. An affair of such magnitude requires the deepest deliberation: and as much time may probably elapse, before any thing conclusive is determined upon, I shall make no apology for submitting my ideas to you upon [6] the

[1] It is to be observed, that many persons have deserved the reward, though only one has stepped forwards to claim it. It would be improper to mention his name: be it sufficient to observe, that his history is an ample justification of the wisdom of the Glocester Gaol Regulation. Months and months elapsed before any impression was made upon him. At length, humanity and tenderness overcame every obstacle, and this hardened piece of marble, as he was for a considerable period, became as ductile and as pliant as the softest wax.

[2] See Frost, Bowyer, and Davis, *passim.* It should be observed, that many articles enter into the Poor Rates, which, strictly speaking, do not belong to them, such as Constables' Bills, Law Expences, Bridge Money, or what is paid to the County Stock, Premiums for destroying Vermin, &c. &c. not to mention that in some Parishes the extraordinary expenditure, for the Repair of the Highways, is included.

[3] Whether we take the population of this kingdom according to Mr. Price's estimate or that of his opponent still the same conclusion will follow. It is also to be observed, that I have totally omitted the thousands which are dispensed by the private hand of charity.

subject, trusting that they may in the interim be of some service, may be the means of reducing your Rates, and mending withal the condition of the Poor.

The source of far the greater part of the mischief seems to me to be the inattention, to give it no harsher name, of your Parish Officers – I mean the Churchwardens and the Overseers of the Poor, who content themselves with executing a part and a very small part too of the statutes, whilst they totally neglect the spirit of them. The laws are good, but the execution is bad. I need not inform you that the leading features of the system of the Poor Laws are these: To provide materials of work for such as are healthy, strong, and unemployed – To relieve with money those only who are aged, impotent or infirm – To hold Monthly Meetings for the sake of investigating the situation and relieving the complaints of the distressed– To be regular in binding as apprentices the children of such parents, as, on account of the numerous families, or other sufficient reasons, are unable to provide for them themselves – And where poverty is occasioned by idleness or dissipation, there to fix a proper stigma upon the offender by withholding assistance, unless he submits to the opprobrium of wearing for a time the Parish badge.[1] All these regulations are founded in the most consummate wisdom, and breathe the purest philanthropy. To how great a degree they have deviated from, and what consequences have ensued upon that deviation, you too well know by fatal experience. In many places, your Churchwardens seem unapprized that the care of the Poor is entrusted to them jointly with the Overseers.[2] The Monthly Meetings are [8] neglected. The Pauper Children are suffered to remain at home, where they are bred up in sloth and ignorance, with their usual wretched concomitants, filth and disease. The Parish badge is unknown. Few materials for work are provided. Little employment is thought of. And the Overseers, fully taken up with their own business, relieve all indiscriminately with Money - the most sure and certain method that could possibly be thought of to encourage future application.[3] At the commencement of a new year (for the office is annual[4]) the new Overseers either proceed [C-9] in the same beaten

[1] As the Act enjoining the badge may admit of two interpretations, I have taken it in its best sense, that which is not repugnant to humanity.

[2] To so great a pitch has this been carried, that I have known an instance of an Overseer positively denying the authority of the Churchwarden to interfere, either in granting relief or making the rate.

[3] Exclusive of this objection, it is too well known, that when Money is given, it is often spent at the Public-house, instead of being appropriated to the relief of the family.

[4] Perhaps this is one of the greatest deficiencies in the Act of Elizabeth. The law has flung the *onus* upon the substantial householders only, and with a view to render this *onus* more even and less perceptible, has limited the duration to one year. It has the appearance of great wisdom and impartiality, but the consequence is, that by the time an Overseer understands his business, and the real situation of his paupers, his office expires, and his

ruinous tract, or perhaps seeing the improvident waste of their predecessors, and wishing to make a reform, withhold the usual weekly allowance; the consequence of which is that the younger part of the Paupers, unaccustomed to labour, ignorant of the proper modes of setting about it, destitute of all principle, religious and moral, and with their appetites rendered keen by want, have immediate recourse to pilfering and thieving; acting cautiously at first for fear of detection, but gradually becoming more and more emboldened by success, till at length [10] discovery ensues, the vengeance of the Law overtakes them, and they find themselves compelled to exchange the wretched walls of their cottage for the still more dreary and melancholy ones of a Prison. I appeal to you, Gentlemen, whether this statement be not too often founded upon fact. To you too I again appeal, to say, whether it be consistent with the feelings of justice or humanity, to be severe in exacting punishment on those unhappy Beings, whose criminality has been the result of ignorance and want of instruction, to provide against which the Legislature has appointed proper Officers, armed with extraordinary powers, but who have neglected those powers entrusted with them for that important purpose. I then call upon you, Gentlemen, to make use of that respectability and influence which you possess to enforce in your respective Parishes an opposite conduct. Regardless of rotation,[1] re-[C 2-11] commended to the choice of your Magistrates for the office of Overseers none but substantial Householders, conscientious men, who, you have reason to believe from their past conduct, will do their duty. Go yourselves to the Monthly Meetings, and insist upon the regular attendance there of both Churchwardens and Overseers, or else let them be fined for their neglect.[2] Enquire diligently into the state of your actual Poor, and of the class but one degree above them, who suffer in silence and with patience, and whom accident, sickness, want of employment, or other causes, are likely to reduce to the same wretched low condition. With respect to [12]

---

successor has all to begin anew. In case the much-talked of Bill, now pending, should not take place, might it not be adviseable to empower Parishes to hire Overseers, payable not out of the Poor Rates at large, but by those persons only who are eligible? There would be a difficulty in drawing the line, and in defining the word substantial householder, which certainly, in this respect, is a comparative term. Still I think it to be practicable. As the Law stands at present, such a practice could not be supported, as is evident from the Cheltenham case – R. *v.* Welch and al.

[1] Whilst the Overseer's Office is attended with so much trouble, it is not to be wondered at, if the Parishioners prefer the apparently equitable mode of taking it by turns. There are, however, many insuperable objections against it, as must be evident to any one, who will think for a moment upon the subject. The same wretched system prevails whith respect to the appointment of Constables and Surveyors of the Highways; and the consequences I need not point out.

[2] 73 [sic] Eliz. c. 2. Overseers, neglecting to meet on a Sunday once a month in the parish church, forfeit 20 shillings.

these latter, adopt that most wise and humane practice of that gentle and peaceable description[1] of men, who, the moment they have reason to believe any of their brethren are making earnest but ineffectual struggles against adversity, instantly stretch out the helping hand, and by thus affording them timely relief, enable them to restore their lost ground. Discriminate between those who become poor through age, infirmity, a numerous family, or the visitation of Heaven, and those who are made so by their own profligacy, dissipation, and idleness. Put a stigma upon the latter, but only till they shew symptoms of reform: the sufferings of the former alleviate by every mode that tenderness can invent or humanity suggest. Keep exact lists of the numbers of your poor families, with the respective ages of the younger part of them, and during that interval which subsists between the period when [12] children are first capable of gentle labour, and that at which the Law directs them to be apprenticed, establish Schools, where they may be taught such work as is suitable to their tender years, and may be instructed in the first principles of their duty to GOD and man. If the parents will not permit their children to be sent to such schools, do you withhold relief. When they are arrived at maturer years, apprentice them out, ever keeping in view the wise provisions of 32 G. 3. c. 57[2]. Calculate the expences of every pauper family with their acknowledged earnings, and where the latter fall short of their necessary expenditure[3], supply the deficiency by a weekly allowance, but withholding that allowance until their own labour has been previously exerted. Compel your Officers[4] to [14] provide

[1] A Pauper Quaker is I believe unknown. – See Dr. Letsom's late Tract.

[2] An act for the further regulation of parish apprentices...Pickering, vol.37.

[3] See on this subject Mr. Davis's publication, wherein is most clearly evinced the insufficiency of the agricultural poor man's wages for the maintenance of his family.

[4] A question of an important nature here presents itself, with respect to those Parishes which are purely agricultural, or wherein no manufactures are established - What employment can be found for the Poor? I think the answer is not difficult. Let the Pauper Children of both sexes, till they are apprenticed, be instructed in spinning and knitting coarse wool and worsted; and although the produce of their labour, if sold, will not amount to the prime cost, yet still I contend, it is an ultimate gain; habits of industry are acquired; temptations to thieving are avoided; emulation is excited; the mind is gratified with the attainment of knowledge and dexterity in trivial matters, which may be the foundation of further acquisitions in more important concerns. The Lincolnshire practice, see Mr. Boyer already quoted, points out the purposes to which the produce of this labour may be applied. Granted, that the stockings are coarse, that the cloth is bad, that the texture is uneven and unequal.- Still the Poor are to be cloathed, and in most parishes there are benefactions of warm garments, &c. to be disposed of. Instead then of going to the shops for these articles, apply to your home manufactory. But what, you will say, shall we do with grown up persons, who have no employment? It is too late for them to learn. Granting you the full force of the objection, which is perhaps stated in rather too strong terms, I would recommend the mode adopted in the North of Oxfordshire. The occupiers of land, by agreement among themselves, employ by turns, in proportion to their estates, all persons who complain of their inability to obtain work. The persons thus employed go by the name

a proper stock of materials to work upon, and permit them to relieve with Money [15] those alone who are unable to work. If you have a Workhouse[1] in your Parish, inspect it frequently; and whilst you exact de-[16] corum, industry, and subordination on one hand, see on the other that authority be tempered with mildness; that government be exerted without severity; that there be plenty without waste, and œconomy without avarice. All these regulations are contained in the spirit and the letter of your Poor Laws, and if duly enforced would make them answer their great design – the comfort and relief of indigence, the encouragement of industry and virtue, and the punishment of idleness and vice.

The conscientious, humane person (and such, Gentlemen, is, I trust, your character) will proceed a few steps further. Anxious to make his fellow creatures happy, because he knows it is the future road to make them good and honest, he will encourage by his influence and example the establishment of Friendly Societies[2]. [D-17] He will, if in the neighbourhood of large towns, be active in supporting Dispensaries for providing Medical Assistance on a plan similar to that laudable one[3] now existing in the Clothing part of this County. If he be in the vicinity of waste and uncultivated Commons[4], he will endeavour to procure liberal

---

of Roundsmen. They are paid by the Task or Great. The advantages resulting from it are many and obvious, not to mention, that by this mode the land obtains frequently an extraordinary degree of culture, which amply repays itself.

[1] A Workhouse, without constant inspection, is too apt to be perverted to bad purposes. – I wish not to cast a general censure, but when left to the sole management of the master, with little or no controul from others, especially where the Poor are farmed, it is a nuisance to the inhabitants. With a view of deterring others from seeking relief, a system of harshness and tyranny is adopted – all relief is refused, unless the whole family consents to come within the house with their little property.- No distinction is made between age, infirmity, and causal distress, and persons of a different denomination.The consequence is, that the Paupers, rather than submit to such treatment, prefer want; but nature must be satisfied, and thieving is the result. – A late Act has most wisely vested in the Magistrate a power of granting relief out of a Workhouse, fetttering it at the same time with such prudent regulations, as to prevent this power from being exerted to improper purposes.

[2] Pure unmixed good is seldom to be obtained. The late humane Act to prevent the vexatious Removal of Paupers will, it is to be feared, operate to the injury of these Societies. As long as the privilege of being unremoveable was confined in a great measure to the Members, it of course was a high encouragement to them.

[3] See the annual account published in the Glocester Paper.

[4] Where the legal Owner has objections to give up his right, without any consideration whatever, perhaps a mode somewhat similar to the following might be adpted. Let the value of the land, in its uncultivated state, be fairly taken, a lease be granted at a nominal rent for 99 years, and a power given to the occupier to purchase at any period, but the price to increase in proportion as the expiration of the lease approaches. For the first ten years, the purchase-money should be little more than the value of the land as a Waste. Could it be possible to prevent alienation, it would be an improvement.- Give a man property of his own, and you of course connect him with the Soil. He soon becomes industrious and generally honest. The fear of retaliation will prevent him from injuring his

portions of them to be [18] allotted for the support of large families, free from all taxes as well as tithe.– He will be punctual in paying his Labourers on the eve of Market-days, in order to enable them to deal for Ready Money.[1] – He will provide that the Weights and Balances of the Shopkeepers be not deficient.– He will discountenance Public-houses, especially in retired solitary situations, as the bane of industry, the destruction of health, and the ruin of morality. – He will frequently visit the Cottages[2] of the Poor, and by gentle modes of [19] persuasion will inculcate the necessity of sobriety, diligence, neatness and cleanliness, together with an œconomical managment of the little earnings they obtain.- He will then see[3] the sufferings of the lower class, the only method of acquiring a [20]proper idea of them, and will be at least as active in removing their miseries, as he will be earnest to punish their vices.[4] If the Laws of Society call upon him to do the latter, those of humanity and compassion will be as loud in behalf of the former. Above all, he will set his face against that barbarous, that wicked and destructive mode, adopted I trust by very few Parishes in this County, the cruel mode of withholding relief from an unhappy man in the time of his distress, 'till he has first pawned or expended his little all, the slow hard-earned savings of an extraordinary course of industrious labour for a

---

neighbour. The present mode of granting leases of wastes for three lives, often impoverishes the Labourer, and enriches the Lord of the Manor alone.

[1] When the poor man deals upon credit, his articles are often bad in quality, the price is high, and he gets so involved as to be unable to extricate himself.- At length a day of reckoning arrives, and the County Court finishes his ruin.

[2] If the non residence of the Clergy be blameable, that of the Gentry is still more so, because the consequences are far worse. The Lady Bountiful of former days no longer exists. Can it be a matter of wonder, that the lower classes are ignorant and brutal, when we see that their superiors have entirely deserted them; that little attention is paid to their sufferings, that there is no example to humanize them, no hospitality to encourage them. Subscriptions for their occasional relief are numerous and great, but these are far from being an adequate remedy to the evil complained of.

[3] I maintain it, that no other method, but that of being an actual eye-witness of their sufferings, can make a true and lasting impression. The mind naturally turns from woe, and is compelled, as it were, in self-defence to eradicate theremebrance. The following anecdote will supply the place of a thousand arguments: – A Lady, at –, returning from church on a remarkably cold day, almost perishing from the severity of the weather, and struck with the idea of the sufferings of her fellow-creatures, who were probably destitute of fire as well as clothing, instantly pulled out of her purse five Guineas, which she directed the Butler immediately to expend in the purchase of coals for the Poor. A warm room, large fire, and a good dinner, in a few hours restored the Lady to her pristine heat; when ringing the bell, she enquired whether the Butler has bought the coals? – Being answered in the negative, she replied, Very well – Give me the money back – The weather is by no means so cold, as in the morning – I think I know a better mode of laying it out for the benefit of the Poor. My readers will easily guess at the occasion of the change of atmosphere, and how far it extended.

[4] Even for a man as well-disposed to the Poor as this clergyman, the idea prevails that they *have* vices, as if they were vicious by definition and virtue of their poverty.

long wearisome period of perhaps many past years. It is a mode as injudicious and impolitic as it is cruel; it defeats its own end, and cuts the very nerves of industry, sobriety, and œconomy.

Gentlemen – I will detain you no longer. – The subject was of too interesting a nature to be compressed within narrower terms. Again, therefore, I say, enforce your Statutes; for this purpose improve upon these imperfect hints, and I dare venture to promise you, that you will not only [21] mend the condition of the Poor, but will better your own. The lower ranks will look up to you as their true and real friends. No Sophistry will prevail on them to consider their interests as distinct and separate from your's; but they will look upon them as so blended, that the destruction of the one will be that of the other also. In short, you will by so doing take the most effectual method to reduce the Poor Rates; will prevent, rather than punish vice; will encourage industry and virtue; will render Gaols themselves less necessary; and establish so firm and compact an union between the different classes of society, as shall render your lives, your persons, and your property more secure; and, what is of no small consequence now, will place you at perfect ease from the turbulent attacks of domestic foes (if any such there be) and from the threatened invasion of foreign enemies.

Charge delivered at Easter sessions, 1797.[1]

Gentlemen of the grand jury,

THE expected alterations in the Poor Laws having not yet taken place, in consequence of the pressure of public business, the ancient system founded upon the 43d of Elizabeth is still to remain in force; and as the annual appointment of the persons principally commissioned to execute that system is now approaching, perhaps a few ob-[c-22] servations upon the nature of their office, and the mode in which they can best peform their duty, may be not altogether useless or unacceptable.

It is a striking and characteristic principle in the British Constitution, that no infringment can be made upon the property of the subject without the consent of his Representative: It has therefore often been a matter of surprise, especially among foreigners, that in every parish throughout the kingdom, a few individuals, should be permitted, under the title of Overseers, to lay a discretionary tax upon the property of their neighbours, and this with little or no controul whatever, either as to the sum they raise, or the mode they expend in, provided only that the assessment is made equally and impartially. The surprize is still further increased by the consideration, that this practice has been suffered to subsist in a kingdom dependent, in a great measure, for the high rank it holds, upon its extensive trade and commerce, wherein the active exertions of all its members seem to be more particularly necessary, and in which, of course, idleness is but one degree removed from vice. Accordingly political writers, both at home and abroad, have not been sparing in their censures upon the subject. The present effect of the English Poor Laws, say they, are the increase of beggars, the destruction of industry, the [C 2-23] encouragement of sloth, and a total want of subordination, and their future consequences must be still worse, the rates increasing so rapidly and enormously, as to threaten destruction to the State itself, inasmuch as they must soon reduce the payers to a level

[1] [I hardly know how, from the omission of a charge which ought not to have escaped my researches, to plead an excuse for those that may be misplaced, or have a wrong date. When, however, you are informed, that few of the Charges were dated by Mr. FOLEY, and that I found them not left in any kind of order, or even together; and when you consider the difficulties of ascertaining the true dates, you will not wonder if some of them should have escaped even the indefatigability and accuracy of our friend Mr. SANDIFORD, to whose kind assistance, not only this publication, but many others relating to the County are so greatly indebted.– W. L. B.] W L B=W. L. Baker who, as one of the executors of the Rev. Foley, edited in 1804 the Charges hereafter given. See introduction.

with those whom they pay, and thereby disable them from providing the necessary supply for the use of Government. On the other hand writers of a different complexion have been equally warm in extolling the system, as bearing the most consummate marks of wisdom, policy, and humanity. Perhaps the truth may lie between the two extremes. No human contrivance can be absolutely perfect: much less can it remain so for any long period. The best planned Laws may be perverted and defeated by changes of circumstances, length of time, and the ingenuity and depravity of mankind. The 43d of Elizabeth was by no means a hasty measure – it was not adopted on the spur of the occasion – it was the result of much serious enquiry and profound deliberation, matured by long experience; and seems rather to have been the consequence, than the cause, of some of those evils which are now laid to its charge. Be this as it may, one thing is certain, and I would wish to press it strongly on your attention, at this particular period. No other nation has a provision of this [24] nature made for its lower classes of society. It is impossible, that a poor man can, *amongst us*, ever perish for want. By this compulsory system of relief, the whole property of the Rich (landed as well as personal) is engaged, and as it were mortgaged, for their support. When therefore you hear it insidiously asserted, that all Governments are the same to the Poor, and that if our happy Constitution were subverted, they might gain, but could not possibly lose, in the general scramble and confusion, you may safely reply, that the assertion is by no means founded. The Poor have indeed in this kingdom much to lose – they would lose that ample support, which is now given them by the Laws, in case of the failure of their labour through age, illness, or misfortune, and would be left, as in the other parts of the universe, to depend upon the charity and benevolence of their richer neighbours, funds totally uncertain and precarious at best, and too often guided by caprice, inclination, or the whim of the moment.

From the extraordinary powers lodged in the hands of the Overseers, you must be sensible how important it is, that proper persons should be placed in the office. The appointment is indeed exclusively in the hands of the Magistrates, but for want of local knowledge, they expect that each parish should elect and return for their choice a [C 3-25] number of substantial householders. At the head of the list are placed the persons to whom the parishoners give the preference, and who therefore are in general made the objects of the Magistrate's choice. Without meaning the most distant disparagement, it is obvious, that the Publicans and inferior Tradesmen should, if possible, be omitted. The properest persons are doubtless those conscientious substantial householders, who, in case they are prevented by the multiplicity of their own business from executing the office in person, are in such easy circumstances, as to enable them to hire a deputy. I shall only add on this head, that to prevent delay, notice should be given to each person intended to be inserted in the list, that he may, should he chuse it, be enabled to state his objections on the day of appointment.

With respect to the persons appointed, I will presume, that henceforward they will observe the directions of the Statutes; that they will hold monthly meetings – apprentice out the Children of the Poor – find employment for the able of all ages – by suitable premiums encourage the industrious – affix the parish badge upon the idle and dissolute – be peculiarly attentive to the aged, and to those who have seen better days – and distinguish between casual assistance, and constant weekly relief, remembering that – whilst they are empowered to [26] give the former, they have no right to dispense the latter, without the order of a Magistrate, or the consent of the Vestry. To many this may seem to be executing the office with sufficient fidelity and diligence. Possibly it may have been so at the commencement of the institution, but the times are now altered, and require far greater exertions. Of this the Overseer will be convinced, if he reflects a moment on his peculiar situation. He must be sensible, that it is with the greatest difficulty some of the inferior payers are able to answer the repeated demands made upon them – that many of them work much harder than those who subsist by their bounty – that the greater part of the burden lies upon the landed property – that though benevolence will never scruple to extend almost her last mite in support of real distress, yet common sense revolts against the absurdity of saddling the frugal and industrious with the maintenance of the idle, the profligate, and the dissolute – and that the generous disdain of being supported at the public expence, which once characterised our Paupers, scarcely excepting the impotent themselves, no longer subsists. Hence he will conclude, that, though he is possessed of almost unlimited powers over the public purse, yet he is, for this very reason, bound to be more strictly economical. On the other hand he will recollect, that he is constituted, [27] as it were, the husband of the widow, the father of the orphan, the friend of the friendless, the sole patron and supporter of the aged and needy – that he is to be eyes to the blind, and feet to the lame– that whilst his humanity stimulates him to remove, or at least to alleviate, their several distresses, he must be upon his guard, as he will often be assailed by artful tales of fictitious woe, and pretended poverty– that it is his peculiar province and duty to discriminate between real misery, and that which assumes the garb of it –and that however difficult may be the task, especially in large districts, he is bound to perform it. Hence he will see the necessity of setting his face with stern severity against every species of imposture, for this amongst other reasons, that he may be the better enabled to afford more liberal relief to the truly necessitous and indigent. Even with respect to this latter class, he will soon be sensible, that the line he has to pursue is far from being always clear and obvious. The least insight into human nature will shew him, that too much liberality may encourage sloth or produce excess, whilst the contrary extreme, a rigid parsimony, will generate careless indifference, or terminate in despair.

Wherever then application is made for relief, let not the Overseer rest satisfied with the mere representation of the pauper, but let him make further [28] enquiry of the neighbours - let him take a personal inspection of the family, their number, their mode of employment, their place of habitation, and the immediate occasion of their distress - let him satisfy himself, whether he can make any effectual call either on parents or filial affection. If this be impossible; - if the Parents or Children be unable to come forward, he must in such case be guided by circustances, and act accordingly. Should the Small-pox break out, he will be sensible of the propriety of taking the opinions of the parishioners on the expediency of a general inoculation for such as chuse it at the public expence; and in all cases of contagious fevers, it is recommended to him, till he can procure medical assistance, to use his utmost endeavours to introduce cleanliness and fresh air into the cottages of the sick, as the best mode of stopping the progress of the disorder. The mere supply of fresh straw for the bedding of the diseased, and frequent sprinklings of vinegar on the floor, will often, during the hour of illness, produce the happiest effects; and upon recovery, scraping and white-washing the walls with hot lime will be found useful to prevent a relapse, and the spreading of the contagion. Policy and œconomy, as well as humanity, dictates the adoption of these measures.

The time will only permit me to drop some few cursory hints in addition to what has been already [29] said. With a view then to prevent uncessary litigations, which too often consume a great part of those sums that should be preserved sacred for the maintenance of the Poor, it is advisable in cases of removals always to give notice[1] to the Overseer of the parish where the settlement is supposed to be, that he may be present at the examination of the Pauper, if he chuses to attend. You will recollect that the Legislature, in order to better the condition of the Poor, and to enable them to take their labour to the best market, has wisely altered the law of removals. None, except persons of particular descriptions, can now be removed, because they are likely to be chargeable; they must actually be so, to give jurisdiction to the Magistrate. Two other statutes have been lately enacted, breathing the same spirit of benevolence and humanity to the lower classes of society. By the first, Workhouses are put under the more immediate inspection and governement of the Justices; and by the latter, a power is given to the Magistrates, in particular cases, to grant relief to such persons as in their judgment ought to be continued

[1] See Burn. – Title Poor, Section 3, Removals.

in their respective habitations at home, notwithstanding a Workhouse may have been provided by the parish.

Mountebanks and Quack Doctors disposing of plate and other articles by way of lottery, have been been [30] found by experience to be dreadful nuisances to the neighbourhood where they erect their stages: The Overseer therefore in these cases should send early information to the neighbouring Magistrates, wo are vested with full powers to punish the offenders.

The Church and Highway rates are on no consideration whatever to be blended with those of the Poor. The last are often censured most unjustly as being too exorbitant, when in fact the blame is to be imputed elsewhere.

The assessments should never be destroyed, but deposited at the end of the year in the parish chest.

The Constables should be directed to bring in their bills quarterly; and in case of refusal, without just cause of excuse, payment should be withheld.

The Overseer, previous to the expiration of his office, and before he applies for the Magistrate's allowance of his accounts, ought to submit them to a vestry meeting duly called. He will also understand, that all relief ordered by a Magistrate, is payable at the beginning of the week.

When firing is scarce, the Overseer will do well to recommend to his more opulent neighbours to lay in a competent stock of fuel during the summer, to supply the Poor with at prime cost. It will prevent depredations upon the hedges and other fences, which in cold severe weather it may ap-[31] pear harsh to punish; but which, if connived at, will undoubtedly lead to greater enormities.

As in most parishes there are two Overseers, if one of them could be induced to accept the office for a second year, it might be of great service to the new officer; but where this is not applicable, the deficiency will be be in some measure supplied, if observations on the state of the Poor were reduced into writing, and handed dow to the successor.

Addressing myself to a Glocestershire Grand Jury, I need not express my indignation at some practices, which have unfortunately been too prevalent elsewhere. No Overseer of this county will, I trust, ever so far forget his own character, as to have any share in, or benefit from, any contract for supplying the Paupers of his parish with the necessaries of life, or even the materials of labour. The same sacred regard to character will never permit him to suffer any parochial meetings to be held, except at the sole expence of the individuals who compose it. For a similar reason he will be strictly conscientious in appropriating the charitable legacies and benefactions, of which his parish is possessed, to the sole purpose for which they were given; remembering that it was the benevolent intention of the donors, not to relieve the pockets of the payers to the rates, but to render more comfortable the condition of the Poor. Actuated by the same motive, he will hold [32] in the highest detestation every effort to ease his own parish, and burthen that of others, by encouraging improper marriages among paupers, idiots, lunatics, or pregnant women. Should any one be so unmindful of his own honour and that of his country, as to be engaged in such nefarious practices, he may be assured, that, if prosecuted to conviction, he will feel the severest treatment of this Court.

These instructions, Gentlemen, you will take, as they are intended, in good part; and your Officers by a due observance of them will, I trust, give equal satisfaction to the Poor and the Rich; they will have the thanks of the one and the prayers of the other, and, what is superior to both, the approbation of their own consciences, together with the assurance of Divine Favour.

CHARGE DELIVERED AT EASTER SESSIONS, 1797.[1]

Gentlemen of the grand jury,

I FIND myself called upon to address you, rather in compliance with established custom, than from any real occasion that requires it. In the several bills to be brought before you, you are aware that you hear only the evidence in behalf of the Crown: you will therefore scrutinize, with a strict but impartial severity, the nature of that evidence, its admissibility, its weight, and its credibility: you will naturally require it to be clear, connected, and nearly certain and positive; and you will be cautious of exposing the accused party to the shame and ignominy, the expence and danger of a trial, from inadequate circumstances, or vague suggestions of probability.

The internal police of the Gaols of the County, Gentlemen, still continues such as to merit, and in- [34][2] deed surpass, the warmest commendations I can bestow upon it. The one great design which pervades and animates the whole, is to amend and reform; and by this means most congenial to humane nature, and therefore most efficacious – instruction and good usage. The unconvicted and the guilty, the criminal and the debtor, are never permitted to associate together. The different sexes are constantly kept asunder. You will also find, on a personal inspection, that the hardest labour required from the most atrocious criminals, has its proper interval of rest and refreshment; that the allowance of food, though plain and simple, is nutritive and amply sufficient; that all confinement underground, or in damp unhealthy cells, is unknown; that the lodging is warm and comfortable; that the rooms are clean, airy, and wholesome; that irons are never used except in cases of great necessity; that the man is never forgot in the prisoner; that the offence, rather than the offender, is the object of animadversion; and, in short, that so great is the attention paid both to the health and the instruction of the prisoners, that it becomes, on their return into society, a difficult matter to determine, whether their moral or their natural constitutions are the most amended and improved. For these regulations, Gentlemen, I need not say to whom you are indebted; regulations which, whilst they reflect [35] the highest honour on the humanity and good

[1] The date is probably wrong, since the previous one already bears 'Easter Sessions, 1797', being hand-numbered 2, whereas the present text is numbered 3.

[2] Again, pages are misnumbered in the original text: p. 33 which begins the 3rd text is not numbered, and the next one is p. 22, and thus down to the end of the book. Page numbers here are corrected accordingly.

sense of the Person who proposed, and the County which adopted them, will, I am persuaded, be most extensively beneficial to the community at large, not only in the present, but also in future generations.

Gentlemen, Admirable as these regulations are, you must be aware that they can affect those persons only who are doomed by the laws of their country to a temporary seclusion from society. But, as innocence is better than penitence, so every wise Legislature wishes to prevent crimes, if possible, rather than punish them. In this most important task, it is incumbent upon every man to take his share, because what is for the good of all, ought to be pursued by all. From those who think themselves unequal to active exertions in this line, a good example is required, or at least that negative virtue of withholding all encouragements to persons who, but for that encouragement, would not think of deviating into the paths of dishonesty. I make this observation principally on account of a practice which, I am sorry to say, prevails much in the extremity of this county, and which, I am persuaded, ultimatemy supplies your Gaols with a greater number of inhabitants, than almost any other crime that can be mentioned: I mean the dishonest practice of buying stolen Venison. Men in other re-[36] spects, of character and reputation; men, who would shudder at being branded with the stigmatizing name of receivers of stolen goods, offend in this instance, without compunction or remorse. They do not consider that the principals in the first degree would never venture on stealing Venison, if they were not certain of selling it. To supply, then, this only motive for committting theft, is to become virtually guilty of that theft: nor can any man of common sense and probity hesitate a moment to determine, that his species of dishonesty is as unjust and atrocious as any other. Whatever is the property of its owner, especially if it be that on which he places any value, it makes no real difference in the crime of depriving him of it, whether it serves his pleasure or his profit: his disappointment, and the expence to which the care of that property subjects him, render it totally unlawful to plunder him of it. Even in the case where the Venison stolen is the property of the Crown, the theft is by no means excuseable; but it is a notorious fact, that this wretched excuse is void of foundation. Few heads of deer are now to be found in the Royal Forests; and, for years past, the whole that has been hawked about for sale has been the property of private individuals. Consider, again, the consequences of encouraging such miscreants. These wretches not only accustom [37] themselves, but also train up numbers, to get their livelihood by this species of robbery. This habit, together with the idleness and debauchery that attends it, by no means confines itself to this one kind of depredation, but leads them also to every species of theft which can endanger the property of a neighbourhood, till at length their lives become forfeited to the violated laws of their country.

To those on whom this reasoning will make no impression – to those who prefer the temporary gratification of their palates to the dictates of reason, honesty, and virtue, let me suggest briefly, that even self-interest calls upon them not to encourage any longer this species of villany: that detection is easy, and may be accomplished with secrecy; that on conviction the penalty is heavy, (and I speak the sense of the Magistrates, when I say, it will be enforced with the utmost severity;) that they expose themselves not only to the poacher, who would secure his own safety by betraying them; but that even lie at the mercy of the lowest of their own menial servants, who, instigated, whether by real or supposed injury, or merely by the love of lucre, have it in their power at any time to hold them out to that ignominy and disgrace which they justly deserve.

Gentlemen, I will detain you no longer: to ay any more upon the subject, would be an insult to [38] the understanding of those who hear me; and to have said less, would not have been consistent with that anxiety which your Magistrates must always feel for the morals, police, and good repute of the County.

CHARGE DELIVERED AT EPIPHANY SESSIONS, 1798.

Gentlemen of the grand jury,

I FEEL particular pleasure in seeing so respectable a body of Jurors assembled on the present occasion; and as none of the criminal cases to be laid before you require any unusual attention, I trust I shall need no apology for submitting to your united deliberation some few hints relative to the lower class of people in your respective neighbourhoods.

It is too obvious a truth to require proof, that the poor man's industry, be it ever so great, is at the present moment utterly inadequate to the supply of his own wants and those of his family. The high price of provisions necessarily causes such inadequacy. The wheat crops last harvest, in many parts of the kingdom, were greatly deficient. Much corn was housed in a bad condition, and part of the remainder was unproductive, neither filling the bushel as usual, nor yielding the accustomed quant-[39] tity of flour. Upon an average, good wheat is worth about 15 s. a bushel in the Gloucester market, and in some parts of the county it bears a higher price. Whilst the weekly wages of the labourer in husbandry seldom exceed eight or nine shillings, how is he to satisfy the cries of an infant family for bread alone, exclusive of the other claims upon him, for rent, clothing, and for fuel? Our laws indeed, with true parental affection, have empowered the Magistrates to grant parochial relief; but, as matters are now circumstanced, there may be a doubt whether this remedy doth not sometimes encrease the evil. Where the Magistrate lives at a distance, consider how much of the pauper's time, as well as that of the Overseer, is expended in journeying backwards and forwards to litigate the points, whether any relief be necessary, or, if necessary, in what proportion it should be allowed. The temper of those whose peculiar province it is to inspect the condition of the poor, is not unfrequently soured by numerous, repeated, and unexpected applications for assistance; and accusations of negligence and idleness on the one hand are so positively denied, and on the other so loudly retorted by recriminations of want of feeling, that the Magistrate is often at a loss to which party he is to give credit. If I may be permitted to speak from my own experience, I can [41] safely aver, that for some time past, the greater part of my mornings has been taken up in adjusting disputes of this kind, and in endeavouring to allot to the respective claimants such a proportion of relief, as should stimulate, not supersede, their own exertions: and after all, I am sorry to say, that the result has been seldom more satisfactory to myself than to the contending parties, principally because the relief directed was to be afforded in money, it being liable to be squandered in ale-houses, and to be expended most unwisely. The question then is, whether, among yourselves, you might not adopt some plan, calculated to prevent, or at least to lessen, both these evils – the granting relief in money, and the loss of time so injurious to the Pauper, to the Overseer, and to the Community? Being of opinion that you may in many, though not in all cases, effectuate these desirable purposes, I submit the following hints to your consideration.

The common food of the labouring poor is principally bread, and that made of the finest wheat flour – a practice which has been often reprobated as neither healthy nor œconomical, by those who, from their abilities and researches into the subject, were most competent to judge. This bread, in the country, is frequently purchased at small retail shops, where, for want of an assize being sent, and a competition [42] between rivals, the loaves are shamefully deficient in weight. Thus the labourer's wages, which, in the best of times, with strict œconomy, are little more than sufficient to breed up his family with decency, become, at dear seasons, by his own improper management and the fraudulent practices of others, barely adequate to his own personal subsistence. To raise his wages would be prejudicial to the public: to enable him by charitable distribution to persist in the same kind of diet, would, in time of scarcity like the present, be an aggravation of the mischief, because the more wheaten bread you assist him to purchase, the more you encrease the demand, and in addition thereto, enhance the price. The want of wheat, which was so sensibly felt about three or four years since, put the thinking and benevolent part of the nation upon making various experiments, to discover whether substitutes for bread might not be used; substitutes equally nutritious, wholesome, and palatable, and withal of a cheaper nature. Fortunately, these exertions succeeded; and it was ascertained that soup in particular had just the best title to all these claims, and especially because barley flour, the best adapted for its basis, abounded in a greater quantity of mucilage than even wheat itself. The prejudices that were at first raised against it, have in a great mesure happily subsided, and shops for the sale of it at reduced [43] prices, have been established, under the patronage of the first characters, not only in different parts of the metropolis, but in various places of the country to the no small comfort, satisfaction, and emolument of the lower classes of society. I submit therefore to you, whether subscriptions for similar establishments in your respective neighbourhoods might not be equally beneficial. Should you resolve to sell it at something about half the price, the following advantages among others would be the consequence:- The poor, by being gradually accustomed to a different, as well as better diet, than that derived from bread alone, would no longer feel that degree of alarm which they now experience upon the scarcity of corn, and therefore would not be disposed to those scenes of riot, violence, and tumult, which on these ocasions are too apt to disgrace the national character. They would have more than an equivalent for that money which they have to expend, and would be free from these impositions practised upon them through the medium of false weights and short measures. The Parish Officer would be assured, that the publican no longer fattened upon the spoils of the pauper; and the pauper, soon finding from experience that the relief afforded him exceeded, both in quality and quantity, that which he could have purchased in other places with the money to be obtained by the Magistrate's order,[44] would rest satisfied, and appropriate the whole of his time to the maintenance of his family. At first, you may possibly have prejudices to contend with; but patience, and mild treatment, and good humour will, I trust, easily surmount them.

Should particular circumstances render this scheme impracticable in some districts, permit me, on such a supposition, to remind you of an Act lately passed, which seems to be little known, and less practised, at least with its concomitant regulations. The Act I allude to, is 36 Geo. III. c. 22, which permits bakers and others to make and expose to sale loaves made of wheat, deducting only 5 lb. weight of bran per bushel, or mixed with other grain. To prevent any impositions upon the purchaser, the loaves are to be marked, and in some conspicuous part of the shop is to be affixed a paper, specifying in large characters the sorts, the mixtures, and their proportions. There are also penalties affixed for the sale of false weights or false markings. A shop of this kind, established and conducted under your own immediate auspices, must be productive of good.

I would suggest another hint; it is relative to the article of fuel. Doth not policy, as well as charity, direct to you to lay in a stock of coals when the roads are good, and to retail it in winter at prime cost to your indigent neighbours? This would preserve your fences, and secure the poor from those [45] shameful impositions now so often practised upon them; would make the small sums they have to expend go much further; and of course would render application for parochial relief less necessary.

Gentlemen, The practices I have taken the liberty to recommend, will, I know, occasion at first to each individual among you some trouble and loss of time; but can you spend part of your time better than in assisting your fellow-creatures? and as to the objection that may be made, relative to the expence thereby incurred, at a time when Government finds itself compelled to call upon you for heavy sacrifices, I pay the less attention to it, when I recollect, that I am addressing myself to Britons, whose characteristic it ever was, and, I trust, ever will be, to reject every idea of indulging themselves in the superfluities, nay even in the comforts and conveniences of life, until they have first supplied the necessities of their Neighbours and Countrymen.

CHARGE DELIVERED AT EASTER SESSIONS, 1798.

Gentlemen of the grand jury,

IT IS with sincere pleasure that I am enabled to congratulate you and the County, on the very small numbers of Prisoners who will at this Sessions engage your time and attention. This desirable effect must undoubtedly, in part, be attributed to the late general Goal Delivery; but I flatter myself, that much is also to be ascribed to that greater degree of care and attention which has been of late years, and still continues to be, paid to the education and morals of the rising generation, and to which the community is much indebted. It is an undoubted truth, that a stricter gravity in the intercourse of daily life; that good order, good manners, and general regularity, must prevail and flourish, in proportion to the encrease of Christian knowlege [47] amongst the different ranks of society. Whilst those who are capable of reading and judging for themselves, must, by the experience of what has passed, and is now passing in review before them, be driven to the reflection, that religion is their only stay and support, and inseparably connected with their best and dearest interests even in this life, they will be readily persuaded to do what in them lies for the advancement and propagation of it among the young members of their poorer brethren. It is natural for me, both from my profession and my situation in this place, to recommend this point, Gentlemen, to your most serious consideration; and I can do it from a sincere conviction of its utility. In many places, where more time cannot conveniently be spared from the ordinary occupations of the poor, we owe much to that care which has been taken to appropriate at least the Sunday to their religious improvement. The advantages of such regulations appear, even to a superficial observer, in that decency and sobriety which many of our villages exhibit: habits of industry and attention are acquired at that season in which alone they can be acquired – in yearly youth: obedience and submission to parents and superiors, on a due sense of which society depends for its subsistence, are then effectually inculcated; and if to this we add the inestimable importance of the knowledge [48] which it is our primary object to instil, subservient not only to their present but also their future welfare, we can surely want no further inducement to persuade us to unite heartily in promoting the religious instruction of the lower orders in our neighbourhood. I should be sorry, that your exertions in this respect should be for a moment checked by the insinuation which you may have heard thrown out, that the poor are inclined to abuse their knowledge; and that by learning to read, they are enabled to imbibe and disseminate the principles of irreligion and sedition. There is undoubtedly no good which may not be abused, and much of the mischief which of late years has overspread the world, has risen up, we readily allow, from the diffusion of improper publications: but the blame is to be attributed, not to the lower classes of society, but to men of higher rank, and far superior education; men accustomed to artifice and deep dissimulation, who, from the darkest and basest designs, have endeavoured, by polluting the minds of others, to eradicate every principle, moral, social, and religious. Whilst, therefore, your care is confined to the promotion of that knowledge only which teaches the fear of God, and the obligations under which men live to each other in society, the objects of it will, I trust, ever shew their gratitude by their obedience, and spend their little leisure in the perusal of such [49] books only as they shall have been taught by you to look up to with reverence, and to consider as the comfort of their daily toils, and their guide to happiness.

I am urged by the aspect of things at this important period, to direct your most serious attention to this expedient, and to every other than can tend to the amelioration of the morals of society. Our circumstances are beyond all example awful and alarming, and they obviously call upon us to practise ourselves, and promote in others, the strictest integrity, and sanctity of manners; these being the only effectual methods of securing the favour of Providence. We are next called upon, by the menaces of our insolent and implacable enemies, to adopt every human means of vigilance and circumspection; that, if their threats of invasion should be put into execution, we may be prepared with heart and hand to oppose to them the most formidable resistance. It would be presumption in me to pretend to offer to you any advice on this head. I can only wish to assist you in promoting an entire union of all ranks; an universal will to repel so unwarranted an aggression; a prompt and ready obedience to the commands of his Majesty's Government; a general disinterestedness and disposition to make any personal sacrifices for the sake of the public good; and a willing co-operation in every measure that the as-[50] sembled sense of the nation may deem expedient for the common safety. Under such precautions, it is the conviction of the wisest and most experienced, that we may still without presumption bid defiance to their threats.

I need not warn you, that in this contest every thing which is valuable in life, is at stake. To maintain it with manly fortitude, even under the heaviest burdens, we have still the most powerful reasons: in the prospect of what we have to lose, should we basely and tamely sublit, as other European States, to their infinite sorrow, have done; and in the retrospect of those extraordinary successes with which Providence hath crowned our naval exertions. Though we have suffered much, yet no diminution of empire hath been hitherto sustained; and every effort to deprive us of any of our most distant dominions, hath been defeated.

May the present wild projects of our enemies against our religion, laws, and liberty, be frustrated with like success; - may this kingdom still remain the asylum of injured innocence and oppressed virtue;- and may this happy constitution, the source of real happiness, and the pride and boast of every intelligent Briton, be daily strengthened and improved, and be perpetuated to our latest posterity!

[D 2-51]

CHARGE DELIVERED AT EASTER SESSIONS, 1800.

Gentlemen of the grand jury,

FROM the short period of time which has elapsed since the last Assize, I was in hopes that you would have had little or no business, and that I should have been enabled to have discharged you at an early hour, with your country's thanks for your attendance. In this I am mistaken, for with real concern I observe, that the gaol has been rapidly filled, and that you will have several criminal cases laid before you. It is difficult to assign an adequate cause of this sudden increase of profligacy. It cannot with reason be attributed to want of employment, for the more numerous part of the prisoners are labourers in husbandry; and it is well known, that the business of agriculture at this season of the year demands a greater quantity of hands than the country can supply. Few of them [52] can plead, in extenuation of their offence, the cries of a numerous family for bread, most of them being single persons, and unburthened with children. The price of provisions of all kinds, indeed, still continues most deplorably high; yet this is no justifiable pretext for theft and depredation. The humanity of the English laws has made ample provision for the poor and impotent. They have but to state and verify their wants, and those wants are immediately supplied. The whole property of the rich is, as it were, mortgaged for their support. Exclusive of the attention paid by those, whose more immediate province it is to superintend the distresses of the lower class; – exclusive of the incessant and indefatigable pains taken by the Magistrates to obtain an accurate knowledge of the real situation of the poor, and to meliorate it by every possible exertion; – exclusive, I say, of these considerations, so ample and extensive have been the charities of the rich, that I very much question, whether a reduction of the price of the several necessaries of life to their usual moderate standard, may not eventually be prejudicial to the poor, insamuch as it will shut up, as being no longer necessary, those avenues of benevolence, through which for months past they have been so materially benefited. It is an object well worthy of your attention, Gentlemen, to ascertain, if possible, the sources of this increased depravity. [53

Should you think that it has proceeded from a neglect of early instruction, let me earnestly recommend your enforcing, to the utmost of your power, both by precept and example, a regular attendance of your children and domestics, and all over whom you have an influence, at their respective places of religious worship on the Sabbath. Should you be of opinon, that it has arisen from idleness, and a want of industrious habits at an early period of life, strenuously insist upon your Churchwardens and Overseers executing that wise institution of the 43d of Elizabeth, whereby the children of such as are unable to maintain their families, are directed to be placed out parish apprentices. Should you discover that the evil has commenced at a later date, from an association with bad company at ale-houses which encourage tippling, you have but to state the matter, and I pledge myself in behalf of all your Magistrates, that the licences of such houses will be withdrawn. Much as I reprobate the conduct of those, who, in consequence of their violating the laws of their country, become at these solemn seasons the objects of your judicial inquiry, I am not without my apprehensions, that part of the criminality of some of them may originate in the neglect and supine indolence of their former employers and masters; who, too often, wink at the absence of their servants upon Sundays; who disregard their [54] sleeping out at nights, provided they are in their places at the usual hours of work; and who are totally inattentive to character at the time when they are hired, a circumstance which, alone, as it tends to confound every quality of the heart, and to put upon a complete level sobriety and drunkenness, honesty and villainy.

Regretting, Gentlemen, as I sincerely do, this abundant profligacy, I feel considerable comfort in telling you, that it has manifested itself principally in petty larcenies, and that it has not, except in one single instance or two, been exerted in any of those shameful outrages, which, a few years since, in a similar scarcity of grain, were attended with most fatal consequences. In general, we do not hear of obstructions to the passage of corn to market, of the plunder of waggons, of impediments to the navigation of vessels on canals or rivers: in one district of the county, indeed, the greater part of which is extra-parochial, and which perhaps, for that reason, is more sensible of the pressure and distress of the times, some misguided men, inattentive alike to the voice of reason and to the laws of their country, have acted in a manner highly improper, which occasioned the military to be called out to controul them. Should any of you, Gentlemen, be situated in their neighbourhood, your endeavour to awaken [D4-55] within them a just sense of their interests, would be an act of true policy of no less than real humanity. Tell them, that the modes they pursue must infallibly tend to defeat their own designs, and to increase the evils of which they complain. Tell them, that the cheapness of a market must depend upon the plenty with which it is supplied; that where there is no security for payment, no commodities will be exposed on sale, except in a scanty measure, at a price far beyond the real value, and in proportion to the risque and danger incurred; that plunder, and taking by violence at reduced prices, can only answer a momentary purpose, and may check, but cannot encourage, the production of grain. Tell them, that a continuance in such nefarious proceedings, will not only insure to them the ill will of every respectable member of society, and particularly of those upon whose good offices and benevolence they depend, but that it will expose them to every danger which can make an impression upon the minds of reasonable beigns, and will subject them, in proportion to the different aggravations of their guilt, to imprisonment, transportation, and death itself with every mark of ignominy. Need I add, Gentlemen, that it is incumbent upon yourselves, upon every man of property, to resist such daring violations of the law in the first instance, in-[56] asmuch as the Hundred wherein such outrages are committed, is compellable to make good all the losses sustained in consequence thereof! But I forbear dwelling any longer upon so melancholy a subject. I hope, that these rash men have seen their error; that they will be grateful for the lenity displayed by their Magistrates, and will offend no more. The names and persons of many of them are well known, and a repetition of the offence will cancel that pardon which is only conditional, and will most undoubtedly call down upon them condign punishment.

You, Gentlemen, will, I am persuaded, persist in that exemplary line of conduct which has hitherto so effectually tended to preserve peace and good order. You will see that poverty, when not the offspring of idleness and profligacy, shall not perish through want. You will encourage industry, and cheerfully relieve the distresses of those who, from illness, large families, misfortune, or advanced years, are unable to supply their own necessities, and who for that reason, have a natural as well as a legal claim upon the benevolence, charity, and humanity of their more affluent fellow-creatures.

CHARGE DELIVERED AT EASTER SESSIONS, 1801.

Gentlemen of the grand jury,

IN consequence of the General Gaol Delivery at the late Assize,[1] you will have few criminal cases laid before you, though some of them are of such a nature as to call for your particular attention. I shall easily be understood to allude to those tumultuous meetings which have been lately held in different parts of the county, for the awoved purpose of redressing a greivance under which the community in general now unhappily labours, that of the high price of provisions. All such meetings are looked upon with an hostile eye, both by the common and the statute law, and this with the greatest reason; for they tend to break the peace, to create terror and confusion, and to introduce plunder and anarchy. Upon this account, by the common law, not only Peace-Officers, but individuals, [58] are called upon to suppress every species of riot, "by staying those whom they shall see engaged therein from executing their purpose, and also by stopping others whom they shall see coming to join them." The statute law has greatly strengthened the authority of the Magistrates. So far back as the time of Edward III. they were authorised to restrain, correct, and imprison rioters. Subsequent Acts of Parliament have given them fuller powers; and, in the reign of George I. it was enacted, that where any number of rioters, to the amount of twelve or more, should presume to continue together for the space of one hour after proclamation had been made for them to depart, they should incur the guilt and penalty of felony, without benefit of Clergy. Criminals of this latter class are not, gentlemen, subject to your jurisdiction, nor will you be called upon to exercise your judgment upon the cases of these who were the ringleaders in the late riots: though all concerned in them are equally guilty in the eye of the law, the lenity of the prosecutors has made a suitable distinction. Whilst the most daring and active are reserved for a more solemn tribunal, armed with higher powers, (the powers of life and death,)[2] it is intended, I understand, to submit to

[1] A characteristic confusion in words, about assize=a special commission to High Judges, and the session of Oyer and Terminer and General Gaol Delivery, generally held at once with the Assizes. Hence, the collective name of Assize for the three commissions. See *Crime in England 1550–1800*, ed. J. S. Cockburn (London: Methuen, 1977), J. H. Baker, "Criminal Courts & Procedure at Common Law," pp. 15–48, and G. Lamoine, *Littérature et justice pénale en Angleterre au XVIIIe siècle* (Paris: Didier-Erudition, 1987) I, 21, on the subject.

[2] This an example of the distinction between the jurisdiction of the Quarter-Sessions, and that of the sessions of Oyer & Terminer, which had a power of passing judgment of death over, in this case, rioters, under the famous Riot Act.

your inquiry, those only whose criminality appears to be of a less dark complexion; those only who ignorantly listened to the persuasions of others, [59] though in hopes of profiting by the general plunder; those who kept themselves in the back ground, and who deserve the appellation perhaps of fools rather than that of knaves. If, upon investigation, you shall find that any three persons or more have thus assembled for an unlawful purpose, and that they have attempted to carry that purpose into execution, the guilt of one becomes the guilt of all, and it is your duty to find the bill preferred to be a true bill.

Whilst I thus call your attention to so painful a part of your duty, let me not be misunderstood, as if I was insensible to the distresses of the poor. In common with the other Magistrates, and with every friend to humanity, I deeply feel and deplore them: but the same principle compels me to contend, that the violent measures adopted by those unthinking persons who thus take the law into their own hands, are not only calculated to defeat the very end proposed, and to encrease in a tenfold proportion the evil complained of, but that they are in this county needless and peculiarly criminal. The Magistrates have the powers of granting relief to every pauper resident within a parish; and those powers your Magistrates have exerted uniformly, upon a scale, it is presumed, to their real wants: and with respect to those who reside in extra-parochial places, (I particularly allude to the inhabitants of the Forest of Dean,) such has been the attention, [60] so great the humanity, of Government, that no sooner were their distresses made known, through a memorial presented by the Grand Jury at the last Assize, than there was an immediate order for a thousand pounds to be issued from the Treasury for their instant relief. The pretences for rioting in this part of the kingdom are entirely done away; and you will excuse me, Gentlemen, if I suggest to you, that it will not be unbecoming your character to endavour, both as members of the Grand Jury and in your individual capacities, to remove the unhappy prejudices which have been one great cause of these riotous proceedings; prejudices which have been industriously circulated, and which have unfortunately taken too deep root. They indeed chiefly affect the farmer and middle-man, the mealman or factor. Be assured, that, in all states of advanced civilization, the latter is a most useful, not to say necessary, member of society. The article exposed for sale, will always be cheaper, in proportion to the greater number of competitors for public favour; and, with respect to the farmer, a reasonable man would be almost enclined to think, from the clamours raised against him, that he had the disposal of the seasons in his own hands. What is to be ascribed solely to the visitation of Heaven, is laid to the charge of individuals; and that real scarcity, which is the result of a deficiency or failure of the last harvest, is pretended to be artificial, and [61] ascribed to the inhumanity of that respectable class of men, whose skill, labours, and capital, are employed in cultivating the earth. However, supposing for a moment that there are individuals among them, who, dead to the calls of humanity, and alive only to the suggestions of their own unfeeling avarice, still continue to hoard up stores of grain, in hopes of obtaining a more advanced price; yet, be assured, the number of these persons is comparatively small, and know not whether, whilst they thus designedly consult their own interest, they are not at the same time, though unknown to themselves, the most useful members of society. Had that unhappy phrenzy a few months since become general, which providentially was merely local, – had the farmers universally been compelled to bring their own stock of corn to market, as they most injudiciously were in some districts;- what, I ask you, would have been the case at this moment? Not a mere scarcity would have existed, but an actual famine, and with it, in all probability, plague, pestilence, and civil war.

Gentlemen of the Grand Jury, It is your duty to remove these prejudices by cool argument and sound reasoning. Act accordingly. Consider how much is at stake. Policy, humanity, and self-interest demand your exertions? Be œconomical as far as relates to your own expenditure; this will enable you to be charitable to the distressed. [62] Above all, see that the regulations of a late Act of Parliament for providing different substitutes for grain be diligently enforced.

Heavy and frequent as must be the calls of the new Overseers of the Poor upon the public purse, till the arrival of the harvest, no good man will, I trust, repine: – he will wait with patience for the more happy moment, when he can enjoy the convenienceies and comforts, without depriving his fellow-creatures of the necessaries, of life; and whilst his first object will be to consult the interests of others, he will rest persuaded that such a conduct must be ultimately beneficial to himself.

CHARGE DELIVERED AT EPIPHANY SESSIONS, 1802.[1]

Gentlemen of the grand jury,

PERSUADED as I am, that you are fully competent, as well from experience as from education, to the due execution of the important office for which you are now assembled, I shall not take up your time with unnecessary observations. I would rather wish to call your attention for a few moments to a subject wherein the community at large seems to me to be deeply interested; a subject wherein your own exertions, and those of gentlemen placed in situations of similar respectabiilty with yourselves, may be of material consequence, inasmuch as upon those exertions will in some mesure depend the comfort and security of the several ranks of society in your respective neighbourhoods.

After an expensive war of many years continuance, in support of the liberties of Europe, as well [64] as of our own, our laws, our religion, and our happy constitution; the sword is at length sheathed, and peace restored to the contending nations of the world. Whether the terms of this peace be such as we had a right to expect; – whether they have afforded any and what indemnity for the past, or provided any and what security for the future; are points beyond your abilities and mine thoroughly to comprehend: leaving, therefore, the consideration of them to those whose more immediate province it is to investigate subjects of this nature, it will be more decorous, useful, and suitable to persons in our situation, to direct our combined efforts towards the rendering this peace as advantageous as possible within the several circles to which our influence may extend.

I need not observe to you, Gentlemen, that one principal consequence of the termination of the war, will be the disbanding many thousands of our fellow-subjects, whose services have been most usefully employed in the army and the navy. The greater number of these persons will naturally return to the places of their respective settlements, as well to enjoy the comforts of domestic life among their families, as to secure a maintenance for themselves. It is reasonable to suppose, that they will return nearly pennyless, and be of course unable to take advantage of

[1] Again a problem of date appears here: the peace of Amiens was signed March 21; we could think this to be at least the Easter sessions, if Easter Day 1802 had not been April 18; as sessions were usually held in the week *after* Easter, it would mean that this sessions is in fact the summer sessions for 1802.

these human statutes which em-[E-65] power them to set up and exercise their respective trades in towns corporate. Those who have been engaged in the sea service, how successful soever they may have been in the acquisition of prize-money seldom lay any share of it for a future emergency; and as to the soldiers, the arrears of pay due to them at the time of their discharge, will be little more than sufficient to carry them to their several homes. When arrived there, the prospect is not the most comfortable. It is not impossible that they may come to a parish, the whole labour of which is pre-occupied, where husbandry is already provided with sufficient hands, and where the loom may be either unemployed from the deadness of trade, or may be at least useless to them through the introduction of machinery, to the management of which they are strangers. But supposing this not to be the case, the persons of the class I am describing, have been for years unaccustomed to the incessant toil necessary both in agriculture and manufactures; they therefore, with some difficulty, will resume their former occcupations, and with still greater difficulty will perform them. Add to this, that many of them will return with maimed limbs, and broken constitutions; that the greater part of them have been habituated to spend the whole out of their pay upon themselves alone, without apportioning any of it to their wives and families; [66] that they have contracted habits of expence, perhaps of dissipation; and that, in consequence of their way of life, they are disposed to be indolent; it being a general and just remark, that military men always prefer danger to labour. Standing therefore in need of, or at least requiring, more ample support than is sufficient for other labourers habituated to toil and seclusion from the world; unable at the same time, by the exertion of their talents, to merit wages to an equal amount, if any employment at all; their situation will be deplorable, and will call for greater attention than can be given to it by a single individual or two, by an Overseer of the Poor, or a Churchwarden of a Parish. It should also be taken into consideration, that whilst every poor man in this kingdom has a legal claim upon his more opulent neighbour, to the extent of providing necessaries for himself and his family, this claim, in the case of soldiers and sailors, becomes undoubtedly of far stronger obligation. It is a claim on their part strictly merited, insamuch as it is to their efforts and fortitude, to the firmness and honesty of their conduct on the most trying times, (I particularly allude to the late partial mutiny at the Nore,) that we are indebted, under the good Providence of God, for the posssession of our laws and property, perhaps even [E 2-67] for our existence as a nation. The great question then is, How and in what manner are these men to be supported? Their own earnings cannot effect this desirable end. You will say, perhaps, that the parish purse must be resorted to. Granted. Still let it be recollected, that the interests of payers to this fund are in some measure to be consulted; that it is not a perpetual fountain, impossible to be exhausted; and upon the supposition that the streams derived from thence should prove inadequate to supply the real or imaginary wants of the day, let me then ask, what will ensue? The probable consequences are too obvious; and I will venture to predict, that in this case private property will soon be invaded, and that to a much greater extent than it experienced during the calamities of the late war, even when heightened by a scarcity almost bordering upon famine.

Sensible of my incompetency to so arduous a task, I pretend not to lay down any particular rules, and shall therefore only suggest a few general hints, leaving the adoption and improvement of them to those possessed of superior abilities, greater leisure, and more local knowledge than myself.

It may perhaps then be advisable, in the first instance, that the principal persons of every parish should associate together, for the purpose of providing employment for the new comers. In places [68] where either new roads are to be formed, new canals to be dug, new inclosures to be made, or wastes to be broken up and turned into tillage, this will not be difficult, but in other districts the case will be different. As the persons in whose behalf I am pleading, will not be very anxious to seek for labour at a distance, labour should be brought to their doors. Where then the advantages just now mentioned are not to be obtained, let the plough occasionally give place to the spade – let machinery sometimes admit manual labour to a participation of its profits;– in other words, let labour be not simplified till there be a deficiency of hands; let it rather be multiplied; for it seems to be sound policy, that the emolument of an individual should never be preferred to that of the public. Wherever labour is scarce, and labourers abound, opulence of every kind, whether commercial or agricultural, should adopt a circuitous mode of attaining its pursuits, and should be contented to divide a greater part of the profits arising from the employment of a large capital among those inferior agents, through whose services those profits are obtained; for it stands to reason, that it is more advisable for a pauper to earn some part of his maintenance by his own industry, than that he should earn none at all.

Gentlemen, it hs been frequently observed, that [E 3-69] as every æra has its characteristic marks, whereby it is distinguishable from other æreas, so also every order of men has its peculiar failings. If the observation be founded on justice, perhaps a propensity to drinking is that to which the military and seafaring men are most addicted. It seems to arise from their course of life, and, though not justifiable, may admit of much excuse. The great exertions which each class is often called upon to make; the fatigue they undergo, their exposure to every vicissitude of weather; their broken repose, and occasionally short allowance of provisions, together with a consciousness of the importance of the services in which they are engaged, and the dangers accruing to their country in case of failure; must impair the strongest constitution, and may require a temporary additional stimulus, both to the mind and body. On such occasions, strong liquors are not improperly resorted to, acting as immediate restoratives, and enabling them to undergo fresh fatigues. Frequent repetitions by degrees grows into a custom, and, thus, what was at first introduced from necessity, becomes at length habitual through practice. It will therefore become an object of no small consequence to you, to remove from them all temptations to improper indulgence in this article. On this account, you should permit no public-houses in solitary retired situations, and a strict eye should be [70] kept upon those which are not so circumstanced. All tippling and drunkenness, when encouraged or connived at by the publican, should be severely animadverted upon; and care should be taken to prevent, as much as possible, those meetings, where drinking is as it were the business of the day; I mean those occasioned by cock-fighting, skittle-alleys, and illegal horse-races.

Having thus provided employment for your new guests, and guarded them against that temptation to which they are most subject, it will be your next object to encourage amongst them that spirit of œconomy and good management so necessary to the inferior classes, but so little observed by them.[1] For this purpose, it would be of great utility were you to introduce village shops, upon the excellent plan recommended by the Society established for bettering the condition of the Poor; by selling at prime cost, and without giving credit, and to act according to it. Where no patriotic persons will set up a shop of this kind, it becomes of greater consequence to pay the hireling his wages on the eve preceding the market day. Ready money has many advantages over credit; and undoubtedly he who has the fewest and least means of providing himself and family with the necessaries of life, should be enabled to purchase them in the best and cheapest [E 4-71] mode that can be devised. On this account too, it is peculiarly incumbent upon you to pay great attention to the weights and balances within your several districts. The frauds practised in this respect, are but too plainly evinced by the numerous convictions which have taken place in every part of the county, where inspectors have been appointed. As the penalty is but trifling, it were to be wished, that for a second offence the Legislature had empowered the publication of the names of the delinquents, as well to fix a greater stigma upon them, as to put the unwary upon their guard.

Could you find it practicable to establish Friendly Societies, they

[1] Once more, the usual complaint against the poor, that they were 'improvident'; in a similar spirit, see the numerous pamphlets of the *Cheap Repository Tracts* series, written by Mrs. Hannah More and her sisters between 1794–95 to counteract the pro-French propaganda against which the J.P.s precisely had been ordered to fight.

would be the means of still farther encouraging that spirit of œconomy and forecast which I am now recommending; and, perhaps, no class of men would be more likely to become members of them than soldiers and sailors, -the weekly allowances which in this case they would be called upon to make for their own advantage, resembling so nearly the deduction from their pay, to which they have been habituated, for the sake of their comrades, in those great national foundations, the Hospitals of Greenwich and Chelsea.

I shall make but one observation more respecting this description of men. If you trace the annals of history, you will be unable to discover any [72] period during which British bravery and intrepidity have shone with greater lustre than in the late war. Without wishing in the least to depreciate from the merit of the private soldier and sailor, still undoubtedly great share of pride is due to the Officers, for the pains they took to discipline and instruct them, and the unremitting attention they uniformy shewed them, at home, in the field, or on the ocean, in sickness and in health. Do you but act the same part with the Officers, and I doubt not but that your efforts will be attended with similar success: they made them equally good soldiers and sailors, and do you make them equally good subjects. Insist with them, if you please, upon the observation of as strict a discipline and severe a police; but, on the other hand, take equal care to provide them with warm cloathing, good provisions, regular pay, and comfortable lodging. Convince them by your kindness, that you do not neglect and discard them as almanacks of a former year's date, but that you hold their past services in grateful remembrance. Shew them that their country has their interests at heart; encourage and reward every degree of merit: the intrepid warrior will then soon learn to be the diligent labourer, the laborious husbandman, or the skilful artizan. Your own property, and that of your neighbours, will receive additional security; [73] and a nation possessed of subjects thus attached to her by ties of mutual interests, and equally habituated to the employments of peace and the toils of war, will have nothing to dread from the intrigues of domestic faction, or the menaces of foreign enemies.

CHARGE DELIVERED AT EASTER SESSIONS, 1802[1].

Gentlemen of the grand jury,

THE relaxed state of morals now so universally and justly complained of, calls loud for the active interference of those who are vested with any degree of authority in the execution of the laws; and indeed of all who wish either to preserve for themselves, or to transmit to their posterity, that security of life and property which they have been hitherto accustomed to enjoy. This increased depravity, among the inferior orders, cannot with propriety be attributed to the distress and indigence [75] arising from the high price of provisions, because never was parochial relief dispensed to so large an amount, in a more discriminating and judicious manner, than it has been done of late years; not to mention the studied exertions made by the hands of private benevolence, to supply any causal deficiency. It can with as little reason be ascribed to the want of due foresight in the Legislature. The Penal Code has kept an increase pace with the increased number of offences; and that to so great degree of late, as to infuse terror into the human mind, which can but recoil at seeing such a multiplication of laws, the enforcing of which, even when attended with banishment or death itself, seems to be no longer productive of its usual effects. Among our fellow-subjects in Scotland, the case is represented to be widely different. Though poverty has not there the same advantages which it possesses in England, (for there are no compulsory laws to provide for the distressed poor,) yet crimes of a deep complexion are seldom perpetrated, and a public execution is rarely witnessed. It should seem, therefore, that in some respect or other, their policy is superior to that of their more southern neighbours. The cause perhaps may easily be explained. Education in the early periods ofd life, is more attended to there than it is with us; it is not confined, as it is here, to the higher or middling [76] classes, but is extended to all, even the lowest, scarcely a parish being without its appropriate schoolmaster, whose province it is to instruct all that are willing to learn. The consequence is obvious. The mind, whilst yet tender and free from any bad tendencies, is impressed with sound principles of

[1] [Some local and temporary circumstances seem to have called our friend's attention to this subject more fully, at a time when he had greater leisure to consider it, as I find by a MSS. wherein many passages are interwoven with the subject matter of this Charge. Their weight will, I feel confident, plead my excuse with you for inserting some of them as notes, although I thereby tender the form of this Charge different from that of the others. – W.L.B.]

virtue, morality, and religion - principles which seldom lie dormant for any length of time, and are rarely, if ever, totally obliterated. In England, numerous as are our Charity Schools, they are far from being adequate to a similar purpose. The great mass of the common people have no other resources, for even first principles, than what they can collect from their parents, nearly as illiterate as themselves, or from their casual attendance on places of divine worship. To supply this defect, Sunday Schools have been established in various places: but how excellent soever this foundation may be to build upon, it is too probable that without some further superstructure, they will not, of themselves, be able to effect the wished-for reformation! It is difficult to suppose, that the wisdom of our ancestors could have omitted a point of so much importance as the early education of the inferior class of the people, and that [77] they could have imagined, that ignorance would be productive of morality and obedience to the laws. The fact is otherwise. They were equally attentive to the moral and to the natural wants of the poor - they had an eye to the improvement of the rising generation, not only in the then present, but in all future ages - and the blame is imputable to their descendants, for not enforcing the provisions which they so judiciously made. The 43d Eliz. c. 2[1], the basis of our Poor Laws, has, in an oblique and indirect manner, guarded against the evil here alluded to, and that by means apparently so harsh and contradictory to the feelings of humanity and natural affection, as to be justified only by considerations of political expediency, and imperious necessity. The Legislature, aware of the evil consequences which must ensue to the individual, as well as to the community at large, if the Children of the Poor were suffered to remain at home in a state of ignorance and idleness; and with a view of giving them that degree of instruction, and those habits of industry, which could alone make them useful members of society, has, with an apparent cruelty, but real benevolence, directed that they should [78] be taken from the arms of their natural parents at that early period when the age of nurture ceases; has substituted the Churchwardens and Overseers of the poor in the place of those natural parents, and empowered them to place them out as Apprentices, wherever they shall see convenient. How far the Parish Officers have deserved the name of parents, or acted as such, is too evident. It is sufficient for me to observe, that often times they have totally neglected their duty, and that, even in those instances where they have put the statute in execution, they have done in so imperfect and garbled a manner, as scarcely to retain any vestige

[1] Though previous to this æra a legal provision was made for the necessities of the poor, yet it is difficult to ascertain to what extent, and by what mode, it was raised. This is made evident by the quotations from the Mirror, as they are to be seen in Blackstone, Burn, and others.

of the original institution. It may therefore not be improper, if I offer you a few observations upon this clause of the Act itself - the mode in which it has been usually enforced- and the manner in which I conceive it ought to be executed.

The statute enacts, "That it shall be lawful for the Churchwardens and Overseers of the Poor, or the greater part of them, by the assent of two Justices, to bind the Children of such of the Poor as are unable to maintain them, Apprentices wherever they shall see convenient." Hereby is repealed that part of 5. Eliz. c.4, which had restricted within narrow limits the power of taking Apprentices in husbandry and other trades therein specified; but, as some doubts probably remained [79] upon the subject, 1 Jac. I. c. 25, further ordained, "that all persons to whom the Overseers should bind any Children Apprentices, may take and keep them as such, any former statute to the contrary notwithstanding." This is confirmed and rendered perpetual by 3 Car. I. c.4. The power, therefore, of taking Apprentices without incurring any of the penalties inflicted by 5 Eliz. c. 4., was now completely established. Still there remained a grand desideratum. Laws without sanctions were little better than nullities. A power of binding Children Apprentices was, indeed, vested in the Parish Officers; a power of receiving was also lodged in those to whom they were so bound; but there was no mode of compelling persons to take Apprentices, and to execute the counterpart of the indentures, except by indictment, a form of proceeding which was tedious, expensive, and often fruitless, in consequence of a failure in those technical forms which are here rigidly expected. To avoid, therefore, this circuitous mode of proceeding, it was enacted by 8 & 9 Will. III. c. 30, entitled, "An act for supplying defects in the Laws for the Relief of the Poor," "that a person refusing to receive such Parish Apprentices, should incur a penalty of £10. to be levied by distress and sale, by warrant under the hands and seals of two Justices." A subsequent Act, 18 G. III. c. 47, makes an altera [80] tion in the priod of binding, and determines that no Male Child shall be bound longer than till he is 21 years of age, instead of 24, as had been originally enacted.[1] And last of all came the 32 G. III. c. 57, which gives enlarged powers to the Magistrates, and

[1] We next meet with 20 Geo. III. c. 36, entitled, " An Act for obviating doubts touching the binding and receiving Poor Children Apprentices, in pursuance of several Acts of Parliament made for the relief of the Poor, within particular incorporated hundreds or districts, &c." Clause 1 ordains, "that after June 4, 1780, persons to whom any Children shall be bound Apprentices, in pursuance of the above-mentioned Acts, shall be obliged to provide for them in like manner as for others, under a similar penalty, i.e. 10 £. Then follows cl. 2, limiting the words of 43 Eliz. and enacting, "that none but inhabitants and occupiers of land, tenements, or hereditaments in the parish where such child belongs, shall be compellable to take an Apprentice."

corrects the deficiencies of the former statutes.[1] Such are the provisions made by the [81] Legislature upon this important point. Let us next see in what mode they have been carried into execution.

In several places within this county, a custom prevails of taking the Children as Apprentices, but without binding them as such by indenture. The reason assigned is, that, when they are able to shift for themselves, they may no longer continue in their own parishes, but get settlements elsewhere, previous to their attaining the age of 21. The evil consequences which arise from hence, are many. For want of a legal connection between the parties, the Child is neither Servant nor Apprentice; and in case of ill behaviour on either side, the Magistrate has no authority. When the service is most wanting, perhaps in the midst of harvest, the Child, from his own caprice, from the solicitations of his parents, who want his assistance in gleaning, from the bad examples of other idle boys, or pehaps from having received proper chastisement for his faults, runs away, and no redress can be obtained. At the return of winter, when employment is scarce, he is no longer useful; covered with rags and disease, and his morals totally impaired, he becomes a fresh burden to the parish, and no creditable family is willing to re-[82] ceive him. Now the foundation upon which this improper conduct is built, is bad. The law which directs Children to be bound for no longer a period than till they are 21 years old, does not absolutely enjoin that they shall be bound till they are so old. It says, you shall not exceed that limit, but it gives you a power of binding for a shorter time. And, accordingly, it has been determined in the Court of King's Bench, that the clause is not imperative and compulsory, but directory and discretional. I therefore do earnestly recommend it to you in all instances, actually to bind the Children by indentures, and, according to the size and age of them when first taken from their Parents, to fix the period of their apprenticeship, namely, till they shall arrive at the age of 17 or 18 years. I need not observe to you, that a Child cannot be bound a Parish Apprentice till he is seven years old, nor will the statute allow of compulsion after he is 15.

[1] From a careful perusal and comparison of these Acts with each other, it appears that the Parish Officers, with the consent of two Justices, have the power of binding out Poor Children – That they are to do it where they see it convenient – That their own discretion, regulated by the laws of common sense, reason, and equity, is to guide them – That, if they bind them to inhabitants or occupiers of either lands, tenements, or hereditaments in their own parish, they may select, a masters or mistresses, whom they please, provided they are capable of maintaining them – That neither the Gentleman, Clergyman, Tradesman, nor Husbandman, has any exemption from the onus – That they are all equally bound to participate of the burden without any priority or predecency – That ability is the first recommendation – That where the parties are dissatisfied with the determination of the Officers and the two Justices, there is given a power of appeal to the General Quarter Sessions – and as the certiorari is not in express terms taken away, that the Court of King's Bench has the ultimate jurisdiction.

The error just now pointed out, is confined only to some particular places; but I fear the next I have to mention pervades the greater part of the county. No natural parent suffers his affection for his child to be totally discarded the moment in which he is placed out apprentice, but is still anxious for his future morals and welfare. Parish Officers, substituted in their room, and constituted by law as their guardians, should have the same feel-[F 2-83] ings, and should by no means think they have discharged the important trust confided to them, when the indentures are executed. It is their bounden duty to have a watchful eye over Apprentices; to see that they have proper food, raiment, and lodging; to make frequent enquiries into the mode in which they are treated; and whether they meet from their Masters or Mistresses with that behaviour which the law enjoins, which humanity dictates, and which our religion calls for: where they see any thing amiss, they ought first to remonstrate; and if their remonstrances prove fruitless, then they should complain to the Magistrates, who are vested with ample powers of redress.[1] [84]

[1] To the doctrine as above laid down, I am aware that many objections have been urged. These I will now mention, and endeavour to obviate them as I go along.

And first it is objected, that 43 Eliz. c. 2., refers to 5 Eliz. c. 4, that they are both made in *pari materia*, and must be construed together. That as in 5 Eliz. only some particular trades are mentioned, and those merely of an inferior kind, Tradesmen of a superior class, Merchants, Gentlemen, Attornies, Clergymen, and others of a similar denomination, are excluded. That Magistrates have no jurisdiction except over the trades there specified; and that of course no redress can be obtained where the Apprentice is guilty of misdemeanors.

To this I answer, that 5 Eliz. c. 4, has nothing to do with 43 Eliz. c. 2; that they were made upon different subjects, without reference to each other; and that this will be evinced by making the most cursory comparison of them. 5 Eliz. c. 4, does not authorize a Husbandman to take an Apprentice, unless he occupies half a plough land; and though it may be difficult to say precisely what was the quantity of a plough land or a hide, yet it probable was that quantity which was sufficient to keep in employ a team of cattle. A modern Act has estimated it at £ 50 a year. See 13 G. III.c. 78 and 84. It marks out the persons who may be compellable to serve in husbandry or particular trades as servants by the year only. It specifies the hours of work in which labourers shall be obliged to attend in the day. It ascertains the wages. It marks the ages wherein women shall be compellable to serve, namely, between 12 and 40 years old; and will not permit a child to be bound in husbandry under 10 years old. It precludes particular prsons from taking Apprentices, unless the Parents of such Apprentices have substance of their own, and are enabled to spend to such an amount. It was in short made, as the title observes, for the ordering of Artificers, Labourers, Servants of Husbandry, and Apprentices, and, agreeably to the preamble, in hopes that by it, they should banish idleness, advance husbandry, and yield to the hired peson, both in the time of scarcity and in the time of plenty, a convenient proportion of wages.

The 43d Eliz. c. 2, is shortly entitled an Act for the Relief of the Poor. It enjoins the Officers of the Parish to apprentice the Children of the Poor where they shall see convenient, without saying a single word of husbandry or trade. It permits Children to be put out at seven years of age, for the age of nurture then ceases. It never notices Servants by the year, their hours of working, their ages, their pay, or their misdemeanors. Instead of permitting a man to take an Apprentice according as his own circumstances or those of the Parents of the Apprentices may be, it compels all men of ability to take Apprentices out of those who

The next point to be considered is, who are bound to take Parish Apprentices? The statute makes use of the expedient, "wherever the Parish Officers shall see convenient, with the assent of two [85] Justices." They in their discretion are to chuse proper Masters and Mistresses, and the law holds all persons proper, who, by their profession or manner of living, have occasion to keep servants. Such are Husbandmen, Tradesmen, Merchants, and Gentlemen, whether of the Laity or Clergy. With [86] respect to the first class, in country places, few others, comparatively speaking, are to be found, and undoubtedly they seem to be most peculiarly proper, as in the various labours of the field, some are perfectly suitable to the tender age of the Children when first apprenticed. The employments of husbandry never cease; they are calculated to improve the health of those concerned, as well as to rear up a hardy race of men, who may useful in various ways to their country; in addition to which, that the morals are less likely to be injured there than in populous cities. Upon this head I would briefly observe, first, that a person occupying an estate on a parish, though resident elsewhere, is as liable to have an apprentice bound to him as if he was an active householder in it: and secondly, that a regard should be had to the real value of the land occupied, rather than to the supposed number of ancient farms which he may cultivate.

With respect to Tradesmen and Merchants, it has been often argued, that there is a degree of hardship in imposing an Apprentice upon a person of this description, when he may have a considerable premium with one of a different sort. But there is fallacy in this argument which is easily [F 4-87] seen through. You do not impose a Parish Apprentice upon him to learn that peculiar art or mystery whereby he gains his living; and the objection is at once removed, by binding a Female

---

are Children of the poor and impotent; and even an occupancy of £ 10. by the year has been adjudged to be sufficient ability. In short, 5 Eliz. c.4, is a repetition of the statutes of Henry VIII. and is, as Dr. Burn observes, in great part obsolete; whereas, 43 Elis. c.2, is now in full force, and continues to be the corner stone of the whole fabric of the Poor Law which have since passed the Legislature to the present moment.

It ought not be omitted, that all these subsequent laws refer by name particularly to 43 Eliz. c. 2; whereas not one of them mentions 5 Eliz. c. 4. But the truth is, all argument upon this point is superseded by the decision of that Court where all proceedings of Parish Officers and Magistrates are cognizable. This is clearly decided in R. v. Saltern, Bott, vol. 1, p. 555, pl. 791. Judge Willes then said, 5 Eliz. c. 4, cannot be connected with 43 Eliz. c. 2. Judge Ashhurst and Judge Buller assented; and to the objection that the Parish Apprentice was only eight years old, they paid no regard whatever. The objection then drawn from the mention of one trade and omission of another, in 5 Eliz. totally ceases, is done away; and with respect to the Magistrates having no jurisdiction over Apprentices, excepting those which are therein mentioned, it has long been since adjudged that the reverse is the truth. But even granting this Act to have been deficient in this particular, 20 G. II. c. 19, and 32 G. III. c. 17, amply supply this deficiency: all Parish Apprentices, their conduct, and that of their Masters, are hereby made subject to the authority of the Magistrate.

Apprentice, in whose indenture the usual covenant is, that she shall be instructed in housewifery.

As to the Gentry and Clergy, it has been sometimes asserted, that they are improper masters, as having no employment for Apprentices; and that, therefore, assigning them Children, the end of the statute is defeated, as they cannot teach them anything useful. The objection is disparaging both to the Gentry and to the Clergy. It is in their power to have the Children taught and instructed to make good servants – a class always in demand, and, when honest and virtuous, always respected. Whilst it was the practice among gentlemen to take children of their poor neighbours, or small tenants, into their families, and to promote them on their good behaviour, they had as many friends, though in an humble sphere, as they had domestics. A burglary then committed through the advice and assistance of a servant, was a phœnomenon that rarely occurred, and which, when it did occur, excited universal detestation. What is now the case, everyman's experience will best inform him. The law makes no exception of the class of persons I am describing, and reason [88] and equity forbid, that the onus of training up Children should be entirely flung from their shoulders, upon those of others which are less able to bear the weight. May I also take the liberty of stating, that at this particular period, to persons thus circumstanced, when the taxes laid upon menial servants, on account of the exigencies of the State, amount nearly to a prohibition from keeping any, the Legislature, still anxious for the encouragement of binding Parish Apprentices, has connected œconomy with domestic comfort, and has granted permission, to those so disposed, to reap all the advantages of having one without being subject to the taxes accruing therefrom; Parish Apprentices being exempted from the duties, on condition of their wearing no liveries. There doubtless may be, and are, many cases, where it would be highly inconvenient for families to take Apprentices. To such families the law has virtually given an alternative. They may pay the penalty of ten pounds, which should be appropriated to the purposes of binding out such of the Poor Children as, by illness or infirmity, are unfit to be placed out in the usual way which the law directs.

To such parishes as, from past neglect, have a number of Children to bind at once, I would recommend the placing them out by ballot, rather than by the mere will and selection of the Officers, [89] with a liberty to the intended Masters to make changes amongst themselves, previous to the actual signing of the indentures, according as they shall judge a Boy or Girl best to suit their convenience.

Upon the whole, I believe that binding out Parish Children is the wisest and most beneficial mode of providing for the Poor. It not only reduces the rates at the present moment, but even to a distant period, as it breeds up those Children, which would otherwise be habituated to ignorance, vice, and idleness, in a manner calculated to enable them, at a future day, to procure their own livelihood, and to instruct their posterity to do the same. It teaches them industry and useful knowledge; and by procuring them proper provision and raiment, not only gives them a relish for these blessings, but points out to them the proper modes of obtaining and securing them, and thus makes them valuable members of the community.[1] It will, if any thing [90] can, check the torrent of vice and wickedness which occasions Gentlemen, standing on your situation, so much trouble and anxiety at these periodical solemnities, and which indeed threatens to overwehlm the whole community in one common ruin, unless checked and restrained. From me it requires no [91] apology to have thus pressed your attention to so important a point as the Education of the Youth of your Inferior Orders, persuaded as I am, that "if your train up a Child, in the way he should go, he will not, when he is old, be inclined to depart from it."

[1] The law which first enjoined it, has been the theme of constant admiration and eulogy among the well-informed writers on the subject. The Judges have ever spoken of it with the highest respect, and have been uniformly strict in enforcing a due observance of it, particularly that clause which substitutes the Overseers and Justices in place of the natural Parents; and have even carried the point so far, as not to permit the Magistrates to form separate judgments, but compelled them to meet together to deliberate on so important a point. In all their decisions upon the the subject, as far as can be collected from the reports of various authors, it appears, from their general reasoning, that they looked upon it as a kind of poor rate, to which all were liable in proportion to their ability. Reason seems to say the same, and to dictate, that as equality is the principle of taxation, so all ought to bear an equal share of the burden, in proportion to their ability. Need I add, that at this particular period, above all others, the argument claims especial attention. In a neighbouring country, once the envy of all other nations, the seat of arts and sciences, and of every thing which was thought to give a peculiar relish to life, one great argument was used with wonderful succcess to overturn their constitution, was the practice among the Aristocracy, or the Optimates, to fling every burden upon the lower classes. The repair of bridges, the payment of taxes, with a variety of other articles, were the exclusive privileges, if I may call them so, of the inferiors. Warned by their example, we should learn wisdom from their folly. The same objection which militates against a Gentleman taking a Parish Apprentice, operates equally against his paying his quotum of the Poor's Levies. In short, the law prescribes to all who are able to afford it, this mode of providing for the exigencies of the Poor. Reason and equity give their sanction to it. Experience has confirmed its wisdom and beneficial effects. Religion and morality are benefited by it. The interests of the community at large, as well as of individuals in particular, require it: and at this moment political motives demand it with so high and imperious a tone, that it is little short of phrenzy to turn a deaf ear to their united voice.

CHARGE DELIVERED AT EPIPHANY SESSIONS, 1803.

Gentlemen of the grand jury,

ON inspecting that class of offences in the Calendar which is subject to your enquiry, I do not perceive any thing, either in their nature or in their number, which requires any particular comment from the Chair. Competent as you are, both from education and experience, to fulfil that important trust for which you are now assembled, any observations from me would be superfluous and unnecessary: I shall therefore detain you no longer on this subject, than merely to remark, that should any unforeseen difficulty occur in the execution of your office, you will, upon communicating it to the Court, receive every assistance which it is in our power to afford.

Gentlemen, A late advertisment in the Provincial Papers having excited a considerable degree of [93] public attention, I thought it incumbent upon me to make some enquiries into the occasion of it. I refer to that advertisement wherein was announced, some months since, the establishment of a Friendly Society in the Manufacturing part of this County, under the name of *The Woollen Cloth Weaver's Society.*[1] I ought previously to apprize you, that in the year 1793, an Act passed the Legislature for the encouragement of Friendly Societies[2]. They had before existed in various parts of the kingdom for a considerable period, and much business had been supposed to be derived from them. By a small voluntary subscription of the Members of such Societies, funds had been raised for their mutual benefit in sickness, old age, and infirmity; and thus both the happiness of individuals was promoted, and the public burthens were very sensibly diminished. Like all other well designed human institutions, they were no exempt, in their infancy, from various errors and deficiencies. The calculations were often wrong, and by a too liberal allowance at first to the indigent Members, the funds were inadequate to the demands made upon them, at a more advanced period. Frauds were often practised by the Stewards, who embezzled the contributions, and against whom it was found difficult, if not impossible, to obtain either civil or criminal redress. The rules themselves were

[1] Various articles appeared in *The Gloucester Journal,* for 11 October 1802, promising a reward for anyone discovering a dishonest weaver; 25 October 1802, explaining their intentions; 13 Dec., signed W. H. Jessop, Solicitor, "the same is established to preserve peace and good understanding between the weavers and their employers..." I owe this information to the kindness of the Divisional Librarian of Gloucester.

[2] Not identified.

frequently ill [94] digested, and, by admitting contrary interpretations, occasioned much controversy; and more than once it happened, that the Societies themselves were suddenly dissolved, when in the most flourishing state, by a majority of members, who, looking only to the advantage of the present moment, insisted upon dividing the stock; and thus they disappointed the hopes of those who had been subscribers for a number of years, and to whom the injury became more distressing, on account of their advanced time of life. The Legislature, therefore, seeing that such Societies, if properly regulated, might be productive of good, interfered in their behalf, invested them with peculiar privileges, and guarded them against those inveniencies to which experience had shewn they were most liable: and, being persuaded that the General Courts of Quarter Sessions of the Peace for the respective counties in which such Societies were established, consisting of the principal Gentlemen of the country, free from prejudice, and anxious for the good of their indigent neighbours, would cheerfully give their utmost attention and assistance in examining the several regulations of these Societies, and in endeavouring to bring them as near to perfection as possible, made it a necessary condition, that all their Rules and Orders should be subject to the inspection, revision, and controul of those respectable Courts. The event has [95] corresponded with the humane design of the Legislature, and every Friendly Society with which I am acquainted in this county, has readily accepted the proffered favour, to their no small emolument and advantage. When, therefore, I first heard of the establishment of the Woollen Cloth Weavers' Friendly Society, I looked forwards wit anxiety to the production of their Rules at the last Sessions.[1] That anxiety was considerably increased upon hearing that the Society consisted neearly of three thousand persons, many of whom, from their inferior situation in life, must naturally be supposed, through want of leisure, abilities, and education, to be incompetent to form a proper judgment for themselves. Where the interests of such numbers are concerned,– numbers sufficient, if their operations are conducted with secrecy, to alarm the jealousy of every well regulated Police, – where the salutary measures recommended by the Legislature to be pursued, as necessary for the well being of such Societies, are wholly unnoticed and unregarded; inattention on the part of that Court, which is entrusted with the more immediate superintendance of them, becomes almost criminal; and the greater share of this criminality would justly attach to that person of whom, in consequence of the confidence reposed in him through the partiality of his Brother Magistrates, might naturally be expected a [96] peculiar degree

[1] *Rules and Articles to be observed and kept by the Members of a Friendly Society or Club, called the Woollen-Cloth Weavers' Society, instituted for the Purposes hereinafter mentioned, and begun the 24th day of September, 1802*. Glocester: D. Walker, 1802. 15 pp. – Gloucester Library, ref. J 11.53.

of vigilance upon so extraordinary an occasion. For this reason, I have endeavoured to get a copy of the Rules of the Society here alluded to; in which having succeeded, though with some difficulty, I now think it my duty to state them publicly, with such observations as the shortness of the time since I obtained them, and my other avocations, have enabled me to make.

The Society, then, in question, seems to have two leading objects in view; one, to protect their privileges, as manufacturers, from any participation by those who are unqualified, as not having served a legal apprenticeship; and the other, to support each other in sickness, infirmity, and the like. Respecting the first object, I say not a word. If their just privileges have been attacked, and if these privileges be not inconsistent with the general good of the commuity at large, the law is open, and they have a right to claim redress. I am concerned with the second object alone, and to that I now require your attention. Here it will be necessary for me, first, to recite the Articles relating to it.

The first Article declares, "That any person throughout the kingdom of Great Britain, who shall have been regularly apprenticed to the trade of a Woollen Cloth Weaver, shall be eligible as a Member of the Society, and no other person; and that a meeting of the Members in each parish [97] shall be holden on the first Monday in every month, at some one public-house in the said parish." The second Article enacts, "That, at the first monthly meeting in each parish, there shall be chosen, by the majority of the Members present, two persons, who shall act as Stewards for the year, and receive the monthly payments." The third Article determines "That there shall be four quarterly meetings of the Stewards of the several parish meetings in the year, who are to assemble together; those for one particular district, and the adjoining parishes, at Stroud; and those for the other district, and the adjoining parishes, at Dursley." The fifth Article determines, "That the Stewards of each parish shall form a Committee, who shall regulate all the proceedings, and transact all the business, of the Society." The sixteenth Article orders, "That whenever a Member becomes incapable of labour, through old age or any other infirmity, or should be wanting relief in any other respect; or if any Member should die, leaving a distressed family, the Steward or Stewards of his respective parish shall make a report of such circumstance at the next quarterly meeting, and the case shall be there considered, and such relief shall be granted, as the major part of the Stewards at such meeting shall deem necessary, so as not to reduce the fund under £200. [98]

These, Gentlemen, are Rules of the Woollen Cloth Weavers's Society - Rules totally subversive of, and contradictory to, the interests of the Members; and such, therefore, as candour itself cannot but reprobate in the most pointed terms.

The first Article contains a mixture of ideas the most extensive, and at the same time the most contracted and narrow. Whilst the Society invites into its bosom the regularly apprenticed weaver, though resident in even in the remotest parts of England and Scotland, it rejects every one who has not served a legal apprenticeship. In both respects it is inconsistent with that true policy which ought to actuate all Friendly Societies. All the Members of such clubs should be resident within a reasonable distance of each other, partly for the purpose of obtaining relief with greater ease, and partly for that of preventing fraud and imposition. To men of property in the neighbourhood the terms of admission should be easy, and they should be solicited to enrol their names as honorary members, for this obvious reason – they increase the public stock, without the probability of diminishing it.

But how, or in what respect, can a Member, whose place of residence is far distant from Stroud or Dursley, be benefited by his admission into the Society? Unless his parish produces two Members, no Steward can be elected for it; and [G 2-99] if so, he is both precluded from sending in his petition, when distressed, to the quarterly meeting, and also from electing a Representative or Delegate to dispose of his own subscription. But waving this objection, suppose him to be taken suddenly ill, to have a fractured limb, or to be in any of those emergencies which require immediate relief - how is he to obtain it? An inhabitant of North Britain may be imagined to enter eagerly into the Society, because it flatters him with those hopes of certain support, which he cannot look for in his own district, no laws being established there for the relief of the poor. But is his condition at all bettered by so doing? No. He is only tantalized with the vain hope of obtaining assistance from a fund to which he had largely contributed. Insult is added to injury, for no assistance can be had, but at a quarterly meeting, and long before that takes place the unhappy object may have been confined to his grave. But, for the sake of argument, let it be granted that the distressed Member is resident near these two seats of government, Dursley and Stroud, still the latter objection prevails. The monthly meeting of his parish has not the power of relieving him. This high privilege is the exclusive right of this quarterly meeting; and he also, may have exchanged this life for a better, before his petition can be received. [100]

Even supposing this not to be the case, what has be to depend upon? The discretion, the generosity of the Committee: a Committee bound by not fixed laws, compelled to allow him no certain sum: a Committe who may grant or reject his petition altogether, without assigning any reason: a Committee who may be liberal or parsimonious, according to the whim of the moment, the caprice of temper, the suggestions of private friendship or individual animosity, or perhaps even the effect of the liquor which they may have drank [sic]. Every man, when he enters into a Friendly Society, should know for certain what he is to expect in the hour of distress. This is the very principle of the Friendly Societies, and that alone which can induce a man, living by the sweat of his brow, to relinquish, for the present moment, part of his hard earned wages, in the hopes of obtaining it with interest, when his strength faileth. In every other Society, the Rules of which have been submitted to this Court, (and many such have fallen under my inspection,) some attention has been paid to the age of the Members at the time of admission; to the period of time during which they shall have continued Members; to the cause, the nature, and the duration of their illness; and to a mode of settling such disputes as may arise without trouble, delay, or expence. In this Society the reverse is the case in every respect. The quarterly meeting has the [101] despotic power of determining every thing secretly and without controul, aided indeed by the talents of a Professional Gentleman, who is appointed to two situations the most incompatible with each other, those of Solicitor and President; situations so totally contradictory, that his interests as Solicitor must ever be at variance with his interests as President.

Part of the sixteenth Article is peculiarly open to objection. That age and infirmity should have relief, is commendable; and may they ever receive it in such ample proportion, as to be sufficient to alleviate the calamities generally attending them! But the following sentence contains a meaning far beyond what at first meets the eye, and may be converted to dangerous purposes, if a Member "should be wanting relief in any other respect." What! Is it the purpose of the Society to grant relief, if wanted solely through idleness, drunkenness, or perhaps a conspiracy not to work but at increased wages, or a combination to strike, unless the master clothiers submit to every improper, perhaps insolent, demand of their journeymen? If this be the meaning, and I am warranted in saying that efforts to that purpose have been made, let the Society at once discard the name of Friendly Societyy, and assume one more appropriate to it – that of an Affiliated Society, in the modern acceptation of the term: let it openly avow its end and design – that of [102] laying the master clothiers at the feet of their servants, which must ultimately terminate in one common ruin to themselves and their employers, together with the destruction of the chief manufacture of this county, and the staple trade of the kingdom.

Gentlemen, I trust no apology will be thought necessary for addressing these observations to you. Resident, as I hope many of you are, in the neighbourhood where this extraordinary scene of fallacy on one part, and folly on the other, is now being carried on, I cannot but earnestly call upon you to exert that influence which you are possessed of, in endavouring to nip the evil in the bud, and to put a stop to its progress: and there are obvious reasons which, with an imperious tone, call upon to interfere in the present instance. To guard the unwary from imposition, and to protect the ignorant from the artifices of deception, is a duty incumbent upon all persons at all times, and more particularly upon Gentlemen possessed of your degree of respectability. The example, if followed, has a most pernicious tendency upon the interests of the kingdom at large. Besides which, it is necessary on your own account, as well as that of those misguided men, who are squandering their property for no purpose whatever, to the great injury of their wives and families, and who, thus endeavouring to catch at a shadown run no small chance of losing the substance. Associate with them, and endeavour [103] by reason and argument to undeceive them. Convince them, that the best mode which they can adopt for their own permanent advantage, is to form a strict union with their employers, and not with those who endeavour to poison their minds and excite their resentment by tales of imaginary grievances, for the purpose of involving them in the expence of protracted law-suits, the issue of which is ever uncertain. Recall to their minds, in short, that truth which they have been in the daily habit of experiencing – that their interests and those of their employers are inseparable, are one and the same; and that diligence, honesty, and fidelity on their part, will never fail of being rewarded by more than proportionate encouragement, liberality, and kindness on that of their masters.

FINIS.

A CHARGE DELIVERED TO THE *Grand Jury*, AT THE QUARTER SESSIONS, at the *NEW BAYLEY COURT-HOUSE*, IN SALFORD APRIL 25th, 1798, *By THOMAS BUTTERWORTH BAYLEY, Esq.* CHAIRMAN. PRINTED AT THE REQUEST OF THE GRAND JURY, MANCHESTER: PRINTED BY J. HARROW. 1798.

TO
Mr. *Richard Alsop*, Foreman,
Mr. *James Meredith*, of Ardwick,
Mr. *Thomas Richardson*, of Great Bolton,
Mr. *James Fletcher*, of same,
Mr. *Longworth Wilding*, of Blackrod,
Mr. *John Crompton*, of Farnworth,
Mr. *John Osbaldeston*, of Worsley,
Mr. *Benjamin Southerne*, of same,
Mr. *Robert Andrews*, of Harpur-Hey,
Mr. *Newman Hyde*, of Manchester,
Mr. *John Wilson*, of same,
Mr. *Edward Best*, of Turton,
Mr. *George Grimshaw*, of Gorton,
Mr. *Robert Lord*, of Halliwell,
Mr. *Otho Hulme*, of Great Bolton,
Mr. *Samuel Ashworth*, of Salford,
Mr. *John Ashton*, of same.
Gentlemen sworn on the Grand Inquest,
at the Quarter Sessions at Salford, April 25th, 1798,
THIS CHARGE
is most respectfully dedicated by their faithful Friend and Servant,
Tho. B. BAYLEY.
Hope, near Manchester, May 1st. 1798.

A CHARGE, &c.

Gentlemen of the grand jury.

IN my Addresses from this Chair to former Grand Juries, I have generally confined my Observations to subjects more immediately connected with the Business of this Court; and have avoided Discussions of what are usually called Political Subjects; which however useful they may be in our free Government, when properly conducted, have here no direct Application to our particular Service and Employment. But now, Gentlemen, we are met at a Season of actual danger, which demands our serious Attention, not to the State of Parties, but to the Security of our Country.

One of the greatest Blessings of Men is their being constituted social Beings, and placed in a State of mutual Dependance and correspondent Duties. Hence the Origin and Progress of all civil Associations from the fabulous Times of Orpheus, to the Establishment of our happy Government, at the Revolution. Perfection belongs not to any Scheme of human Wisdom; but from the Æra above named, Britons have every Reason to love [6] and venerate their Constitution. We may say that it is the Production of the successive Wisdom of Ages; that it connects the Honour and Efficacy of Royalty, with the Happiness and Liberty of the People; and that it is perfectly competent (as we constantly experience) by its own efficient Powers, and by Measures at once legal and peaceable, to correct its Errors and supply its Deficiencies.

This Court of Justice which is now met to administer our wise and excellent Laws for our common Protection, "for the Punishment of evil Doers, and the Praise and Reward of them that do well," is a striking Proof of my Assertion. Can it then be unseasonable, when we are about to discharge our several Functions in this interesting Occasion; to call to mind the inestimable Blessings we enjoy from our excellent Constitution and the benignant Reign of a Sovereign, who is in truth, the Father of his People.

Cicero says, that dear as are to us our Parents, our Children, our Friends – yet all these tender personal Ties and Connections, are comprehended in, and must be given up, *to the Love of our Country.* Let us attend to what this prescribes. [7]

First, *Union* – a Sacrifice of former Disputes and Animosities, on the Altar of Concord: And in Consequence, our utmost Exertions in the Defence of our King and Country.

The Crisis of Britain fast approaches, and soon it must be (I trust most happily) determined, whether she is to maintain her Security and Honour as a free and independent Nation, or crouch to the detested Tyranny of the Republic of France. This insulting Foe openly declares its fixed Purpose to destroy our most beloved Sovereign and his Royal Family; to abolish our Government and Laws; to root out our Religion; and lay prostrate our whole Estate; in short, 'it aims to possess our Sinews, our Marrow, and our Blood."

Menaced as we thus are from abroad, what is our internal Situation?

Gentlemen, I have not the smallest Apprehension of counteracting what I have before said of the Duty of general Union, by my Observations of this Head. The good Sense and manly Honour of our Countrymen will ever retain a great Majority of them – steady in their Loyalty, and active in the Country's Cause. But we [8] have too much reason to believe that we have amongst us, some Men wicked enough to betray it; who are most subtle to devise, and industrious to put in practice, every Machination, which may delude the credulous and unwary, divide and weaken the very means of our Defence, and even instruct, encourage and assist our invading Enemy. Gentlemen, we are under the greatest Obligations to his Majesty's wise and vigorous Measures to detect and to punish these Plotters of their Country's Ruin; I hope they will not be too late to enlighten the Understandings of deluded and mistaken Men, and wholly to frustrate the Imaginations and Hopes of Traitors.

You will excuse the Warmth with which I express the honest Feelings of my Heart, but these are not Times for base and cowardly Neutrality; this is not a political Squabble, or a party Question; – It is for our Country – Our Duty is plain, it cannot be mistaken; we must not halt between two Opinions; he that is not with us is against us.

If there shall remain amongst us, Men whose political Depravity may be Proof against the Calls of Duty, or the Suggestions of Fear, and who, with their accustomed Wiles may still pursue their dark Plans of Sedition and of Treason, be [9] it your Care, and that of every loyal true- hearted Englishman to discover these Men, that their evil Practices may receive their merited Punishment. Such of you as are engaged in Trades, and employ many Labourers in different Branches of the Manufactures, will do well to make yourselves acquainted with their Characters and Behaviour, that a proper Discrimination may be made, and timely Notice given of all who are chargeable with seditious Practices.

For our general Defence against Invasion, we are now called upon by Authority to offer our personal Services. Let us make ourselves acquainted with the Particulars of the Requisition, that we may avoid a hasty and indiscreet Zeal, and a timid Indifference, which may equally frustrate the Measures of Government.

Patient Subordination, and a steady Trust in the executive Departments of the State, are peculiarly necessary. Each Man's Duty and Place will be assigned to him; there let him be active, watchful, and sober. If we would save our Country, we must imitate the Spartan Self-denial and Temperance: We must go forth, not with the luxury of a Persian Host, but with the simple and unincumbered Arrangement of the Macedonian Phalanx. [10]

We must, on this Occasion, be content to give up the Pride, Pomp and Circumstance of "*glorious War*," the more effectually to serve our King and Country.

In the circular Letter from Mr. Secretary Dundas to the Lords Lieutenants of Counties, respecting the arming more Volunteer Corps, it is stated as an essential Condition that they should consist of "none but known, or respectable Householders, or Persons who can bring, at least, two such Householders to answer for their *good Behaviour.*"

The Emissaries of France, with incredible Industry and Perseverance, have first deluded and divided, and thus subdued mighty Nations. Their Efforts of this kind are unceasing in this Kingdom.

Let us all endeavour to check the progress of this delusion, and guard our Countrymen against the Snares, Misrepresentations and Falshoods of the disaffected. Let us shew them their present happy State, and what must be the dreadful Con-[11] sequences, should the Invasion of the French be successful. Let us present to their View, the unavailing repentance of Flanders, Holland, Italy, and Switzerland; in all which Countries the Tree of Liberty is watered by the bitter Tears of the wretched Subjects of French Deceit and Tyranny. Holland once the Emporium of Commerce, has lost its Trade and all its Sources of Wealth. Its Inhabitants were duped by the Pretences of the French to free them from Taxes, - But such is the Rapacity of these Deliverers, that they have already plundered the poor Dutchmen of nearly one half of all their Property, real or personal.

Infidelity, the malignant Star which now sheds over us its baneful Rays, would deprive us of all Sanctions of Duty, and all Hopes of a World to come. Under its Influence, the French abroad, and their seditious Friends in this Country, are most active to disperse wicked Books, which pretend there is no Truth in the Bible; no God for them to fear; no future State; no final Judgment. From their Success in this horrible Attempt, their best hopes are formed of destroying this Country; but, I trust, Englishmen will never forget that the Fear and Love of God, (whose Power no Creature is able to resist) are the beginning, and the consummation of all their Du-[12] ties, and all their Happiness. Christianity is the Law of England, it is its Foundation and its Defence. Let us all therefore steadfastly adhere, to this Anchor of our Hope, in principle, and in act.

FINIS.

THE **CHARGE** OF THE HONOURABLE DENIS GEORGE, LATE RECORDER OF DUBLIN, AND NOW ONE OF THE BARONS OF HIS MAJESTY'S COURT OF EXCHEQUER IN IRELAND, *DELIVERED BY HIM AT THE NEW SESSIONS-HOUSE ON THE 20TH DAY OF OCTOBER, 1798,* to the GRAND JURIES FOR THE CITY OF DUBLIN and COUNTY OF DUBLIN, AND NOW PUBLISHED AT THEIR REQUEST. DUBLIN: PRINTED BY JOHN EXSHAW, PRINTER AND STATIONER TO THE GRAND JURY OF THE CITY OF DUBLIN, N° 8, GRAFTON-STREET.

[3]

THE CHARGE OF THE HONOURABLE DENIS GEORGE, &C.

Gentlemen of both Grand Juries,

ON this day, for the first time, are opened here new Commissions of Oyer and Terminer and General Gaol Delivery; which we now proceed to execute.

I have often before had the honor to preside as Recorder of the city of Dublin, or as Judge, where most of you have acted as Grand Jurors.- I know that the general outline of your duty, so well marked out to you by your oath, is fully understood by you; I therefore shall not delay you upon that topic, but call your attention to the species of crimes, which now prevail, and may be submitted for your consideration.[4]

The offences formerly contained in the Dublin calenders, were for the most part such as flowed from individual depravity; having for their end the destruction or the injury of the individual life of the subject; or the violent invasion of the liberty and property of a single man, and such crimes were mischievous and alarming; but the offences prevalent of late have had for their object a mischief more extended. - The subversion of the Kingly power - the overthrow of our ancient Constitution - and the murder, or at least the banishment and ruin of every man attached to it; and the crimes which at present disfigure and disgrace our country shew but too plainly, that the dregs of the disorders with which we have been afflicted still remain; however, it is not be doubted, but that our Government will by the most wise and effectual remedies prevent all danger of relapse.

Our calamities however, having been local, have possibly produced one good effect, they have served to shew rash and inconsiderate men, who lived apart from the scenes of misery, the horrors which would have been universal, if rebellion had succeeded; and to convince them without bitter personal experience, of truths which otherwise they might not have believed.

This kingdom surrounded as it is by seas, and defended as it is, by victorious fleets, presented a place of security where much of the talents and riches of Europe would have concentered, in taking refuge from the oppressions of France; and thus should we have flourished amidst the wreck of empires, becoming daily more rich and more prosperous had our people been "let to themselves" and allowed to judge of their condition by their own feelings, and their own senses.

But the reverse of things within a few years past has been sad indeed! and that reverse has been [5] produced by the unrelenting perseverance of a wicked faction calling themselves United Irishmen in the endeavour to disengage the people from their allegiance to the King, under whose mild government they have lived eight and thirty years, who during all that time has made the happiness of his subjects and the prosperity and glory of his kingdoms the objects of his fondest care.

Every considerate man must know that the oath of allegiance which the subject owes to the King is an obligation of a most salutary nature. The King when he accepts his Crown, does in the most solemn and public manner by his coronation oath, bind himself to the safety and happiness of his subjects, and to make the known laws of the land the rule of his conduct. – That oath he has fulfilled, and we have seen, and I hope, shall long enjoy a patriot King at the head of our free Constitution.

We, his natural born subjects, on our part are bound to him in duty, even though we had never taken any oath of allegiance. – The oaths enjoined by our statutes in this particular are only declaratory of the duty which obliges us "to bear fair and true allegiance to his Majesty King George and him to defend to the utmost of our power against all traitorous conspiracies and attempts whatsoever which shall be made against his person, crown or dignity, and do out utmost endeavour to disclose and make known to his Majesty, all treasons and traitorous conspiracies which we shall know to be against him." Such is our primary duty in society as Irish subjects, and to break or withhold this duty is, according to the circumstances, either high-treason or misprision of treason.

We cannot bear faith and true allegiance to his Majesty, without defending him to the utmost [6] of our power against all traitorous conspiracies and attempts which we know to be made against his person, crown or dignity; and this duty the loyal yeomen of our counties have well, effectually and gallantly fulfilled. – Nor, gentlemen, is this all, a less important duty remains – we are also bound to disclose and make known to his Majesty, all treasons and traitorous conspiracies which we shall know to be against him, and this duty, they who give true information to the Magistrates, and afterwards give full and true evidence in Courts of Justice against traitors, do fulfil.

Such as value the applauses of immoral men, and court a base and criminal popularity, will be alone wanting in this branch of duty, which when honestly fulfilled is no less laudable, and likely to be more useful than the observance of any other.

They whose plans are deranged or whose hopes or wishes are lost by such disclosures, call all, who fulfil this branch of their allegiance, spies and informers, and wickedly compare them with certain monsters which history has deservedly branded with infamy. – By such arts the sense of shame which has given to promote what is virtuous, is perverted; and men are made to blush when they set about a duty the most indispensable, and which nothing less than the profligacy of these times could prevent from the being the most popular also.

The duty of allegiance to the King is so blended with our own welfare, that in supporting the throne we but defend ourselves and our families, we are well held together in our society by our political connection with him, and he cannot be deposed by treasonable practices without involving the whole nation in blood, and confusion, and experience has shewn us that *every stroke at the Throne is necessarily levelled at the public safety and tranquility.* [7]

The conspiracy that has been formed against our lives, liberties, and properties, has been by God's blessing exposed, and it is now held up by the Reports of both Houses of Parliament, to public condemnation.

These Reports have shewn us the foul means that were made use of for our Destruction, and the unworthy instruments of treason, who vainly hoped to raise themselves to power on the ruins of the Kingly authority; and to riches, by the plunder of his Majesty's good and faithful subjects.- It is not to be wondered at that such numbers had engaged in the plot- a conspiracy which attracted to it the ambitious, the impatient, the disappointed, the discontented, the idle, the profligate, and politically fanatic of a populous country must ever be numerously supported - but the discomfiture and disgrace that has attended their designs, will, I trust, in future induce men to seek rank and opulence, by cultivating those talents that are always seen in the train of the virtues; by learning, by sober industry; by patience and perseverance in useful and honourable pursuits; by promoting a ready obedience to the laws, and by paying the respect that is due to the King and Constitution, from which they derive security and protection. Rank and distinction so acquired are dignified - riches so earned are our own, and will prosper with our posterity.

The two Houses of our Parliament in the full exposure, they have made in their reports, of the various impositions under which this conspiracy grew to be formidable, will render it difficult in any future period for treason to continue to personate public spirit until the very eve of insurrection.

We shall not be told, that men closeted in dark cabals, who affect to bind themselves to political measures by unlawful and equivocal oaths - [8] whose orders and proceedings are wrapped up in secrecy, who by every sort of libel circulate discontent in order to prepare the minds of men for disaffection.

We shall not, I say, again be told that these men have no other view than parliamentary reform; all who are not wilfully blind shall acknowledge the imposture and the parliamentary reformer of a future day, such as I describe shall stand exposed the wild revolutionist.

Among the monsters produced by this faction, one of the greatest is the attempt made by them to seduce all descriptions of men, and amongst them, the Roman Catholic of Ireland, into an unnatural confederacy with the Government of France – a Government whose earliest act of dominion was to overthrow all Roman Catholic establishments within its own country – a government which profaned its own Christian churches, and offered up to Reason the incense that lay upon the altars of religious worship – a Government which chased the Pope himself with insult out of Rome – stripped its churches of their decorations, pillaged their treasuries, and polluted their sanctuaries.

And still stranger must it be, if after such well known treatment of their church, and also of him who is at their head, any of the Roman Catholic clergy of this country should be led to take a part with the French against our Government; under whose auspices, Catholic Colleges were built up in Ireland as they were thrown down in France, and whilst the French Government (in its eagerness for the possessions of the church) was occupied in France in the unfeeling extermination of their clergy, by hundreds, and thousands; here it was the public care to perpetuate their Order, and this has been done, without exercising any control over its tuition or interfering with its discipline. [9] Every history I have met with has shewn that the most ambitious and most self-interested philanthropers have set out, in all ages, and in all countries, by professing to be the poor man's friend; and this sort of philanthropy all the founders of the Irish Union did of course at first put on; and how have they manifested their friendship? In our towns and cities they have called off men from their useful labours to consult on plans of ideal Republics and visionary Commonwealths; the artizans and manufacturers desist from their occupations – they collect, and conceal, mortal weapons – all is alarm – the speculations and improvements of the affluent which used to distribute employment and abundance among the lower orders, are postponed until more favourable times shall hold out the prospect of more permanent security. The profession of arms, for public and private defence, is almost the only visible occupation; and it is much to be regretted, that the inconvenience and distress which has followed, is not confined to the criminals who occasioned it; this is no more than a faint sketch of what has been very lately the state of our towns but the Union did not confine itself to their limits; it has sent its emissaries through a peaceable industrious, and improving country; and amongst the laborious, and contented, it has created wants and desires which were never before felt, and which in the scale and order of civilized life, are suited only to the higher ranks of society: it has excited in them vain hopes, and bad passions – it has awakened their fears, and roused up their revenge by imaginary dangers – and the peasant (who attends with credulity to whatever may draw him into mischief) is abused by false news, and strange prophecies: with unforeseen and alarming offences, they first make strong laws necessary, and then calumniate and vilify the acts of the le-[10] gislature: hence it was, that men who loved their country, and were ready to defend it with their lives, soon after submitted to be sworn to betray it over to French adventurers: hence it is that in many parts of this once happy kingdom, the sincere, the kind-hearted, and the hospitable Irish character is no more to be found, and no longer serves to sweeten and to enliven human intercourse: and hence is that where innocence was once used to repose, guilt now stalks restless and undisturbed – where all was harmony it is now become the scene of discord – and where there was a cheerful wife and playful family, there is now a houseless widow left to curse the wretches who seduced, or perhaps forced the father of her children from his home to rush on his own destruction. – Such, and still worse, is the afflicting view which the disturbed parts of our country present to the eye of sensibility.

What infatuation! that any man but the outlaw or the outcast, should put his life and fortune under the orders of a Directory, composed of men, whom he never saw or knew – of whose talents in Revolutionary emergency there never was any trial; with whose ability to fill the station of a law-giver, and with whose moderation and wisdom in the exercise of power he is utterly unacquainted.

Of the various motives which men have for embarking in Revolution - the desire of plunder is perhaps that which seduces the greatest numbers. But see how much against the dictates of plain reason he acts, who would overturn the law which secures to his opulent neighbour, his life and property. Let me ask what is life without the security of the law? It is a precarious existence held only till another person is by interest, or by enmity tempted to take it away. And what is property without the security of the law? It is that possession, which we hold only whilst we are stronger [11] than those who covet it. – If then the law and the constitution were overturned, and the strong allowed to plunder the weak, how long would he enjoy the goods he so acquired? And what security would he in his turn have for his misgotten wealth? – Would the riches he had obtained by pillage cease to be covetted by others, because they had changed owners? – Surely no.

A second and third set of spoilers would not be wanting, to strip, and perhaps to slay, the men who were early and active in the works of depredation – let not therefore any one who would preserve life or liberty, or who either has or ever hopes to have, property, tempted to rise against the constitution and the law; their value as well to the poor, as to the rich, is, (as many of our greatest blessings are) seldom fairly appreciated until the enjoyment of them is interrupted.

These observations on the uncommon extent, and nature of the treasons of the present times having been submitted to you; the sort of evidence that may be expected to shew the guilt, or innocence, of the culprits charged with this offence is well deserving of your consideration.

It is notorious, that these offenders are bound to each other by oaths; and however these oaths may in other respects vary, in all of them there is a clause of secrecy, and an engagement not to give evidence against each other in Courts of Justice- Thus we see that the public justice of the land is the foremost in their apprehensions – and they most providently prepare for trial, and lay a ground for acquittal, as soon as they meditate, and resolve to commit the crime,

From the very nature of treasonable conspiracy, written papers and the testimony of accomplices, or persons considered so to be, are the proof from which conviction, in general, can reasonably be ex-[12]pected. The United Men were fully aware of this – to the dishonour of their profession they appear to have had amongst them, some Barristers, and they have doubtless under the advice of such associates, as much as possible, and studiously avoided committing any proofs of their guilt to paper – but to secure themselves against the vast host of accomplices engaged, and to lead unseen, and unknown, was a work requiring the most ingenious management – however their contrivances served only to diminish the danger, but could not wholly remove it, and without individual confidence the noxious parts could not be connected into one destructive system. Thus it appears that the danger arising from the desertion or remorse of accomplices was inevitable, and therefore every terror, that might affright the heart; and every personal abuse that might wound the feelings of the man, according to his rank, were stored up for such as might relent – and besides this, a flagitious sort of false honor was inculcated, that might prevent men from hearkening to the voice of nature, and so putting a stop to the intended carnage; hence it was that whilst many did from their souls, hate, and abhor this new tyranny, and languished to declare that hatred and abhorrence, but a few men had the courage, or the virtue, to break loose from the toils in which they were entangled, to confess their own, and in order to stop the mischief prosecute the guilt of their accomplices. Whoever submits himself to be sworn and become a member in conspiracy, does thereby not only make a bare surrender of all character, but make himself also, whether present or absent, a principal or accessory in all the various crimes of his accomplices committed in furtherance of the common end. The criminality in which he may be involved, and the legal punishments to which he is thus [13] deservedly exposed, are to the last degree, alarming - yet many have of late acted as if these plain rules of the law and justice had not existed. Some there were thus implicated in crime, who have happily merged all their criminality in public service.

We can well conceive that an unfortunate man, under the continual pressure of malign influence, may be led on, step by step, near to a horrible extremity – but there the abused feelings of the man revolt against further seduction; and he will follow no farther – there he stands, anxious for nothing but the best means of making the fullest atonement to God and his country, and this I trust is the general feeling of multitudes, who are now no longer United Irishmen.

You must be sensible that a prosecutor of this sort, must be the most circumstancial detector of secret treason. Crimes must in our Courts be proved by facts within the knowledge of the witnesses, and if any man does seriously and in good earnest look for better parol evidence, of a treasonable conspiracy than this, his notion of conspiracy must be singular, and his experience must be slender of the caution and circumspection of this sort of guilt. Again, persons prosecuting under such circumstances, are charged by their former associates and their adherents, to be guilty of perjury against the wicked oaths they had taken as United Men, and on that account they would have such witnesses, held to be infamous and incompetent – and very convenient had it been to the Union, if such doctrine had found a favourable reception in Courts of Law. – The danger which conspirators must dread had then been wholly removed. – The guilty would no longer regard each other with distrust, and treason would be hatched in the most perfect security.

But, gentlemen, when criminals, confederated to overset the constitution, cause an outcry to be [14] raised against such persons in such circumstances; that should only recommend them to the countenance, protection, and gratitude of all others.

It would give the most lively joy to every good man, if these offenders could be reclaimed by measures of mercy and forgiveness – such have lately been tried; and their efficacy has since been most powerfully seconded – I mean by the splendor and effect of Naval Victory, and by the loyalty of the country, now supported by the force and spirit of the British army.

When they who are privates in the ranks of our conspirators, now look at the miserable remnant of this rebellion, their own observation must convince them, that the criminal chimæras which they formed, are altogether impracticable; and it will require only a moderate share of reflection, to induce them to abandon an enterprise which is at once wicked, perilous, and hopeless.

But as to such as had attained to place and rank in the conspiracy - As to men who have been for years past tormenting themselves and their hearers with seditious disputation.

As to men who were the most enamoured of French principles, and French manners, when French butcheries were most disgusting.

As to men who have caused more violent deaths, and greater human misery, than ever was heard of in Ireland; and yet have such rare talents as can persuade the common people even to this day, that they are their best friends.

As to men who would at any time cheerfully devote the lives of a thousand foolish followers rather than sacrifice one of their head-strong opinions.

As to men whose pride is suited to the high station, which in their visions they had allotted to themselves, under their new-fangled constitu [15] tion; and whose honor, now stands bound to the enemy, by the stately obligation of an Imperial treaty.

As for men who seat themselves, as it were, upon thrones, and from thence deliver lectures pleasing to simple minds, upon the doctrines of equality;

It is hard task I fear for such men, together with their habits, to lay down their more than princely expectations, and become good and dutiful subjects.

As this great evil ought wholly to engross the public mind, until it is totally removed - I have thought it right to direct your attention on this occasion to it alone.

The vigilance and valour of the loyal in every department of the community, is still wanted to restore and secure the peace, and to retrieve the character of our country.

And finally, let every man whether he be placed in an exalted station, and endowed with transcendant talents, or whether with modest merit in his humble line, he renders any service honorable to himself, and useful to his King and Country let him I say, after the example of the pious and victorious Lord Nelson, not omit to ascribe to the blessing of Almighty God, all the merit of the achievement.

A **CHARGE** DELIVERED TO THE GRAND JURY, *AT THE ASSIZES HOLDEN AT ELY,* ON WEDNESDAY THE 27TH DAY OF MARCH 1799. By HENRY GWILLIM, Esq. CHIEF JUSTICE OF THE ISLE OF ELY. PUBLISHED AT THE REQUEST OF THE MAGISTRATES AND GRAND JURY. LONDON: PRINTED FOR J. BUTTERWORTH, · IN FLEET STREET. 1799

[A 2 -3]

A CHARGE, &c. &c. &c.

Gentlemen of the Grand Jury,

ALTHOUGH your Calendar exhibits a greater number of offences than we are usually called upon to examine upon these occasions, and some of them are of a very dark complexion; yet I am not aware of any difficulties that lie in the way of your duty, nor that you need any directions from me to guide you in your inquiries. The difficulties ought indeed to be striking and prominent, before I should venture to interpose unsolicited assistance. I have had too long experience of the ability of the Grand Jurors of this franchise, I am too well acquainted with the propriety and correctness with which they conduct themselves in the execution of their office, to hold it necessary, or even decent, to insist upon the ordinary topicks in addresses of this kind. It would only be to point out to them what they already see; to tell them what they already know. And if I were to look no farther, Gentlemen, than the business immediately before you, I would most certainly not obtrude myself upon you for a moment: but, when I consider the wide extent of your duty, [4] and the claims which your country has upon persons of your description, as well in your private, individual characters, as in this your publick, collective capacity, I think it cannot be altogether improper, nor inconsistent wit the object of our meeting, to direct your attention to the circumstances of the present crisis.

Perhaps, Gentlemen, there never was a time when more caution, more vigilancy, more exertion, more enquiry were necessary on the part of those who are anywise concerned in the administration of the government, than at the present awful moment. The contest in which we are now engaged is no common contest; it is not a question of territory, of aggrandisement, or succession, which the sword is to decide: but the question now at issue is, whether we are to retain our old habits, our old usages, our old laws, our old government, our old liberties; or whether we are to give up all these, and exchange them for notions, the effects of which we have never tried; for speculations, we have not had time to examine; for theories, which have never been reduced into practice. To hazard, nay more, to part with all we have, in the expectation of gaining some *possible* advantage, is an act, not of wisdom, but of desperation. Innovation, in all cases, is dangerous: but it is more particularly so in states, where nothing can justify it but urgent necessity and evident utility.[1]

The truth is, that the fabrick of government is a work of time: it must be built upon, and moulded into, the temper, the dispositions, the habits, the circumstances of the people for whose use it is intended. Laws must be made for men, not men for laws. Laws must be given *populo volenti*; the scheme of legislation must adapt itself to the genius of the people else, the machine can never be brought to act. The idea of establishing one form, one system [5] of government over the world is chimerical and absurd: it is a notion which can originate only, as we see it now doth, in a spirit of domination, and which conquest only can affect to realize. Such a state of things (if we can suppose such a state to exist) would be a violence upon Nature, and the mere effect of force and coercition. It could not be lasting: but the moment the pressure was taken off, the elastick power of Nature would restore her to her original and proper state. Uniformity is no more to be expected, as it is no more to be desired, in the political, than in the natural world. As long as men differ from one another, as long as human nature is what it is, there must be different systems of government. The very accidents of climate and situation produce a different temperament, which requires a different regimen. What might well suit a temperate region, would be ill adapted to a tropical climate: the same draught of liberty which would barely exhilarate the inhabitants of one, would drive the natives of the other into an absolute phrenzy. In the making of laws, too, the state of society must be attended to. In an early state of society, the laws, like the wants of the people, will be few and simple: but in a more advanced state, as population increases; as the means of subsistence become more difficult; as invention grows more active; as the desires of men become more numerous and more diffuse, and the scheme of government more complex: the legislator will find himself compelled to narrow the rights of one part of the people, and to enlarge the privileges and grant additional indulgences to another part.

It is manifest, then, Gentlemen, that all abstract notions of government

[1] It would be interesting to compare this paragraph with Burke's *Reflections on the present Revolution in France*, nearly ten years old when this Charge was delivered.

are absurd;[1] and that to attempt to enforce them is an act [6] equally of violence and temerity. It is manifest, also, that that form of government must be the best, which is the best adapted to the genius of the people to whom it is applied; and will most easily accommodate itself to those alterations and improvements which the varying circumstances of those people, and the exigencies of their situation, may from time time require.

It was a wise answer that was made by the great Athenian legislator, when he was asked whether he had prescribed good laws for the Athenians: *They are best*, said he, *which the Athenians are able to bear.* Gentlemen, you will do well to keep this answer always in your mind; when the imperfections of your own government are pressed upon you, consider whether they are not the consequence of, whether they are not necessary to, that state of things to which you must submit, and which in truth you wish for: whether that which, simply considered, may appear to be wrong, will not, in its relative situation, be found to be right: examine too the proposed improvements, consider whether you could bear them, whether the attempt to introduce them would not universally provoke resistance, and resistance lead to anarchy.

The form of government which you are invited to accept, which is held up to you in exchange for that which you now enjoy, is called a pure republick; that is, where the sovereign power is lodged in the whole body of the people. If virtue, (and by virtue is meant a disinterested regard for the commonwealth, and an invariable consent in the whole people to postpone all private considerations to the publick good;) if this be the principle of such a form of government, as a great writer[2] has stated it to be, then [7] you will consider whether this principle exist among you; whether a nation in that state of society we are now arrived at; whether a people so fertile of inventions, with so many artificial wants, with such notions of exclusive rights and exclusive enjoyments, with the selfishness consequent to wealth and commerce, with the desire of pre-eminence and distinction natural to man, and confirmed in us by long habit; whether a people in such a state be capable of a species of government which professeth to move only upon equality, disinterestedness, forbearance, and self-denial; whether they could bear it.

An attempt was made in the last century to introduce democracy into this country, and we all know, Gentlemen, with what success: we know that those who had been the most active in destroying the machine of the old government, were glad to collect the scattered pieces and put them together again, and were forced to acknowledge that no other could be so well adapted to this country. Sir Bulstrode Whitlocke, who

[1] Again, the criticism levelled at the new French institutions, of being abstract, is derived from Burke.

[2] Montesquieu, Sp. of Laws, book iii. c. 3.

was a regularly educated and professed lawyer, who held the great seal in the time of the commonwealth, and who had taken a considerable part in all the miserable vicissitudes of the times, is stated to have said at a meeting of Cromwell and his officers about the settlement of the nation[1], "That the laws of England are so interwoven with the power and practice of monarchy, that to settle a government without something of monarchy in it, would make so great an alteration in the proceedings and practice of our law, that they had scarce time to rectify it; *nor could they well foresee the inconveniencies that would arise thereby.*" And we are told[2] that, [8] Whitlocke was so firmly persuaded that his country could receive no other form of government, that he often renewed his instances with Cromwell to that effect. In truth, Gentlemen, there is something in the regularity of a monarchy which is admirably suited to the gravity of an Englishman, whilst the limitations which our constitution prescribes to it, favour his love of freedom. The Protector was, no doubt, well convinced of the justness of Whitlocke's advice, but he had neither the courage nor the honesty to restore the diadem to its rightful owner, and he durst not assume it himself: he had sacrificed truth too long to the lust of power to make an open avowal of his real sentiments, and he was obliged to submit to be fettered in the exercise of his powers by the falsehoods which he had used to attain it. But in addition to so important a testimony as that of a man so conversant with the constitution of his country as Sir Bulstrode Whitlocke, who acted so considerable a part under the commonwealth, and whose opinion therefore is clear of all suspicion of being influenced by partiality or prejudice in favour of the crown; in addition to such a testimony of the congeniality of our present form of government with the temper and habits of our fellow-subjects, we may further remark its aptitude to accommodate itself to the exigencies of circumstances, its capacity to receive improvements without danger to its principle, or affecting its identity. Old rights have been secured to the people, and now privileges have been granted to them, and yet the original form of government remains unimpaired. The Reformation, so far as that great event may be politically considered; the petition of right in the time of Charles the First; the *Habeas Corpus* Act in the time of his son; the Triennal Act, that is, the act to oblige the King to call a parliament once in three years at the least[3] [9] these confirmations of original rights, and grants of further privileges, with many others that must occur to you, were made without the slightest detriment to the constitution itself.

[1] See Dr Morton, the Editor's, Preface to the Parliamentary Writ, p. 33. -[See *Memoirs, Biographical and Historical of B. Whitelocke*, ed. R.H. Whitelocke (London: Routledge, Warne, & Routledge, 1860.)]

[2] Id, p. 34.

[3] St. W. & M. ch. 2

Our present scheme of government, Gentlemen, is not only the most happily adapted to the genius of this country, is not only admirable relatively considered, but is in itself perhaps the most stupendous system of polity that ever was devised by human wit. A system like ours, that should combine in itself the benefits of the three regular forms of government, which mankind have acknowledged; of monarchy, aristocracy, and democracy; of the one, the few, and the many; was treated by the most philosophical historian of antient Rome as visionary[1]; as what we could never hope to see realized; or, if by accident it should be brought into being, what could never be of any long duration. A system that should unite with the vigour and energy of a monarchy, the wisdom, the temper, the moderation of an aristocracy, and that generous concern for the common interest, that disinterested regard for the general welfare, the virtue of a republick; that by combining the benefits, should exclude the evils generally consequent to each form of government; is a state which certainly seems rather to be desired, than expected. Gentlemen, I have said, a system that should combine the *benefits* of the three forms of government; for it is a political error leading to very dangerous consequences, to suppose that our system actually combines the three forms of government themselves: had it been so, it certainly could not have been lasting: three jarring interests, three powers co-ordinate and co-equal in the state, must soon have terminated in anarchy and confusion. No; the beauty of our form of government, the in-[10] genuity of the contrivance, is, that whilst it unites the benefits of each, it is in itself one and simple: it is a monarchy; the power, and dominion, and sovereignty are lodged in one only: the king reigns, the king is supreme, the whole scheme of government is carried on by the king only, and in the king's name: the king only acts in all cases; not indeed arbitrarily and without controul, but under certain checks and limitations. These checks are, that he must act in all cases with the *advice* of his subjects; in some cases with their *consent* as well as *advice*. His powers in matters of legislation is qualified by the *consent* of his parliament, the constitutional representatives of the three estates in the realm, of the whole people of his kingdom: he can make no law which they have not previously agreed upon as proper to be propounded by him, which they do not authorize him to make. His power in the executive part of his government is qualified by the *advice* of certain counsellours, whom the laws have assigned to him, and who are responsible to the country for every act which he does. Thus, while a complex effect is produced, the machine itself is perfectly simple; while the interests of all are provided for, the unity and entierty of the monarchy are preserved: the states affect no

[1] *Cunctas nationes et urbes populus, aut primores, aut singuli regunt: delecta ex his et consociata republicæ forma laudari facilius, quam evenire; vel, si evenit haud diurturna esse potest.* Tacit. Annal. lib.4.

quality or co-ordination with the sovereign; though they limit his power, they acknowledge his supremacy: the subject is not distracted where to pay his allegiance: he findeth the whole power of the state concentrated in one only: " he hopeth for protection from the crown," to use the words of Sir Michael Foster, "and he payeth his allegiance to it in the person whom he seeth in full and peaceable possession of it. – He seeth the fountain whence the blessings of government, liberty, peace, and plenty flow to him; and there he payeth his allegiance.[1]" [B 2 -11]

Beware then, Gentlemen, of all attempts to make any alteration in this most stupendous machine: beware how you affect to vary its direction, or to abridge it any of any of its parts as useless. The attempt at reform, will end most probably, as it is most commonly intended it should end, in its ruin. Depend on it, the system is so complete, so perfect within itself, that you cannot strip it of any parts without endangering the whole.

One of the popular objections of the present day is the aristocratical part of our constitution. Hereditary distinctions and hereditary privileges are treated by modern reformers as infringements upon the natural rights of man, and inconsistent with all just notions of government. Gentlemen, give not ear to such objections: if the objectors are sincere in them, they are ignorant of human nature; if they are not, what their true intention is, you cannot doubt. Gentlemen, there is a natural aristocracy among mankind: one man is endued with superior talents and superior powers to another: he feels his superiority, and that sense of superiority gives him a claim to the lead and control of those whom he finds inferior to him: and if great talents were accompanied with great virtue, and the world were always disposed to yield to the guidance and direction of superior merit, the legislator might trust to the disposition of nature; the stags with the largest heads would ever be the foremost in the herd. But as things are not so constituted; as the claims of merit are not always attended to; as virtue and talent are not always found together; the legislator feels himself obliged to interpose, and fix a political aristocracy which shall correct the mischiefs and disturbances to which the pretensions of the natural aristocracy must perpetually give occasion. He selects there-[12] fore a part of the people to whom he grants hereditary honours and hereditary privileges, and upon whom also he lays hereditary duties: though he selects a part only of the people, yet he at the same time excludes no man from the hope of participating in these immunities: the doors of the temple of honour are always open to virtue and ability. By this means, while he secures the quiet of the state, and prevents the publick business from being interrupted by the difficulty of election, and the rivalry of power, he does not repress the natural

[1] 1 Cr. Law, 8vo edit. p. 399.

aristocracy, he only regulates its direction. He excites a stronger emulation; he gives an additional stimulus to exertion in the publick cause; he points to a pre-eminence that shall survive the grave, and live in the descendant; and thus artfully interests in the preservation of the whole, the individual pride and feelings of a parent. Nor does the advantage stop here; the descendant is piqued to emulate the deeds of his ancestor, and to shew himself not unworthy of the distinction which he inherits.

If moderation be, as it is said to be[1], the principle of an aristocracy, then has that principle been most religiously adhered to by the aristocracy of this country. For whoever will carefully peruse the pages of our history, and, in particular, will examine the proceedings of that period[2], which is generally, though perhaps not very properly, called the Revolution, will perceive how many obligations we owe to, and how much the success of that important event depended upon, the calmness, the temper, the deliberation, the wisdom of the House of Peers. No man wished for the abolition of that august assembly, or for an abridgment of their privileges, who does not also wish for an abolition of the whole government. Abolish, says Montesquieu, (and he is alluding to this country,) *abolish, in a monarchy, the prerogatives of the lords, the clergy, the nobility, and the cities; you will presently have a popular state, or a despotick government.* For the privileges which are granted to the nobles, the clergy, and to corporate bodies, operate as a check upon the crown and the people; and by stopping the encroachments of either, keep the whole system together. A publick, political, artificial interest, which shall always be the same, is an admirable contrivance to counteract the effects of the private, individual, and therefore variable, interest of the crown and the people. These political beings, these creatures of the state, can only exist while things continue as they are: they have equally to dread the licentiousness of the people and the tyranny of the prince. Any change in the system, is inconsistent with a uniform interest founded upon the system, as it exists. If the monarch exceed his proper limits, and become despotick, the privileges of these bodies must be odious to him, and of course be annihilated: on the other hand, if the licentiousness of the people prevail, and the state become democratick, such privileges must be alike odious, and alike annihilated. Despotism and democracy equally abhor all distinctions: the one will not be advised; the other will not be controlled. The necessity of this bond of union to the existence of our government was well understood in the last century, and accordingly the first step that was taken by those who aimed at the destruction of their country, was to strip the clergy of their prerogatives, and to declare the House of Lords useless. That barrier being removed, the people had only to choose between [14]

[1] Sp. of Laws, Book iii, c. 4.

[2] See the Journals of the Lords and Commons.

despotism and democracy, between the tyranny of the one and of the many. The extremes, no longer kept distinct and separate, clashed and instantly the fabrick fell.

Gentlemen, I have perhaps insisted too long upon these topicks; many, if not all, of my observations have, no doubt, often occurred to you: but it may not be wholly improper, at these times, to recollect our old notions, and to review the foundations of our old opinions; for, as in religion, we are often pertly and flippantly called upon *to give a reason for the faith that is in us*: so, in civil matters, we are now boldly require to state and explain the grounds of that just admiration which we feel for our constitution; to account for – good Heaven! is it possible? – we are required to account for our love to our country. And to whom can I so properly, so emphatically address myself upon such a subject, as to the Grand Jurors of the country; to that council, which the constitution hath assigned to the sovereign, in the just maintenance of his laws, and in the inquiry into offences committed against his peace, his crown, and his dignity? You are not only charged, Gentlemen, to inquire of those things which are propounded to you at the time of your meeting, which are submitted to your consideration upon the representation of others; you are also bound to communicate to one another, and to present for publick investigation and correction, whatever you may have discovered to be injurious to the government under which you live, to the general security and happiness of your fellow-subjects. The obligation to institute such an inquiry implies a previous obligation upon the party to make himself acquainted with those things which are likely to become the objects of it. When you undertake to pre-[15] sent all such offences as have come to your knowledge, your country has a right to suppose that you have not neglected the means of information; that you do not enter into such an engagement unprepared, not wholly incompetent to state to one another the true situation of those parts of the country where you severally reside, the general dispositions of the people, the offences which are most prevalent, the dangers which most immediately threaten the peace of the society. Communications of this kind, made by active and intelligent men to one another, are productive of infinite advantage; they enable them to ascertain the temper of the times, to discover the evil that is epidemick, and to trace its true causes; and the evil bring [read: being] once known, the proper remedy can be freely and easily applied.

I have already said, Gentlemen, that vigilance and inquiry were never more necessary on the part of those who are anywise concerned in the administration of the government, than at the present moment. The same arts which have been used, the same engines which have been employed, to destroy and dissolve the several governments upon the Continent, and have too well succeeding in reducing the greater part of them to a shapeless ruin, are now turned against the government of this country. It is not by force of arms merely that the enemy seeks to destroy us; he has recourse to means more subtle, more secret, and far more certain. He attempts to shake all our received opinions; to sap all our religious notions. He well knows, that if a people can once be prevailed with to despise what they have long justly revered; to question what they have long justly believed; doubt, and uncertainty, and indecision, and anarchy, and confusion, must inevitably follow. There will be no longer a common end; no [16] longer a common interest; no longer any bond of union. A people, who can at once be persuaded to disclaim all dependance upon their God, to renounce all the great truths which he has been graciously pleased to reveal to them, can find no resting-place, but will be the sport of every wind that may chance to blow, and the easy conquest of every foe that may invade them. The relations of society can only be supported by law; and the sure foundations of the law of man must be deeply laid in the law of God.

Such, Gentlemen, being the means which are taken to effect our destruction, you cannot be too eager to inquire into, nor too anxious to suppress, all those publications which tend to unsettle the political and religious opinions of your fellow-subjects, and to excite a disregard and contempt of that government by which they have been long generously protected. At the same time that I press this inquiry upon you, I beg leave, Gentlemen, to be understood as not wishing to check or discourage, in the slightest degree, a fair and liberal discussion of all those measures which the king's ministers may from time to time propose. I am most desirous that all persons, to whom any office of trust in this country is delegated, should be narrowly and unceasingly watched; that their mistakes, misrepresentations, and misconduct should be exposed and subjected to publick review. God forbid, Gentlemen, that a manly opposition should not always exist among us! But there are publications industriously circulated among us, to the object of which no man can affect to be a stranger; and the mischievous effects of which no man can doubt - there are publications which, on the one hand, vindicate the injustice, soften the vices, palliate the cruelties, justify the [C-17] atrocities, magnify the resources, and blazon the successes of the enemy; while, on the other hand, they depreciate the merit of our victories, ridicule the generous patriotism of our fellow-subjects, represent our constitution as not worth preserving, declare our liberties to be extinguished, treat our holy religion as priestcraft, and its ministers as tools in the hands of the civil power, insult our Sovereign, and blaspheme our God. – To assist in, or even to countenance, the circulation of such publications, is to aid the cause of rebellion and impiety: to tolerate them is an argument of weakness in the government, and of criminal indifference in those who are entrusted with the administration of it – and yet of this description are some of our publick newspapers. I cannot flatter myself that those mischievous publications may not have found their way into this country. Their circulation has been anxiously promoted; and I fear that there is no part of the kingdom, however remote, which they have not visited. They are most frequent at our inns and publick-houses; for care is generally taken to place them there, where they are likely to meet with the greater number of readers, and, of course, to do the greater mischief. I have no difficulty, Gentlemen, in thus publickly declaring, that I think the magistrates will be fully justified in with-holding a licence from any publican who may admit papers of this sort into his house, and communicate them to his guests. The magistrates will, no doubt, act, in this case, with the temper, the caution, and the candour which mark their general conduct. They will first endeavour, by gentle means, to prevail with the publican to discontinue his encouragement to the obnoxious publication; they will advise him of the mischief he is doing, and warn him of the danger he incurs. Should these means prove ineffectual; [18] should he disregard their kind advice, and obstinately continue to act in opposition to all their remonstrance; I have no difficulty, I repeat it, in thus publickly declaring that they will be justified in with-holding a licence from such a man: nay more; I say, that it will be their bounden duty so to do. It is not to be endured, Gentlemen, that the poison of sedition and irreligion should be vended under the licence of publick authority.

It is not only to publications, Gentlemen, that your attention must be directed; it behoves you also to check that licentiousness of conversation which so much obtains at present. Let not the truths which have been delivered down to us by our ancestors be cast aside with a sneer; not let the maxims which we have imbibed from our early youth, and which the experience of our forefathers has given us as infallible guides for our conduct, be condemned as prejudices. Let us not be alarmed by the word *prejudices*. In our journey through life, it is absolutely necessary that we should occasionally act from prejudice. A prejudice, *quatenùs* a prejudice, is not therefore wrong: it is at the most no more than an opinion which we have taken up rather hastily and without thorough examination. It is as likely to be right as to be wrong: it is in most cases likely to be right. Our ancestors have acted upon it, and they have acted well; we feel and enjoy those, though perhaps we cannot trace it to its source. Besides, the more maxims we collect; the more we avail ourselves of the wisdom of our ancestors, and the more we shorten our own labour. We should never act at all, if we staid to probe and examine every maxim; neither would every mind be equal to the examination, not capable of satisfying itself. In morals and in politicks, as in [19] the arts and sciences, we must take some things for granted; we must proceed upon some truths as self-evident, and requiring no demonstration. If every workman were to be expected to enquire into the principle upon which his rule was founded, before he applied it, our mechanick employments were be all at a stand: if every subject is to satisfy himself, before he yields obedience to the laws, that all the maxims upon which the government of his country proceeds are consonant to his imperfect notions of the relations between the governors and governed, the machine of government can never move.

Gentlemen, you will also discourage all disquisitions into the abstract rights of man. Man is not to be confined as a solitary being, as a being that never looks beyond himself; but he is to be considered as a member of society, and as a member of that society in which he is placed. There he is to look for his duties, and there he is to look for his rights: the former will lead him to the latter. He who is practically right, is seldom theoretically wrong: we shall in general find that our interest and our duty go together; that we best consult our happiness and that of our species, when we conscientiously and punctually discharge the general duties of life; that he who is the best father, the best son, the best husband, the best master, the best neighbour, the best subject, is also the best friend to himself and to his country. If the governed are good, the governors cannot be otherwise.

Permit not, Gentlemen, any debates upon questions, the discussion of which outrages all decency; where one of the disputants must avow and maintain the principles of a rebel and traitor, of an infidel or an atheist. In matters of state, Gentle-[20] men, familiarize not yourselves to discuss the conduct you are to observe in extreme cases; nor busily affect to ascertain the point where obedience ends, and resistance begins. In matters of religion, Gentlemen, presume not, in the freedom of conversation and the heat of convivial argument, to touch upon the mysteries of our redemption, or the attributes of our Creator. When I press these things, Gentlemen, upon your consideration, as I do with all seriousness and earnestness, I feel a well-grounded confidence that I shall not press them in vain. I know that I am not addressing myself to men who are indisposed to exert themselves in our present difficulties; but who, on the contrary, glow with the same patriot zeal which animates the rest of their countrymen; who have displayed the same magnanimity and heroism, and the same determined resolution to assert their rights, and preserve their liberties, which have been manifested in every other part of the kingdom; and who, seeing whence in this country "the blessings of government, peace, liberty, and plenty flow," have joined in that generous emulation we now behold among our fellow-subjects, "contending who shall first and best express their duty and gratitude to their sovereign, at this time especially, when the seditious endeavours of unreasonable men have made it necessary to assert the ancient loyalty of the English nation; and make the world sensible that we do not degenerate from those prime glories of our ancestors, love and allegiance to our prince*."

* See the Address of the University of Cambridge to King Charles the Second in 1683. *Collier*'s Ecclesiastical History, vol. ii. p. 903, 904.

THE END.

INDEX

[Surnames are given in block capitals; subject matters in lower case type; only place names have capital initials. Because of the profusion of allusions to, or quotations from, statutes, texts are only referred to in the simplest manner under Statutes.]